ASCENT
CENTER FOR TECHNICAL KNOWLEDGE

Autodesk® Civil 3D® 2026
Beyond the Basics for Grading

Learning Guide
Imperial Units - Edition 1.0

ASCENT - Center for Technical Knowledge®
Autodesk® Civil 3D® 2026
Beyond the Basics for Grading
Imperial Units - Edition 1.0

Prepared and produced by:

ASCENT Center for Technical Knowledge
630 Peter Jefferson Parkway, Suite 175
Charlottesville, VA 22911

866-527-2368
www.ASCENTed.com

Lead Contributor: Jeff Morris

ASCENT - Center for Technical Knowledge (a division of Rand Worldwide Inc.) is a leading developer of professional learning materials and knowledge products for engineering software applications. ASCENT specializes in designing targeted content that facilitates application-based learning with hands-on software experience. For over 25 years, ASCENT has helped users become more productive through tailored custom learning solutions.

We welcome any comments you may have regarding this guide, or any of our products. To contact us please email: feedback@ASCENTed.com.

Contents

Chapter 8: Managing Surfaces	8-1

Preface

The Autodesk® Civil 3D® 2026 software enables the creation of intelligent relationships between objects to support various civil engineering tasks. *Autodesk Civil 3D 2026: Beyond the Basics for Grading* is intended for users who create or manage site grading plans using Autodesk Civil 3D.

The topics cover the use of feature lines, grading tools, and corridors to design a commercial site, which includes a parking lot, building pads, pond, and a simple sewage lagoon. A road is included in the survey, with existing conditions collected by a survey team. The practice exercises allow you to practice grading the lots in a small residential subdivision.

The course content assumes that the existing conditions have already been processed. To learn how to create these existing conditions, refer to the content in *Autodesk Civil 3D 2026: Essentials for Surveyors*.

Topics Covered

- Introduction to grading

- Traditional grading tools and the grading optimization tool

- Parcel grading

- Grading using feature lines

- Grading using grading objects and grading groups

- Grading using corridors

- Grading using the grading optimization tool

- Managing surfaces

- Visualization in Autodesk® InfraWorks®

Prerequisites

- Knowledge of AutoCAD basics as taught in *AutoCAD Essentials*, or equivalent experience.

- Knowledge of Civil 3D basics as taught in *Autodesk Civil 3D: Essentials*, or equivalent experience.

- A sound understanding and knowledge of civil engineering terminology

- Access to the 2026.1 version of the software and the Grading Optimization extension, to ensure compatibility with this guide. Future software updates that are released by Autodesk may include changes that are not reflected in this guide. The practices and files included with this guide might not be compatible with prior versions (e.g., 2025).

Note on Learning Guide Content

ASCENT's learning guides are intended to teach the technical aspects of using the software and do not focus on professional design principles and standards. The practices aim to demonstrate the capabilities and flexibility of the software, rather than following specific design codes or standards, which can vary between regions.

Note on Software Setup

This guide assumes a standard installation of the software using the default preferences during installation. Lectures and practices use the standard software templates and default options for the Content Libraries.

Lead Contributor: Jeff Morris

Specializing in the civil engineering industry, Jeff authors learning guides and provides training and implementation support for all Autodesk infrastructure solutions.

Jeff has over 25 years of experience in the civil engineering industry. His diverse work experience includes multiple roles as a Trainer, Application Specialist, Implementation and Customization Consultant, CAD Coordinator, and CAD/BIM Manager in civil engineering and architectural firms. He has worked in different countries, from small private firms to large multinational corporations and government organizations. Through his extensive experience in Building and Infrastructure design, Jeff has acquired a thorough understanding of CAD Standards and Procedures and an in-depth knowledge of CAD and BIM.

Jeff studied Architecture and holds a diploma in Systems Analysis and Programming. He is an Autodesk Certified Instructor (ACI) and an Autodesk Certified Professional for Civil 3D and Revit.

Jeff Morris is the Lead Contributor for *Autodesk Civil 3D: Beyond the Basics for Grading*. This title was formerly part of *Autodesk Civil 3D: Fundamentals for Land Developers (Grading)*, for which he was the lead contributor since 2019.

In This Guide

The following highlights the key features of this guide.

Feature	Description
Practice Files	The Practice Files page includes a link to the practice files and instructions on how to download and install them. The practice files are required to complete the practices in this guide.
Chapters	A chapter consists of the following: Learning Objectives, Instructional Content, Practices, Chapter Review Questions, and Command Summary.
	• **Learning Objectives** define the skills you can acquire by learning the content provided in the chapter.
	• **Instructional Content**, which begins right after Learning Objectives, refers to the descriptive and procedural information related to various topics. Each main topic introduces a product feature, discusses various aspects of that feature, and provides step-by-step procedures on how to use that feature. Where relevant, examples, figures, helpful hints, and notes are provided.
	• **Practice** for a topic follows the instructional content. Practices enable you to use the software to perform a hands-on review of a topic. It is required that you download the practice files (using the link found on the Practice Files page) prior to starting the first practice.
	• **Chapter Review Questions**, located close to the end of a chapter, enable you to test your knowledge of the key concepts discussed in the chapter.
	• **Command Summary** concludes a chapter. It contains a list of the software commands that are used throughout the chapter and provides information on where the command can be found in the software.
Appendices	Appendices provide additional information to the main course content. It could be in the form of instructional content, practices, tables, projects, or skills assessment.

Practice Files

To download the practice files for this guide, use the following steps:

1. Type the URL *exactly as shown below* into the address bar of your Internet browser to access the Course File Download page.

   Note: If you are using the ebook, you do not have to type the URL. Instead, you can access the page by clicking the URL below.

   https://www.ascented.com/getfile/id/pogoniaPF

2. On the Course File Download page, click the **DOWNLOAD NOW** button, as shown below, to download the .ZIP file that contains the practice files.

3. Once the download is complete, unzip the file and extract its contents.

   The recommended practice files folder location is:
   C:\Civil 3D Grading

   Note: It is recommended that you do not change the location of the practice files folder. Doing so may cause errors when completing the practices.

Stay Informed!
To receive information about upcoming events, promotional offers, and complimentary webcasts, visit:
www.ASCENTed.com/updates

Grading: Beyond the Basics

Throughout the grading process, it is important for designers to be able to visualize the effects of ground reshaping. Understanding how water flows across the surface helps identify where adjustments may be needed.

You will explore how to create styles that make it easier to visualize ground surfaces and their impact on water movement.

Learning Objectives

- State the purpose of grading and reshaping the earth's surface.
- List the tools in the Autodesk® Civil 3D® software that can be used for grading.
- Identify the required settings to set up a new grading project.
- Set up feature line styles.
- Set up a grading group style for easy viewing of grading objects.
- Create grading criteria sets for multiple types of grading tasks.
- Create surface styles that make the effects of your grading easier to see and adjust.
- Create sites for managing common topology, such as parcels, alignments, grading groups, and feature lines.
- Create a drawing template specifically for grading.

1.1 Overview

Grading is used in construction to create the proper slope conditions for drainage, transportation, landscaping, and more. Its purpose is to provide stability for the site by minimizing soil erosion and sedimentation. When reshaping the ground surface, engineers and designers strive to prevent drainage problems, such as standing water on roads, flooding of homes and businesses, and having the ground wash away with storms, as shown in Figure 1–1. A properly graded project establishes drainage areas, directs drainage patterns, and affects runoff velocities.

Figure 1–1

Before creating a grading plan, the existing conditions of a site must be gathered. Land surveys, soil investigations, and storm data should all be studied before starting to consider where to create cut or fill areas. Another consideration is the newly created hard surfaces that create additional runoff.

Roads and Right-of-ways

Existing roads offer access points to the property and usually lie beyond the property limits. Even if the roads directly border the property, there are usually right-of-ways which must be respected. It is fair to assume that the limit of such right-of-ways will form the development (grading) limit for the property.

Proposed roads are usually part of the overall design. In many cases, Civil 3D corridors are designed to accommodate the access and vehicular traffic flow within the development site. These corridors are typically designed over the existing ground surface to form a basis for other grading.

Figure 1–2 shows the development site for this course.

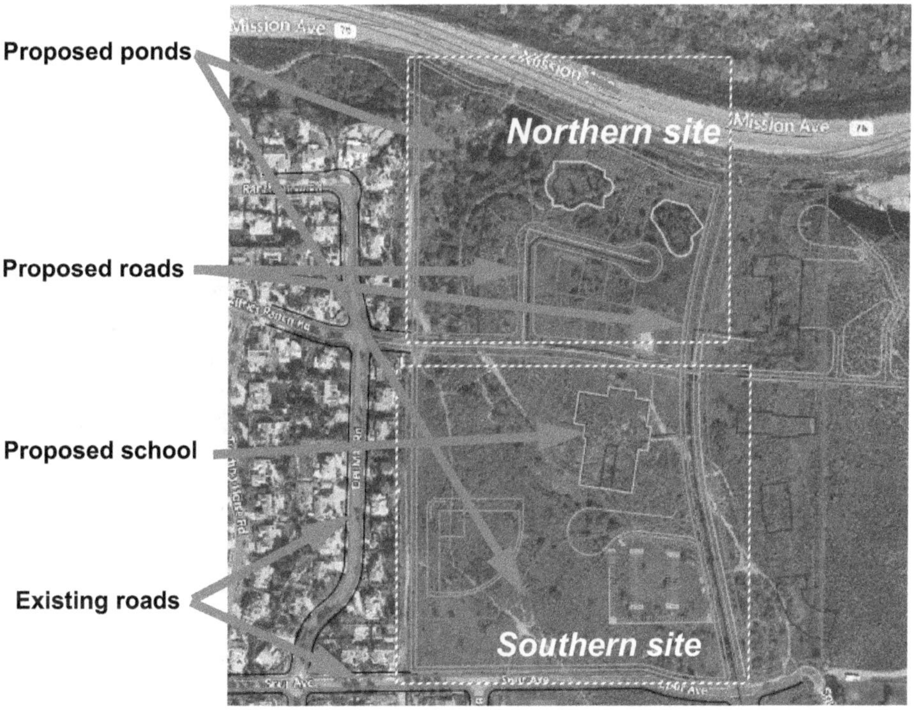

Figure 1–2

The lecture part and the practices will focus primarily on the Northern Site, with the Southern Site available for additional practices with minimal instructions.

Standard Civil 3D Grading Tools vs Grading Optimization

Grading can be an arduous process. Although it sounds simple that "water runs downhill", the tasks involved in conceptualizing, designing, and calculating proper drainage on a site are complex and involved.

Civil 3D has some great grading tools to help with such tasks. The more traditional Civil 3D tools were the best options before the 2022 release of Civil 3D. With that release, grading tasks were complimented with an additional tool known as the Grading Optimization Program.

It is an alternate approach to grading solutions. It is an external program designed to find several different grading scenarios based on a variety of input data. Once a preferred solution is found, it is imported into Civil 3D as a surface along with optional points and breaklines. It is considered a tool primarily for initial site studies, layouts and conceptual grading, as shown in Figure 1–3.

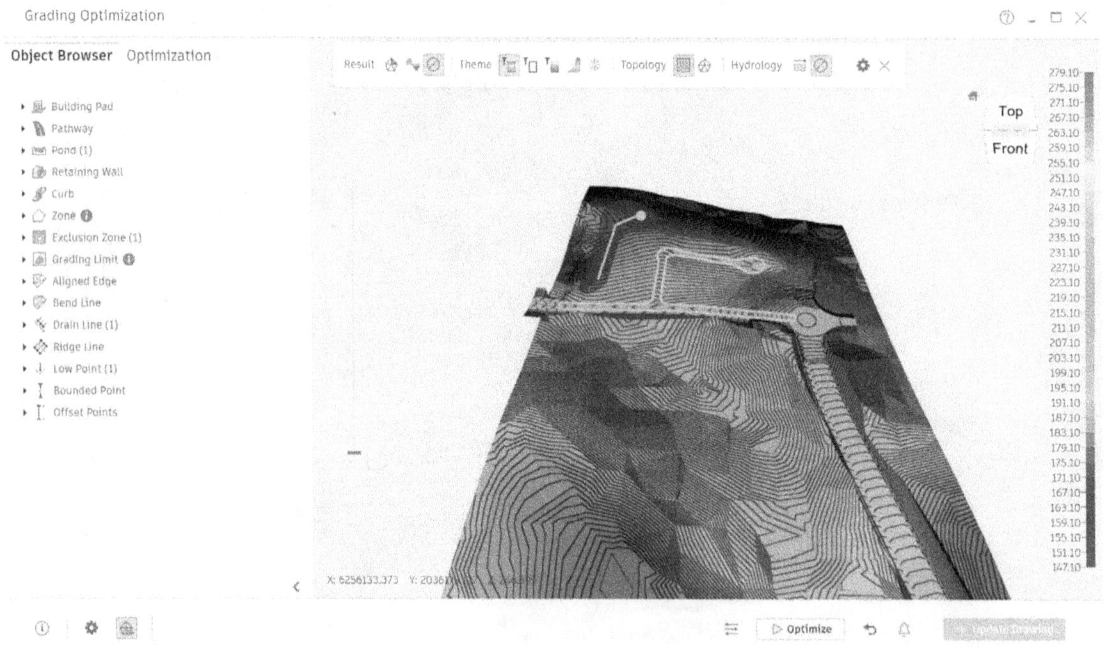

Figure 1–3

This program works well in conjunction with the traditional Civil 3D tools.

Parts of the Grading Object

Grading objects contain several components. A basic grading object contains a footprint or base line, projection lines, daylight or target lines, and faces. Each of the parts are shown in Figure 1–4.

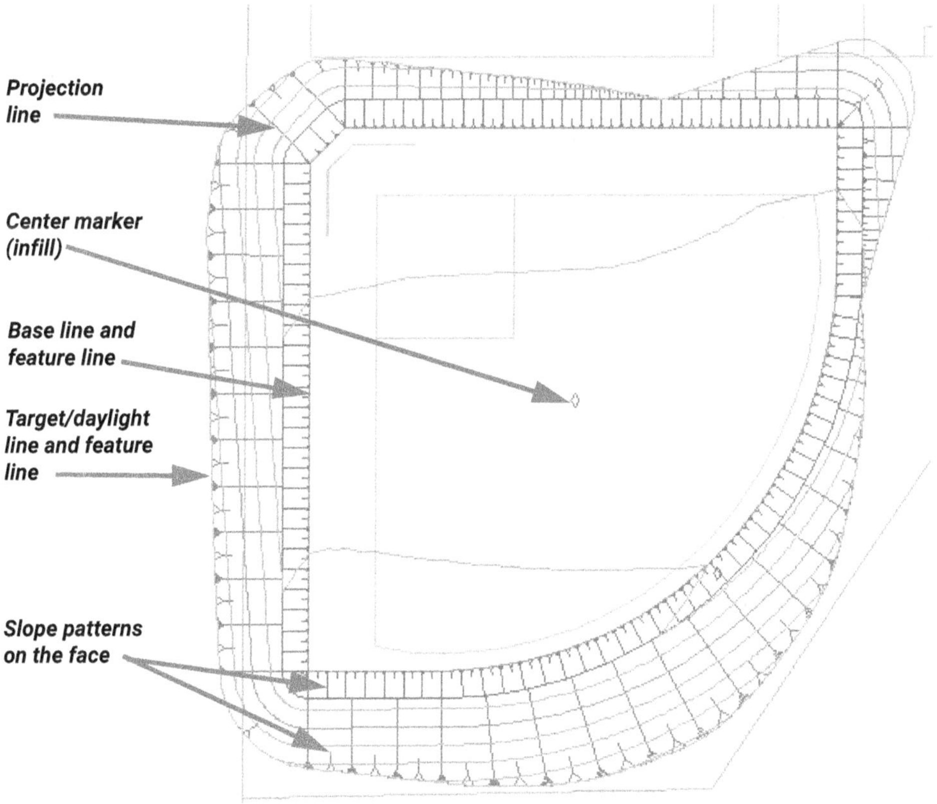

Figure 1–4

- **Base lines** act as the footprint for the grading object. They can be a parcel line or any open or closed feature line. Feature lines can represent ridge or swale lines, building footprints, parking lots, and a number of other design features.

- A **target line** is the end result of a grading object. It can be defined by a distance, elevation (relative or absolute), or surface. If a surface is used as the target, the result is a daylight line. In all cases, the target line will be a feature line that can then be used as the base line for another grading object.

- A **face** is the slope area created by the application of a grading criteria. Depending on the grading object's specified style, slope patterns might be displayed on each face according to the type of grading solution. The slope pattern for a distance grading object might look different than the slope pattern on a cut or fill slope, as shown in Figure 1–4.

- **Projection lines** define the face edges within a region of a grading object and are used for the facets along curves and break points on the base line and target line.

- The **center marker** is a diamond that marks a graded face's center and is used for display and selection purposes. When you edit each grading object, select the center marker that displays the *Grading* contextual tab in the ribbon. In most cases, this center marker designates a grading infill.

A **grading group** is a collection of grading objects that is used to organize gradings and make surface creation and volume calculations easier. By setting a volume base surface in the grading group properties (as shown in Figure 1–5), grading volume tools can be used to calculate a quick volume between the new grading surface and the existing ground surface.

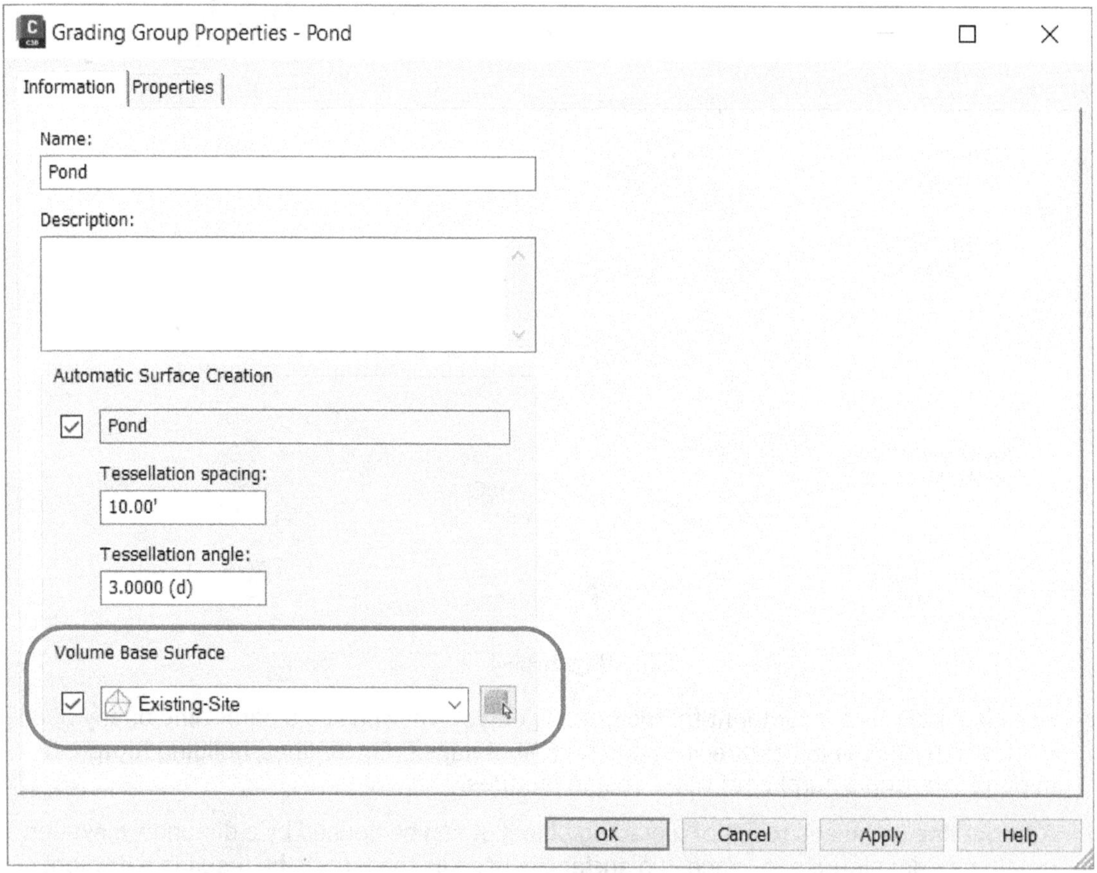

Figure 1–5

Grading Workflow

Setting Up Gradings

In the preliminary phase of a project, you can save a lot of time and effort if your drawing is set up beforehand with the settings and styles needed to convey design intent effectively. Then save it as a template.

1. **Establish Grading Settings:** This is where you will define units of measurement to be used throughout the project for gradings.
2. **Create Grading Styles:** Styles determine how feature lines, surfaces, and grading groups display in the drawing and on the printed sheet.
3. **Define Grading Criteria:** Predefining the methods and projections for grading saves time and ensures that the proper standards are followed.

Designing and Creating Gradings

The process used to create gradings might vary from one project to another. The list of tasks below is intended to be a high-level overview.

1. **Create a Site:** A site is where the grading information created resides in Civil 3D. This is where the interaction between Feature Lines and Grading Groups occur.
2. **Create Feature Lines:** Parcel lines can be used to create feature lines or convert existing linework into feature lines. Nearly every grading project contains at least one feature line.
3. **Create Grading Groups:** The interaction between feature lines can be controlled along with grading projections using grading groups.
4. **Create the Grading:** By creating multiple grading objects, you can determine the slope of the ground from the base line to the target line.
5. **Modify the Grading as Required:** Editing commands can be used to make easy adjustments to grading objects and feature lines as the design changes.

Outputting Grading Information

It is important to be able to convey the grading design to others. During the design phase, community leaders and the public might need to be able to visualize the finished project. Creating renderings for the public makes visualizing the project easier for them. However, contractors are more familiar with reading contour data with cut and fill slopes labeled or shaded to indicate how much ground needs to be moved from one area to another. They might also need cut and fill reports to help them order the correct volume of material for the site.

1. **Select the Grading Group Surface Creation:** Once the grading group satisfies your grading specifications, you need to create contours for it. This is only accomplished by creating a surface.
2. **Edit Grading Styles:** Viewing the surface in various ways assists in finding problems and communicating design intent.

3. **Plot and Publish the Drawings:** Drawings can be plotted onto paper or published electronically to send to interested parties more efficiently.

4. **Produce Reports:** Reports complement drawings to communicate design intent and volumes to interested parties.

1.2 Tools in Autodesk Civil 3D

The Autodesk Civil 3D software is a powerful application for civil engineering design. Although it runs in the familiar AutoCAD® environment, the software is based on a dynamic engineering model that contains all of the core geometry and integrates all of the data. When you make a change to the design, the Autodesk Civil 3D software automatically updates the related objects, views, annotations, tables, etc.

The objects used for grading in the Autodesk Civil 3D software establish intelligent relationships. The following table lists items that can be used for grading and shows the relationships and how a change made to one object is reflected in others.

When you edit these objects...	These objects are updated...
Points	Surfaces
Surfaces	Grading Groups, Profiles, Pipe Networks, and Corridors
Parcels	Grading Groups and Corridors
Alignments	Grading Groups, Corridors, Profiles, Parcels, Sections, and Pipe Networks
Profiles	Grading Groups, Corridors, Parcels, Sections, and Pipe Networks
Grading Groups	Surfaces and Corridors
Subassembly	Assembly, Corridors, and Surfaces
Assembly	Corridors and Surfaces
Feature Lines	Grading Groups, Alignments, Profiles, Corridors, and Surfaces
Sample Lines	Sections and Corridors

1.3 Drawing Settings in Detail

The values in Drawing Settings influence every aspect of the drawing environment. Each tab has values affecting a specific drawing area: for example, layer naming properties, coordinate systems, default precisions, input and output conventions, abbreviations for alignment, volume units, etc. After the Autodesk Civil 3D software is correctly configured, you should only need to access the first two tabs for your everyday work.

To access the Drawing Settings, in the *Toolspace>Settings* tab, select and right-click on the drawing name (at the top), and select **Edit Drawing Settings**.

Units and Zone

In the *Drawing Settings* dialog box, the *Units and Zone* tab (as shown in Figure 1−6) sets the Model Space plotting scale and coordinate zone for the drawing. The scale can be a custom value or selected from a drop-down list. A zone is selected from a drop-down list of worldwide categories and coordinate systems.

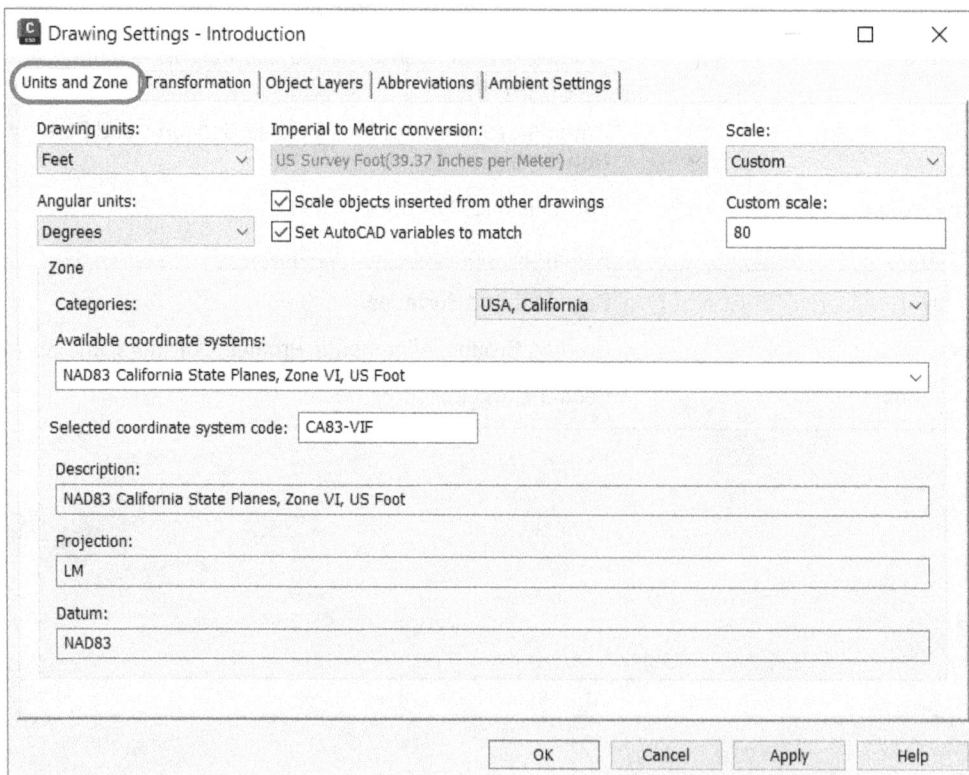

Figure 1−6

Note: If you work predominantly in one Coordinate Zone, you can set your template to that zone.

A drawing which has been assigned a coordinate system enables points to report their grid coordinates, longitude, and latitude. Conversely, when assigning a coordinate system, grid coordinates and Longitude and Latitude data can create points in a drawing.

Object Layers

The *Object Layers* tab (shown in Figure 1–7) assigns layer names to Autodesk Civil 3D objects. A modifier, which can be a prefix or a suffix, is associated with each layer's name. The value of the modifier can be anything that is typed into its *Value* field. Traditionally, the value is an * (asterisk) with a separator (a dash or underscore). The Autodesk Civil 3D software replaces the asterisk with the name of the object of the same type. For example, the base surface layer name is **C-TOPO** with a suffix modifier of -* (a dash followed by an asterisk). When a surface named **Existing** is created, it is placed on the layer **C-TOPO-EXISTING**, and when a surface named **Base** is created, it is placed on the layer **C-TOPO-BASE**.

The last column of the *Object Layers* tab enables you to lock the values. When a value is locked at this level, the Autodesk Civil 3D software does not permit it to be changed by any lower style or setting.

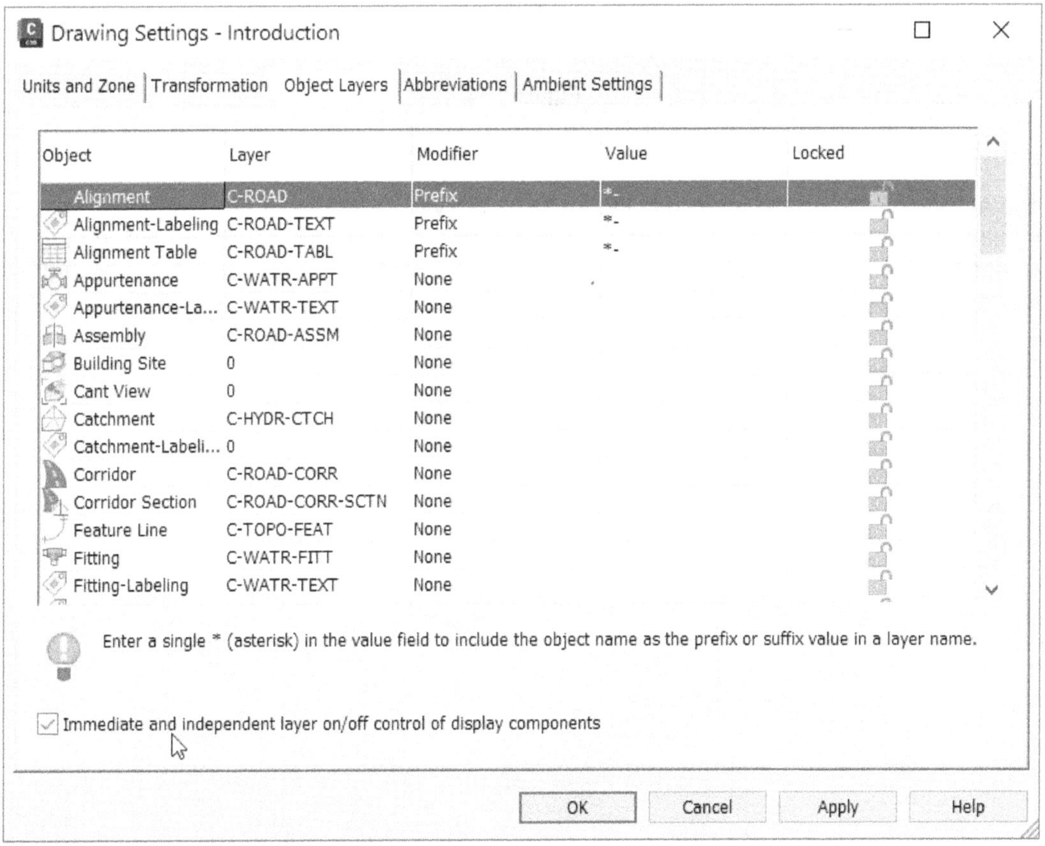

Figure 1–7

To change the listed object layers, double-click on a layer name. In the *Layer Selection* dialog box (shown in Figure 1–8), select the layer from the list. If the layer does not exist, click **New** in the *Layer Selection* dialog box. This opens a second dialog box, in which you can define a new layer for the object type.

Layer Selection

Layer source:
C:\Civil 3D for Surveyors\References\DWG\Intro   New...

Layers:

Layer	Color	Linetype	Lineweight	Plot Style	Plot
0	white	Continuous	Default	Color_7	Yes
A-BLDG	white	Continuous	Default	Color_7	Yes
A-BLDG-FPRT	white	Continuous	Default	Color_7	Yes
A-BLDG-SITE	white	Continuous	Default	Color_7	Yes
A-BLDG-UTIL	white	Continuous	Default	Color_7	Yes
A-BREAKLINE	red	Continuous	Default	Color_1	Yes
A-PROP-LINE	white	Continuous	Default	Color_7	Yes
A-Property	white	Continuous	Default	Color_7	Yes
A-Property-Exist...	yellow	Continuous	Default	Color_2	Yes
A-SITE-BOUNDA...	red	Continuous	Default	Color_1	Yes
A-TOPO-MAJR	9	Continuous	Default	Color 9	Yes

Figure 1–8

Ambient Settings

In the *Ambient Settings* tab (shown in Figure 1–9), the values influence prompting and reports. For example, the *Direction* area affects the prompting for direction input: **Decimal Degrees**, **Degrees Minutes and Seconds** (with or without spaces), or **Decimal Degrees Minutes and Seconds**. Any value set at this level affects everything (labels and commands) in the drawing.

Drawing Settings - Introduction

Units and Zone | Transformation | Object Layers | Abbreviations | Ambient Settings

Property	Value	Override	Child Override	Lock
General				
Plotted Unit Display ...	decimal			
Set AutoCAD Units	Yes			
Save Command Cha...	Yes			
Show Event Viewer	Yes			
Show Tooltips	Yes			
Imperial to Metric co...	Use US Survey F...			
New Entity Tooltip St...	On			
Driving Direction	Right Side of th...			
Drawing Unit	foot			
Drawing Scale	80.000			
Scale Inserted Objects	Yes			
Independent Layer On	No			

Figure 1–9

Command Settings

In the *Edit Command Settings* dialog box (shown in Figure 1–10), you can set the default object and label styles used when creating objects with a specific command. Each object type contains a unique set of commands. Typical values in these dialog boxes include the naming format template (surface 1, parcel 1, etc.), design criteria (minimum area, frontage, length of vertical curve, and minimum horizontal curve), etc.

To open the dialog box, expand a collection in the *Toolspace>Settings* tab until the commands display. Right-click on the command to which you want to assign default settings and select **Edit Command Settings**.

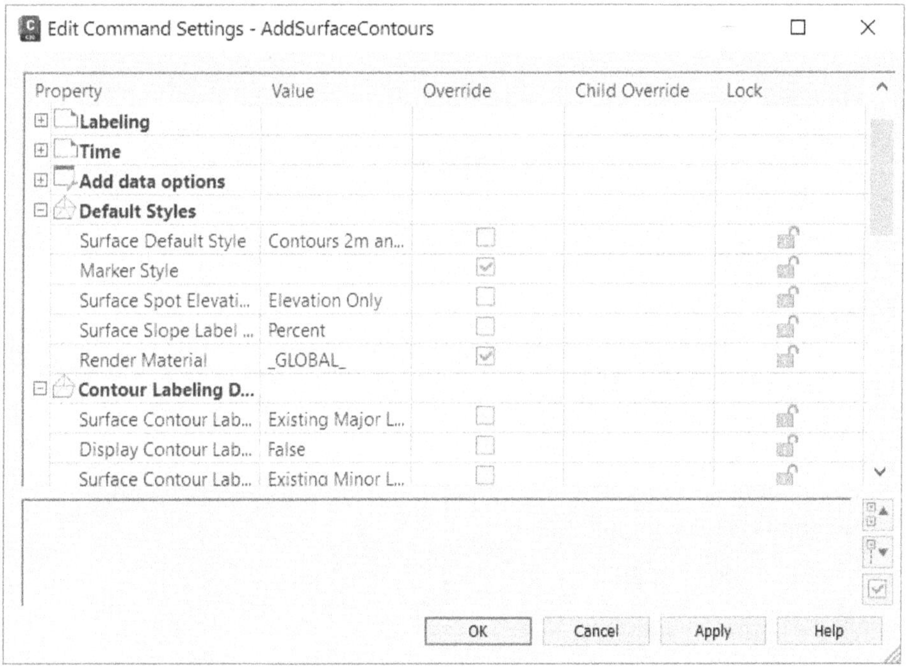

Figure 1–10

💡 Hint: Style and Setting Overrides

In the *Edit Label Style Defaults*, *Feature Settings* and similar dialog boxes, a downward pointing arrow in the *Child Override* column indicates that a setting or style lower in the settings tree has a different value than the one displayed. Selecting the arrow (which creates a red **x** over the icon) and clicking **OK** removes the variant settings and makes all lower settings and styles match those assigned in the dialog box. This can be a quick way of standardizing multiple settings dialog boxes and styles at the same time.

For example, in the *Surface Label Style Defaults* window (shown in Figure 1–11), some surface label styles are assigned a layer other than 0 and a visibility of false, because an arrow is present in the *Child Override* column. Since an arrow is not shown for the Text Style property, all surface label styles are using a text style of **Standard**.

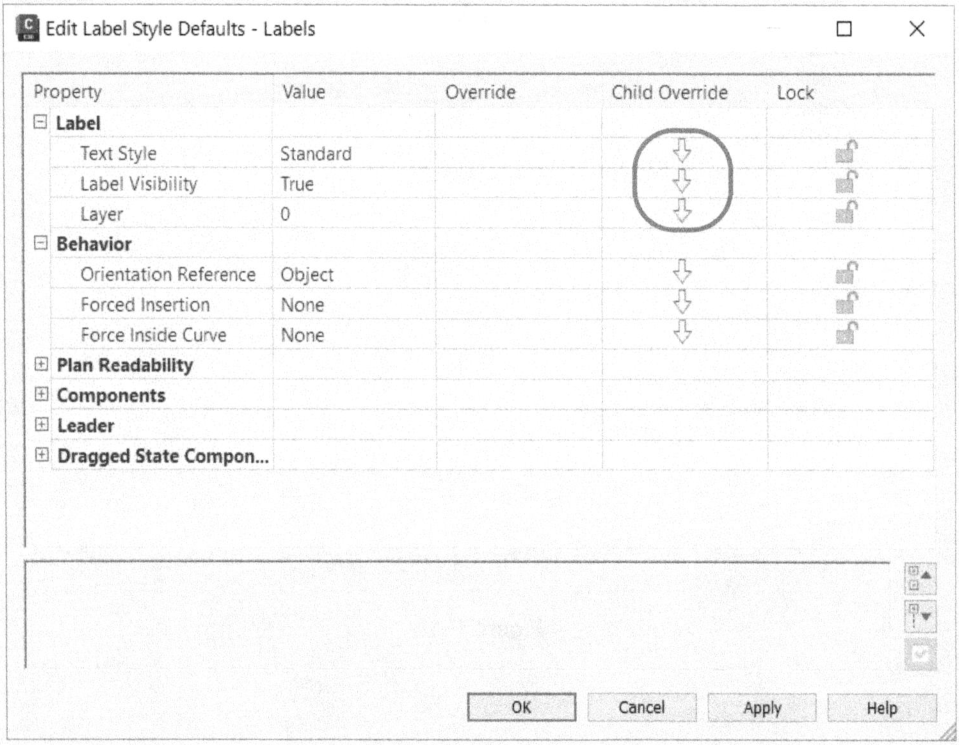

Figure 1–11

The *Override* column indicates whether a value in this window is overriding a higher settings dialog box. Clicking the **Lock** icon prevents you from changing that value in a lower setting's dialog box or style.

Practice 1a
Settings and Defaults

Practice Objectives

- Create a customized drawing template for grading.

- Identify the required settings to set up a new grading project.

In this practice, you will create a template based on National CAD Standards to include the correct settings and defaults for the types of grading done in the project.

Task 1: Create preliminary drawing template.

1. Open the Autodesk Civil 3D software. In the *Start* tab, click the **New** drop-down arrow and select **Autodesk Civil 3D (Imperial) NCS.dwt**, to start a new drawing using this template. This is one of the standard templates that come with the software.

2. Click ![C] (Application Menu) and select **Save As>Drawing Template**, as shown in Figure 1–12.

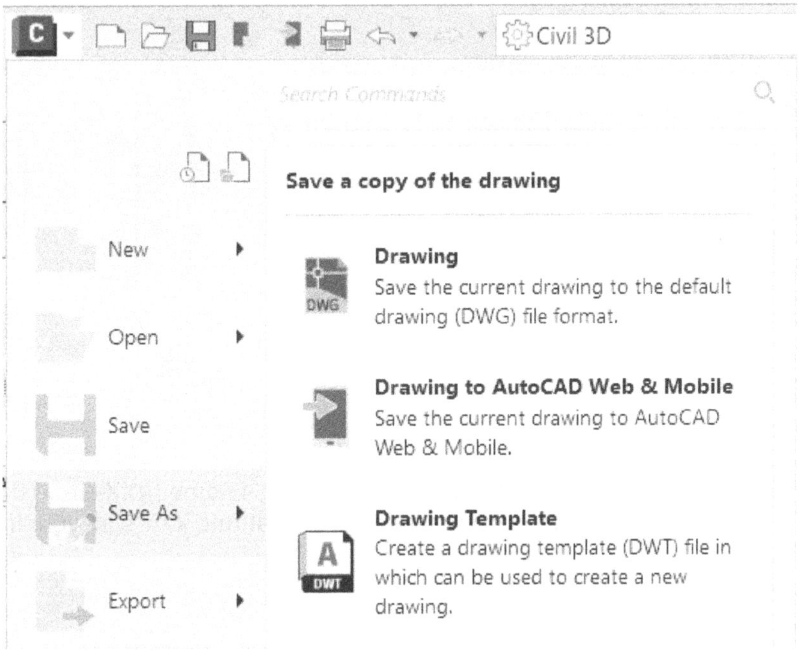

Figure 1–12

Note: Having project files stored in a common folder structure emulates proper CAD procedures. For training purposes, these folders reside on the local C drive, but in practice, these folders should be on a shared network drive so that the entire project team has access to them. GRD is for Grading; CA83-VIF designates the coordinate zone we will set this template up for.

3. Browse to the *C:\Civil 3D Grading\Ascent-Config* folder and type **XXX-GRD (CA83-VIF) NCS.dwt** as the template file name (replacing XXX with your initials). Click on the **Save** icon.

4. In the *Template Options* dialog box, add an appropriate description for this newly created template, for example: **Civil 3D Training template for Land Development**.

5. Select the *Toolspace>Settings* tab, as shown in Figure 1–13.

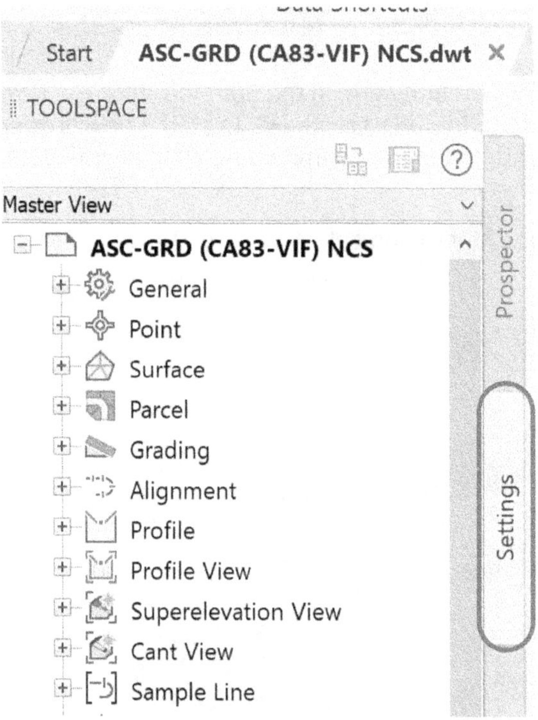

Figure 1–13

6. In the *Toolspace>Settings* tab, right-click on the drawing's name (**XXX-GRD (CA83-VIF) NCS**) at the top, and select **Edit Drawing Settings**. (Substitute XXX with your initials.)

7. In the *Drawing Settings* dialog box, select the *Units and Zone* tab, as shown in Figure 1–14.

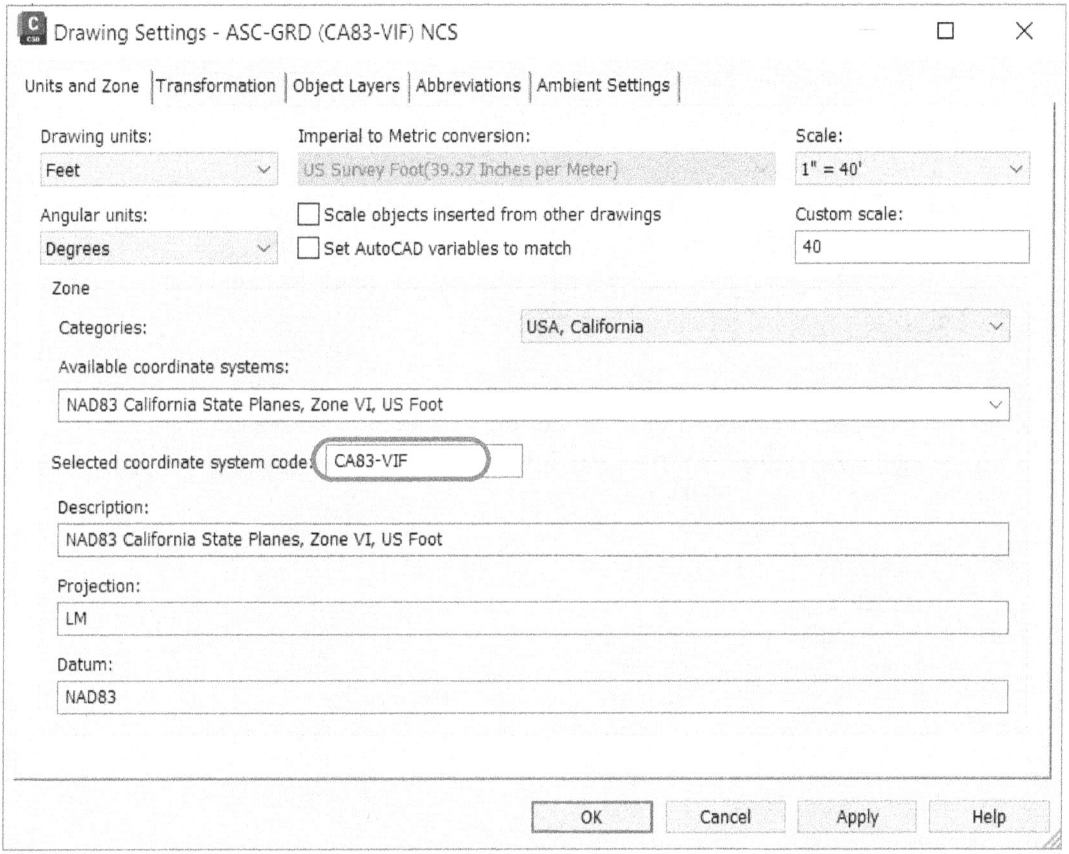

Figure 1–14

8. In the *Selected coordinate system code* field, type in **CA83-VIF**. This is the code for *NAD83 California State Planes, Zone VI, US Foot*. These coordinates are in the vicinity of the *CA83-VIF* coordinate zone.

9. Click **OK** to close the *Drawing Settings* dialog box.

10. Note the coordinates of the drawing are near 0,0. In the Command Line, type **Zoom** and press <Enter>, then type **C** (for Center) and press <Enter>. For the coordinates, type **6256700, 2036200**. At the ensuing *magnification or height* prompt, type **5300** and press <Enter>.

11. Start the **Single Line text** command (type in **DTEXT** in the Command Line or select in the ribbon>*Annotate* tab, *Multiline Text* drop down), then select the center of the display as the insertion point.

12. Set the *text height* to **150** and the *rotation angle* to **33**.

13. Type the following, pressing <Enter> after each line (when done typing the last line, press <Enter> twice to finish):

    "GRADING TEMPLATE...

    DRAWING SET TO CA83-VIF COORDINATE SYSTEM.

    GO TO DRAWING SETTINGS TO MODIFY IF NEED BE.

    DELETE THIS MESSAGE."

14. Zoom extents.

15. Save the drawing template.

Task 2: Establish typical settings for grading.

1. In the *Toolspace> Settings* tab, right-click on the drawing's name (**XXX-GRD (CA83-VIF) NCS**) at the top, and select **Edit Drawing Settings**. (Substitute XXX with your initials.)

2. In the *Object Layers* tab, set the *Tin Surface Modifier* to a **Suffix**, and type **-*** (dash, asterisk) in the *Value* field, as shown in Figure 1–15.

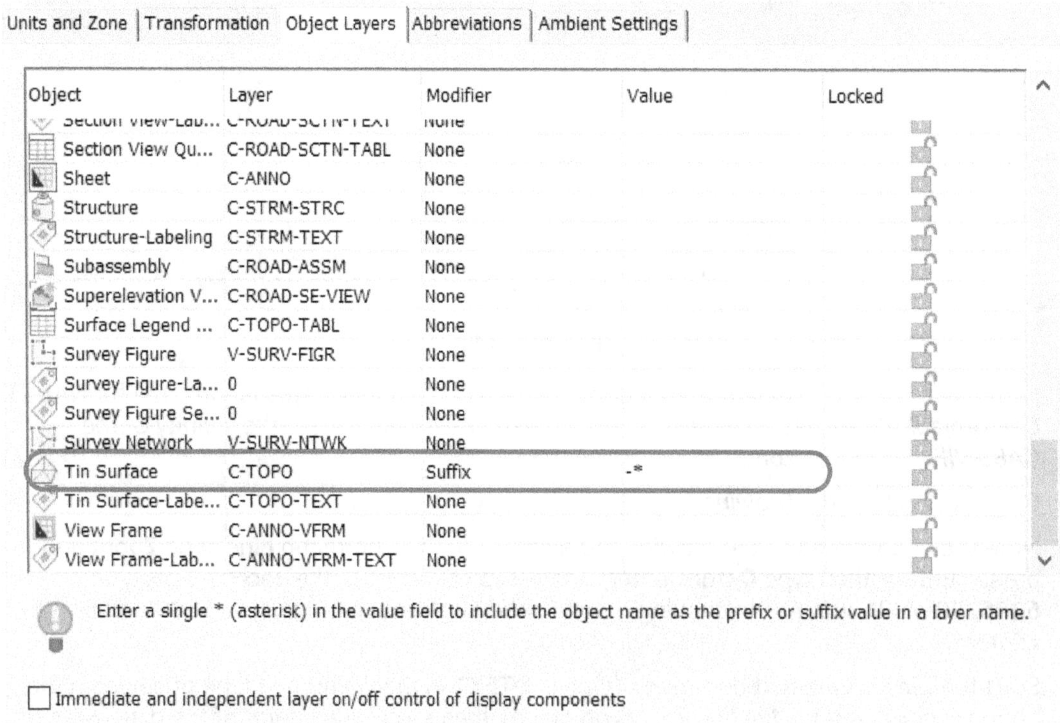

| Units and Zone | Transformation | Object Layers | Abbreviations | Ambient Settings |

Object	Layer	Modifier	Value	Locked	
Section View-Lab...	C-ROAD-SCTN-TEXT	None			
Section View Qu...	C-ROAD-SCTN-TABL	None			
Sheet	C-ANNO	None			
Structure	C-STRM-STRC	None			
Structure-Labeling	C-STRM-TEXT	None			
Subassembly	C-ROAD-ASSM	None			
Superelevation V...	C-ROAD-SE-VIEW	None			
Surface Legend ...	C-TOPO-TABL	None			
Survey Figure	V-SURV-FIGR	None			
Survey Figure-La...	0	None			
Survey Figure Se...	0	None			
Survey Network	V-SURV-NTWK	None			
Tin Surface	C-TOPO	Suffix	-*		
Tin Surface-Labe...	C-TOPO-TEXT	None			
View Frame	C-ANNO-VFRM	None			
View Frame-Lab...	C-ANNO-VFRM-TEXT	None			

Enter a single * (asterisk) in the value field to include the object name as the prefix or suffix value in a layer name.

☐ Immediate and independent layer on/off control of display components

Figure 1–15

3. In the *Ambient Settings* tab, verify that the following values are set, as shown in Figure 1–16.

- *Volume Unit:* **Cubic yard**
- *Grade Format:* **percent**
- *Slope Format:***run:rise**

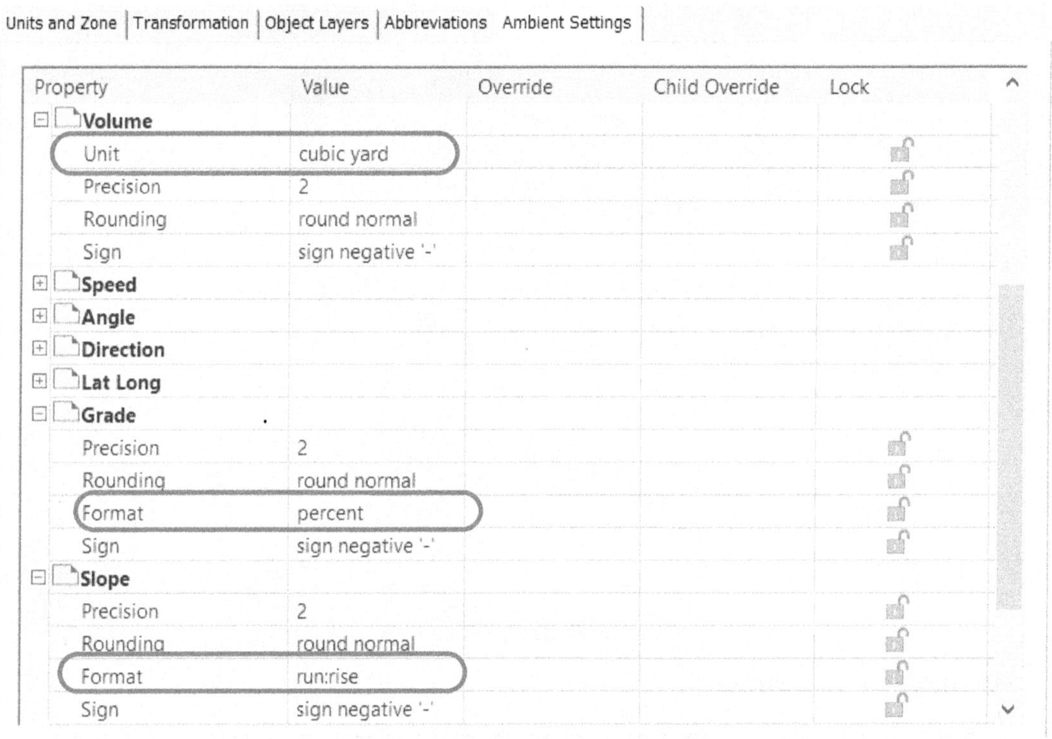

Figure 1–16

4. Click **OK** to close the dialog box.
5. In the *Settings* tab, complete the following:

- Expand **Grading>Commands.**
- Right-click on *CreateFeatureLines.*
- Select **Edit Command Settings.**

Note: You can also double-click on CreateFeatureLines.

6. In the *Edit Command Settings* dialog box, complete the following, as shown in Figure 1–17:

   - Select the Plus symbol next to *Feature Line Creation* to expand it.
   - In the *Feature Line Name* and *Use Feature Line Style* fields, select **True**.
   - Expand *Default Styles* and set the *Feature Line Style* to **Basic**.
   - Click **OK**.

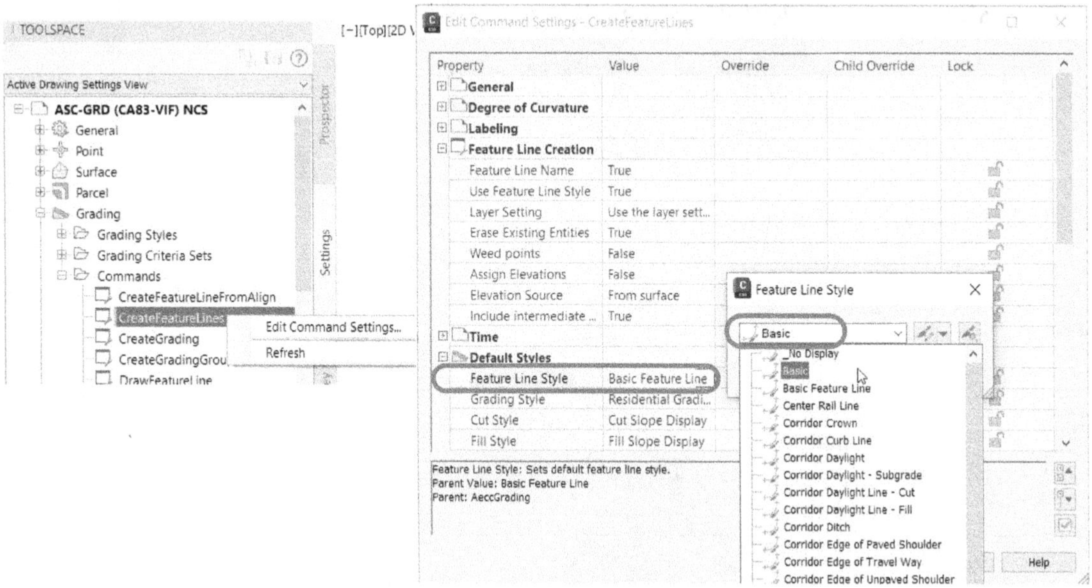

Figure 1–17

7. Save the drawing template.

End of practice

1.4 Feature Line Styles

Styles assist you in creating the design documentation required for construction documents so that you can focus on the design rather than drafting standards.

Feature lines are complex, linear 3D objects that define a string of known or proposed elevations. Feature lines can be used as breaklines (or folds) in surfaces or as grading object baselines and are created during the corridor creation process. Corridor feature lines can be extracted for use in grading groups. When a drawing is created using one of the standard Autodesk Civil 3D templates, it contains a large number of feature line styles, as shown in Figure 1–18.

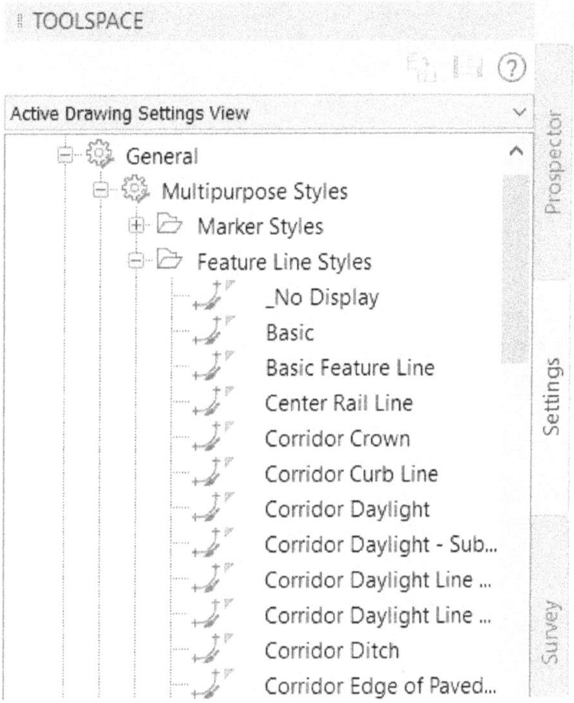

Figure 1–18

Additional feature line styles can easily be created. In the *Settings* tab, expand **General>Multipurpose Styles,** right-click on *Feature Line Styles* and select **New**. The *Feature Line Styles* dialog box opens, as shown in Figure 1–19.

The *Information* tab assigns a name and description. It also indicates who created the style and when it was last modified.

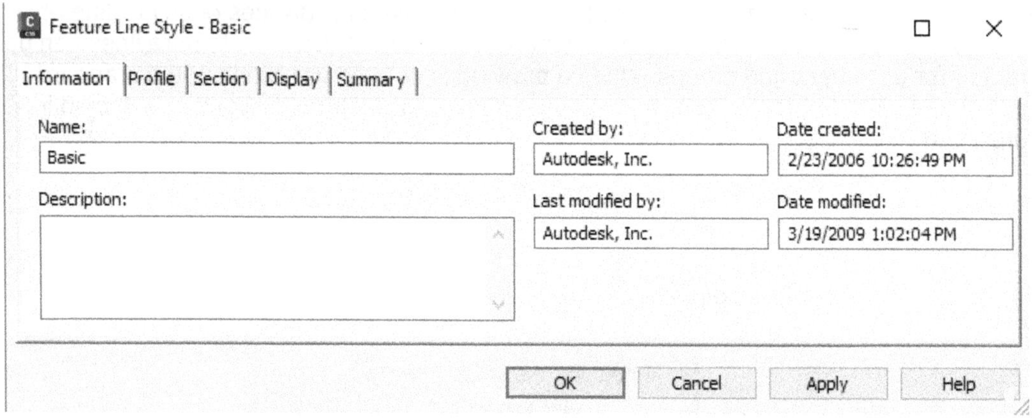

Figure 1–19

The *Profile* tab sets the marker symbol that displays at the end points and internal vertices of the feature line in the profile view, as shown in Figure 1–20. The markers are set to not display when the **_No Markers** style is selected.

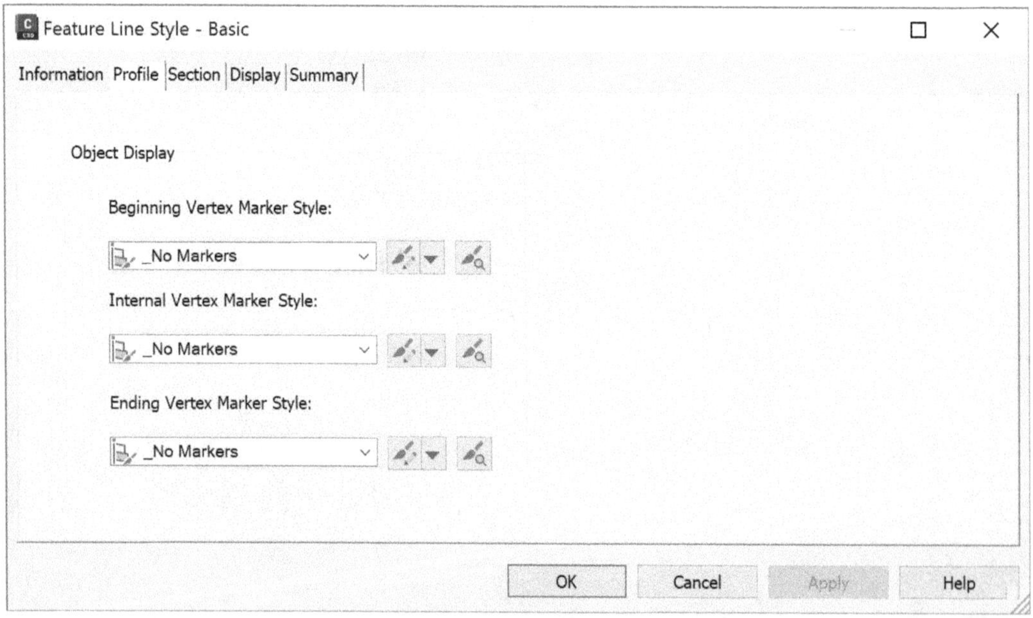

Figure 1–20

The *Sections* tab sets the marker symbol that displays in the section view, as shown in Figure 1–21. The markers are set to not display when the **_No Markers** style is selected.

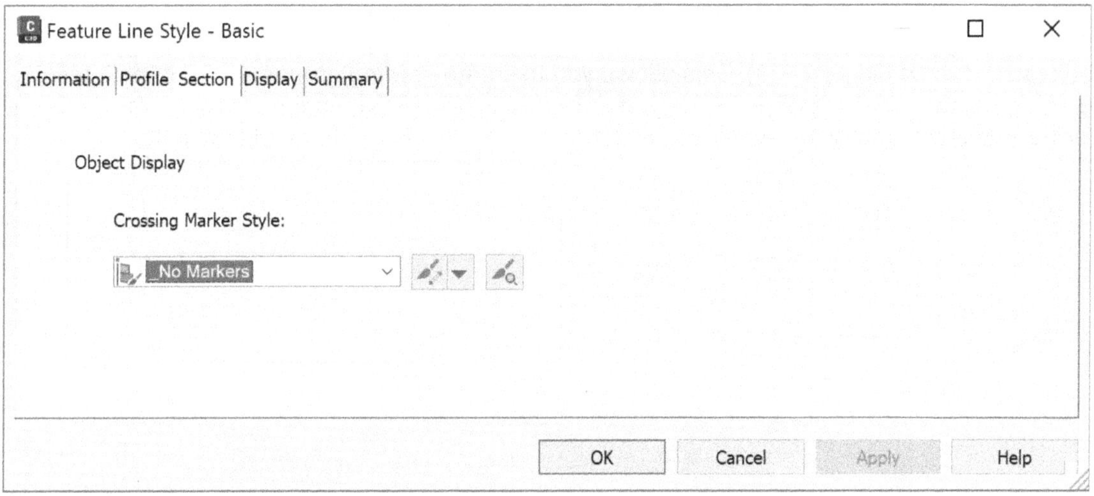

Figure 1–21

The *Display* tab is where you set the layer, color, linetype, visibility, etc., of the feature line in the various views, as shown in Figure 1–22. If the layer is set to layer **0** (zero), the drawing settings determine the layer on which the feature line is located. If it is set to any other layer in the *Feature Line Style* dialog box, it overrides the drawing settings.

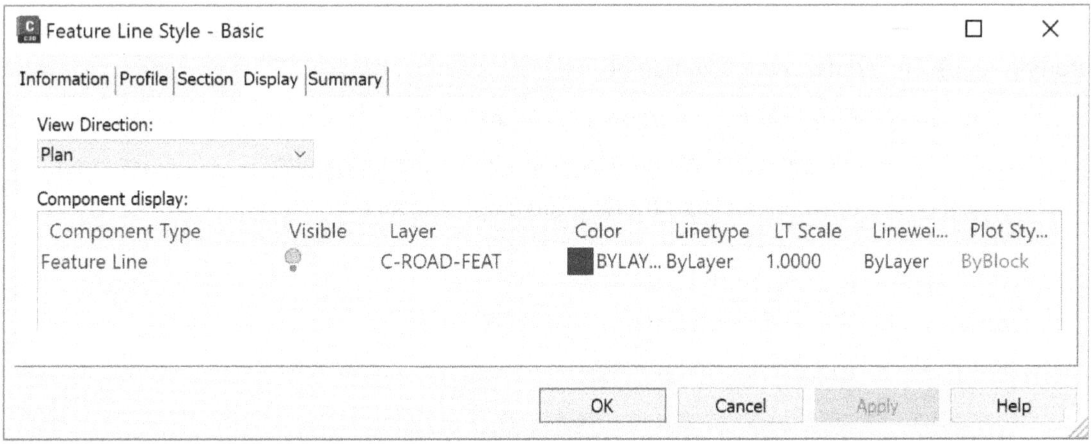

Figure 1–22

The *Summary* tab displays the settings that are set on all of the other tabs and is useful for quickly referencing what is happening in a specific style.

1.5 Grading Group Styles

The grading group style determines what is displayed in the drawing. You can set the layers for the various grading components to a no plot layer in the *Display* tab of the *Grading Style* dialog box (as shown in Figure 1−23). This allows you to create grading groups, which enable the grading objects to be displayed while you are working and not when the drawing is printed or plotted. Therefore, only the contours and labels are displayed on the printed sheet.

Compone...	Visible	Layer	Color		Linetype	LT Scale	Lineweight	Plot Style
Center Marke		C-TOPO-GR...		BYLAYER	ByLayer	1.0000	ByLayer	ByLayer
Daylight Line		C-TOPO-GR...		BYLAYER	ByLayer	1.0000	ByLayer	ByLayer
Projection Lir		C-TOPO-GR...		BYLAYER	ByLayer	1.0000	ByLayer	ByLayer
Internal Edge		C-TOPO-GR...		BYLAYER	ByLayer	1.0000	ByLayer	ByLayer
Solid Shadinc		C-TOPO-GR...		BYLAYER	ByLayer	1.0000	ByLayer	ByLayer
Slope Pattern		C-TOPO-GR...		BYLAYER	ByLayer	1.0000	ByLayer	ByLayer

Figure 1−23

The *Center Marker* tab determines the size of the center mark (diamond at the center of the grading face). The center mark size can be:

- a percentage of the screen, as shown in Figure 1−24.
- a fixed size (using feet or meters) according to the drawing units.
- based on the drawing scale so that it plots a specific size.

Figure 1−24

The *Slope Pattern* tab determines the patterns used to mark the grading slopes. If you select the option to display a slope pattern, an additional style needs to be created to define the number of components to use and the length of each of those components. To access this style, select the **Edit Current Selection** option as shown in Figure 1–25.

Alternatively, you can go to the *Settings* tab and expand **General>Multipurpose Styles>Slope Pattern Styles**. This enables a symbol to be placed at the beginning of the slope. The symbol can be a block, triangle (opened or closed), or tapered lines (with or without a gap). You can also have multiple components for the slope pattern with different symbols and line lengths for each.

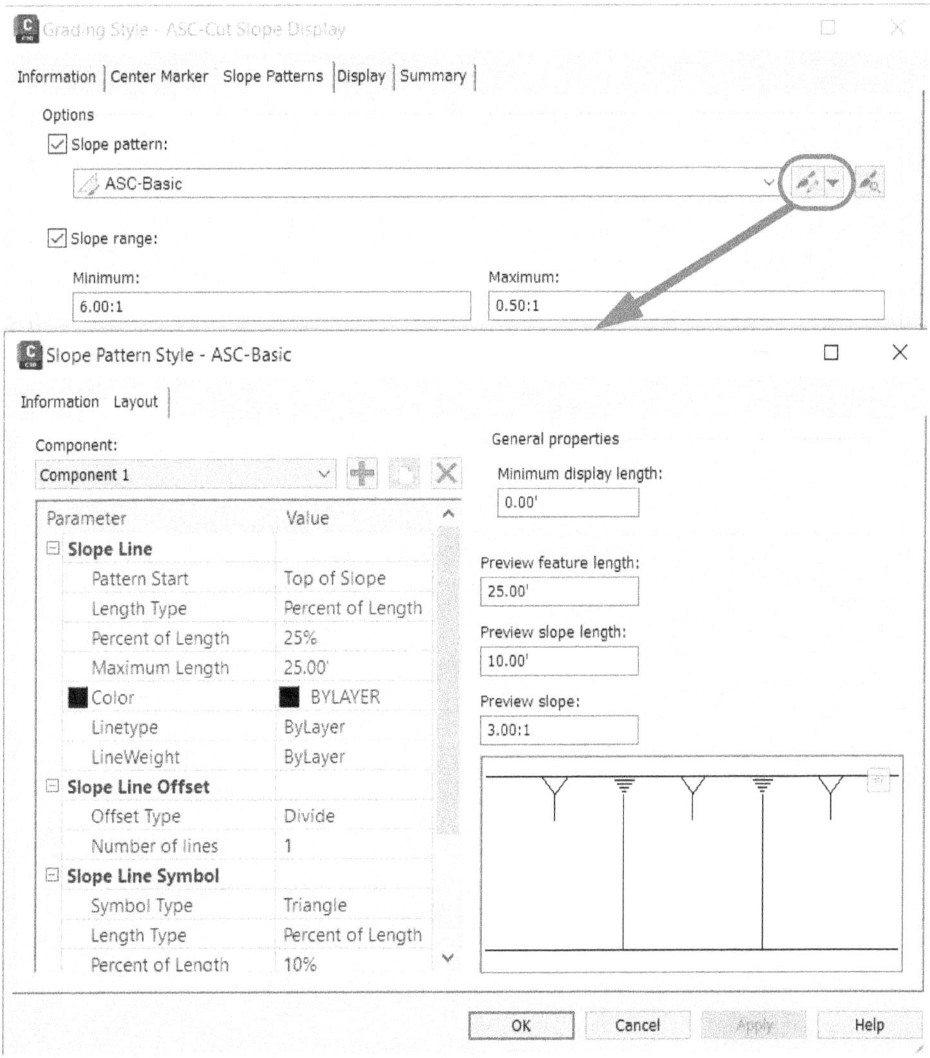

Figure 1–25

In the *Grading Style>Slope Pattern* tab, the slope ranges can also be turned on. This enables you to apply the slope patterns to a limited range of slope values that you specify.

In the *Display* tab, you can set the layer, color, linetype, visibility, etc., of the various components in the plan or model views, as shown in Figure 1–26. If the layer is set to layer **0** (zero), the drawing settings determine the layer on which the grading group components are placed. If it is set to any other layer in the *Grading Style* dialog box, it overrides the drawing settings.

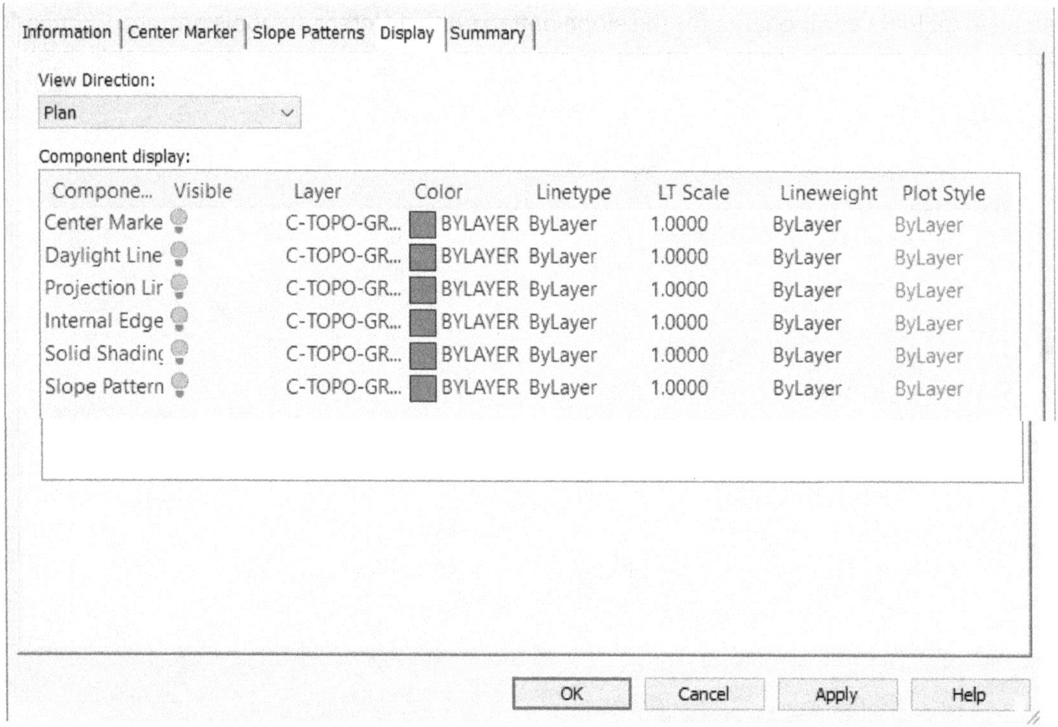
Information
Center Marker
Slope Patterns
Display
Summary
View Direction:
Plan
Component display:
Compone... Visible Layer Color Linetype LT Scale Lineweight Plot Style
Center Marke C-TOPO-GR... BYLAYER ByLayer 1.0000 ByLayer ByLayer
Daylight Line C-TOPO-GR... BYLAYER ByLayer 1.0000 ByLayer ByLayer
Projection Lir C-TOPO-GR... BYLAYER ByLayer 1.0000 ByLayer ByLayer
Internal Edge C-TOPO-GR... BYLAYER ByLayer 1.0000 ByLayer ByLayer
Solid Shadin(C-TOPO-GR... BYLAYER ByLayer 1.0000 ByLayer ByLayer
Slope Pattern C-TOPO-GR... BYLAYER ByLayer 1.0000 ByLayer ByLayer
OK
Cancel
Apply
Help

Figure 1–26

The *Summary* tab is a quick way of determining which center marker and slope pattern styles were set on previous pages, as shown in Figure 1–27.

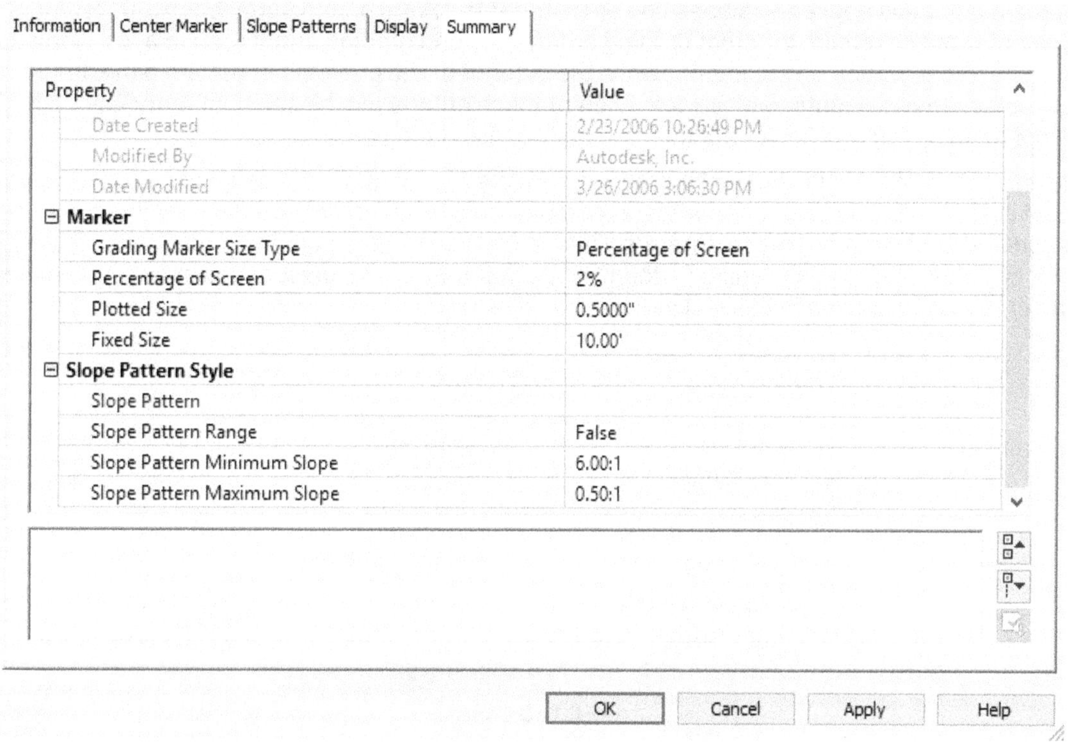

Information | Center Marker | Slope Patterns | Display | Summary

Property	Value	^
Date Created	2/23/2006 10:26:49 PM	
Modified By	Autodesk, Inc.	
Date Modified	3/26/2006 3:06:30 PM	
⊟ **Marker**		
Grading Marker Size Type	Percentage of Screen	
Percentage of Screen	2%	
Plotted Size	0.5000"	
Fixed Size	10.00'	
⊟ **Slope Pattern Style**		
Slope Pattern		
Slope Pattern Range	False	
Slope Pattern Minimum Slope	6.00:1	
Slope Pattern Maximum Slope	0.50:1	∨

OK   Cancel   Apply   Help

Figure 1–27

1.6 Grading Criteria Sets

Grading criteria is applied to a base line or footprint to create grading projections. Different types of projects require different grading criteria. A pond grading might require a 2:1 slope up to a specific elevation on the interior while the exterior of the pond might require a maximum of a 3:1 slope that daylights to a surface. Each of these criteria can be set in an Autodesk Civil 3D template to speed up and control the grading process during design.

Design criteria can be locked in the criteria to ensure that predefined design specifications are used every time. This also permits faster completion of grading projects by reducing the redundant typing of grading parameters. Once each type of grading criteria has been created, they can be included in a Grading Criteria Set so that they are in one location, making them easier to use (as shown in Figure 1–28).

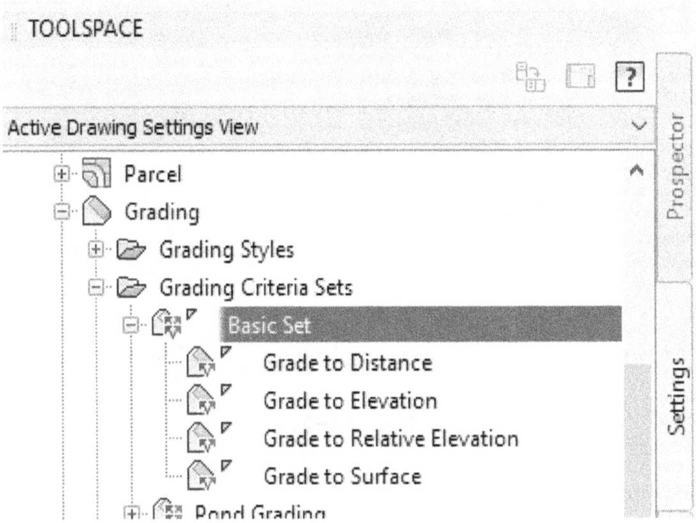

Figure 1–28

There are four different types of grading criteria:

1. **Grade to Distance**
2. **Grade to Elevation**
3. **Grade to Relative Elevation**
4. **Grade to Surface**

Grade to Distance

When you need to keep a specific grade or slope for a specified horizontal distance, you use the **Grade to Distance** criteria (as shown in Figure 1–29). For example, a building pad for a house might require that the ground slopes away from the house at a 2% grade for a specified distance to ensure that standing water is directed away from the foundation. Use this criteria to set the target at a specific distance and then lock that distance so that it cannot be changed.

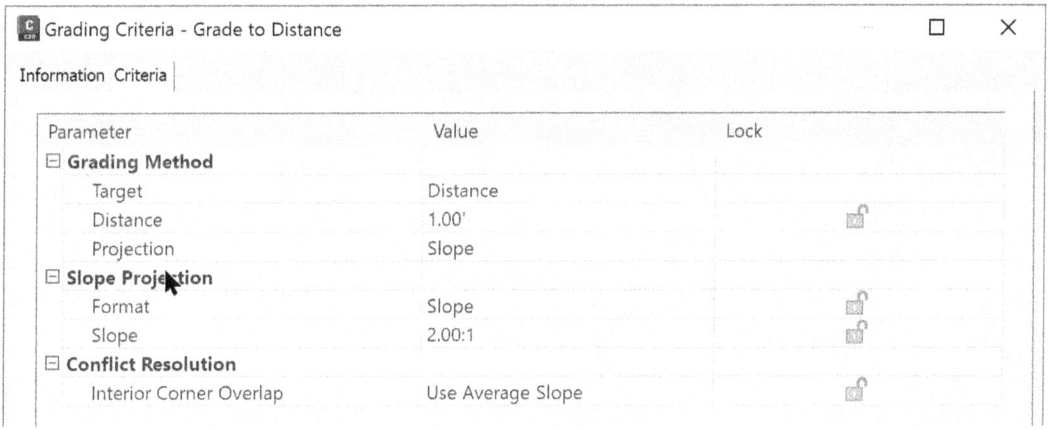

Parameter	Value	Lock
⊟ **Grading Method**		
Target	Distance	
Distance	1.00'	🔓
Projection	Slope	
⊟ **Slope Projection**		
Format	Slope	🔓
Slope	2.00:1	🔓
⊟ **Conflict Resolution**		
Interior Corner Overlap	Use Average Slope	🔓

Grading Criteria - Grade to Distance — Information / Criteria

Figure 1–29

Grade to Elevation

When you need to keep a specific grade or slope to an absolute elevation, you need to use the **Grade to Elevation** criteria (as shown in Figure 1–30) to set the target to be a specific elevation. You can then decide which slope or grade to use for the fill slopes separate from the cut slopes. This is useful in pond grading since the top of the pond needs to be level.

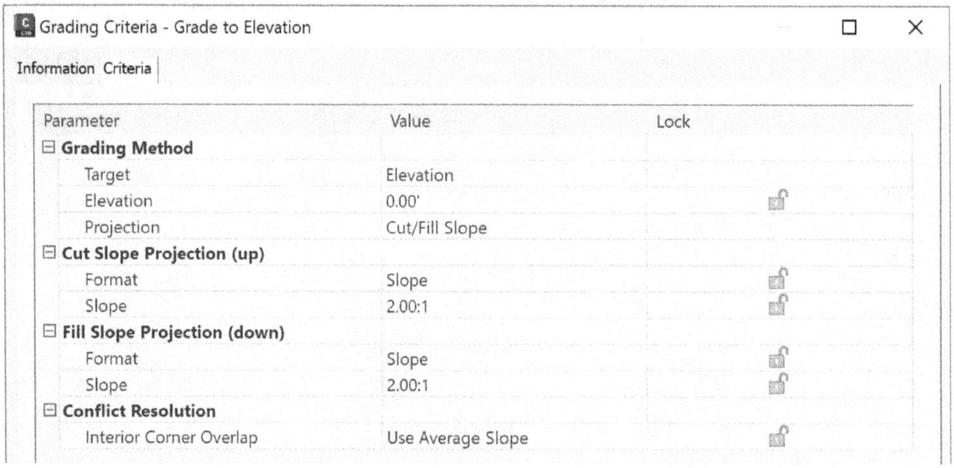

Figure 1–30

Grade to Relative Elevation

Sometimes it is necessary to project a grade up or down a specific vertical distance. This strategy requires using the **Grade to Relative Elevation** criteria (as shown in Figure 1–31), which enables you to set the target to a specific vertical distance and the slope or grade for that relative elevation. You can then lock the relative elevation so that it cannot be changed.

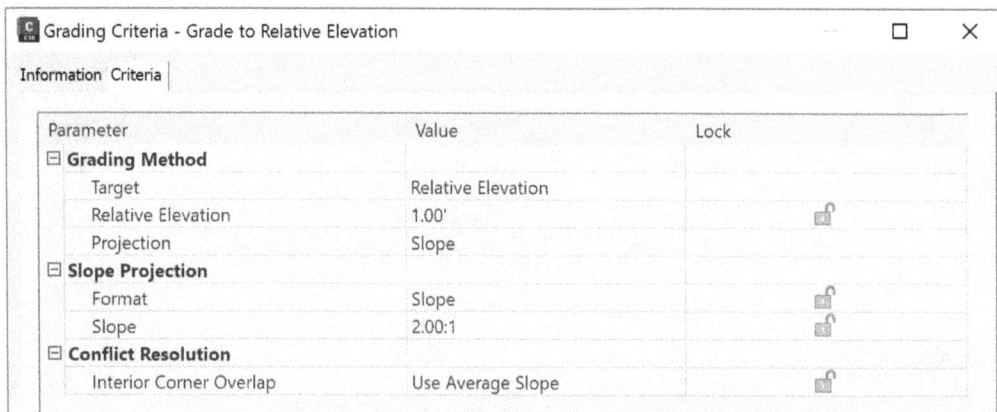

Figure 1–31

Grade to Surface

When you need to keep a specific slope until the projection finds daylight, you need to use the **Grade to Surface** criteria (as shown in Figure 1–32). It enables you to set the target to be a specific surface name. You can then decide which slope or grade to use for the separate fill and cut slope solutions. This criteria is typically used last to finish the grading solution.

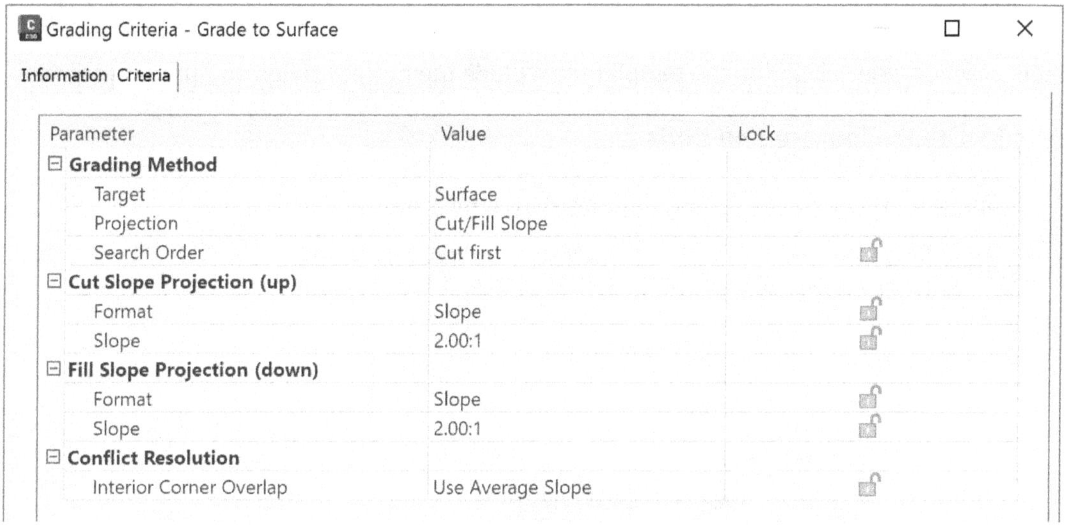

Figure 1–32

- When locking grading criteria parameters, note that once they are locked, they cannot be changed (not even during the editing process). If you change the design parameters, you might need to redefine the grading group rather than just edit it as you would if the grading criteria was not locked.

Practice 1b
Grading Styles

Practice Objective

- Create feature line styles, grading group styles, and a grading criteria set to be used in the project.

In this practice, you will add to the template to include the correct styles and grading criteria.

Task 1: Create feature line styles.

1. Continue working in the drawing template from the previous practice.
2. In the *Settings* tab, expand *General tree>Multipurpose Styles*, then right-click on **Feature Line Styles** and select **New**, as shown in Figure 1–33.

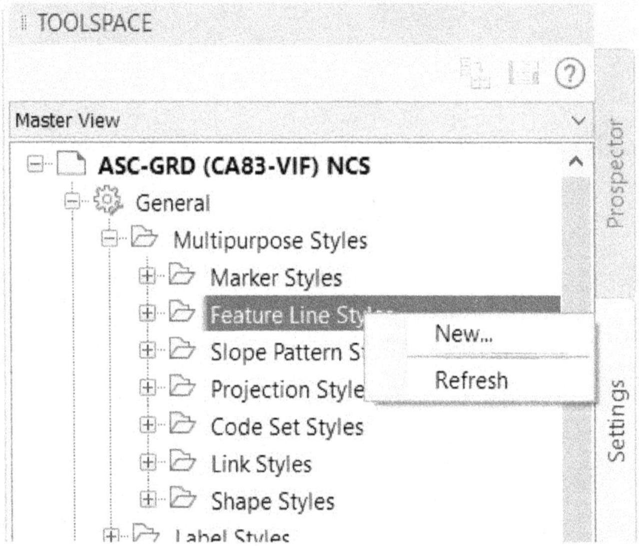

Figure 1–33

3. In the *Information* tab, for the *Name*, type **ASC-Parking Lot**. For the *Description*, type **Parking lot foot print**.

4. In the *Profile* tab, set each of the *Vertex Marker Styles* to **_No Markers**, as shown in Figure 1–34.

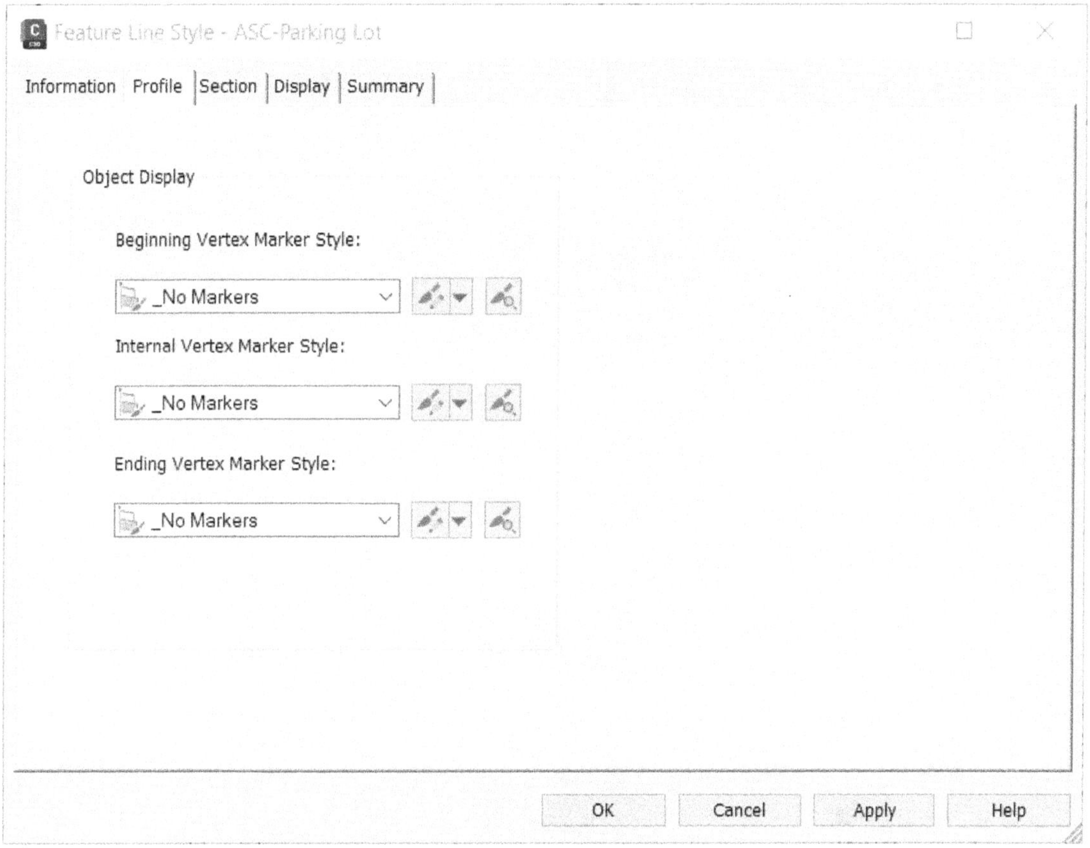

Figure 1–34

5. In the *Section* tab, set the *Crossing Marker Style* to **_No Markers**, as shown in Figure 1–35.

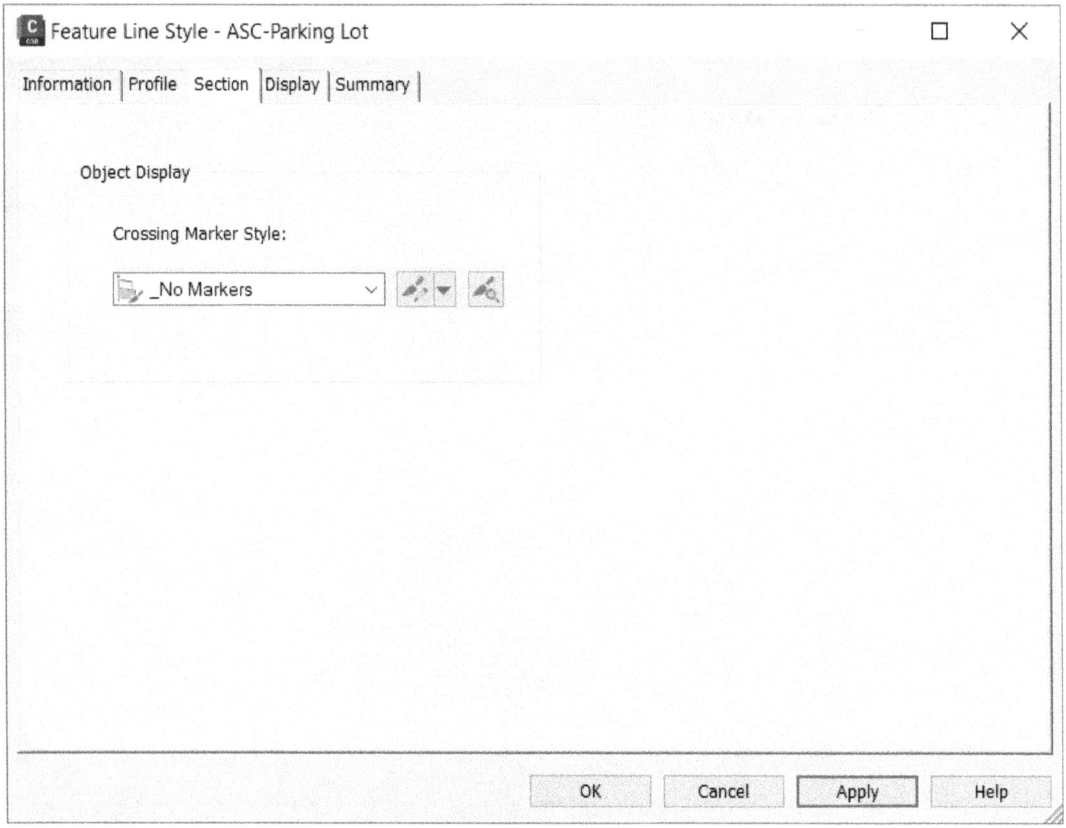

Figure 1–35

6. In the *Display* tab, select the Layer **0** to the right of the *Feature Line* component. In the *Layer Selection* dialog box, click the **New** button as shown in Figure 1–36.

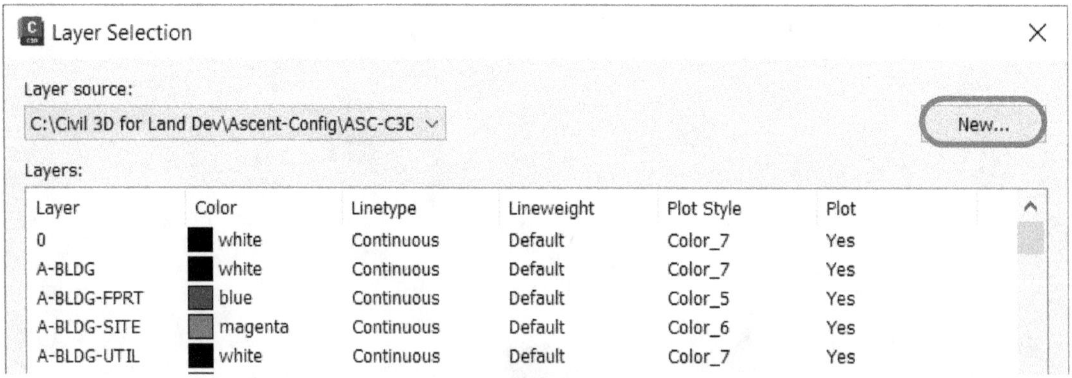

Figure 1–36

7. For the *Layer name*, type **C-GRAD-PARK** and set the *Color* to **40**, as shown in Figure 1–37. Click **OK** three times to close all of the dialog boxes.

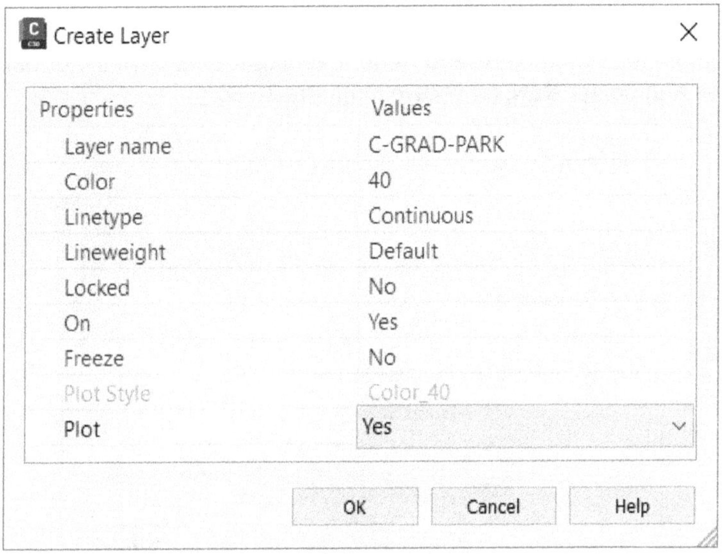
Create Layer
Properties
Values
Layer name
C-GRAD-PARK
Color
40
Linetype
Continuous
Lineweight
Default
Locked
No
On
Yes
Freeze
No
Plot Style
Color_40
Plot
Yes
OK
Cancel
Help

Figure 1–37

8. Repeat Steps 2 to 7 to create additional feature lines for the design objects listed in the following table. Keep the same settings unless otherwise noted.

Feature Line Style Name	Layer Name	Color
ASC-Building Pad	C-GRAD-BLDG	Blue (5)
ASC-Pond	C-GRAD-POND	Yellow (2)
ASC-Lagoon	C-GRAD-LGON	Green (3)

9. Save the drawing template.

Task 2: Create grading group styles.

1. Continue working in the drawing template from the previous task.

2. In the *Toolspace>Settings* tab, expand *General>Multipurpose Styles*, right-click on **Slope Pattern Styles** and select **New**, as shown in Figure 1–38.

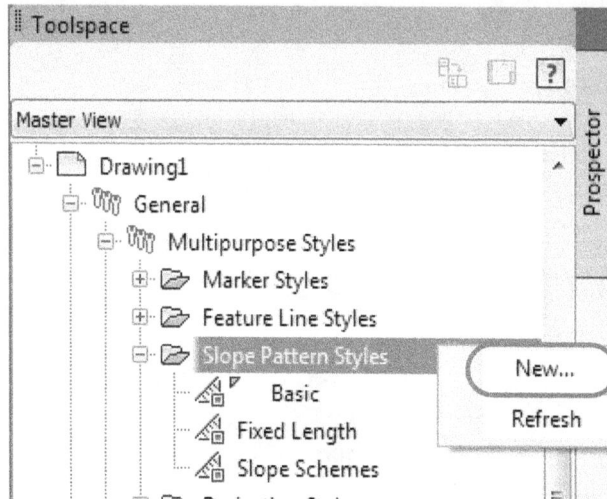

Figure 1–38

3. In the *Information* tab, type **ASC-Easy Viewing** for the name.

4. In the *Layout* tab, for Component 1, in the *Slope Line Symbol* area, set the following:

    *   *Symbol Type*: **Triangle**
    *   *Percent of Length*: **10%**

5. Set the *Component* to **Component 2**, as shown in Figure 1–39.

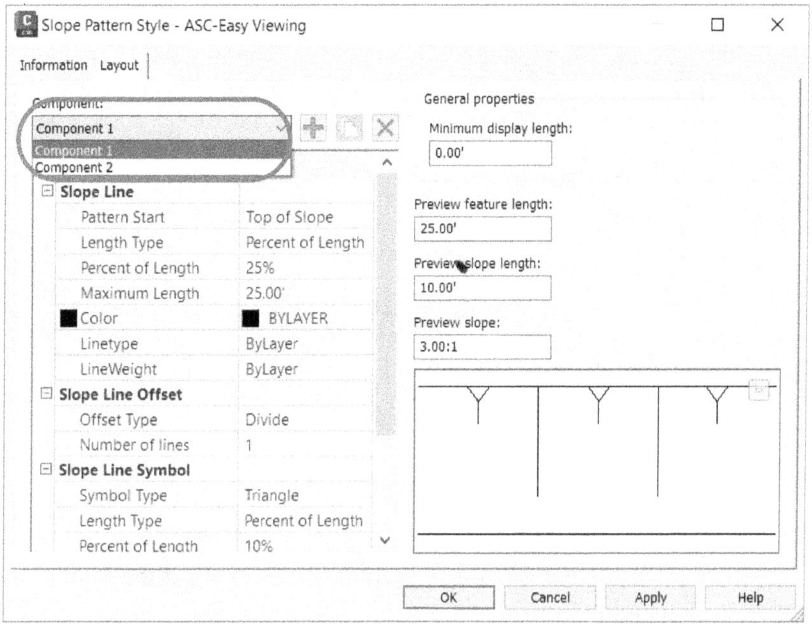

Figure 1-39

6. For Component 2, in the *Slope Line* area, set the *Percent of Length* to **75%**, as shown in Figure 1-40. This will ensure that the slope lines are not mistaken for projection lines.

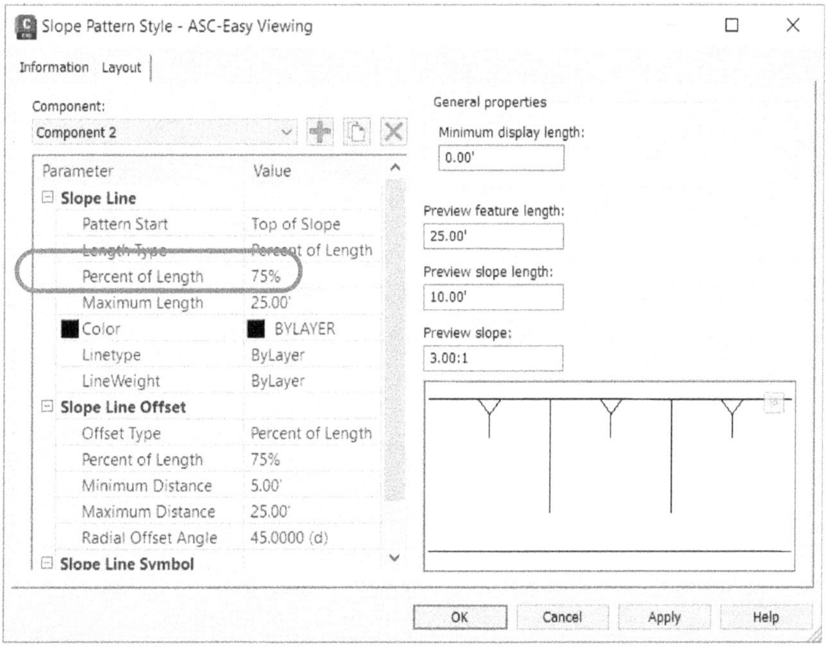

Figure 1-40

7. Click **OK**.

8. In the *Settings* tab, expand *Grading*, then right-click on **Grading Style**s and select **New**, as shown in Figure 1–41.

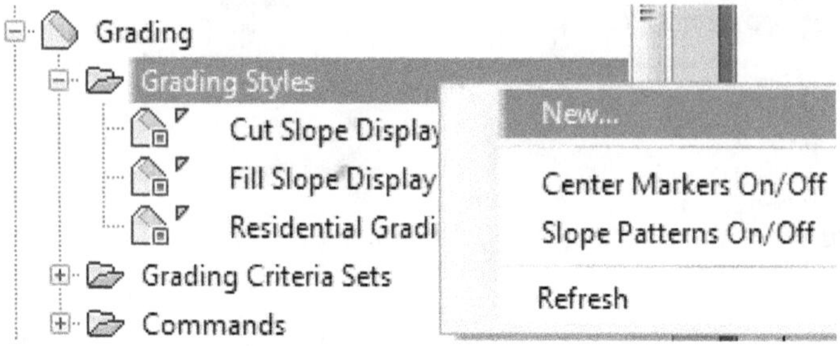

Figure 1–41

9. In the *Information* tab, type **ASC-Pond Grading Display**.

10. In the *Center Marker* tab, type **5** for the *Percentage of Screen* size.

11. In the *Slope Patterns* tab, select the **Slope pattern** option and set the *Style* to **ASC-Easy Viewing**, as shown in Figure 1–42.

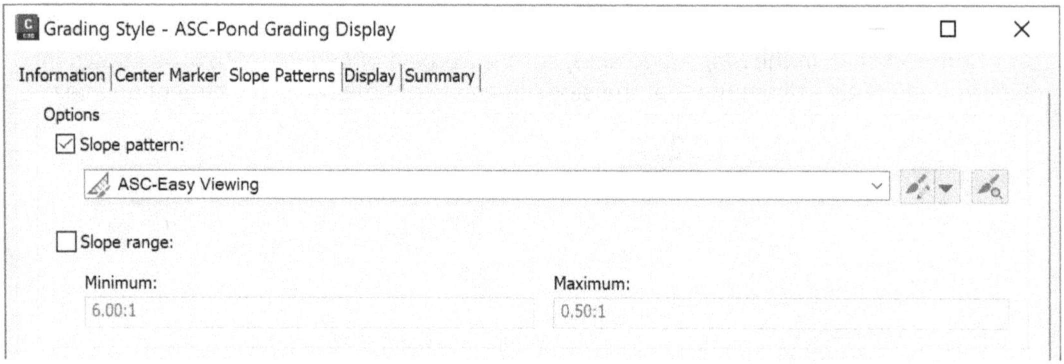

Figure 1–42

12. In the *Display* tab, select all of the components using <Shift>, and then select a **0** (zero) in the *Layer* column. In the *Layer Selection* dialog box, click the **New** button. For the *Layer name*, type **C-GRAD-NPLT** and set *Plot* to **No**, as shown in Figure 1–43.

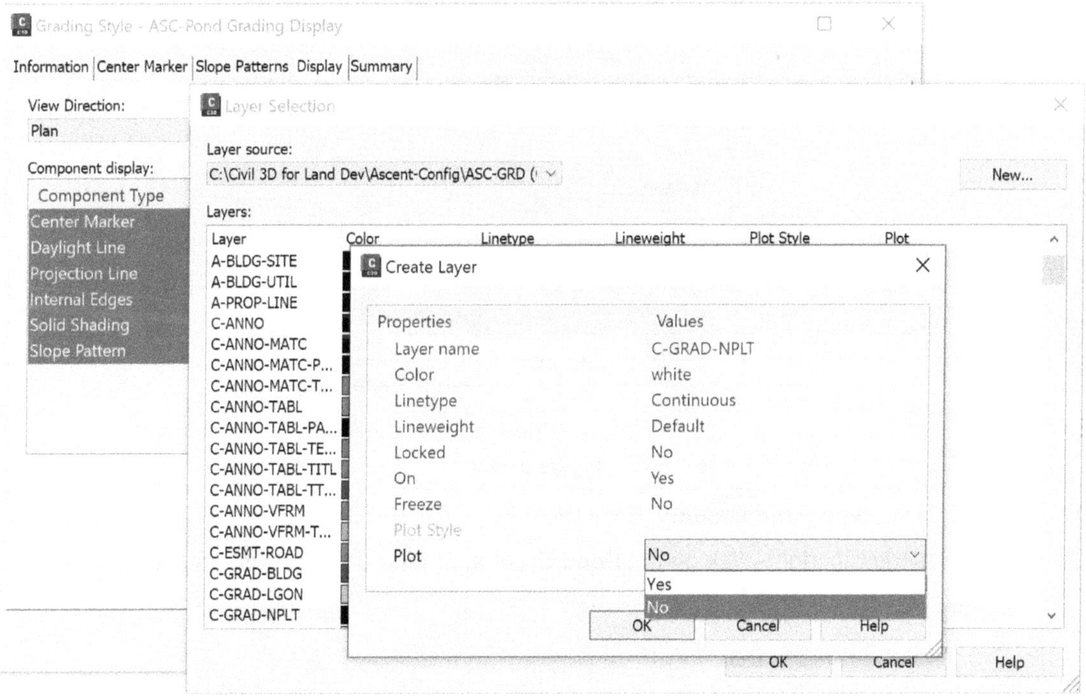

Figure 1–43

13. Click **OK** three times to close all of the dialog boxes.

14. Save the drawing template.

Task 3: Create grading criteria sets.

1. Continue working in the drawing template from the previous task.

2. In the *Settings* tab, expand *Grading>Grading Criteria Sets>Basic Set*.

    - Note that it includes the criteria for each type of projection that can be created in the Autodesk Civil 3D software. When this set is used, the designer can select which slope/grades to use and the distance to which to grade. For *Pond Grading*, you will want more control of the slopes to ensure that the correct specifications are used.

3. Right-click on **Grading Criteria Sets** and select **New**, as shown in Figure 1–44.

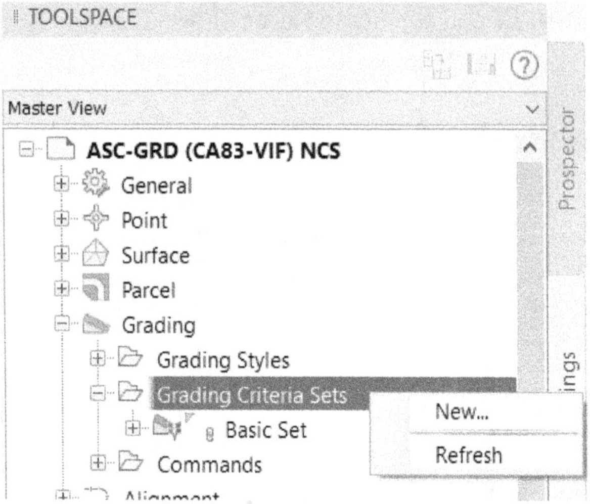

Figure 1–44

4. For the *Name*, type **Pond Grading**. Click **OK**.

5. In the *Settings* tab, right-click on the **Pond Grading** criteria that you just created and select **New**, as shown in Figure 1–45.

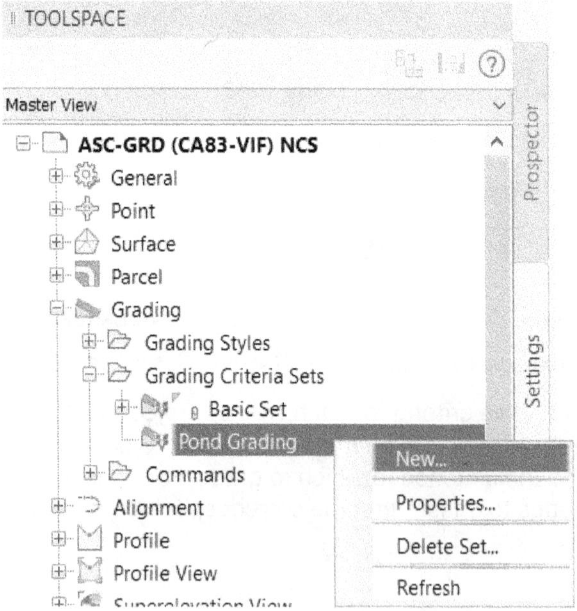

Figure 1–45

6. In the *Information* tab, for the *Name*, type **Interior**.

   Note: You might have to save the drawing for the new criteria to be displayed.

7. In the *Criteria* tab, complete the following, as shown in Figure 1–46:

   • Set *Target* to **Elevation**.

   • For *Elevation*, type **160**.

   • For both Cut Slope and Fill Slope Projections, set *Format* to **Slope**.

   • For both Cut Slope and Fill Slope Projections, set *Slope* to **3**.

   • Select each **Lock** icon to lock each parameter and ensure that it cannot be changed when used in a grading.

   • Click **OK**.

Parameter	Value	Lock
⊟ **Grading Method**		
Target	Elevation	
Elevation	160.00'	🔒
Projection	Cut/Fill Slope	
⊟ **Cut Slope Projection (up)**		
Format	Slope	🔒
Slope	3.00:1	🔒
⊟ **Fill Slope Projection (down)**		
Format	Slope	🔒
Slope	3.00:1	🔒
⊟ **Conflict Resolution**		
Interior Corner Overlap	Use Average Slope	🔒

Grading Criteria - Interior

Information Criteria

Figure 1–46

8. Repeat Steps 5 to 7 to create the following grading criteria. Keep the same settings unless otherwise noted in the following table and shown in Figure 1–47.

Grading Criteria Name	Grading Method	Slop Projection	Lock
Rim	Distance, 6', Slope	Grade, 2%	Yes
Outer Slope to Surface	Surface, Cut/Fill Slope, Cut first	Slope, 3:1 cut, 3:1 fill	Yes

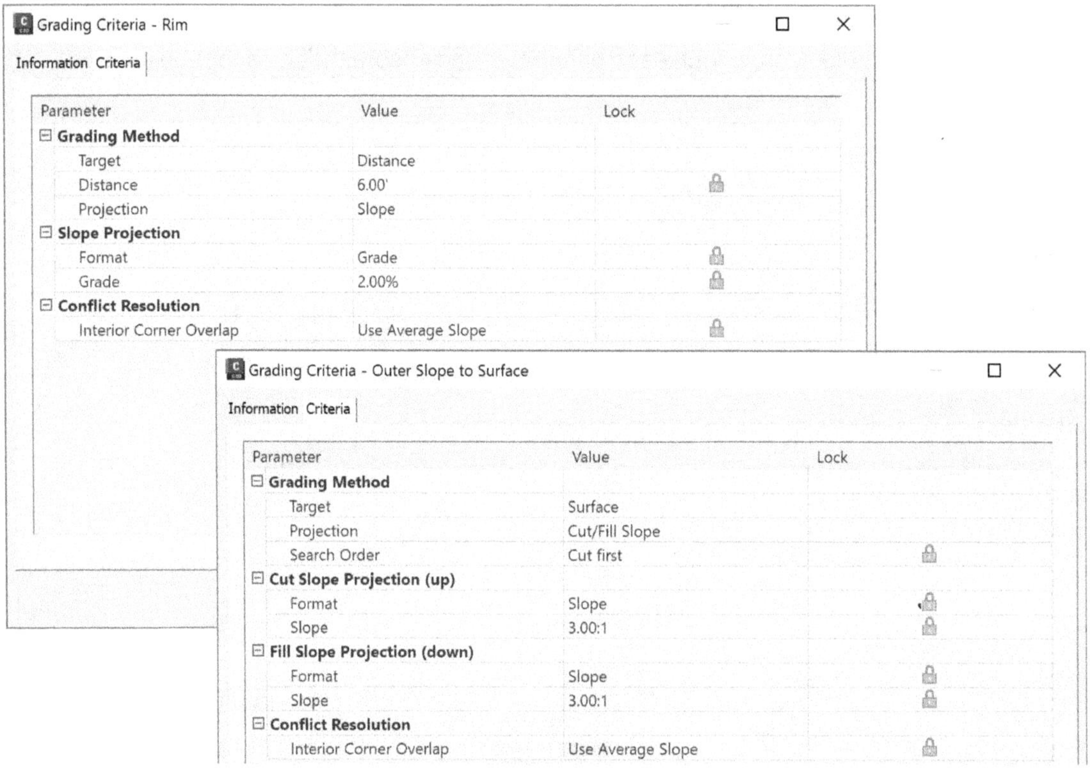

Figure 1–47

9. Save the drawing template.

End of practice

1.7 Surface Styles

The Surface Civil 3D (AEC) object is a complex object composed of irregular (TIN) or regular (DEM) triangles, as shown in Figure 1–48. Such an object contains valuable data pertinent to design and decisions making.

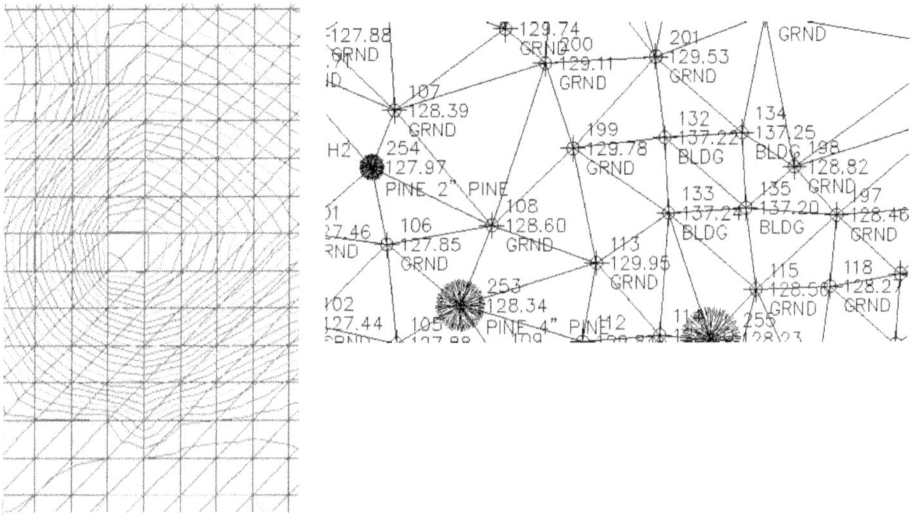

Figure 1–48

Such data can be displayed through *Surface Styles*. In the *Surface Style* dialog box, the *Display* tab enables you to toggle on or off triangles, borders, contours, and other items, as well as define the layer, color, linetype, etc. that are assigned, as shown in Figure 1–49.

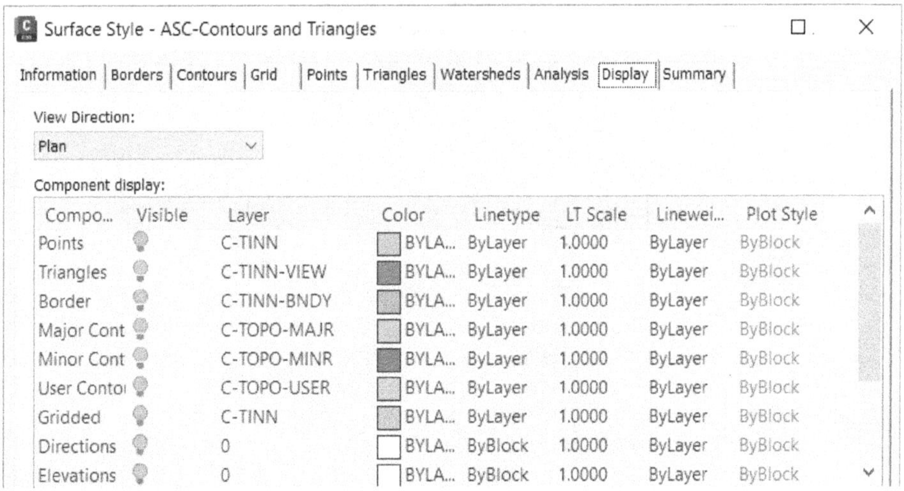

Figure 1–49

The *Contours* tab sets the contour interval, smoothing, and other settings, as shown in Figure 1–50.

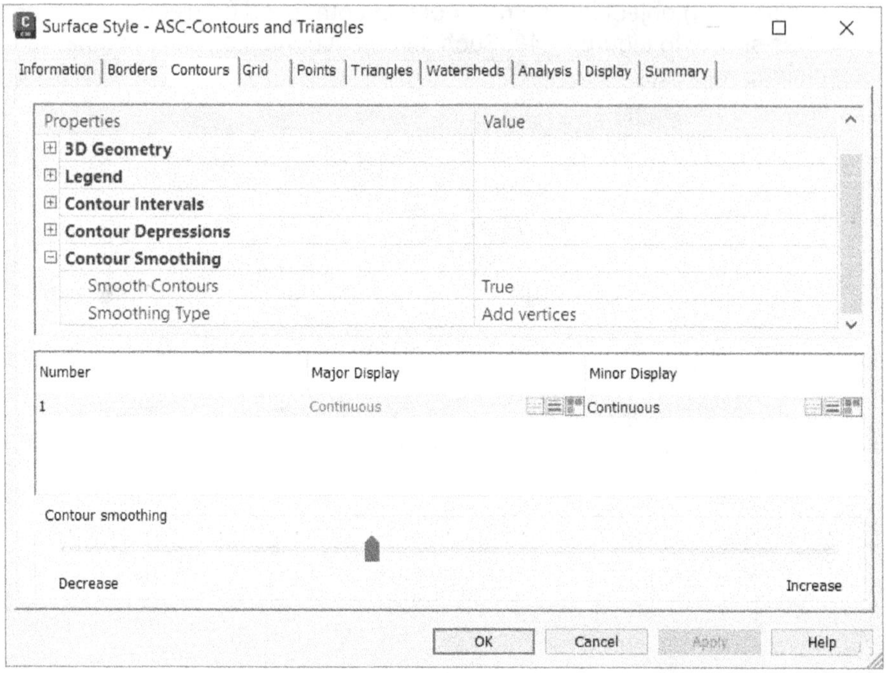

Figure 1–50

The *Display* tab controls the layers that the different components of the surface reside on, including **Slopes, Slope Arrows** and **Watersheds**, etc. as shown in Figure 1–51.

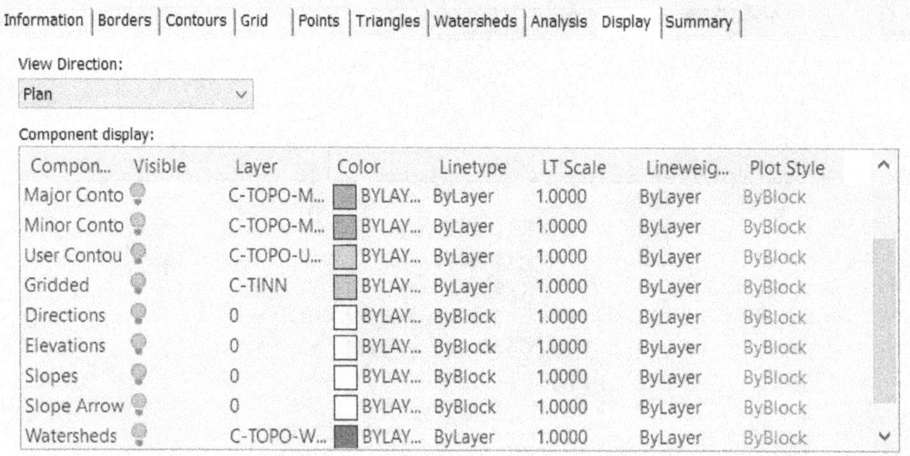

Figure 1–51

1.8 Sites Overview

In the Autodesk Civil 3D software, sites are used as a collection point for common topologies that share relationships with each other. When an alignment and a parcel reside in the same site, they interact with each other. An alignment that resides in the same site as a parcel subdivides the parcel. Grading groups and feature lines also reside in sites and interact with each other when they share the same site. Each drawing can have multiple sites for various purposes, as shown in Figure 1–52.

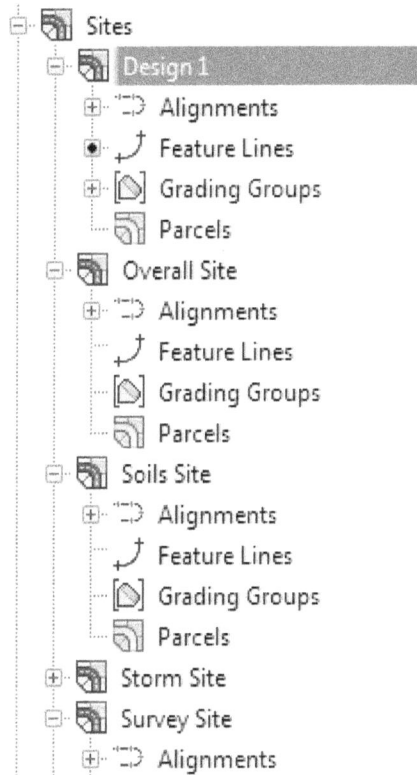

Figure 1–52

Sites for Design Options

It is recommended that you always start your project with an overall site in which you place all of the existing parcel linework. Then before adding alignments, feature lines, and grading groups to your design, you can create another site, label it **Design option 1**, and copy the parcels with which you are going to be working into that site, as shown in Figure 1–53.

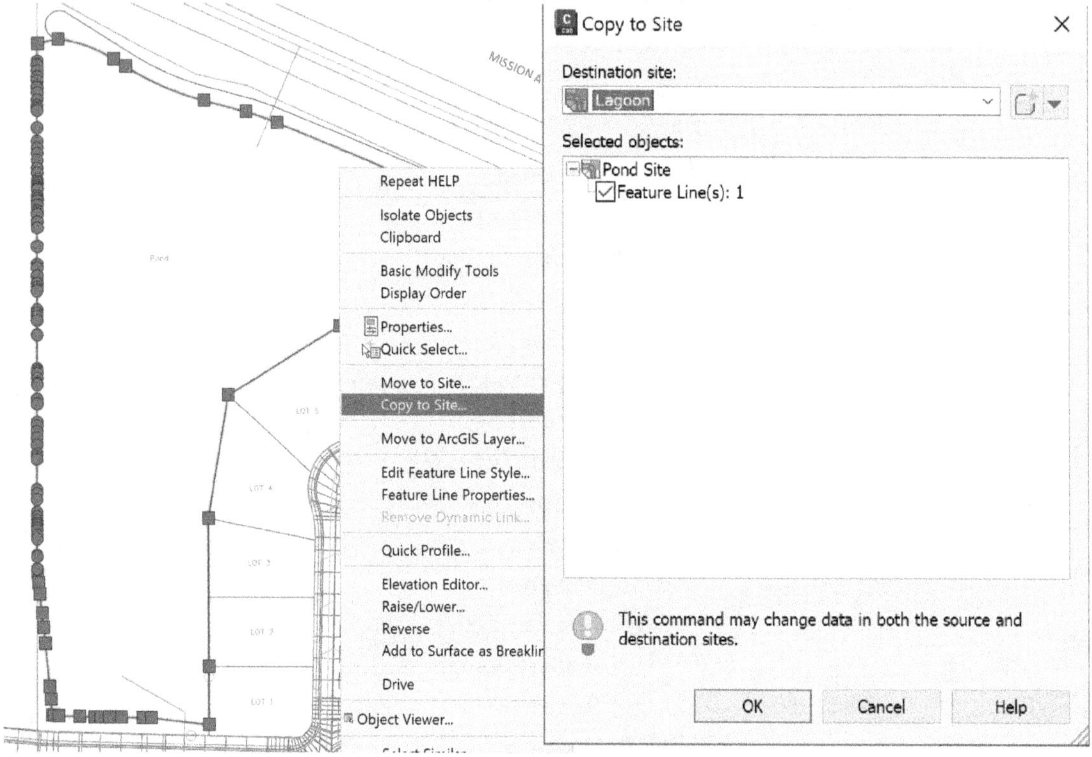

Figure 1–53

This enables you to provide more options to your clients without having many file versions in multiple drawings on a server. Once a client decides which design option to pursue, the other sites can easily be deleted, removing all of the design components within it at the same time, as shown in Figure 1–54.

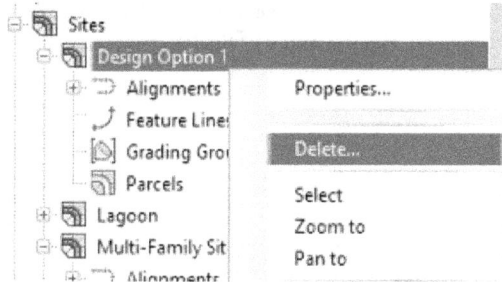

Figure 1–54

Creating Sites

To create a new site, select the *Prospector* tab in the *Toolspace*, right-click on *Sites* and select **New**. In the *Information* tab, type a name that is relevant to the entire team. In the *3D Geometry* tab, set the *Site Display Mode*, as shown in Figure 1–55.

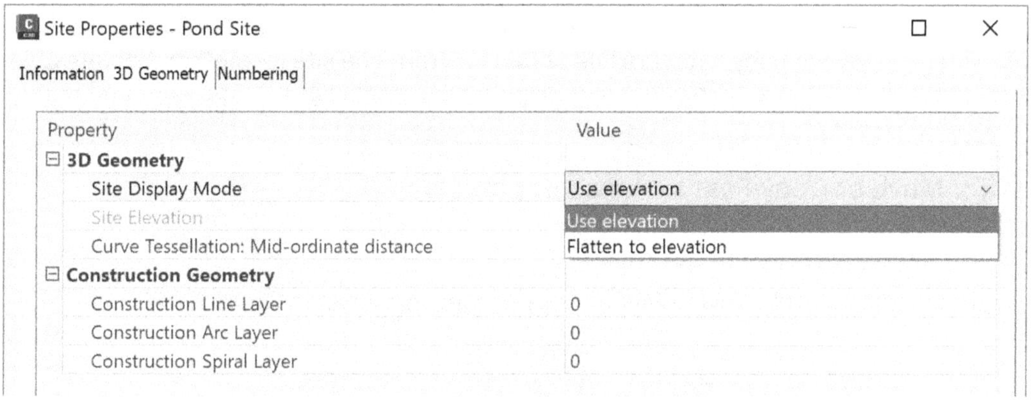

Figure 1–55

- It is recommended that you leave the default option as **Use elevation** so that the site's linework displays at its actual elevations, making it easier to view design intent from any direction in the Object Viewer or Model Viewer.

  Note: If you do not take the time to create the project site(s) before starting to create feature lines, parcels, or grading groups, a default site is created automatically, called Site 1. By default, alignments are placed in the alignments tree rather than in a specific site.

- The optional **Flatten to elevation** option causes all of the site's linework to become 2D and to be located at the elevation that you set.

- In the *3D Geometry* tab, you can also set the layers on which the construction geometry is to be located.

The *Numbering* tab enables you to set the Automatic number for parcels and the counting interval to use for the next number, as shown in Figure 1–56.

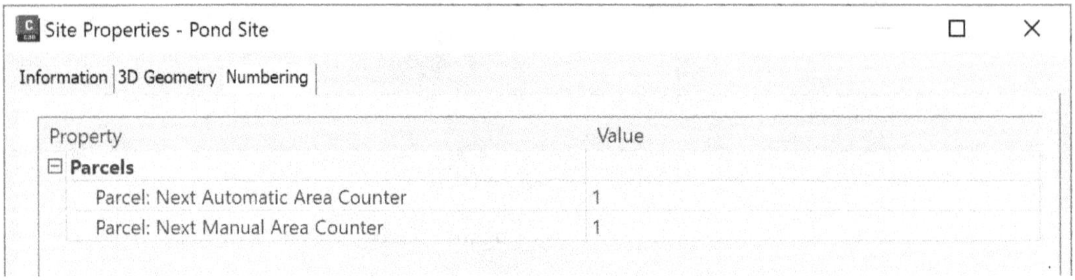

Figure 1–56

Copy or Move Objects from One Site to Another

Feature lines and parcels must reside in a site to be created and used. If you use feature lines for grading, it is important that they reside in the same site as their grading group. Sometimes feature lines or parcels are created in the wrong site or need to be reused in other sites. In such cases, you can move or copy a feature line or parcels from one site to another. You are able to copy or move the contents of an entire site (alignments, grading groups, parcels, and feature lines) to another site.

How To: Move or Copy Feature Lines or parcels

1. Select the object(s) to move or copy.

2. Right-click and select **Move to Site** or **Copy to Site**, as shown in Figure 1–57.

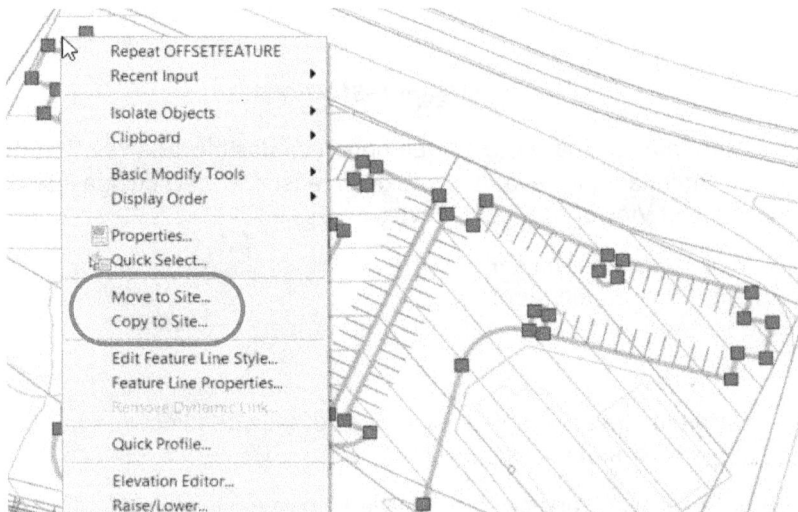

Figure 1–57

- Another option is to select **Move to Site** or **Copy to Site** on the *Feature Line* or *Parcels* contextual tab>*Modify* panel, as shown in Figure 1–58.

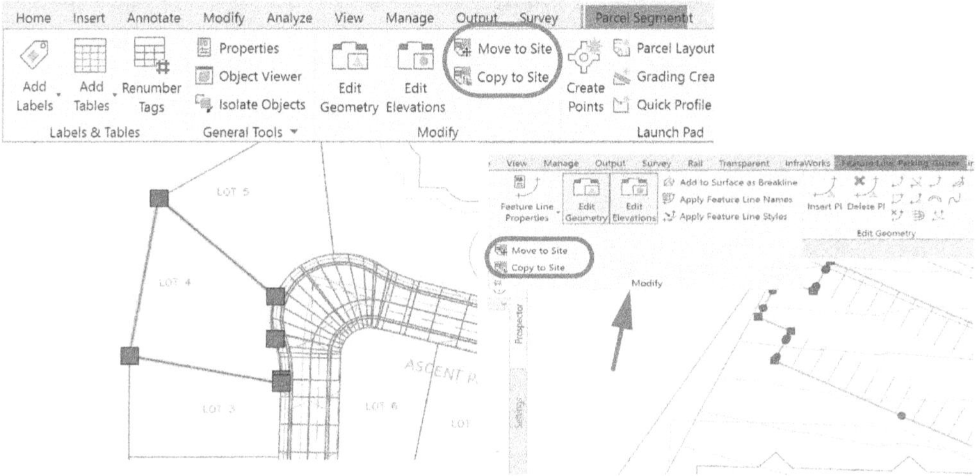

Figure 1–58

3. In the dialog box, select an option for the *Destination site*, as shown in Figure 1–59.

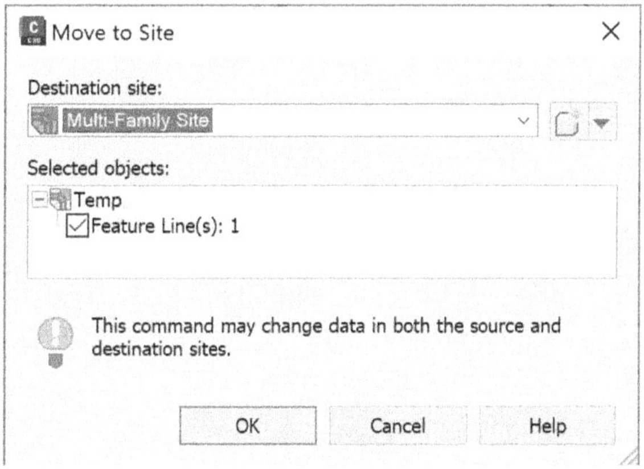

Figure 1–59

Civil 3D appends the name with a (1) (or the next available number) so as to ensure that the feature line name remains unique. This is true of moving or copying the features line to another site.

> *Note: Copying the parcels and placing them in a new site causes them to lose any interaction they have with other objects, such as feature lines, alignments, or grading groups. To ensure that you are working with the correct site's parcels when adding elevations and making other edits, it is recommended that you create a style that turns off the display of parcel segments, and set the parcels in the unrequired sites (i.e., sites that you are not currently working with) to that style.*

Practice 1c
Prepare for the Project

Practice Objective

- Create a surface style and sites in preparation for the grading project.

In this practice, you will add a surface style to the template to make it easier to display the site grading. You will also create some sites to give multiple design options to the client.

Task 1: Create a surface style.

1. Continue working in the drawing template from the previous practice.

2. In the *Settings* tab, expand **Surfaces>Surface Styles**. Right-click on **Contours 2' and 10' (Design)** and select **Copy**, as shown in Figure 1–60.

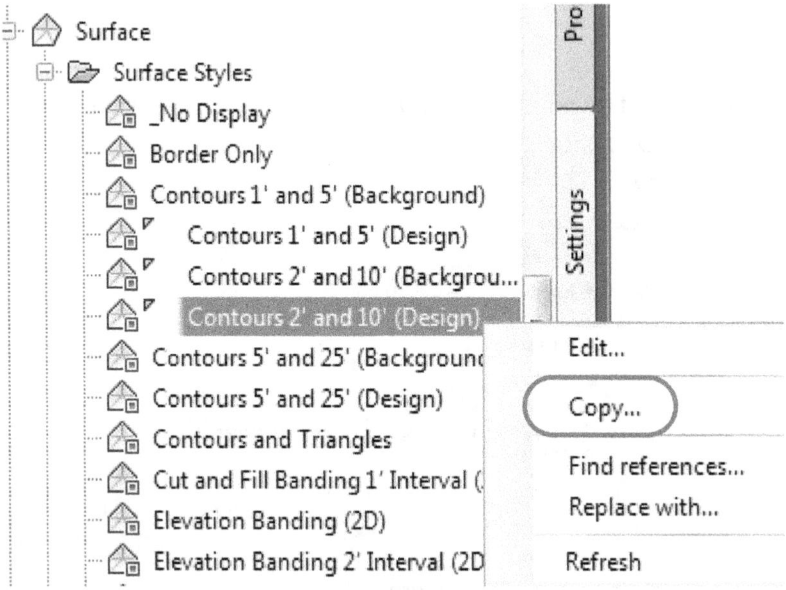

Figure 1–60

3. In the *Information* tab, type **ASC-Temporary Grading View**.

4. In the *Display* tab, turn on the layers **Slope Arrows** and **Watersheds**, as shown in Figure 1–61.

| Information | Borders | Contours | Grid | Points | Triangles | Watersheds | Analysis | Display | Summary |

View Direction:

| Plan | ∨ |

Component display:

Compon...	Visible	Layer	Color	Linetype	LT Scale	Lineweig...	Plot Style
Major Conto	◉	C-TOPO-M...	▨ BYLAY...	ByLayer	1.0000	ByLayer	ByBlock
Minor Conto	◉	C-TOPO-M...	▨ BYLAY...	ByLayer	1.0000	ByLayer	ByBlock
User Contou	◉	C-TOPO-U...	▨ BYLAY...	ByLayer	1.0000	ByLayer	ByBlock
Gridded	◉	C-TINN	▨ BYLAY...	ByLayer	1.0000	ByLayer	ByBlock
Directions	◉	0	□ BYLAY...	ByBlock	1.0000	ByLayer	ByBlock
Elevations	◉	0	□ BYLAY...	ByBlock	1.0000	ByLayer	ByBlock
Slopes	◉	0	□ BYLAY...	ByBlock	1.0000	ByLayer	ByBlock
Slope Arrow	◉	0	□ BYLAY...	ByBlock	1.0000	ByLayer	ByBlock
Watersheds	◉	C-TOPO-W...	▨ BYLAY...	ByLayer	1.0000	ByLayer	ByBlock

Figure 1–61

5. In the *Watersheds* tab, expand 3D Geometry. Verify that *Watershed Display Mode* is set to **Use Surface Elevation**, as shown in Figure 1–62.

| Information | Borders | Contours | Grid | Points | Triangles | Watersheds | Analysis | Display | Summary |

Watershed properties	Value
⊟ **3D Geometry**	
Watershed Display Mode	Use Surface Elevation
Flatten Watersheds to Elevation	0.00'
Exaggerate Watersheds by Scale Factor	0.000
⊞ **Point Size**	
⊞ **Surface**	

Figure 1–62

6. Click **OK** to close the dialog box.

7. Save the drawing template.

Task 2: Create sites.

1. In the *Prospector* tab, right-click on **Sites** and select **New**.
2. In the *Information* tab, for the *Name*, type **Multi-Family**. For the description, type **Parcels, building pads, and parking lots for multi-family property**.
3. Click **OK** to close the dialog box and accept the defaults on the other tabs.
4. Repeat Steps 1 to 3 to create the following sites. Keep the same settings unless otherwise noted in the following table.

Site Name	Description
Pond Site	Storm water retention pond
Lagoon	Lagoon and wetland grading
Residential Grading	Single family lot grading

5. Save the drawing template.

End of practice

Chapter Review Questions

1. What geometric shape is the Center Mark of a grading object?

   a. Diamond

   b. Circle

   c. Triangle

   d. Rectangle

2. Figure 1−63 shows each of the parts of a grading object. Match the numbers with their corresponding names.

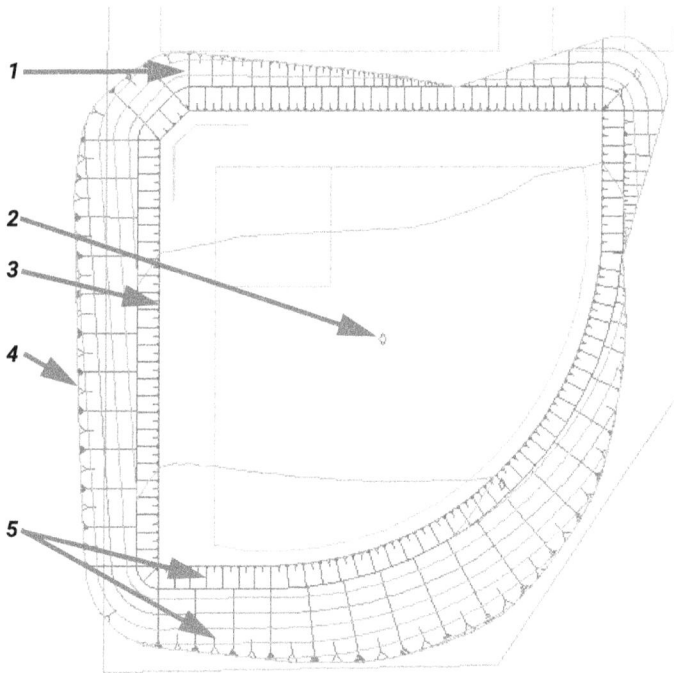

Figure 1−63

   a. Slope Pattern

   b. Center Mark (Infill)

   c. Target Line

   d. Projection Line

   e. Base Line

3. When you edit a grading group, which of the following objects are updated?

   a. Feature Lines, Alignments, and Surfaces.

   b. Points, Surfaces, and Corridors.

   c. Surfaces and Corridors.

   d. Assemblies, Profiles, and Feature Lines.

4. How can you have the software automatically use one style when creating a feature line from objects and a different style when creating a feature line from scratch?

   a. Set it in Drawing Settings, in the *Ambient Settings* tab.

   b. Set it in Command Settings.

   c. Set it in Drawing Settings, in the *Object Layers* tab.

   d. Set it in the grading group style.

5. If you create a grading criteria with locked parameters, you can still change the parameters during the editing process.

   a. True

   b. False

6. What are sites used for? (Select all that apply.)

   a. To group the collection of common topology that share relationships with each other.

   b. To provide different design options within the same project.

   c. To house the sample sections for a grading design.

   d. To set the settings and styles to use for grading projects.

Feature Lines

Feature lines play a key role in grading with Civil 3D. They are frequently used as the foundation for building grading models. Throughout this course, feature lines are often used as the starting point for grading in various practices.

Assigning elevations to feature lines speeds up the creation of a grading model and ground surfaces and streamlines the grading process. You will create and edit multiple feature lines using different methods for later practices in this course.

Learning Objectives

- List the five ways in which feature lines can be created.
- Creating a Feature Line for parking lots.
- Creating a Feature Line from objects in an XREF for building pads.
- Creating a Feature Line from surface and design elevations for a pond.
- Drawing a Feature Line.
- Editing Feature Line geometry.
- Editing Feature Line elevations.

2.1 Feature Lines

Feature lines can be thought of as folds or creases in a surface. Curb and crown lines, tops and toes of slope, streams and brooks, etc. can all be represented by feature lines.

Feature lines are complex, linear 3D objects that define a string of known elevations. Feature lines can be created by converting AutoCAD® lines, arcs, or polylines. Feature lines can also be extracted from Corridors. Site properties enable you to assign elevations to lot lines or treat them as 2D representations of parcels. They can also be used to create temporary grading surfaces or delineate curbs for parking lots, or the outline of a pond.

The Autodesk® Civil 3D® software uses 3D polylines known as *Feature Lines* for grading footprints, corridor modeling, and surface breaklines. A feature line can represent a building footprint, parking lot perimeter, swale, or ridgeline. The benefit of using a feature line over an AutoCAD 3D polyline is its ease of editing and its ability to support arcs without tessellation. Tessellated curves are undesirable in grading because of their many small grading faces around radial corners.

To access commands for creating feature lines, select the *Home* tab>*Create Design* panel and select **Feature Line**, as shown in Figure 2–1.

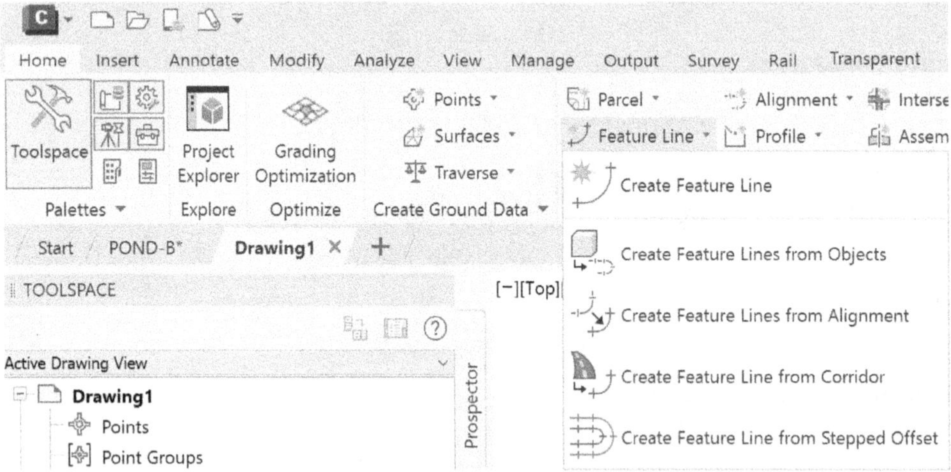

Figure 2–1

Feature lines can be created in five different ways:

1. Create Feature Line manually
2. Create Feature Lines from Objects
3. Create Feature Lines from Alignment
4. Create Feature Line from Corridor
5. Create Feature Line from Stepped Offset

2.2 Create Feature Lines

Like most other Civil 3D objects, feature lines can be created manually or from existing objects.including some Civil 3D objects such as alignments and corridor elements, as shown in Figure 2–2.

Figure 2–2

Create Feature Lines from objects

Designs often start out as 2D conceptual drawings to help determine where to locate design components. In these cases, you can easily convert existing 2D or 3D polylines, lines, or arcs into feature lines. During the conversion process, a name and style are assigned to the feature line along with elevations for each of the vertices. To edit the elevations of a feature line, you use the same tools used for editing parcel segment elevations.

How To: Create a Feature Line from Existing Objects

1. In the *Home* tab>*Create Design* panel, expand the *Feature Line* drop-down list, as shown in Figure 2–3.

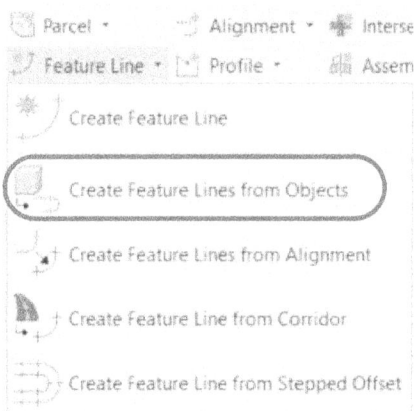

Figure 2–3

2. Select the arcs, lines, or polylines in the drawing to convert or type **X** and press <Enter> to select objects in an external reference file.

3. In the *Create Feature Lines* dialog box, set the **Site** to ensure that other feature lines, parcels, and grading groups interact with the new feature line. Type a name for the feature line. Set the *Style*, *Layer*, and *Conversion options*, as shown in Figure 2−4.

Figure 2−4

4. For *Conversion options*, if the **Assign elevations** option is selected, a dialog box opens for you to assign elevations to the vertices, as shown in Figure 2−5.

   • Select the **Elevation** option and type the required elevation value or set the vertex elevations to be assigned from other gradings or surfaces that exist in the drawing.

   • Select the **Insert intermediate grade break points** option to add more elevation points to the feature line, anywhere the line crosses a surface triangle.

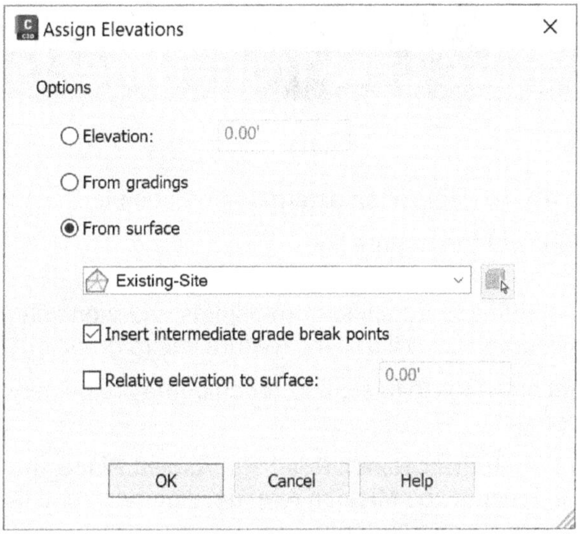

Figure 2–5

5. For *Conversion options*, if the **Weed Points** option is selected, a third dialog box opens, as shown in Figure 2–6.

- Set the minimum angle, grade, or length that is required between the elevation points. This causes any points closer than the set minimums to be removed.

- You can also set the minimum 3D distance between elevation points.

- At the bottom of the dialog box, an information line indicates how many vertices are going to be weeded out.

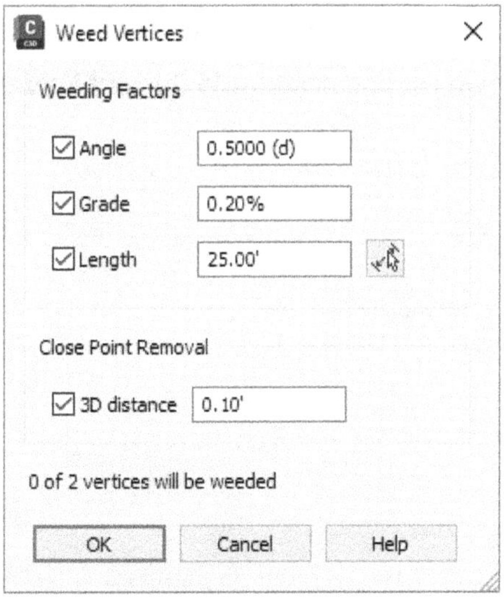

Figure 2–6

Practice 2a
Create a Feature Line from Objects in an XREF

Practice Objectives

- Create a feature line from objects in an external reference file.
- Modifying the elevations of the feature lines.

In this practice, you will create a feature line from objects and then edit the feature line elevations. Later in this course, you will use the feature line to grade out building pads.

For the land development drawings in this guide, much of the preliminary work has already been done for the site development.

The completed corridors for **Jeffries Ranch Road** and **Ascent Place**, the **Ascent Place knuckle** and **cul-de-sac target** alignments, the **Mission Avenue** alignment, and the **Existing-Site** surface have been referenced through *Data Shortcuts*.

A Residential Grading surface has been referenced as well; its surface style is set to **_No Display**. This surface will be created in the *Parcel Grading* chapter.

Task 1: Create a feature line from objects.

In this task, you will convert a drawing's polyline into a grading feature line. The feature line is the basis for the future grading object baseline. There are two building platforms to be converted, one for the office building, the other for the hotel.

1. In the *Start* screen, click **Open...**, or expand [C] (Application Menu) and select **Open**.
2. In the *Select File* dialog box, browse to the *C:\Civil 3D Grading\Working* folder.
3. Expand the *Tools* drop-down list and select **Add Current Folder to Places**, as shown in Figure 2–7.

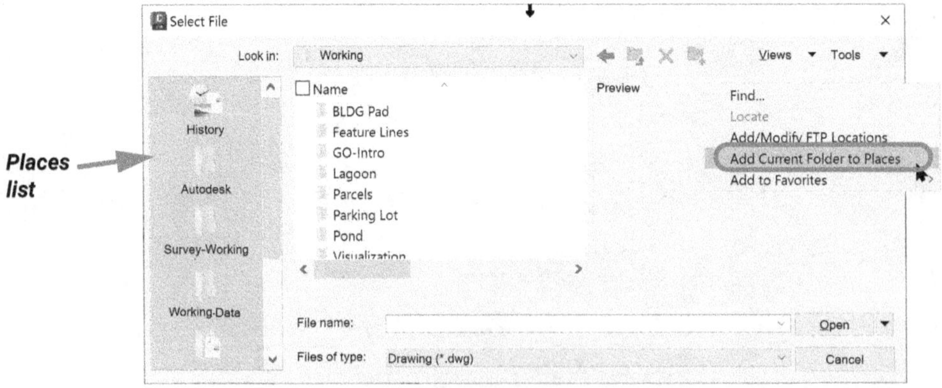

Figure 2–7

4. After you create the new entry into your *Places*, select the **Feature Lines** folder.

5. Open **BLDG-FL**.dwg.

6. Hover over *Data Shortcuts* and look at the tooltip that displays, as shown in Figure 2−8. Ensure that your **Data Shortcuts Working Folder** is set to *C:\Civil 3D Grading\Data Shortcuts\Fundamentals* and the **Data Shortcuts Project Folder** to *Ascent-Development*.

   • If not, right-click on Data Shortcuts to set the **Working Folder to** *C:\Civil 3D Grading\Data Shortcuts\Fundamentals* and the **Data Shortcuts Project Folder** to *Ascent-Development*.

Figure 2−8

7. In the *View* tab>*Named Views* panel, select **Office** as the view to zoom into the outline that represents the office building platform surrounding the office building, as shown in Figure 2−9.

Figure 2−9

8. In the *Home* tab>*Create Design* panel, expand the *Feature Line* drop-down list and select ⬛ (Create Feature Lines from Objects), as shown in Figure 2–10.

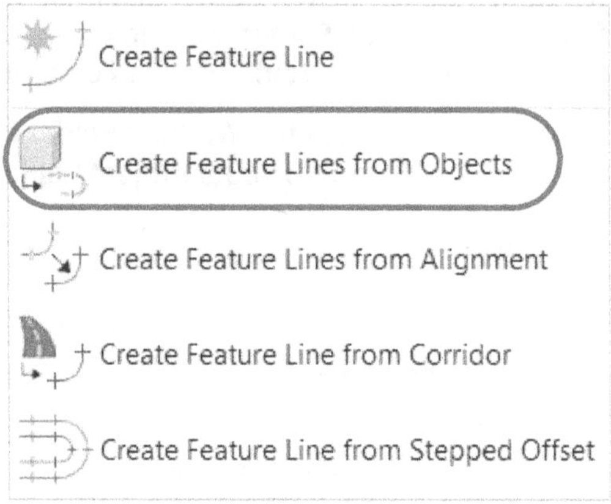

Figure 2–10

9. In the Command Line, select **Xref** to select linework from the XREF.

10. Select the cyan polyline, as shown in Figure 2–11. Press <Enter> to end the object selection process.

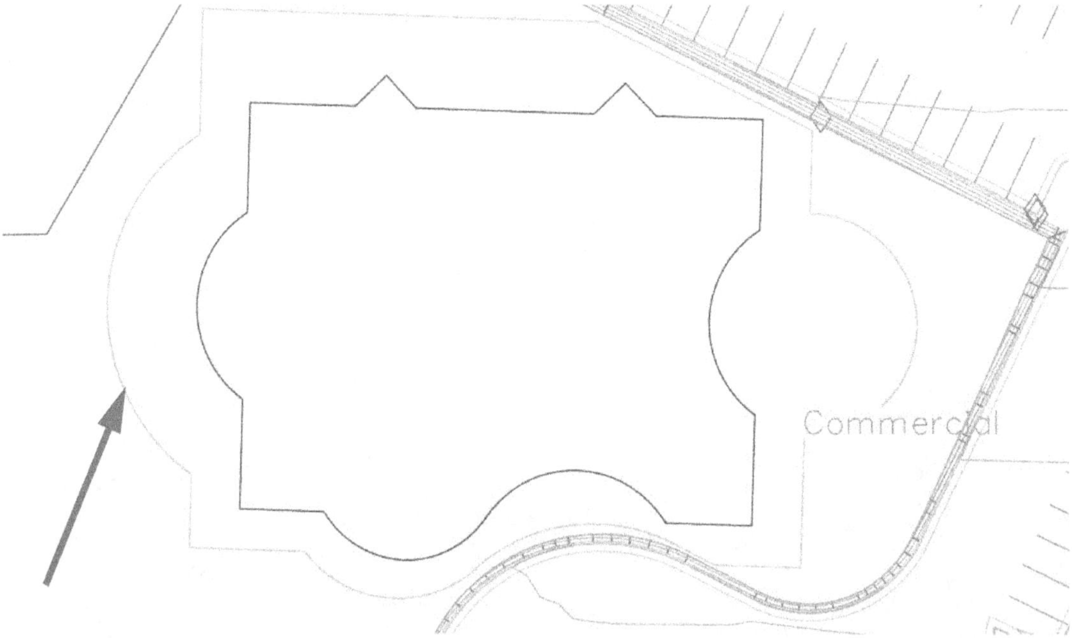

Figure 2–11

11. In the *Create Feature Lines* dialog box, complete the following, as shown in Figure 2–12:

- Set *Site* to **Multi-Family Site**.
- For *Name*, type **Office**.
- Set *Style* to **ASC_Building Pad.**
- Set *Conversion options* to **Assign elevations**.
- Click **OK** to close the dialog box.

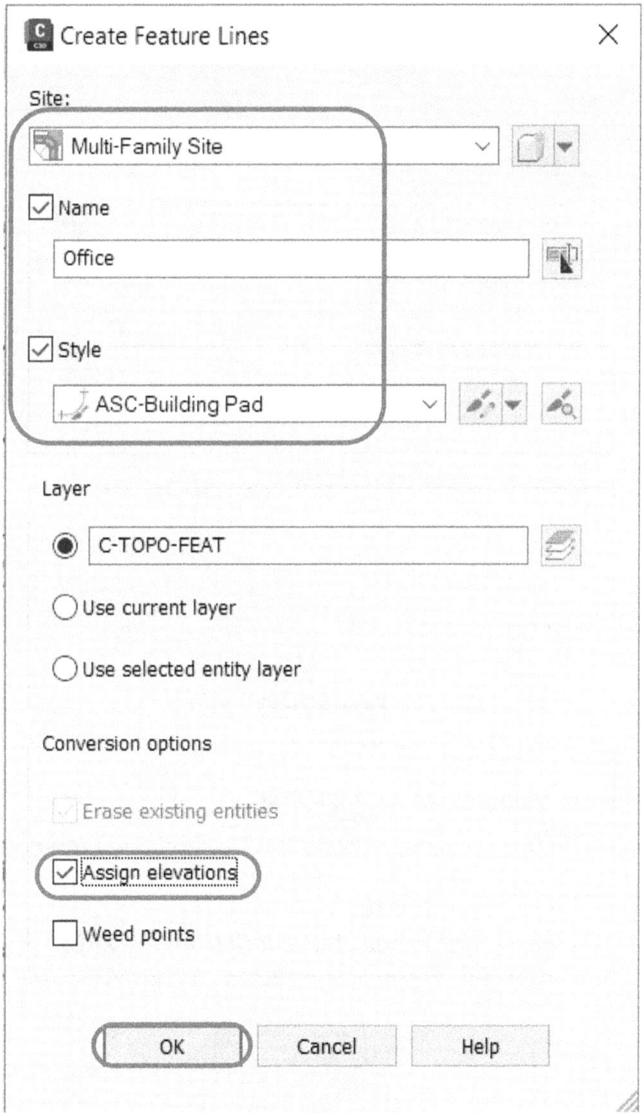

Figure 2–12

12. In the *Assign Elevations* dialog box, complete the following, as shown in Figure 2–13:

- Select **From Surface** for the surface.
- Select **Residential Grading**.
- Clear the **Insert intermediate grade break points** and **Relative elevation to surface** options.
- Click **OK** to close the dialog box.

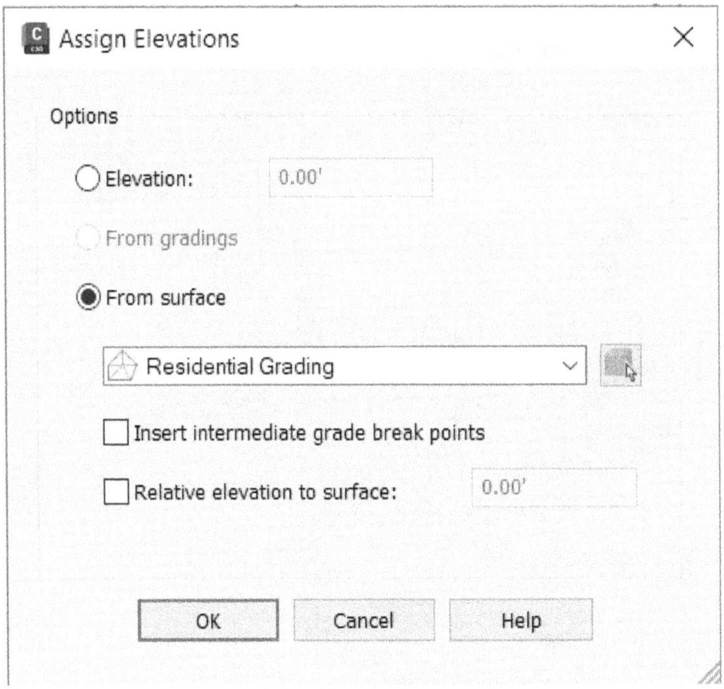

Figure 2–13

Repeat steps for the hotel, as follows:

13. In the *View* tab>*Named Views* panel, select **Hotel**.

14. In the *Home* tab>*Create Design* panel, expand the *Feature Line* drop-down list and select (Create Feature Lines from Objects).

15. In the Command Line, select **Xref** to select linework from the XREF.

16. Select the cyan polyline representing the pad for the hotel and pool, as shown in Figure 2-14. Press <Enter> to end the object selection process.

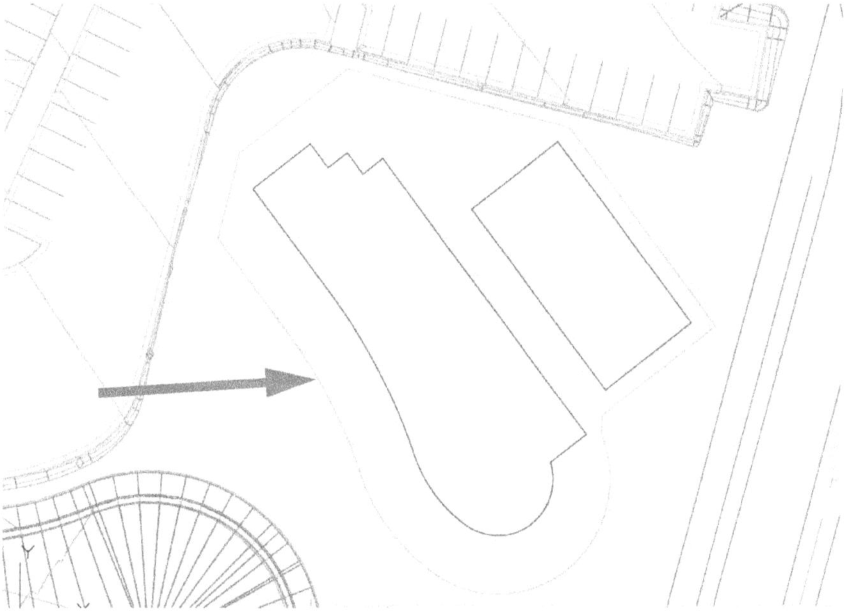

Figure 2-14

17. In the *Create Feature Lines* dialog box, complete the following:

    • Set *Site* to **Multi-Family Site**.

    • For *Name*, type **Hotel**.

    • Set *Style* to **ASC_Building Pad.**

    • Set *Conversion options* to **Assign elevations**.

    • Click **OK** to close the dialog box.

18. In the *Assign Elevations* dialog box, complete the following:

    • Select **From Surface** for the surface.

    • Select **Residential Grading.**

    • Clear the **Insert intermediate grade break points** and **Relative elevation to surface** options.

    • Click **OK** to close the dialog box.

19. Save the drawing.

Task 2: Edit the feature line elevations.

In this task, you will edit the elevations of the feature line. The feature lines acquired the elevations at each vertex from the surface. These elevations need to be flattened to a constant elevation. You will use parts of the *Elevation Editor*. Note that the *Elevation Editor* will be discussed in much greater detail later in this chapter.

1. Continue working in the drawing.

2. Select the Office feature line created in the previous task. (In the *Feature Line* contextual tab>*Modify* panel, select **Edit Elevations**, as shown in Figure 2−15.

Figure 2−15

3. In the *Edit Elevations* panel, select **Elevation Edito**r, as shown in Figure 2−16.

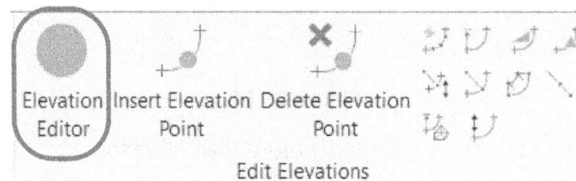

Figure 2−16

4. In the *Elevation Editor* panorama, select any row and hold down <Ctrl> as you type **A** to select every row, as shown in Figure 2−17.

   Note: Alternatively, you don't have to select any rows and can go straight to the next step. When none of the rows are selected, the Elevation Editor acts on all rows.

Figure 2–17

5. In the *Elevation Editor*, click (Flatten Grade or Elevation). Select **Constant Elevation**, as shown in Figure 2–18. Click **OK** to close the dialog box.

Figure 2–18

6. In the *Elevation Editor*, click (Raise/Lower). In the *Input* field, type **180** and press <Enter>, as shown in Figure 2–19.

Figure 2–19

7. Click ✔ to close the *Elevation Editor* panorama.

8. Repeat the same steps for the Hotel pad, with the elevation of **179.0.**

9. Save the drawing.

End of practice

2.3 Draw Feature Lines

When creating feature lines, ↻↑ (Create Feature Line) creates both straight and curved segments. Elevations are assigned at each vertex by typing an elevation value or by assigning an elevation from a surface that exists in the drawing.

How To: Draw a Feature Line

1. In the *Home* tab>*Create Design* panel, click ↻↑ (Create Feature Line).
2. In the *Create Feature Lines* dialog box, set the site, enter a name for the feature line, and select a style for the feature line, as shown in Figure 2-20. Click **OK**. Note that the conversion options are unavailable since the feature line is being drawn rather than created from an existing object.

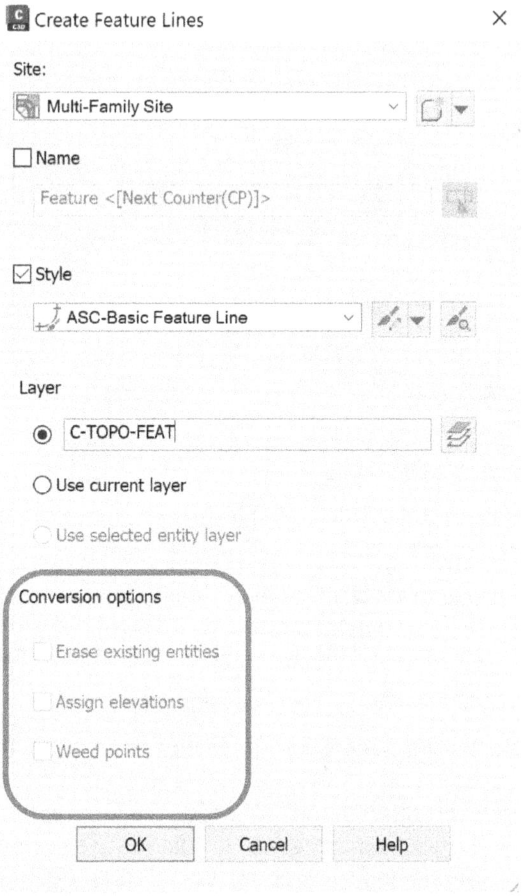

Figure 2-20

3. In the Command Line, you are prompted to *Specify start point*. Pick a point in the drawing or type a coordinate value where the feature line starts.

4. In the Command Line, you are prompted to *Specify elevation*. You can either type an elevation value or type **S** and press <Enter> to obtain a surface elevation at that point.

5. In the Command Line, you are prompted to *Specify the next point*. Pick a point in the drawing or type a coordinate value to define the next end point.

6. Type the capital letter(s) from the following options to set the elevation:

Option	Description
Grade	A grade percentage is applied between the previous point and the next point.
SLope	A rise:run slope is applied between the previous point and the next point.
Elevation	The typed elevation is given to the next point.
Difference	An elevation is calculated for the next point by adding an amount to the previous point's elevation value.
SUrface	Obtain the elevation from a selected surface at the next point in the drawing.
Transition	Skips setting the elevation of the next point and subsequent points by pressing <Enter> until an elevation is assigned to the last point. The elevations for all intermediate vertices is calculated from a grade based on the distance between the first and last point and the change in elevation.

7. In the Command Line, you are prompted to *Specify the next point*. Type **A** and press <Enter> to draw an arc.

8. Type the capital letter from the following options to create the arc according to the required design parameters.

Option	Description
Arc end point	Pick an arc end point to complete the arc. The arc is automatically tangential to the previous segment.
Radius	Enter a radius and then pick the end point of the arc or type **L** to enter the arc length. The arc is automatically tangential to the previous segment.
Secondpnt	Pick a point to specify the second point through which the arc must pass. Then specify the arc endpoint by picking another point or typing **L** to set the arc length. This enables the arc to not be tangential to the previous segment.
Line	Returns to drawing straight line segments.
Undo	Undoes the last segment of the feature line.

Using feature line arcs avoids creating tessellated arcs. This is preferred when working with grading footprints because it creates many small grading faces joined by radial corners. If you use 3D polylines as surface breaklines for grading, tessellation occurs and slows down your drawing. You can use the **Fit Curve** command to convert tessellated arcs to true arcs.

Practice 2b
Feature Lines from Elevations

Practice Objective

• Create and edit feature lines using various tools.

In this practice, you will define the perimeter of the pond using two methods of defining a feature line: you will create a feature line from a surface and then create a feature based on design elevations. For this practice (and the subsequent practices involving the Pond design), the *Jeffries Ranch Rd* corridor has been replaced with the **Jeffries Rand Rd** for *Pond* corridor.

Task 1: Create a feature line from a surface.

Mission Avenue is the northern boundary of the site and an existing subdivision bounds the eastern side. To establish a design control line for the north and west perimeters of the site, you will create a feature line that extracts elevations from the existing surface.

1. Open **POND-FL1.dwg** from the *C:\Civil 3D Grading\Working\Feature Lines* folder.

2. In the *View* tab>*Named Views* panel, select the preset view **Storm Pond**. A red polyline displays along the north and west property lines, as shown in Figure 2–21.

   *Note: You might need to type **Regen** in the Command Line to display this polyline.*

Figure 2–21

3. In the *Home* tab>*Create Design* panel, expand the *Feature Line* drop-down list and click

   ⬜ (Create Feature Lines from Objects).

4. When prompted to *Select the object*, select the red polyline shown above in Figure 2–21. Press <Enter> when done.

5. In the *Create Feature Lines* dialog box, complete the following, as shown in Figure 2–22:

   - For *Site,* select **Pond Site.**

   - For *Name,* type **North-West-Boundary.**

   - In the *Conversion options* area, select the **Erase existing entities**, **Assign elevations**, and **Weed Points** options.

   - Accept all of the other defaults and click **OK** when done.

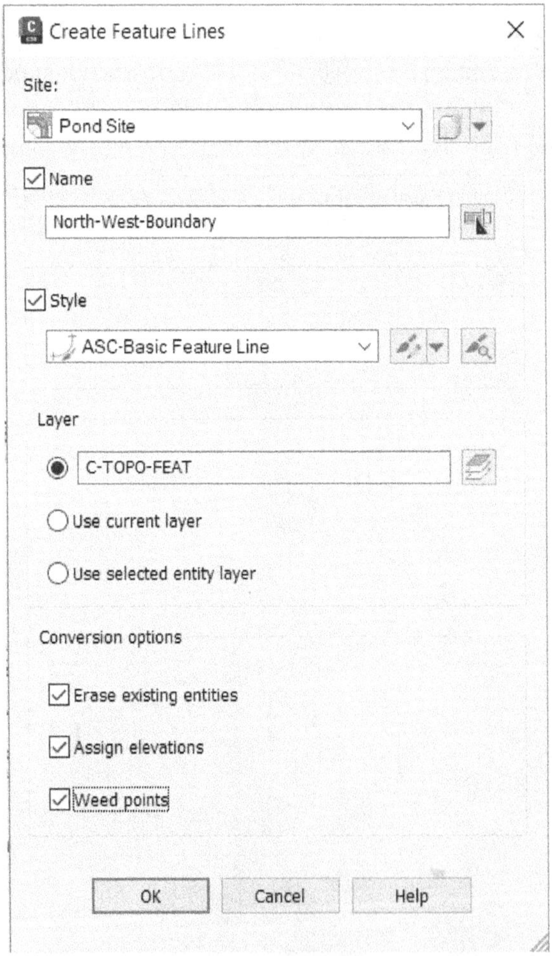

Figure 2–22

6. In the *Assign Elevations* dialog box, complete the following, as shown in Figure 2–23:

    -   Select the **From surface** option.
    -   In the drop-down list, select **Existing-Site**.
    -   Select the **Insert intermediate grade break points** option.
    -   Click **OK** to accept the changes and close the dialog box.

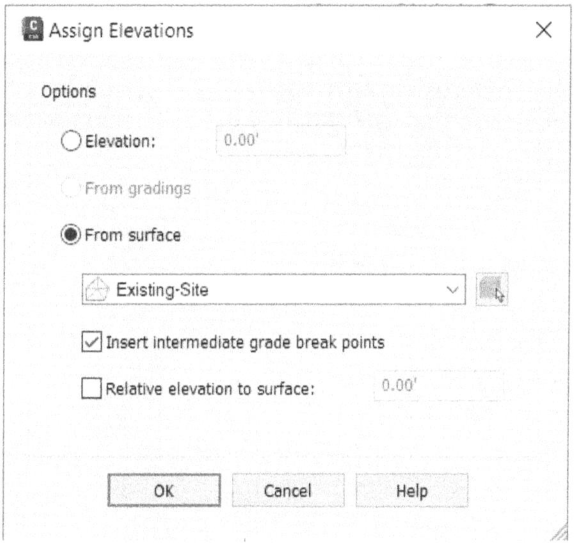

Figure 2–23

7. In the *Weed Vertices* dialog box, accept the defaults as shown in Figure 2–24, and click **OK**.

Figure 2–24

8. A feature line has been created for the north and west property lines of the site, with elevations matching the existing ground surface. Save the drawing.

Task 2: Create a feature based on design elevations.

In this task, you will create a feature line of the east perimeter of the pond. The grades at the east perimeter of the pond are governed by the rear grades of the lots or parcels.

1. Continue working with the drawing from the previous task.

   Based on the street grades and types of lots that are required (Walkout Basements), elevations for the east property line have been roughly calculated. The last point (Pt. 7) ties into the existing ground elevation that is controlled by Mission Avenue, as shown in Figure 2–25.

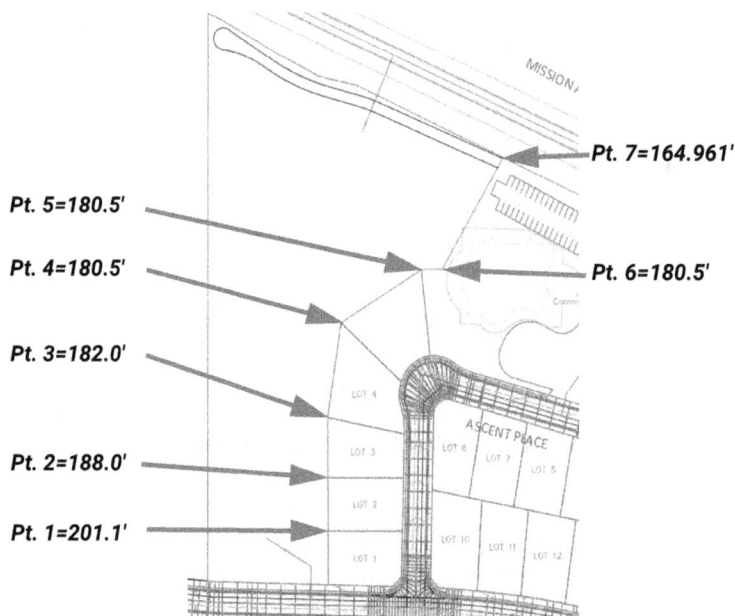

Figure 2–25

2. In the *Home* tab>*Create Design* panel, expand the *Feature Line* drop-down list and click (Create Feature Line).

3. In the *Create Feature Lines* dialog box, complete the following:

   • Select **Pond Site** for the site and select the option to name it.

   • For the *Name*, type **East-Boundary**.

   • Accept all of the other defaults.

   • Click **OK**.

4. When prompted for the feature line points, using the **Endpoint** Osnap, select **Pt. 1**, as shown above in Figure 2−25.

5. When prompted to *Specify elevation or [surface] <0.000>*, type **201.1** and press <Enter>.

6. When prompted for the next point, using the **Endpoint** Osnap, select **Pt. 2**, as shown above in Figure 2−25.

7. You are prompted to *Specify grade or [SLope/Elevation/Difference/SUrface/Transition] <0.00>*. If the option is not set to accept elevations, type **E** and press <Enter> to set the default as the elevation.

8. Once the option has been set to accept elevations, you are prompted to *Specify elevation or [Grade/SLope/Difference/SUrface/ Transition] <61.300>*. Type **188.0** and press <Enter>.

9. Continue selecting endpoints and entering elevations for all of the points as shown in Figure 2−25. When finished entering the elevation for the last point, Pt. 7 (**164.961**), press <Enter> to exit the command.

10. Save the drawing.

End of practice

Practice 2c
Draw a Feature Line

Practice Objective

- Create a feature line and assign elevations to the vertices to the feature line.

In this practice, you will create a temporary site, draw a feature line. This will be used later to create a temporary surface for a parking lot.

Task 1: Create a temporary site.

1. Open **PKLOT-FL.dwg** from the *C:\Civil 3D Grading\Working\Feature Lines* folder.

2. In the *View* tab>*Named Views* panel, select **Parking Lot** as the view to zoom into the parking lot area, as shown in Figure 2–26.

Figure 2–26

3. In the *Prospector* tab, right-click on **Sites** and select **New**, as shown in Figure 2–27.

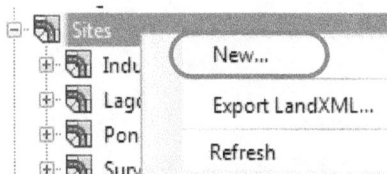

Figure 2–27

4. In the *Information* tab, for the *Name*, type **Temp**. Click **OK**.

Task 2: Draw a feature line.

1. Continue working in the drawing from the previous task.

2. In the *Home* tab>*Create Design* panel, click ⬩ (Create Feature Line).

3. In the *Create Feature Lines* dialog box, complete the following, as shown in Figure 2–28:

   * For *Site*, select **Temp**.
   * For *Name,* type **CenterLine**.
   * For *Style,* select **ASC-Basic Feature Line**.
   * Click **OK**.

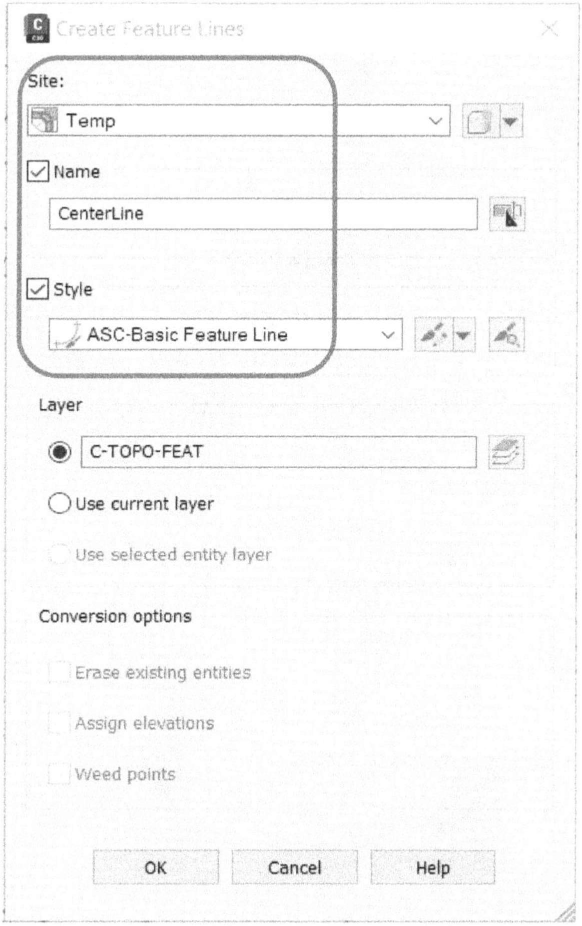

Figure 2–28

4. At the Command Prompt, you will be prompted to pick a point. Using the **Endpoint** Osnap, click point one on the parking lot center line, as shown in Figure 2−29.

Figure 2−29

5. Type **S** and press <Enter> to have it find the elevation of a surface at that point.

6. When prompted for the surface, select **Road-Tops**, as shown in Figure 2−30, and click **OK**.

    *Note: If this dialog box does not open, type **S** and press <Enter> to select the surface.*

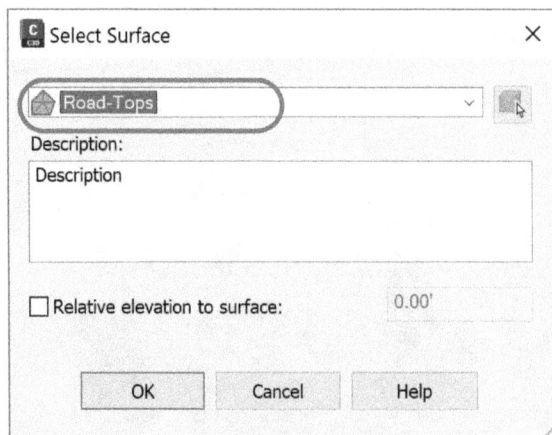

Figure 2−30

7. For the next point, use the **Endpoint** Osnap to pick point 2, as shown in Figure 2–29.

    *Note: If grade is not the default, type **G** and press <Enter> before setting the negative 2% grade.*

8. For the elevation, the default will be to set the grade. Type **-2 (minus 2)** and press <Enter> to set the grade at 2% going down.

9. For the next point, use the **Endpoint** Osnap to pick point 3, as shown in Figure 2–29.

10. For the grade, verify that the option is set the **Grade** and not **Slope**. Type **-2 (minus 2)** and press <Enter> to set the grade at 2% going down.

11. For the next point, use the **Endpoint** Osnap to pick point 4, as shown in Figure 2–29.

12. For the elevation, the default will be to set the grade. Type **-4 (minus 4)** and press <Enter> to set the grade at 4% going down.

13. Press <Enter> to end the command.

14. Save the drawing.

End of practice

2.4 Create Feature Lines from Corridors

When corridors are created, the sub-assemblies' point codes create feature lines. These feature lines can be used in grading groups but they must be extracted from the corridor for the

Grading command to recognize them. ✏️ (Create Feature Line from Corridor) in the *Feature Line* drop-down list in the *Home* tab>*Create Design* panel extracts the feature lines from a corridor model. During the extraction process, you determine whether the new feature line automatically updates if the corridor changes. The **Create dynamic link to the corridor** option in the *Create Feature Line from Corridor* dialog box creates this dynamic link.

How To: Create a Feature Line from a Corridor

1. In the *Home* tab>*Create Design* panel, expand the *Feature Line* drop-down list and click

   ✏️ (Create Feature Line from Corridor), as shown in Figure 2–31.

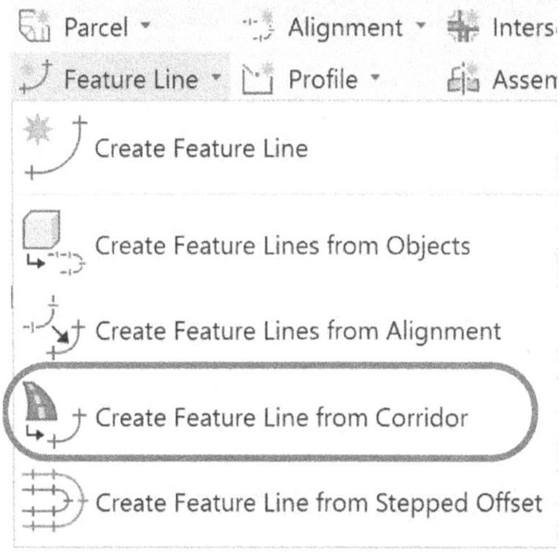

Figure 2–31

2. When prompted, select the corridor that you want to use.

3. When prompted, select the corridor feature line that you want to use, as shown in Figure 2–32.

4. In the *Extract Corridor Feature Line* dialog box, select a *Site*.

5. Click **Settings** and determine whether you want to have the feature line automatically update or not with the **Create dynamic link to the corridor** option, as shown in Figure 2–32.

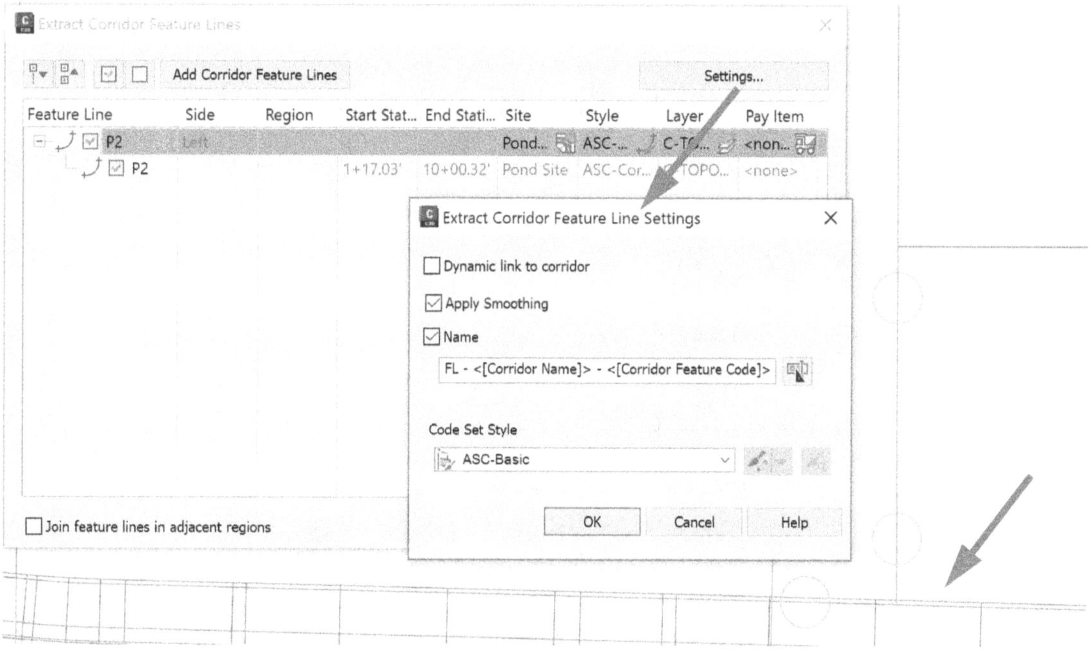

Figure 2–32

Note: It is recommended to name feature lines in complex models for easy identification.

6. If you want to give the feature line a name, select the **Name** option and type a name in the *Name* field.

7. Click **OK** to accept and close the dialog box.

8. A message displays in the Command Line indicating that a feature line has been created. Press <Enter> to exit the **Selection** command.

2.5 Edit Feature Line Geometry

Working with feature lines is similar to working with standard AutoCAD lines and polylines. The differences are with the tools that are used to make the required changes. To access the tools, select a feature line. In the *Feature Line* contextual tab>*Modify* panel, click 🔲 (Edit Geometry). The *Edit Geometry* panel displays, as shown in Figure 2–33.

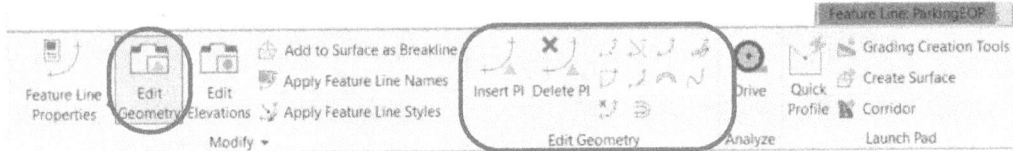

Figure 2–33

The tool functions are as follows:

Icon	Command	Description
	Insert PI	Adds a new vertex to a feature line, survey figure, parcel line, polyline, or 3D polyline, giving you additional horizontal and vertical control.
	Delete PI	Removes a selected vertex from a feature line, survey figure, parcel line, polyline, or 3D polyline.
	Break	Creates a gap or break in a feature line, survey figure, or parcel line. The location selected when picking the object is the first point of the break, unless otherwise specified.
	Trim	Removes part of a feature line, survey figure, or parcel line at the specified boundary edge.
	Join	Combines two feature lines, survey figures, parcel lines, polylines, or 3D polylines that fall within the tolerance distance set in the command settings.
	Reverse	Changes the direction of the stationing along a feature line, survey figure, parcel line, polyline, or 3D polyline.
	Edit Curve	Changes the radius of a feature line arc, parcel line arc, or survey figure arc.
	Fillet	Creates a curve between two segments of selected feature line(s), survey figures, parcel lines, or 3D polylines.
	Fit Curve	Places a curve between the selected vertices of a feature line, survey figure, parcel line, or 3D polyline while removing vertices between the selected vertices. Useful for converting tessellated lines to true arcs.
	Smooth	Adds multiple arcs to feature lines or survey figures to assist in smoothing tessellated lines.

Icon	Command	Description
	Weed	Removes unnecessary vertices along feature lines, polylines, or 3D polylines based on defined angle, grade, length, and 3D distance values.
	Stepped Offset	Creates copies of a selected feature line, survey figure, polyline, or 3D polyline at a specified horizontal and vertical distance away from the original object.

Delete PI

Reshaping a feature line is easily done by removing vertices where lines intersect or where lines connect to arcs. This is similar to removing vertices in regular polylines.

How To: Modify a Feature Line Using the Delete PI Command

1. In the Drawing, select a feature line.

2. In the *Feature Line* contextual tab>*Modify* panel, click 🔲 (Edit Geometry). In the *Edit Geometry* panel that displays, click ⤳ (Delete PI).

3. In the drawing, click near the vertex you wish to remove.

Stepped Offsets

When working in the standard AutoCAD® software, you can use the **Offset** command to make copies of lines, arcs, and polylines at a specific horizontal distance away from the original object. However, when working in 3D, a horizontal and vertical offset is often required. Therefore, the **Stepped Offset** command is available in Civil 3D for feature lines. You can use it to make copies of feature lines, survey figures, and parcel lines at a specified distance away from the original object both horizontally and vertically.

How To: Create Stepped Offsets

1. In the *Home* tab>*Create Design* panel, expand the *Feature Line* drop-down list and click ⛁ (Stepped Offset), as shown in Figure 2-34.

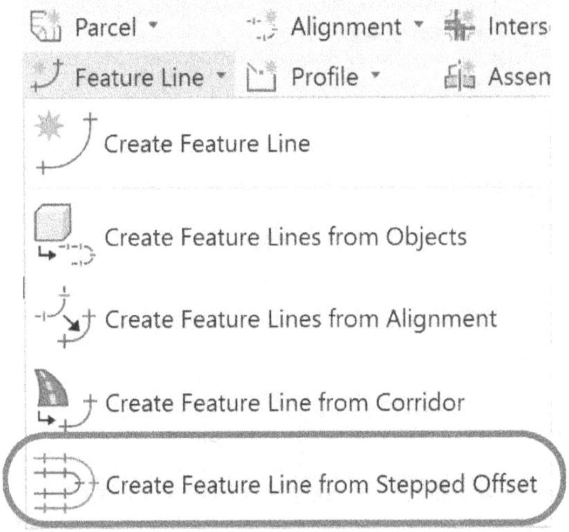

Figure 2-34

2. Specify the distance to offset the new object by typing a numeric value or type **T** (for Through) to specify the point the new object should pass through.

3. Select the feature line, survey figure, or parcel line to offset from the drawing.

4. Specify which side to offset to by picking a point in the drawing.

5. Type the capital letter from the following options to set the elevation of the new object.

Option	Description
Grade	A grade percentage is applied between the original object and the newly offset object.
Slope	A rise:run slope is applied between the original object and the newly offset object.
Elevation	The typed elevation is assigned to the new object.
Difference	An elevation is calculated for the new object's vertices by adding the amount entered to the original feature line, parcel line, or survey figure's vertex elevations.
Variable	A variable is added for a new elevation or a difference in elevation for each vertex along the new feature line, survey figure, or parcel line.

- The default option is set to **Difference** or the last option used.

© 2025 ASCENT - *Center for Technical Knowledge*

Break Feature Lines

Feature lines can be broken into two or more segments in order to have more control over surface elevations. It is common for existing ground surface contours or corridor feature lines to be used in a finish ground grading plan. However, the entire feature line might not be

required. It is in these instances that it becomes necessary to use the feature line ⌁ (Break) or

⌁ (Trim) commands. The **Break** command allows you to break the feature line at selected points, as shown in Figure 2–35.

Broken feature line

Figure 2–35

How To: Break a Feature Line

1. In Model Space, select the feature line that needs to be split into two feature lines.

2. In the *Feature Line* contextual tab>*Modify* panel, click ⌁ (Edit Geometry) to display the *Edit Geometry* panel.

3. In the *Edit Geometry* panel, click ⌁ (Break), as shown in Figure 2–36.

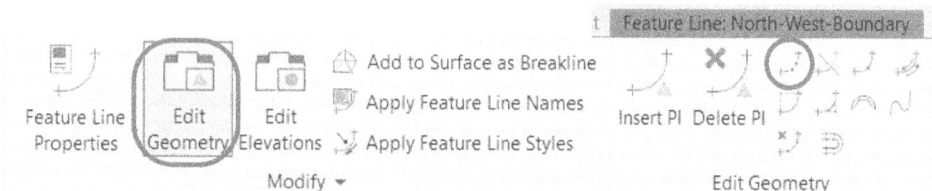

Figure 2–36

4. When prompted to select an object to break, select the feature line at the location where you want to place the first break point.

5. When prompted to select the second break point, click on the line at the second point.

   - If you need to provide a different first point, type **F** and press <Enter>. Click on the feature line to re-select the first break point, and then click on the feature line at the second break point location.

Trim Feature Lines

Feature lines can be trimmed at specified cutting edges. This allows you to ensure that feature lines do not go beyond a specific boundary. The specified boundary becomes the cutting edge, and then the feature line is removed up to the cutting edge, as shown in Figure 2-37.

Figure 2-37

How To: Trim a Feature Line

1. In Model Space, select the feature line requiring trimming.

2. In the *Feature Line* contextual tab>*Modify* panel, click ⬒ (Edit Geometry) to display the *Edit Geometry* panel.

3. In the *Edit Geometry* panel, click ⤬ (Trim), as shown in Figure 2-38.

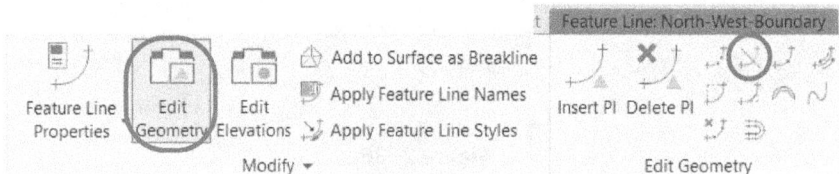

Figure 2-38

4. When prompted to select the cutting edge, select an object to trim to and press <Enter>.

5. When prompted to select the object to trim, select the feature line to trim on the side you wish to remove from the drawing.

Join Feature Lines

When two feature lines touch each other, end to end, at the same elevation, you can join them into one feature line, as shown in Figure 2–39. This is especially useful when you have used various commands such as **Create Feature Line from Objects** or **Create Feature Line from Corridor** to create the base feature lines.

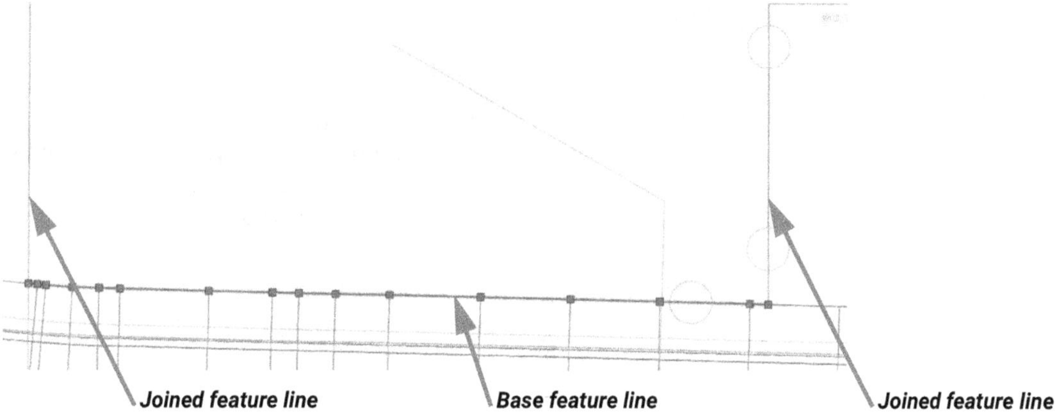

Joined feature line   *Base feature line*   *Joined feature line*

Figure 2–39

How To: Join Feature Lines Together

1. In the *Feature Line* contextual tab>*Modify* panel, click 🗔 (Edit Geometry) to display the *Edit Geometry* panel.

2. In the *Edit Geometry* panel, click ↵ (Join), as shown in Figure 2–40.

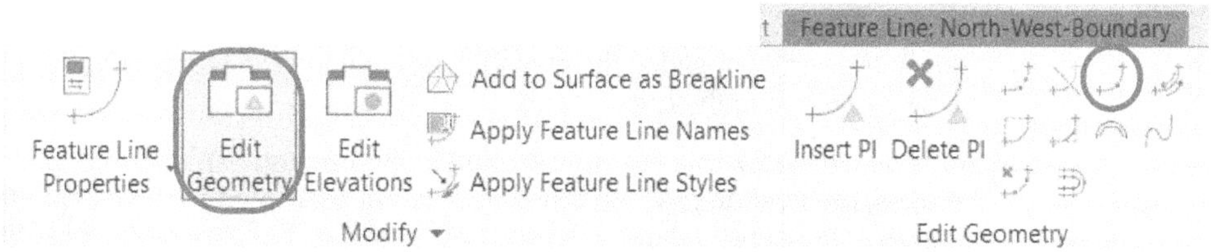

Figure 2–40

3. When prompted, select all the feature lines in the drawing that you want to join.
4. Press <Enter> to end the command.
5. Press <Esc> to exit the feature line selection.

> **💡 Hint: Fixing Feature Lines Which Fail to Join**
>
> If the ⌐ (Join) command does not join the selected feature lines, some grip editing might be required where lines do not intersect perfectly.
>
> Alternatively, you can change the command settings to set a tolerance factor. Changing the tolerance factor allows feature lines with a gap between them to join together as long as the gap is within the selected tolerance.

Grip edits for feature lines

When you select a feature line, blue grips are displayed. Square grips represent vertices of a feature line and circular grips represent elevation points on the feature line. If you hover over a grip, it turns red and a tooltip menu is displayed, as shown in Figure 2–41. If you select a grip by clicking it, you will begin moving the vertex or stretching the elevation point along the feature line, and the menu will not be displayed. Be sure to hover, not select, if you want to see the menu.

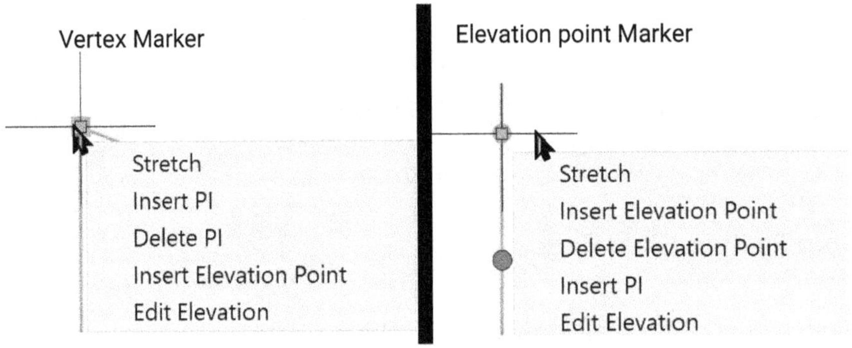

Vertex Marker

Stretch
Insert PI
Delete PI
Insert Elevation Point
Edit Elevation

Elevation point Marker

Stretch
Insert Elevation Point
Delete Elevation Point
Insert PI
Edit Elevation

Figure 2–41

The options are as follows:

Command	Description
Stretch	Moves the vertex or slides the elevation point along the feature line. This is the same as selecting the grip.
Insert PI	Adds a new vertex to a feature line, survey figure. You can add multiple vertices, press <Enter> when finished. You are prompted for an elevation for each PI you insert.
Delete PI	Removes the selected vertex from a feature line, survey figure.
Insert Elevation Point	Adds a new elevation point to a feature line, You can add multiple elevation points, press <Enter> when finished. You are prompted for an elevation for each elevation point you insert.

Command	Description
Delete Elevation Point	Removes the selected elevation point from a feature line.
Edit Elevation	Prompts you at the command line for a new value for the elevation of the vertex or elevation point.

Note: If you alter survey figures, these will have to be updated in the Survey Database as well.

Practice 2d
Edit Feature Lines

Practice Objectives

- Edit feature line elevations by adding additional elevation points at locations other than the vertices.
- Create feature lines from corridors to speed up the creation process and ensure design coordination.

In this practice, you will modify feature line elevations, create a feature line from a corridor, and edit feature line geometry. You will use parts of the *Elevation Editor*. Note that the *Elevation Editor* will be discussed in greater detail later in this chapter.

Task 1: Modify feature line elevations.

In the *Grading Elevation Editor* vista, you can make changes to the feature line design. Due to the grade difference between **Jeffries Ranch Rd** and the adjacent lot grade, the start of the feature line must be adjusted to display a **1:1** slope.

1. Open **POND-FL2.dwg** from the *C:\Civil 3D Grading\Working\Feature Lines* folder.
2. In Model Space, select the **East-Boundary** feature line you created in *Practice 2b - Feature Lines from elevations*, as shown in Figure 2–42).

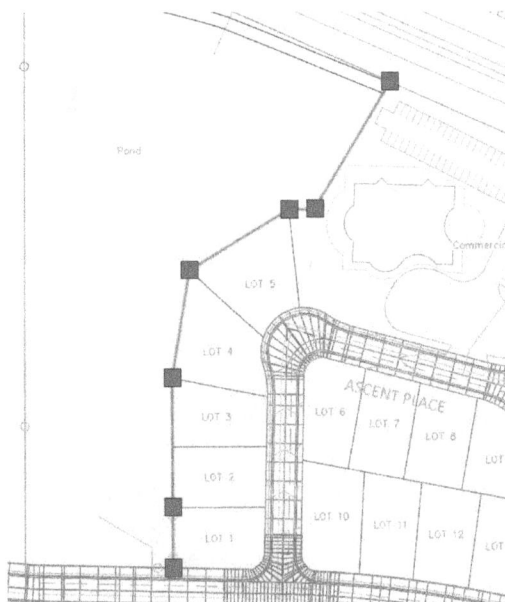

Figure 2–42

3. In the *Feature Line* contextual tab>*Modify* panel, click ⬛ (Edit Elevations) to display the *Edit Elevations* panel, and then click ⬛ (Insert Elevation Point).

4. When prompted for a point, type **13** and press <Enter> in the Command Line (this is the distance/station along the feature line).

5. When prompted for the *Elevation*, type **188.0'** and press <Enter>.

6. Press <Enter> to finish the command.

7. In the *Feature Line* contextual tab>*Edit Elevations* panel, click ● (Elevation Editor) to open the vista. The new station should display with a circle icon (as shown in Figure 2–43) indicating that it is an elevation point rather than a vertex.

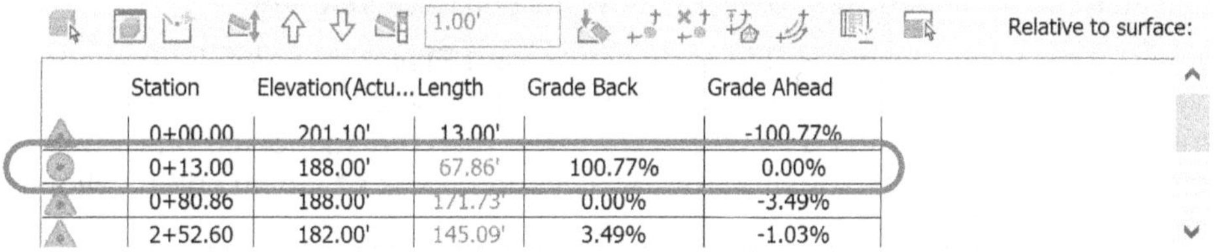

Station	Elevation(Actu...	Length	Grade Back	Grade Ahead
0+00.00	201.10'	13.00'		-100.77%
0+13.00	188.00'	67.86'	100.77%	0.00%
0+80.86	188.00'	171.73'	0.00%	-3.49%
2+52.60	182.00'	145.09'	3.49%	-1.03%

Relative to surface:

Figure 2–43

8. Close the *Elevation Editor* vista using the green check mark in the right corner.

9. Turn the Osnap off (you can use the <F3> keyboard shortcut).

10. Select the blue feature line that marks the outline of an access path, then hover over the blue square grip as indicated. The grip turns red and a tooltip menu is displayed, as shown in Figure 2–44.

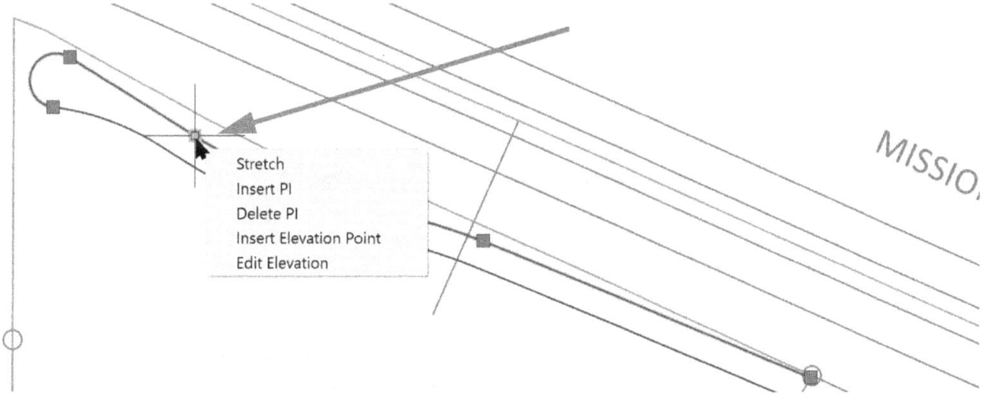

Stretch
Insert PI
Delete PI
Insert Elevation Point
Edit Elevation

MISSIO

Figure 2–44

11. Use the **Stretch** option to move the vertex toward the South East and select a point for the new vertex location. The grip turns blue again.

12. Hover over the same grip, and this time, click to select it. The grip turns red again but no tooltip appears, and you can move (stretch) the vertex. Move it back to approximately its original position.

13. Next, hover over the same vertex and select **Insert PI** from the tooltip menu.

14. Insert a new PI (which is a vertex) on the upper side of the feature line. When prompted for an elevation, press <Enter> to accept the default calculated value suggested by Civil 3D.

15. You are prompted to insert another vertex point—select anywhere, as the exact location does not matter because you will be deleting these PIs in the upcoming steps. Press <Enter> when finished inserting new PIs.

16. Now, hover over one of these newly added PIs and select **Delete PI** from the tooltip menu to remove it. Repeat this process for all the new PIs you have inserted.

17. Afterward, hover over the original PI and select **Insert Elevation Point**. Select a point below the vertex; notice how you cannot pick a point off the line, as you could with PIs. When prompted for elevation, enter a value slightly lower than the suggested one. You are prompted to select another location for the elevation point; so, again enter a slightly lower elevation. Press <Enter> when done.

18. In the *Feature Line* contextual tab>*Edit Elevations* panel, click ⬤ (Elevation Editor) to open the vista.

19. Note the circle icons (as shown in Figure 2–45) showing the new elevation points, their elevations, and the grades ahead and behind.

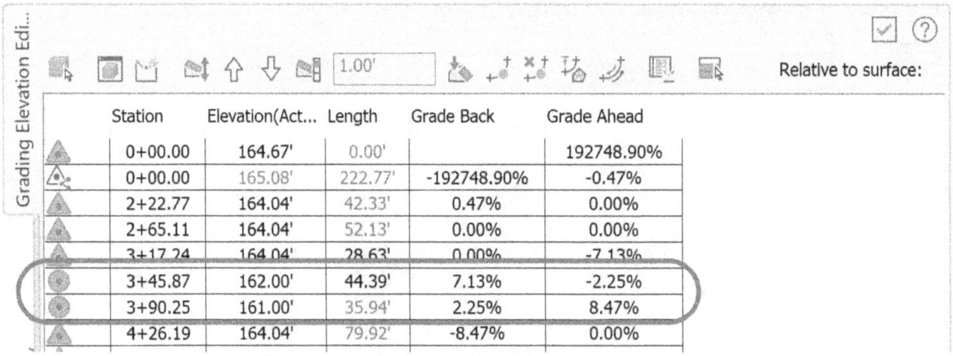

	Station	Elevation(Act...	Length	Grade Back	Grade Ahead
⚠	0+00.00	164.67'	0.00'		192748.90%
⚠	0+00.00	165.08'	222.77'	-192748.90%	-0.47%
⚠	2+22.77	164.04'	42.33'	0.47%	0.00%
⚠	2+65.11	164.04'	52.13'	0.00%	0.00%
⚠	3+17.24	164.04'	28.63'	0.00%	-7.13%
⦿	3+45.87	162.00'	44.39'	7.13%	-2.25%
⦿	3+90.25	161.00'	35.94'	2.25%	8.47%
⚠	4+26.19	164.04'	79.92'	-8.47%	0.00%

Relative to surface:

Figure 2–45

20. In the drawing, hover over another elevation point and use the **Stretch** option to move it. Check the Elevation Editor—note that the elevation value remains the same, but the grades ahead and behind have changed.

21. Now use the **Edit Elevation** option on the elevation point to raise it slightly. Notice the changes in the *Elevation Editor*.

22. In the *Elevation Editor*, select the row of the first elevation point, and use the ⤬ (Delete Elevation Point) to remove it.

23. Close the *Elevation Editor* vista using the green check mark in the corner to the right.

24. Hover over the remaining elevation point and use the **Delete Elevation Point** option in the tooltip menu to remove it as well.

25. Save the drawing.

Task 2: Create a feature line from corridor.

The grades at the south end of the pond are controlled by **Jeffries Ranch Rd for Pond**. In this task, you will extract a feature from the corridor to establish the elevation of the south property line.

1. Continue working with the drawing from the previous task.

2. In the *View* tab>*Named Views* panel, select the preset view **Storm Pond**.

3. In the *Home* tab>*Layers* panel, ensure that the **C-ROAD-CORR** layer is toggled on. Regen the drawing by typing **RE** in the Command Line.

4. In Model Space, select the **Jeffries Ranch Rd** for *Pond corridor* object, right-click, and select **Display Order>Bring to Front** or toggle on the selection cycling.

5. In the *Home* tab>*Create Design* panel, expand the *Feature Line* drop-down list and click

   (Create Feature Line from Corridor), as shown in Figure 2–46.

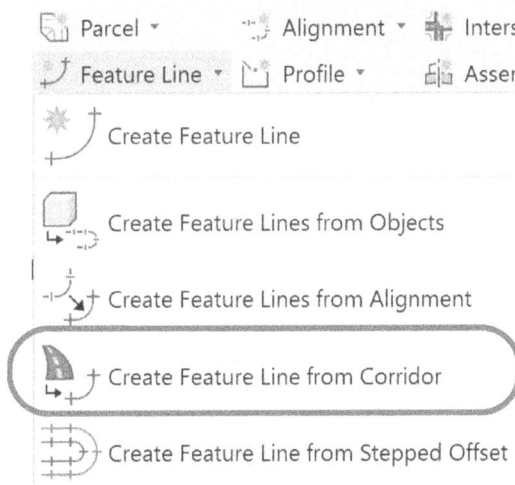

Figure 2–46

6. When prompted to select the corridor, click on **Jeffries Ranch Rd for Pond**.

7. When prompted to select the feature line, hover over the **north edge** line, which highlights in red. A tooltip appears with a **P2** designation, as shown in Figure 2–47. Select that line and press <Enter>.

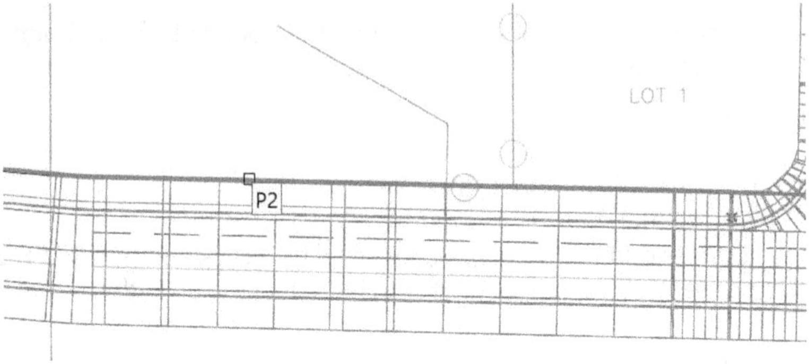

Figure 2–47

8. In the *Extract Corridor Feature Lines* dialog box, complete the following, as shown in Figure 2–48:

   • In the *Site* column, select **Pond Site**.

   • Click **Settings**.

   • In the *Extract Corridor Feature Line Settings* dialog box, clear the **Dynamic link to corridor** option, accept the remaining defaults, and click **OK** to close the dialog box.

   • Click **Extract**.

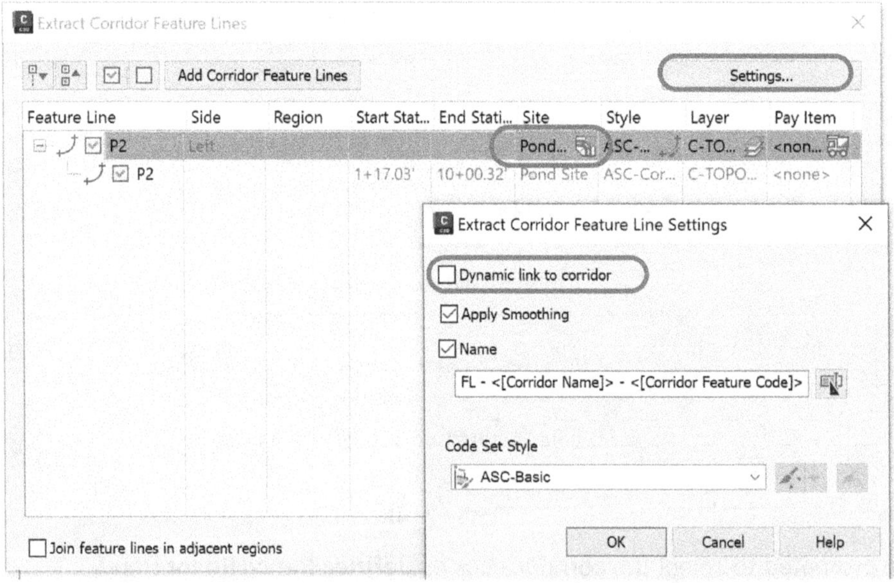

Figure 2–48

Note: A message displays in the Command Line indicating that a feature line from <P2> has been created.

9. Save the drawing.

Task 3: Edit feature line geometry.

1. Continue working with the drawing from the previous task.

2. In Model Space, zoom in to the southern edge of the pond, then select the newly created feature line, as shown in Figure 2–49. In the *Feature Line* contextual tab>*Modify* panel, click

    ![Edit Geometry icon] (Edit Geometry). In the *Edit Geometry* panel, click ![Trim icon] (Trim).

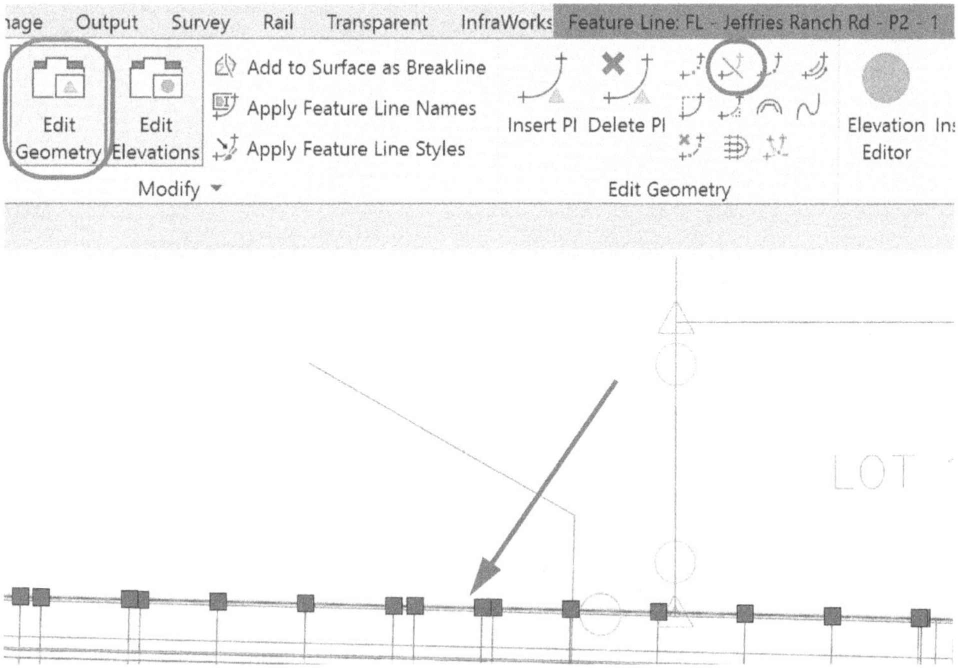

Figure 2–49

3. Complete the following, as shown in Figure 2–50:

   a. When prompted to select the cutting edge, select the east and west property lines of the pond and press <Enter> when done.

   b. When prompted to select the object to trim, select the feature line at a point outside the pond property lines, west of the west cutting edge.

   c. For the second object, select east of the east cutting edge. Press <Enter> when done.

   d. Press <Esc> to exit the feature object selection.

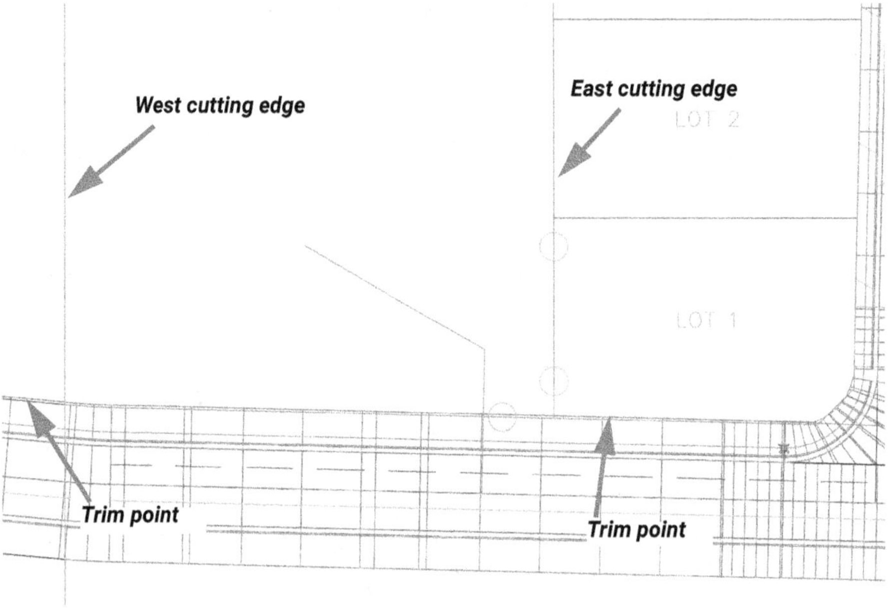

Figure 2–50

A feature line based on the corridor road design has now been created.

4. To ensure it has been properly trimmed, select the feature line once again and note the grips that indicate the extent of the feature line, as shown in Figure 2–51. If the grips extend beyond the green lines, repeat the trimming.

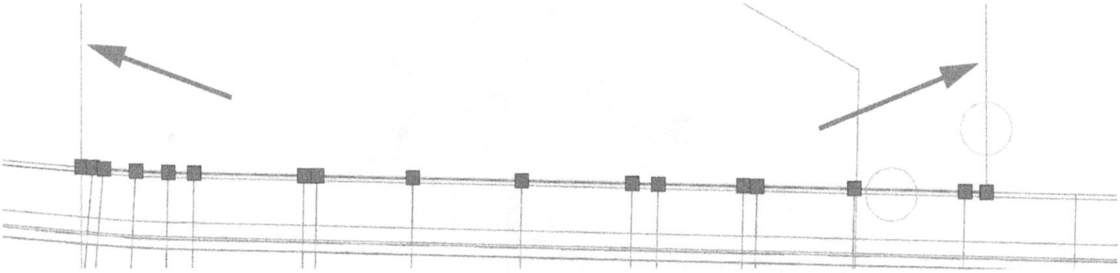

Figure 2–51

5. Press <Esc> to release the selection.

6. In the *View* tab>*Named Views* panel, select the preset view **Pond Corner SW** to zoom to the southwest corner of the pond.

7. Select the **North-West Boundary** feature line, and note by the grips that it extends beyond the **Jeffries Ranch Rd for Pond** corridor. The grips extend beyond the feature line you just trimmed, as shown in Figure 2–52.

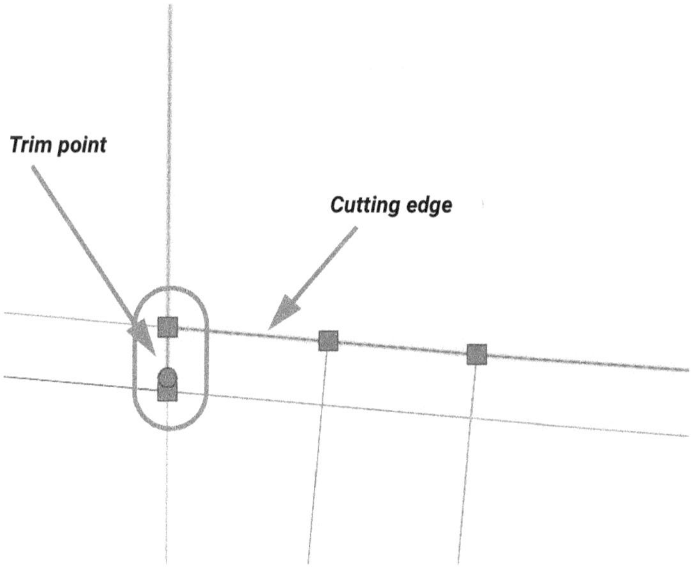

Figure 2–52

8. In the *Feature Line* contextual tab>*Modify* panel, click ⬚ (Edit Geometry) to open the *Edit Geometry* panel if not already open.

9. In the *Edit Geometry* panel, click ⤬ (Trim), then trim the **North-West Boundary** feature line as shown above in Figure 2–52.

10. In the *View* tab>*Named Views* panel, select the preset view **Pond Corner SE** to zoom to the southeast corner of the pond.

11. Select the **East Boundary** feature line, and note by the grips that it also extends beyond the **Jeffries Ranch Rd for Pond** corridor, as shown in Figure 2–53.

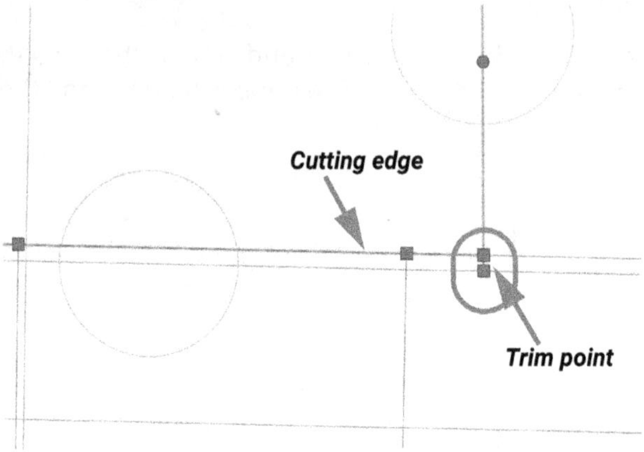

Figure 2–53

12. Repeat the trimming, picking the cutting edge and the trim point as shown above in Figure 2–53.

13. In the *View* tab>*Named Views* panel, select the preset view **Pond Edge South** to zoom to the southern edge of the pond.

14. To join the three feature lines, select the **North-West Boundary** feature line at the west side of the pond.

15. In the *Feature Line* contextual tab>*Modify* panel, click ▢ (Edit Geometry) to display the

    Edit Geometry panel, and then click ⌐ (Join), as shown in Figure 2–54.

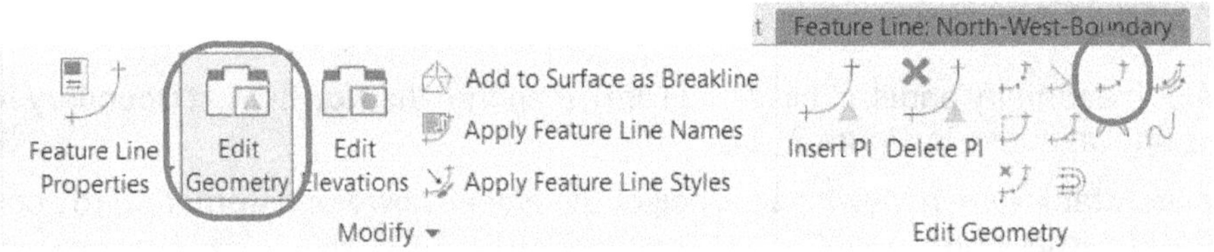

Figure 2–54

Note: If the feature line fails to join any lines in this process, some grip editing might be required where lines do not intersect completely.

16. When prompted, select the feature line to the south and select the feature line to the east. Press <Enter> to end the command and press <Esc> to exit the feature line selection.

17. Save the drawing.

End of practice

2.6 Edit Elevations Panel

Select a parcel segment. In the *Parcel Segment* contextual tab>*Modify* panel, click ⬚ (Edit Elevations) to display the *Edit Elevations* panel. The tools in the *Edit Elevations* panel are as follows:

Icon	Command	Description
●	**Elevation Editor**	Opens the *Elevation Editor* vista in which you can edit each vertex elevation of feature lines, survey figures, and parcel lines.
⌐	**Insert Elevation Point**	Adds an elevation control to the feature line. Elevation points provide an elevation control without creating a whole new vertex. These points are Z-controls without X- or Y-components.
⌐	**Delete Elevation Point**	Permits vertical grade breaks to be removed anywhere other than horizontal vertices.
⌐	**Quick Elevation Edit**	Displays elevation values at vertices and elevation points along a feature line or parcel line. Selecting one of these points enables you to edit it in the Command Line.
⌐	**Edit Elevations**	Edits elevations at vertices along a feature line, parcel line, or 3D polyline as you step through each vertex in the Command Line.
⌐	**Set Grade/Slope Between Points**	Sets the grade or slope between two points on a feature line, parcel line, or 3D polyline. The elevations of the points between the two selected points are interpolated to maintain the grade/slope/elevation/elevation difference entered.
⌐	**Insert High/Low Elevation Point**	Inserts a high or low break point where two grades intersect on a feature line, survey figure, parcel line, or 3D polyline.
⌐	**Raise/Lower by Reference**	Raises or lowers a feature line, survey figure, parcel line, or 3D polyline at a specified grade or slope from a selected COGO point or surface elevation.
⌐	**Set Elevation by Reference**	Sets a single vertex elevation on a feature line, survey figure, parcel line, or 3D polyline at a specified grade or slope from a selected COGO point or surface elevation.
⌐	**Adjacent Elevations by Reference**	Sets elevations of one feature line, survey figure, parcel line, or 3D polyline, based on a grade/slope/elevation/elevation difference from points, on another feature running alongside the first feature.

Icon	Command	Description
	Grade Extension by Reference	Extends the grade of one feature line, survey figure, parcel line, or 3D polyline across a gap to set the elevations of another feature and maintain the same slope.
	Elevations from Surface	Takes the elevations of all of the vertices from the surface if no vertices are selected. If a vertex is selected, it takes the surface elevation for just that vertex.
	Raise/Lower	Raises or lowers all of the feature line vertices by the elevation entered.

The second location where parcel line elevations can be assigned is in the *Elevation Editor* vista. To access these tools, select a parcel segment. This displays the *Parcel Segment* tab in the ribbon, as shown in Figure 2–55.

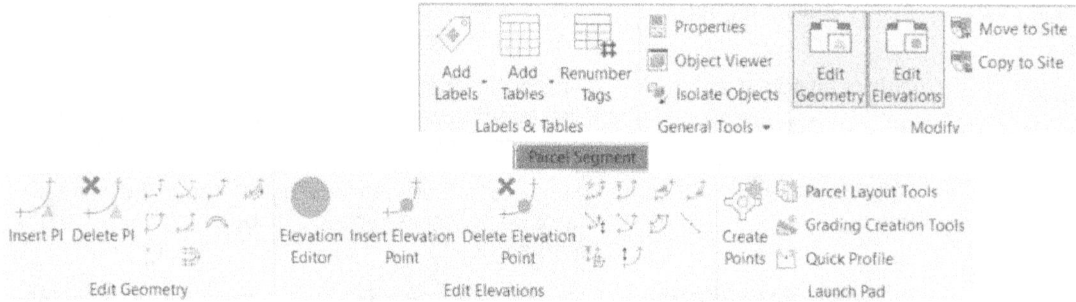

Figure 2–55

In the *Modify* panel, select **Edit Elevations** to display the *Edit Elevations* panel.

In the *Edit Elevations* panel, select the **Elevation Editor** to open the *Elevation Editor* panorama, as shown in Figure 2–56.

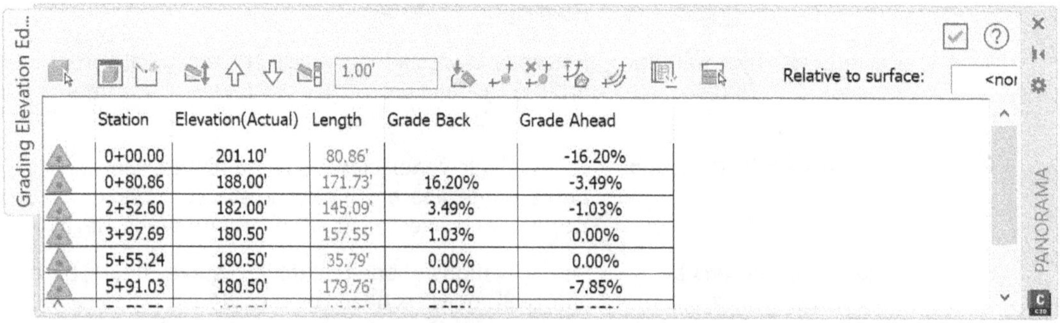

Station	Elevation(Actual)	Length	Grade Back	Grade Ahead
0+00.00	201.10'	80.86'		-16.20%
0+80.86	188.00'	171.73'	16.20%	-3.49%
2+52.60	182.00'	145.09'	3.49%	-1.03%
3+97.69	180.50'	157.55'	1.03%	0.00%
5+55.24	180.50'	35.79'	0.00%	0.00%
5+91.03	180.50'	179.76'	0.00%	-7.85%

Figure 2–56

The *Elevation Editor* contains the properties of the vertices of the selected feature lines or lot lines. The properties for each vertex include a station, elevation, length, grade ahead, and grade back. To make changes to a station's elevation, select the row in which it is located. Selecting one or more rows in the panorama causes a green triangle to display in the drawing indicating which vertex (or vertices) you are working with, as shown in Figure 2–57.

- Stations displaying a ◬ triangular symbol to the left of their station can be edited horizontally and vertically.

- Stations displaying a ◉ circular symbol to the left of their station are elevation points and can only be edited vertically.

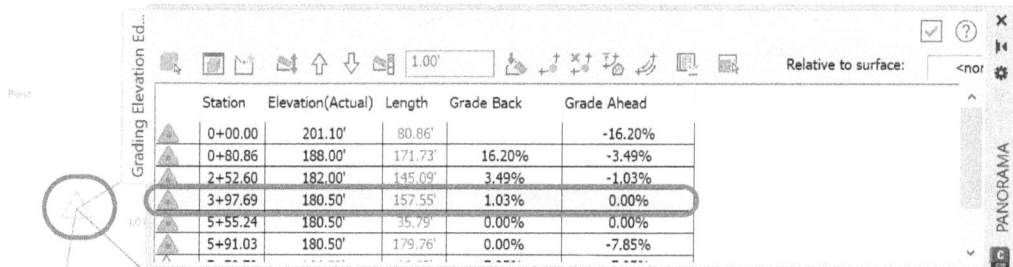

Figure 2–57

Once the required vertices have been selected, you can use the tools at the top of the panorama to change the elevation of each vertex or the slope between vertices. The function of each tool is as follows:

Icon	Command	Description
	Select Feature Line	Selects the feature line, parcel line, or survey figure.
	Zoom To	Zooms to the selected vertex or vertices.
	Quick Profile	Creates a profile view of the selected feature line.
	Raise/Lower	Enables you to type an elevation value in the input field to raise or lower selected vertices to the specified elevation.
	Raise Incrementally	Raises the vertex or vertices selected by the increment set in the input field.
	Lower Incrementally	Lowers the vertex or vertices selected by the increment set in the input field.
	Set Increment	Enables you to type a distance value in the input field to raise or lower selected vertices by a specified increment.
	Input Field	Type a distance or elevation to raise or lower selected vertices.

Icon	Command	Description
	Flatten Grade or Elevations	Flattens selected vertices to a constant elevation or sets a constant grade.
	Insert Elevation Point	Enables you to add additional vertical grade breaks without having to add additional horizontal vertices.
	Delete Elevation Point	Permits vertical grade breaks to be removed anywhere other than horizontal vertices.
	Elevations from Surface	Takes the vertex or vertices elevations from the specified surface.
	Reverse the Direction	Changes the direction from which the feature line is stationed.
	Show Grade Breaks Only	Reduces the number of vertices displayed in the table by only displaying feature line stations where the grade changes.
	Unselect All Rows	Removes all rows from the current selection.

How To: Use Elevations from Surface

1. In the *Modify* tab>*Design* panel, click (Parcel) to open the *Parcel* contextual tab.

2. In the *Parcel* contextual tab>*Modify* panel, click (Edit Elevations) to open the *Edit Elevations* panel.

3. In the *Parcel* contextual tab>*Edit Elevations* panel, click (Elevations from Surface) to assign surface elevations to the vertices of the parcels.

4. In the *Set Elevations from Surface* dialog box, select the surface from which to set the pull elevations.

5. Determine whether intermediate grade break points are required. If not, do not select the **Insert intermediate grade break points** option, as shown in Figure 2–58. Click **OK** to close the dialog box.

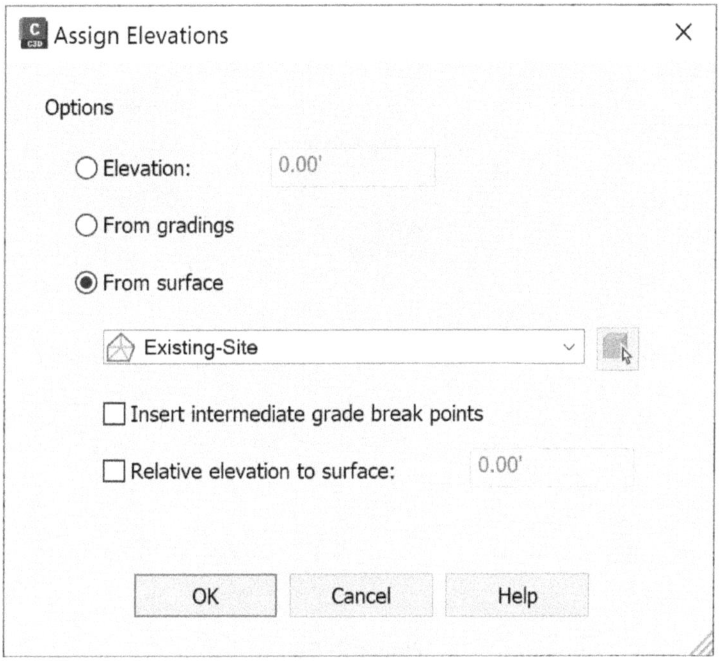

Figure 2–58

6. In the drawing, select the parcel segments that need to be changed.

How To: Use Edit Elevations

1. In the *Modify* tab>*Design* panel, click (Parcel) to display the *Parcel* contextual tab.

2. In the *Parcel* contextual tab>*Modify* panel, click (Edit Elevations) to open the *Edit Elevations* panel.

3. In the *Parcel* tab>*Edit Elevations* panel, click (Edit Elevations).

4. In the drawing, the current vertex is highlighted with a green triangle, as shown in Figure 2–59. In the Command Line, you have the following options: **Elevation**, **Previous**, **Grade**, **SLope**, **SUrface**, **Insert**, or **eXit**.

Figure 2–59

5. If the option is set to **Elevation** (the default until a different option is selected), the current elevation displays in brackets <188.000>. In the Command Line, you can press <Enter> to accept the elevation and go to the next vertex, type an elevation to override the current elevation, or type the capital letter(s) for the required option. The expected results for the selected options are as follows:

Type	Option	Description
E	**Elevation**	Sets the elevation to a typed-in value.
P	**Previous**	Changes the selected vertex to the vertex just before the current one.
G	**Grade**	Sets the slope out to the percent typed in the Command Line.
SL	**Slope**	Sets the slope out to the rise/run ratio typed in the Command Line. (Note that you type the rise and the run is a default value of 1.)
SU	**Surface**	Sets the elevation at the selected surface value for that location.
I	**Insert**	Inserts a new vertex between the current and next vertex along the feature line, survey figure, or parcel.
X	**Exit**	Ends the command.

How To: Use Set Elevation by Reference

1. In the *Modify* tab>*Design* panel, click ⬚ (Parcel) to open the *Parcel* contextual tab.

2. In the *Parcel* contextual tab>*Modify* panel, click ⬚ (Edit Elevations) to open the *Edit Elevations* panel.

3. In the *Parcel* tab>*Edit Elevations* panel, click ⬚ (Set Elevations by Reference).

4. In the drawing, pick a point to reference (from a surface, feature line, another parcel, survey figure, or corridor model).

    Note: Setting elevations by reference does not create a link to the referenced point. If the referenced point changes, the parcel lines, feature line, or survey figures need to be updated manually.

5. In the drawing, select the parcel segment, feature line, or survey figure to edit.

6. In the drawing, specify the vertex or elevation point to adjust by clicking near it.

7. In the Command Line, enter a grade or select one of the other two options for setting the elevation. You can type **S** to set the slope or **D** to set a difference in elevation.

8. Press <Esc> to end the command.

How To: Insert Elevation Points

1. In the *Feature Line* contextual tab>*Modify* panel, click ⬚ (Edit Elevations).

2. In the *Elevation Editor* or in the *Feature Line* contextual tab>*Edit Elevations* panel, click ⬚ (Insert Elevation Point).

3. Either pick a point along the feature line or enter a station where you want the new elevation point to be located.

4. In the Command Line, type the station and press <Enter>, then type the elevation and press <Enter>.

5. In the *Grading Elevation Editor* vista, the new station should be displayed, as shown in Figure 2–60.

Station	Elevation	Length	Grade Ahead	Grade Back
0+00.00	201.100'	13.000'	-100.77%	100.77%
0+13.00	188.000'	67.863'	0.00%	0.00%
0+80.86	188.000'	168.805'	-3.55%	3.55%
2+49.67	182.000'	147.637'	-1.02%	1.02%

Figure 2–60

Practice 2e
Set Parcel Line Elevations

Practice Objective

- Assign elevations to parcel lines using the Edit Elevation tools.

In this practice, you will review the site and prepare the drawing. You will then set the parcel elevations to a surface.

Task 1: Review the site and prepare the drawing.

1. Open **PARCELS-FL.dwg** from the *C:\Civil 3D Grading\Working\Feature Lines folder*.

2. In the top-left corner of the drawing window, select **Top**, then expand *Custom Model Views* and select **Site**, as shown in Figure 2−61. This will zoom into a preset view of the entire site. You can also select the view in the *View* tab>*Named Views* panel.

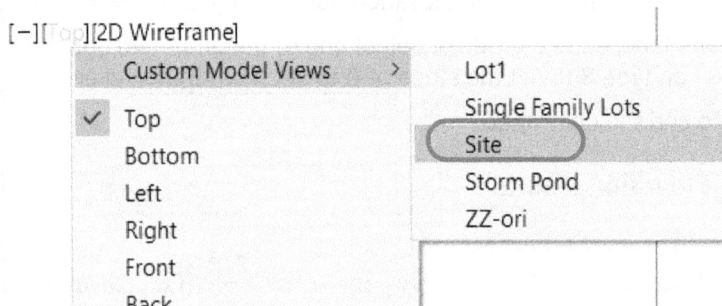

Figure 2−61

3. In the *Prospector* tab, select the **Residential Grading** site, expand the *Parcels* branch and select the **Commercial parcel**, then press and hold <Ctrl> as you select the **Pond** and **ROW** parcels. Right-click and select **Select**, as shown in Figure 2−62.

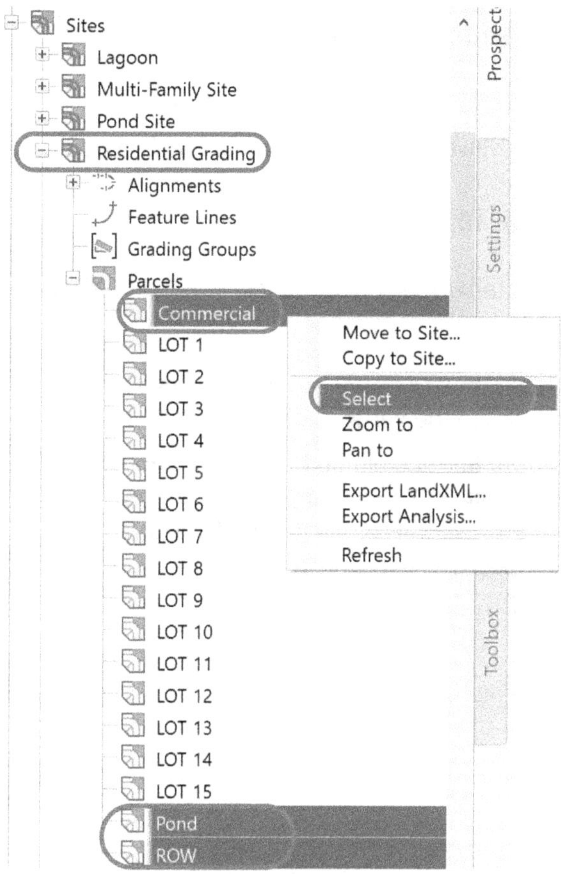

Figure 2-62

4. In the *Parcels* contextual tab>expanded *General Tools* panel, click ⬚ (Send to Back), as shown in Figure 2-63.

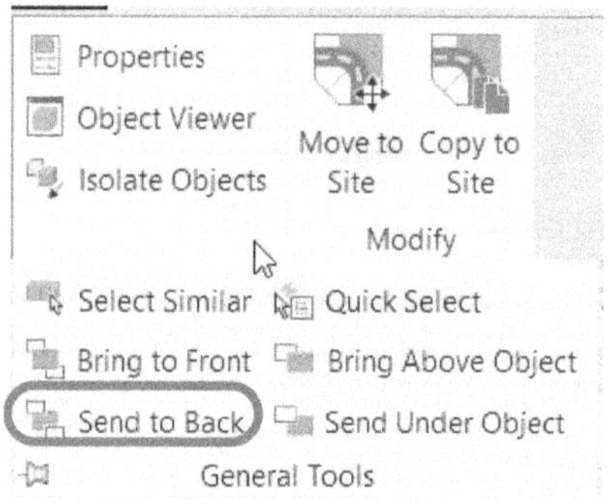

Figure 2-63

5. Press <Esc> to release the selection.

Task 2: Set parcel elevations to a surface.

1. Continue working in the drawing from the previous task.

2. In the *View* tab>*Named Views* panel, select **Single Family Lots** to zoom in on the residential area to be graded.

3. In the drawing, select **Lot 10** by selecting its area label.

4. In the *Parcel* contextual tab>*Modify* panel, click 🖼 (Edit Elevations) to open the *Edit Elevations* panel.

5. In the *Parcel* contextual tab>*Edit Elevations* panel, click 🖼 (Elevations from Surface) to assign surface elevations to the vertices of the parcels.

6. In the *Set Elevations from Surface* dialog box, select **Road-Tops** for the surface. Do not select the **Insert intermediate grade break points** or **Relative elevation to surface** options, as shown in Figure 2-64. Click **OK** to close the dialog box.

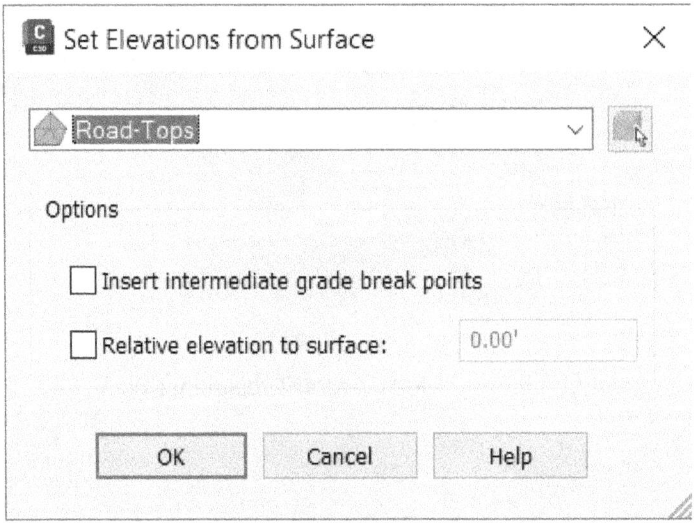

Figure 2-64

7. Select a parcel segment of **Lot 10**.

8. In the Command Line, you are prompted to select objects. Type **M** and press <Enter> to permit crossing window selections. Select all 15 single family lot segments, the Commercial parcel segments, and the Pond parcel segments (17 Total), as shown in Figure 2-65.

Figure 2–65

9. Press <Enter> to end the selection and exit the command.

10. Press <Esc> to clear the selection set.

11. In the drawing, select **Lot 10** by selecting its area label again.

12. In the *Parcel* contextual tab>*Edit Elevations* panel, click ⬤ (Elevation Editor) to open the *Elevation Editor* vista to see which elevations were assigned to the parcel segments.

13. When prompted to select objects, select the parcel segments of **Lot 10**. Note that elevations are assigned to each vertex along the roads but not on the interior, as shown in Figure 2–66. This is because the road surfaces do not extend into the interior.

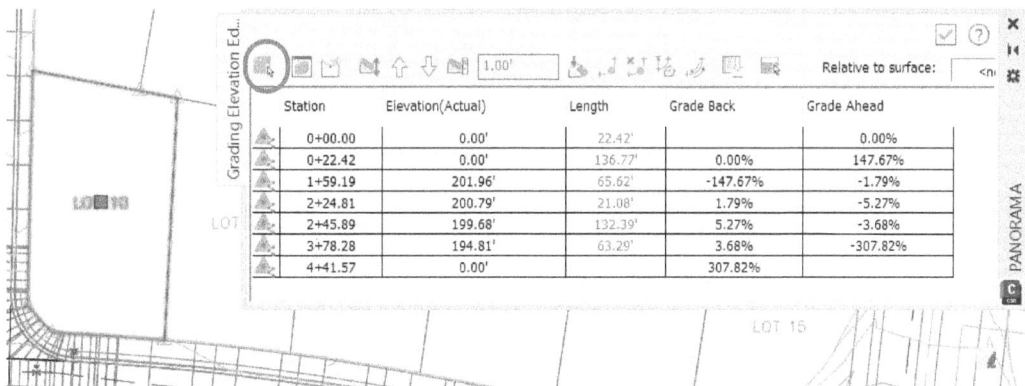

Station	Elevation(Actual)	Length	Grade Back	Grade Ahead
0+00.00	0.00'	22.42'		0.00%
0+22.42	0.00'	136.77'	0.00%	147.67%
1+59.19	201.96'	65.62'	-147.67%	-1.79%
2+24.81	200.79'	21.08'	1.79%	-5.27%
2+45.89	199.68'	132.39'	5.27%	-3.68%
3+78.28	194.81'	63.29'	3.68%	-307.82%
4+41.57	0.00'		307.82%	

Figure 2–66

14. Check other parcels by clicking 🔲 (Select Feature), as shown above in Figure 2–66, to select them without closing the *Elevation Editor* vista.

15. In the *Edit Elevations* vista, click ☑ to close the vista.

16. The *Parcel* contextual tab should still be available since the parcel is still selected. In the *Edit Elevations* panel, click 🖉 (Quick Elevation Edit).

17. Hover over a lot line and notice the grade which appears in a tooltip, as shown in Figure 2–67. Notice that if you are beyond the midpoint of the lot line, the grade changes from positive to negative, and the small green arrow changes direction.

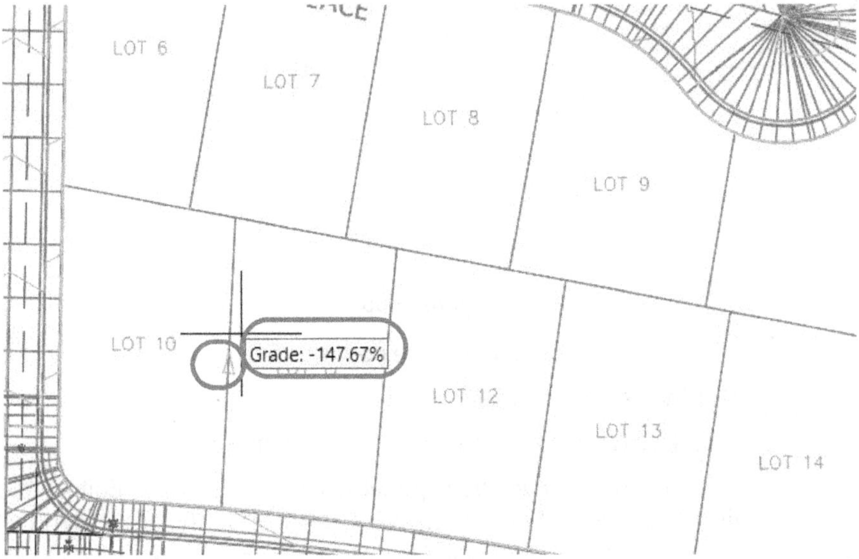

Figure 2–67

18. Ensure that the green arrow is pointing to the rear of the lot and click it, then type **-2 (minus 2)** to have the lot line lower with a 2% grade.

19. Hover over the endpoint of the rear of the lot line. Note that the elevation is no longer zero, but approximately **199**, as shown in Figure 2-68.

Figure 2-68

20. Select the lot line between **Lot 6** and **Lot 7** near the rear of the lot and set that grade to **8**. Hover over the rear endpoint and note that the elevation is about **198.8**.

21. Change all lot lines running north-south of lots (near the rear of the lots) **10** through **15** to grade **-2 (minus 2)**.

22. Change all lot lines running north-south of lots (near the rear of the lots) **6** through **9** to grade up **8%**.

23. Hover over the rear lot lines (running east-west) and note that the grades are acceptable.

24. Press <Enter> to finish.

25. **Lot 10** should still be selected. If not, select it by clicking its area label again.

26. In the *Parcel* contextual tab>*Edit Elevations* panel, click ⬤ (Elevation Editor) to open the *Elevation Editor* vista to see which elevations are now assigned to the parcel segments.

27. When prompted to select objects, select the parcel segments of **Lot 10.** Note that the elevations and grades are acceptable, as shown in Figure 2–69.

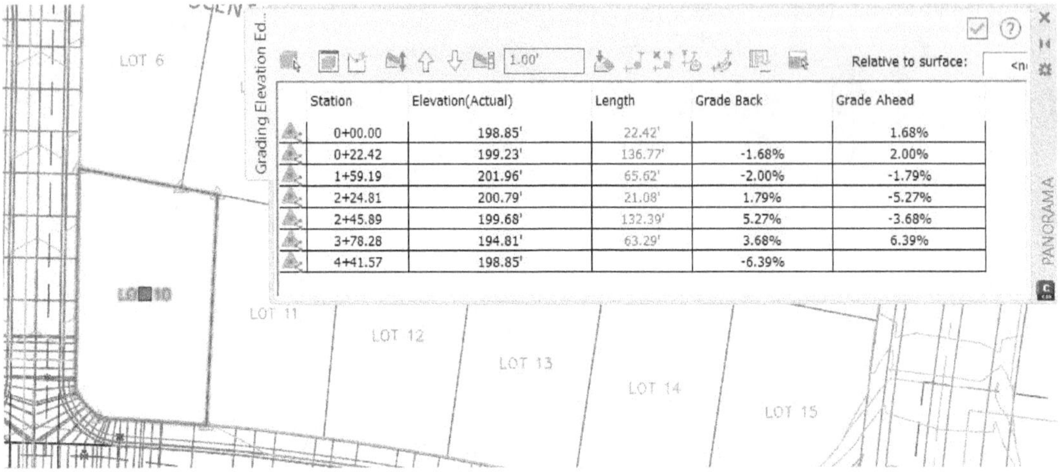

Station	Elevation(Actual)	Length	Grade Back	Grade Ahead
0+00.00	198.85'	22.42'		1.68%
0+22.42	199.23'	136.77'	-1.68%	2.00%
1+59.19	201.96'	65.62'	-2.00%	-1.79%
2+24.81	200.79'	21.08'	1.79%	-5.27%
2+45.89	199.68'	132.39'	5.27%	-3.68%
3+78.28	194.81'	63.29'	3.68%	6.39%
4+41.57	198.85'		-6.39%	

Figure 2–69

28. If time permits, check the other lots 6 though 15. Ensure that **Lot 9** (or **Lot 13**) has no vertices at elevation 0. If it has, set the elevation to **198**.

29. Save the drawing.

End of practice

Chapter Review Questions

1. Which is not an option for creating a feature line?
   a. Create Feature Lines from Objects
   b. Create Feature Lines from Alignment
   c. Create Feature Line from Corridor
   d. Create Feature Lines from Profile

2. When creating a feature line from objects, which object cannot be used?
   a. Lines
   b. Circles
   c. Arcs
   d. Polylines or 3D Polylines

3. Which icon in the *Feature Line* contextual tab>*Modify* panel enables you to edit feature line geometry?

   a.
   b.
   c.
   d.

4. Which icon in the *Feature Line* contextual tab>*Modify* panel enables you to edit feature line elevations?

    a.

    b.

    c.

    d.

5. Which icon in the *Feature Line* contextual tab>*Edit Geometry* panel enables you to trim a feature line at selected cutting edges?

    a.

    b.

    c.

    d.

6. Which icon in the *Feature Line* contextual tab>*Edit Elevations* panel enables you to insert a high/low elevation point?

    a.

    b.

    c.

    d.

7. Feature lines can be extracted from corridor models.

    a. True

    b. False

Building Pad Design

Setting the elevation of a building pad and grading out a specified slope from that pad is important to fully understand how much cut and fill a site is going to have. You will explore how to assign elevations to a building footprint, and then create a simple grading object to calculate how much cut/fill is going to be required for the building at that elevation.

Learning Objectives

- Create a feature line from objects in a drawing or external reference file.
- Project a specific slope from a baseline to a specific target in a drawing.
- Change the grading criteria of an existing grading solution.
- Calculate the earthwork volumes for a grading group or a single grading object using the Grading Volume Tools.

3.1 Grading Creation Tools

This section focuses on grading to a surface. To start the **Grading** command, go to the *Home* tab>*Create Design* panel, expand the *Grading* drop-down list, and select a command in the *Grading Creation Tools* toolbar, as shown at the top of Figure 3–1.

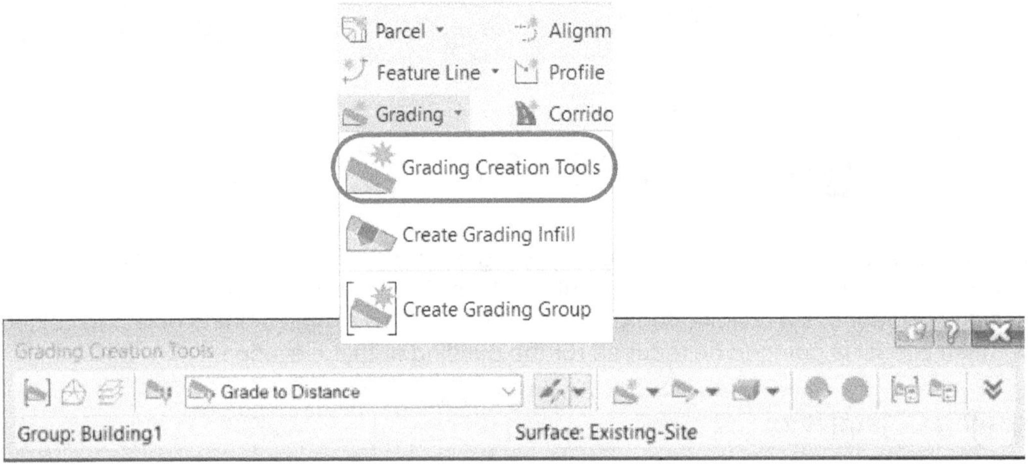

Figure 3–1

It is recommended that you start on the left and work to the right in command specific toolbars. The *Grading Creation Tools* toolbar is no exception to this recommended process. Therefore, the first thing you need to do is define or set the Grading Group.

Grading Groups

A grading object consists of a base line, projection lines, target lines, and faces. Combining multiple grading objects into a group enables you to create complex grading schemes. A grading group calculates a volume for an entire grading area, rather than one object at a time. Figure 3–2 shows each part of a grading group.

Each time a grading object is created, a new feature line is created as a projected target line. The resulting target line can then be used as a baseline for a new grading object within the same group.

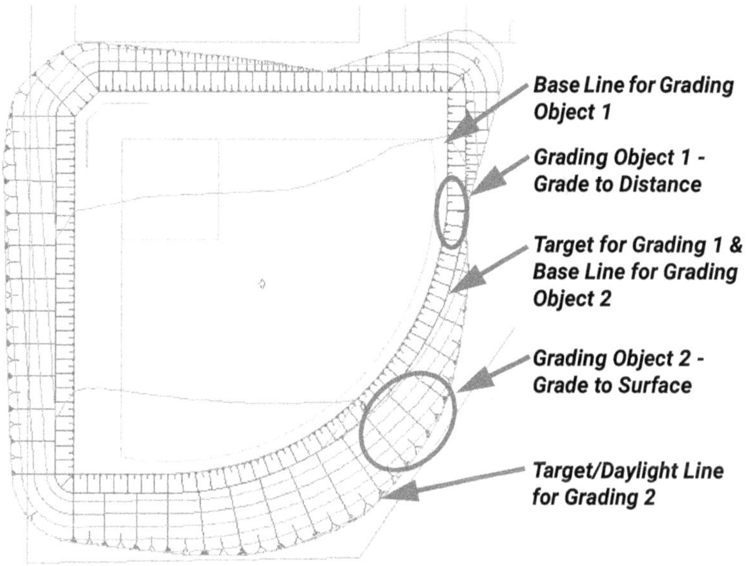
Base Line for Grading Object 1
Grading Object 1 - Grade to Distance
Target for Grading 1 & Base Line for Grading Object 2
Grading Object 2 - Grade to Surface
Target/Daylight Line for Grading 2

Figure 3–2

To create a new grading group, click (Set Grading Group) in the *Grading Creation Tools* toolbar. The first entry is the site in which you want to work, as shown in Figure 3–3. Sites can be created in the template to keep constancy across all of the projects. If a site does not already exist, a new site named **Site 1** is created automatically.

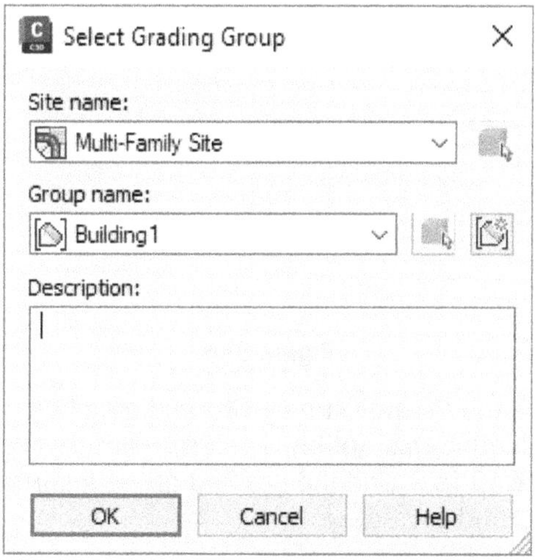
Select Grading Group
Site name:
Multi-Family Site
Group name:
Building1
Description:
OK
Cancel
Help

Figure 3–3

Once the site has been set, another dialog box opens enabling you to create a grading group, as shown in Figure 3–4. The first task is to type a name and a description. Next you decide whether you want to predefine a surface for the grading group. If simple grading groups are being created with one or two projections, creating a surface immediately should not be a problem. However, if a grading group is complex with three or more grading objects, it is recommended that you wait until the grading group is complete before creating the group's surface.

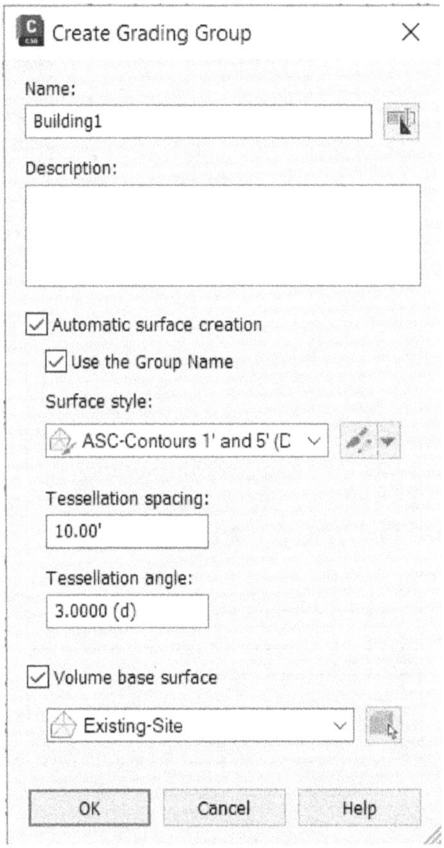

Figure 3–4

The last option to consider in the *Create Grading Group* dialog box is whether or not to set a Volume base surface. By selecting this option, a volume for the entire grading group can be calculated between this base surface and the grading group's surface. The base surface is usually set to the existing ground surface.

If the **Automatic surface creation** option is selected, a *Create Surface* dialog box opens, as shown in Figure 3–5. If you also selected the **Use the Group Name** option, the surface name field is already filled in with the grading group's name. Using the grading group's name as the surface ensures consistency and makes communication between other team members easy because they recognize that the grading group and surface are the same. As with any Autodesk Civil 3D surface, you can assign a style to the grading group surface.

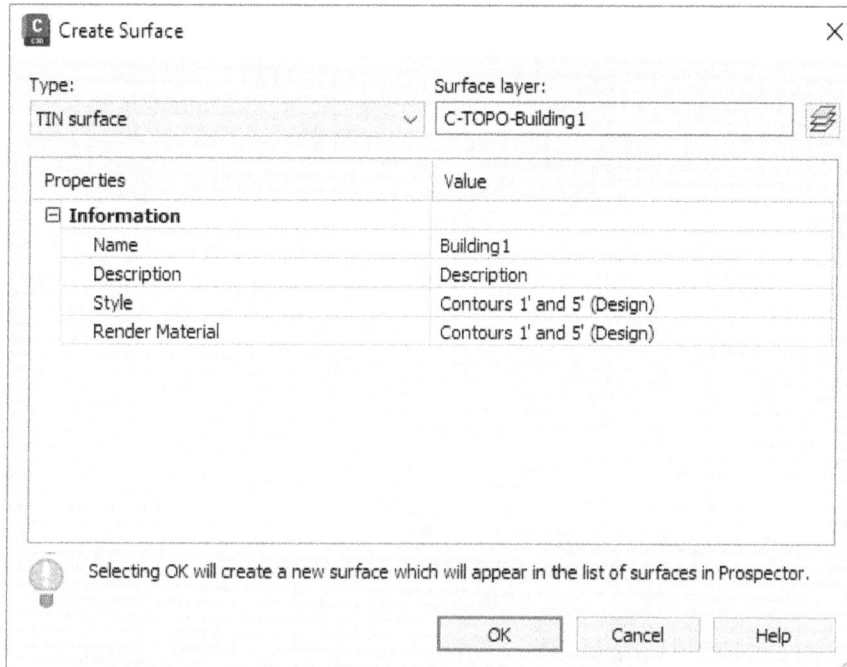

Figure 3–5

Grading Setup

The next task in the *Grading Creation Tools* toolbar is to set the target surface ⬦ . This is especially important if you want to grade to a surface because this surface is the Grade to Surface criteria's target. If a volume base surface was set in the *Create Grading Group* dialog box, the surface is set in the *Grading Creation Tools* toolbar, as shown in Figure 3–6.

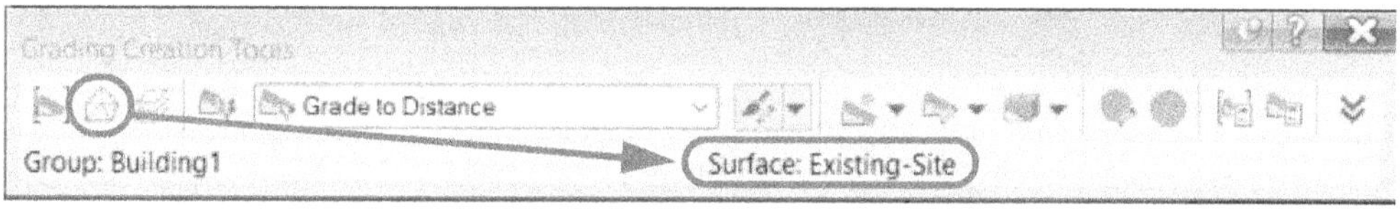

Figure 3–6

The next tool in the *Grading Creation Tools* toolbar is ⬦ (Set Grading Layer). Although you can use this tool to set the *Layer* for the grading objects, it is recommended that you use the drawing settings and grading styles to set the layer.

The next tool is ![icon] (Select a Criteria Set). The standard Autodesk Civil 3D template includes a Basic criteria set that incorporates all four grading criteria without any locks toggled on. If you or someone in your company has added additional grading criteria sets to prevent unnecessary parameter entries, you can select the grading criteria set that you want to use, as shown in Figure 3–7.

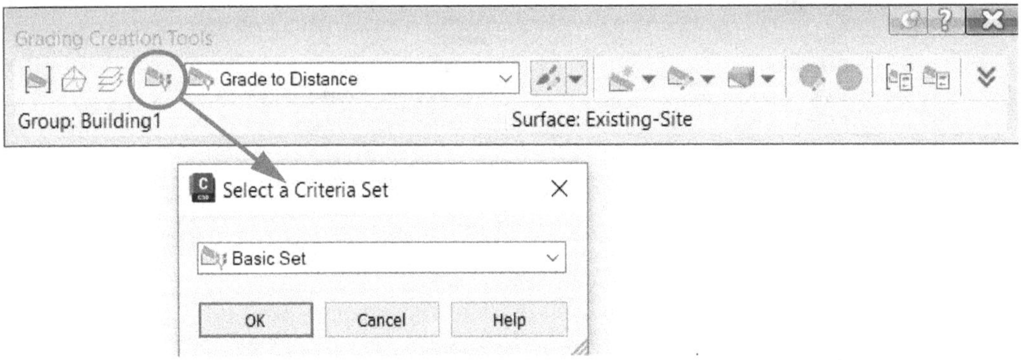

Figure 3–7

Depending on the selected Criteria Set, different grading criteria might be available. Figure 3–8 shows the criteria available in the Basic Set. Select the required criteria for the type of project you are doing. If the required criteria is not available, you can create new criteria on the fly by clicking ![icon] (Create New Criteria).

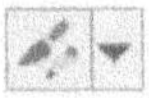

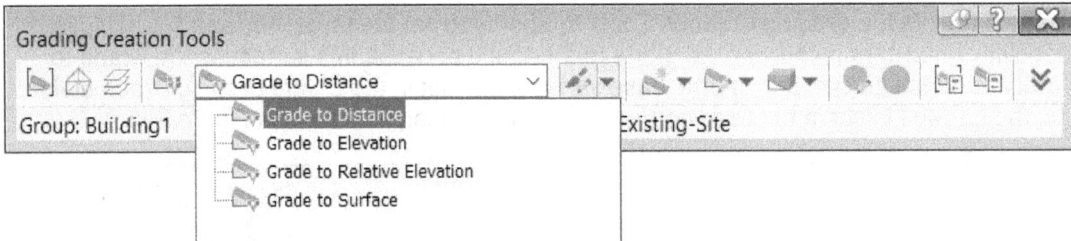

Figure 3–8

Create Grading

After setting the above parameters, you are ready to start grading. Click ![icon] (Create Grading) and select the feature line that you want to use as the baseline. Next you are prompted for the side to which to grade if you want the grading to apply to the entire length of the feature line. After you have set the length to apply the grading criteria, the next prompt is for the grading parameters. This only occurs if the criteria you are using is not locked. Grading can be done on either side even if you have an open feature line or a closed feature line. If you are grading to the inside of a closed feature line, projections continue until the target is reached or the grading grades to itself, as shown in Figure 3-9.

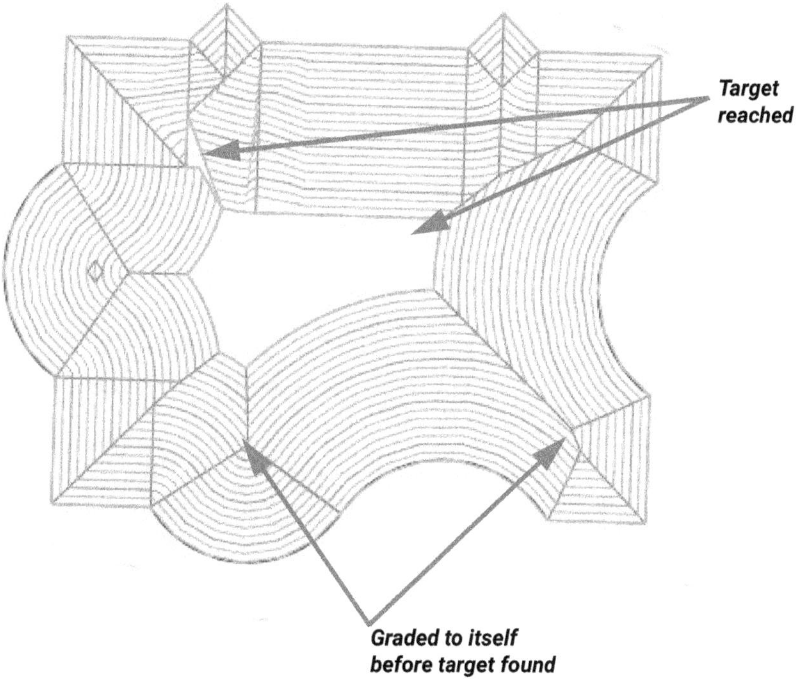

Target reached

Graded to itself before target found

Figure 3-9

Grading Infill

Sometimes there is a need to fill in an area between two grading objects or feature lines. A grading infill is a grading face that eliminates holes in grading groups and ensures that the finished ground surface covers the entire grading area. To create an infill, click  (Create Infill) in the *Create Grading* drop-down list in the *Grading Creation* toolbar. The routine prompts you to pick a point in the open area to infill with a grading face (similar to picking a point to hatch an area), as shown in Figure 3–10.

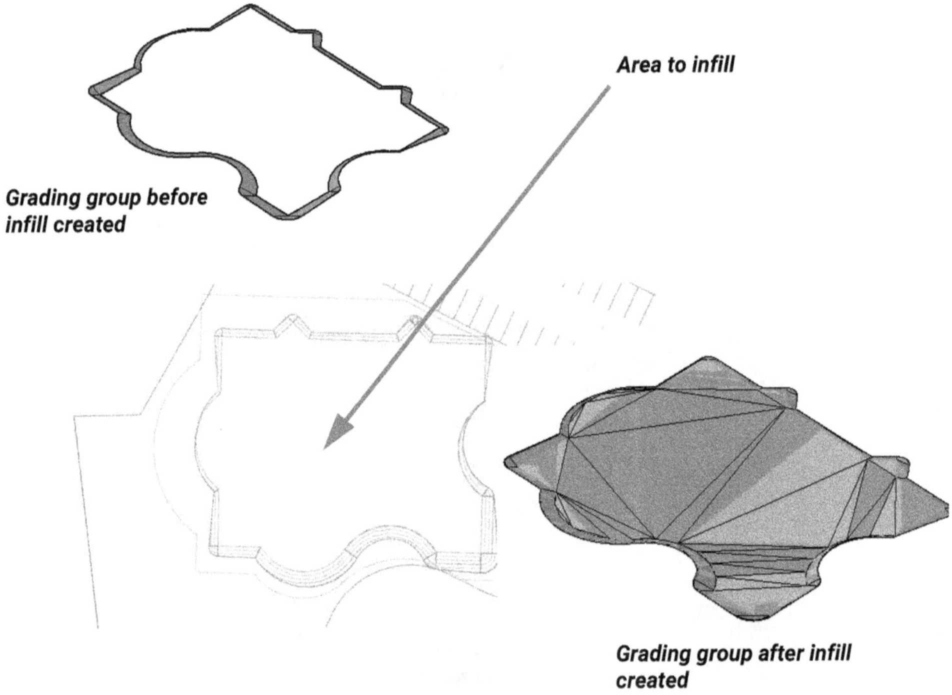

Area to infill

Grading group before infill created

Grading group after infill created

Figure 3–10

3.2 Editing the Grading

After creating a grading group, you might need to change one or more of the grading parameters. Some changes are required due to a mistake when creating the original grading place or due to a design change. In either case, the grading criteria used during the creation of the grading object determines what can change. If you used a *Grade to Distance* criteria but meant to use a *Grade to Surface* criteria, then you must delete the original grading object and replace it with a new grading object.

Delete Grading Objects

To delete a grading object and not corrupt your drawing, you should first select the grading object and, in the *Grading* contextual tab>*Modify* panel, click ✎ (Delete Grading), as shown in Figure 3-11. It is important that you delete the outer most grading object before deleting the interior grading objects. This is because if an interior grading object is used by other grading objects as a baseline, the exterior grading object becomes corrupt and unusable.

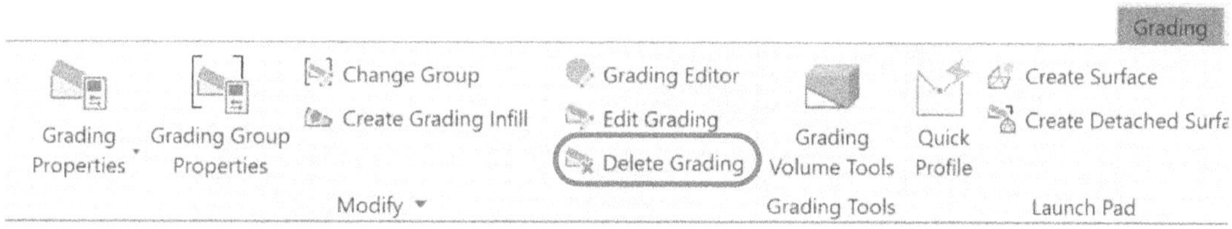

Figure 3-11

Modify Grading Object Criteria

To modify the input parameters of a grading object, you must first ensure that the criteria used was not locked, as locks prevent editing. To check this and make the required changes at the same time, you use the *Grading Editor*. In the *Grading* contextual tab>*Modify* panel, click

🔊 (Grading Editor), as shown in Figure 3-12.

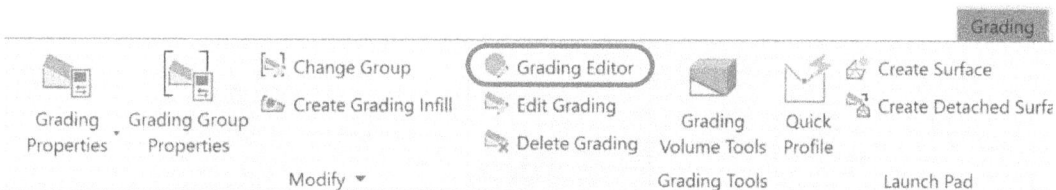

Figure 3-12

The Panorama's *Grading Editor* vista enables you to modify a grading's parameters. Any parameters that were locked when creating the grading object have a lock symbol to the left indicating that they cannot be changed. Anything without a lock can be changed by selecting the value field to the right of the parameter, as shown in Figure 3–13.

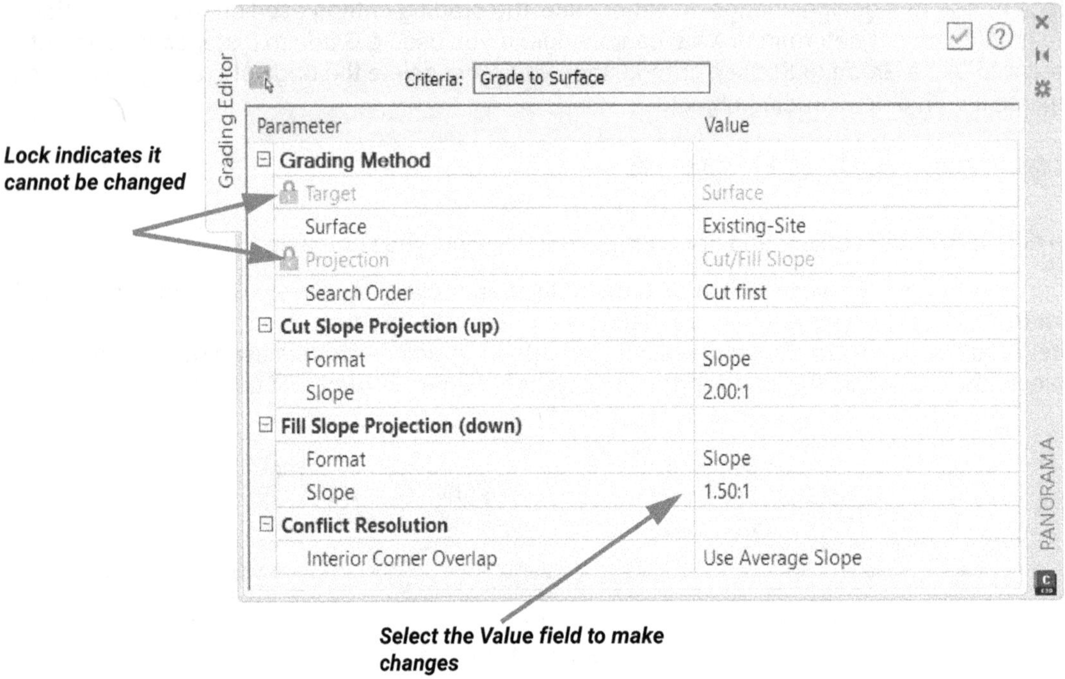

Figure 3–13

Alternatively, you can click ⬛ (Edit Grading) on the *Grading* contextual tab>*Modify* panel to use the *Grading Editor* to change the grading parameters, as shown in Figure 3–14. This routine prompts you for the parameters in the Command Line. Note that you are only prompted for parameters that are not locked.

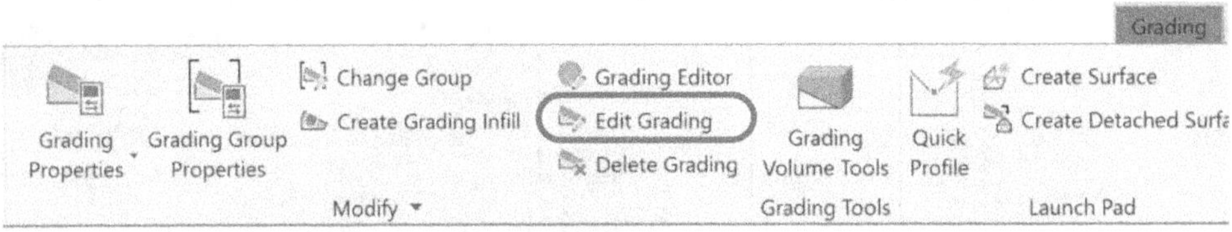

Figure 3–14

Practice 3a
Grading Creation Tools

Practice Objectives

- Project a feature line at a specific slope to a surface.
- Project another feature line to a surface on a temporary site.
- Adjust the grading.
- Create infills.

In this practice, you will grade to a surface, create infills, and modify the grading criteria.

Task 1: Grade to a surface.

In this task, you will use the feature line created in an earlier practice as a baseline for your Grading Object and use the *Grading Creation Tools* toolbar to create a grading that slopes into the existing ground surface.

1. Open **BLDG-A.dwg** from the *C:\Civil 3D Grading\Working\BLDG Pad* folder.

2. In the *Home* tab>*Create Design* panel, expand the *Grading* drop-down list and click

   (Grading Creation Tools). The *Grading Creation Tools* toolbar displays.

3. In the *Grading Creation Tools* toolbar, click (Set the Grading Group). Select

   Multi-Family Site, and click (Create a Grading Group) as shown in Figure 3–15.

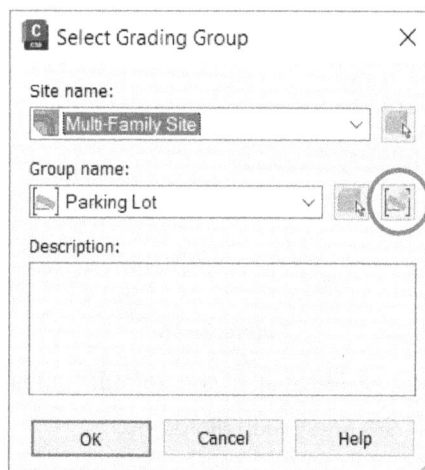

Figure 3–15

4. In the *Create Grading Group* dialog box, set the following, as shown in Figure 3–16:

- For the *Name*, type **Building Pads**.
- For the *Description*, type **Commercial building platforms**.
- Select the option to automatically create a surface.
- Set the *Volume base surface* to **Residential Grading**.
- Click **OK** to close the dialog box.

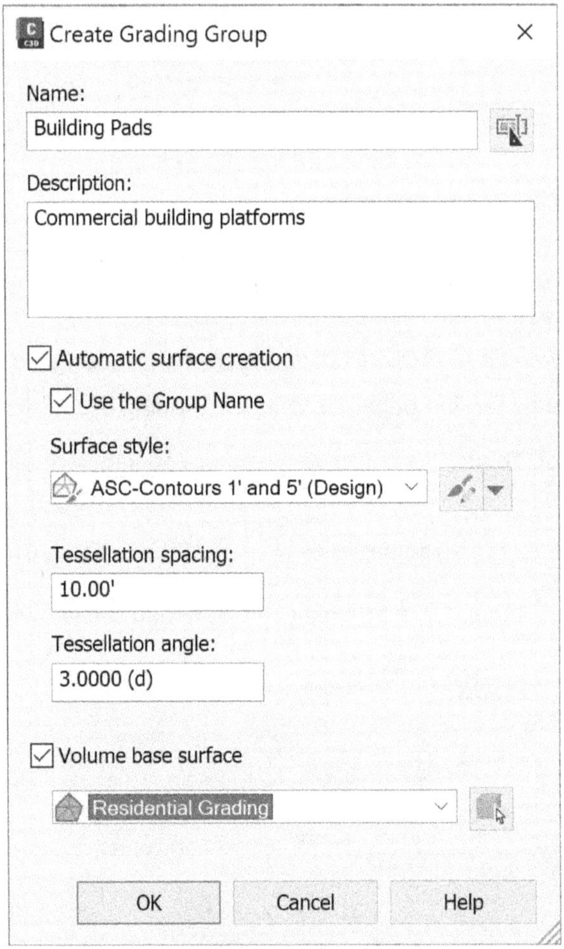

Figure 3–16

5. In the *Create Surface* dialog box, leave all of the default values and click **OK**.
6. Click **OK** to close the *Select Grading Group* dialog box.

7. In the *Grading Creation Tools* toolbar, verify that the *Criteria Set* is set to **Basic Set** by hovering over ▱ (Select a Criteria Set). Set the grading criteria to **Grade to Surface**, as shown in Figure 3-17.

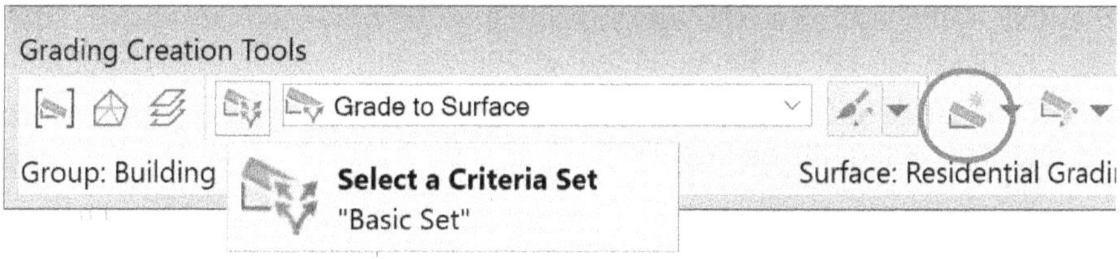

Figure 3-17

8. In the *Grading Creation Tools* toolbar, click ▱ (Create Grading), as shown in Figure 3-17.

9. In the model, select the blue hotel pad feature line marked as **B** in Figure 3-18.

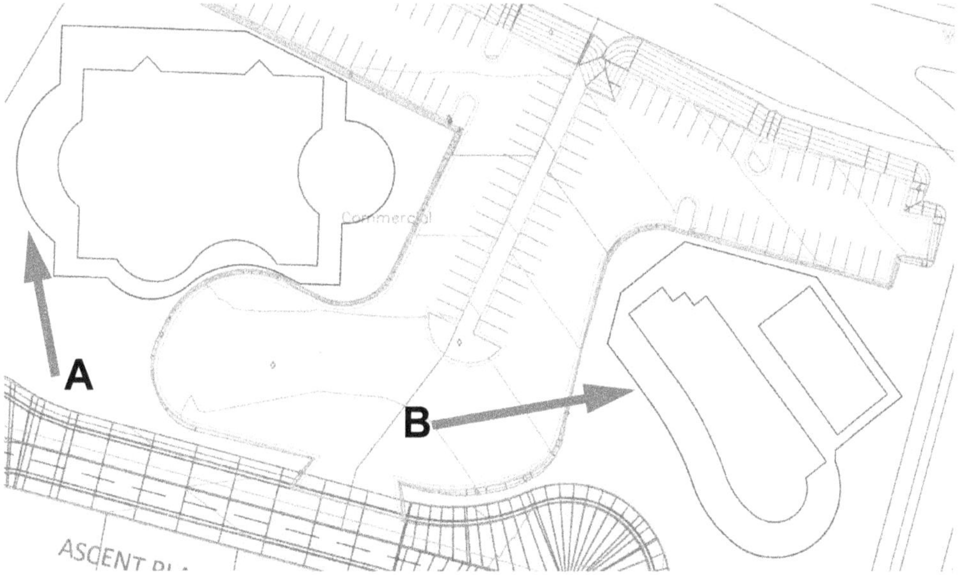

Figure 3-18

10. When prompted for a grading side, pick a point outside the building footprint.

11. When prompted to apply it to the entire length, press <Enter> to accept the default of **Yes**.

12. Press <Enter> to accept the default format of slope for both cut and fill.

13. Press <Enter> to accept the default 2:1 slopes for both cut and fill.

14. Click ✔ to close the *Events* vista if it displays. Press <Esc> to end the command. The drawing should display as shown in Figure 3–19.

15. Press <Esc> to finish the grading command.

16. Note that the grading between the parking curb and the hotel pad neatly coincides, as shown in Figure 3–19. This is because both grading groups reside in the same site.

17. There are issues with this solution, as shown in Figure 3–19 where it gets too close to the property line. This will get fixed later in this practice.

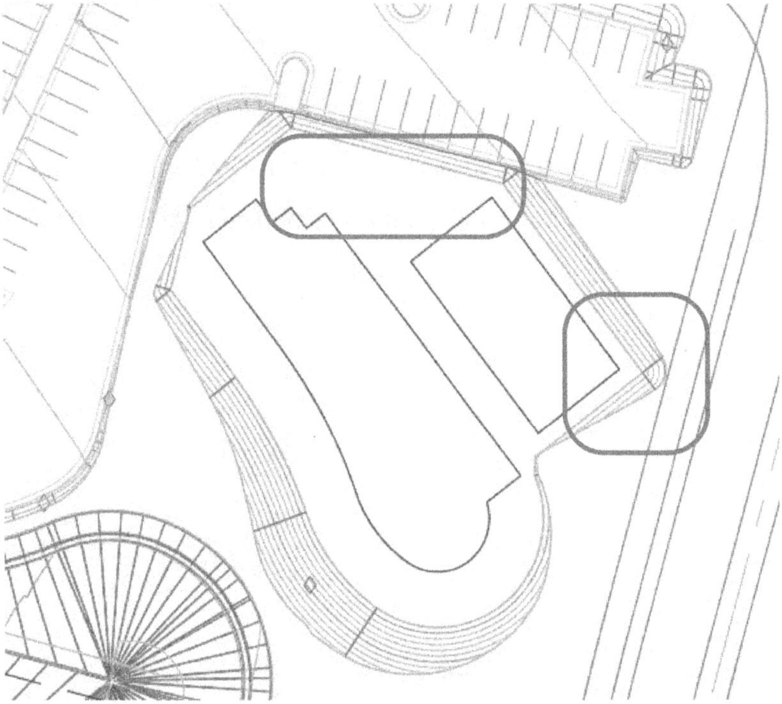

Figure 3–19

18. Save and close the drawing.

Task 2: (Optional) Attempt to grade the office pad.

Civil 3D's grading tools and procedures as well as creating surfaces from grading groups can be somewhat unpredictable at times. When grading scenarios get complex and other grading groups within the same site are present, Civil 3D may not be able to solve the grading and either give unexpected results or even crash the program.

Such is the case when trying to grade the office pad as you have done with the hotel pad. You can attempt to perform this task in the following steps, but if there are time constraints or your system becomes too unstable, you can review the result by opening **BLDG-A1-Complete.dwg** from the *C:\Civil 3D Grading\Working\BLDG-Pad* folder.

The next task (3) will start with the completed drawing from the previous task (1).

Repeat the same steps you did in the previous task for the office pad feature line, as follows:

1. Open **BLDG-A1.dwg** from the *C:\Civil 3D Grading\Working\BLDG Pad* folder.

2. In the *View* tab>*Named Views* panel, select **Office**.

3. In the *Home* tab>*Create Design* panel, expand the *Grading* drop-down list and click

    (Grading Creation Tools).

4. Ensure that the Grading Group is set to **Building Pads**. If not, click on (Set the Grading Group). For *Site name*, select **Multi-Family Site**, and to set the *Group Name* to **Building Pads**, then click **OK**, as shown in Figure 3–20.

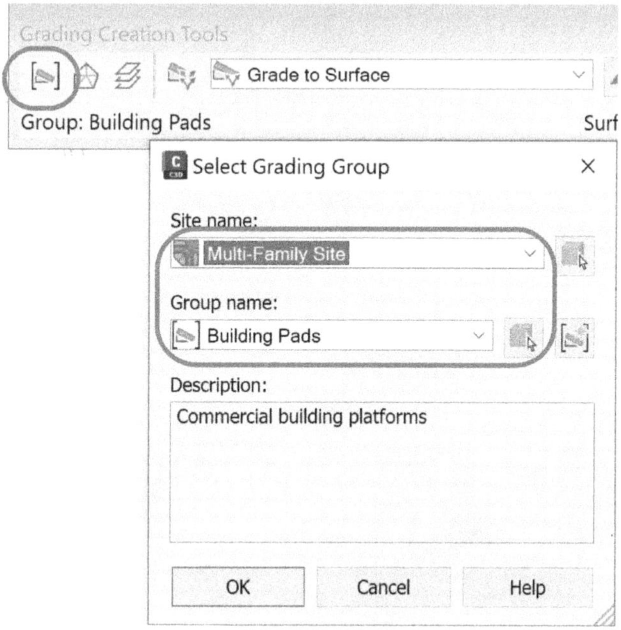

Figure 3–20

5. In the *Grading Creation Tools* toolbar, verify that the grading criteria to **Grade to Surface**.

6. In the *Grading Creation Tools* toolbar, click (Create Grading).

7. In the model, select the blue office pad feature line, marked as **A** in Figure 3–18. When prompted for a grading side, pick a point outside the building footprint.

8. When prompted to apply it to the entire length, press <Enter> to accept the default of **Yes**.

9. Press <Enter> to accept the default format of slope for both cut and fill.

10. Type **1 (One)** to set the slope to 1:1 for both cut and fill.

11. Click ✔ to close the *Events* vista if it displays. Press <Esc> to end the command. The drawing should display, as shown in Figure 3–21.

12. Press <Esc> to finish the grading command.

13. There are major issues with this solution, as shown in Figure 3–21. Initially they may not be apparent, except where the grading is incomplete in the North-west corner of the office pad, marked as **A**. However, notice what has happened to the surface over at the hotel pad and in the parking area north of the hotel, marked as **B**. This is unacceptable.

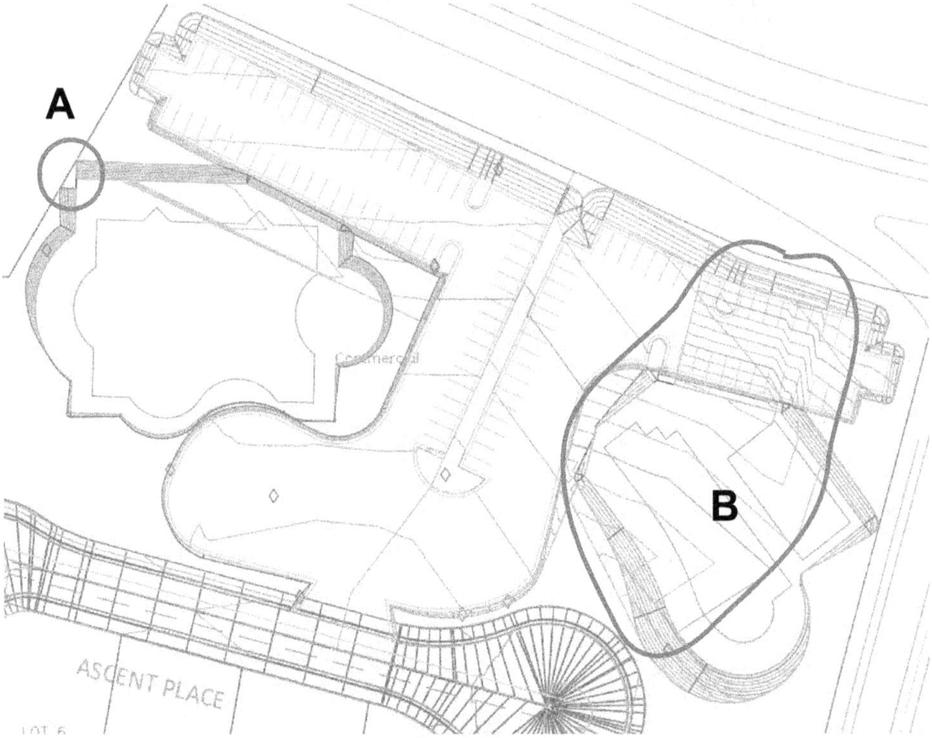

Figure 3–21

14. We will find another solution in the next task. For now, quit the drawing without saving.

Task 3: Alternative way to grade the office pad.

While it is convenient to have grading groups interact when they belong to the same site, at times it can become impossible for Civil 3D to grade properly with such interdependent grading groups. When this occurs, it is advisable to create the grading groups on different sites (usually a temporary site) and later paste the resulting surfaces together to form a combined surface.

1. Open **BLDG-B**.dwg from the *C:\Civil 3D Grading\Working\BLDG Pad* folder.

2. In the *Prospector* tab, right-click on **Sites** and select **New**, as shown in Figure 3–22.

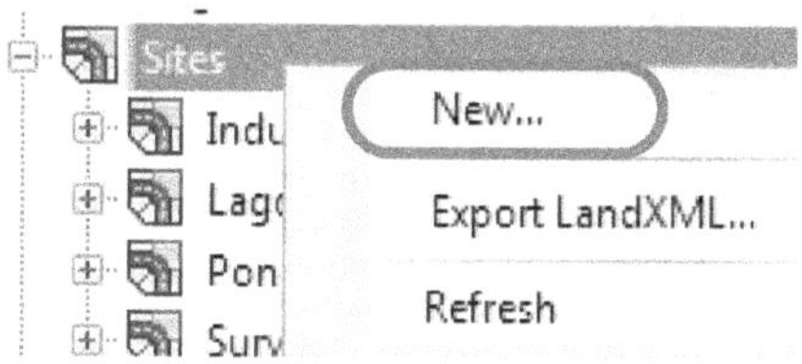

Figure 3–22

3. In the *Information* tab, for the *Name*, type **Temp** and click **OK**.

4. In the *View* tab>*Named Views* panel, select **Office**.

5. Select the **Office** feature line and in the right-click menu, select **Move to Site...**, as shown in Figure 3–23.

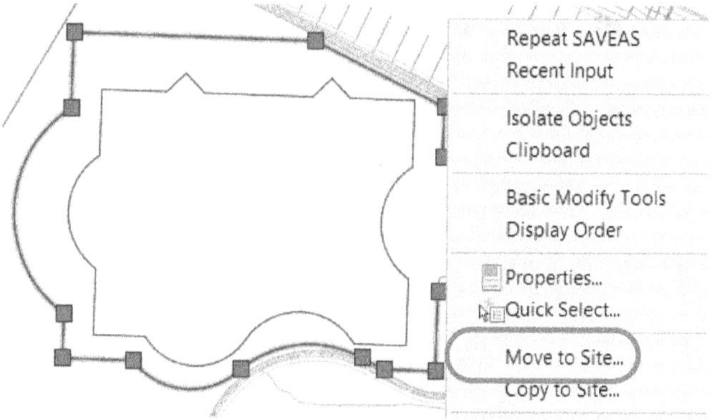

Figure 3–23

6. In the *Move to Site* dialog box, use the drop-down arrow to select the **Temp** site, as shown in Figure 3–24.

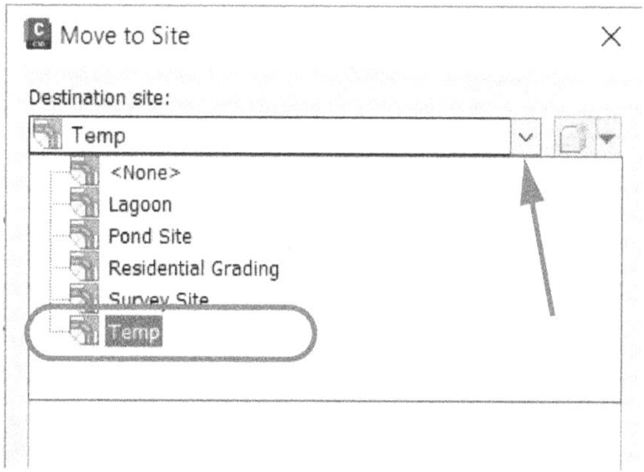

Figure 3–24

7. Click **OK** to dismiss the *Move to Site* dialog box.

8. Note that after the move, the name of the feature line has changed to **Office (1)**.

Repeat the same steps you did in Task 1, as follows:

9. If need be, in the *Home* tab>*Create Design* panel, expand the *Grading* drop-down list and click ![icon] (Grading Creation Tools).

10. In the *Grading Creation Tools* toolbar, click ![icon] (Set the Grading Group).

11. The *Select Grading Group* dialog box opens. Select the **Temp** site, then click ![icon] (Create a Grading Group), as shown in Figure 3–25.

Figure 3–25

12. In the *Create Grading Group* dialog box, set the following, as shown in Figure 3-26:

    - For the *Name*, type **Office Pad**.
    - Select the **Automatic surface creation** option.
    - Set the *Volume base surface* to **Residential Grading**.
    - Click **OK** to close the dialog box.

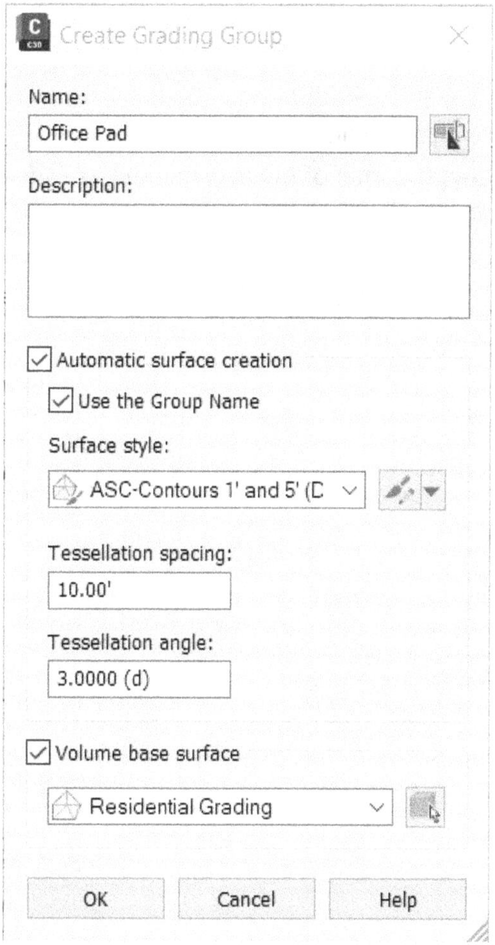

Figure 3-26

13. In the *Create Surface* dialog box, leave all of the default values and click **OK**.

14. Click **OK** to dismiss the *Select Grading Group* dialog box.

15. In the *Grading Creation Tools* toolbar, make sure that grading criteria is **Grade to Surface**.

16. In the *Grading Creation Tools* toolbar, click  (Create Grading).

17. In the model, select the **Office (1)** feature line. When prompted for a grading side, pick a point outside the building platform footprint, as shown by the arrows in Figure 3–27.

18. When prompted to apply it to the entire length, press <Enter> to accept the default of **Yes**.

19. Press <Enter> to accept the default format of slope for both cut and fill.

20. Type **1 (One)** to set the slope to 1:1 for both cut and fill.

21. Click ✓ to close the *Events* vista if it displays. Press <Esc> to end the command. The drawing should display, as shown in Figure 3–27.

22. Press <Esc> to finish the grading command.

23. There are some issues with this solution, as shown in Figure 3–27. The grading is incomplete in the North-west corner of the pad, marked as **A1**. This can be solved with transitional grading tools, which will be covered later in this guide.

24. The grading between the parking lot and the office pad overlaps since they are on different sites, marked as **A2**. This will get resolved later when pasting the separate surfaces into a combination surface.

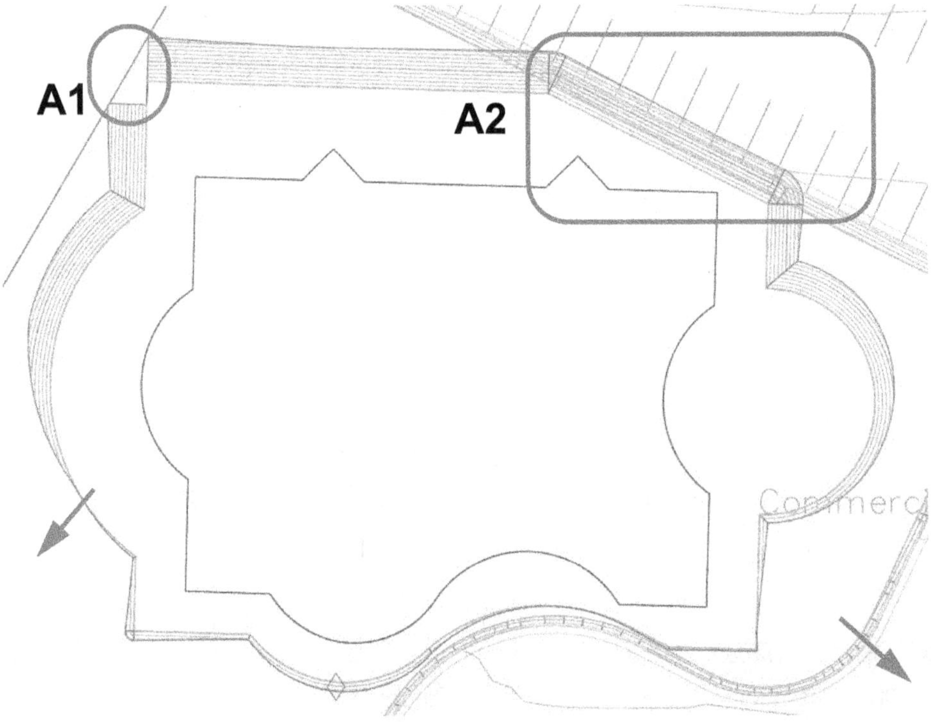

Figure 3–27

25. Save the drawing.

Task 4: Create infill.

1. Open **BLDG-C.dwg** from the *C:\Civil 3D Grading\Working\BLDG-Pad* folder. Do not continue working in the drawing from the previous practice; the office building pad grading has been fine-tuned in this drawing. The transitional grading tools used will be covered later in this guide.

2. If need be, in the *Home* tab>*Create Design* panel, expand the *Grading* drop-down list and click ▨ (Grading Creation Tools).

3. In the *Grading Creation Tools* toolbar, verify that the *Grading Group* is set to **Office Pad**, as shown in Figure 3–28.

Figure 3–28

4. In the *Grading Creation Tools* toolbar, expand the *Create Grading* drop-down list and click

   ◣ (Create Infill). Pick a point in the center of the office pad, marked as **A** in Figure 3–29.

   Note: A green diamond indicating that the area now has a grading face should display.

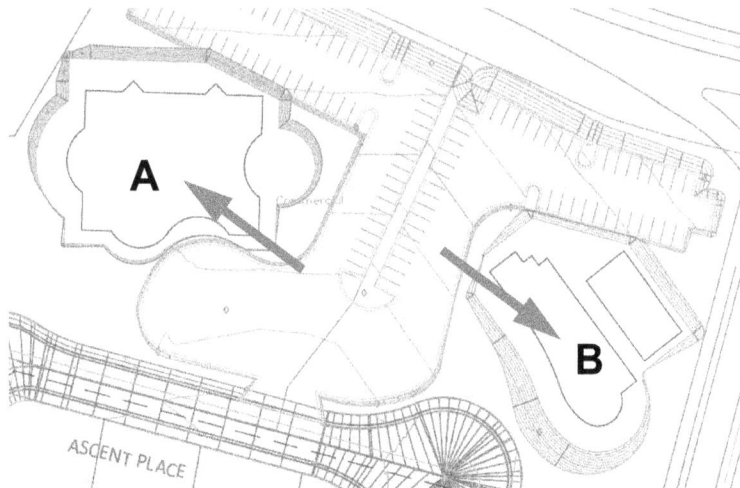

Figure 3–29

5. Press <Enter> to end the command. If the *Events* vista displays, click ✔ to close it.

6. In the *Grading Creation Tools* toolbar, change the *Grading Group* to **Building Pads**, as shown in Figure 3−30.

Figure 3−30

7. In the *Grading Creation Tools* toolbar, expand the *Create Grading* drop-down list and click

   (Create Infill). Pick a point in the center of the Hotel pad, marked as **B** in Figure 3−29.

8. Press <Enter> to end the command. If the *Events* vista displays, click ✓ to close it.

9. Save the drawing.

Task 5: Modify the grading criteria.

After completing the grading, for the office pad, note that the fill slope on the northwest side of the building pad is encroaching the property line, and the other fill slopes are a bit too steep. Rather than moving the building or the pad, you will decrease the corner grading to **0.3** and increase the other fill slope to **1.50:1**.

1. Continue to work in the drawing from the previous task.

2. Select the grading object center mark (diamond symbol) created by grading, marked as **A1** in Figure 3−31.

   *Note: If you have problems finding the diamond grip, zoom out and **REGEN** the drawing. This will resize the diamond grips.*

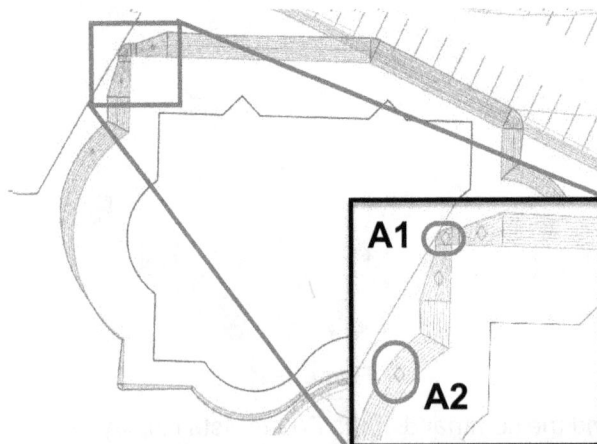

Figure 3−31

3. In the *Grading* contextual tab>*Modify* panel, click ◈ (Grading Editor).

4. In the *Grading Editor* panorama, change the *Fill Slope* to **0.3:1**, as shown in Figure 3-32, and press <Enter>. Note that the results are immediate; the grading recalculates after you press <Enter>.

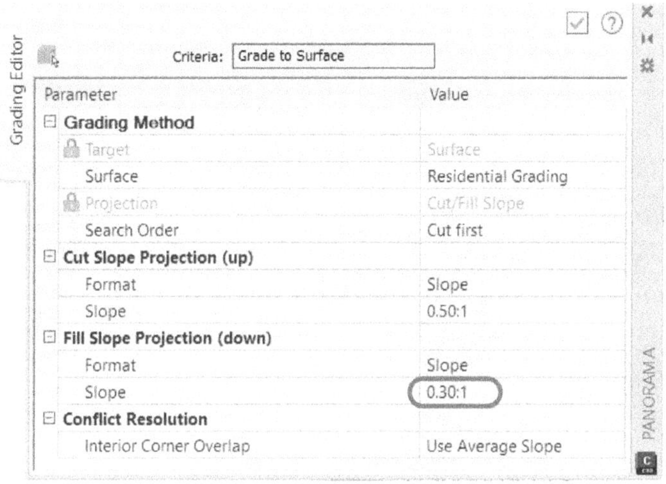

Figure 3-32

5. Click ✓ to close the *Grading Editor* panorama. Press <Esc> to release the grading object.

6. Repeat steps with the grading object center mark marked as **A2** in Figure 3-31. Give this a fill slope of **1.50:1.**

7. The final result is displayed in Figure 3-33.

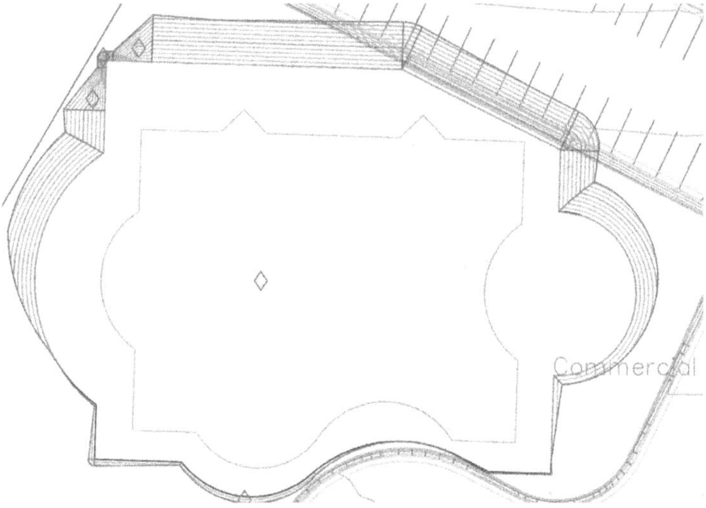

Figure 3-33

8. Zoom out to see both building pads.

9. Select the Building Pads surface (select one of its contour lines) and the Office Pad surface.

10. In the right-click menu, click **Add to Model Viewer**. Using the Viewcube, set the view direction to **SW Isometric**, as shown in Figure 3–34.

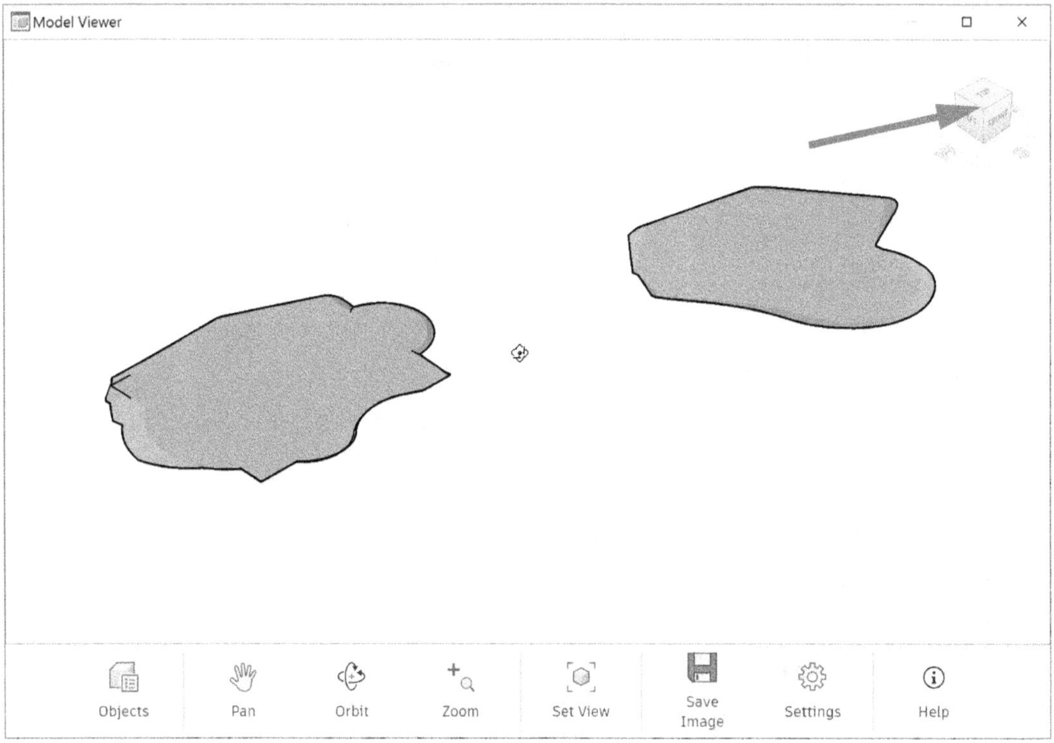

Figure 3–34

11. Close the *Model Viewer*.

12. Press <Esc> release the selection.

13. Save the drawing.

End of practice

3.3 Grading Volume Tools

The biggest benefit to using grading groups to create future grading plans is the ease with which they can be modified and their volumes calculated. The Grading Volume Tools assist in calculating the earthwork volumes for the grading group and assist in balancing the cut and fill volumes.

Calculate Volumes

Selecting a grading object displays the *Grading* contextual tab. You also access this tab by going to the *Modify* tab>*Design* panel and clicking (Grading). In the *Grading* tab>*Grading Tools* panel, click (Grading Volume Tools) to access the *Grading Volume Tools* toolbar, as shown in Figure 3−35.

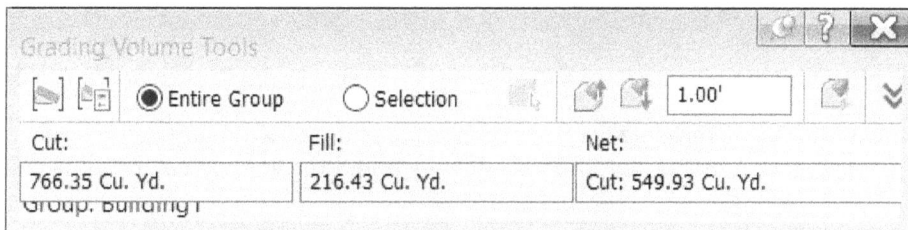

Figure 3−35

The group whose calculation displays in the toolbar is listed in the bottom left corner. To change which group is being calculated, click (Set Group) at the top left. By default, the **Entire Group** option is set so that the volume for all of the grading objects within the group is calculated as one item. To find the volume of a single grading object, change the option to **Selection** and pick a grading object in the drawing by clicking , as shown in Figure 3−36.

Figure 3−36

Balance Volumes

Grading groups can be adjusted vertically using the Grading Volume Tools to balance the cut and fill volumes and reduce the cost of hauling material in or out of the site. To do so, the **Entire Group** option must be selected. The option to raise or lower the group becomes available, as shown in Figure 3–37.

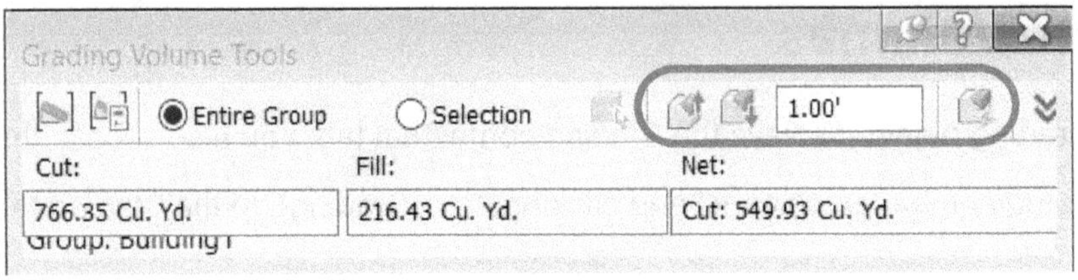

Figure 3–37

Incremental Changes

Typing an increment in the input field and clicking ⎘ (Raise Entire Group) or ⎗ (Lower Entire Group) enables you to incrementally raise or lower the entire grading group. Clicking ⏷ displays the history of how the incremental changes affect the volume calculations, as shown in Figure 3–38.

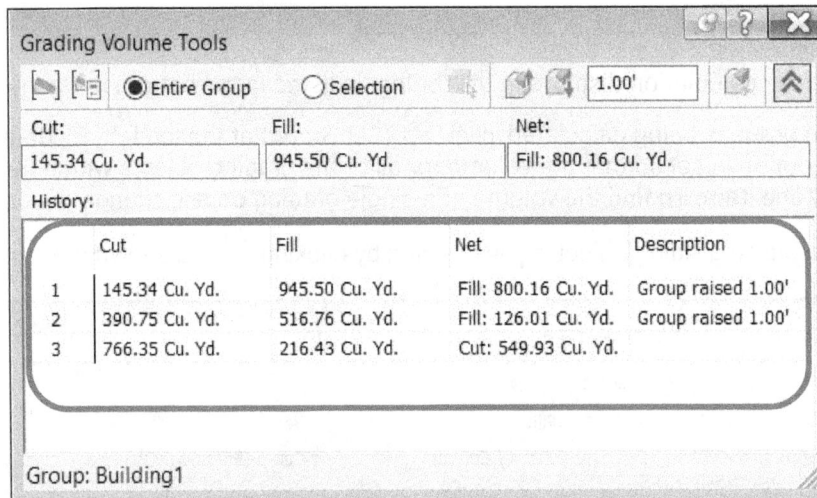

Figure 3–38

Automatically Balance Cut and Fill

Many projects require that the cut and fill for the project be minimized as much as possible to reduce costs. If that is the case on your project, you can use ⬚ (Auto Balance) to automatically raise or lower the entire grading group to balance the volumes. If this option is selected, a dialog box opens prompting you to set the required volume, as shown in Figure 3–39.

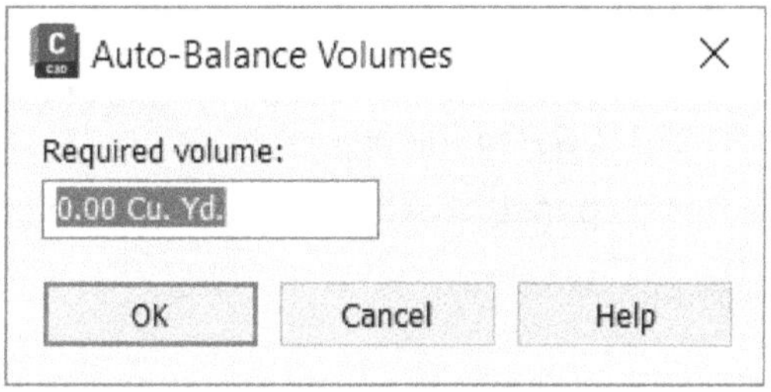

Figure 3–39

If you enter a specific volume in the *Required volume* field and click **OK** but the resulting volume does not match your entered target volume, you can click ⬚ (Auto Balance) again to get it closer. There might be times when you need to click this option more than once to get the required result.

Practice 3b
Grading Volume Tools

Practice Objectives

- Calculate and balance the cut and fill volumes of a grading group.

In this practice, you will calculate the grading group volume.

1. Continue working in the drawing from the previous practice or open **BLDG-D**.dwg from the *C:\Civil 3D Grading\Working\BLDG Pad* folder.

2. In the *Home* tab>*Create Design* panel, expand the *Grading* drop-down list and click

   ![icon] (Grading Creation Tools).

3. In the *Grading Creation Tools* toolbar, click ![icon] (Grading Volume Tools), as shown in Figure 3–40.

Figure 3–40

4. In the *Select Grading Group* dialog box, ensure that the **Office Pad** group in the **Temp** site is selected, as shown in Figure 3–41.

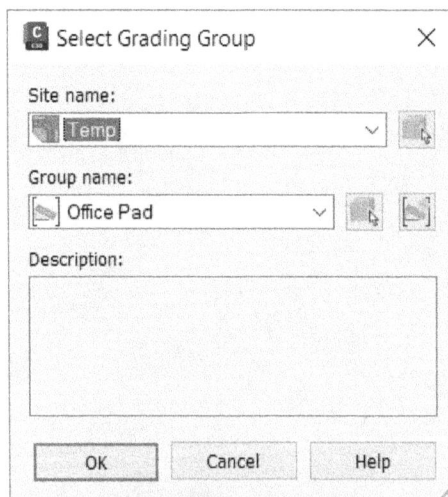

Figure 3–41

5. Click **OK** to dismiss the *Select Grading Group* dialog box.

6. Click ⬆ (Raise Group) to raise the entire group by **1'**, as shown in Figure 3–42.

7. Click ⌄ (Expand Toolbar) to display the grading calculation history, as shown in Figure 3–42.

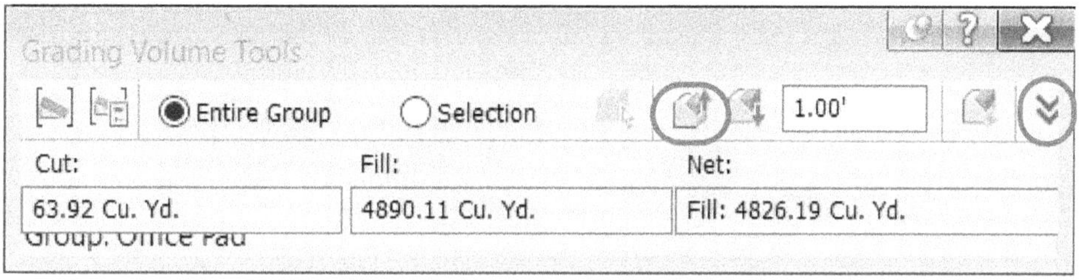

Figure 3–42

8. Click ⬆ (Auto-Balance) to automatically balance the cut and fill volumes for the entire group. Take the default of **0.00 Cu. Yd.** (zero), as shown in Figure 3–43. Click **OK** to close the dialog box.

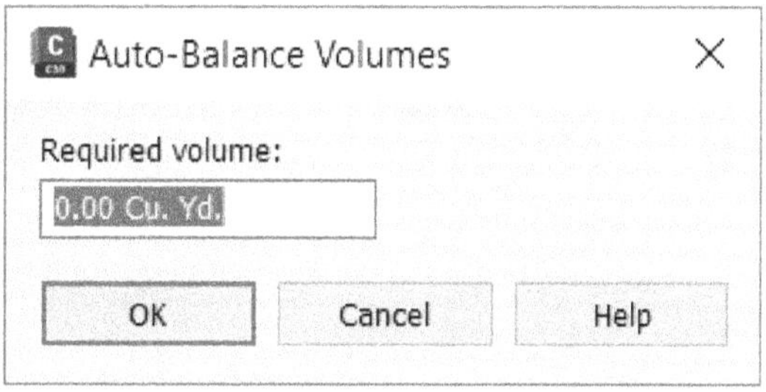

Figure 3–43

9. Click ✓ to close the *Events* vista if it displays.

10. Review the final volume calculation, as shown in Figure 3–44 and Figure 3–45.

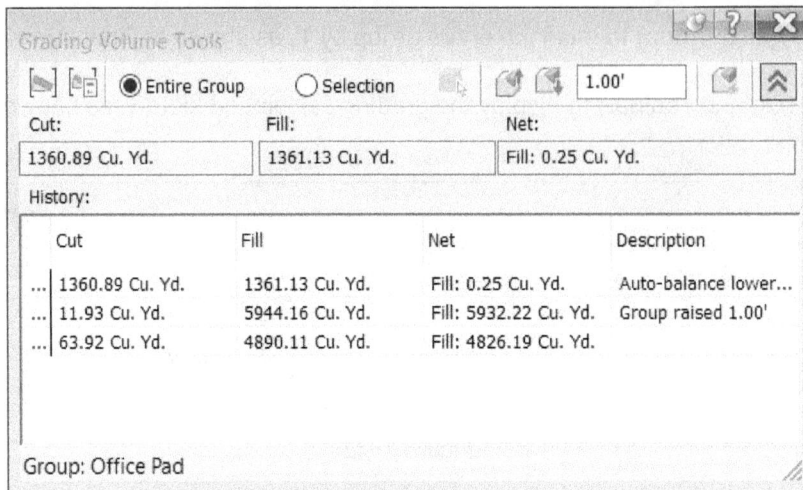

Figure 3–44

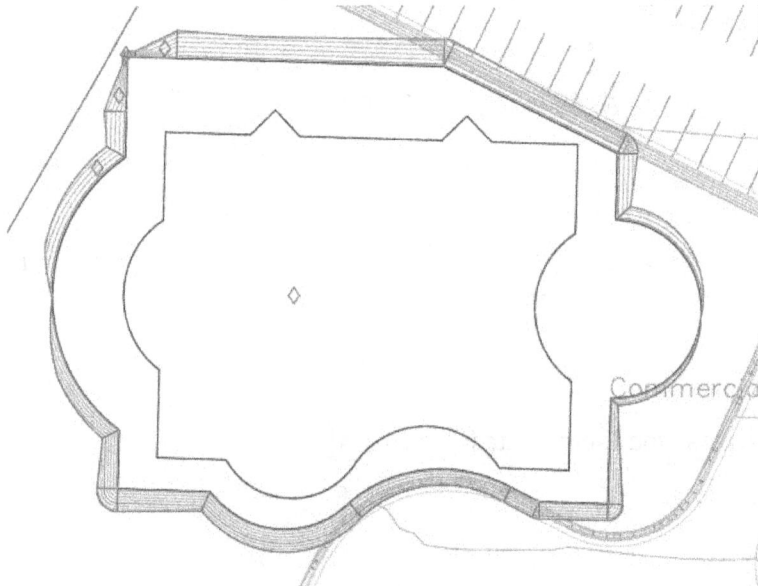

Figure 3–45

11. Save the drawing.

End of practice

Chapter Review Questions

1. Which icon in the *Elevation Editor* represents an elevation point?

   a. (Circle)

   b. (Triangle)

2. Which icon fills in an area that has not been graded with a grading face?

   a.

   b.

   c.

   d.

3. Which icon in the *Grading Volume Tools* toolbar enables you to display a history of the grading volume calculations?

   a.

   b.

   c.

   d.

Command Summary

Button	Command	Location
	Auto-Balance	• **Toolbar**: Grading Volume Tools (*contextual*)
	Create Feature Lines from Objects	• **Ribbon**: *Home* tab>*Create Design* panel, expand *Feature Line* drop-down list and click **Create Feature Lines From Objects** • **Command Prompt**: CreateFeatureLines
	Create Grading	• **Toolbar**: Grading Volume Tools (*contextual*)
	Create Grading Infill	• **Toolbar**: Grading Volume Tools (*contextual*) • **Ribbon**: *Home* tab>*Create Design* panel, expand *Grading* drop-down list and click **Create Grading Infill** • **Command Prompt**: CreateGradingInfill
	Elevation Editor	• **Ribbon**: *Feature Line* contextual tab> *Edit Elevations* panel>*Elevation Editor* • **Command Prompt**: GradingElevEditor
	Grading Creation Tools	• **Ribbon**: *Home* tab>*Create Design* panel, expand *Grading* drop-down list and click **Grading Creation Tools** • **Command Prompt**: GradingTools
	Grading Volume Tools	• **Ribbon**: *Grading* contextual tab> *Grading Tools* panel>**Grading Volume Tools** • **Command Prompt**: GradingVolumeTools
	Lower Grading Features	• **Toolbar**: Grading Volume Tools (*contextual*)
	Raise Grading Features	• **Toolbar**: Grading Volume Tools (*contextual*)
	Set Group	• **Toolbar**: Grading Volume Tools (*contextual*)
	Set Surface	• **Toolbar**: Grading Volume Tools (*contextual*)

Introduction to Grading Optimization

Grading is often more complicated than it appears. Even though the idea that "water runs downhill" seems straightforward, planning, designing, and calculating site drainage require careful consideration and expertise.

Civil 3D offers useful tools for handling grading tasks efficiently. In addition to its traditional features, Civil 3D includes the Grading Optimization Program, which enhances the overall grading process when used together with the standard tools.

Learning Objectives

- Understand the traditional Civil 3D grading tools.
- Understand the Grading Optimization tools.
- Explore the Grading Optimization interface.
- Create grading boundary zones.
- Create the Interim Design Grade.

4.1 Grading Optimization

In the 2022 Civil 3D release within the Autodesk AEC Collections, the Grading Optimization program was introduced. It is an alternate approach to grading solutions. It is an external program designed to find several different grading scenarios based on a variety of input data. Once a preferred solution is found, it is imported into Civil 3D as a surface along with optional points and breaklines. It is considered a tool primarily for initial site studies, layouts and conceptual grading, as shown in Figure 4–1.

> **Note:** Since the 2024 release of Civil 3D, the Grading Optimization program is available as an extension from the Autodesk account.

Figure 4–1

You then create more grading objects to develop and refine the design, and to test and probe your solutions by running them through the **Grading Optimization**. When you reach the limits of refinement with the **Grading Optimization**, you can use the exported feature lines, points, and surfaces to employ the traditional grading tools within Civil 3D for the finish detail.

As you become more confident with the use of the **Grading Optimization** program, the line between grading with the Optimization Program and the traditional Grading methods will get pushed more towards the finished design.

Grading Optimization Workflow

The best way to consider proper workflow for the Grading Optimization is to apply real-world site-development procedures and sequencing. When you consider the following, the general workflow will make sense:

- overall site and topology for the project
- general grading arrangement, where buildings, parking, pond(s) and landscaping may go
- high points and low points for the overall water flow across the site
- drainage areas and direction, for proper discharge and possible pond locations
- access to the site - from existing travel ways if suitable or from new ones that will need to be created
- construction (excavation) sequencing, storage pits and borrow sites etc.

There are a few other requirements to enable the **Grading Optimization** program to work. These are:

- **A surface** - usually a modified existing surface of the entire site, to base the grading process on.

- **Specialized Grading Objects** within the Grading Optimization program with defined parameters, such as curbs, drain lines, ponds, etc.

- Overall **Grading Optimization** options to control the earthwork volumes, the number of iterations, etc.

Grading Surface

Every land development project needs some type of Existing Surface to act as a base for the project. Of course, the more precise the surface, the better.

If the site is relatively flat with minor undulations, then such an existing surface can serve as the base for the Grading Optimization. When the surface of the existing conditions is complex with many grade changes, it is recommended to generate a simplified interim surface as a base for the Grading Optimization. This is done by running the entire site through the grading optimization process, with the site boundaries as the grading limit, and giving adequate design parameters for the intended design.

Figure 4–2 shows the difference between the existing conditions surface and an interim design grade surface used in this course.

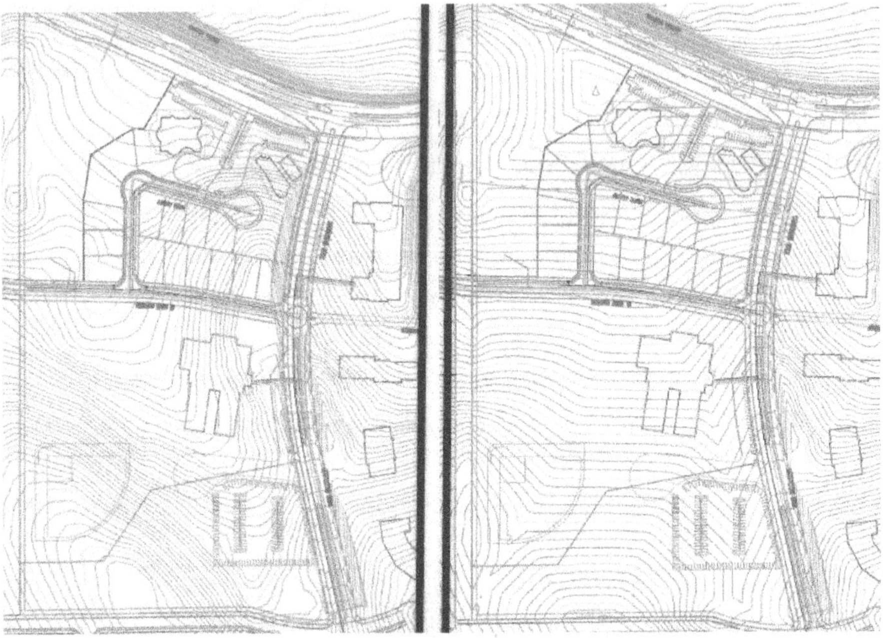

Figure 4–2

Depending on the conceptual plan, corridors may be created based on such an interim design grade. Such corridor surfaces can be added to the base surface for the Grading Optimizer, as shown in Figure 4–3.

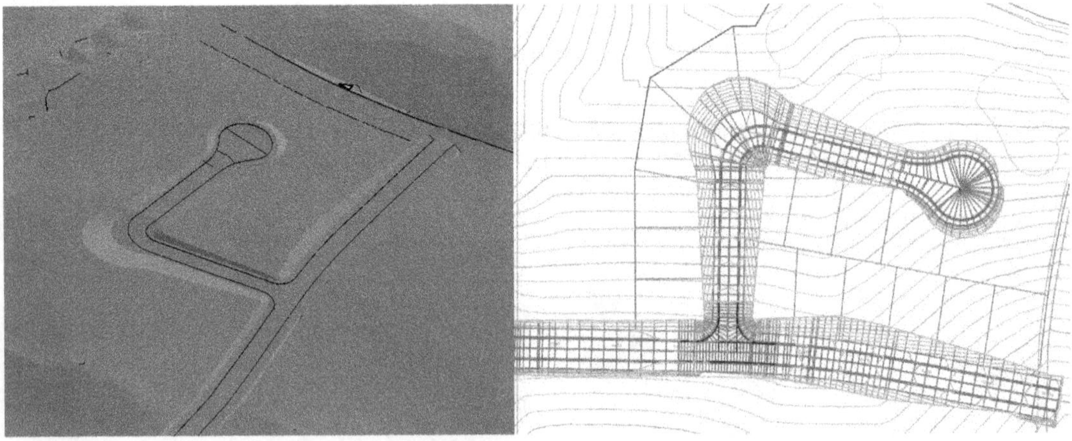

Figure 4–3

Grading Optimization Objects

The Grading Optimization programs requires a variety of input data in order to search for grading solutions. These objects are defined within Civil 3D along with the proper design parameters. These parameters can be changed in the Grading Optimization program, but not the geometry of the objects.

Within Civil 3D, the Grading Objects are accessible through tool palettes. There are separate tool palettes for Metric Grading Objects and Imperial Grading Objects, as shown in Figure 4-4.

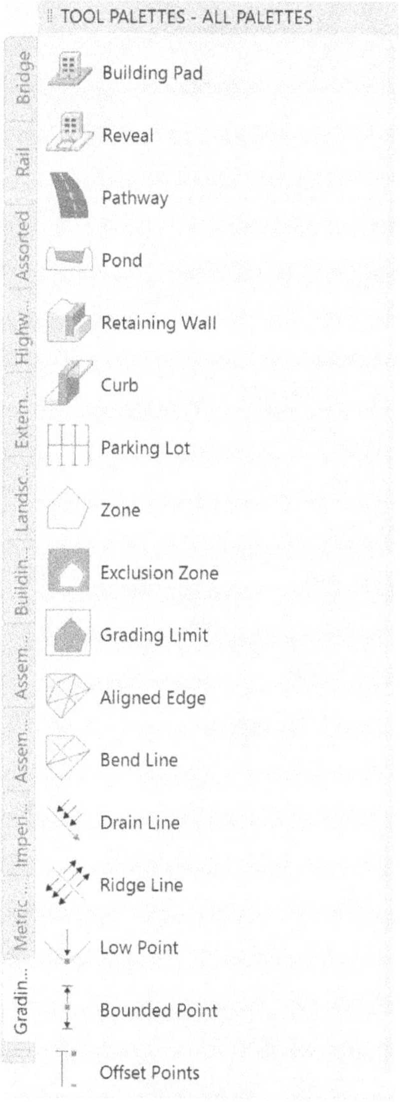

Figure 4-4

The proper tool palette can be launched by clicking on the [icon] (Grading Object Tools) in the *Grading Optimization* panel of the *Analyze* tab, as shown in Figure 4–5. If the tool palette is already open and set to a different palette, then clicking on the icon will make the *Grading Objects* palette current.

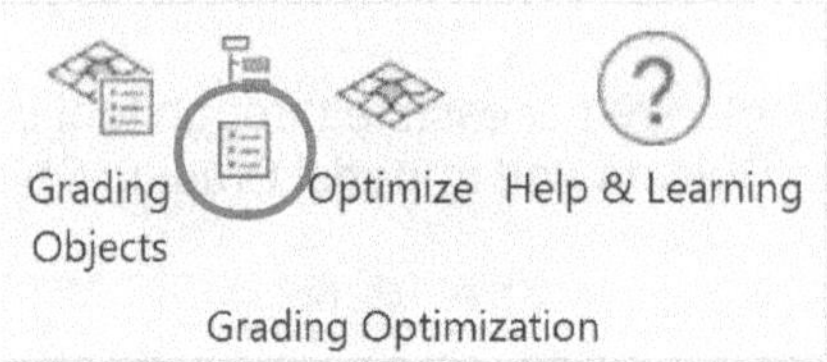

Figure 4–5

Note: If the icon has a light blue sheen background, this means it is already active.

You assign these grading objects to Civil 3D COGO points, regular open or closed AutoCAD (2D) polylines, or Civil 3D feature lines, as follows:

Three Types of Grading Elements		
Points (COGO Points)	**Lines (Polylines for Feature Lines)**	**Areas (Closed Polylines or Feature Lines)**
Low Point	Aligned Edge	Zone
Bounded Point	Bend Line	Exclusion Zone
	Drain Line	Isolation Zone
	Ridge Lines	Pond
	Curb	Curb
	Retaining Wall	Retaining Wall
	Offset Points	Building Pad
	Reveal	Grading Limit
	Pathways	Parking Lot
		Discontinued:
		Sidewalk*
		Accessible Path*

*Note: * In previous versions of the Grading Optimization for Civil 3D, there were pre-configured zone tools for sidewalks and accessible paths. These have been removed from the Grading Object Tool Palette and replaced with the Pathways Grading Element. Any previous instances of these zones in a drawing are still applicable but will not possess the features of a pathway.*

Once a grading object is attached to an object, parameters need to be entered in the Civil 3D Tool Properties window, as shown in Figure 4–6. These parameters differ for the different types of grading objects.

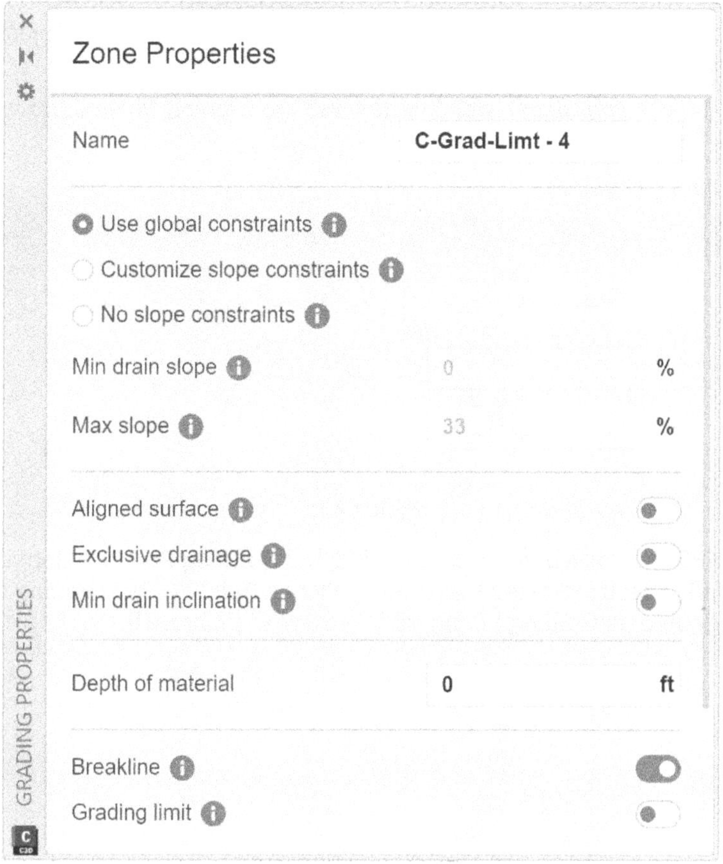

Figure 4–6

All grading objects defined within the Civil 3D drawing are listed in the *Grading Objects Browser*, as shown in Figure 4–8. Beside each Grading Object class is a count in parenthesis as to how many such objects are defined within the drawing. You can expand that object and get a listing of the names of all such objects.

The *Grading Objects Browser* can be opened by clicking on ▣ (Grading Objects Browser) in the *Grading Optimization* panel of the *Analyze* tab, as shown in Figure 4–7.

If you want both the *Grading Object* tool palettes and the *Grading Objects Browser* launched,

click on ▣ (Grading Objects).

> *Note: If the icon has a light blue sheen background, this means it is already active.*

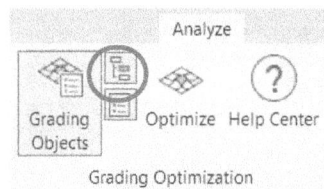

Figure 4–7

Notice in Figure 4–8 the **Zone** branch is expanded, but **Building Pad** is collapsed. The (1) next to the **Building Pad** branch indicates that it has only one Building Pad Grading Object. There is also a Zone designated as Grading Limits, so it is a separate branch.

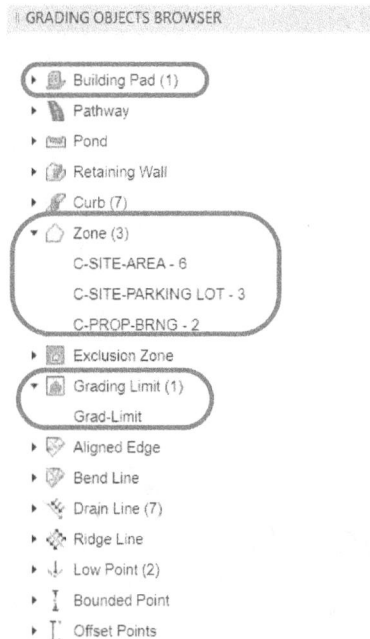

Figure 4–8

When you select a grading object by its name in the *Grading Objects Browser* window, the polyline (or COGO point) is selected in the drawing and the appropriate Tool Properties window, as shown in Figure 4–9.

Figure 4–9

Launching the Grading Optimization Program

Once a proper surface and the appropriate grading objects are defined, the Grading Optimization Program can be launched directly from within Civil 3D, by clicking

(Optimize) in the *Grading Optimization* panel of the *Analyze* tab, as shown in Figure 4–10.

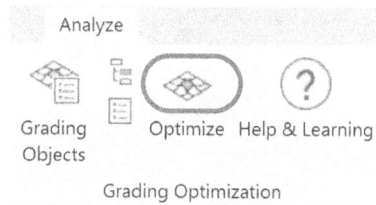

Figure 4–10

Note: *If the Grading Optimization program is already running, a message stating that is displayed in the Command Line.*

If there are multiple Civil 3D surfaces present in the drawing, you are prompted for the EG surface, which is the surface the Grading Optimization program will use for its calculations. If you have already run the Grading Optimization program previously in the current drawing, you can simply press the <Enter> key to reselect the same surface, otherwise you can select another surface. It may take a while for the Grading Optimization Program to launch.

The Grading Optimization Help Center

The *Grading Optimization Help Center* is a panel that contains a variety of items intended to guide the user through the Grading Optimization process. It is available by clicking ⑦ (Help Center) in the *Grading Optimization* panel of the *Analyze* tab, as shown in Figure 4-11.

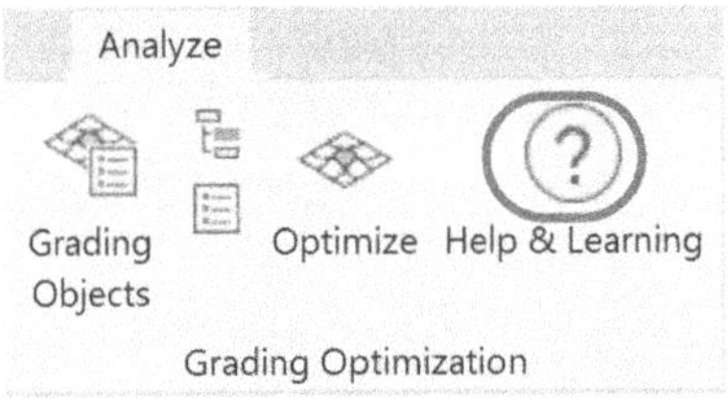

Figure 4-11

The *Grading Optimization Help Center* panel can be docked on the main Civil 3D screen, as shown in Figure 4-12.

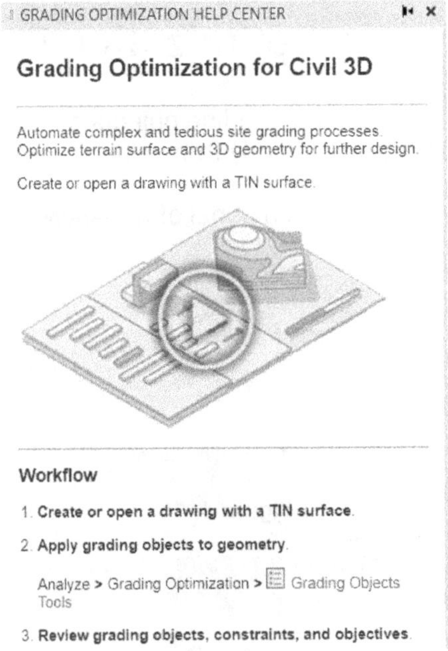

Figure 4-12

When you launch the *Grading Optimization* window for the first time, you are greeted with a *Help and Learning* side panel, as shown in Figure 4–13. It contains similar topics as the e *Grading Optimization Help Center*. You can close this panel by clicking the **X** in the upper right corner of

the panel. To relaunch it, click on ⌕ in the upper right corner of the *Grading Optimization* window.

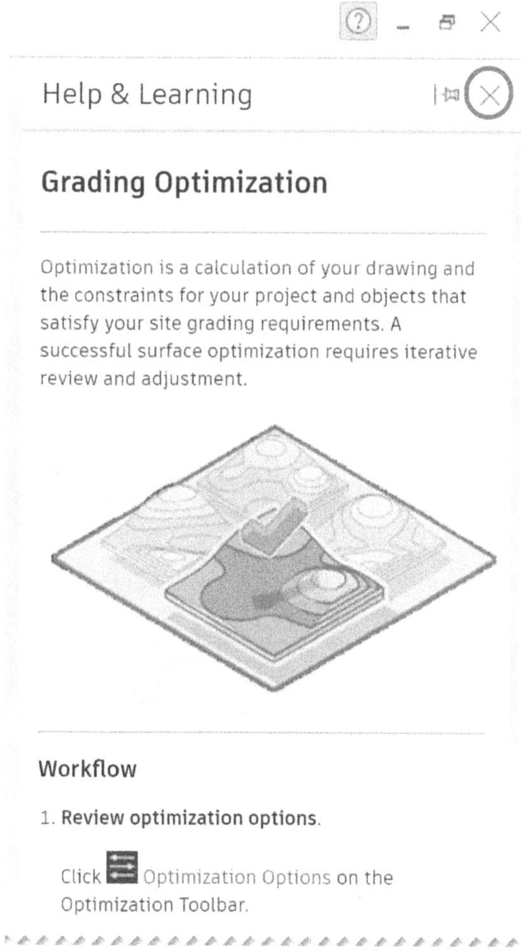

Figure 4–13

Grading Optimization Interface

The Grading Optimization program is a stand-alone program. It is launched from within Civil 3D, but has its own interface. The program can be moved to another computer screen. When the Grading Optimization program is running, you can switch back to Civil 3D and continue to work on the drawing, or you can even open another drawing. However, if you exit the Civil 3D program, the Grading Optimization will also shut down.

When launched, you are greeted with the *Grading Optimization* interface as shown in Figure 4–14.

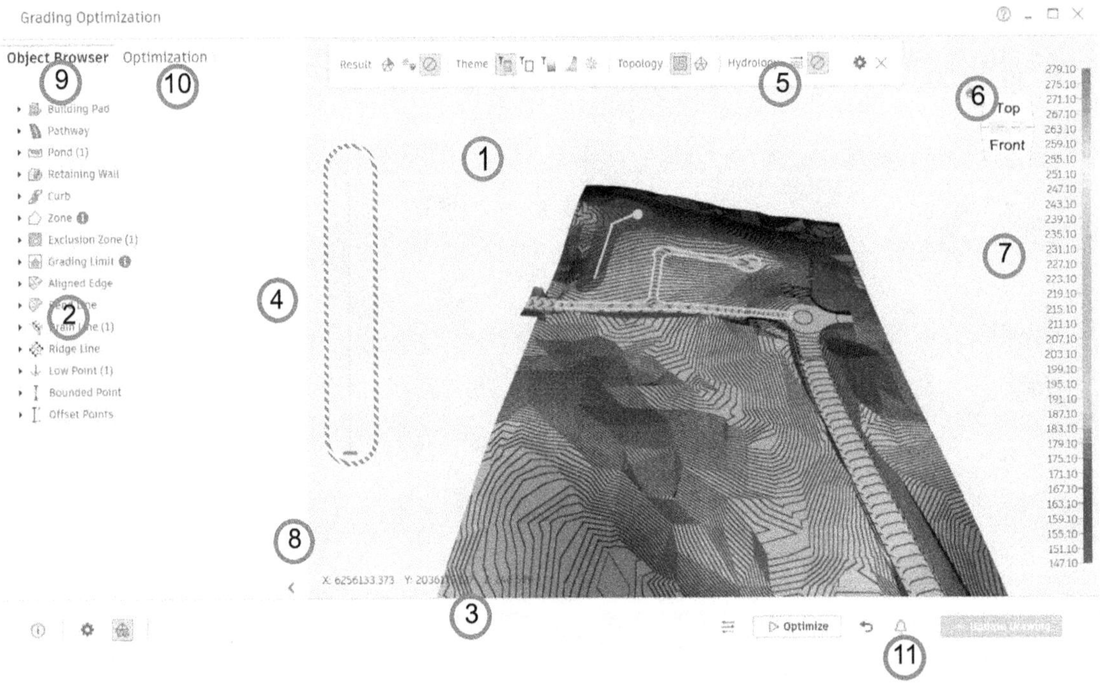

Figure 4–14

1 - Visualization Display	2 - Grading Objects Browser	3 - Optimization toolbar	4 - Vertical Exaggeration
5 - Visualization toolbar	6 - Viewcube	7 - Legend Bar	8 - Cursor Position
9 - Object Browser	10 - Optimization tab	11 - Notifications	

Color Theme

By default, the display of the interface uses the Dark color theme, which is controlled by the Civil 3D configuration, as shown in Figure 4–15.

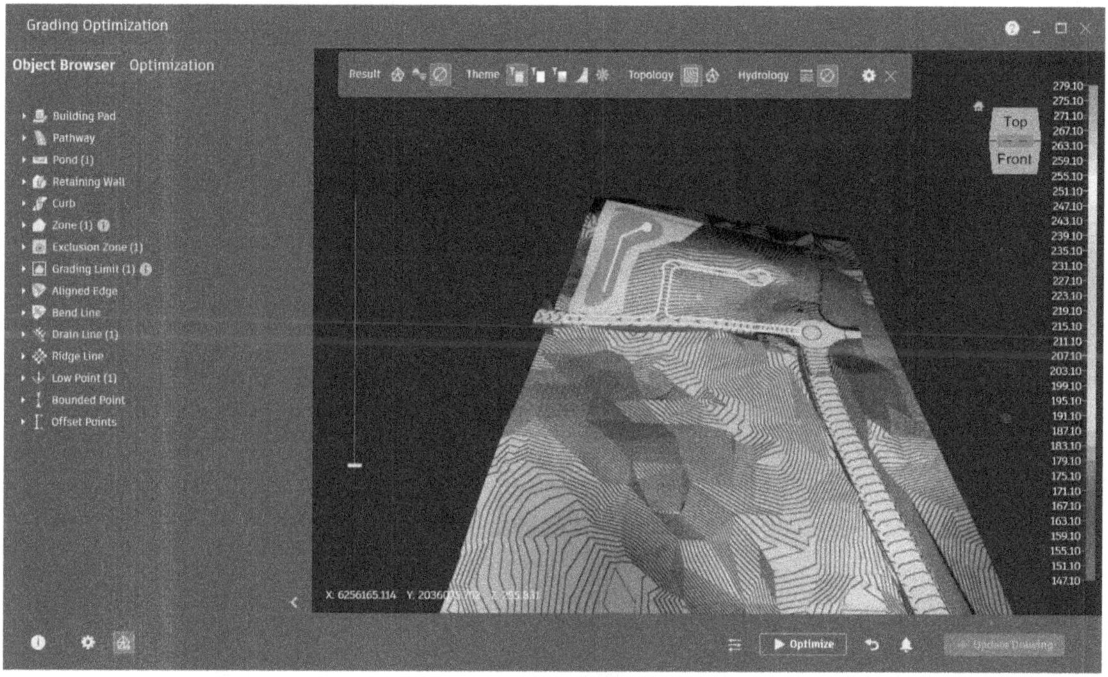

Figure 4–15

You can change it to the Light color scheme by clicking **[C]** (Application Menu) to expand it and then clicking **Options** at the bottom of the list to open the *Options* dialog box. In the *Display* tab, in the *Window Elements* area, expand the *Color theme* drop-down list and select **Light**, as shown in Figure 4–16. Then, click **OK** for the background color of the interface components to change to light. The light color scheme is used throughout this guide for printing clarity.

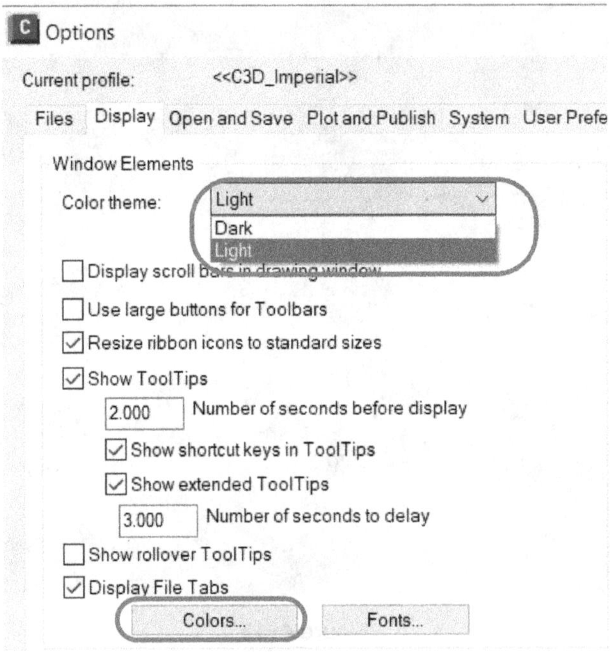

Figure 4–16

1 - Visualization Display

The *Visualization Display* is the main viewing area of the program.

2 - Grading Objects Browser

The *Grading Objects Browser* is basically the same as in the Civil 3D interface. All parameter settings configured in Civil 3D carry through; however, they can be changed in the Grading Optimization program. If changes are made, they move back into Civil 3D. They are displayed by default or can be displayed by clicking on the *Object Browser* tab (see Item #9 in Figure 4–14).

3 - Optimization Toolbar

The *Optimization toolbar* spreads across the bottom of the *Visualization Display*. It contains a variety of tools for visualization, configuration and monitoring the Grading Optimization process, as shown in Figure 4–17.

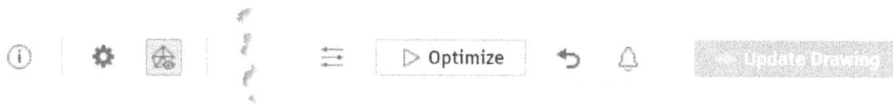

Figure 4–17

The following tools are included:

- ⚙ *Model Settings* - To set or change the preferences for the Grading Optimization's surface generation

- ⬡ *Visualization toolbar* - Toggles the *Visualization* toolbar

- ⇌ *Optimization Options* - To set or change the options for the Grading Optimization for cut/fill calculations, the amount of iterations, etc.,

- ▷ Optimize *Optimize* - Initiates the optimization process. When it is optimizing, the icon changes to ☐ Stop , allowing you to stop and terminate the process.

- ↺ *Reset* - Resets the optimization process.

- 🔔 Notification - During optimization, various messages may appear which warrant attention, along with suggestions on how to resolve issues, as shown in Figure 4–18.

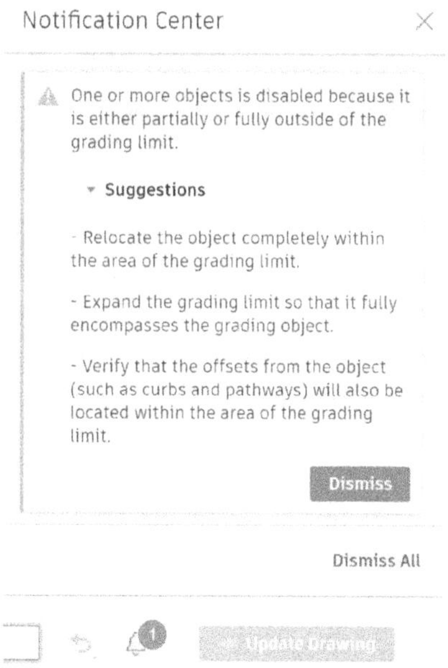

Figure 4–18

- **Update Drawing** *Update Drawing* delivers the optimized surface, and optional feature lines and points to the drawing in Civil 3D that had initiated the Grading Optimization process.

*Note: If the Optimization process determines inconsistencies which trigger notifications, a warning dialog box appears as shown in Figure 4–19. It can be dismissed by clicking the **Close** button, or you can open the Notification Center panel (as shown in Figure 4–18), by clicking **Stop and fix**.*

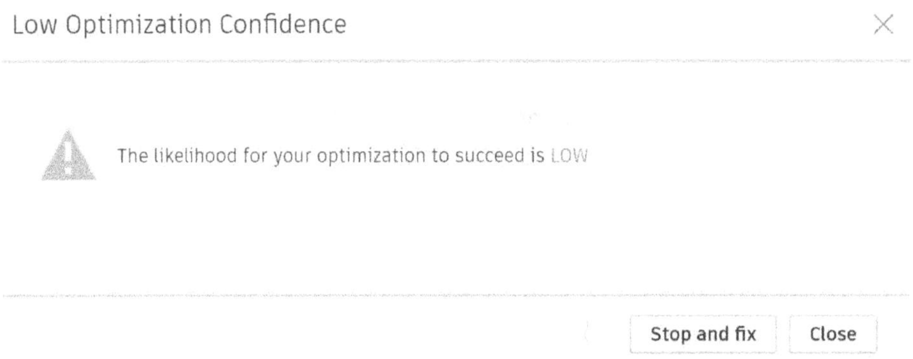

Low Optimization Confidence   ✕

⚠ The likelihood for your optimization to succeed is LOW

Stop and fix   Close

Figure 4–19

These toolbars and dialog boxes are modeless, which means they can remain open while working in other sections of the program. If there is a cyan sheen to the icon, then the dialog box or toolbar is open.

Object properties appear in panels along the right side of Grading Optimization.

The progress meter on the *Optimization* toolbar has been enhanced to display stages to indicate what has completed and what is currently processing.

4 - Vertical Exaggeration Slide

The *Vertical Exaggeration Slide* is located on the left side of the *Visualization Display*. It changes the vertical exaggeration of the terrain. By default, it is set to 1:1 (no exaggeration), but can be increased for a more detailed view of the grading process, for flatter areas, as shown in Figure 4–20.

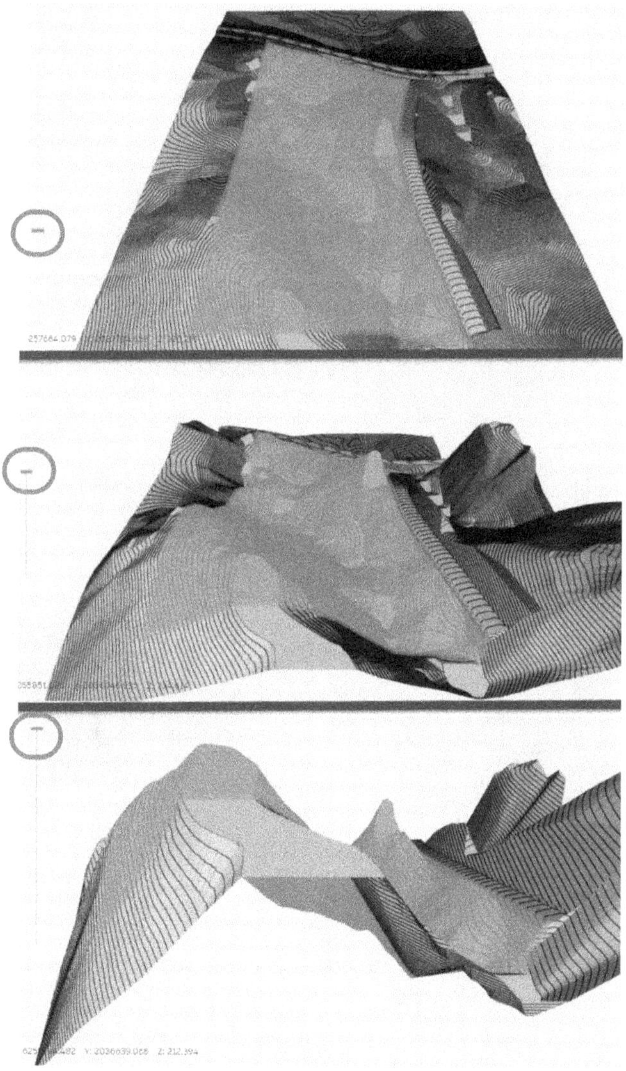

Figure 4–20

5 - Visualization Toolbar

The *Visualization toolbar* is a collection of tools for changing the display of the surface for a variety of purposes, as shown in Figure 4–21 (for example, the surface can display themes for elevations, slopes or orientation). These will be discussed later in the course as required.

Figure 4–21

Note: A cyan sheen on the icon means that this is the current option.

6 - Viewcube

The *Viewcube* provides quick access to many different predefined views. As you move the cursor over it, each face or corner highlights. Once highlighted, you can click the face or corner to reorient the model to the highlighted predefined view, as shown in Figure 4–22.

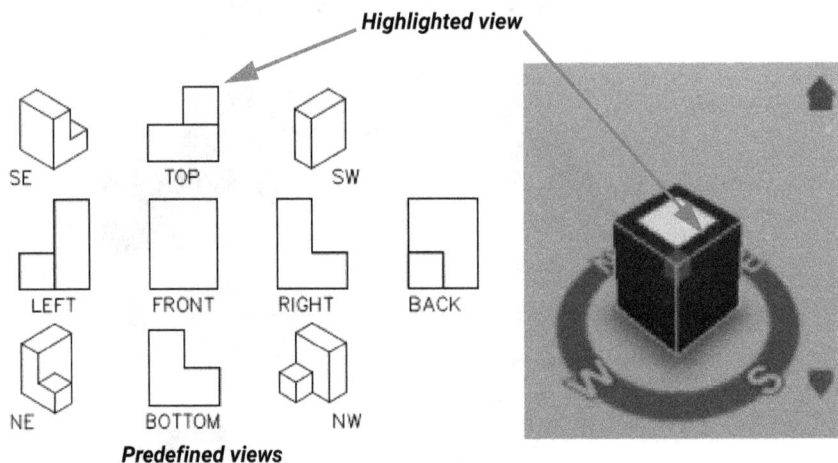

Figure 4–22

7 - Legend Bar

The *Legend Bar* is located on the right side of the *Visualization Display*. It lists the different ranges based on the visualization theme.

8 - Cursor Position

The *Cursor Position* is in the lower left corner of the *Visualization Display*. It displays the position in X, Y, and Z coordinates of the cursor as it travels over the surface. (The Z coordinate is not affected by the *Vertical Exaggeration*.)

9 - Object Browser Tab

The *Object Browser* tab displays the *Grading Objects Browser*.

10 - Optimization Tab

The *Optimization* tab displays the *Optimization* panel, as shown in Figure 4–23.

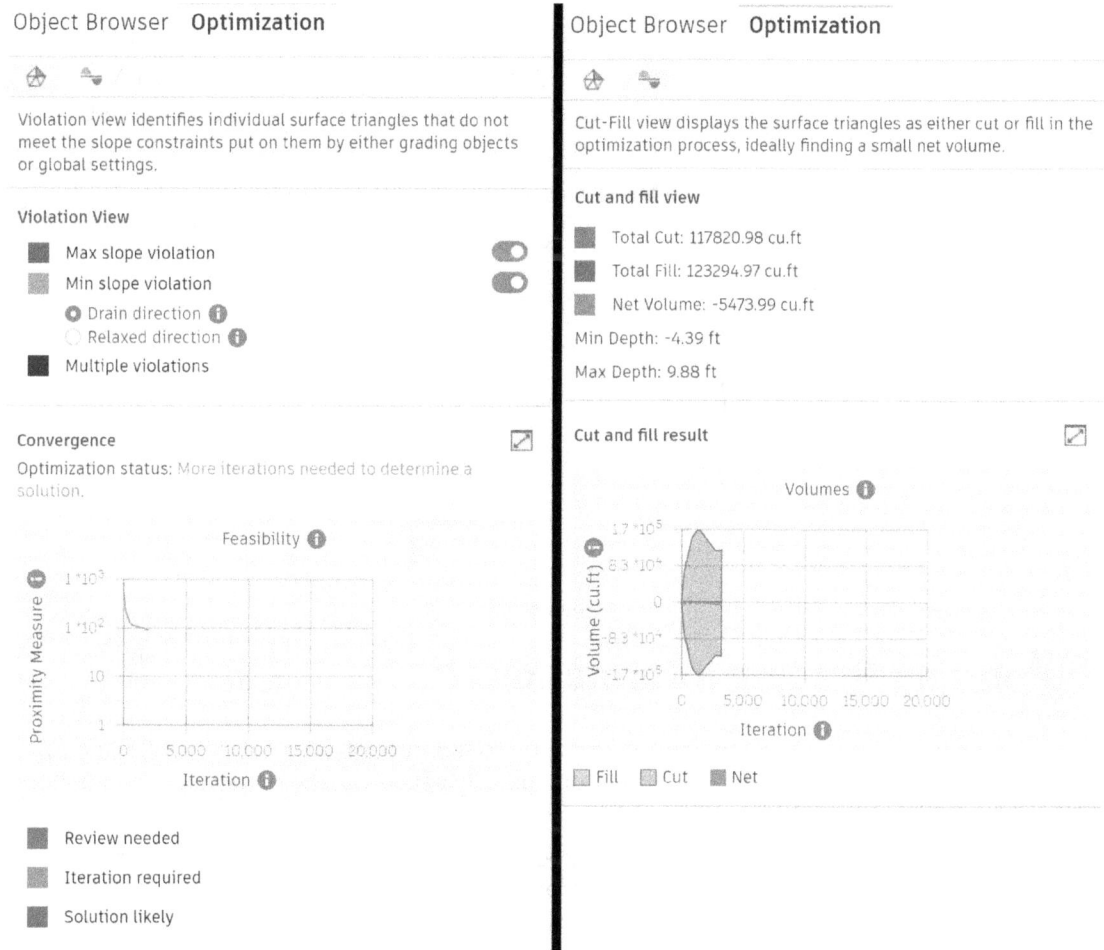

Object Browser **Optimization**

Violation view identifies individual surface triangles that do not meet the slope constraints put on them by either grading objects or global settings.

Violation View

- Max slope violation
- Min slope violation
  - Drain direction ⓘ
  - Relaxed direction ⓘ
- Multiple violations

Convergence

Optimization status: More iterations needed to determine a solution.

- Review needed
- Iteration required
- Solution likely

Object Browser **Optimization**

Cut-Fill view displays the surface triangles as either cut or fill in the optimization process, ideally finding a small net volume.

Cut and fill view

- Total Cut: 117820.98 cu.ft
- Total Fill: 123294.97 cu.ft
- Net Volume: -5473.99 cu.ft

Min Depth: -4.39 ft

Max Depth: 9.88 ft

Cut and fill result

☐ Fill ☐ Cut ■ Net

Figure 4–23

11 - Notifications

The *Notification* icon displays the number of warnings generated during the Optimization Process.

Navigating the Model

Navigation commands are critical for working efficiently in any drawing program. When navigating the **Grading Optimization** surface, you can change the camera position to obtain a better view of the design.

Mouse

The mouse is the main model navigation tool. A three-button mouse can be used to pan around the model, zoom in/out, and orbit the model in 3D, as shown in Figure 4–24. Unlike in an AutoCAD-based software, holding the mouse wheel to pan does not work in the Grading Optimization program.

Hold the mouse wheel to zoom in and out.

Hold the right mouse button to pan around.

Scroll the mouse wheel toward you to zoom out, and away from you to zoom in.

Hold the left mouse button to orbit in 3D

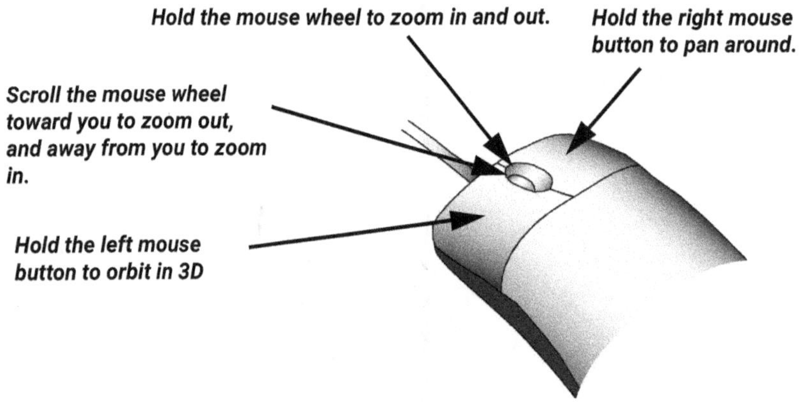

Figure 4–24

Outputting Grading Information

It can take a long time for the Grading Optimization to run through all the iterations and come up with a solution. In real-world applications, one usually sets up all the parameters and options and then initiates the optimization to run over lunch time or even over night.

When the optimization is complete or if it has been interrupted, you can send the results back to the source Civil 3D drawing that initiated the process. If you do, all changes made to the parameters of the grading objects in the Grading Optimization program will be updated in the Civil 3D drawing.

When you initiate this process, (by clicking [Update Drawing] button), the Grading Optimization program closes and you are returned to Civil 3D, to the drawing that had launched the Grading Optimization program in the first place. The *Save Optimization Result* dialog box opens, providing the following choices, as shown in Figure 4–25:

- Save the Surface
- Create Feature Lines
- Create Points

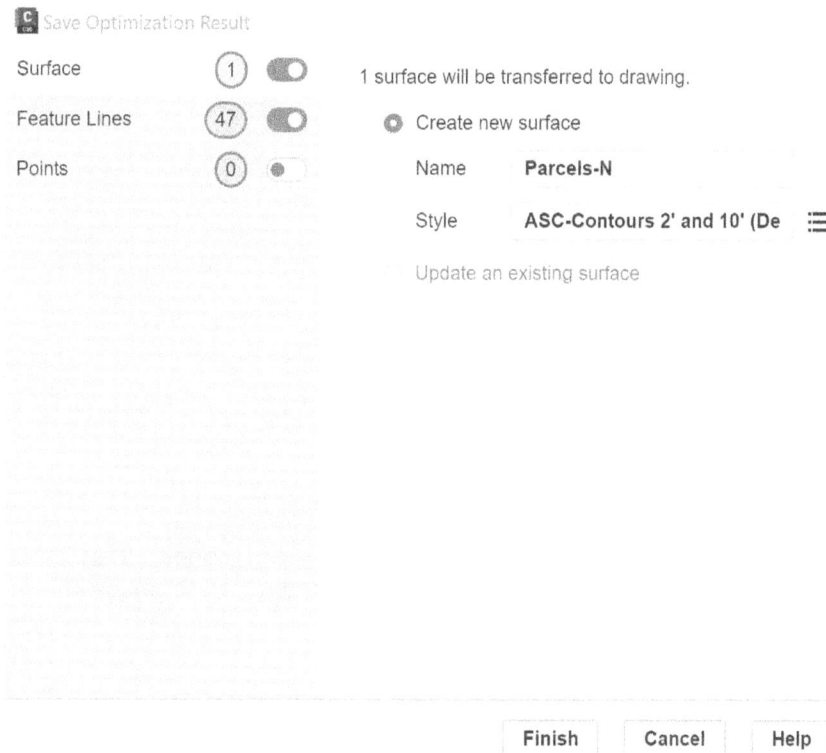

Figure 4–25

With each of these choices, you have the option of creating new Civil 3D objects (Surfaces / Feature Lines / Point groups) or updating existing ones. When creating new ones, you can change the name / site / point group and select a style for the objects, as shown in Figure 4-26.

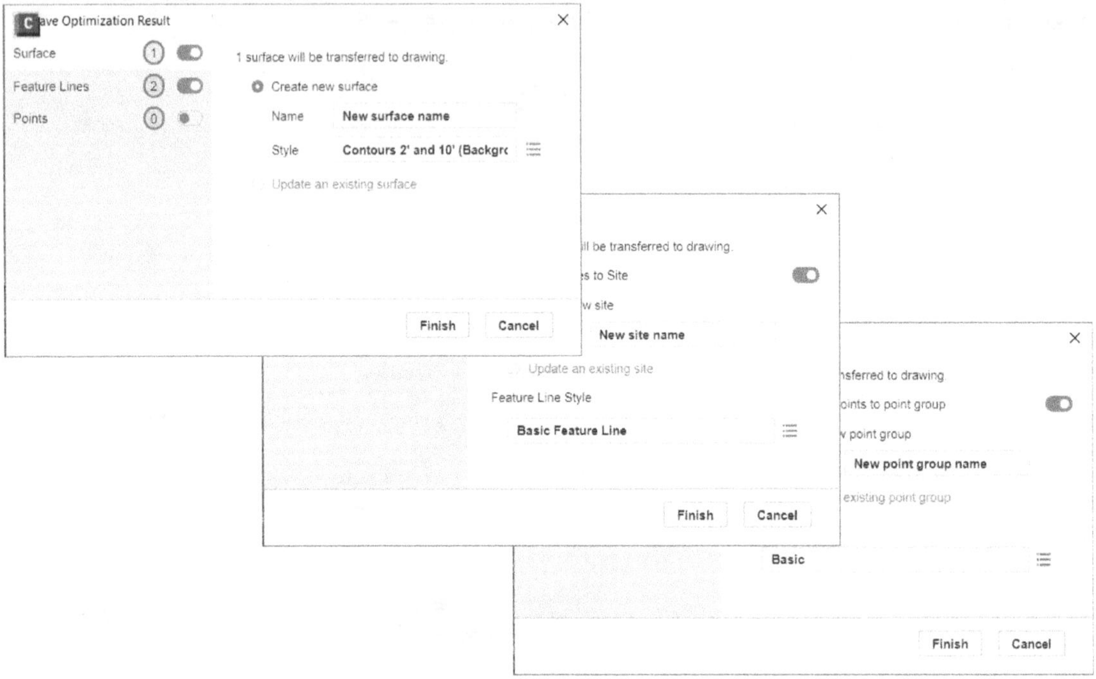

Figure 4-26

In order to keep this course to an acceptable time frame, the practices set up in this course are designed to run over a short duration. In most cases, the optimization can be interrupted before completion and the subsequent practice will start off with what the result of the Optimization would be.

Practice 4a
Grading Optimization Interface

Practice Objectives

- To get familiar with the Grading Optimization process interface.

- To work within Civil 3D and launch the Grading Optimization program.

- Identify the required settings to set up a new grading project.

Note: The Grading Optimization process can be time consuming, and you may require additional time to complete the process than the estimated 20 minutes.

In this practice, you will examine an existing drawing with Grading Objects. You will add and modify some grading objects, then launch the Grading Optimization program. You will get familiar with its interface, and finally bring the results back into Civil 3D.

Task 1: Examine the grading objects in Civil 3D.

1. Open **Intro-GO-1.dwg** from the *C:\Civil 3D Grading\Working\GO-Intro* practice files folder.

2. If the *Geolocation - Online Map Data* dialog box displays, click on **Remember my choice**, then click **No** because you do not want to use online map data, as shown in Figure 4–27.

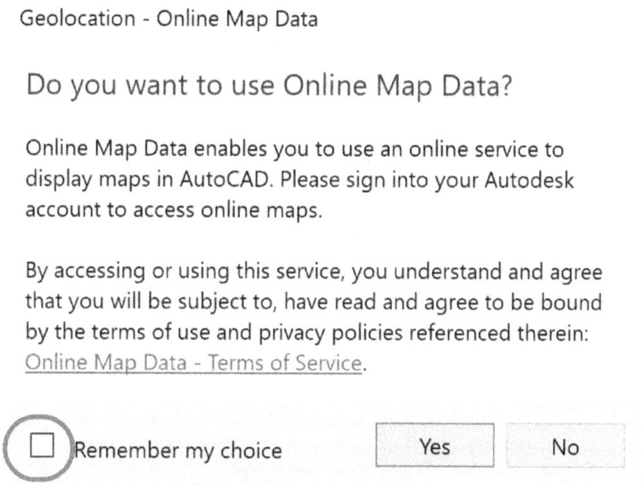

Geolocation - Online Map Data

Do you want to use Online Map Data?

Online Map Data enables you to use an online service to display maps in AutoCAD. Please sign into your Autodesk account to access online maps.

By accessing or using this service, you understand and agree that you will be subject to, have read and agree to be bound by the terms of use and privacy policies referenced therein: Online Map Data - Terms of Service.

☐ Remember my choice | Yes | | No |

Figure 4–27

3. The Online map was already captured on a layer. For clarity, freeze the ZZ-Image layer.

4. Use the **<Ctrl> W** keyboard shortcut to enable the AutoCAD Selection Cycling, or toggle the

    (Selection cycling) on the status bar.

5. A lot of the grading objects have already been added to this drawing. Zoom in and click on the orange periphery with selection cycling on. Note that there are two polylines on top of each other, as shown in Figure 4–28.

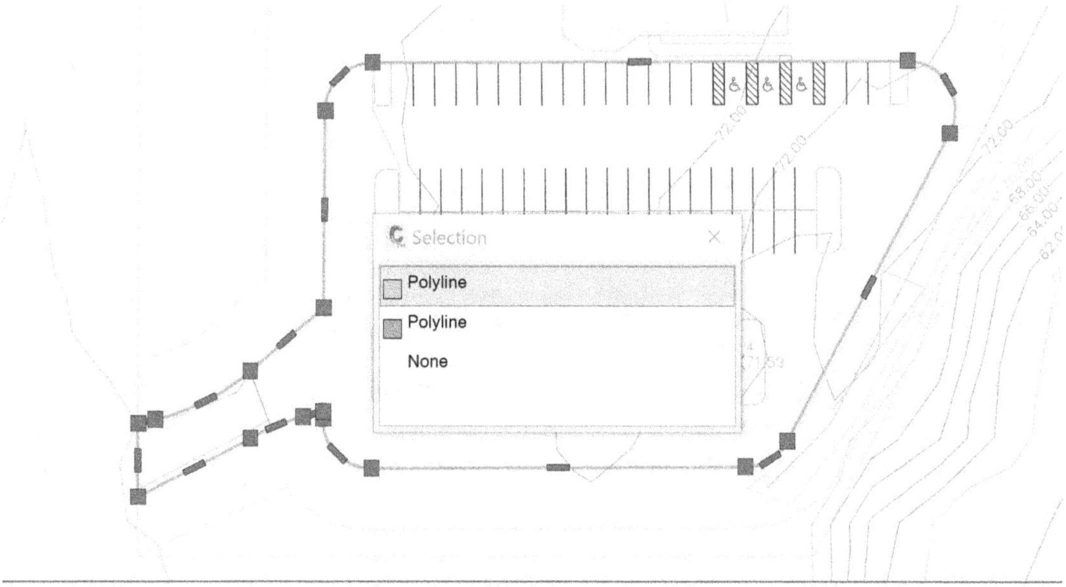

Figure 4–28

6. Select the top polyline for the parking. In the *Zone Properties* dialog box, note that the *Max slope* is set to **5%** and the *Min drain slope* is set to **1%**.

7. Press <Esc> to clear the selection and to close the dialog boxes.

8. Click on the orange polyline. In the *Curb Properties* dialog box, note that this polyline is a curb with a specific *Height* and *Width*, as shown in Figure 4–29.

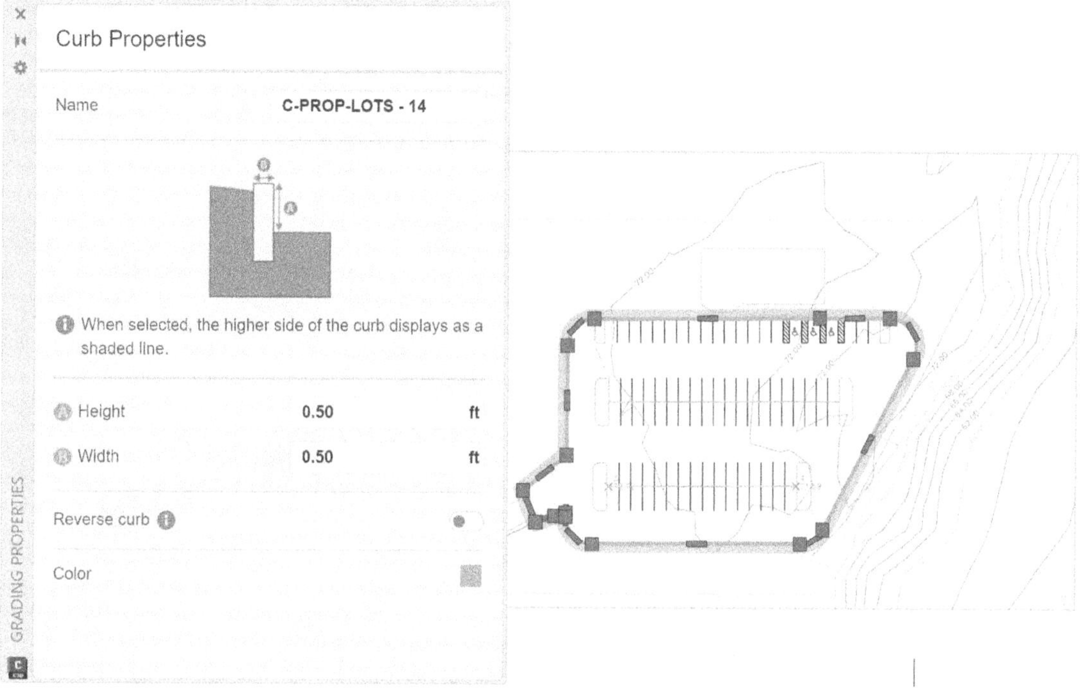

Figure 4–29

- Note that there are two tones to this curb and the higher side of the curb is displayed with a shaded line.

9. Reverse the curb and note that the shaded line changes.

10. Reverse it again to ensure that the shaded line is on the outside. The curb will step down from the outside into the parking lot.

11. Press <Esc> to clear the selection.

12. Save and close the drawing.

Task 2: Launch the Grading Optimization program.

In this task, you will investigate the properties and procedures for the Grading Optimization program.

1. Do not continue working on the same drawing from the previous task, but open **Intro-GO-2.dwg** from the *C:\Civil 3D Grading\Working\GO-Intro* practice files folder. More grading objects have been created in this drawing which will make the grading optimization process more thorough and realistic.

2. In the *Analyze* tab>*Grading Optimization* panel, click ⬥ (Optimize). You are not prompted to select an EG (Existing Grade) surface since there is only one surface in the drawing.

3. It may take a while for the Grading Optimization program to launch. Once it launches, the *Get started* guide may appear (if this is the first time the program is launched). If it does, close the *Get started* guide by clicking on the **X** in the upper right corner.

4. The grading objects will be listed in the *Grading Optimization* browser on the left-hand side, as shown in Figure 4–30.

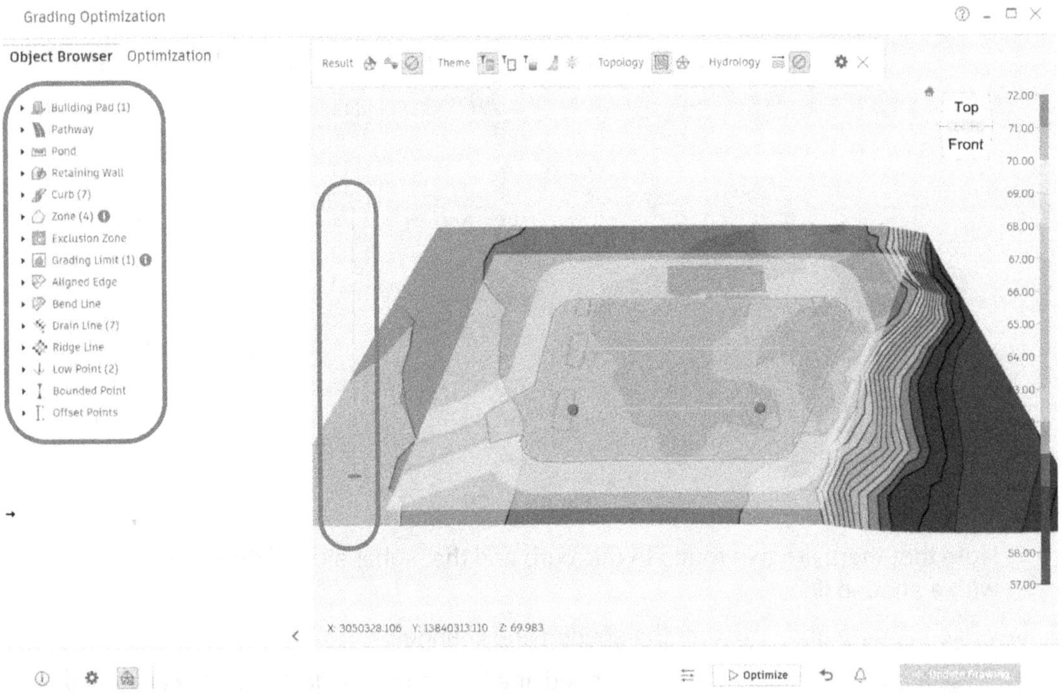

Figure 4–30

5. Navigate around the drawing area of the *Grading Optimization* window. Hold the left mouse button down to orbit, hold the right mouse button down to raise the drawing up or down, and hold the wheel mouse button down to zoom in and out.

6. Adjust the vertical exaggeration bar on the left-hand side (as shown in Figure 4–30) up and down and note how the terrain changes. Adjust the bar back down to the lowest level to continue.

7. In the *Grading Optimization* browser, expand **Building Pad** and select **Office**. Note how the office is highlighted in the drawing area and the Building Pad Properties are listed, as shown in Figure 4–31.

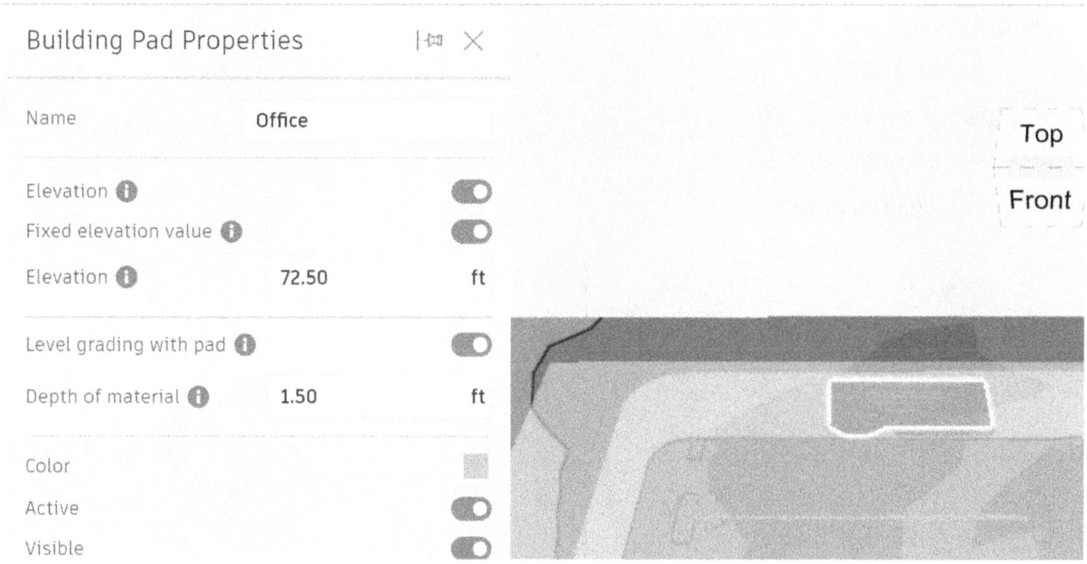

Building Pad Properties

Name	Office
Elevation	
Fixed elevation value	
Elevation	72.50 ft
Level grading with pad	
Depth of material	1.50 ft
Color	
Active	
Visible	

Top

Front

Figure 4–31

8. Change the *Elevation* of the building pad to **73.0** and press <Enter>.

9. In the *Grading Optimization* browser, right-click on **Office** and click **Zoom To**. Your display is zoomed to the building pad.

10. At the bottom of the *Grading Optimization* window, click ⇌ (Optimization Options), as shown in Figure 4–32.

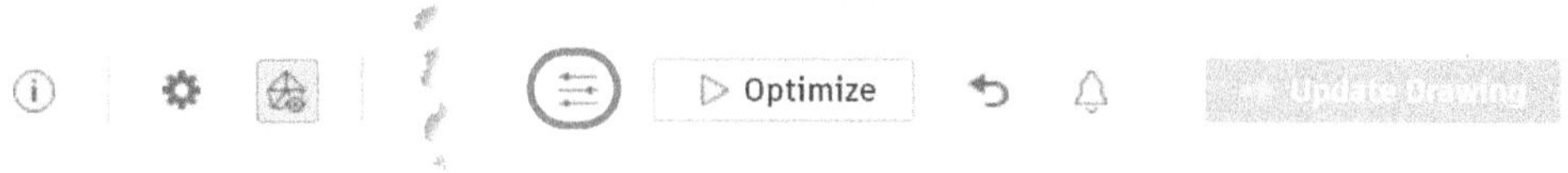

ⓘ ⚙ ⬡ ⇌ ▷ Optimize ↩ △ Update Drawing

Figure 4–32

11. In the *Optimization Options* window, set the following, as shown in Figure 4–33:

- *Min drain slope*: **0.05**
- *Max slope*: **33**
- *Cut and fill constraint*: **None**
- *Iteration*: **10000**
- *Balance cut and fill*: **20**
- *Minimize earthwork*: **50**
- *Smooth surface*: **75**

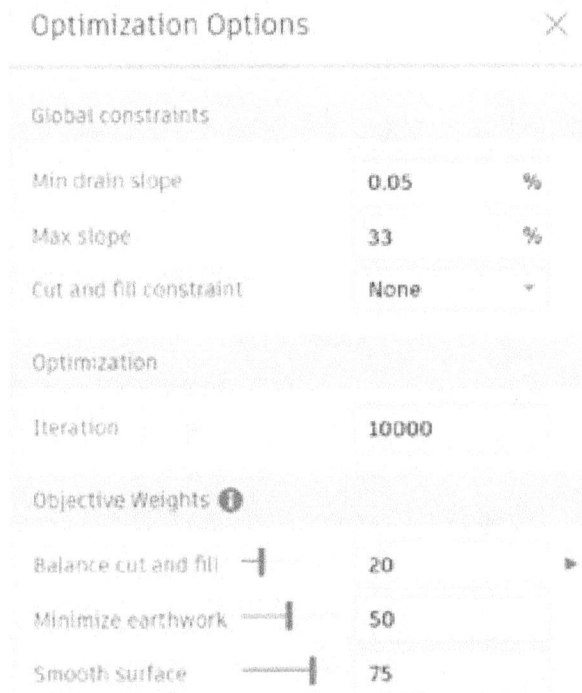

Figure 4–33

12. Close the *Optimization Options* window by clicking on the **X** in the top-right corner.

13. At the bottom of the *Grading Optimization* window, click **Optimize**. For now, you can ignore the alert in the notification center.

14. Notice how the number 1 displays in the notification area during the optimization process.

    Click on ⌂ (Notification Center) to open the **Notification Center** read the Alert. Expand **Suggestions** and read the various suggestions. Click on **Dismiss**, as shown in Figure 4−34.

Notification Center   ✕

⚠ One or more objects is disabled because it is either partially or fully outside of the grading limit.

▾ Suggestions

- Relocate the object completely within the area of the grading limit.

- Expand the grading limit so that it fully encompasses the grading object.

- Verify that the offsets from the object (such as curbs and pathways) will also be located within the area of the grading limit.

Dismiss

Dismiss All

Figure 4−34

15. It can take some time to go through these iterations. If you do not have enough time, you can click ☐ Stop (Stop) and close the Grading Optimization program, then move on to the next task in this practice.

16. Once the optimization is complete, a notification displays in your system tray, as shown in Figure 4−35.

Grading Optimization
Optimization is complete.
5:04 PM

Figure 4−35

17. Click **Update Drawing**, as shown in Figure 4–36. This will send the optimization results back to the Civil 3D drawing where Grading Optimization was originally launched from.

Figure 4–36

18. In the Civil 3D drawing, in the *Save Optimization Result* window, ensure that the **Create new surface** option is selected to create a new surface. Enter **Parking Lot** for the *Name* and click

☰ (Surface Style) to select a surface *Style*. In the *Surface Styles* dialog box, select **ASC-Contours 2' and 10' (Design)** and click **Finish** to close the *Surface Style* selection box, as shown in Figure 4–37.

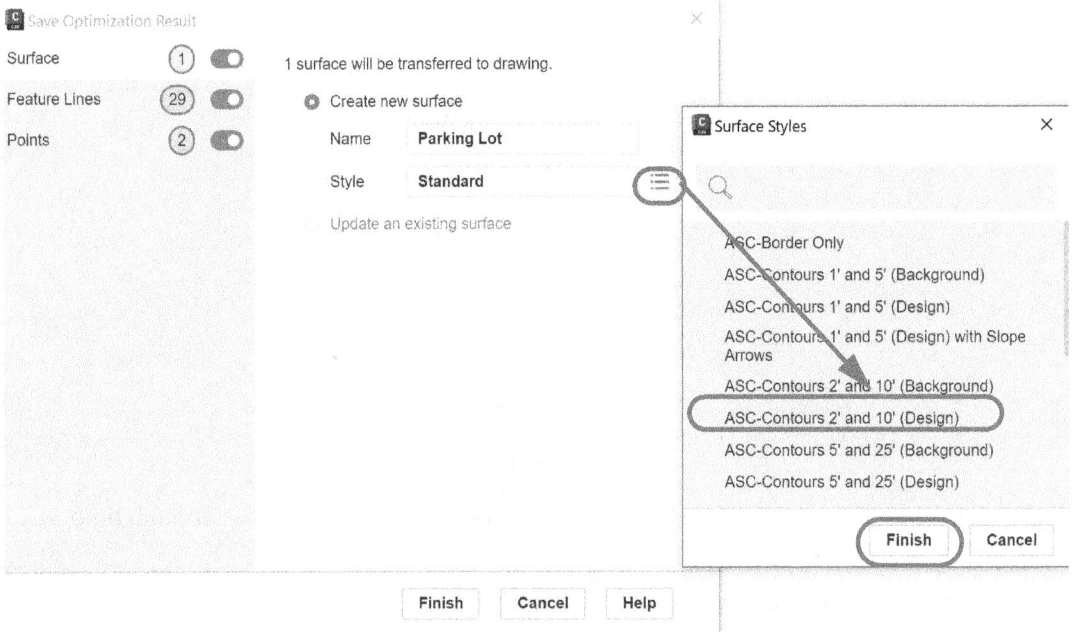

Figure 4–37

19. In the *Save Optimization Result* window, click **Create new feature lines,** and enter **PARK-** as a prefix, as shown in Figure 4–38.

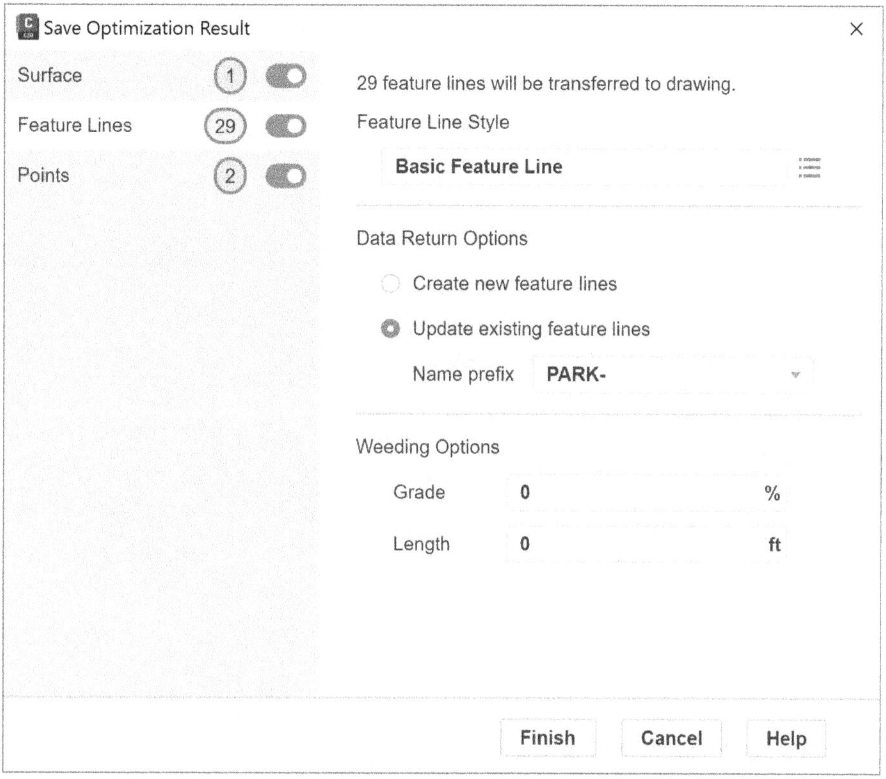

	Save Optimization Result		×
Surface	① ⬤	29 feature lines will be transferred to drawing.	
Feature Lines	29 ⬤	Feature Line Style	
Points	② ⬤	**Basic Feature Line**	

Data Return Options

○ Create new feature lines

◉ Update existing feature lines

Name prefix   **PARK-**

Weeding Options

Grade	0	%
Length	0	ft

Finish   Cancel   Help

Figure 4–38

20. In the *Save Optimization Result* window, click **Points**. Select the **Create new point group** option to create a new point group and name it **Parking Lot**.

21. Click **Finish**. Civil 3D will create a new surface, site, and point group for the information retrieved from the Grading Optimizer.

Note: It can take some time to create a new surface, point group, and site.

22. When finished, expand **Surfaces** in the *Prospector* tab and note the new surface called **Parking Lot**. Expand **Site** and note the new site called **Parking**, then expand **Point Groups** and note the new point group called **Parking**, as shown in Figure 4–39.

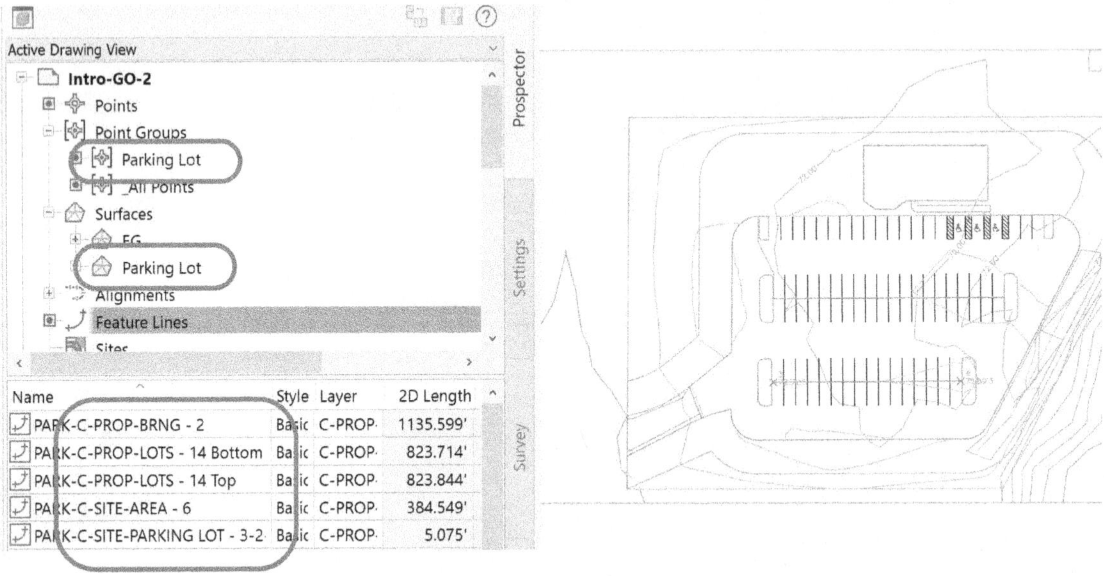

Figure 4–39

23. Save the drawing.

Task 3: Review the Grading Optimization results.

1. Continue to work with the same drawing as the previous task. If you did not complete the previous task, open **Intro-GO-3.dwg** from the *C:\Civil 3D Grading\Working\GO-Intro* practice files folder.

2. In the *Prospector* tab, expand the *Surfaces* branch. Right-click on **Parking Lot** and click **Select**.

3. Select the **Parking Lot** surface and launch the *Object Viewer* (or *Model Viewer*, if you prefer) either from a contextual ribbon or from the right-click menu, as shown in Figure 4–40.

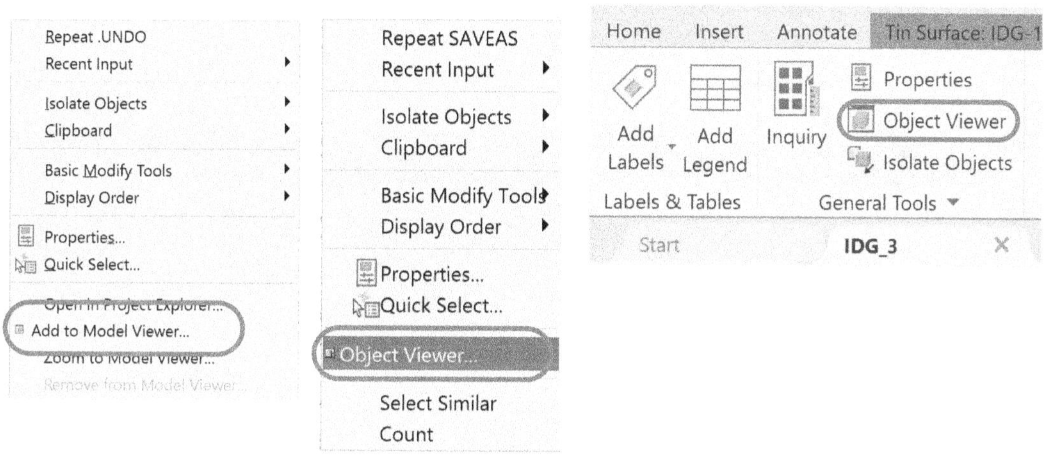

Figure 4–40

4. The Object Viewer is displayed as in Figure 4–41. Set the visual style to **Conceptual** and the preset view to **SW Isometric**.

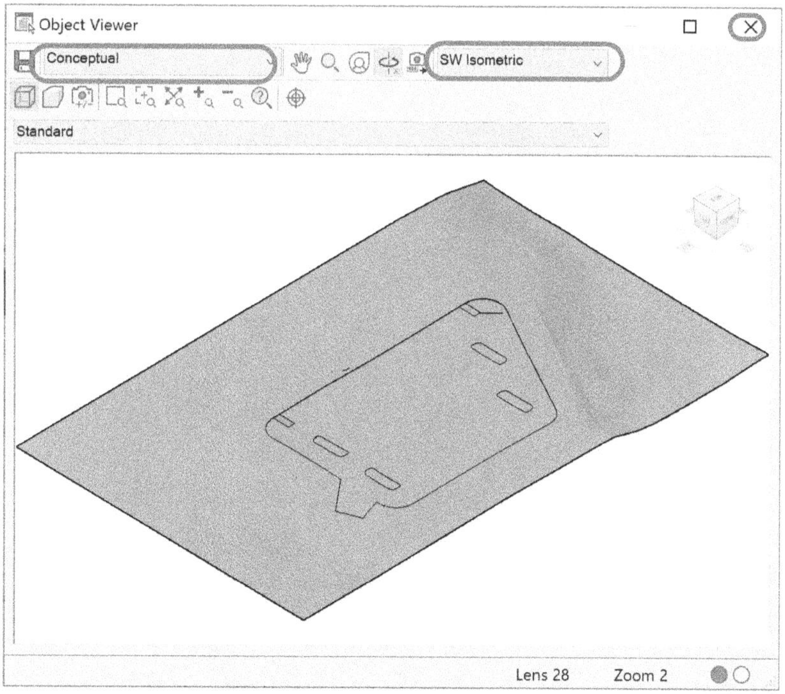

Figure 4–41

5. Close out of the Object Viewer through the **X** in the top right corner.

6. In the *Prospector* tab, expand the *Point Groups* branch and select the **Parking Lot** point group and note the two points that are shown in the *Preview* section.

7. In the Prospector tab, click on *Feature Lines* and note all the newly created feature lines that are shown in the *Preview* section.

8. Save and close the drawing.

End of practice

4.2 Grading Optimization Zones

The **Grading Optimization Zones** are the most common of the Grading Optimization objects. Zones can be used for paved areas, excavations, defining limits, etc. There are many type of zones:

- Building Pad

- Pond

- Curb and Retaining Wall (can also be a linear object)

- Pathways

- Zone:

  - (General)

  Note: *There is no "General" Zone in Grading Optimization. The term is used only to distinguish this zone from other zone types.*

- Parking Lot

- Exclusion Zone

- Isolation Zone

- Grading Limit

In the *Grading Objects* tool palette, the *Parking Lot* is present, but it is not separate Grading Objects, merely general zones with predefined parameters. When defined, it is listed under "Zones" in the *Grading Objects Browser*.

When any zone is defined as a *Grading Limit*, as shown in Figure 4–42, then that zone will automatically move from the **Zones** branch to the **Grading Limit** branch within the *Grading Objects* window.

Figure 4–42

Since a typical Grading Optimization project will have many zones, it is important to understand their relationship. Zones can be directly adjacent, can overlap or can be apart. Therefore, zones of the same type can be re-arranged in terms of priority, but only in the Grading Optimization program, not in the Civil 3D *Grading Object* window, as shown in Figure 4–43.

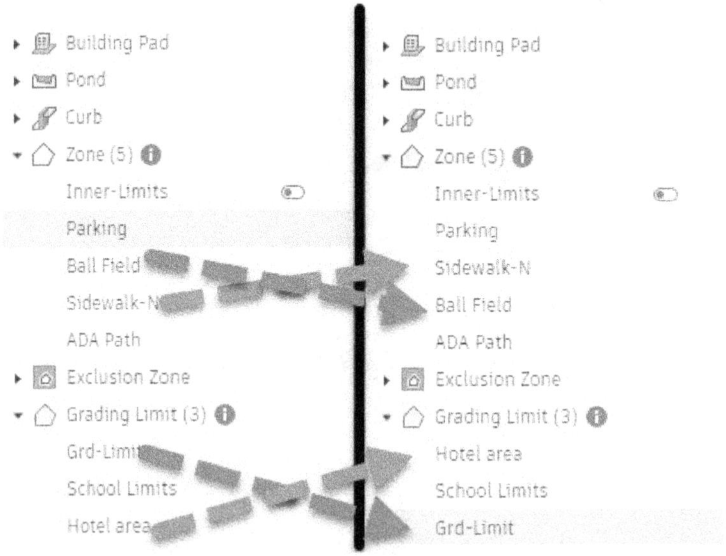

Figure 4–43

However the order of processing of the grading object types is set and cannot be rearranged. The order is as listed, as shown in Figure 4–44.

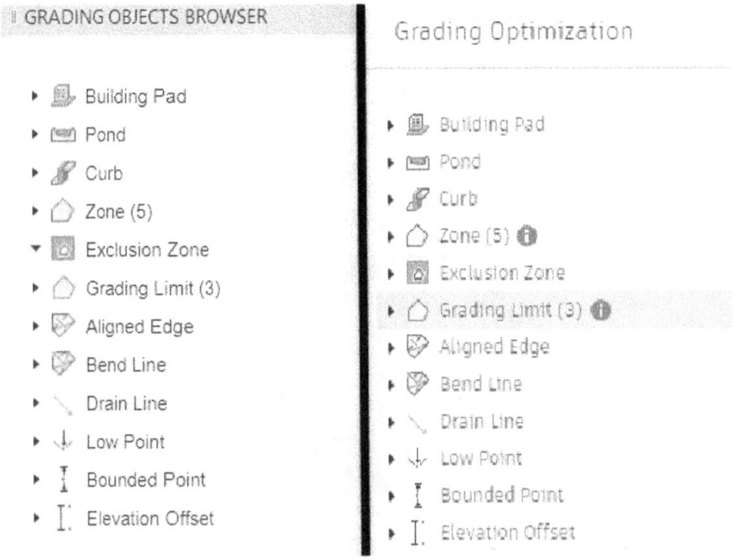

Figure 4–44

A single polyline or feature line can only contain one Grading Optimization object. If there are grading object parameters already assigned, these will be wiped out if you assign a different grading object to that element.

To remove a Grading Object's definition from an object, select the object and right-click. The right-click menu has an option to remove the Grading Objects, as shown in Figure 4-45.

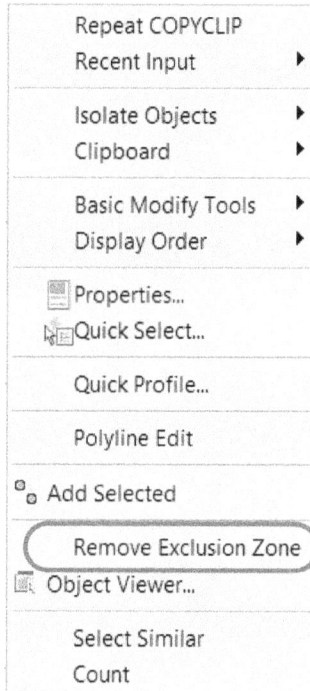

Repeat COPYCLIP
Recent Input ▶
Isolate Objects ▶
Clipboard ▶
Basic Modify Tools ▶
Display Order ▶
▦ Properties...
▧ Quick Select...
Quick Profile...
Polyline Edit
ᵒₒ Add Selected
⟨ Remove Exclusion Zone ⟩
▨ Object Viewer...
Select Similar
Count

Figure 4-45

In this chapter, we will only be dealing with the General Zone, Exclusion Zone, and Grading Limit.

Creating Grading Objects

Zones are area objects and must be defined by a closed polyline (pline) or a closed feature line. The elevation of the plines and feature lines are irrelevant, since Grading Optimization will be assigning the elevation of the zones based on its base surface.

Note: Do not click and drag Grading Objects from the palette onto the drawing.

The defining polyline or feature line must be closed and cannot self overlap (butterfly) itself. To create grading objects, select the type of Grading Objects from the Grading Objects tool palette by clicking on it, then select the polyline or feature line that defines the area, as shown in Figure 4–46.

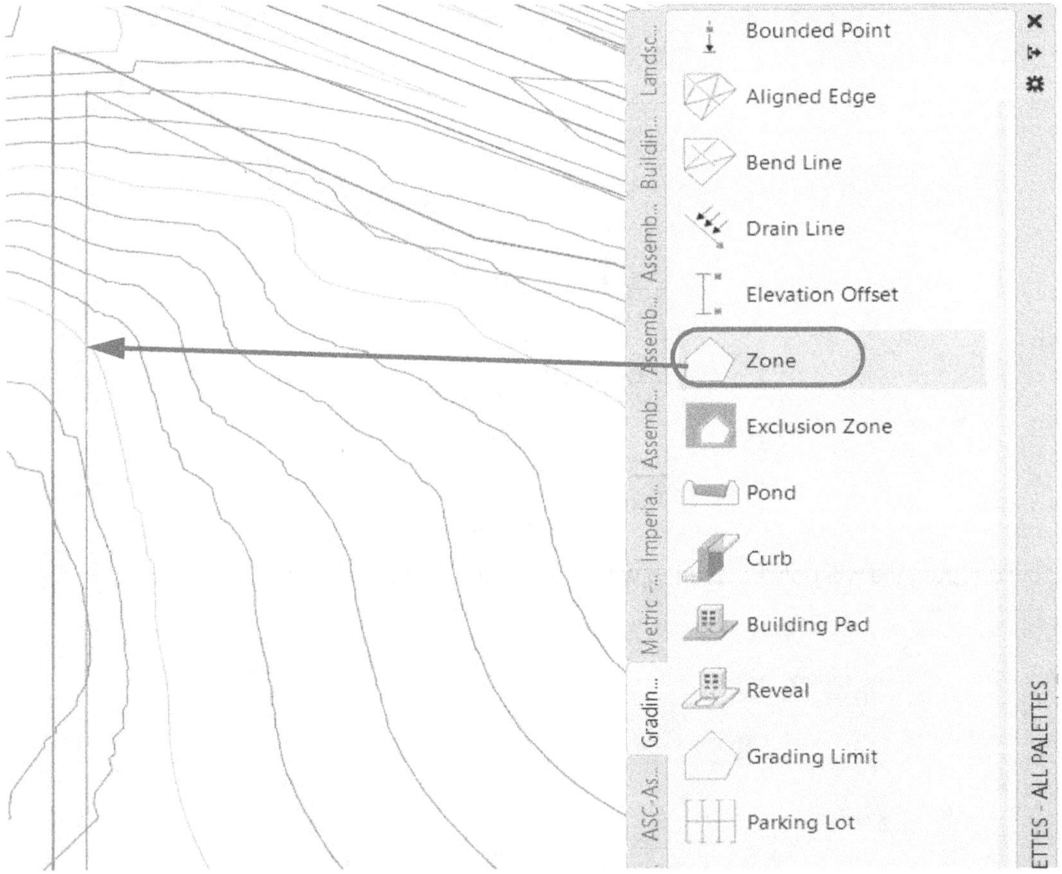

Figure 4–46

You can select multiple plines (feature lines) at the same time and they will all be assigned to that Grading Object with the default parameters.

If you want to assign many objects simultaneously with certain parameters, prior to assigning the object, change the parameters in the Tool Palette object by right-clicking on it and selecting Properties, as shown in Figure 4–47.

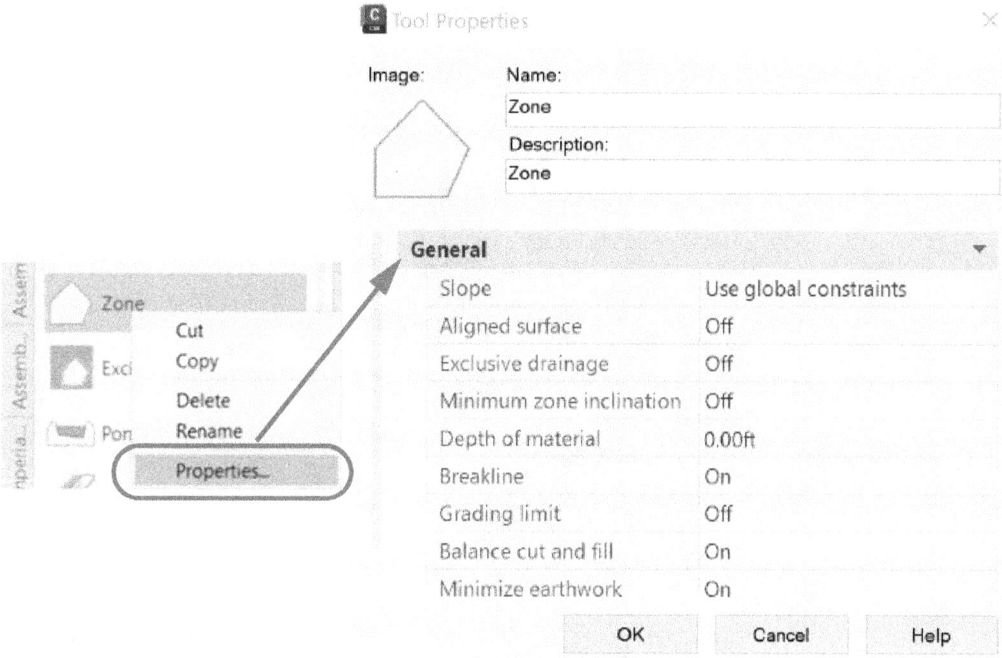

Figure 4–47

Once you assign Zone Grading Objects to the polyline or feature line, the *Zone Properties* dialog box displays in which you can change its parameters, as shown in Figure 4–48.

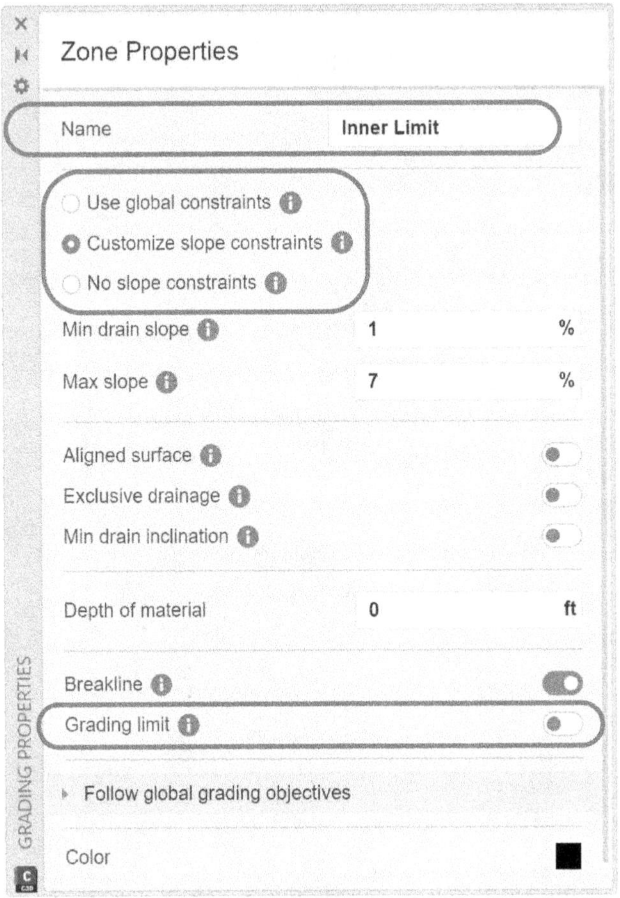

Figure 4–48

These parameters can be changed in the Civil 3D drawing or later in the Grading Optimization program. When these parameters are changed in the Grading Optimization interface, these changes will be ported back into the Civil 3D drawing.

There are many parameters, options, and setting to be considered in this dialog box. Many will be covered in more detail later in this course.

Zone Properties

Zones require various parameters in order for Grading Optimization to proceed. These are listed in the *Zone Properties* dialog box.

Name

It is good practice to name the zone with a meaningful name for easy identification. The default name is the layer name along with a sequential number, unless the pline resides on Layer 0, in which case the default name is the Grading Object's type along with a sequential number.

Constraints

A zone requires slope parameters for Grading Optimization to be able to process them. There are three choices:

a. **Global constraints**

The global constraints are only accessible in the Grading Optimization interface by clicking

on ≡ (Optimization Options). In the upper part of the *Optimization Options* dialog box, you can set the minimum drain slope and maximum slope globally as well as the **Cut and fill constraint** option, as shown in Figure 4–49.

Figure 4–49

The **Cut and fill constraint** options available in the *Optimization Options* dialog box allow you to specify **Cut Only, Fill Only,** or **None**. If **None** is specified, then the cut and fill can be balanced based on the *Objective Weights*. The Cut and fill constraint is stored within a drawing and for other optimizations.

If you need to specify a desired amount of either cut or fill, click on the small arrow to expand the panel to reveal the **Cut - fill =** section, as shown in Figure 4–50.

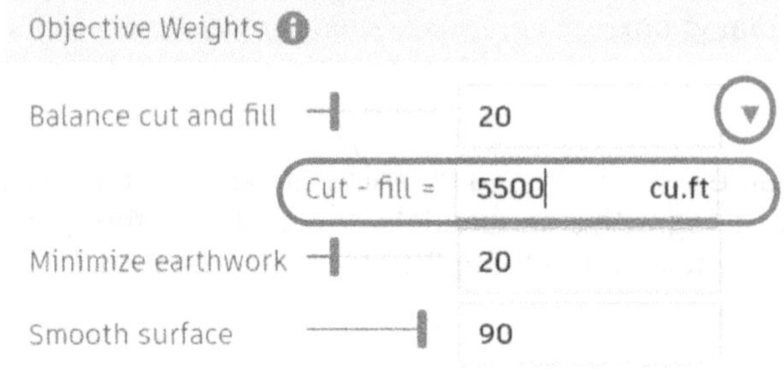

Figure 4–50

b.   Customize slope constraints

When **Customize slope constraints** is toggled **on**, the lower part of the dialog box becomes editable and you can enter the maximum slopes and minimum drain slopes for this particular zone, as shown in Figure 4–51.

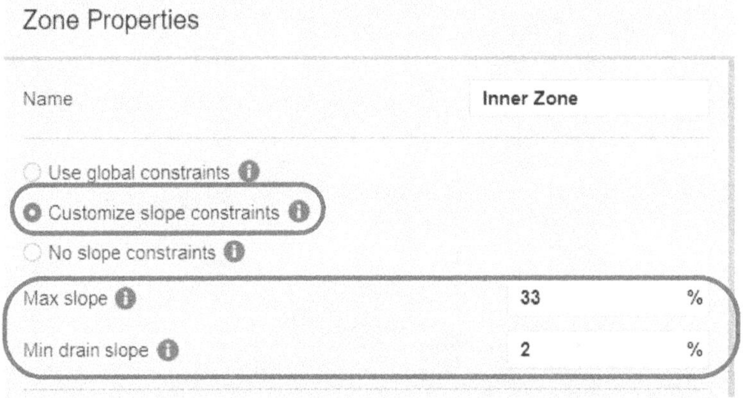

Figure 4–51

c.   No slope constraints

Disables any slope constraints for this zone. This means that the minimum slope is zero and the maximum infinite. When the **No slope constraints** option is toggled **on**, the customized slope areas are disabled.

Aligned Surface

The underlying structure of surfaces are triangles. In most cases, the surfaces are Triangulated Irregular Network (TIN) surfaces. When the **Aligned Surface** is toggled **on**, it will force the edges of these triangles to get aligned with a flat or asymmetrical plane, as shown in Figure 4–52.

Aligned surface is ON   *Aligned surface is OFF*

Figure 4–52

Exclusive Drainage

There are elements in Grading Optimization that are designed to control the drainage of the site (as defined by the Grading Limit), such as Low Points and Drain Lines. When the **Exclusive Drainage** is toggled **on**, then such drain elements are only used within its zone and not to other zones. When it is toggled **off**, the drain elements affect all zones, as shown in Figure 4–53.

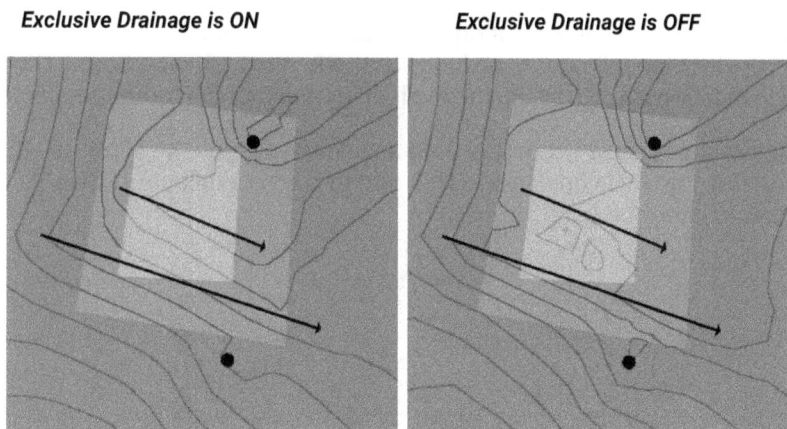

Exclusive Drainage is ON   *Exclusive Drainage is OFF*

Figure 4–53

Exclusive Drainage gets toggled **off** whenever **Aligned Surface** is toggled **on**. They both cannot be toggled **on** at the same time.

Minimum Drain Inclination

The **Minimum** Drain Inclination toggle allows you to control the minimum direction of every triangle within the zone. This way, you can control the drainage and water flow across the surface. When disabled, the drain elements affect all zones, as shown in Figure 4–54. Notice the direction of the red flowline arrows.

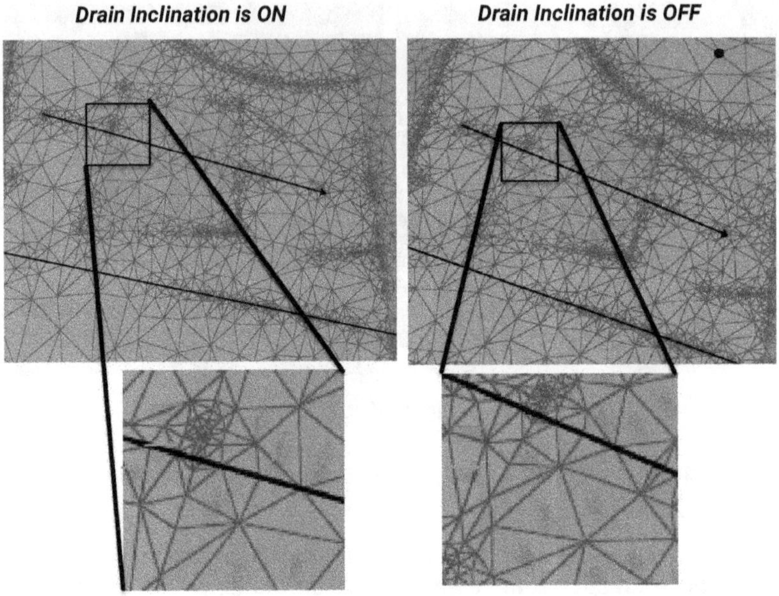

Drain Inclination is ON   **Drain Inclination is OFF**

Figure 4–54

The term *Inclination* in Grading Optimization refers to compass angle (or Aspect). **0** is East and it runs in a counter-clockwise direction, making North **90**, West **180** and South **270**. When the **Minimum** Drain Inclination is toggled **on**, the Inclination direction becomes available, where you

can type in the appropriate value (from 0 to 360) as shown in Figure 4–55, or use the ✏ button to graphically indicate the angle on screen. This option is only available in Civil 3D, not in the Grading Optimization interface.

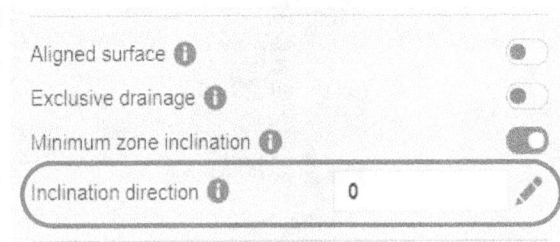

Aligned surface ⓘ

Exclusive drainage ⓘ

Minimum zone inclination ⓘ

Inclination direction ⓘ   0

Figure 4–55

Aligned Surface

The underlying structure of surfaces are triangles. In most cases, the surfaces are Triangulated Irregular Network (TIN) surfaces. When the **Aligned Surface** is toggled **on**, it will force the edges of these triangles to get aligned with a flat or asymmetrical plane, as shown in Figure 4–52.

Aligned surface is ON *Aligned surface is OFF*

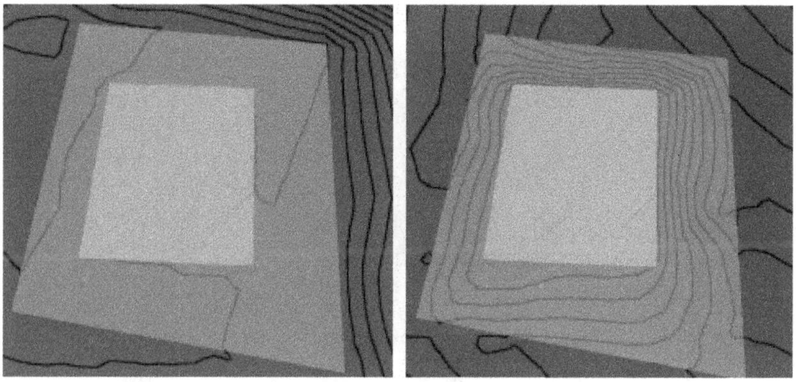

Figure 4–52

Exclusive Drainage

There are elements in Grading Optimization that are designed to control the drainage of the site (as defined by the Grading Limit), such as Low Points and Drain Lines. When the **Exclusive Drainage** is toggled **on**, then such drain elements are only used within its zone and not to other zones. When it is toggled **off**, the drain elements affect all zones, as shown in Figure 4–53.

Exclusive Drainage is ON *Exclusive Drainage is OFF*

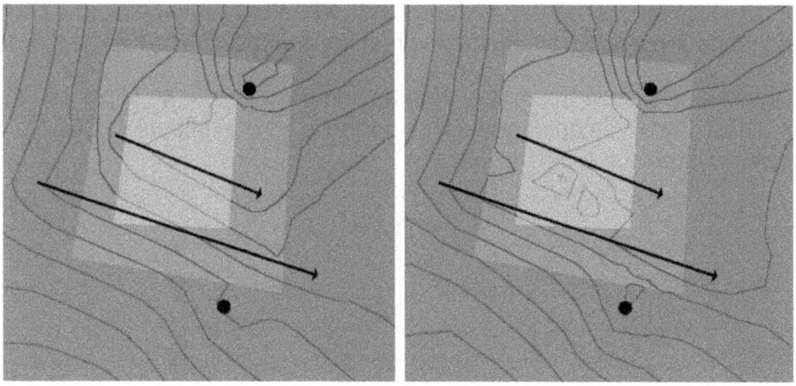

Figure 4–53

Exclusive Drainage gets toggled **off** whenever **Aligned Surface** is toggled **on**. They both cannot be toggled **on** at the same time.

Minimum Drain Inclination

The **Minimum** Drain Inclination toggle allows you to control the minimum direction of every triangle within the zone. This way, you can control the drainage and water flow across the surface. When disabled, the drain elements affect all zones, as shown in Figure 4–54. Notice the direction of the red flowline arrows.

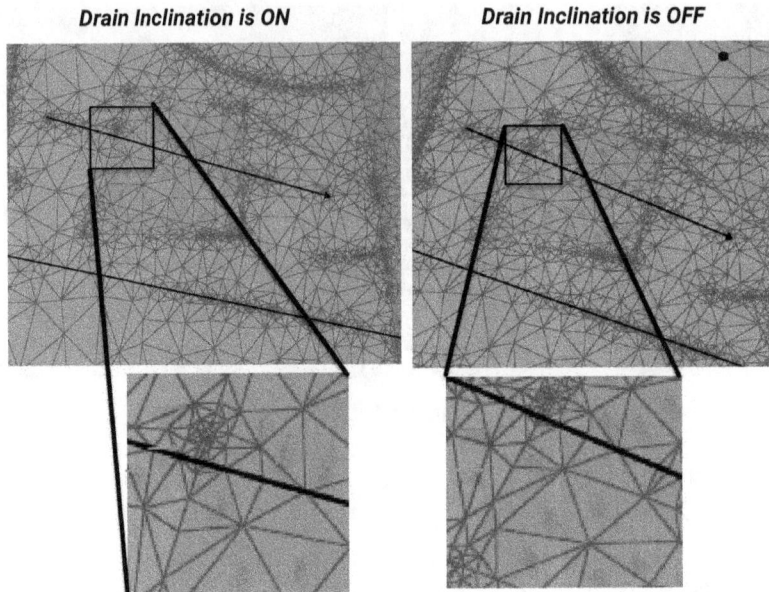

Figure 4–54

The term *Inclination* in Grading Optimization refers to compass angle (or Aspect). **0** is East and it runs in a counter-clockwise direction, making North **90**, West **180** and South **270**. When the **Minimum** Drain Inclination is toggled **on**, the Inclination direction becomes available, where you

can type in the appropriate value (from 0 to 360) as shown in Figure 4–55, or use the ✏ button to graphically indicate the angle on screen. This option is only available in Civil 3D, not in the Grading Optimization interface.

Figure 4–55

Depth of Material

The **Depth of Material** value is the material depth in cut and fill situations that should not be considered in cut/fill calculation. It can be considered the grubbing surface of unsuitable material for construction purposes. Enter a positive value, as shown in Figure 4–56. If you do enter a negative value, Grading Optimization will simply revert to its previous value.

Depth of material	2	ft

Figure 4–56

Follow global grading objectives

When you expand the *Follow global grading objectives* region of the *Zone Properties* dialog box, you can choose if this particular zone will follow the *Optimization Options* set up in the Grading Optimization interface, as shown in Figure 4–57.

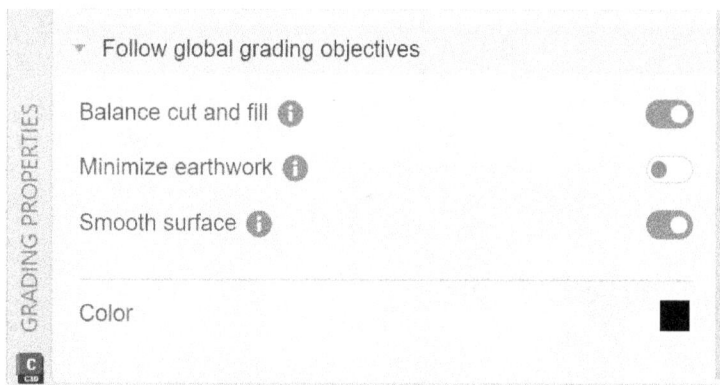

Figure 4–57

You can toggle the following:

- **Balance cut and fill**
- **Minimize Earthwork**
- **Smooth Surface**

When toggled **off**, this zone will ignore the values set in the *Optimization Options* dialog box, as shown in Figure 4–58.

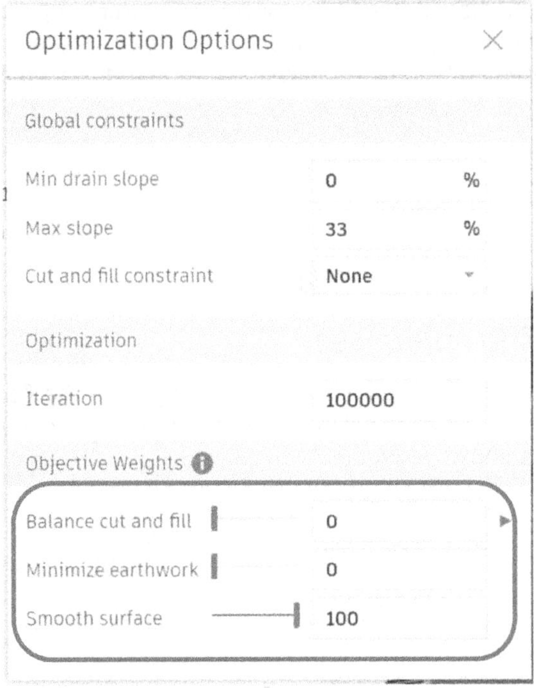

Figure 4–58

Layers and Civil 3D Styles

The default name of a Grading Object refers to the layer name of the object. Thus it is recommended that the defining polylines reside on specific layers reserved for the Grading Optimization process. These layers can then be filtered for easier manipulation such as locking or freezing.

Note: For ease of distinction, the layer names were created with Title case, whereas the standard layer names are upper case.

In the **ASC-Grading-Styles.dwg** reference template included in the dataset for this course, the following layers have been included:

Layer Name	Color	Description
C-Grad-Bend	70	Bend Lines
C-Grad-Bldg-Revl	1 (red)	Reveals
C-Grad-Bldg-Pads	4 (cyan)	Building Pads
G-Grad-Dran	4 (cyan)	Drain Lines

Layer Name	Color	Description
C-Grad-Curb	30	Curb (either lines or zones)
C-Grad-Edge	6 (magenta)	Aligned Edge
C-Grad-Limt	50	Grading Limit
C-GRAD-NPLT	7 (white)	No plot information
C-Grad-Pnts	3 (green)	Low and Bounded Points
C-Grad-Offs	3 (green)	Offset Points
C-Grad-Park	40	Parking Lots
C-Grad-Path	120	Accessible Path
C-Grad-Pond	5 (blue)	Ponds
C-Grad-Walk	140	Pathways
C-Grad-Wall	210	Retaining Walls
C- Grad-Zone	2 (yellow)	General Zones
C-Grad-Zone-Excl	60	Exclusion Zones
C-Road-Prof	1 through 5	Various - Road Profile Options

In addition, there is a point style for creating Grading Optimization point groups. Its style is an

argyle pattern (⊠).

It is recommended that you use your reference style template in order to incorporate the special Grading Optimization layers in your working drawings, according to your organization's CAD standards.

Note: The dataset for this course has layers and style templates already set.

Grading Limits

Any of the "General" zones (including the *Parking Lot* zone) can be defined as representing a Grading Limit. For the initial Grading Optimization studies, the grading limit represents the site boundaries beyond which no grading can occur. This is also known as the *Limits of Disturbance*.

As the Grading Optimization process gets more refined and it establishes one or more design surfaces, the grading limits may change. For example, if specific areas of interest or intent are being evaluated, such as ponds or building pads, the grading limits can be changed to speed up the Grading Optimization process. Consider how far out the grading process for the particular scenario may go and then establish the grading limits there. The term *Limits of Disturbance* is appropriate when considering this.

Therefore, Grading Optimization projects can have multiple zones defined as Grading Limits, and you can activate whichever grading limit zone is required for the particular iteration you are studying.

To enable the Grading Limit parameter, toggle it **on** in the *Zone Properties* dialog box, as shown in Figure 4–59. To activate or deactivate a Grading Limit, toggle it **on** or **off** in the Grading Optimization interface. This cannot be done in the Civil 3D interface.

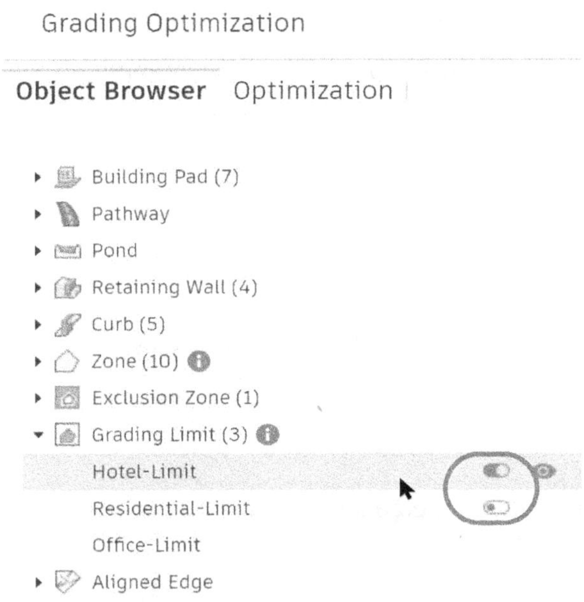

Figure 4–59

💡 Hint: Grading Limit Zone

During a Grading Optimization process, only one grading limit zone should be activated. If there are multiple grading limits active, the one that is highest up in the Grading Limit branch becomes the active one, and the others are ignored.

Exclusion Zones

Exclusion zones are self-explanatory. The area contained within the defined exclusion zone will not be optimized, and any Grading Object within the exclusion zone will be ignored during the optimization process.

When a polyline or feature line is selected as an Exclusion Zone, the *Exclusion Zone* dialog box that displays is quite simple, as shown in Figure 4–60. As always, it is recommended that you give the zone a meaningful name for easier identification, and optionally give it a different color. The default color is yellow.

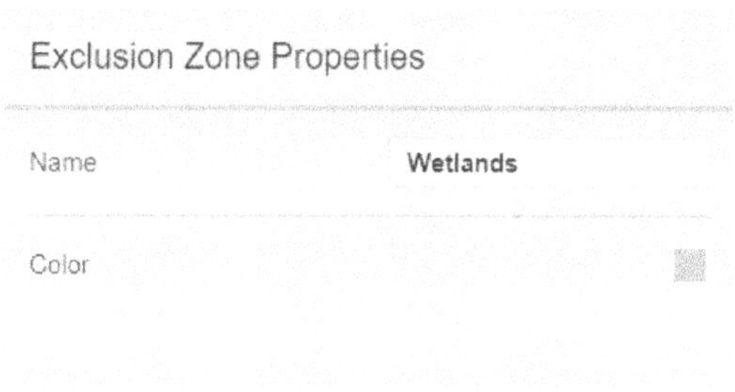

Exclusion Zone Properties

Name	Wetlands
Color	

Figure 4–60

Practice 4b
Create the Interim Design Surface

Practice Objectives

- Create Grading Optimization zones.
- Create an interim design grade as a base for the grading.

The Grading Optimization process can be time consuming, and you may require additional time to complete the process than the estimated 15 minutes. In this drawing, the existing surface is a combination of survey data and breaklines. Corridors were previously created and their top surfaces have been pasted into this existing surface. A variety of AutoCAD plines were copied from the Base xref drawings, and other plines were created to serve as the basis to create the required zones, as shown in Figure 4–61.

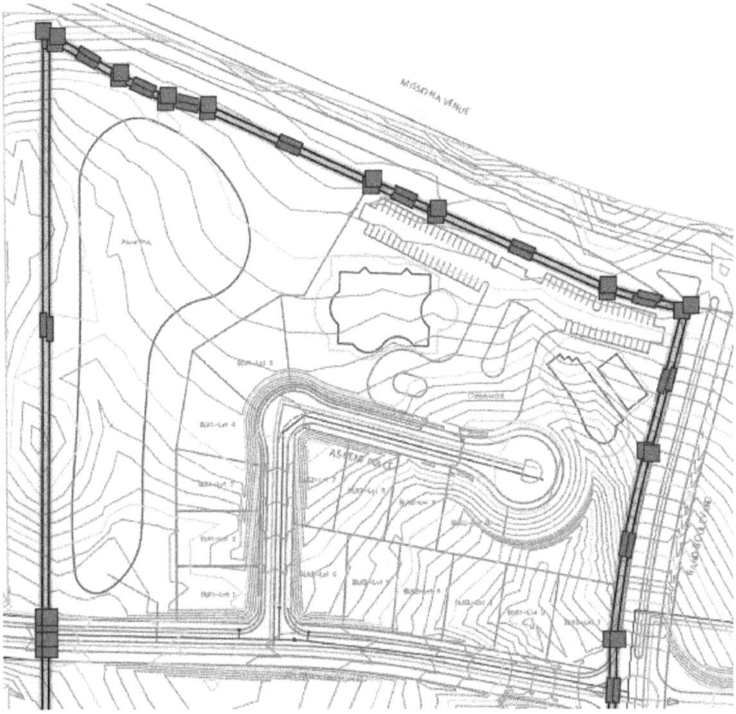

Figure 4–61

Task 1: Examine drawing setup.

1. Open **IDG_1.dwg** from the *C:\Civil 3D Grading\Working\GO-Intro* folder. Do not continue from the previous drawing.

2. In the *Prospector* tab of the Civil 3D *Toolspace*, expand the *Surface* branch and note that the **GO-EG** surface is the only surface.

3. In the *View* tab>*Named Views* panel, select **North-Site**. This will zoom into the northern portion of the site.

Task 2: Examine Polylines needed for defining zones.

1. A variety of AutoCAD Polylines (plines) have been created in this drawing through various means, some of which will be covered in subsequent practices in this course.

2. Select the various plines, and their intended function is shown in Figure 4–62. Use the Selection Cycling to select the proper one.

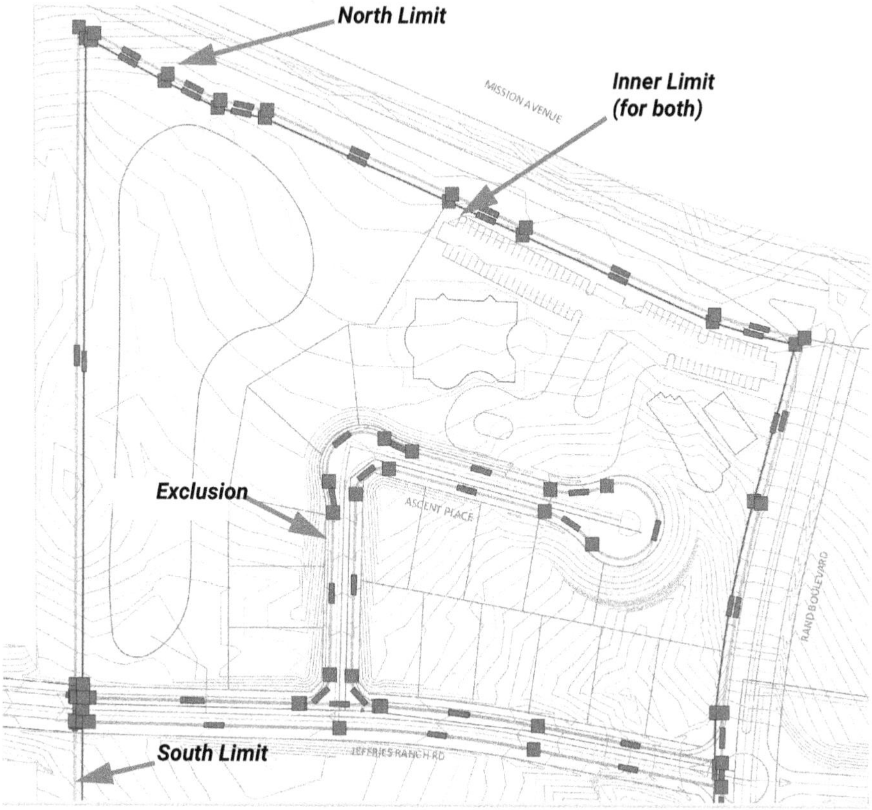

Figure 4–62

3. In the AutoCAD *Properties* dialog box, note that these plines are closed, and see the layers they reside on.

4. Go to the *Analyze* tab>*Grading Optimization* panel, and select ⬚ (Grading Objects Browser).

5. Note that there are no Grading Objects defined in the drawing, because there are no numbers listed after the branches, as shown in Figure 4–63.

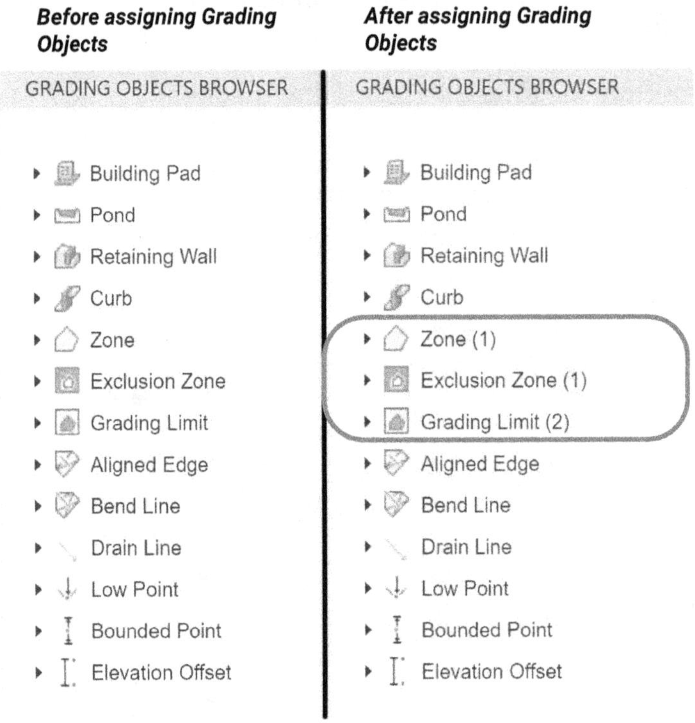

Figure 4–63

6. In the *Viewport control* area, select **Custom Model Views**, and then select the **Pick-Zone** view to make it current.

7. In the *Analyze* tab>*Grading Optimization* panel, select ⬚ (Grading Objects Tools). This will open the Tool Palettes in the *Grading Object Imperial* tab.

8. In the Tool Palette, select ⬭ (Grading Limit). Civil 3D will prompt you to select objects to set as a zone. Select the pline labeled *North Limit* as shown in Figure 4−64. Press the <Enter> key to finish the selection.

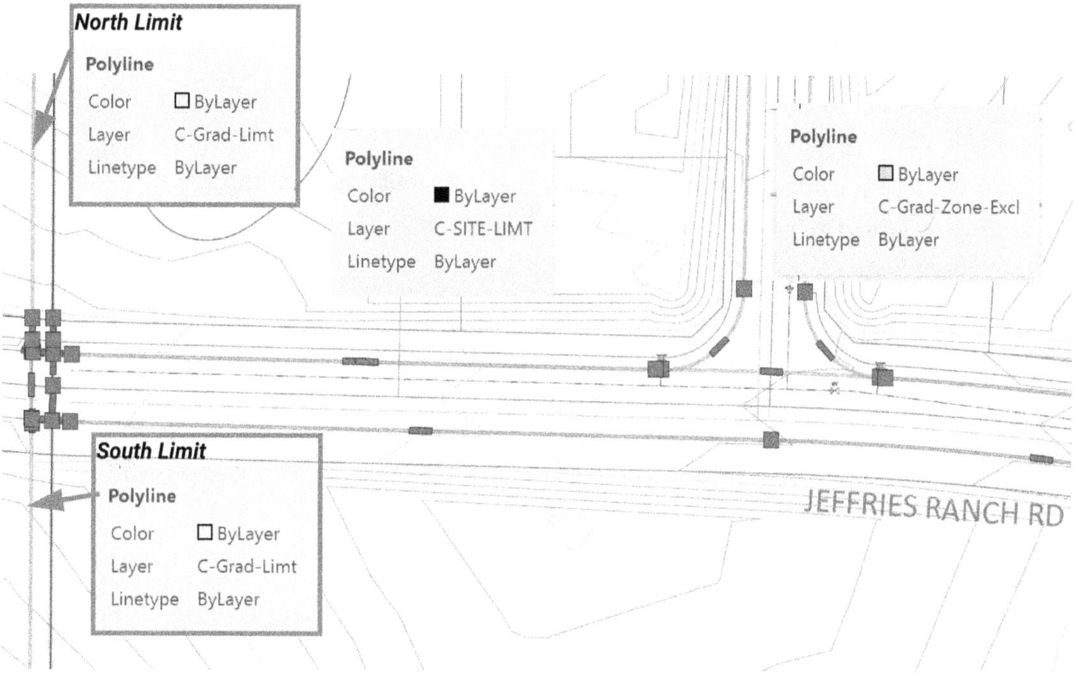

North Limit

Polyline

Color	☐ ByLayer
Layer	C-Grad-Limt
Linetype	ByLayer

Polyline

Color	■ ByLayer
Layer	C-SITE-LIMT
Linetype	ByLayer

Polyline

Color	☐ ByLayer
Layer	C-Grad-Zone-Excl
Linetype	ByLayer

South Limit

Polyline

Color	☐ ByLayer
Layer	C-Grad-Limt
Linetype	ByLayer

JEFFRIES RANCH RD

Figure 4−64

9. In the *Grading Limit Properties* dialog box that opens, set the following, as shown in Figure 4–65:

   - *Name*: **North Limit**
   - **Customize slope constraints**: toggle **on**
   - *Min drain slope*: **2%**
   - *Max Slope*: **50%**
   - *Depth of material*: **0** (which is the default)
   - *Breakline*: **Off** (Option is only displayed if Grading Limit has been toggled off)
   - **Grading limit**: **On** (which is the default - because you picked the **Grading Limit** tool)
   - Color: **2 (Yellow)**

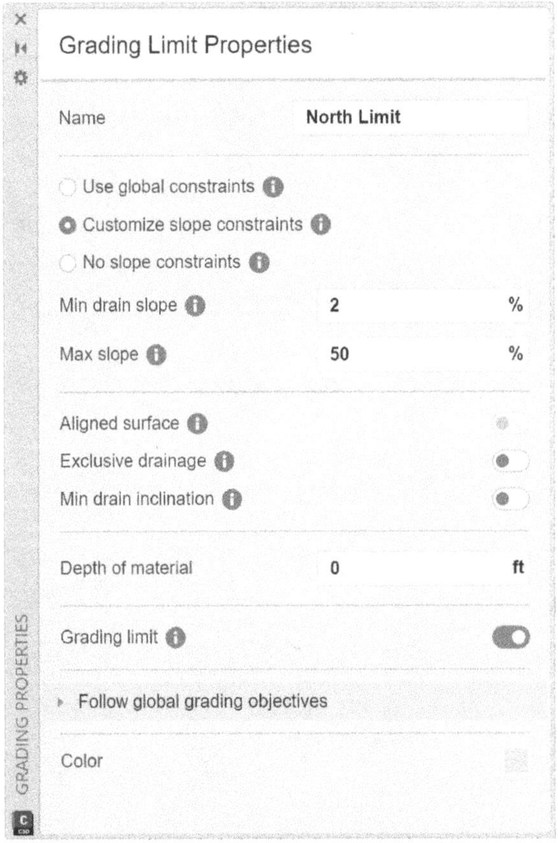

Figure 4–65

10. Press the \<Esc\> key to clear the selection and close the *Grading Limit Properties* dialog box.

11. *Optional*: Repeat the same procedure for the South Limit.

12. In the Tool Palette, select ⬜ (Exclusion Zone). Civil 3D will prompt you to select objects to set as a zone. Select the pline labeled *Exclusion* as shown in Figure 4–66. Press the <Enter> key to finish the selection.

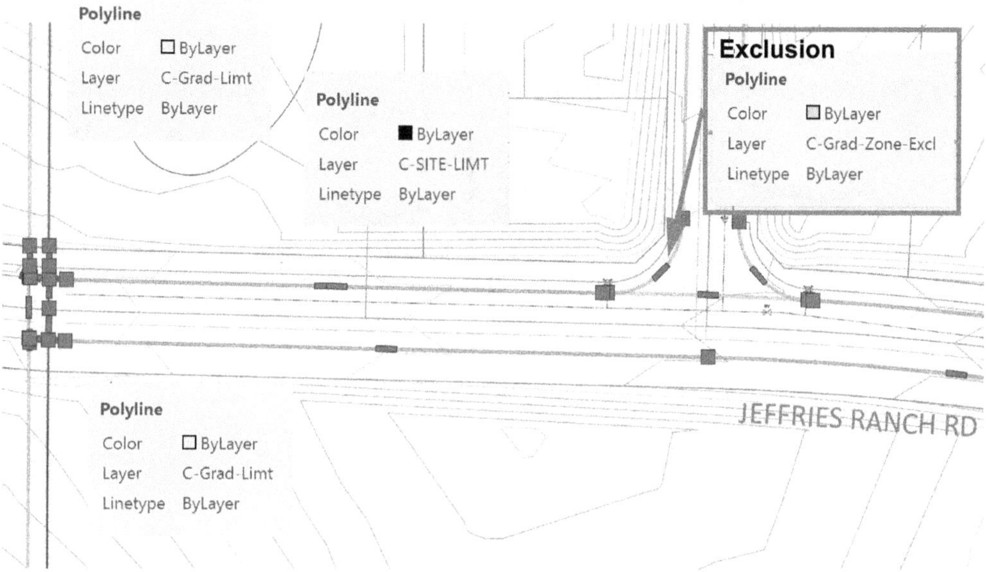

Polyline
Color   ☐ ByLayer
Layer   C-Grad-Limt
Linetype   ByLayer

Polyline
Color   ■ ByLayer
Layer   C-SITE-LIMT
Linetype   ByLayer

Exclusion
Polyline
Color   ☐ ByLayer
Layer   C-Grad-Zone-Excl
Linetype   ByLayer

Polyline
Color   ☐ ByLayer
Layer   C-Grad-Limt
Linetype   ByLayer

JEFFRIES RANCH RD

Figure 4–66

13. In the *Exclusion Zone Properties* dialog box, enter the following, as shown in Figure 4–67:

- Name: **Road Exclusion**
- Color: **Magenta** (pick from Select Color box)

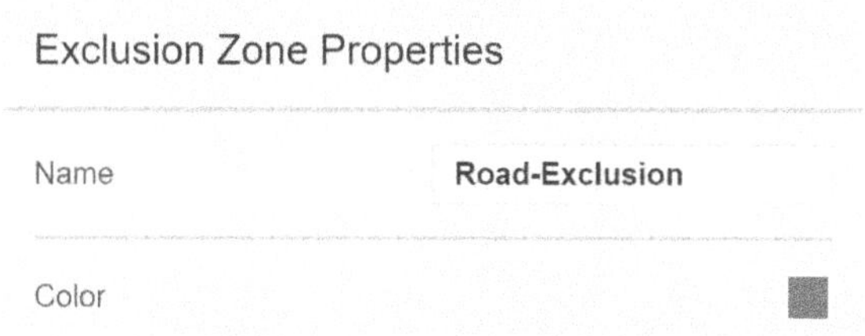

Exclusion Zone Properties

Name	**Road-Exclusion**
Color	■

Figure 4–67

14. Press the <Esc> key.

15. In the Tool Palette, select ⬠ (Zone). Civil 3D will prompt you to select objects to set as a zone. Select the pline labeled *Inner Limit (for both)* as shown in Figure 4–68. Press the <Enter> key to finish the selection.

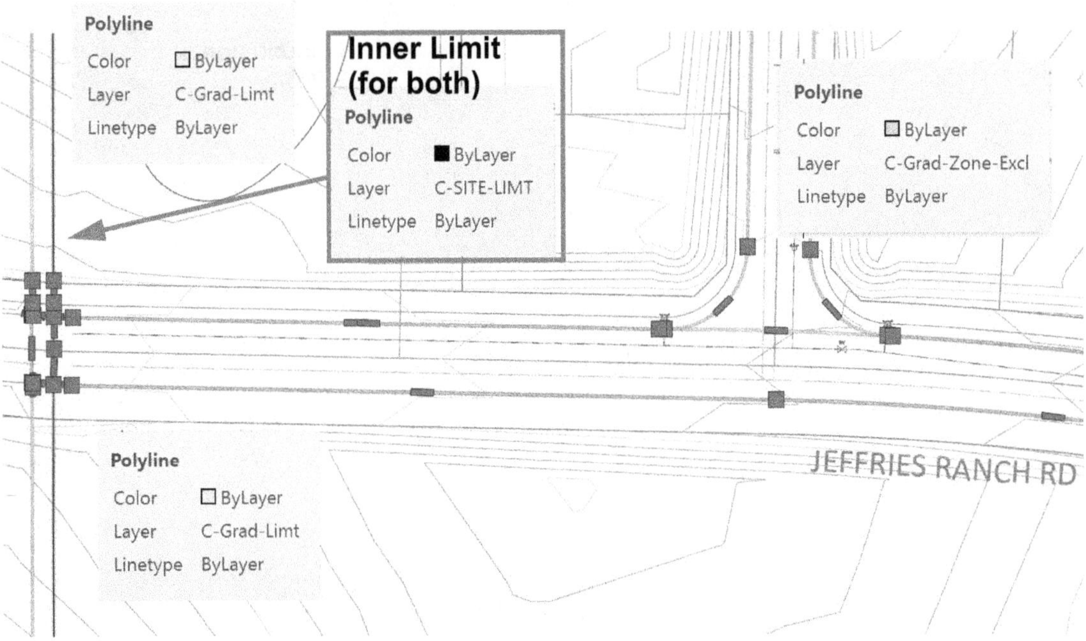

Polyline

Color	☐ ByLayer
Layer	C-Grad-Limt
Linetype	ByLayer

Inner Limit (for both)

Polyline

Color	■ ByLayer
Layer	C-SITE-LIMT
Linetype	ByLayer

Polyline

Color	☐ ByLayer
Layer	C-Grad-Zone-Excl
Linetype	ByLayer

Polyline

Color	☐ ByLayer
Layer	C-Grad-Limt
Linetype	ByLayer

JEFFRIES RANCH RD

Figure 4–68

16. In the *Zone Properties* dialog box, set the following, as shown in Figure 4–69:

- *Name:* **Inner Limit**
- **Customize slope constraints**: toggle **on**
- *Min drain slope:* **1%**
- *Max Slope:* **7%**
- *Depth of material:* **0** (which is the default)
- **Breakline**: **on** (which is the default)
- **Grading limit**: **off** (which is the default - because you picked the **Zone** tool.)
- Expand the Follow global grading objectives by clicking on the down arrow.
- **Minimize Earthwork**: toggle **off**

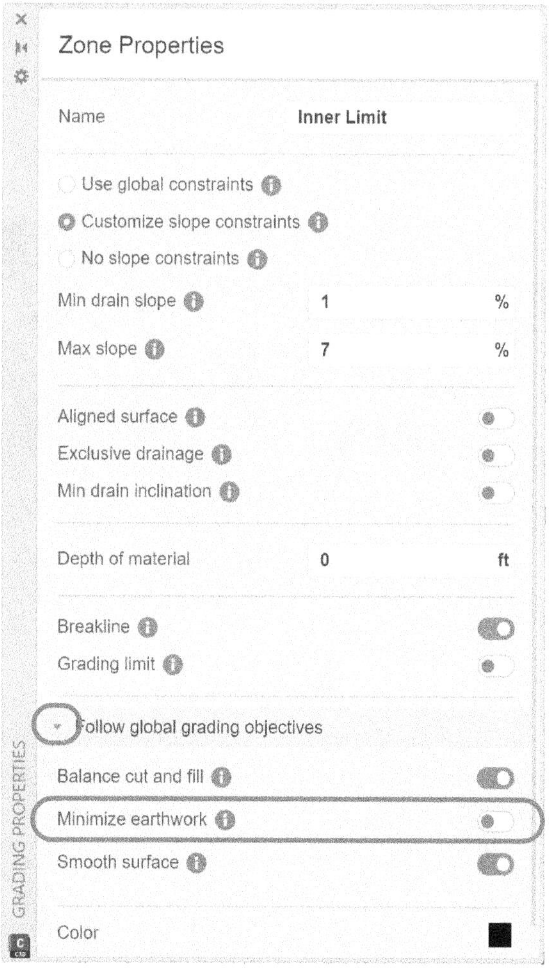

Figure 4–69

17. Press the <Esc> key.

18. Save the drawing.

Task 3: Create an Interim Design Grade Surface.

1. Continue working with the drawing from the previous practice or open **IDG_2.dwg** from the *C:\Civil 3D Grading\Working\GO-Intro* folder.

2. Go to the *Analyze* tab>*Grading Optimization* panel, and select ◈ (Optimize). This launches the Grading Optimization program, as shown in Figure 4–70.

Note: Since there is only one surface present in the drawing, you are not asked to select an EG (Existing Ground) surface for the Grading Optimization to use.

Figure 4–70

3. On the left side, expand the *Zone, Exclusion Zone,* and *Grading Limit* branches, and then click on the Grading Objects listed. You will note that this contains the same information that you had entered in Civil 3D.

4. If you created a South Limit in the previous task, click on the **South Limit** Grading Limit object. In the *Grading Limit Properties* dialog box, set the toggle for **Active** to **off**, as shown in Figure 4–71. Since you will only be optimizing the northern site, the South Limit is not required.

Color

Active

Visible

Figure 4–71

5. In the *Optimization* toolbar at the bottom, click on ⇌ (Optimization Options).

6. In the *Optimization Options* dialog box, set the following, as shown in Figure 4–72.

   - *Iteration:* **15000**
   - *Balance cut and fill:* **10**
   - *Minimize earthwork:* **35**
   - *Smooth Surface:* **100%**

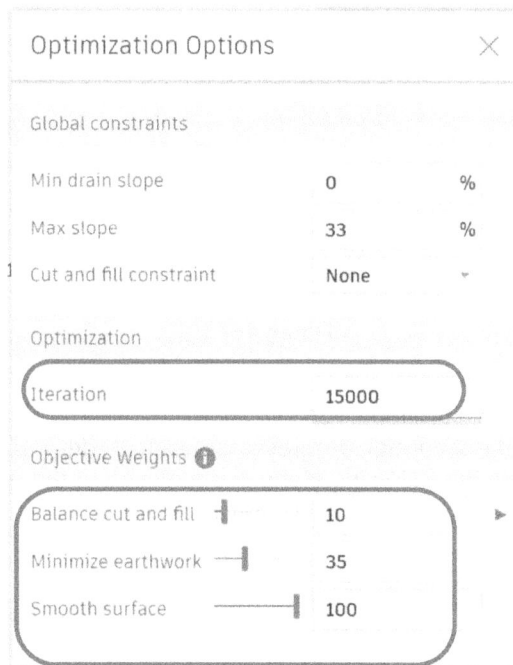

Optimization Options ✕

Global constraints

Min drain slope	0	%
Max slope	33	%
Cut and fill constraint	None	˅

Optimization

Iteration — 15000

Objective Weights ⓘ

Balance cut and fill	10	▶
Minimize earthwork	35	
Smooth surface	100	

Figure 4–72

7. Click on the ▷ Optimize (Optimize) button to begin the optimization.

8. A warning will show up stating that the edges of the grading limit exceed the maximum slope allowed. This warning will disappear after a short while.

    Note: During the optimization process, you can even go back to Civil 3D and continue your design development, or even open another drawing.

9. While the optimization is progressing, you can navigate in the graphics window to see the changes taking place. There is a tally of the cuts and fills in the lower left window. Also, the optimization progress bar in the *Optimization* toolbar slowly moves from left to right showing how far along the optimization is, as shown in Figure 4−73. Press the <Enter> key to finish the selection.

Figure 4−73

10. If the optimization is taking too long, you can click on [Stop] (Stop) to interrupt the optimization process. If not enough progress has been made, you can close the Grading Object program and skip the following steps and move on to the next practice, where you can open the next drawing where the optimization has been completed, as shown in Figure 4−74.

Figure 4−74

11. Once the Optimization has been completed (or interrupted), the ![Update Drawing] button is active. Click on it to send the results from the Grading Optimization back to the Civil 3D drawing that launched the Grading Optimization process.

12. Back in Civil 3D, you will find the *Save Optimization Result* dialog box displayed, as shown in Figure 4–75.

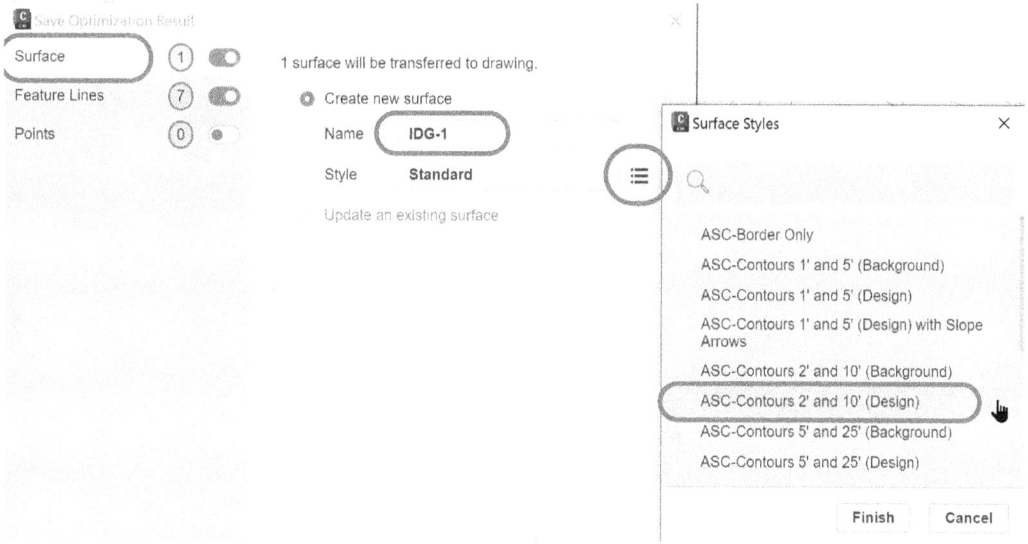

Figure 4–75

13. Name the surface **IDG-1**. Click on the ⦂ (Select) button to select the surface style from the list and select **ASC-Contours 2' and 10' (Design)**.

14. Click **Finish** to close the *Surface Styles* selection panel.

15. Click on the Feature Lines listing on the left side.

16. For the *Feature Line Style*, click on the ⦂ (Select) button to select the surface style from the list, and select **ASC-Basic**.

17. Provide a *Name prefix* for the feature lines and name it **IDG-1-** as shown in Figure 4–76.

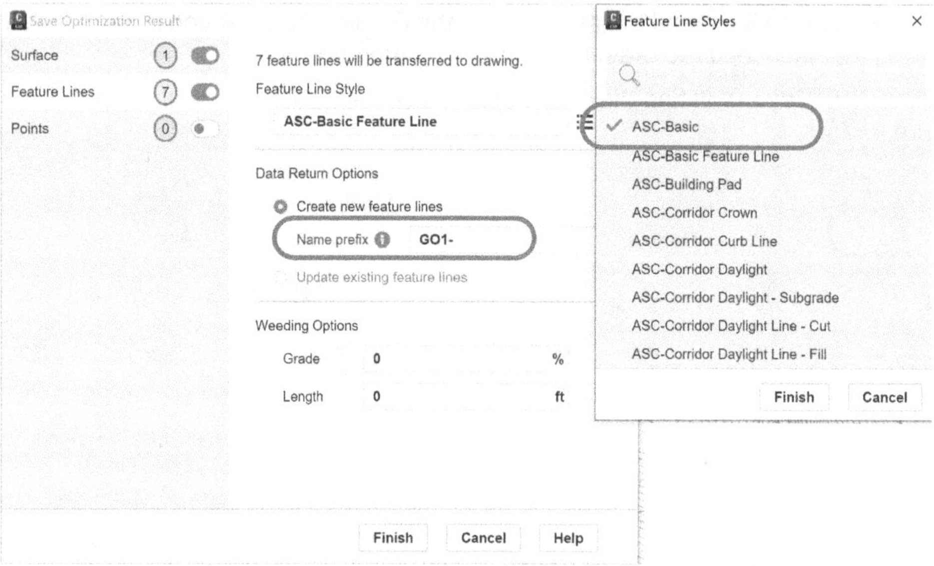

Figure 4–76

18. Click **Finish** to close the *Feature Line Styles* selection panel.

19. Click **Finish** to close the *Save Optimization Result* dialog box.

20. The new surface is built and displayed. It is also listed in the *Surfaces* branch of the Prospector.

21. The *Events* panel of the Panorama may open to warn of duplicate points which are ignored.

Dismiss the Event Viewer by clicking on the green check mark ☑.

22. Save the drawing.

Task 4: More practices for the Southern Site (Optional).

1. Repeat the same process for the Southern site to create an Interim Design Grade.

2. Remember to click on the **North Limit** Grading Limit object. In the *Grading Limit Properties* dialog box, set the toggle for **Active** to **off**, since you will only be optimizing the southern site.

3. Toggle on the **South Limit** Grading Limit object.

4. Name the resulting surface and site (for the feature lines) **IDG-South-1**.

5. Save the drawing as **South-IDG.dwg** in the *C:\Civil 3D Grading\Working\GO-Intro* folder.

Chapter Review Questions

1. Which of the following is NOT a member of the *Grading Optimization* tool palette?
    a. Retaining Wall
    b. Building Pad
    c. High Point
    d. Parking Lot

2. Which of the following needs to be defined from a linear object (not a closed object)?
    a. Exclusion Zone
    b. Bounded Point
    c. Offset Points
    d. Pathways

3. Which of the following can be defined by a linear or a closed object (select all that apply)?
    a. Reveal
    b. Curb
    c. Aligned Edge
    d. Retaining Wall
    e. Accessibly Path

4. How can you exaggerate the elevations in the Grading Optimization program?
    a. You cannot.
    b. The surface must be vertically exaggerated in Civil 3D before launching the Grading Optimization.
    c. By using the Vertical Exaggeration slide in the Grading Optimization program.
    d. Through *Optimization Options*.

5. In the Grading Optimization program, what are the display themes (select all that apply):

    a. Elevations

    b. Cut and Fill

    c. Slopes

    d. Orientation

    e. Site Lines

6. Which of the following is NOT a member of the Zone Grading Optimization?

    a. Parking Lot

    b. Isolation Zone

    c. Building Pad

    d. Pathways

7. How do you display cut/fill areas in a surface (Check all that apply)?

    a. Through the *Analyze* tab in the Surface Properties.

    b. You cannot.

    c. Setting the proper Cut/Fill surface style.

    d. Through the *Volumes* dashboard.

8. Can you have more than one Grading Limit for the Grading Optimization to process (Check all that apply)?

    a. No, an error will occur if you have more than one Grading Limit.

    b. Yes, but only one Grading Limit should be enabled.

    c. No Grading Limit is required for the Grading Optimization.

    d. Yes, but only the top Grading Limit in the browser will be used.

Parking Lot Design

Parking lots can be more challenging to grade than buildings because it is important to ensure proper drainage across the parking surface. Here, you will learn how to easily set slopes along the perimeter of a parking lot using a temporary surface. The first of three grading approaches is introduced, along with steps to create feature lines for the curb returns, grading them to the existing ground at different slopes.

The other two grading options (discussed in later topics) use the same base feature line for the back of the curb: one approach involves creating a corridor for the curb, while another explores how the Grading Optimization tool can help design parking lots.

Learning Objectives

- Create a temporary surface to assist in setting feature line elevations and slopes.
- Create a grading group that transitions from one grade to another along a feature line.
- Create a surface from a grading group.
- Create feature lines that affect the grading group surface.

5.1 Create a Temporary Surface

Creating a temporary surface can help set elevations of a complex feature line. For example, a feature line that has to follow a specific slope across a site can be created from the elevations of a temporary surface. Parking lots are examples of this strategy because they often slope to one side or to the center for drainage management.

To create a temporary surface, it is recommended that you create a temporary site for the temporary feature lines and grading groups. Once the design feature line is created, it is used for the final grading and the elevations are obtained from the temporary surface. You can then delete the temporary site without losing any design information. This helps to keep the drawing clean and efficient.

How To: Create a Temporary Surface

1. Create a temporary site for all of the feature lines and grading groups that are going to be deleted later. Define the site by navigating to the *Prospector* tab, then right-clicking on *Sites* and selecting **New**.

2. Decide whether you start from the center and grade out in both directions or start on one side and create multiple grading objects going in the same direction at different slopes. Figure 5–1 shows an example of grading from the center out in both directions.

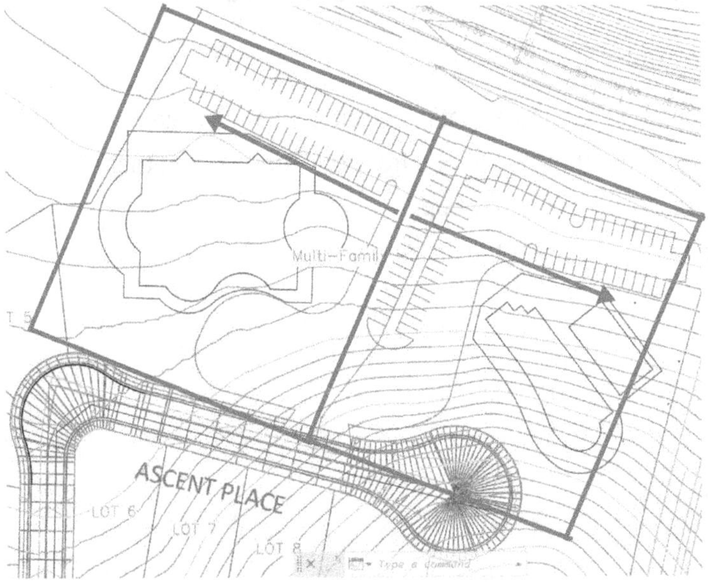

Figure 5–1

3. Create the base feature line.

4. Create a grading group with the **Automatic surface creation** option selected, as shown in Figure 5–2.

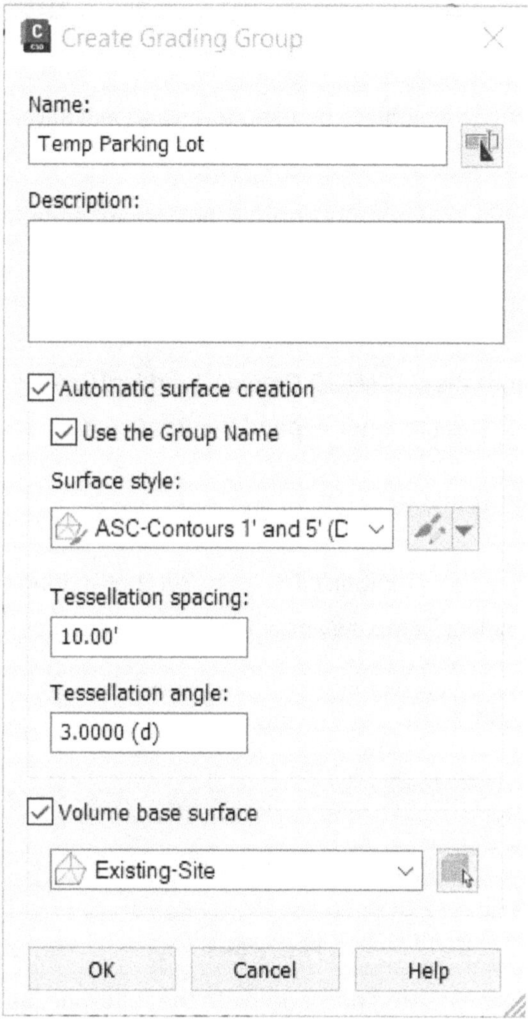

Figure 5–2

5. Create grading from the base feature line out, on each side at a required distance to cover the entire site. Set a grade in each direction to provides the required slopes.

6. Use the surface elevations from this temporary surface to assign elevations for the actual grading design feature line.

Practice 5a
Create a Temporary Surface

Practice Objective

- Create a temporary surface which will be used to assign elevations to the vertices of another feature line.

In this practice, you will create a temporary surface, and create a feature line and set elevations by grading.

Task 1: Create a temporary site.

1. Open **PKLOT-A.dwg** from the *C:\Civil 3D Grading\Working\Parking Lot* folder.

2. In the *Home* tab>*Create Design* panel, expand the *Grading* drop-down list and click

    (Grading Creation Tools).

3. In the *Grading Creations Tools* toolbar, click (Set the Grading Group).

4. In the *Site* dialog box, select **Temp**, as shown in Figure 5–3. Click **OK**.

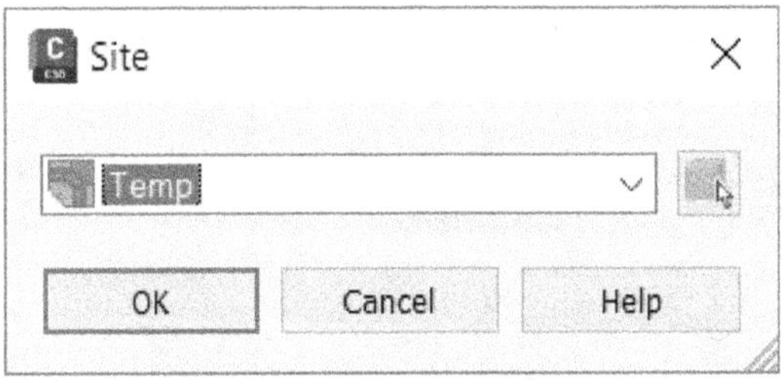

Figure 5–3

5. In the *Create Grading Group* dialog box, complete the following, as shown in Figure 5–4:

    - For the *Name*, type **Temp Parking Lot**.
    - Select the **Automatic surface creation** option.
    - Select the **Volume Base Surface** option and ensure that *Existing Site* is listed.
    - Click **OK**.

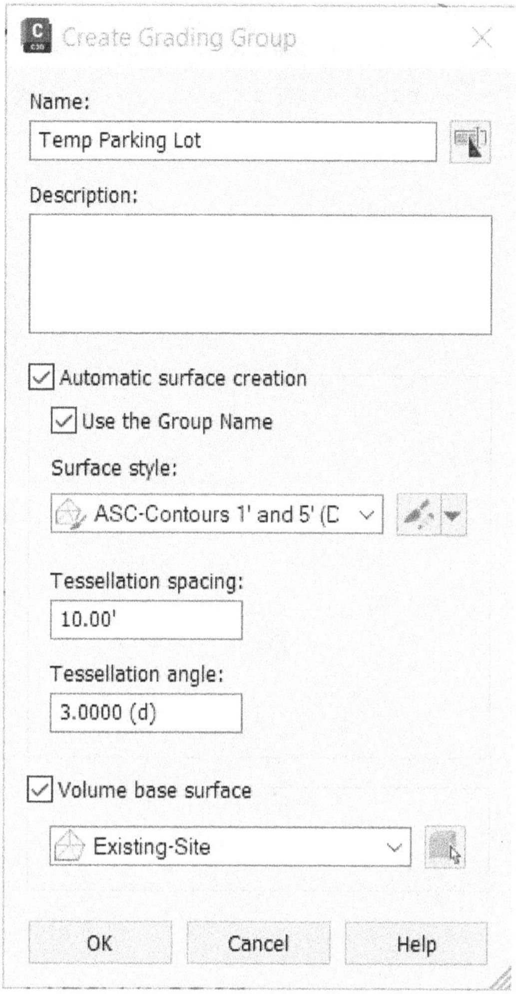

Figure 5-4

6. In the *Create Surface* dialog box, click **OK** to the defaults.

7. In the *Grading Creation Tools* toolbar, select **Grade to Distance** for the criteria, as shown in Figure 5-5.

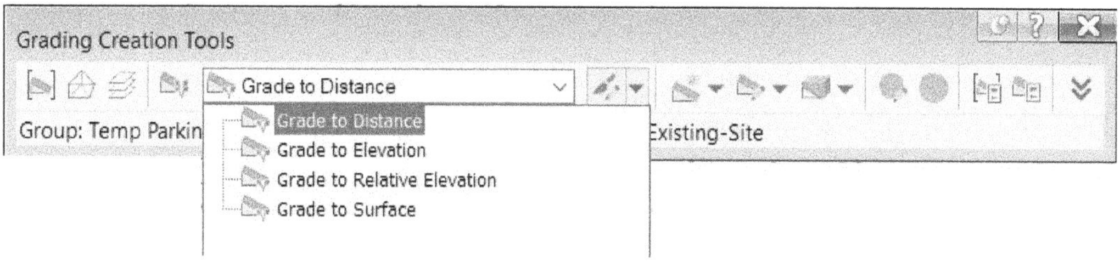

Figure 5-5

8. In the *Grading Creation Tools* toolbar, click ![icon] (Create Grading.

9. In the drawing, select the **CenterLine** feature line, as shown in Figure 5−6.

Figure 5−6

10. When prompted for a side to which to grade, pick a point in the drawing to the right of the feature line. Press <Enter> to accept the default to grade the entire length of the feature line.

   - For the *Distance*, type **235** and press <Enter>.
   - For the *Format*, type **G** and press <Enter> for grade.
   - For the *Grade*, type **-2 (Minus 2)** for a negative 2% slope.

11. Repeat Steps 3 to 10 to grade to the left side **265'** at a **-2%(minus 2)** grade.

   Note: If selecting the feature line is difficult, you might need to set the drawing order of the grading surface to the back or use the Selection Cycling feature.

12. Press <Esc> to end the command.

13. Close the *Grading Creation Tools* toolbar.

14. Save the drawing.

Task 2: Create a feature line and set elevations by grading.

1. Continue working in the drawing from the previous task.

2. In the *Home* tab>*Create Design* panel, expand the *Feature Line* drop-down list and click

   (Create Feature Line from Objects).

3. Type **X** and press <Enter> (or pick the **Xref** option from the Command Line) to select linework from the external reference file. Select the magenta line that represents the parking lot perimeter, as highlighted in blue in Figure 5–7. Press <Enter> to continue.

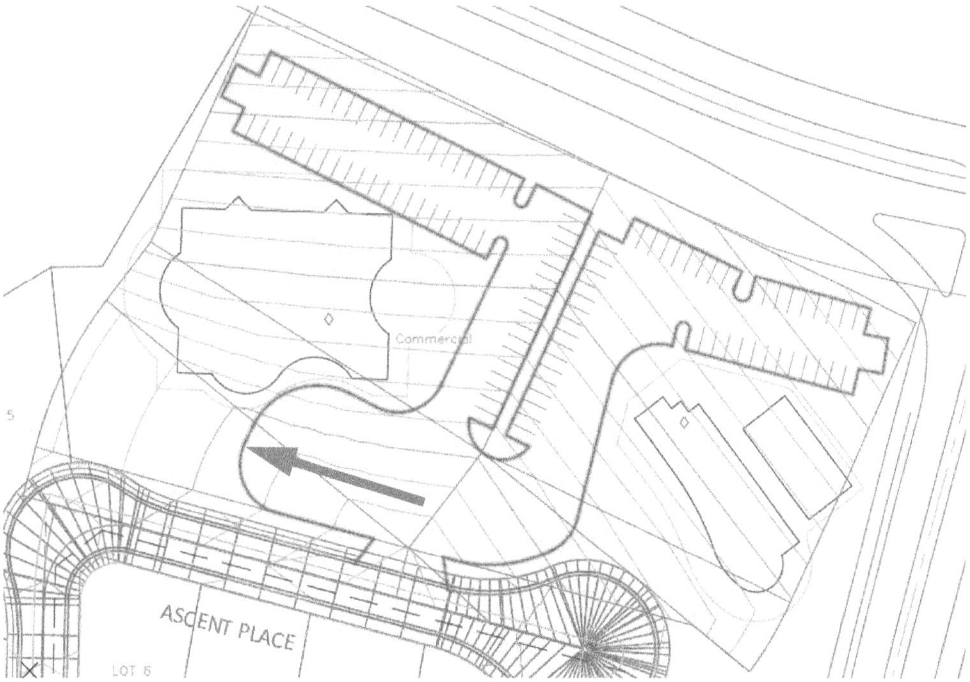

Figure 5–7

4. In the *Create Feature Lines* dialog box, complete the following, as shown in Figure 5–8:

    - Leave the *Site* set to **Temp**.
    - For the *Name*, type **Parking-Gutter**.
    - Set the *Style* to **ASC-Parking Lot**.
    - Verify that **Assign elevations** is selected.
    - Click **OK**.

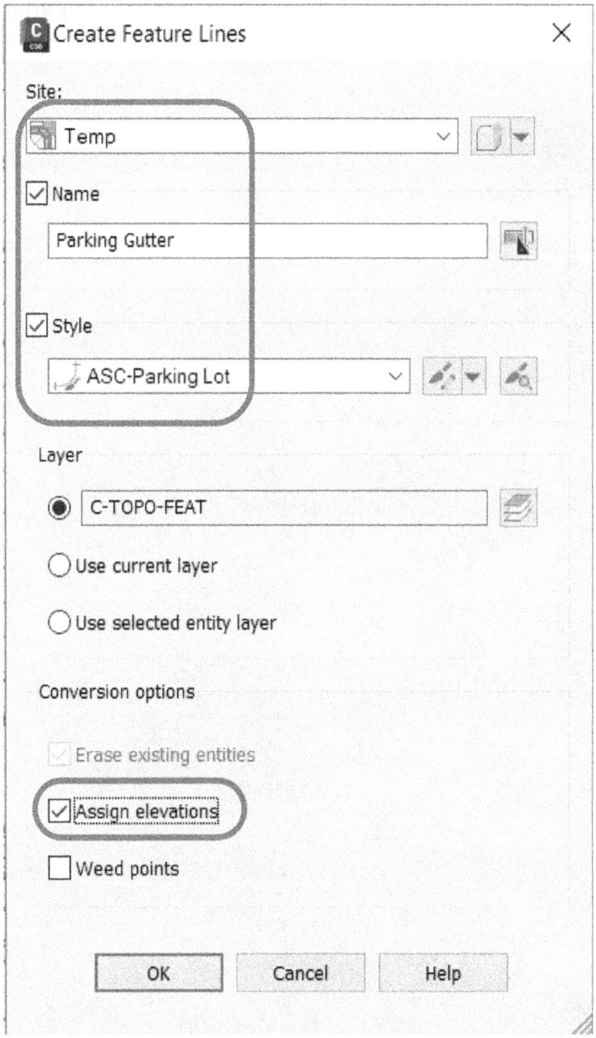

Figure 5–8

5. In the *Assign Elevations* dialog box, select **From gradings**, as shown in Figure 5–9. Click **OK**.

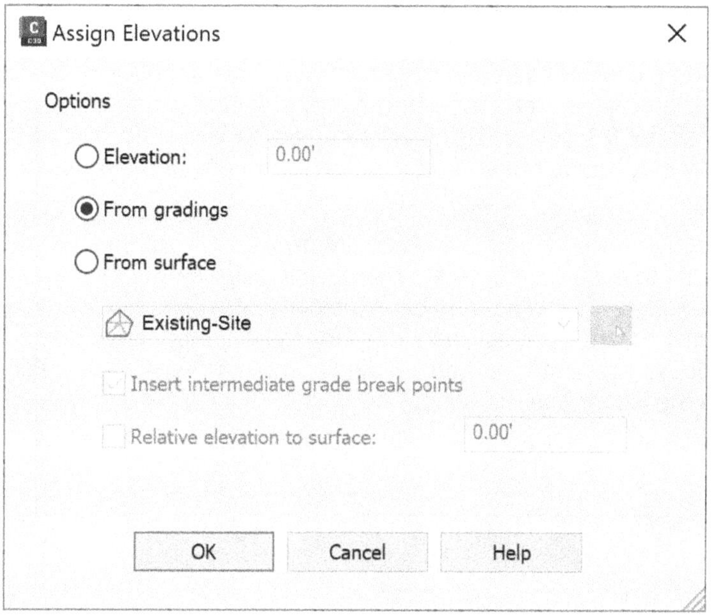

Figure 5–9

6. Save the drawing.

End of practice

5.2 Create a Transitional Grading Group

So far you have only created grading groups that follow the same slope for the entire length of the feature line. Some designs require a transition from one slope to another to accommodate differences in elevation without an ample amount of grading area. For example, you have a target slope for a site of 5:1, but can grade as steep as 2:1 if needed. You might need to use a 2:1 slope to ensure that you do not encroach on an easement, another building, or a property line.

To fit a building on the property, you can grade the front to the preferred slope of 5:1, and then grade the back at 2:1 to ensure that you stay within the property line. In between the two slopes, you use a transitional grading object and have the computer calculate the transitional slopes between the building's front and back, as shown in Figure 5–10. In this example, you had to change grading slopes to ensure that the building to the north is not encroached on by the cut or fill slopes from the building to the south.

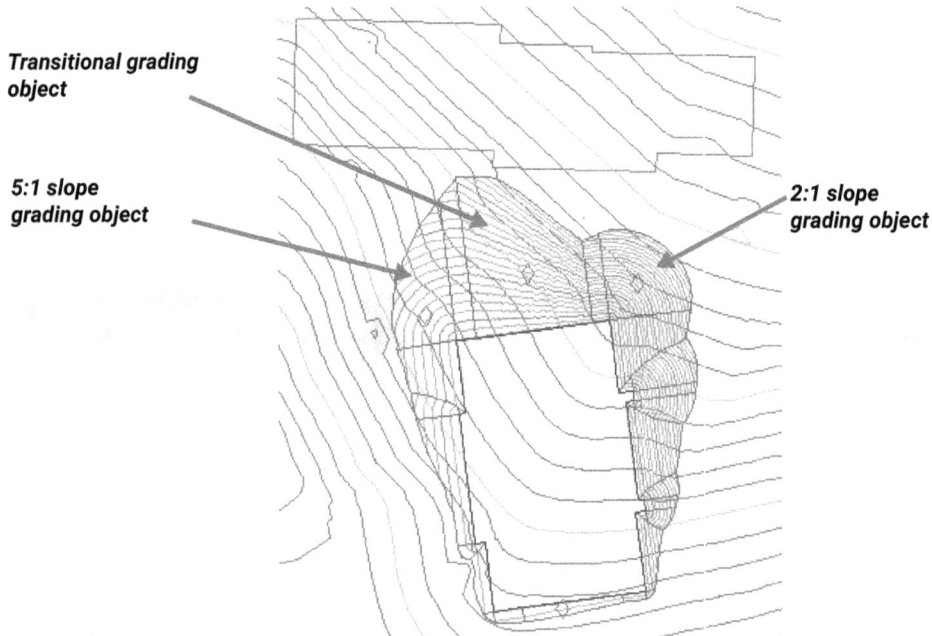

Figure 5–10

How To: Create Transitional Grading Groups

1. In the *Home* tab>*Create Design* panel, expand the *Grading* drop-down list and click

    (Grading Creation Tools).

2. In the *Grading Creation Tools* toolbar, click   (Set Group) on the far left. Select the *Site name* in which you want to work, as shown in Figure 5–11.

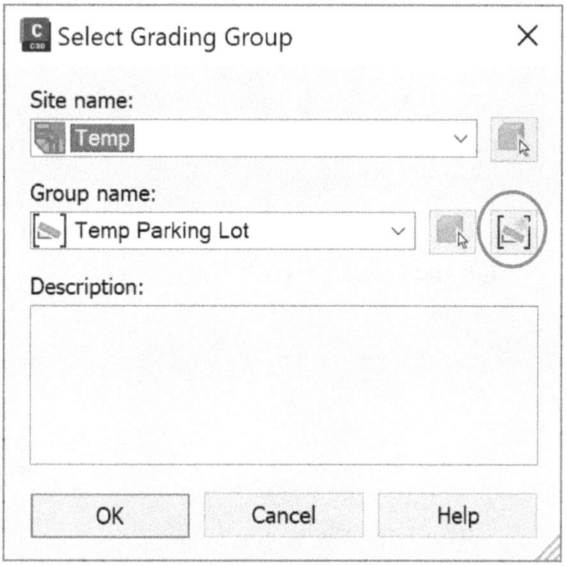

Figure 5–11

3. To create a new grading group, click   (Create a Grading Group), as shown above in Figure 5–11.

4. In the *Create Grading Group* dialog box, type a name in the *Name* field. Do not select the **Automatic surface creation** option, as shown in Figure 5–12. Click **OK**.

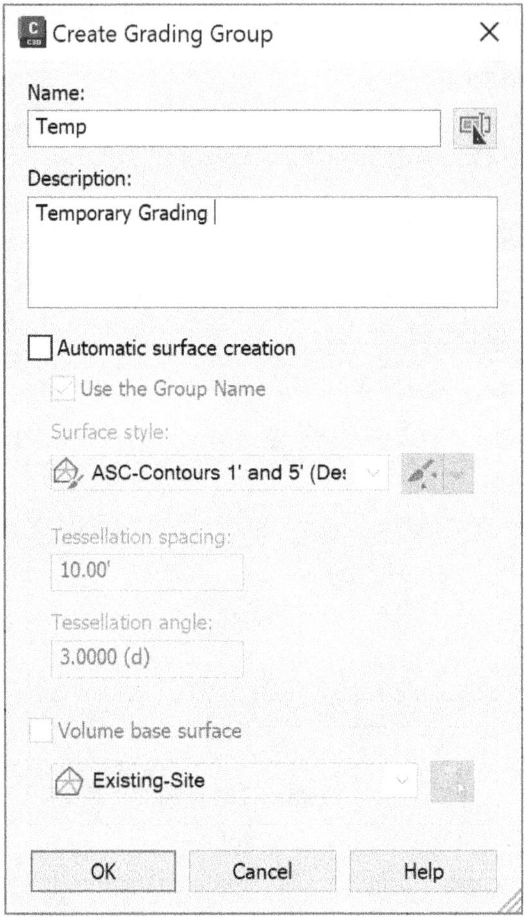

Figure 5–12

5. In the *Grading Creation Tools* toolbar, click ![icon] (Select a Criteria Set) to select the grading criteria set that is required for the project.

6. Set the required grading criteria, as shown in Figure 5–13.

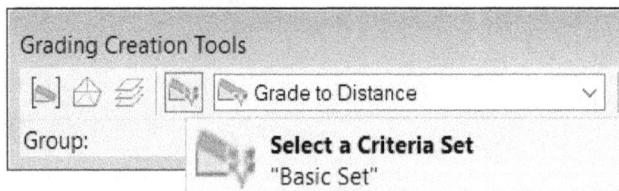

Figure 5–13

7. In the *Grading Creation Tools* toolbar, click ▣ (Create Grading). Select the feature line to use as the baseline.

8. When prompted for a grading side, pick a point in the drawing.

9. When prompted to apply it to the entire length, type **N** (for No) and press <Enter>.

10. In the Command Line, the routine prompts you to *Select the start point*. In the drawing, an arrow displays pointing in the direction of the feature line stations to help you pick the point to start your first slope, as shown in Figure 5−14.

    Note: You can use any Osnap commands or type the feature line station value.

Station:1+92.50', Elevation:237.00'

Figure 5−14

11. In the Command Line, the station you selected displays for your verification (this occurs even if you are typing the station). Press <Enter> to accept.

12. In the Command Line, you are prompted to specify the end point for the grading. You can either pick a point in the drawing (as you did in Step 10), or proceed as follows:

    *   Type a feature line station.

    OR

    *   Type **L** and press <Enter> to set the length of the grading.

    In the drawing, an arrow displays pointing in the opposite direction as the starting point for the grading, as shown in Figure 5−15.

Station:2+20.61', Elevation:237.00'

Figure 5−15

13. In the Command Line, the station displays for verification even if you are typing the station value. Press <Enter> to accept it.

14. Repeat Steps 1 to 12 to set another grading criteria on the same feature line. Your results should be similar to those shown in Figure 5–16.

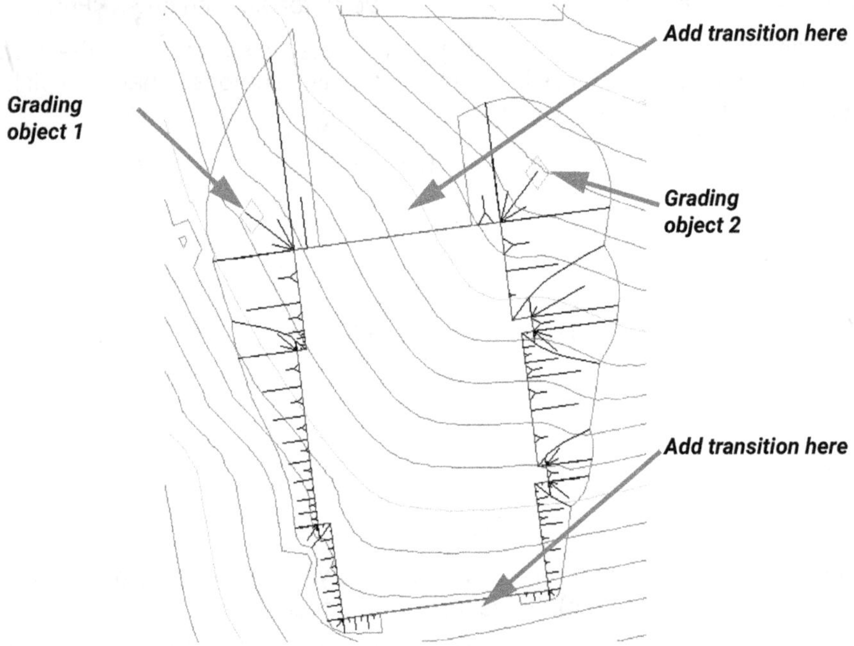

Figure 5–16

15. In the *Grading Creation Tools* toolbar, expand the *Create Grading* drop-down list and click ⬡ (Create Transition).

16. In the Command Line, you are prompted to *Select the feature*. Select the feature line that has been partially graded.

17. In the Command Line, you are prompted to pick a point between the gradings. Select between any previously created grading objects, as shown in Figure 5–16.

18. Repeat Steps 15 and 16 as needed to complete all of the transitions.

19. Press <Esc> to end the command.

Practice 5b
Create Stepped Offsets and Transitional Gradings

Practice Objective

*   Create curb returns using stepped offsets and incorporate them into a parking lot grading group.

In this practice, you will create stepped offsets. You will also move feature lines to a different site, grade to a surface with varying slopes along one feature line, and create transitions between predefined grading objects along the same feature line.

Task 1: Create stepped offsets.

1. Continue working in the drawing from the last practice or open **PKLOT-B.dwg** from the *C:\Civil 3D Grading\Working\Parking Lot* folder.

2. In the *Prospector* tab, expand **Sites>Temp** and select the feature lines. In the preview window in the lower part of the *Prospector*, select **Parking-Gutter**, then right-click and select **Select**, as shown in Figure 5–17.

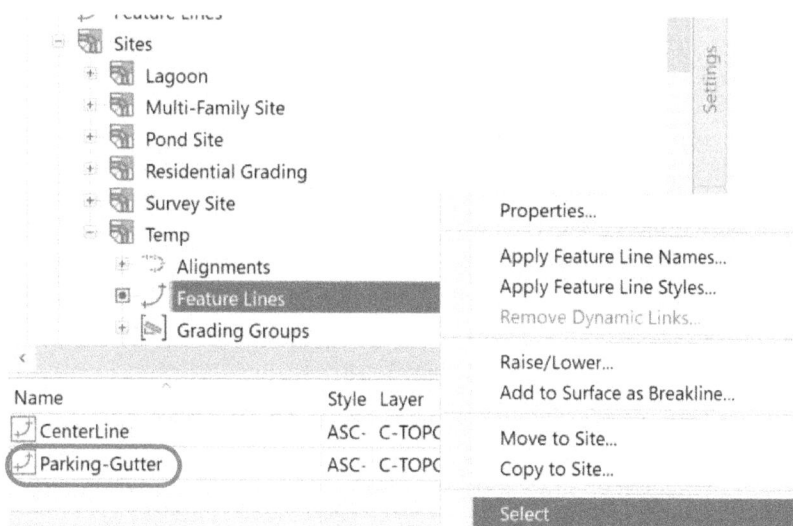

Figure 5–17

3. In the *Feature Line* contextual tab>*Edit Geometry* panel, click 🔲 (Stepped Offset). If the *Edit Geometry* panel is not displayed, click 🔲 (Edit Geometry) in the *Feature Line* contextual tab>*Modify* panel.

4. For the *Offset Distance*, type **2** and press <Enter>.

5. In the drawing, pick a point inside the parking area for the side to which to offset.

6. To set the elevation, type **G** and press <Enter> for grade.

7. For the grade, type **2** to set the grade at 2%. (This will act as the lip of curb.)

8. Press <Esc> to end the command.

9. In the preview window in the lower part of the *Prospector*, select the lowest feature line, then right-click and select **Properties**, as shown in Figure 5–18.

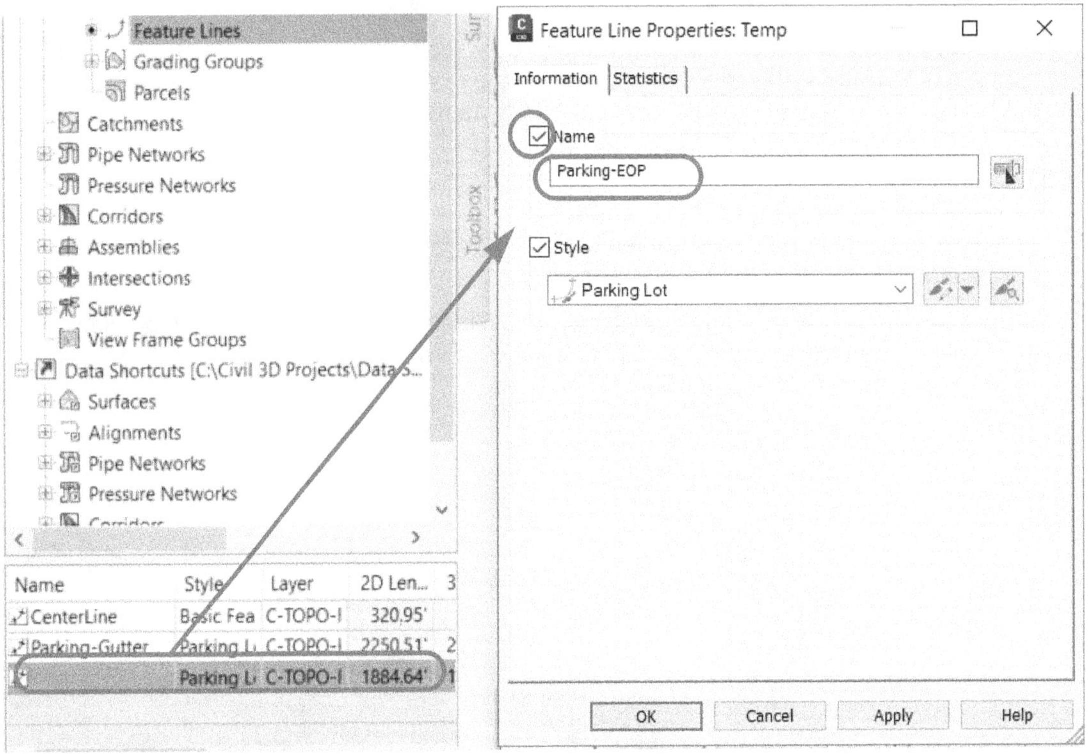

Figure 5–18

10. It is recommended that you rename the newly created feature line with a meaningful name so you can easily identify it later. In the *Feature Line Properties* dialog box, click on the *Name* check mark (which enables the *Name* box) and name the newly created feature line **Parking-EOP**, as shown in Figure 5–18.

    You are going to start the **Stepped Offset** command again in the next step, but first you have to exit and then restart the command to set a different offset value for the next feature line.

11. In the *Prospector* tab, expand **Sites>Temp**, and select the feature lines. In the preview window, select **Parking-Gutter**, then right-click and select **Select**, as shown in Figure 5–19.

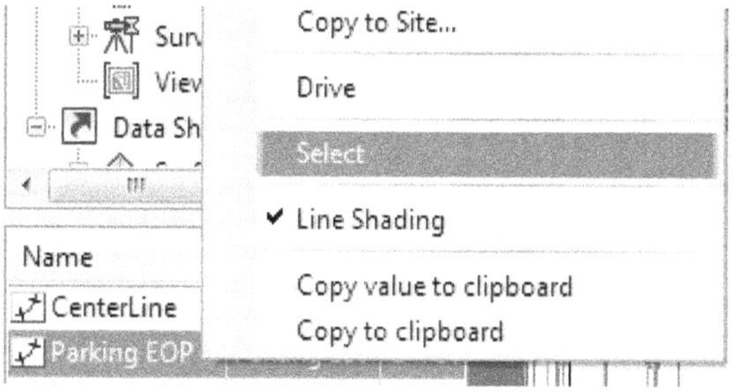

Figure 5-19

12. In the *Feature Line* contextual tab>*Edit Geometry* panel, click ⬚ (Stepped Offset).

   * For the *Offset Distance*, type **0.1**.
   * In the drawing, pick a point outside the Parking-Gutter feature line for the side to which to offset.
   * Type **D** for *Difference* and press <Enter>.
   * For the difference in elevation, type **0.5** to set the new feature line 6" above the other one. (This creates the curb face for the parking lot.)
   * Press <Esc> to end the command.
   * Press <Esc> again to release the selection.

13. In the *Prospector* tab, expand **Sites>Temp** and select **Feature Lines**. In the preview window, select the last feature line without a name, double-click in the *Name* field (as shown in Figure 5-20), and type **Top of Curb** and press <Enter>.

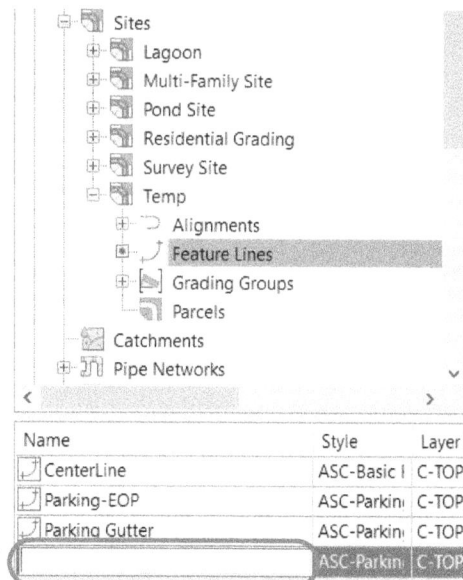

Figure 5-20

14. Select the **Top of Curb** feature line.

15. In the *Feature Line* contextual tab>*Edit Geometry* panel, click ⬚ (Stepped Offset).

- For the *Offset Distance*, type **0.5**.
- In the drawing, pick a point outside the Parking-Gutter feature line for the side to which to offset.
- Note that it already asking to specify the elevation difference since that was option you chose previously.
- For the difference in elevation, type **0** to set the new feature line at the same elevation as the other one. (This creates the top back of curb for the parking lot.)
- Press <Esc> to end the command.

*Note: You could also select **G** for Grade and **0** for the grade, the result will be the same.*

16. Name the feature line **Back of Curb**, using either method as done previously.

17. If you zoom in, the four lines representing the curb are displayed, as shown in Figure 5−21.

Figure 5−21

18. Save the drawing.

Task 2: Move feature lines to a different site.

You now have all of the necessary feature lines in the Temp site. However, you need to move them to the Multi-Family site so they interact when grading the building pads (done in earlier practices).

1. Continue working in the drawing from the previous task.

2. Select the last feature line created from the stepped offset (**Back of Curb**), as shown in Figure 5–22.

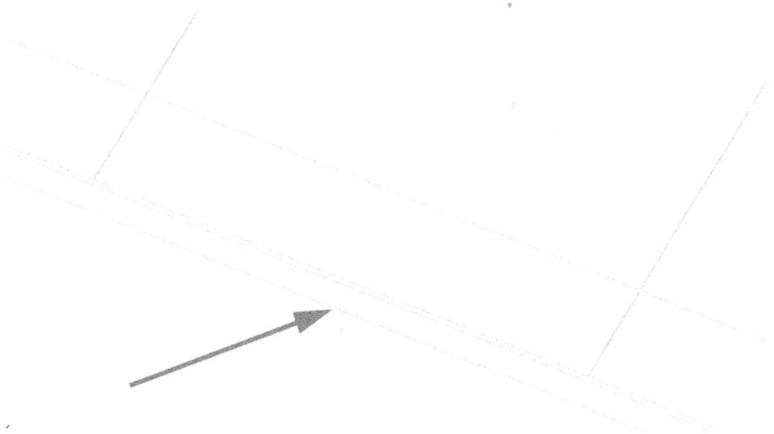

Figure 5–22

3. Right-click and select **Move to Site**, as shown in Figure 5–23.

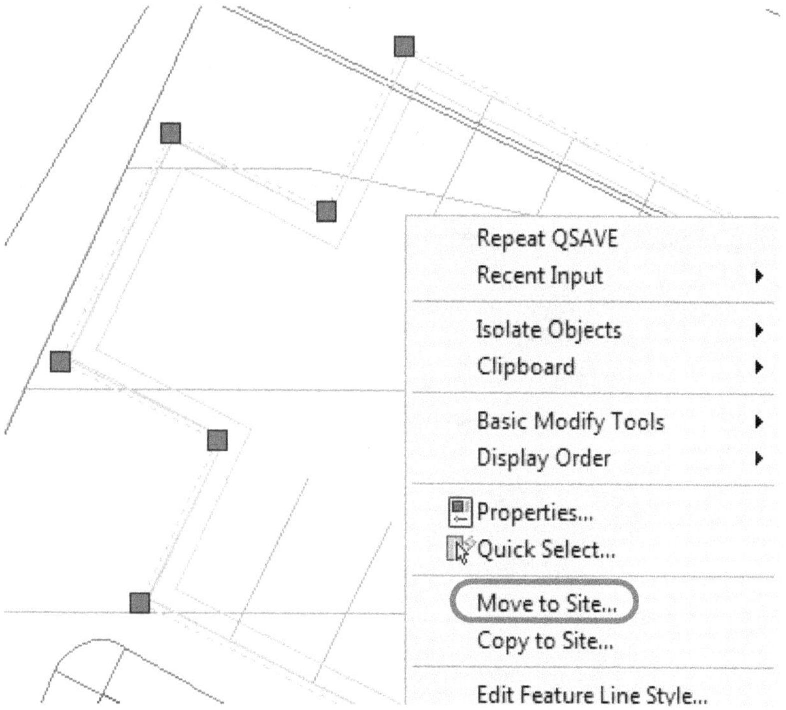

Figure 5–23

4. Set the *Destination site* to **Multi-Family Site**, as shown in Figure 5–24. Click **OK**.

Figure 5–24

5. Note that the name of the feature line is now **Back of curb (1)**. Rename the feature line to **Back of Curb.**

6. In the drawing, select the **Back of Curb** feature line.

7. In the *Edit Geometry* panel that displays, click ⚒ (Delete PI). If the *Edit Geometry* panel is not displayed, in the *Feature Line contextual tab>Modify* panel, click 🗂 (Edit Geometry).

8. In the drawing, remove the ten vertices circled in Figure 5–25.

Figure 5–25

9. Delete the vertex marked **A** in Figure 5–26. (The vertex marked **B** will be moved in the next step.)

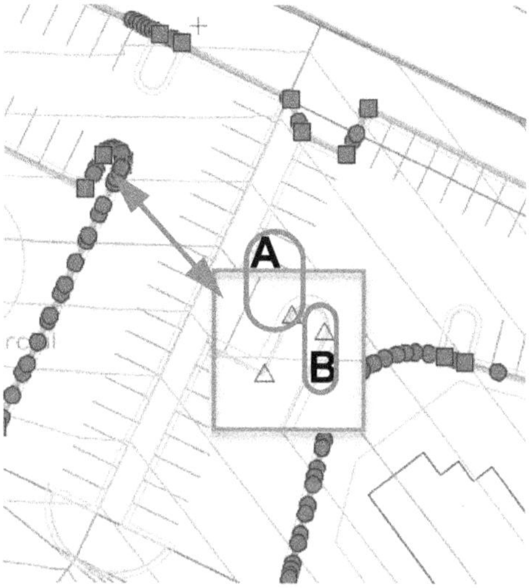

Figure 5–26

10. Press <Esc> to clear the selection and finish the command.

11. Move the vertex marked **A** in Figure 5–27. You can use the Extension Osnap to make it perpendicular to be precise.

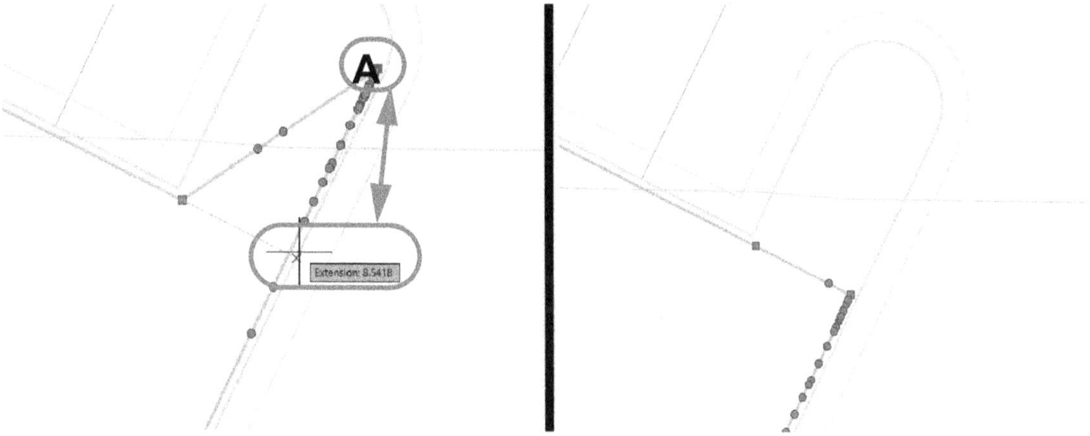

Figure 5–27

12. Press <Esc> to clear the selection.

13. The final result is shown in Figure 5–28.

Figure 5–28

14. Select the **Temp Parking Lot** surface and set the surface style to **_No Display**, as shown in Figure 5–29.

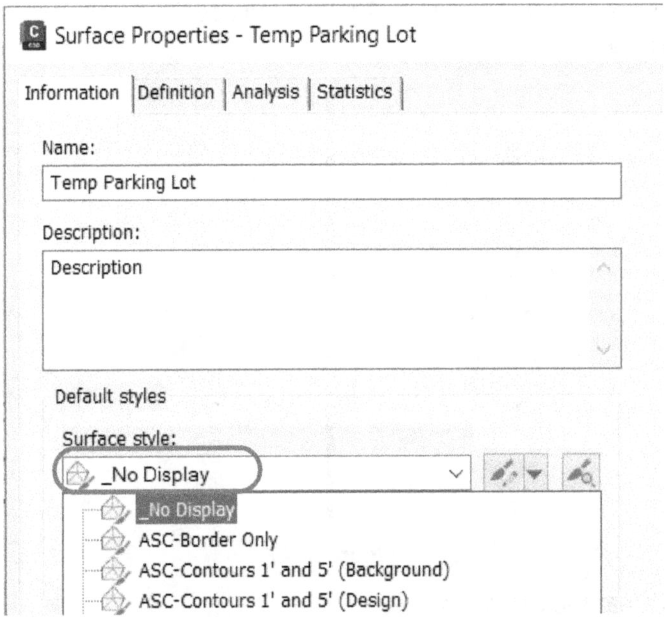

Figure 5–29

15. Save the drawing.

Task 3: Grade to a surface with varying slopes along one feature line.

This task is quite intensive for computer processing. It is recommended that you save often, as well as audit your drawing on a regular basis. You will grade only the beginning of the parking lot, with the rest being optional, depending on your time and your computer's performance.

If you are unable to complete this task, you can skip to the next task, where the grading has been completed for you.

1. Continue working in the drawing from the last practice or open **PKLOT-C.dwg** from the C:\Civil 3D Grading\Working\Parking Lot folder.

2. In the Home tab>Create Design panel, expand the Grading drop-down list and click

   (Grading Creation Tools).

3. In the Grading Creation Tools toolbar, click (Set the Grading Group) on the far left to open the Select Grading Group dialog box.

4. In the Select Grading Group dialog box, select the **Multi-Family Site** and click (Create Grading Group), as shown in Figure 5–30.

Figure 5–30

5. In the *Create Grading Group* dialog box, complete the following, as shown in Figure 5–31:

   - In the *Name* field, type **Parking Lot**.
   - Do not select the **Automatic surface creation** option.
   - Click **OK** twice to return to the *Grading Creation Tools* toolbar.

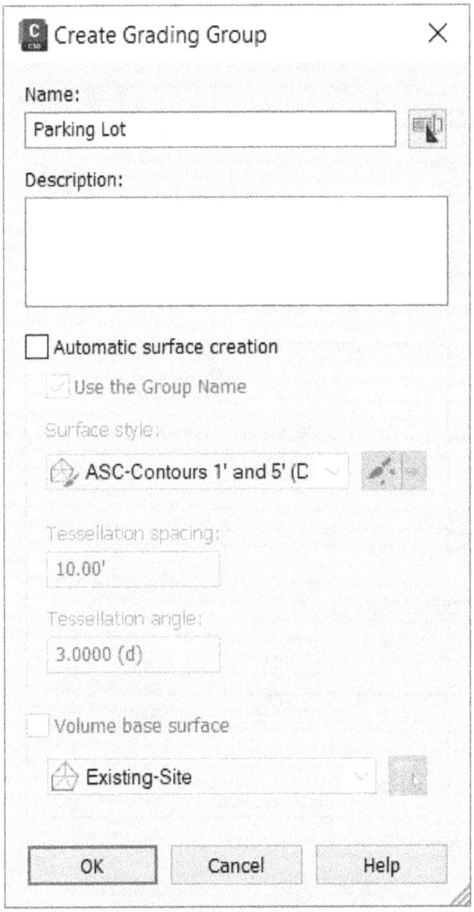

Figure 5–31

6. In the *Grading Creation Tools* toolbar, click (Set Surface).

7. In the *Select surface* dialog box, select **Residential Grading**. Click **OK**.

8. In the *Grading Creation Tools* toolbar, verify that the grading criteria set is set to **Basic Set**. Then set the grading criteria to **Grade to Surface**, as shown in Figure 5–32.

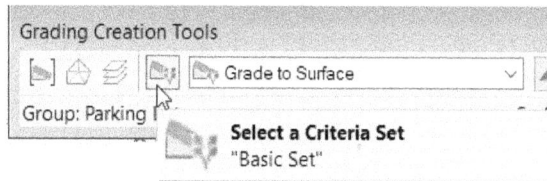

Figure 5–32

9. In the *Grading Creation Tools* toolbar, click (Create Grading). Select the **Back of Curb** feature line to use as the baseline, as shown in Figure 5–33.

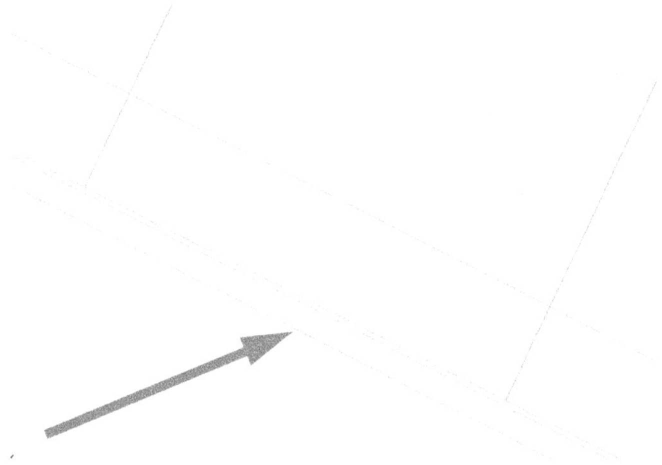

Figure 5–33

10. In the *Grading - Weed Feature Line* dialog box, select **Weed the feature line**, as shown in Figure 5–34.

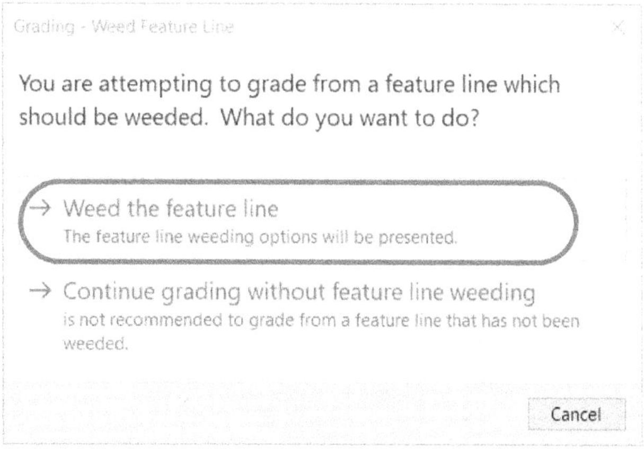

Figure 5–34

---

11. In the *Weed Vertices* dialog box, set the *3D distance* to **1.00'**, as shown in Figure 5–35. Note that 95 vertices will be removed (number of vertices may vary).

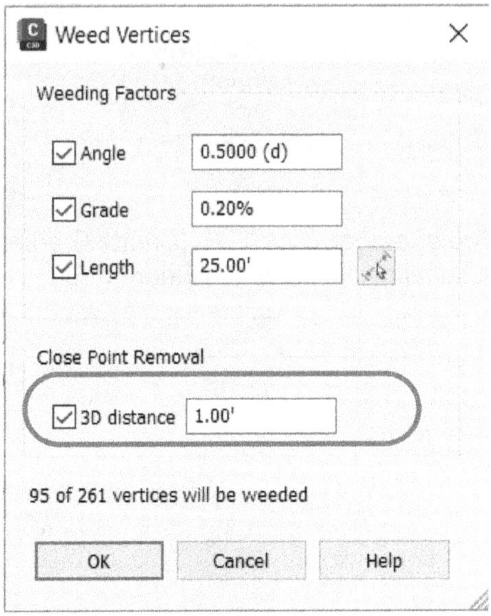

Figure 5–35

12. Click **OK** to continue.

13. When prompted for a grading side, pick a point on the outside of the parking lot.

14. When prompted to apply it to the entire length, type **N** (for No) and press <Enter>.

15. Using the **Endpoint** Osnap, select the endpoint at the beginning of the feature line. Press <Enter> to accept <0+00.00> as the beginning value.

16. Using the **Midpoint** Osnap, select the midpoint of the first curve, as shown in Figure 5–36. Press <Enter> to accept <0+70.54'> as the ending value.

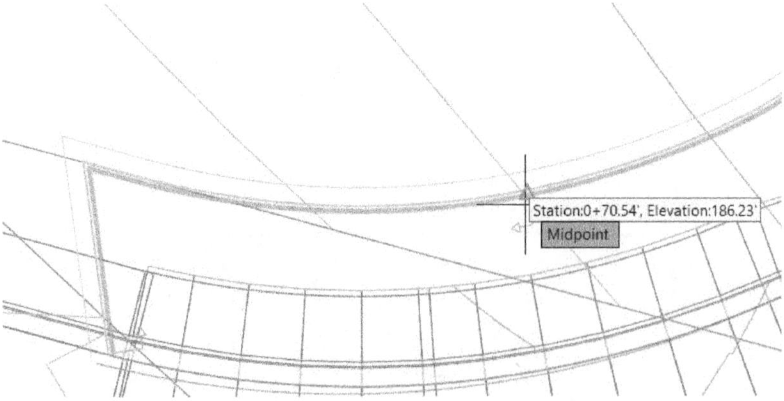

Figure 5–36

17. Press <Enter> to accept **Slope** as the cut format. Type **1** for a 1:1 slope.

18. Press <Enter> to accept **Slope** as the fill format. Type **1** for a 1:1 slope.

Note: The command continues until you press <Esc>. Rather than end the command, select the same feature line again to continue grading until prompted to press <Esc>.

19. Select the **Back of Curb** feature line again.

20. Select a point on the outside of the parking lot to which to grade.

21. In the Command Line, type **135** for the start point. Press <Enter> to accept the beginning value. This is near the beginning of the building 2 footprint.

22. Using the **Endpoint** Osnap, select the south corner of the parking lot north of building 2 for the endpoint, as shown in Figure 5–37. Press <Enter> to accept <4+01.70'> as the end value.

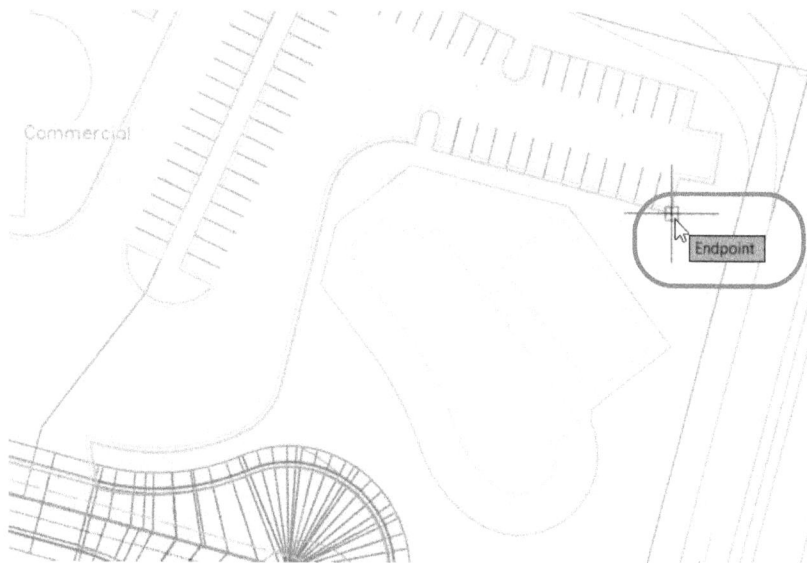

Figure 5–37

23. Press <Enter> to accept **Slope** as the cut format. Type **0.5** for a 0.5:1 slope.

24. Press <Enter> to accept **Slope** as the fill format. Type **0.5** for a 0.5:1 slope.

Optional steps:

The following steps are optional. In the next task, you can open a drawing where these optional steps have been completed.

25. Select the **Back of Curb** feature line again.

26. Select a point on the outside of the parking lot to which to grade.

27. For the beginning point, select the endpoint at the top right corner of the parking lot north of the last endpoint selected, as shown in Figure 5–38.

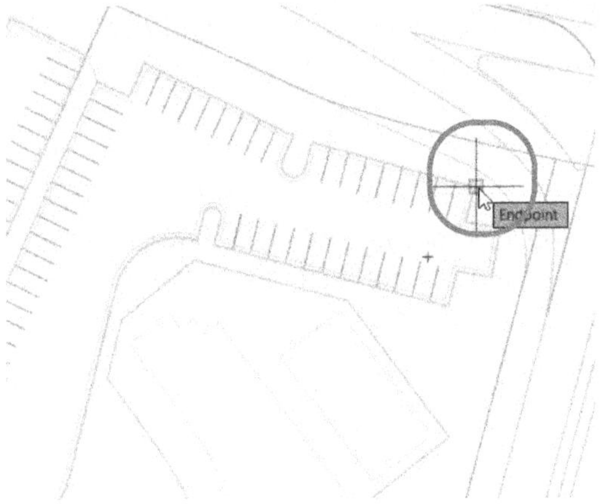

Figure 5–38

28. Press <Enter> to accept <4+96.39'> as the station.

29. For the ending point, select the endpoint at the top left corner on the far north west side of the parking lot, as shown in Figure 5–39.

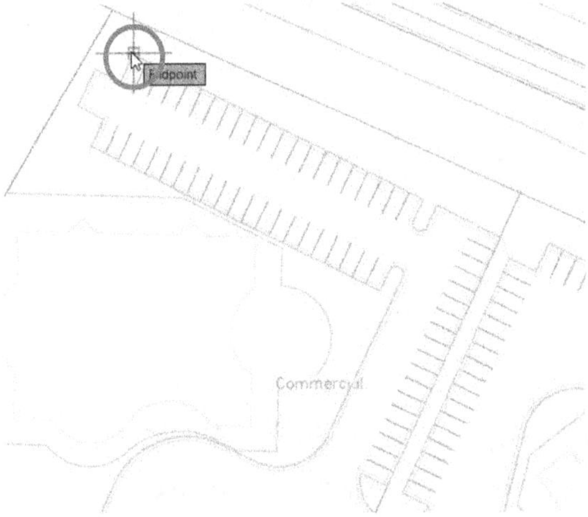

Figure 5–39

30. Press <Enter> to accept <9+66.94'> as the station.

31. Press <Enter> to accept **Slope** as the cut format. Type **2** for a 2:1 slope.

32. Press <Enter> to accept **Slope** as the fill format. Type **1.5** for a 1.5:1 slope.

33. Select the curb feature line again and select a point on the outside of the parking lot to which to grade.

34. Using the **Endpoint** Osnap, select the south corner of the parking lot north of building 1 as the start point, as shown in Figure 5–40. Press <Enter> to accept <10+61.87'> as the start point.

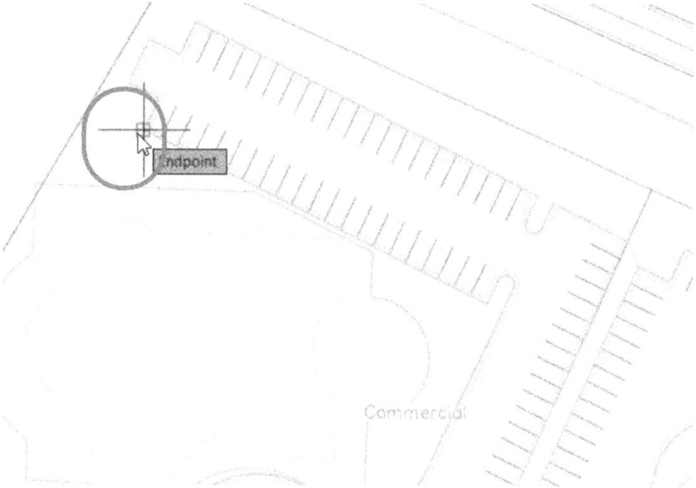

Figure 5–40

35. In the Command Line, type **1500** for the end point. Press <Enter> to accept it.

36. Press <Enter> to accept **Slope** as the cut format. Type **0.5** for a 0.5:1 slope.

37. Press <Enter> to accept **Slope** as the fill format. Type **0.5** for a 0.5:1 slope.

38. Select the curb feature line again and pick a point on the outside to which to grade.

39. Using Osnaps, select the endpoint of the last curve near the parking lot entrance, as shown in Figure 5–41.

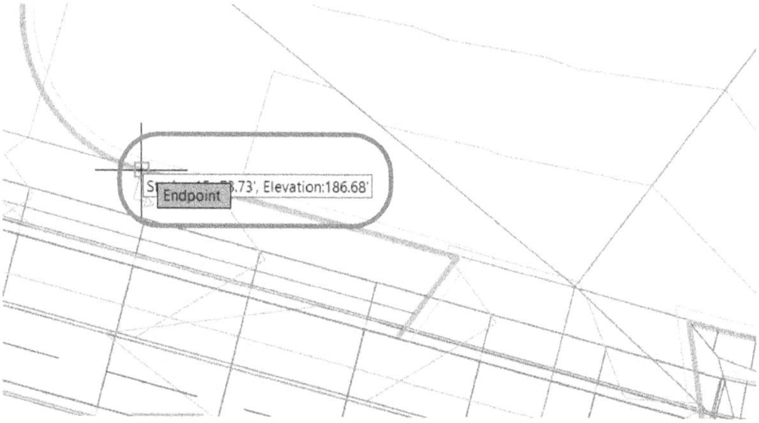

Figure 5–41

40. Press <Enter> to accept <15+73.77'> as the station.

---

41. Using Osnaps, select the endpoint of the feature line at the parking lot entrance, as shown in Figure 5–42.

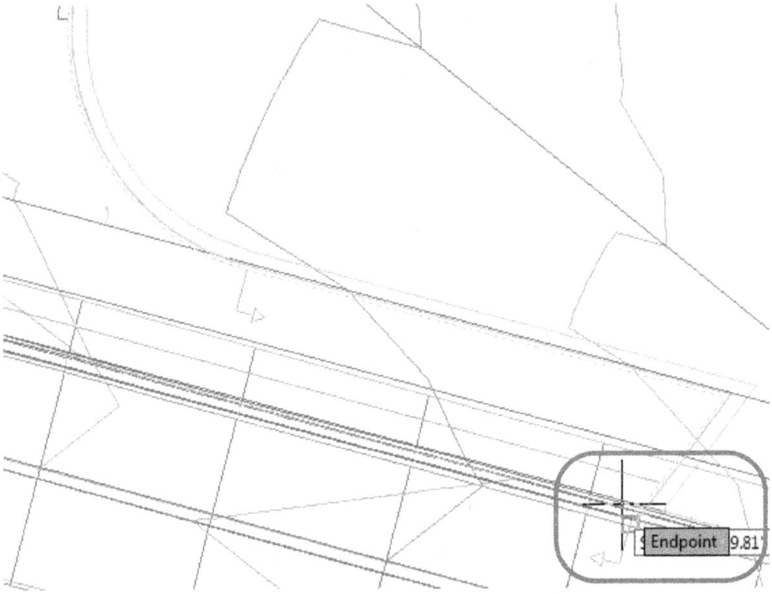

Figure 5–42

42. Press <Enter> to accept the value given.

43. Press <Enter> to accept **Slope** as the cut format. Type **2** for a 2:1 slope.

44. Press <Enter> to accept **Slope** as the fill format. Type **2** for a 2:1 slope.

45. Press <Esc> to end the command.

46. Save the drawing.

Task 4: Create transitions between predefined grading objects along the same feature line.

1. Continue working in the drawing from the previous task, or open **PKLOT-D.dwg** from the C:\Civil 3D Grading\Working\Parking Lot folder.

2. In the *Home* tab>*Create Design* panel, expand the *Grading* drop-down list and click

    (Grading Creation Tools).

3. In the *Grading Creation Tools* toolbar, set the grading group to **Parking Lot within the Multi-Family site,** and the surface to **Residential Grading**, if necessary.

4. Expand the *Create Grading* drop-down list and click (Create Transition).

5. Select the curb feature line that contains the previously created grading objects.

6. In the Command Line, you are prompted to pick a point between the gradings. Select between two previously created grading objects, as shown in Figure 5–43.

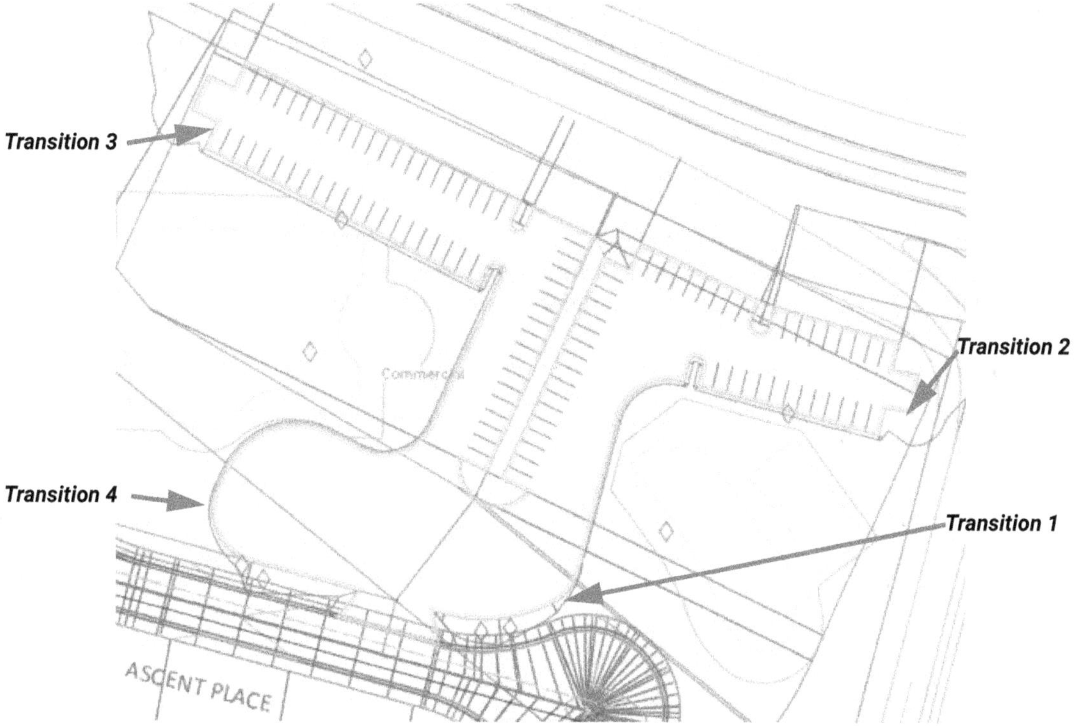

Figure 5–43

7. Repeat Steps 5 and 6 as needed to complete all four transitions.
8. Press <Esc> to end the command.
9. Save the drawing.

End of practice

5.3 Create a Grading Surface

When working with complex grading objects, it is better to completely design the grading group before creating its surface. In most design workflows, as you first create the grading group, you clear the option to create a surface automatically and then build a surface from the grading group at a later time.

When you are ready to build the surface, you can select any part of the grading group. In the

Grading contextual tab, click  (Grading Group Properties). In the *Grading Group Properties* dialog box, select the **Automatic Surface Creation** option to create a surface and click **OK**, as shown in Figure 5–44. You can also select the **Volume Base Surface** option if needed.

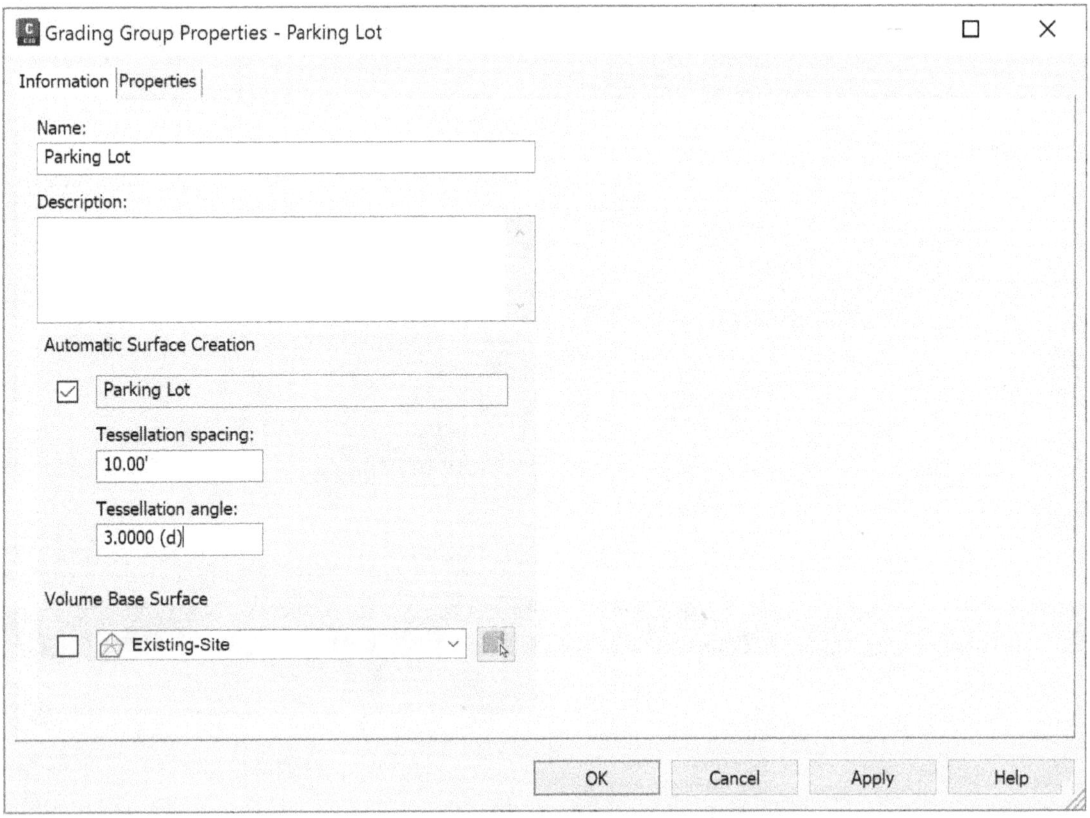

Figure 5–44

The *Create Surface* dialog box opens and you enter a surface name (the grading group name is the default surface name), type a description, set a style, and set a render material. Clicking **OK** creates the surface and displays the contours.

5.4 Add Feature Lines to a Grading Surface

After creating a grading group, any feature lines in the same area affects the surface that was created by the grading group. The key to making this work is to ensure that the grading group and feature lines are in the same site. Figure 5–45 shows what happens when feature lines are drawn on top of a grading object in the same site.

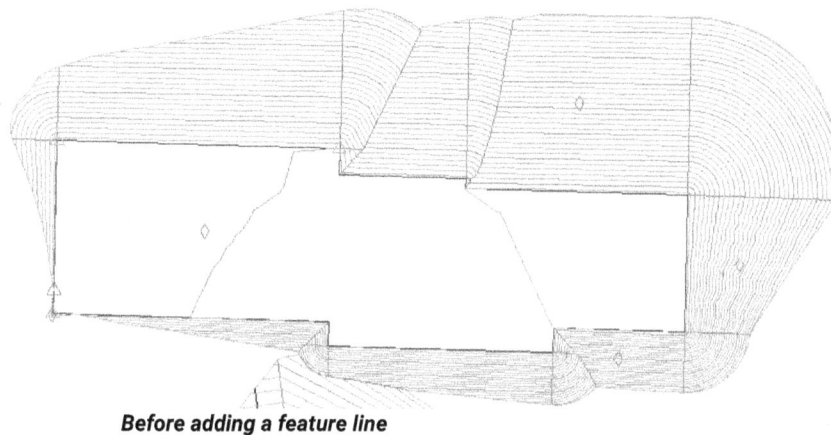

Before adding a feature line

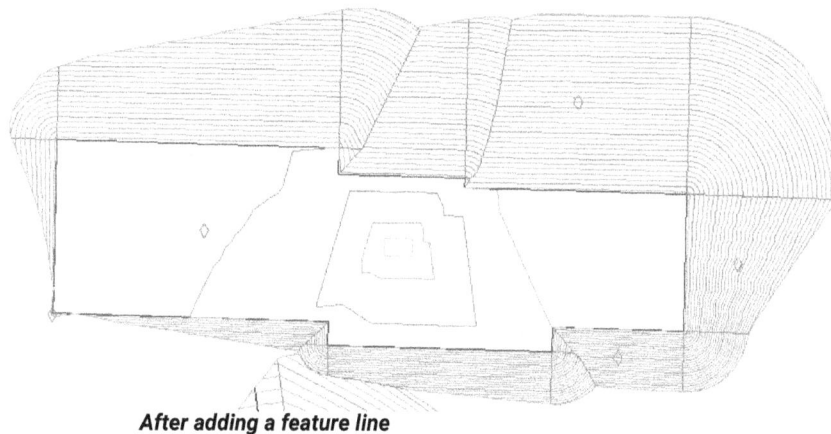

After adding a feature line

Figure 5–45

Practice 5c
Create a Surface with Proper Drainage

Practice Objective

- Create a grading group surface and add feature lines for proper drainage.

In this practice, you will prepare to create a grading surface, create the grading surface, and add feature lines to a grading surface.

Task 1: Prepare to create a grading surface.

Before creating a finished ground surface, you need to clean up and finish the grading group. So far you have created multiple feature lines to represent the curb and gutter of the parking area.But during the offset procedure, you never "capped" off the feature lines. You have also created grading objects all the way around the parking lot. Next, you need to draw a feature line to close the parking lot off, then infill the center of the parking lot to add the pavement's grading.

For convenience, the Parking-EOP feature line has been trimmed back to the Ascent Place EOP. Therefore, you need to open the next drawing. More elevation points were weeded as well.

1. Open **PKLOT-E.dwg** from the *C:\Civil 3D Grading\Working\Parking Lot* folder. Do not continue working in the drawing from the previous practice.

2. In the *View* tab>*Named Views* panel, select **Parking-Entrance** to zoom to the entrance of the parking lot.

3. In the *Home* tab>*Create Design* panel, click ⁂ (Create Feature Line).

4. In the *Create Feature Lines* dialog box, complete the following:

    - For the *Site*, select **Multi-Family Site**.

    - For the feature line *Name,* type **Parking-Endcap**.

    - For the *Style,* select **ASC-Parking Lot**.

5. Click **OK**.

6. Use the endpoint Osnap to snap to the following eight points at the end of the feature lines, as shown in Figure 5–46. Accept the elevations and grades that are calculated.

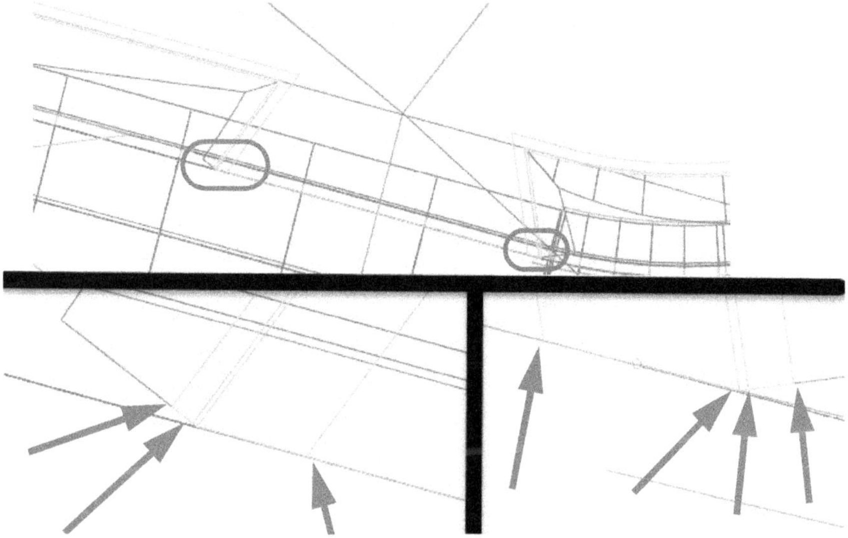

Figure 5–46

7. In the *View* tab>*Named Views* panel, select **Parking-Lot**.

8. In the *Home* tab>*Create Design* panel, expand the *Grading* drop-down list and click

     (Create Infill).

9. In the *Select Grading Group* dialog box, ensure that the **Parking Lot** grading group (in the Multi-Family Site) is set, as shown in Figure 5–47.

Figure 5–47

10. Click **OK** to close the *Select Grading Group* dialog box.

11. In the *Grading Style* dialog box, accept the default and click **OK**.

12. Pick a point in the center of the parking lot area, as shown in Figure 5–48.

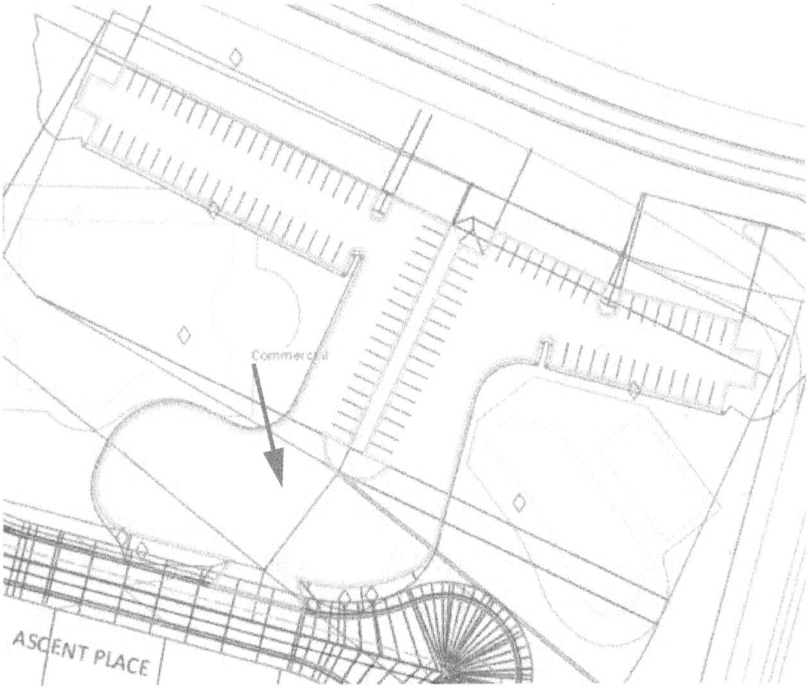

Figure 5–48

13. Press <Esc> to end the command.

14. Save the drawing.

Task 2: Create the grading surface.

1. Continue working in the drawing from the previous task.

2. Select the diamond shape representing the infill center mark of the parking lot (or any part of the grading group). In the *Grading* contextual tab>*Modify* panel, click [icon] (Grading Group Properties).

3. In the *Grading Group Properties* dialog box, in the *Information* tab, select the **Automatic Surface Creation** option, as shown in Figure 5–49.

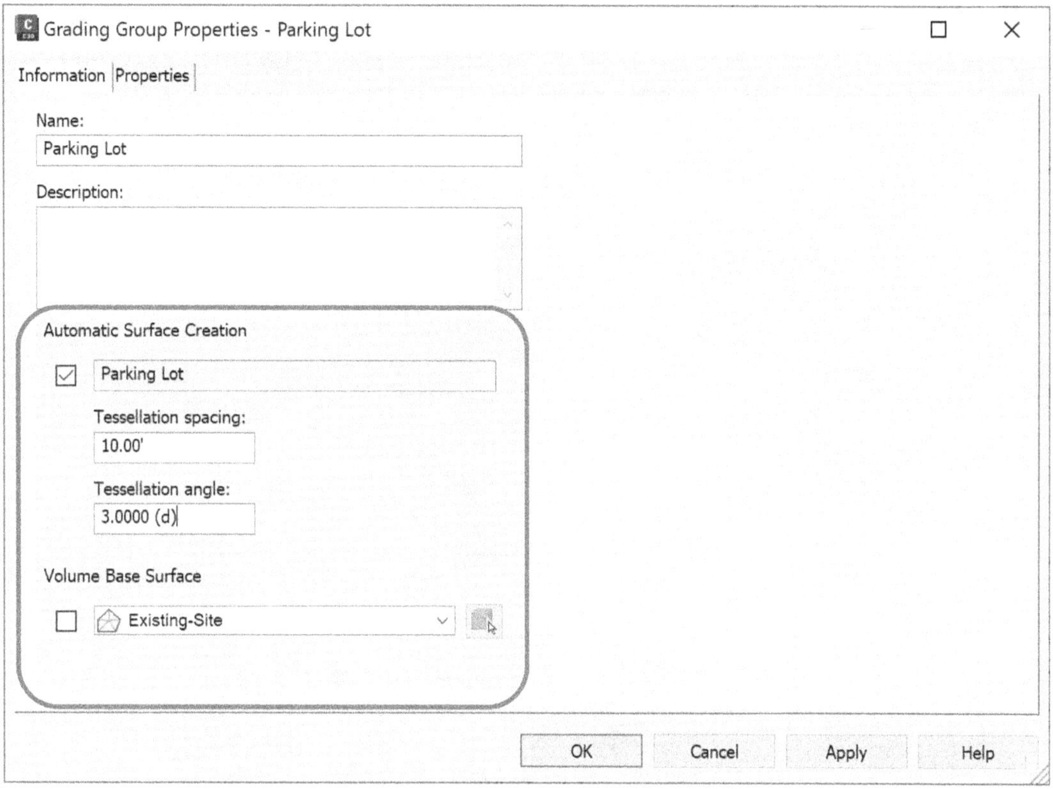

Figure 5–49

4. When the *Create Surface* dialog box opens, click **OK** to accept the defaults.

5. Select the **Volume Base Surface** option and select **Existing-Site** for the base surface.

6. Click **OK** and save the drawing.

Task 3: Add feature lines to a grading surface.

1. Continue working in the drawing from the previous task.

2. In the *Prospector* tab, expand **Sites>Temp**. Select the **Feature Lines** collection to view them in the preview. Select all of the feature lines except **CenterLine**, right-click, and select **Move to Site**, as shown in Figure 5–50.

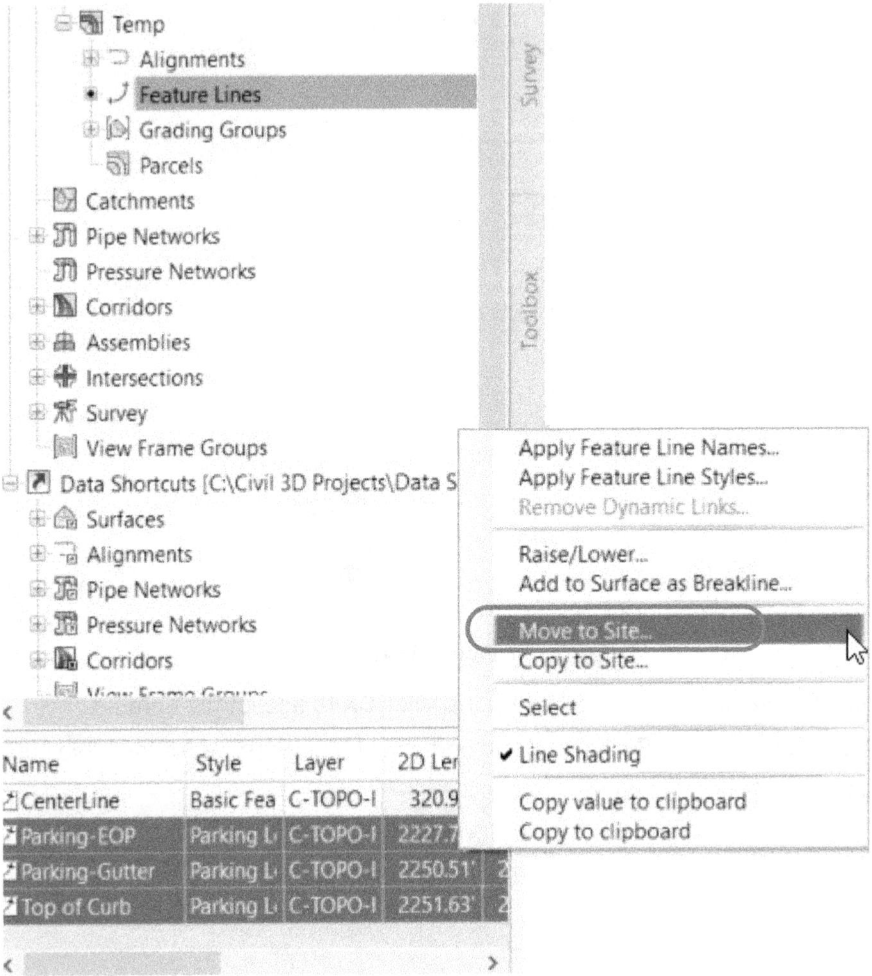

Figure 5–50

3. In the *Move to Site* dialog box, select **Multi-Family Site** as the *Destination site,* as shown in Figure 5-51, and click **OK**.

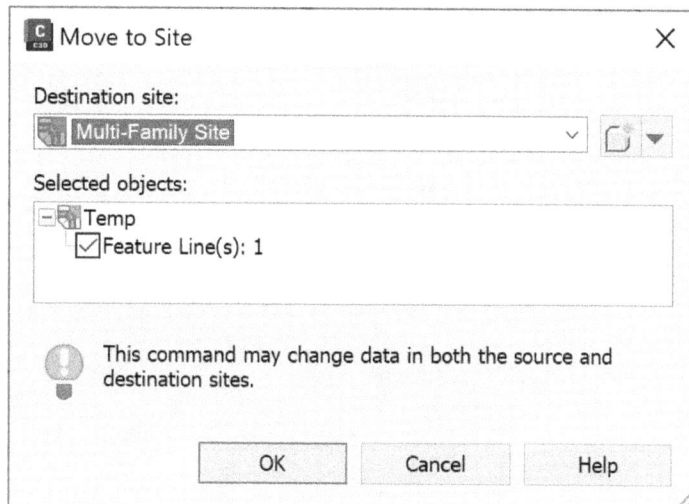

Figure 5-51

The original infill grading object automatically fills in the center island of the parking lot. You need to add additional infill grading objects to fill in the surface of the asphalt and the curbs.

4. In the *Home* tab>*Create Design* panel, expand the *Grading* drop-down list and click

    (Create Infill).

5. Pick a point in the center of the parking lot area, as shown in Figure 5-52.

Figure 5-52

6. Repeat Steps 4 and 5 to add infill between each of the curb lines. When you are done, you should see that the grading is slightly affected along the edge of the parking lot where the feature lines have caused more definition, as shown in Figure 5–53.

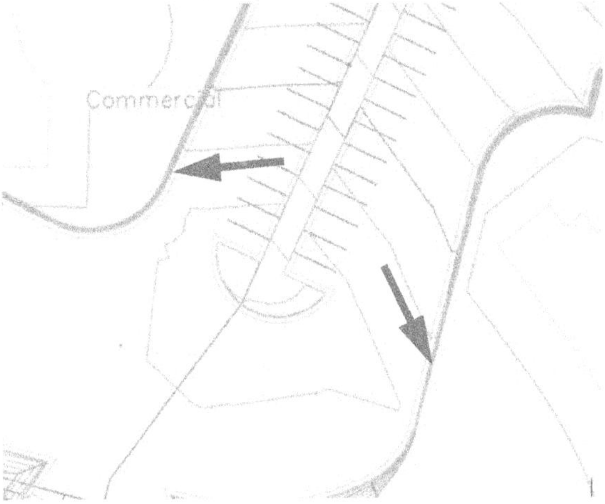

Figure 5–53

7. You can now delete the Temp site. In the *Prospector* tab, expand **Sites**. Right-click on **Temp** and select **Delete**, as shown in Figure 5–54. Confirm **Yes** in the alert box.

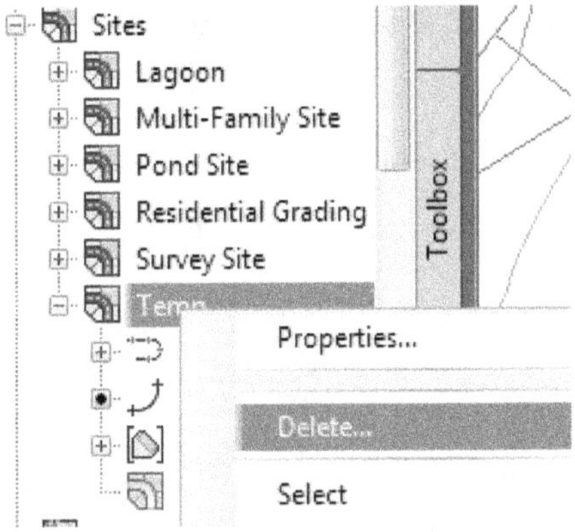

Figure 5–54

Note: If you wish to keep the Temp site for later use, you can freeze the following layers instead:

- C-TOPO-GRAD
- C-TOPO-GRAD-CUTS
- C-TOPO-GRAD-FILL
- C-TOPO-GRAD-TEXT

8. Select the **Parking Lot** surface (select one of its contour lines).

9. In the right-click menu, click **Add to Model Viewer**. Using the Viewcube, set the view direction to **SW Isometric**. Note the hole in the surface, as shown in Figure 5–55.

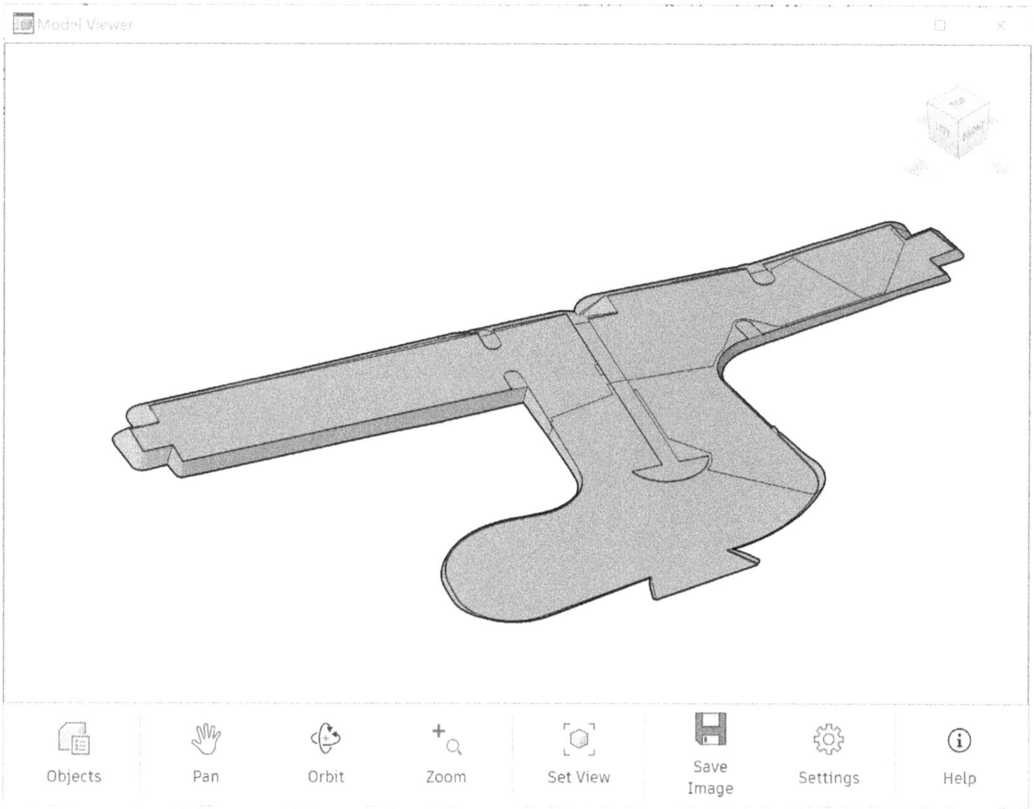

Figure 5–55

10. Close the *Model Viewer*.

11. Press <Esc> release the selection.

12. Save and close the drawing.

End of practice

Chapter Review Questions

1. Which of the following is NOT an option for setting the elevation a feature line vertex as you draw it?

   a. Slope

   b. Transition

   c. Surface

   d. Grading Object

2. Which of the following is NOT an option for creating curves within feature lines as you draw them?

   a. Secondpnt

   b. Diameter

   c. Radius

   d. Arc end point

3. The **Stepped Offset** command is the same as the AutoCAD **Offset** command. These commands can be used interchangeably.

   a. True

   b. False

4. Which of the following is not an option for setting elevations when using the **Stepped Offset** command?

   a. Grade

   b. Slope

   c. Difference

   d. Surface

5. Which icon in the *Grading Creation Tools* toolbar enables you to create transitions between two grading objects of varying slopes?

a.

b.

c.

d.

Command Summary

Button	Command	Location
	Create Feature Line	• **Ribbon**: *Home* tab>*Create Design* panel, expand *Feature Line* drop-down list • **Command Prompt:** DrawFeatureLine
	Create Infill	• **Ribbon**: *Home* tab>*Create Design* panel, expand *Grading* drop-down list • **Toolbar**: *Grading Creation Tools* (*contextual*), expand *Create Grading* drop-down list
	Delete PI	• **Ribbon**: *Grading* contextual tab>*Edit Geometry* panel • **Command Prompt:** DeleteFeaturePI
	Grading Group Properties	• **Ribbon**: *Grading* contextual tab>*Modify* panel
	Stepped Offset	• **Ribbon**: *Feature Line* contextual tab>*Edit Geometry* panel • **Command Prompt:** GradingElevEditor

Parking Lot Grading Options

Parking lots can also be designed using corridors. By placing linework for the back of the curb on an XREF, you create feature lines and a corridor for the curb, then build a surface from the corridor.

Corridors are 3D representations of road designs. To design the curb, first create a typical cross-section (an assembly). Apply the assembly to the back of curb feature line created earlier and then create the parking surfaces.

To complete the parking lot layout, copy the designs from an XREF base drawing into your working drawing and attach curb Grading Objects to them. Review the Grading Optimization results with the convergence plots and finalize the preliminary parking layout.

Learning Objectives

- Create feature lines from an XREF file.
- Create a corridor representing the parking lot.
- Clear bowties from the corridor.
- Edit the feature line.
- Create a surface from the corridor.
- Create a boundary for the corridor surface.
- Check the direction of open and closed polylines.
- Define Curb Grading Objects.
- Change parameters of Grading Objects in the Tool Palette.
- Optimize the Parking Lot grading.
- Study the Convergence Plots.
- Create an interim design surface containing the preliminary parking areas.

6.1 Corridors

A corridor is a 3D model of a proposed design based on alignments and profiles (or feature lines) and assemblies. Corridors can be used to create terrain models (such as a finished ground terrain model) and generate section data. Corridors display as complex drawing objects consisting of individual cross-sections, feature lines that connect marker points (locations where point codes are assigned), and other related data, as shown in Figure 6–1.

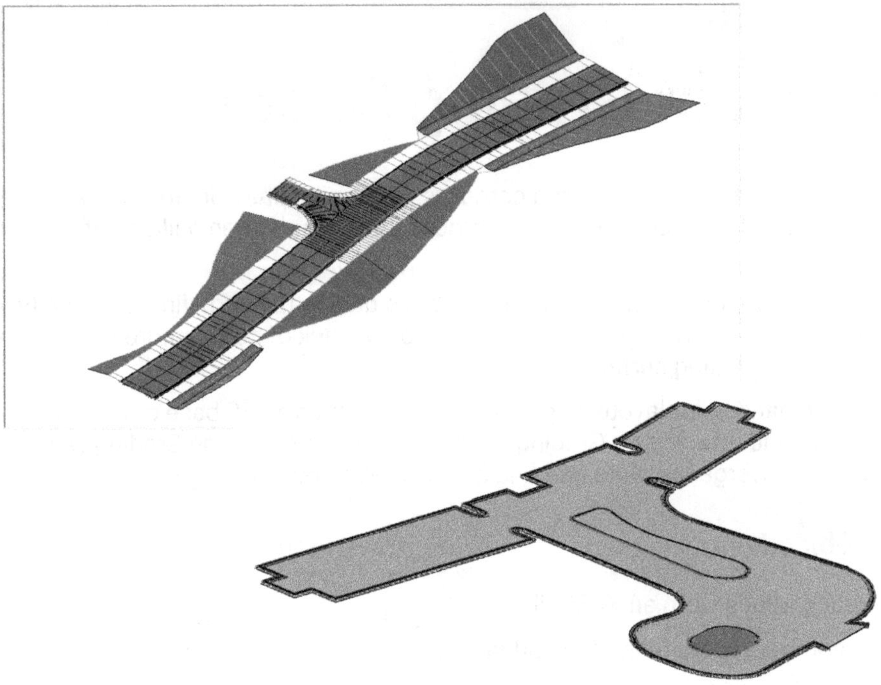

Figure 6–1

To create a corridor, click ▨ (Corridor) in the *Home* tab>*Create Design* panel. A dialog box opens in which you can enter a description, corridor style, layer, alignment or feature line, profile, assembly, and target surface, as shown in Figure 6–2. It also has an option that enables you to set the baseline and region parameters. By selecting this, when you click **OK**, a second dialog box opens, as shown on the lower right of Figure 6–2.

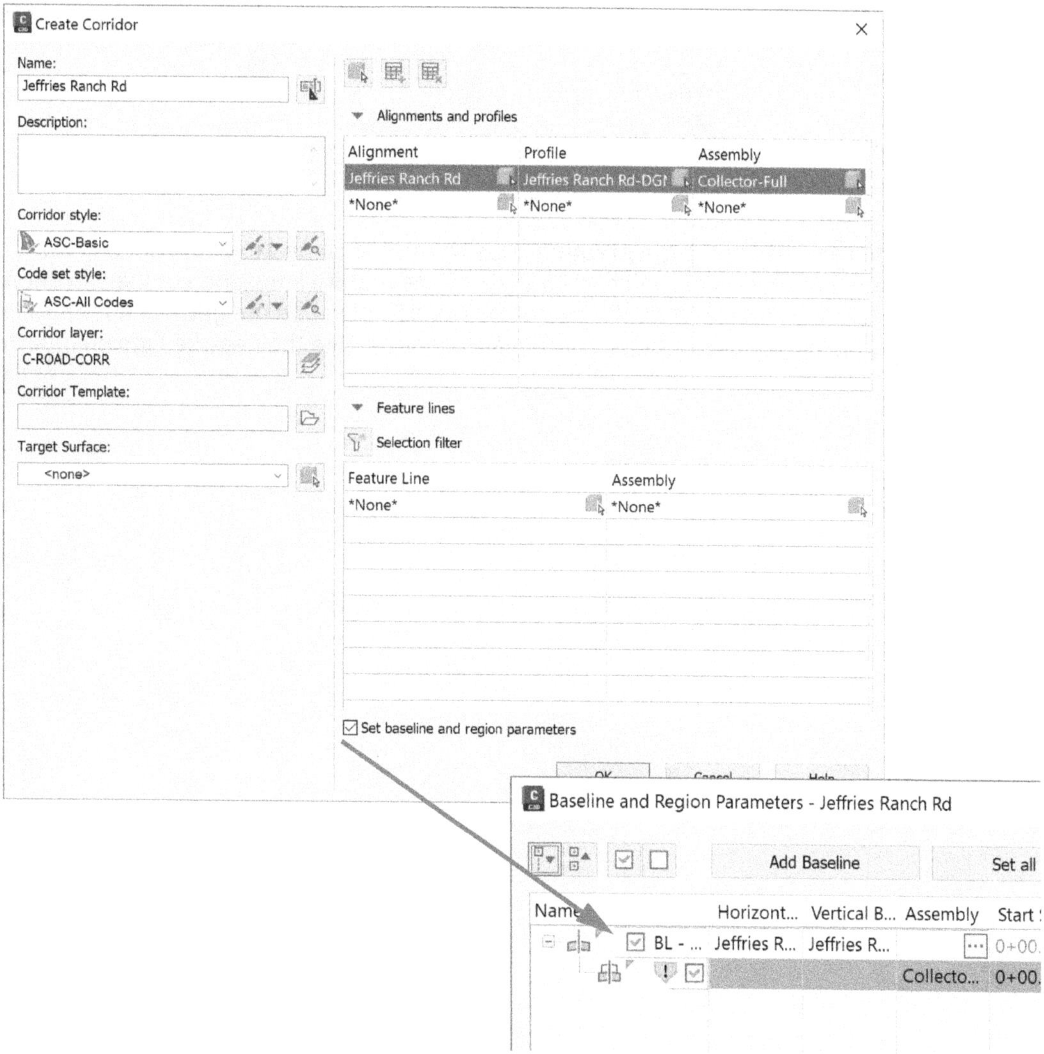

Figure 6–2

Note: Figure 6–2 is from the Civil 3D 2026 version. In the releases before Civil 3D 2025, a different dialog box was used for creating corridors.

6.2 Feature Line Contextual Tab

The *Feature Line* contextual tab (shown in Figure 6–3) contains commands that enable you to edit and modify feature lines. These include tools to edit feature line elevations and feature line geometry, such as **Break**, **Trim**, **Join**, and **Fillet** (which creates a true 3D curve).

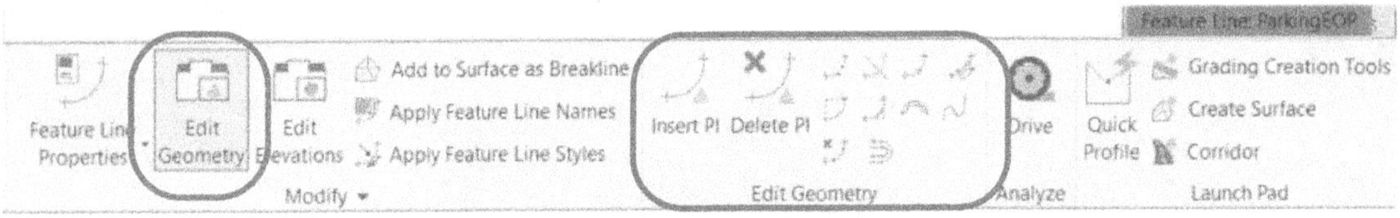

Figure 6–3

These commands can be used to draw feature lines from scratch and to establish an elevation at each vertex. You can also use existing objects to create feature lines and set the elevations of their vertices from surfaces and grading objects. You can also use the grips of a feature line for adding, removing, or altering vertices and elevation points. See the Feature Line chapter for more information.

Practice 6a
Create a Feature Line and Set Elevations by Grading

Practice Objective

- Create split points along parcel lines by adding elevations to adjacent parcel segments.

In this task, you will create feature lines representing the back of curbs of the alternate parking lot and set elevations by grading. While the previous parking lot layout was designed to slope downward toward Mission Ave, this layout explores another drainage option of the parking lot sloping towards Ascent Place.

1. Open **PKCOR-A.dwg** from the *C:\Civil 3D Grading\Working\Parking Corridor* folder.

2. In the *Home* tab>*Create Design* panel, expand the *Feature Line* drop-down list and click

   (Create Feature Line from Objects).

3. Type **X** and press <Enter> to select linework from the external reference file. Select the line that represents the Back of Curb of the parking lot perimeter, designated as **A** in Figure 6−4. Press <Enter> to continue.

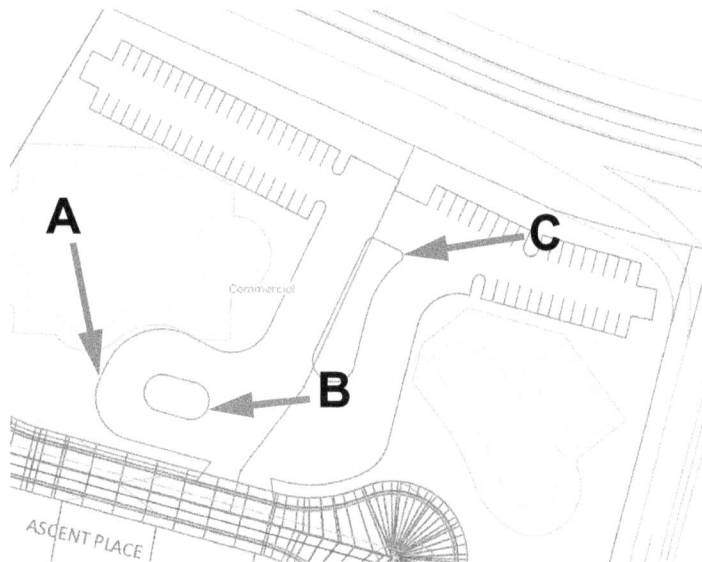

Figure 6−4

*Note: Be sure you select the **Name** option to enable you to type in a name for the feature line.*

4. In the *Create Feature Lines* dialog box, complete the following, as shown in Figure 6–5:

- Set the *Site* to **Multi-Family Site**.
- For the *Name*, type **Perimeter-BOC**.
- Set the *Style* to **ASC-Parking Lot**.
- Ensure that **Assign elevations** is selected.
- Click **OK**.

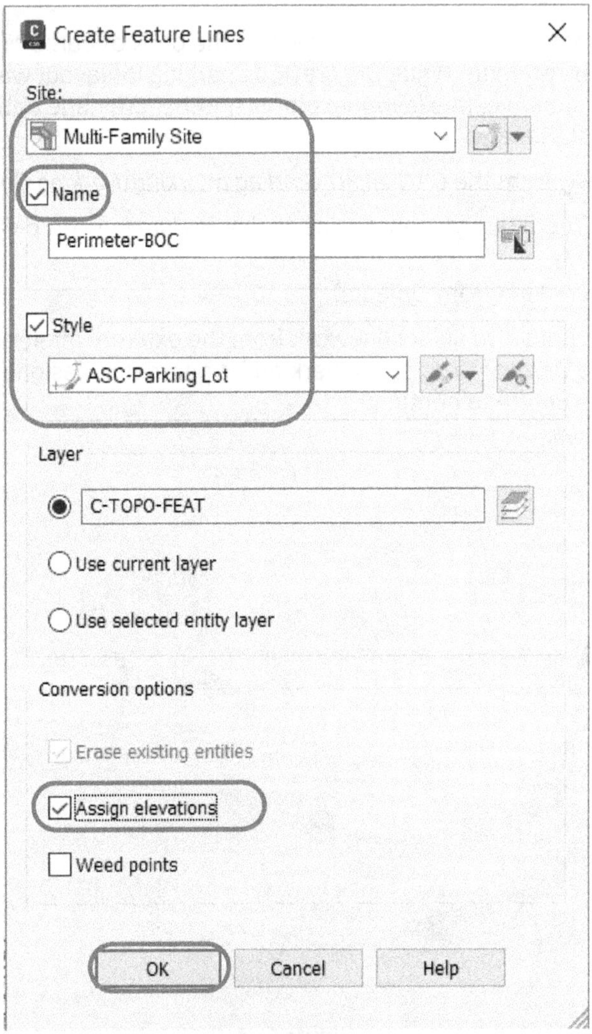

Figure 6–5

5. In the *Assign Elevations* dialog box, select **From surface**, then select **Temp Parking Lot** from the list, as shown in Figure 6-6.

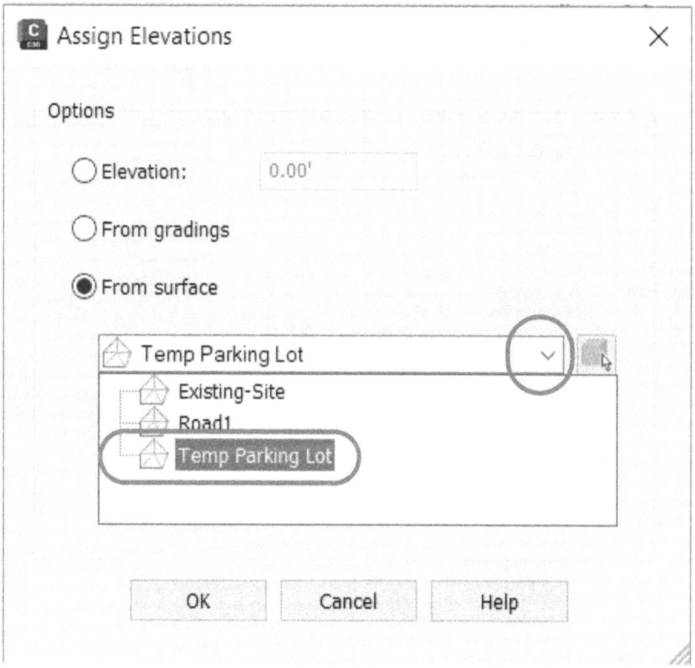

Figure 6-6

6. Select **Insert intermediate grade break points**, and then click **OK**.

7. Repeat Steps 2 to 6 to create:

    *   **B** (as shown in Figure 6-4): Name it **Island-1-BOC** and click **Insert intermediate grade break points**.

    *   **C** (as shown in Figure 6-4): Name it **Island-2-BOC** and click **Insert intermediate grade break points**.

8. Freeze the **C-TOPO-GRAD** layer, on which the grading objects reside.

9. Save the drawing.

End of practice

6.3 Create Corridor

Corridors can be created from alignments and profiles or from Feature lines, or a combination thereof. In the *Create Corridor* dialog box, you can select any number of alignments / profiles or feature lines to create the corridor,

You can expand or collapse the *Alignment and profiles* table or the *Feature lines* table by clicking on the arrow, as shown in Figure 6-7.

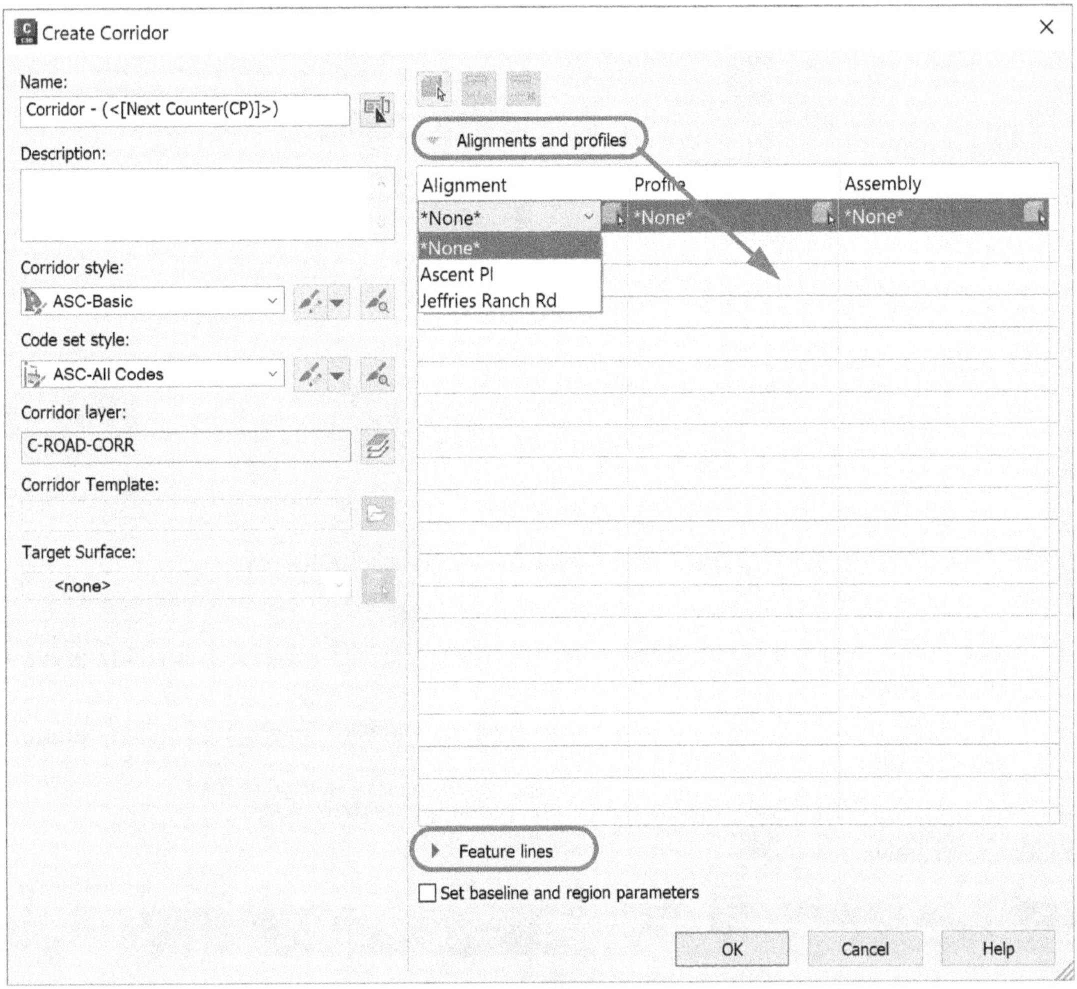

Figure 6-7

You can select any of the objects (alignments, profiles, assemblies or feature lines) from the drawing by picking [icon] (Pick from drawing), or by using the drop-down lists, as shown above in Figure 6−7. The corridor will be created with as many baselines as the alignments / feature lines that were included, each with one region for the corresponding assembly. You can add multiple alignments to create the corridor, and even combine alignments and feature lines to create a single corridor. The corridor will be created with as many baselines as alignments / feature lines were included, each with one region for the corresponding assembly.

Baselines and Regions

Baselines are considered the control line of a corridor. Depending on the nature of the corridors, a baseline can represent a centerline of the path, a median for divided highways, the top of slope for a breakwater, etc. For cul-de-sacs and intersections, baselines are part of curb lines as shown in Figure 6−8.

Figure 6−8

Baselines are either based on a combination of an alignment (the horizontal component) and an associated profile (the vertical component) or a feature line, which represents both the horizontal and vertical. A typical corridor usually contains more than one baseline.

A baseline is made up of one or more regions. Each region contains an assembly. If other assemblies are required for different corridor conditions, other regions need to be created in that baseline. Hence a corridor can have different shapes at different locations for different situations.

Corridors can be created with multiple baselines right from the start, or baselines or regions can be added after the initial corridor is created. Baselines and regions can be added from the *Corridor Properties* dialog box or from the contextual ribbon, as shown in Figure 6–9.

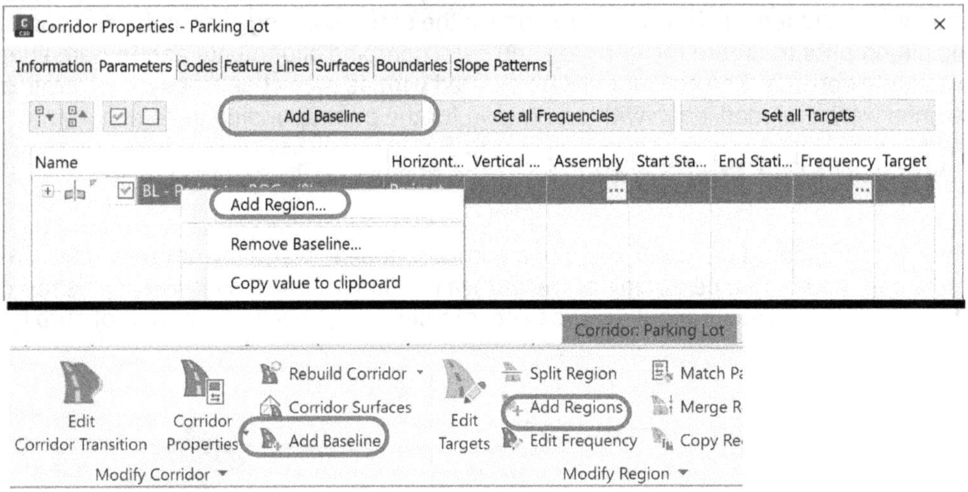

Figure 6–9

In the *Add Baselines* dialog box, you can add multiple alignments/profiles and / or feature lines, as shown in Figure 6–10.

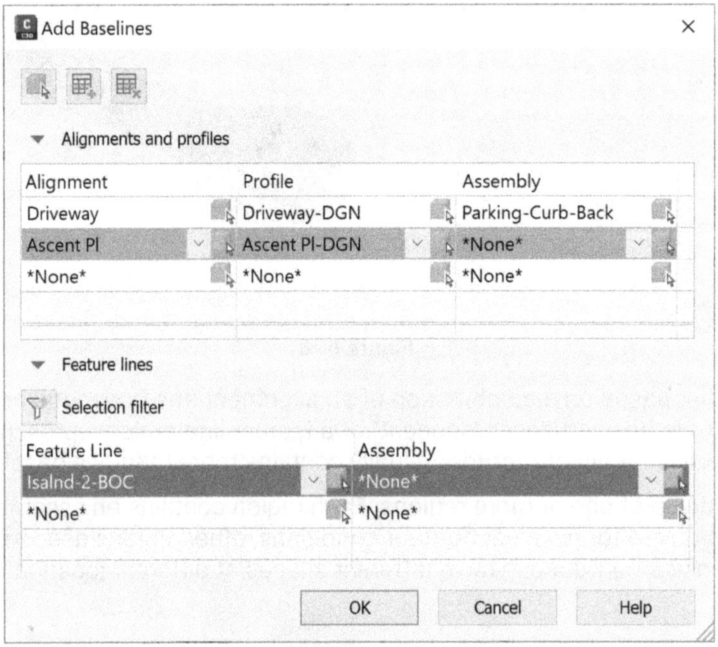

Figure 6–10

You can select any of the objects (alignments, profiles, assemblies or feature lines) from the drawing by picking ▦ (Pick from drawing), or by using the drop-down lists, as shown above in Figure 6–10. When you pick an alignment from the drop-down menu, Civil 3D finds the most appropriate profile, however you should verify that it is the correct profile. If you pick the alignment from the drawing, Civil 3D will display a list in the drawing of the available profiles for that alignment, as shown in Figure 6–11.

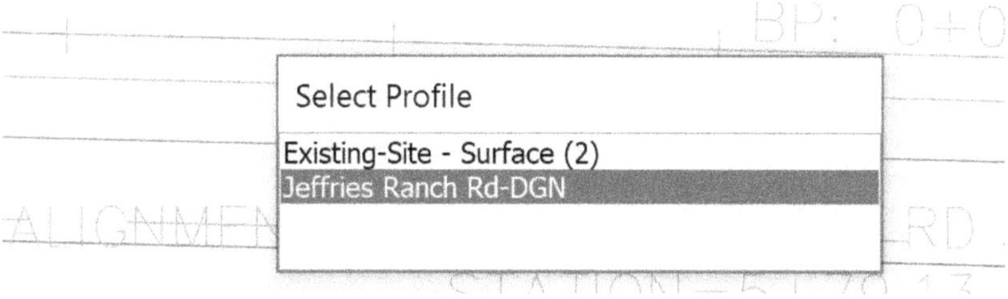

Select Profile

Existing-Site - Surface (2)
Jeffries Ranch Rd-DGN

Figure 6–11

Corridor Contextual Ribbon

Most of the functions performed in the *Corridors Parameters* tab are also available in the ribbon in the *Corridor* contextual tab>*Modify Region* panel, as shown in Figure 6–12. For many users, this is the preferred option; they find it more intuitive because they can pick the regions of the corridor in the drawing and view the results.

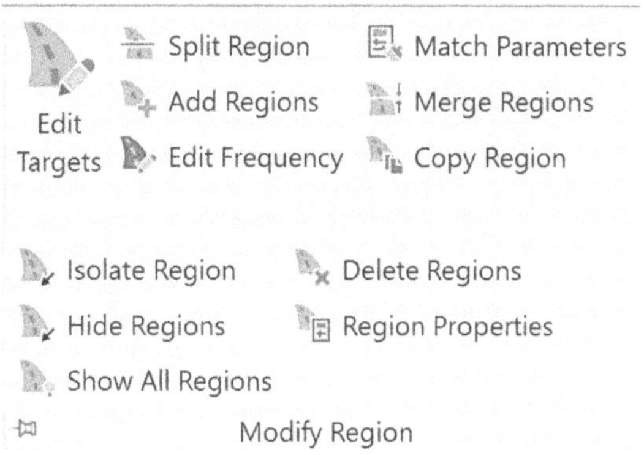

Figure 6–12

The *Corridor* contextual tab>*Modify Corridor* panel also has **Corridor Surfaces**, **Code Sets**, *Feature Lines*, and *Slope Patterns*, as shown in Figure 6–13.

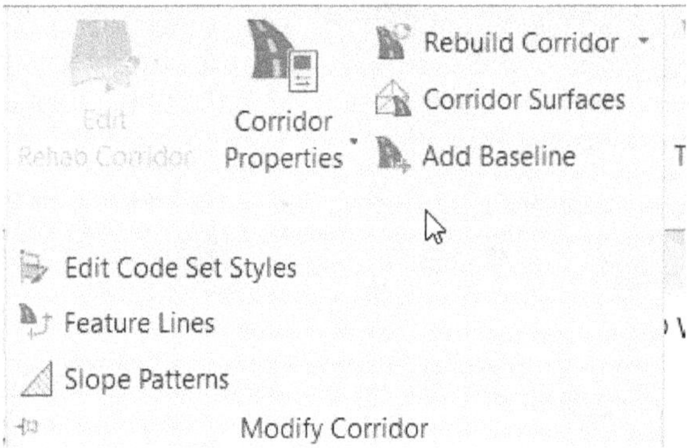

Figure 6–13

Practice 6b
Create the Corridor

Practice Objectives

- Create a corridor model using previously created feature lines and assemblies.
- Add baselines and regions for the islands using Corridor Parameters.

In this practice, you will use the perimeter feature line to create a corridor for the overall parking lot. You will create the initial corridor first, then create the additional baselines after it is built.

Note: The multi-phase corridor creation process shown in this practice is only for training purposes; the entire corridor with all the baselines can be built at the same time.

Task 1: Create a corridor representing the overall parking lot.

1. Continue working with the drawing from the previous practice or open **PKCOR-B.dwg** from the C:\Civil 3D Grading\Working\Parking Corridor folder.

2. In the *Home* tab>*Create Design* panel, click ![Corridor icon] (Corridor). Set the following (as shown in Figure 6–14):

   - For the *Name*, type **Parking Lot**.
   - Ensure that the *Feature line* panel is expanded.
   - For the *Feature line*, from the drop-down menu, select **Perimeter-BOC.**
   - For the *Assembly*, from the drop-down menu, select **Parking-Curb-Back.**
   - Ensure that the *Target Surface* is set **<none>**.
   - Verify that the **Set baseline and region parameters** option is *not* selected.

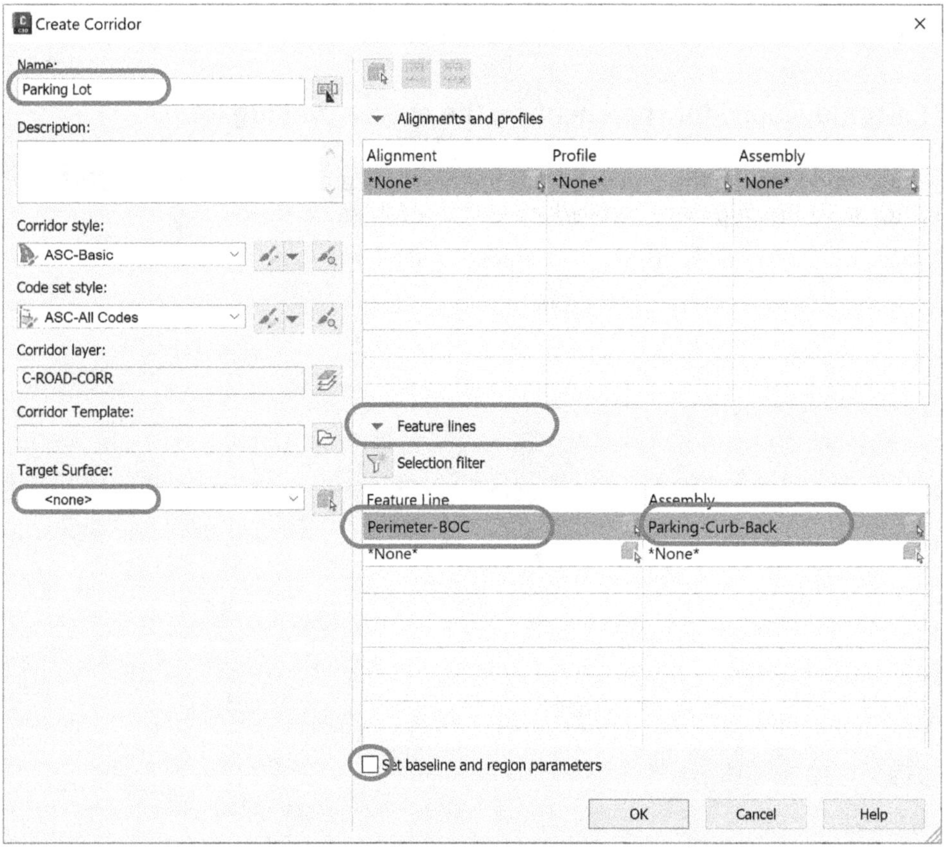

Figure 6–14

3. Click **OK**.

4. The corridor is built. For now, ignore any inconsistencies within the corridor. They will be fixed later.

5. Save the drawing.

Task 2: Add islands to the corridor.

1. Select the corridor. In either the right-click menu or the contextual ribbon, select **Corridor Properties**.

2. In the *Corridor Properties* dialog box, in the *Parameters* tab, click the **Add Baseline** button, as shown in Figure 6–15.

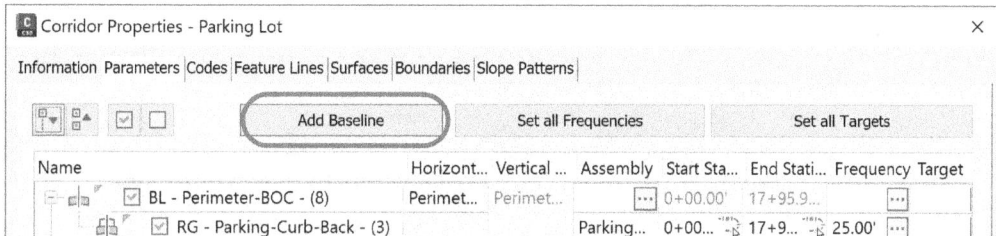

Figure 6–15

3. In the *Add Baselines* dialog box, complete the following, as shown in Figure 6–16:

   • Collapse the *Alignment and profiles* area.

   • In the first row, use the drop-down list for *Feature Line* and select **Island-1-BOC**.

   • Use the drop-down list for *Assembly* and select **Parking-Curb-Back**.

   • In the second row, for *Feature Line*, use ⬚ (Select in drawing) and pick the middle island as shown.

   • Use the drop-down list for *Assembly* and select **Parking-Curb-Back**.

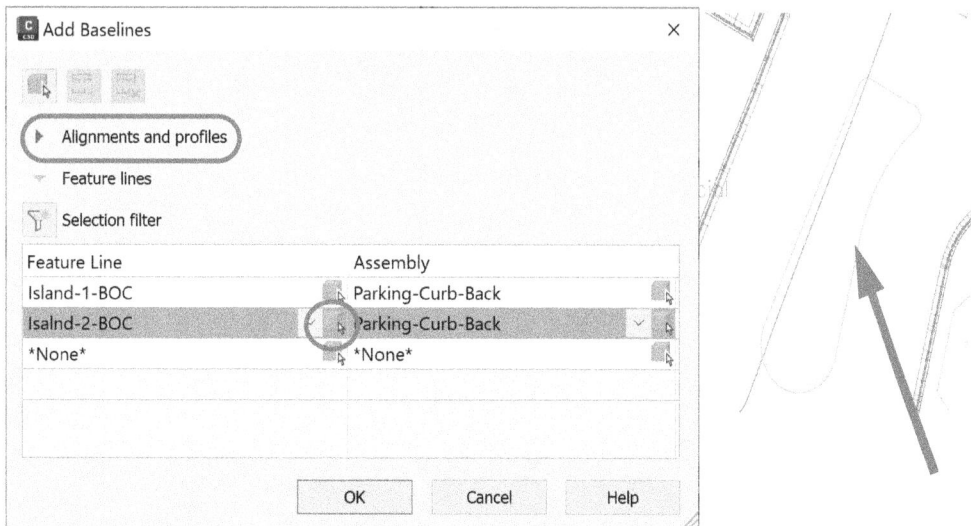

Figure 6–16

4. Click **OK** to close the *Add Baselines* dialog box.

5. The *Corridor Properties* dialog box, in the *Parameters* tab, now includes the two new baselines and regions, as shown in Figure 6-17.

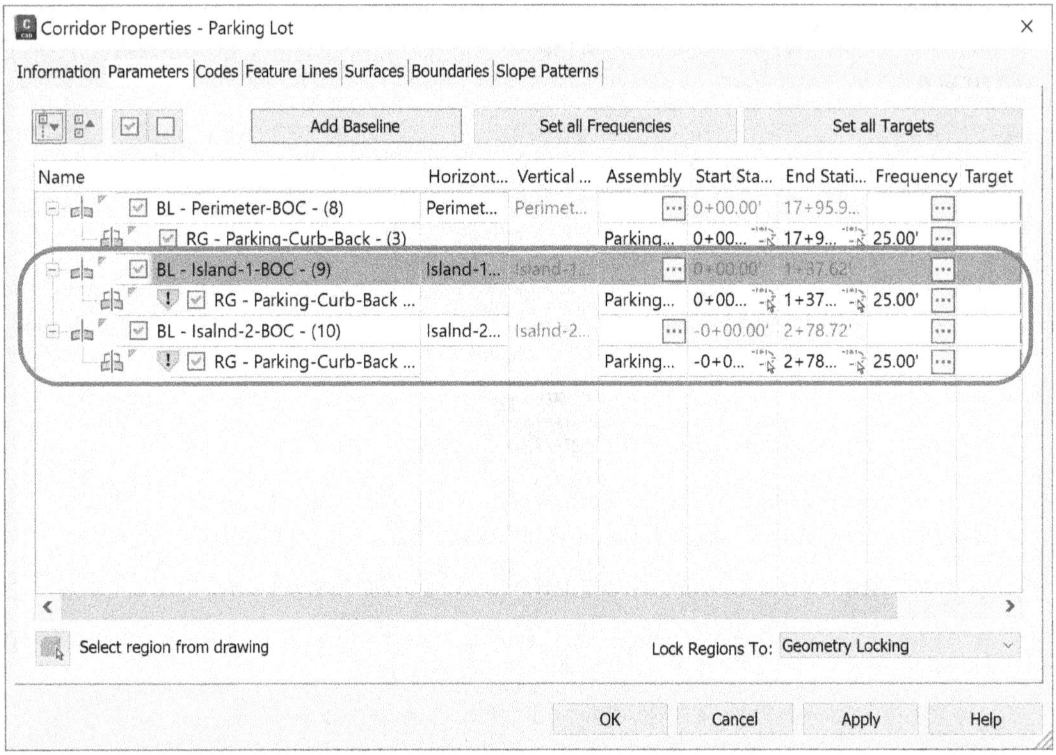

Figure 6-17

6. Click **OK** to close the *Corridor Properties* dialog box. When the warning box displays, select the **Rebuild the corridor** option, as shown in Figure 6−18.

Figure 6−18

Note: For now, ignore any inconsistencies within the corridor. They will be fixed next.

7. Save the drawing.

End of practice

6.4 Corridor Editing

In the typical Civil 3D workflow, you create the initial corridor, then edit and refine it. Corridors are perhaps the most complicated of all the Civil 3D (AEC) objects, with a multitude of settings and defaults. These settings are available in the different tabs of the *Corridor Properties* dialog box.

Corridor Bowties

In situations where there are tight curves or abrupt direction changes (such as corners) in the control line of the corridor, the corridor links can cross each other, resulting in links resembling bowties.

You can edit the feature settings of corridors to automatically clean bowties in corridors, as shown in Figure 6–19.

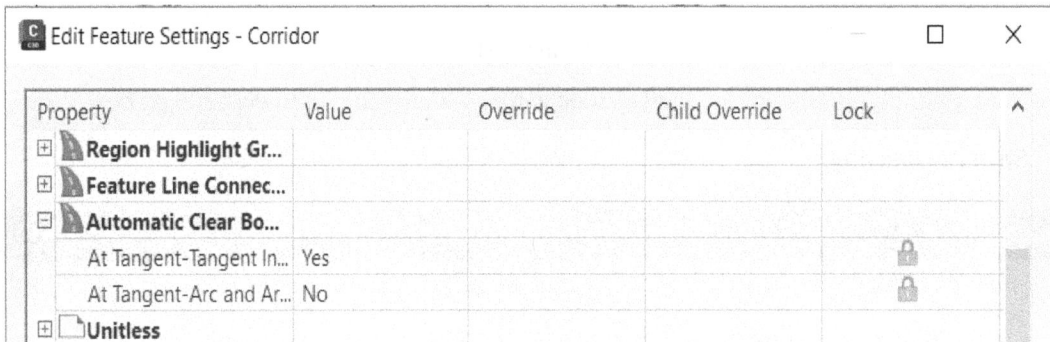

Figure 6–19

But bowties may still persist. In the *Corridor* contextual ribbon, there is a tool to fix such bowties, as shown in Figure 6–20.

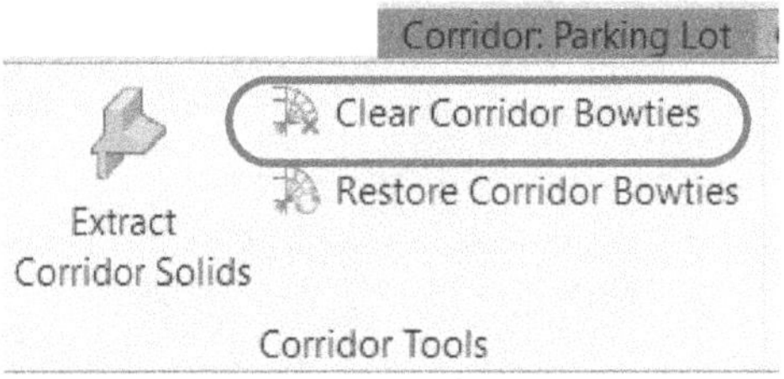

Figure 6–20

How To: Fix Bowties

1. In the *Corridor* contextual tab>*Corridor Tools* panel, click ⟳ (Clear Corridor Bowties), as shown previously in Figure 6−20.

2. You are prompted to select the corridor baseline (either an alignment or a feature line). See **A** in Figure 6−21.

3. You are prompted for the starting subentity. Select the same baseline as you did previously, just *before* the bowtie. Take care that you understand the direction of the corridor and that the stationing of the starting subentity is lower than the ending subentity (next step). See **B** in Figure 6−21. The selected line segment highlights in red.

4. Specify the ending subentity, then select the baseline just *after* the bowtie. See **C** in Figure 6−21.

5. Next you determine where you want the resulting corridor feature lines to intersect. See **D** in Figure 6−21.

6. If there are more bowties to be cleared, you can move on to the next starting entity, or press <Enter> to rebuild the corridor and see the results.

Before the fix   *After the bowties are cleared*

Figure 6−21

Sometimes when the baselines change directions, the cleared bowties will remain and result in unsatisfactory conditions. For this reason, you can restore the original bowtie conditions.

It is the adding of an elevation point at the POTENTIAL intersection point of the flange point of the incoming and outgoing flange. It is not always perfect, but by adding elevation points almost all bowties are removed.

How To: Restore Bowties

1. In the *Corridor* contextual tab>*Corridor Tools* panel, click (Restore Corridor Bowties), as shown in Figure 6−22.

Figure 6−22

2. Since you invoked this command from the contextual corridor ribbon, Civil 3D already knows how many bowties have been cleared and highlights the first one. On the command line, it informs you how many bowties are cleared and the number of the current one.

3. You can choose to restore the current bowtie by simply pressing <Enter>, and it will move on to the next bowtie.

4. You can choose to ignore the bowtie by clicking **Skip** and it will move on to the next bowtie.

5. Once you are done selecting the bowties to be restored, select **Rebuild and restore** at the command line. The command terminates and the selected bowties are restored.

6. You can choose all bowties by clicking **All**. The command terminates and the bowties are restored.

6.5 Reversing Feature Lines

Working with feature lines is similar to working with standard AutoCAD polylines and, like polylines, the direction of feature lines can be reversed. However, it is not the standard AutoCAD **Reverse** command, but a specialized command specific to feature lines, which is accessible through a contextual ribbon.

The direction of the feature line that is the baseline of a corridor will determine the stationing of the corridor as well as the "left" and "right" sides of attached assemblies. When picking objects to create feature lines, it is difficult to know the direction of the picked objects and the resulting feature lines.

How To: Reverse a Feature Line

1. Select the feature line.

2. In the *Feature Line* contextual tab>*Modify* panel, click 🗁 (Edit Geometry). The *Edit Geometry* panel displays, as shown in Figure 6−23.

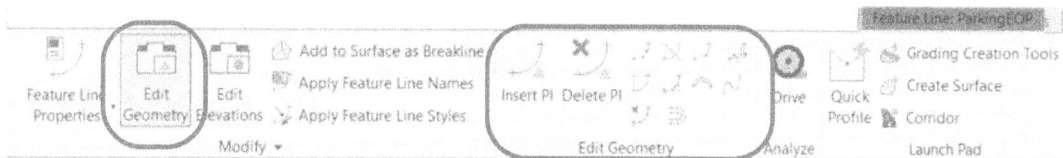

Figure 6−23

3. Click the ⬦ (Reverse) command.

4. Each time you click the command, the feature line changes direction. When assemblies are attached to the feature line (baseline of the corridor), they will change sides.

Practice 6c
Corridor Editing

Practice Objectives

- Change the frequency of the corridor.
- Clean up the various bowties along the perimeter.
- Reverse the direction of the Island feature lines.

In the previous practice, you created the preliminary corridor. In this practice, you will fine tune the corridor by cleaning up the bowties and modifying some feature lines so the curbs are created correctly.

Task 1: Changing corridor frequencies.

In this practice, the frequencies were preset through the *Edit Command Settings* dialog box for the various **Create Corridor** commands. You will change them to see the results.

1. Continue working with the drawing from the previous practice or open **PKCOR-C.dwg** from the *C:\Civil 3D Grading\Working\Parking Corridor* folder.

2. Select the corridor. In either the right-click menu or the contextual ribbon, select **Corridor Properties**. In the *Corridor Properties* dialog box, select the **Set all Frequencies** button. In the *Frequency to Apply Assemblies* dialog box, change the *Horizontal Baseline>Along curves* to **Both** (using the drop-down list), as shown in Figure 6−24.

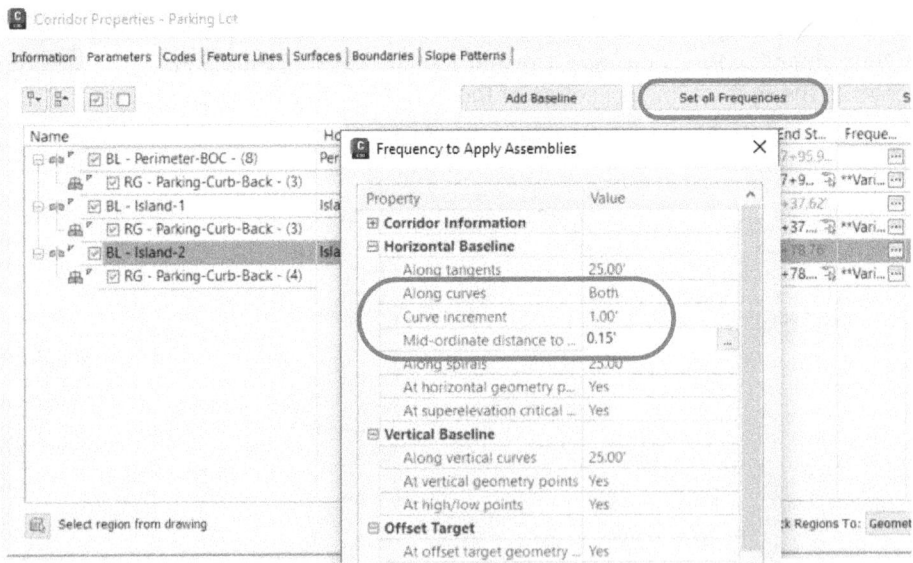

Figure 6−24

3. Change the *Curve increment* to **1.00'** and the *Mid-ordinate distance* to **0.15'**.

4. Click **OK** to close the *Frequency to Apply Assemblies* dialog box.

   Note: The increased placement along the curves, causing a smoother curve.

5. Click **OK** to close the *Corridor Properties* dialog box. When the warning box displays, select the **Rebuild the corridor** option.

6. Save the drawing.

Task 2: Clearing bowties.

In this task, you will clean up the corridor's bowties in the problem areas, as shown in Figure 6–25.

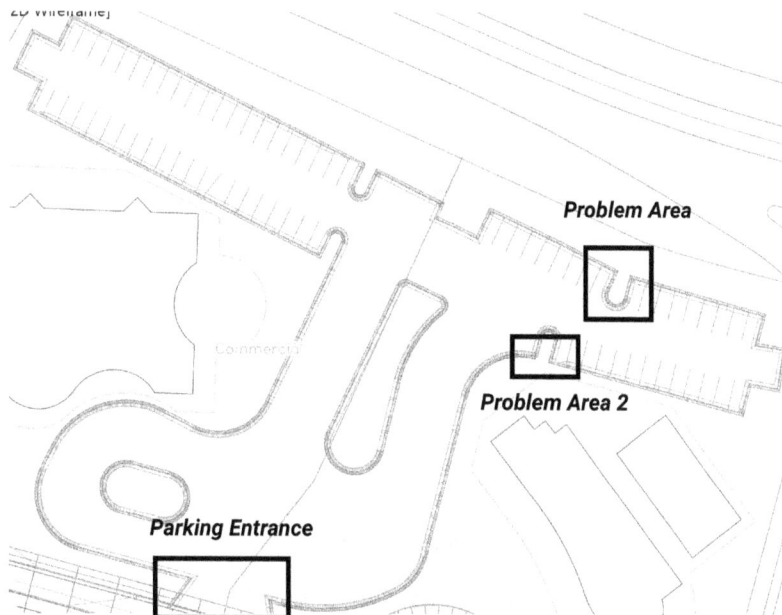

Figure 6–25

1. In the *View* tab>*Named Views* panel, select **Problem Area** to view where some bowties might have occurred.

2. Select the corridor and using either the right-click menu or the *Corridor* contextual tab>*General Tools* expanded panel, send the corridor to the back. This will simplify picking the corridor baseline when clearing bowties.

   Note: Your corridor and bowties may differ from the figure, depending on how the corridor is built. Therefore, adjust the following steps as needed.

3. In the *Corridor* contextual tab>*Corridor Tools* panel, click ![icon] (Clear Corridor Bowties), as shown in Figure 6–26.

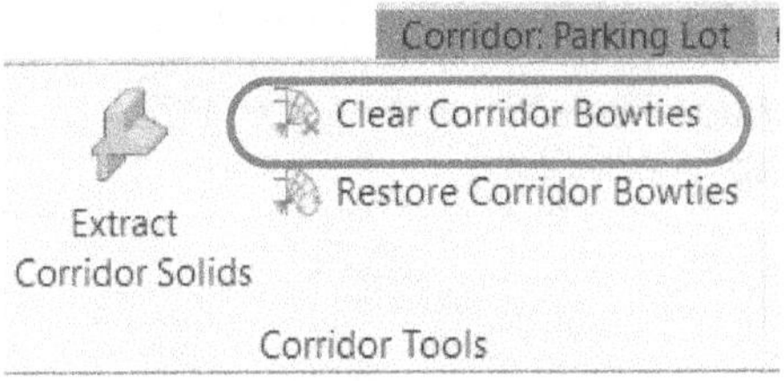

Figure 6–26

4. Select the corridor baseline **A**, as shown in Figure 6–27.

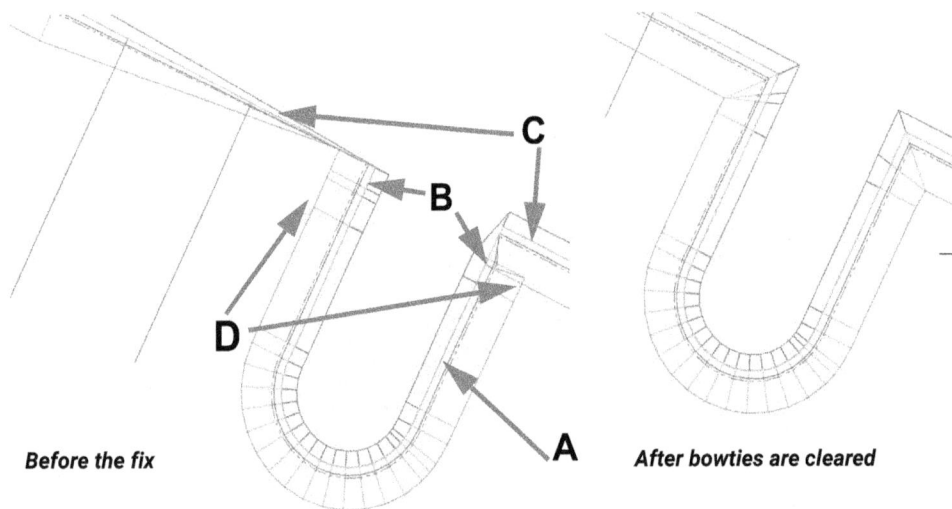

Before the fix   *After bowties are cleared*

Figure 6–27

5. When prompted to specify the starting subentity, select the same baseline as you did previously, just *before* the bowtie. See **B** in Figure 6–27. The selected line segment highlights in red.

6. When prompted to specify the ending subentity, select the baseline just *after* the bowtie. See **C** in Figure 6–27.

7. Next select the point where the resulting corridor feature lines are to intersect. See **D** in Figure 6–27.

8. At the command line, click **Specify another bowtie** to move on to the next corner. Repeat the same steps.

9. Press <Enter> to rebuild the corridor and study the results.

10. In the *View* tab>*Named Views* panel, select **Problem Area 2** to view where other bowties might have occurred.

11. Try to fix these as you did above. Chances are the left one will not clear properly. In the *Corridor* contextual tab>*Corridor Tools* panel, click ⅀ (Restore Corridor Bowties), as shown in Figure 6−28.

Figure 6−28

12. To move to the errant bowtie, keep selecting **Skip** (on the command line) until it is highlighted. You can pan and zoom to keep up with the bowties, then select **Rebuild and restore** at the command line, as shown in Figure 6−29.

Figure 6−29

13. Select the feature line. The circular grips are *Elevation Points* of the feature line and reveal the problem of why the bowtie will not clear properly. As seen in Figure 6−30, the elevation point just after the intersection is too close to the intersection and needs to be eliminated.

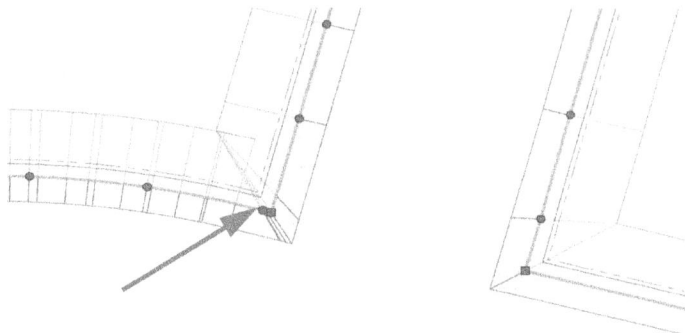

Figure 6−30

14. In the *Feature Line* contextual tab>*Modify* panel, click 📷 (Edit Elevations) to display the *Edit Elevations* panel.

15. In the *Edit Elevations* panel, click ✕ (Delete Elevation Point), as shown in Figure 6–31.

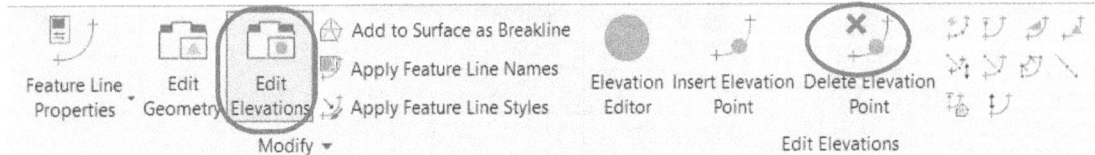

Figure 6–31

16. You can also the **Delete Elevation Point** option from the right-click menu when hovering over the elevation point, as shown in Figure 6–32.

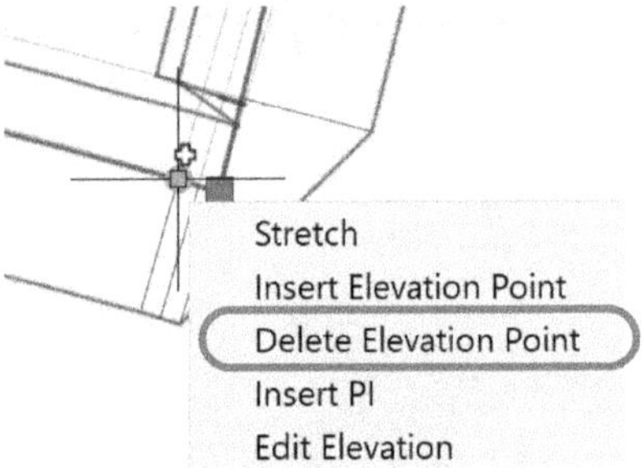

Figure 6–32

17. Select the errant elevation point and press <Enter> twice. You will notice that the circular grip has now been eliminated.

18. In the *Prospector* tab, note that the **Parking Lot** corridor is marked Out of Date (the yellow warning sign). Right-click on the name and select **Rebuild**, as shown in Figure 6–33.

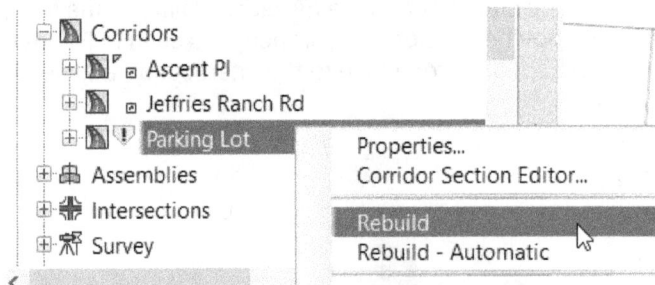

Figure 6–33

19. Click ☑ to close the *Events* vista if it displays. Press <Esc> to end the command.

20. Clear the bowtie as done previously.

21. In the *View* tab>*Named Views* panel, select **Problem-Area2**.

22. Select the **Perimeter-BOC** feature line and note the elevation points (circular grips), as shown in Figure 6–34. They are quite sparse.

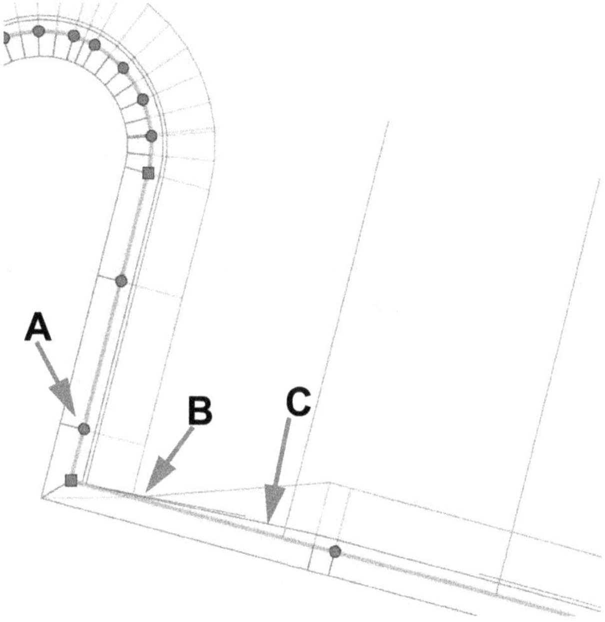

Figure 6–34

- It is the lack of such elevation points at corners that can create the bowties. Often, by adding an elevation point near the overlapping flange, bowties can be removed.

23. Select the elevation point, marked as **A** in Figure 6–34 above, and move it above the intersection of the gutters, as shown in Figure 6–35.

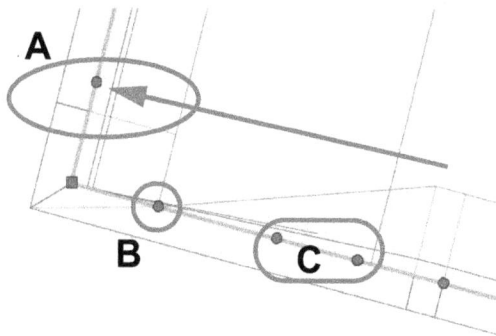

Figure 6–35

24. In the *Feature Line* contextual tab>*Edit Elevations* panel, click ⬚ (Insert Elevation Point). You can also the **Insert Elevation Point** option from the right-click menu when hovering over the elevation point.

25. For the point, select the endpoint of the green EOP (Edge of Pavement) line, marked as **B** in Figure 6–35 above. When prompted for the elevation, accept the default.

26. Add two more elevation points, marked as **C** in Figure 6–35 above. When prompted for the elevation, accept the default.

27. Press <Enter> to finish adding elevation points.

28. In the *Prospector* tab, note that the **Parking Lot** corridor may be marked Out of Date (the yellow warning sign). If it is, right-click on the name and select **Rebuild**, as shown in Figure 6–36.

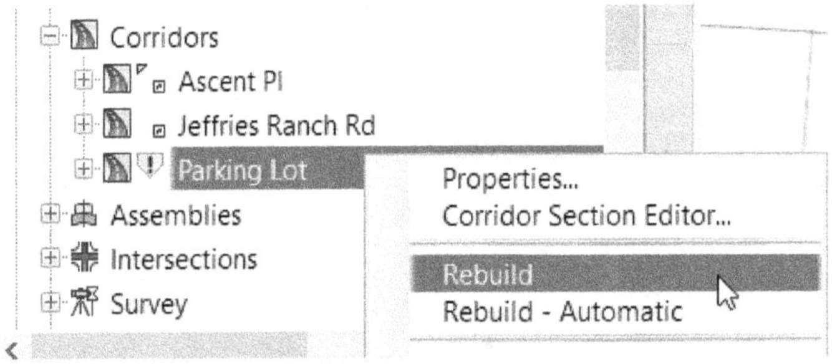

Figure 6–36

29. The bowtie gets resolved, as shown in Figure 6–37.

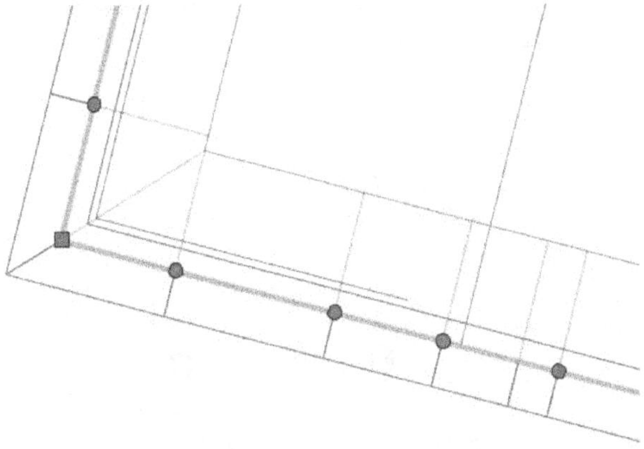

Figure 6–37

30. In the *View* tab>*Named Views* panel, select **Parking Entrance** to view another troubling bowtie.

31. Clear the bowtie in the regular manner, but select the point on the outside where the resulting corridor feature lines are to intersect, as shown in Figure 6-38.

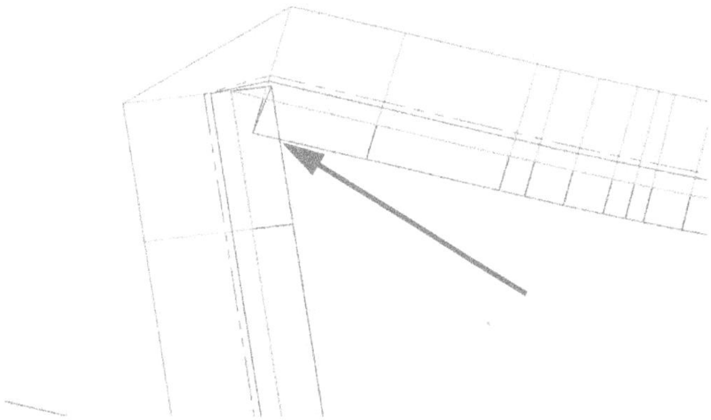

Figure 6-38

32. Continue clearing the rest of the bowties.

33. Save the drawing.

Task 3: Reversing feature lines.

Careful inspection will reveal that the assemblies in the two island regions are attached to the wrong side (the curbs are facing inward). The feature lines need to be reversed and the corridor updated.

1. Note that the magenta links of the corridor representing the **LinkWidthAndSlope** subassembly, as shown in Figure 6-39, fall on the wrong side in the islands.

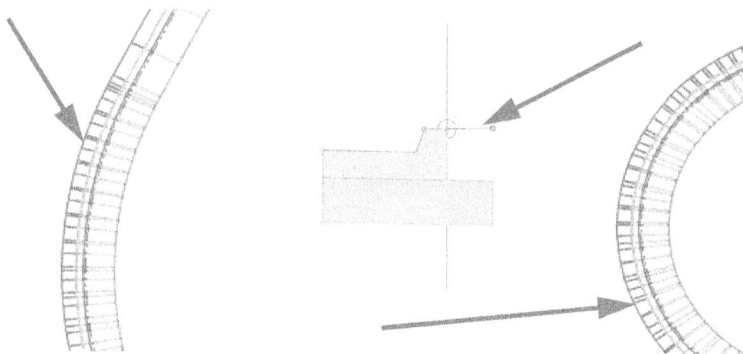

Figure 6-39

2. You need to reverse the island feature lines. Select the first feature line (you need to reverse them one at a time).

3. In the *Feature Line* contextual tab>*Modify* panel, click ⬛ (Edit Geometry). The *Edit Geometry* panel displays, as shown in Figure 6–40.

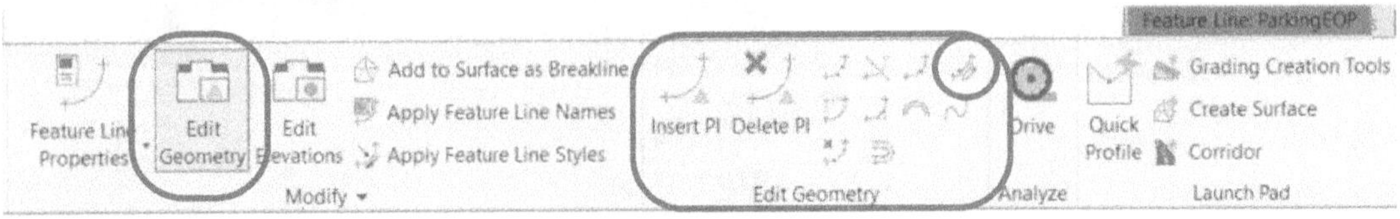

Figure 6–40

4. Click the ⬛ (Reverse) command. The assemblies swap sides but are not yet connected (until the corridor is rebuilt).

5. Press <Esc> to clear the first feature line, then repeat the procedure for the other island feature line.

6. As before, rebuild the **Parking Lot** corridor.

7. Click ☑ to close the *Events* vista if it displays. Press <Esc> to end the command.

8. Save the drawing.

End of practice

6.6 Corridor Surfaces

The *Surfaces* tab in the *Corridor Properties* dialog box enables you to build the proposed surfaces based on corridor geometry. You can create these surfaces from corridor links or from feature lines based on marker points (point codes). As the corridor changes, its surfaces automatically update.

The two most common types of corridor surfaces are **top** and **datum** surfaces.

- **Top surfaces** follow the uppermost geometry of the corridor. These are useful for many purposes, such as in the display of finished ground contours or as a way of determining rim elevations of proposed utility structures.

- **Datum surfaces** generally follow the bottommost corridor geometry, where the corridor and the existing surface meet. These can be used in both Surface-to-Surface volume calculations and Section-based Earthworks calculations to determine site cut and fill totals (when compared to existing ground).

Other surfaces may be created and assigned materials for rendering purposes. Rendering can be done in Civil 3D; however, better results are achieved when using rendering-specific programs like Autodesk® 3DS Max®, Autodesk® Navisworks®, etc.

- **Corridor surfaces:** As with all Autodesk Civil 3D surfaces, these cannot contain vertical elements. Include slight offsets so that vertical curbing and similar geometry are not absolutely vertical.

Overhang Correction

In some configurations, Autodesk Civil 3D assemblies might have top or datum points or links in locations that might lead to incorrect surfaces, such as the datum surface represented by the heavy line in Figure 6–41.

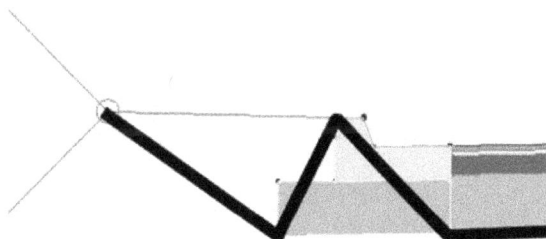

Figure 6–41

In these cases, the **Overhang Correction** option forces these surfaces to follow either the top or bottom of the corridor geometry, as shown in Figure 6−42. This setting is typically only required for top and datum surfaces.

Figure 6−42

Surface Boundaries

Corridor surfaces, as with all Autodesk Civil 3D surfaces, often benefit from a boundary to remove unwanted interpolation between points. The *Boundaries* tab in the *Corridor Surfaces* dialog box enables you to add these boundaries in a couple of ways: by selecting a closed polyline or by interactively tracing the boundary using a jig.

The best option for top and datum surfaces is often to automatically add a boundary that follows the outermost edge on both sides. This can be done using the **Create Boundary from Corridor Extents** command.

For rendering specific surfaces (such as Asphalt, Concrete, etc.), you need to either trace the boundary or pick a polyline representing the boundary.

Practice 6d
Add Surfaces and Boundaries

Practice Objectives

- Adding the top surface to the corridor.
- Extracting a feature line from the corridor.
- Add a boundary to the corridor surface.

In this practice, you will create the finished parking surface from the corridor and apply a boundary.

Task 1: Creating the top surface of the corridor.

1. Continue working with the drawing from the previous practice or open **PKCOR-D.dwg** from the C:\Civil 3D Grading\Working\Parking Corridor folder.

2. Select the corridor. In either the right-click menu or the contextual ribbon, select **Corridor Properties**.

3. In the Corridor Properties dialog box, select the Surfaces tab.

4. Click ⬛ (Create a Corridor Surface). In the *Corridor Surfaces* dialog box, set the following, as shown in Figure 6–43:

  - Name it **Parking Lot Surface - TOP**.
  - Set *Overhang Correction* to **Top Links**.
  - Change *Data type* to **Feature Lines**.

  - In the *Specify code* section, select **Back_Curb** and click ⬛ (Add Surface Item).
  - Repeat for the **Flange**, **Flowline_Gutter**, and **Top_Curb**, one by one.
  - Click **OK**.

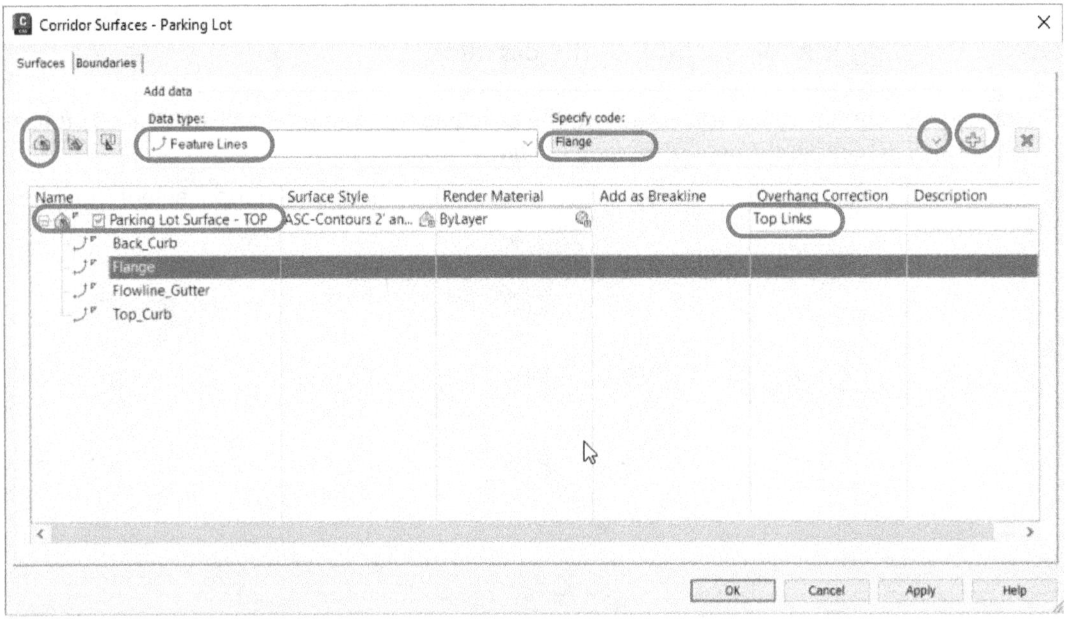

Figure 6–43

5. Click **OK** to close the *Corridor Properties* dialog box. When the warning box displays, select the **Rebuild the corridor** option.

6. The top surface is built, as shown in Figure 6-44.

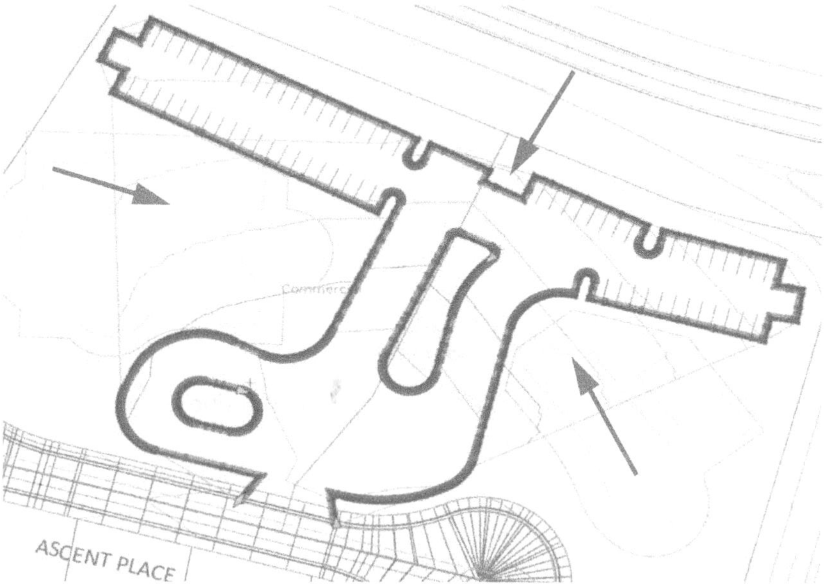

Figure 6-44

7. Save the drawing.

Task 2: Extract corridor feature line.

The top surface expands beyond the parking lot and triangulates across the outer concave curves of the corridor. A boundary needs to be added to trim the surface back. In order to create the boundary, you will extract a feature line from the corridor and convert it to a closed polyline, which then can be chosen as the boundary of the surface.

1. Select the corridor. In the contextual ribbon>*Launch Pad* panel (far right), select

    (Feature Lines from Corridor), as shown in Figure 6-45.

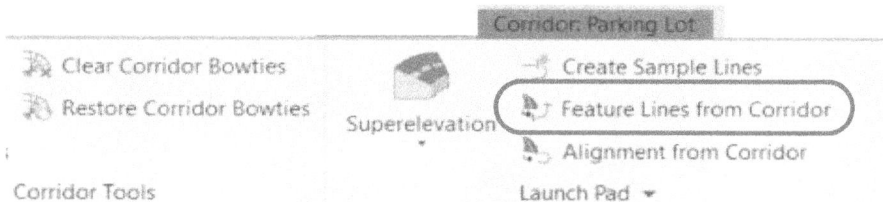

Figure 6-45

2. Hover over the outer edge of the corridor until you see the tooltip displaying **P2** and the outer edge highlights in red, as shown in Figure 6-46.

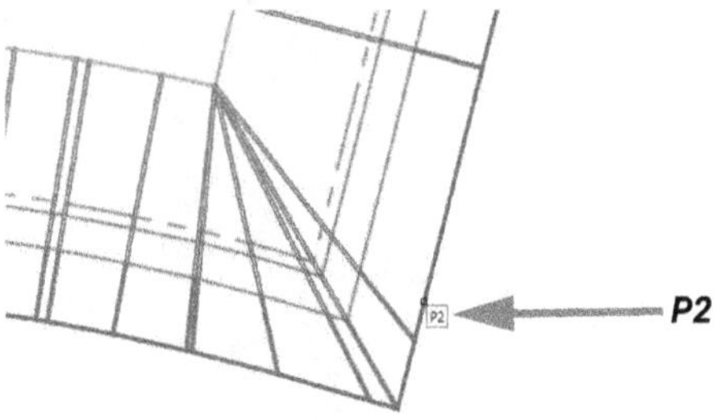

Figure 6-46

3. In the *Extract Corridor Feature Lines* dialog box, click the **Settings...** button in the upper-right corner.

4. In the *Extract Corridor Feature Line Settings* dialog box, set the following, as shown in Figure 6-47:

   • Clear the *Dynamic link to corridor* checkbox.

   • Clear the *Apply Smoothing* checkbox.

   • Select the *Name* checkbox and name it **FL-Outer Limits**.

   • Click **OK** to close the *Extract Corridor Feature Line Settings* dialog box.

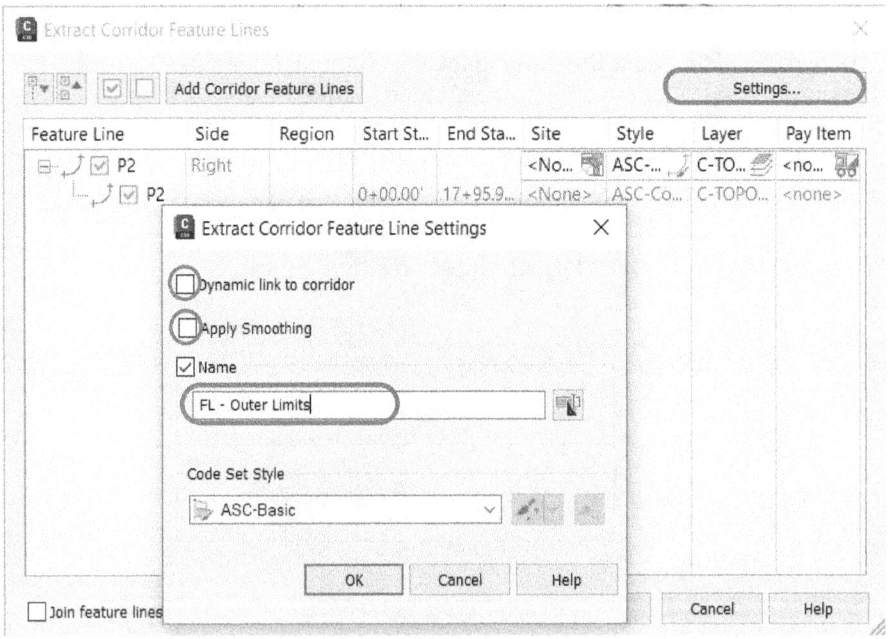

Figure 6-47

5. In the *Extract Corridor Feature Lines* dialog box, click **Extract**.

6. Invoke the AutoCAD Explode command (type **X** at the command line and press <Enter>) and select the extracted feature line. It becomes an AutoCAD 3D polyline.

7. Select the 3D polyline and, in the AutoCAD Properties palette, close the polyline (as shown in Figure 6–48).

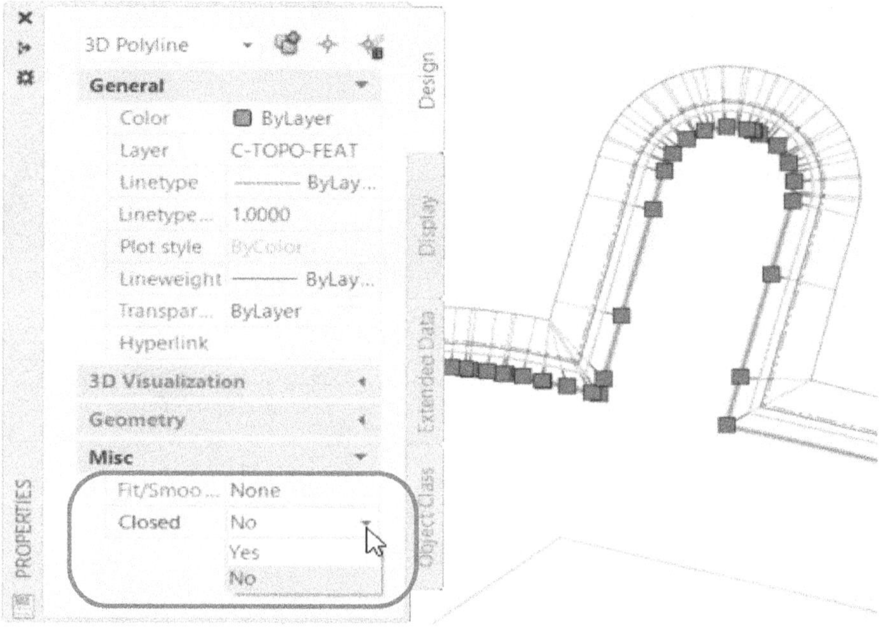

Figure 6–48

8. Save the drawing.

Task 3: Create the corridor surface boundary.

1. Select the corridor. In either the right-click menu or the contextual ribbon, select **Corridor Properties**.

2. In the *Corridor Properties* dialog box, select the *Boundaries* tab.

3. Right-click on **Parking Lot Surface - TOP** and select **Add From Polygon...**, as shown in Figure 6-49.

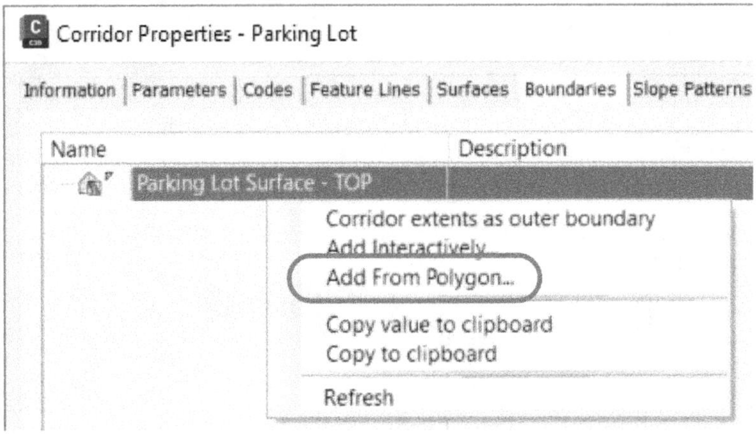

Figure 6-49

4. Select the 3D polyline from the previous task.

5. Click **OK** to close the *Corridor Properties* dialog box. When the warning box displays, select the **Rebuild the corridor** option.

6. Select the **Parking Lot Surface - TOP** surface (select one of its contour lines).

7. In the *Surface* contextual tab, click ⬛ (Object Viewer). Set the view direction to **SW Isometric** and the style to **Conceptual**. Note the hole in the surface, as shown in Figure 6–50. If you prefer, you can also view it through the *Model Viewer* by selecting **Add to Model Viewer** via the right-click menu.

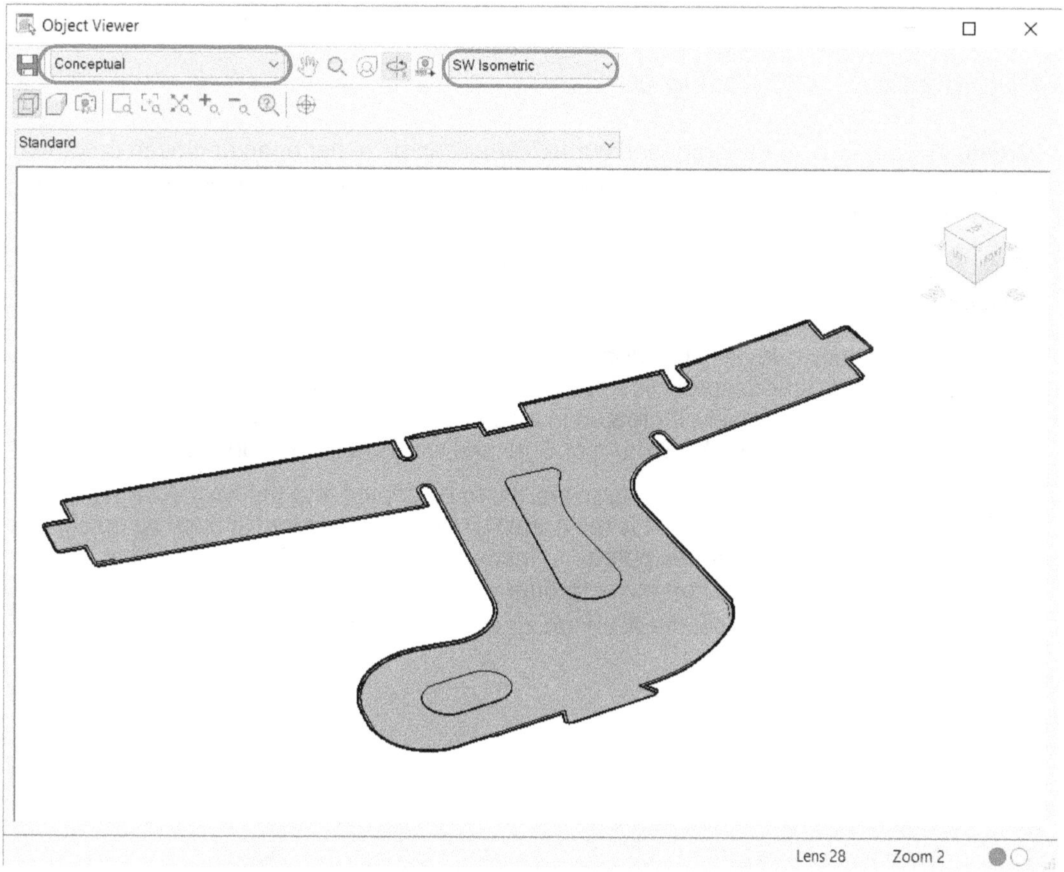

Figure 6–50

8. Press <Esc> twice to close the Object Viewer and release the selection.

End of practice

6.7 Grading Optimization: Parking Lots and Drainage

With Grading Optimization, 2D linework representing the proposed parking lot layout, you can create Curb Grading Objects.

How To: Create a Curb Grading Object

1. Create 2D linework for the proposed curbs. These can be either open or closed polylines, lines, or Civil 3D feature lines. Elevations are not required and will be ignored by Grading Optimization if present.

   *Note: You can always reverse the direction of such objects through the AutoCAD **Reverse** command (or with Civil 3D feature line editing).*

2. When creating linework, pay attention to the direction of the lines. If created in a clockwise direction, Grading Optimization will treat it as the *Top of Curb* and will project the curb object downward. Conversely, if created in a counter-clockwise direction, Grading Optimization will treat it as the *Bottom of Curb* and will project the curb object upward.

3. If linework already exists in an xref drawing, it can be copied into the host drawing by various means. The most efficient is the AutoCAD **NCopy** command. If copying objects, you can use the AutoCAD **Properties** palette to inspect the vertices of the pline under the *Geometry* section. Then you can move through the vertices with the up and down arrows by **Current Vertex**, and note how the **X** on the screen moved, as shown in Figure 6–51.

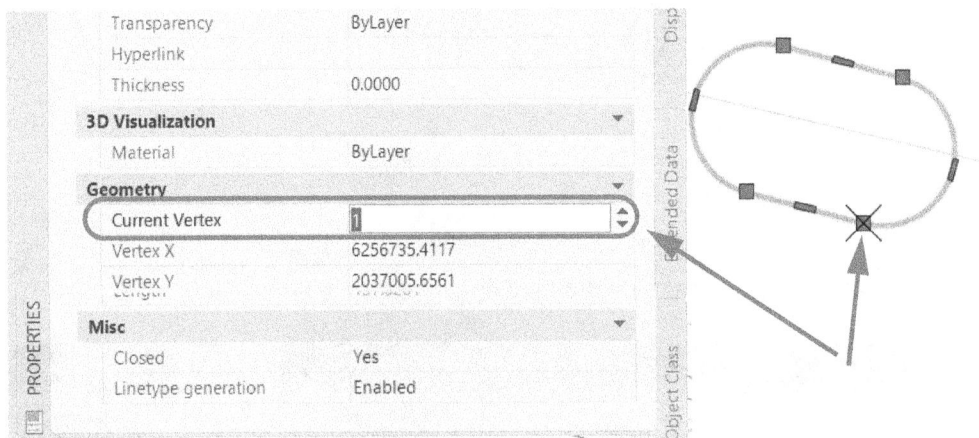

Figure 6–51

4. With the linework for the curbs defined, you assign the  (Curb Grading Object) to the linework by selecting it from the Grading Optimization Tool Palette. You can either select all the linework first and then select the Curb Grading Object in the palette, or vice versa.

5. Once objects have been assigned as Curbs, they have an additional shaded outline to them representing the higher side of the curb, as shown and accentuated in Figure 6–52.

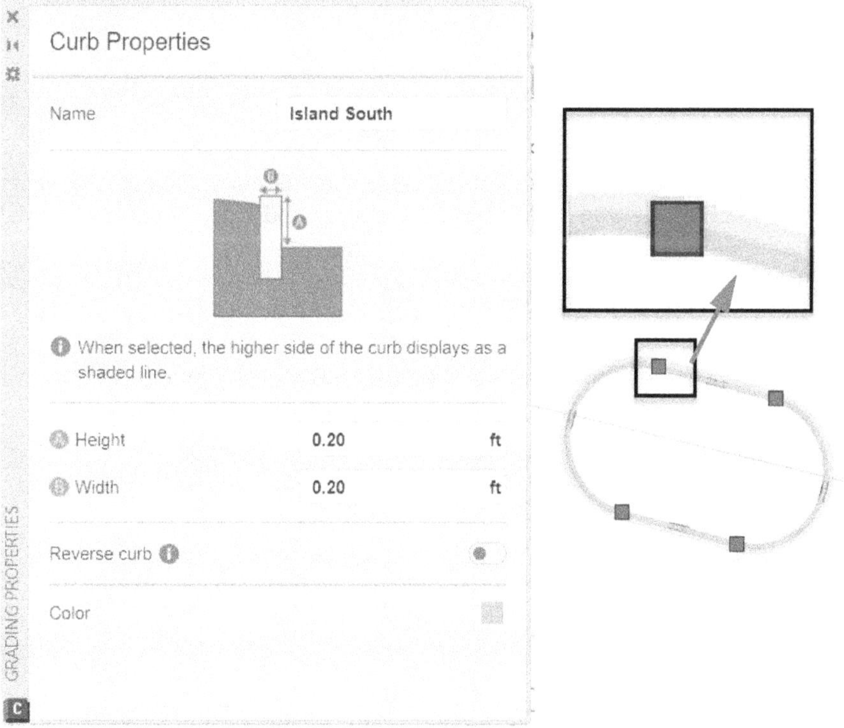

Figure 6–52

> ## 💡 Hint: Shaded Outlines
>
> It can be difficult to discern which is the shaded outline. The pline grips are placed on the lower (unshaded) side of the curb.

6. If assigning objects individually, you can name them for easier identification and reverse the curb direction, if need be. If multiple objects are selected, you will need to edit each one separately and name them and reverse their directions.

7. You can change the *Curb Height* and *Curb Width* in the *Curb Properties* dialog box, either individually or with multiple selected. **Note:** If you need to change many of them, see additional options below.

8. If need be, you can right-click on the object assigned as a curb and remove the Curb definition, as shown in Figure 6–53.

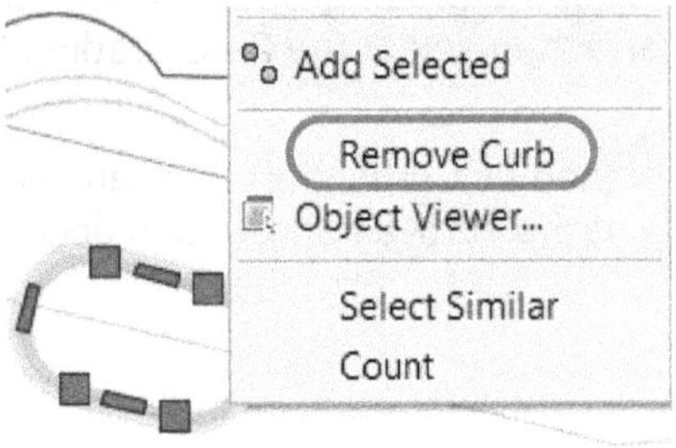

Figure 6–53

As previously stated, you can change the properties of any Grading Object by selecting it on screen or through the *Grading Objects Browser* once assigned. You can also change the default values in the Tool Palettes.

How To: Change or Copy Grading Objects in the Grading Object Tool Palette

1. In the *Grading Object* Tool Palette, hover over the Grading Object you want to manipulate and right-click.

2. In the right-click menu, select **Properties**, shown in Figure 6–54.

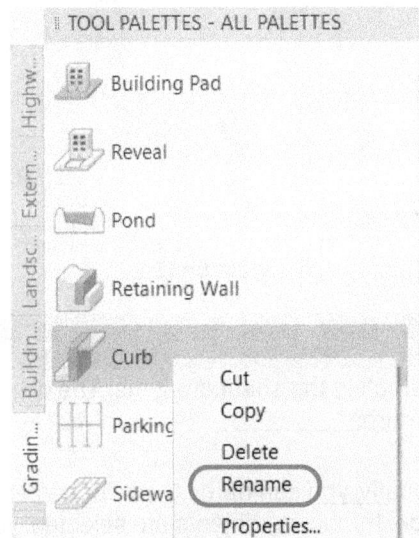

Figure 6–54

3. In the *Tool Properties* dialog box, make the changes to the defaults as required.

4. If you need to change a toggle, you can do that by picking the down arrow to see the available choices and pick the desired one, as shown in Figure 6-55.

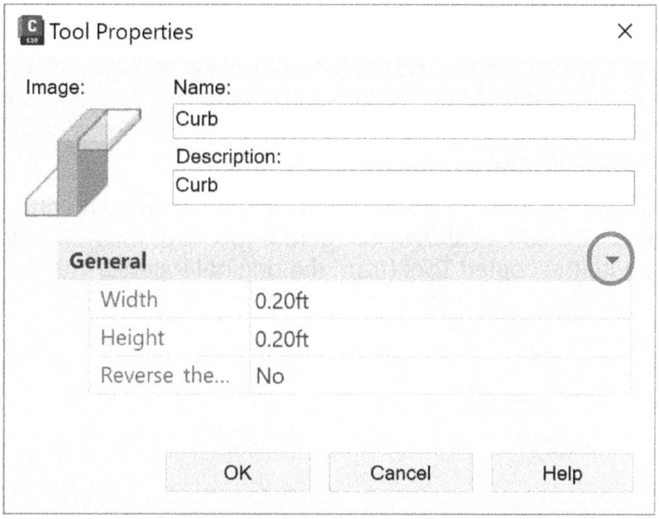

Figure 6-55

5. You can also rename the Tool, however it is not recommended to rename an existing Tool. It is better to make a **copy** of an existing Tool through the right-click menu, then right-click again anywhere in the Tool Palette and select **Paste**, as shown Figure 6-56.

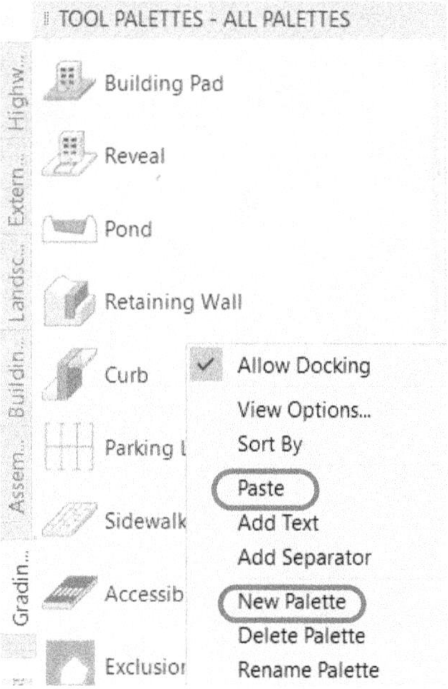

Figure 6-56

6. The copied Tool gets situated at the bottom of the palette and has the same name as the original. Rename it using the right-click menu, or the *Tool Properties* dialog box, as already explained. You will need to change the other properties as well, since you made a copy of the original.

7. You can rearrange the tools within the palette using drag and drop. Click on a tool and drag it up or down to its desired location in the palette. When your cursor reaches the location where the tool can be dropped, a light blue horizontal line appears and you can release the mouse button to drop the tool.

8. If there are many new Tools to be created, you can also create an entire new palette through the right-click menu as shown in Figure 6–56. Give the new palette an appropriate name and then paste the copied Tool (from the original Palette) into the new palette.

Retaining Walls

Civil 3D had a Breakline type named "Wall", which one can add to a surface. This is ideal for defining such "walk-out basement" scenarios. Grading Optimization does not have such elements to be defined. Instead there is the **Retaining Wall** Grading Object, which acts similar to the Curb Grading Object previously discussed.

The **Retaining Wall** Grading Object can be defined from either open or closed polylines, lines or Civil 3D feature lines. Elevations are not required and will be ignored by Grading Optimization, if present.

Once an object has been assigned as a **Retaining Wall**, it receives an added shaded outline. This represents the higher side of the wall, as shown and accentuated in Figure 6–57. It is the direction the wall object was drawn in that decides the high and low side. If drawn in a clockwise direction, Grading Object will treat it as the low side and will grade upward, and vice versa. This can be reversed by either reversing the object with the AutoCAD **Reverse** command, or in the *Retaining Wall Properties* dialog box.

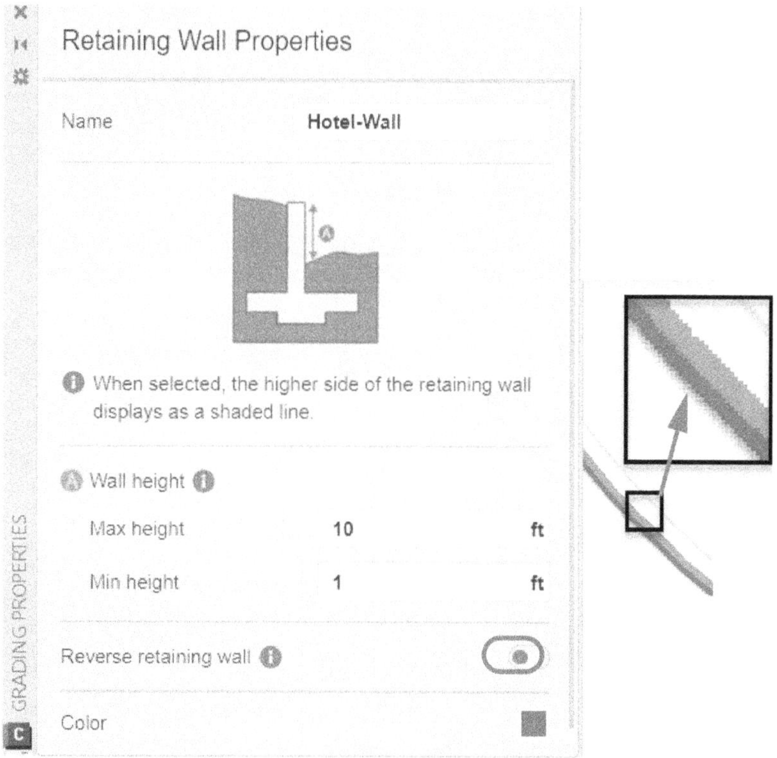

Figure 6–57

If you are assigning objects individually, you can name them for easier identification and reverse the curb direction, if required. If multiple objects are selected, you will need to edit each one separately after they are assigned to give names and reverse directions.

Drain Lines

In order to direct the water flow within the pond (or between basins) to the proper discharge point, drain lines can be set. They are represented by AutoCAD lines or polylines or Civil 3D Feature Lines.These linear objects must be open and cannot contain closed objects. It is recommended that they be put on specific layers for proper CAD standards; however, this will not affect Grading Optimization's processing of drain lines.

The start point of the line will be the high point at the surface elevation at that point, and it will drain towards the endpoint of the linear feature. The minimum and maximum slopes of the drain line are dictated by the **Optimization Options** in the *Grading Optimization* interface, as shown in Figure 6–58. The *Minimum Drain Slope* must be greater than **0.0**.

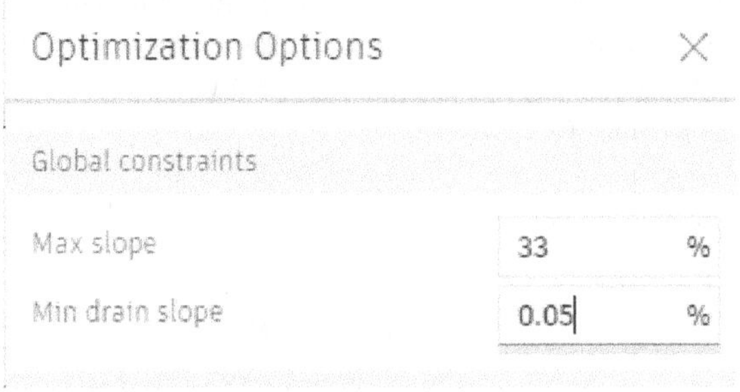

Figure 6–58

The dialog box of the **Drain Line** Grading Object is quite simple, as shown in Figure 6–59. It asks for a name (for easier identification, its color, and whether it will become a feature line once it is processed and returned to Civil 3D.

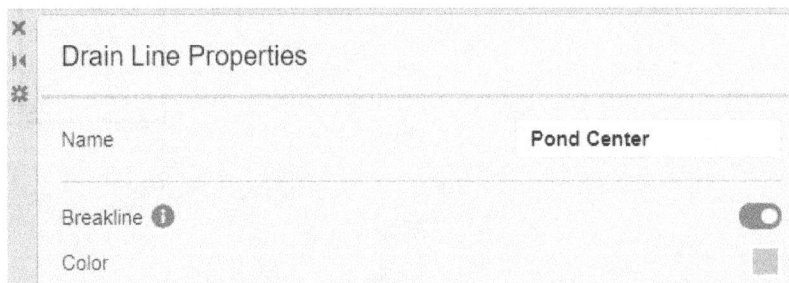

Figure 6–59

Remember that the underlying structure of Civil 3D surfaces are triangles. When a drain line is created, it will divide the triangles and form a crease in the surface to accommodate the drainage.

Low Points

The **Low Point** Grading Object is just that, a low point in the surface. As with drain lines, it reshapes the underlying triangles of the surface to control drainage, as shown in Figure 6–60.

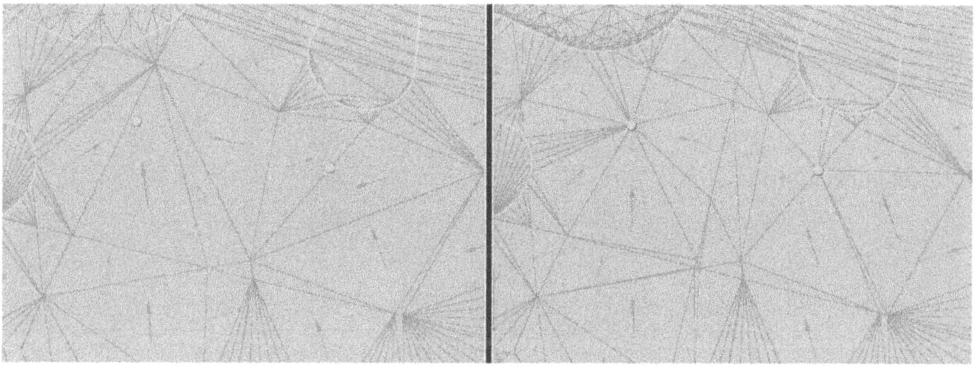

Figure 6–60

Its slopes are also controlled by the Optimization Options.The point you pick must be a Civil 3D COGO or Survey point, it cannot be an AutoCAD point.

The dialog box of the **Low Point** Grading Object is quite simple, as shown in Figure 6–61. It asks for a name (for easier identification), and its color. Another option is to enable the Diamond Shape, which will cause the contours surrounding the low point to form a diamond shape pattern. With this option, you can give the angle of rotation for the contours.

Without this option, the contours will form circular patterns, concentric to the low point.

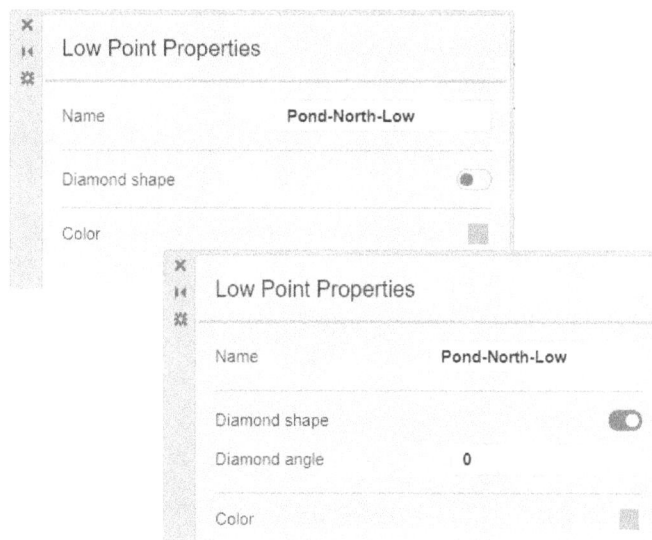

Figure 6–61

Ridge Line

The **Ridge Line** Grading Object can be considered the opposite of a drain line in that it represents a linear elevation that directs drainage away from its placement. As with drain lines, it reshapes the underlying triangles of the surface to control drainage, as shown in Figure 6–62.

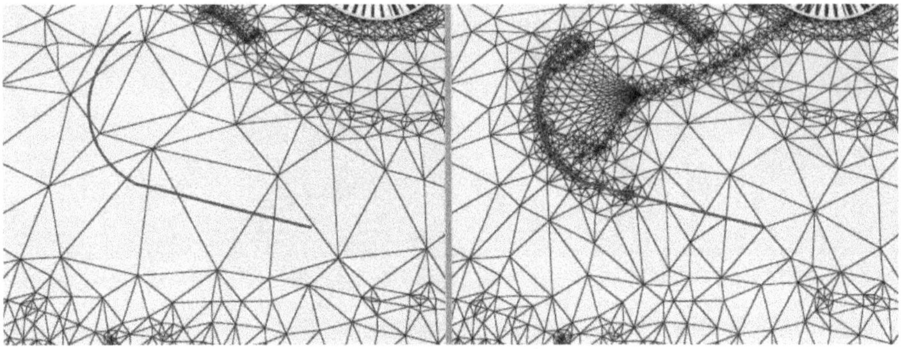

Figure 6–62

> 💡 **Hint: Visualizing tips**
>
> In order to understand how the drain lines, ridge lines and low points work, it is recommended that you turn on the **TIN Topology** and the **Hydrology** in the *Visual* toolbar, as shown in Figure 6–63.

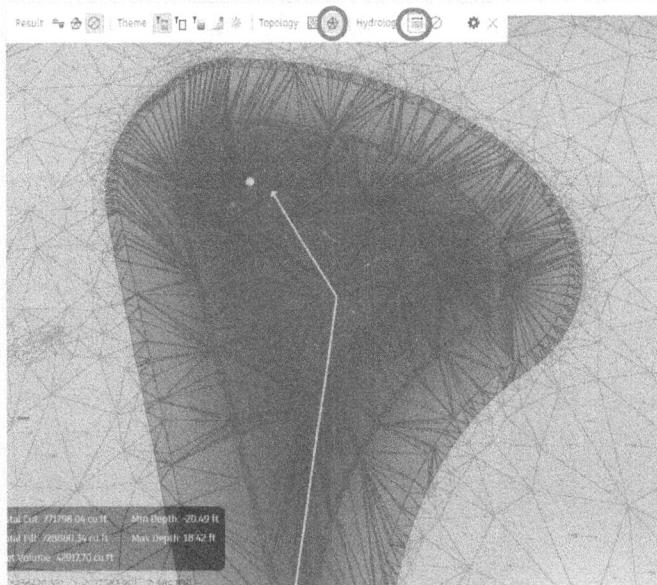

Figure 6–63

Bend Line

The **Bend Line** Grading Object can be compared to the **Drain Line** Grading Object previously discussed. Both are defined by linear objects and force the triangulation of the TIN surface to align with the defined line, as shown in Figure 6–64. It is defined by an AutoCAD line, or polyline, or a Civil 3D feature line. The linear object can contain curves and/or vertices, and can even be a closed object. Any elevations assigned to the linear object will be ignored by the Grading Optimization.

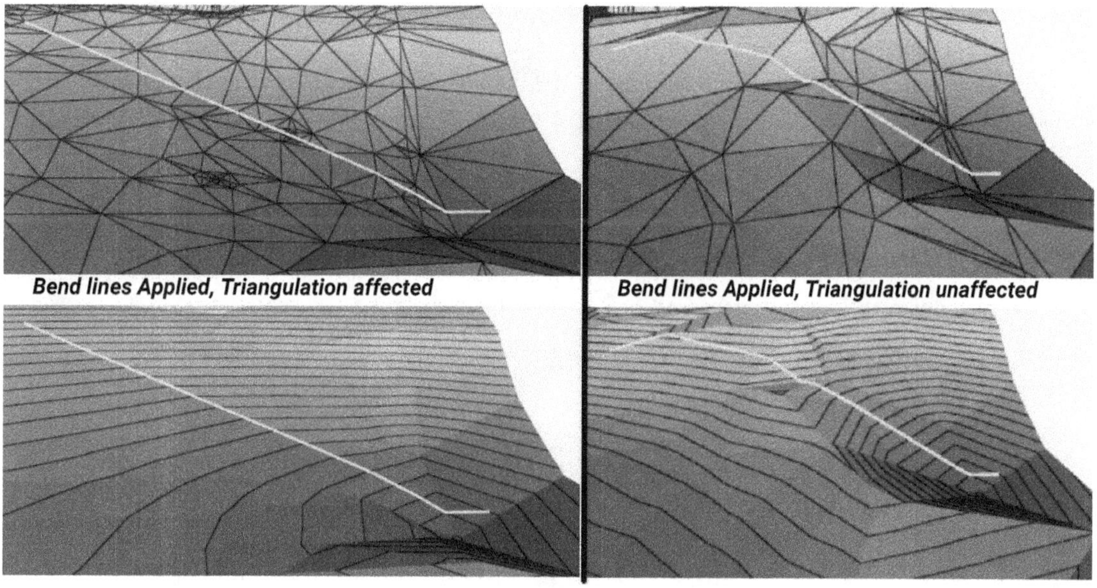

Bend lines Applied, Triangulation affected

Bend lines Applied, Triangulation unaffected

Figure 6–64

The Bend Line object eases the smoothing of the surface on the TIN triangles that touch or intersect the Bend Line. During the optimization, any slope constraints are disregarded for all surface triangles that contact the bend line. The Drain Line acts similarly, except that the drain line will slope downward from the start point to the endpoint of the line, whereas the Bend Line is simply "draped" on the surface like a rope, as shown in Figure 6–64.

Bend Line objects in Grading Optimization can be used to control where slope constraints should be relaxed to help reduce unnecessary earthwork.

Bounded Points

Bounded points are constrained points. You can assign an elevation range for such points to adhere to, thus in effect creating a vertical line within that elevation range to which the optimized surface must pass at that given point, as shown in Figure 6–65. Bounded Point properties can only be assigned to Civil 3D Point objects, not AutoCAD points.

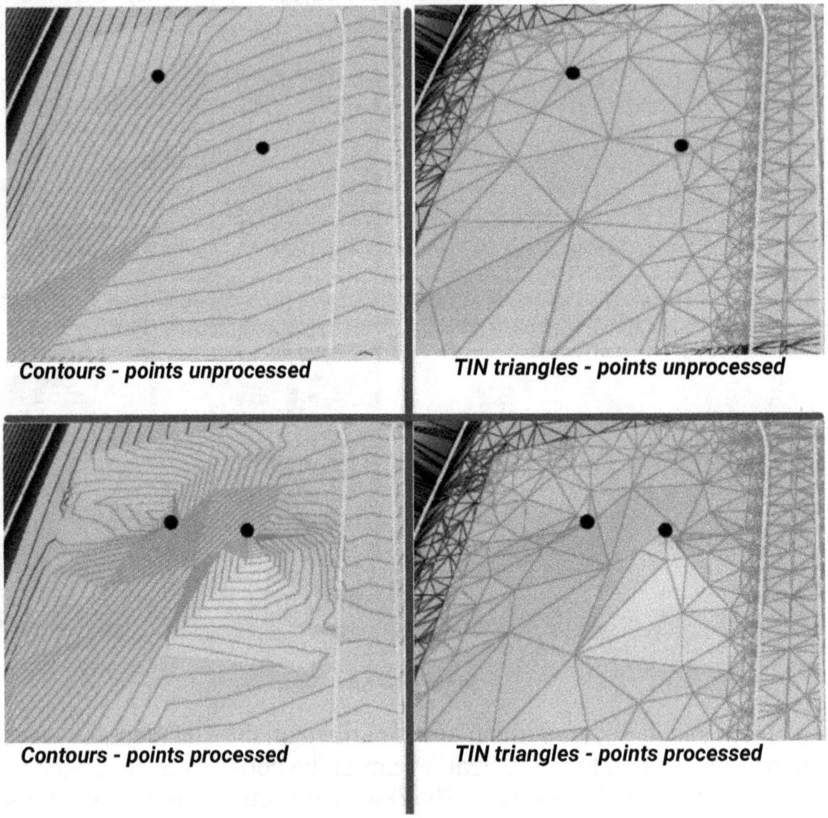

Contours - points unprocessed

TIN triangles - points unprocessed

Contours - points processed

TIN triangles - points processed

Figure 6–65

It is a nice tool for certain situations:

- Fixed points of neighboring parcels to be met, such as points of access, swale centerlines.
- Points representing variable elevations for certain zones.

How To: Create a Bounded Point Grading Object

1. Create Civil 3D COGO or Survey points for the desired Bounded Points.

2. Description and elevations are not important for Grading Optimization, however it is recommended you attribute proper descriptions for the points and assign no elevation to them.

3. It is recommended that you create a special point group for all points created for the Grading Optimization.

4. In the *Grading Optimization* Tool Palette, select the ⁙ Bounded Point (Bounded Point). You can either select all the points first and then select the **Bounded Point** Grading Object in the palette, or vice versa. When done, the *Bounded Point Properties* dialog box displays, as shown in Figure 6–66.

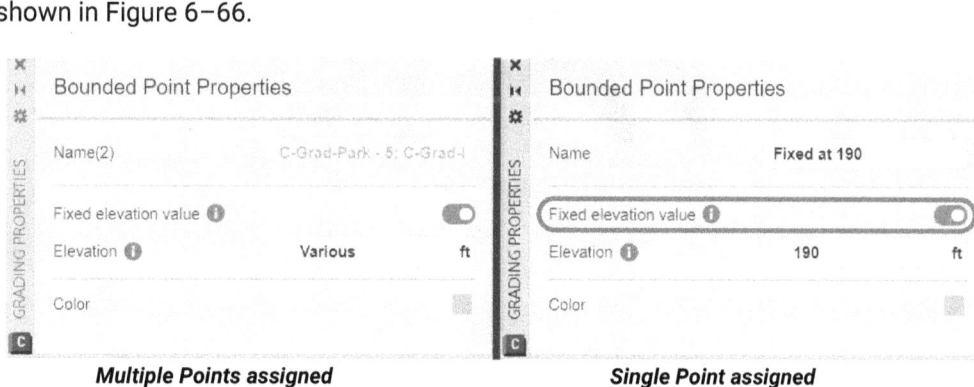

Bounded Point Properties		Bounded Point Properties	
Name(2)	C-Grad-Park - 5; C-Grad-I	Name	Fixed at 190
Fixed elevation value ⓘ	⬤	Fixed elevation value ⓘ	⬤
Elevation ⓘ	Various ft	Elevation ⓘ	190 ft
Color	▨	Color	▨
Multiple Points assigned		***Single Point assigned***	

Figure 6–66

5. If multiple points are assigned at once, you cannot change the names, but you can assign the same elevations (or elevation ranges) to all points.

6. Bounded points should be named for easier identification.

7. If an elevation range is required, toggle **off** the **Fixed elevation value** and the dialog box will expand to allow entry of *Min elevation* and *Max elevation*, as shown in Figure 6–67.

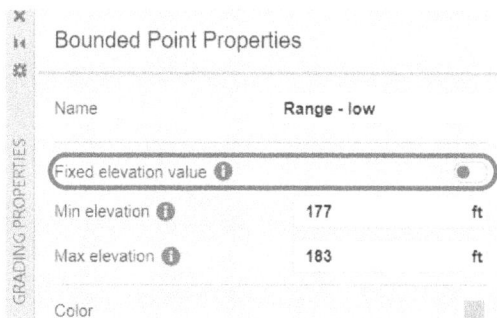

Bounded Point Properties	
Name	Range - low
Fixed elevation value ⓘ	⬤
Min elevation ⓘ	177 ft
Max elevation ⓘ	183 ft
Color	▨

Figure 6–67

💡 Hint: Limit use of Bounded Points

Do not use too many Bounded Points in your project, they can bog down the processing of Grading Optimization. Furthermore, **Bounded Point** properties can readily conflict with the *Max* and *Min* drain slope in **Optimization Options**, as shown in Figure 6–68. So use them sparingly!

Figure 6–68

6.8 Convergence Plots

The Grading Optimization process is very visual and enticing to watch. There is a process bar at the bottom of the screen, and a running total for cuts and fills are displayed as well, as shown in Figure 6-69.

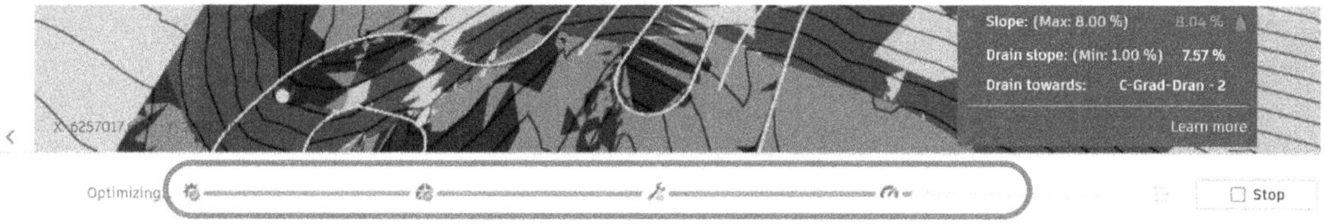

Figure 6-69

However, there is another way of studying the process of the Grading Optimization, focusing more on data and figures. Click on the *Optimization* tab on the upper left corner to switch from the *Object Browser* tab to the *Optimization* tab, as shown in Figure 6-70.

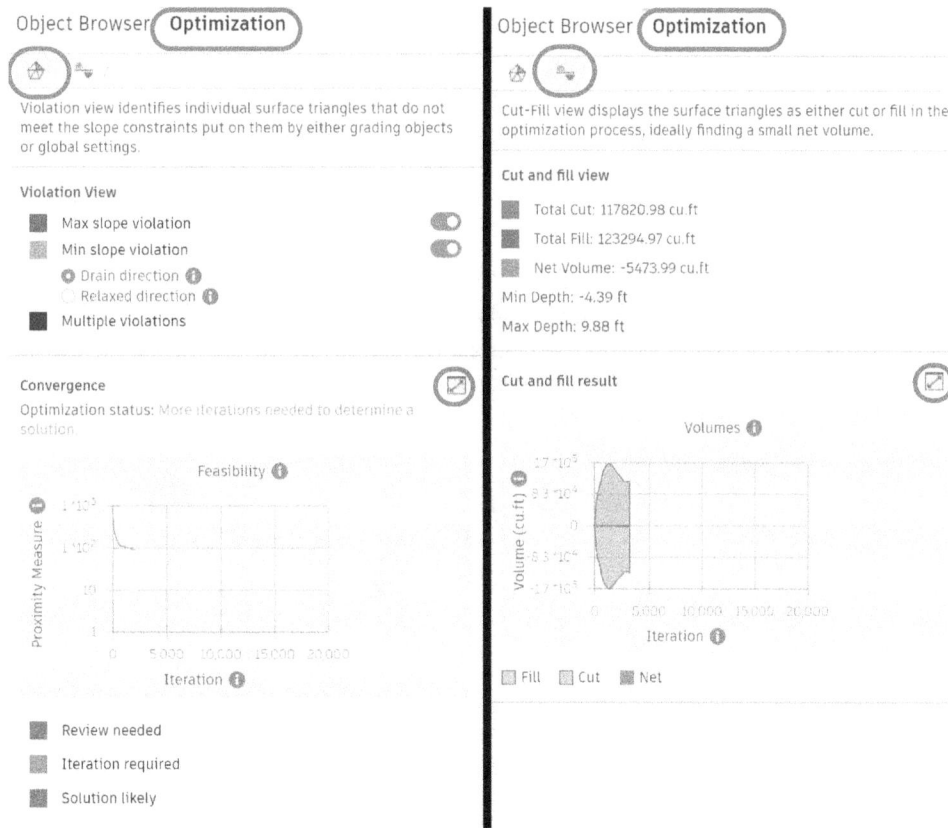

Figure 6-70

You can also open these as modeless, floating panel by clicking on ⬈ (Convergence Plots). This opens the *Convergence Plots* window, as shown in Figure 6–71.

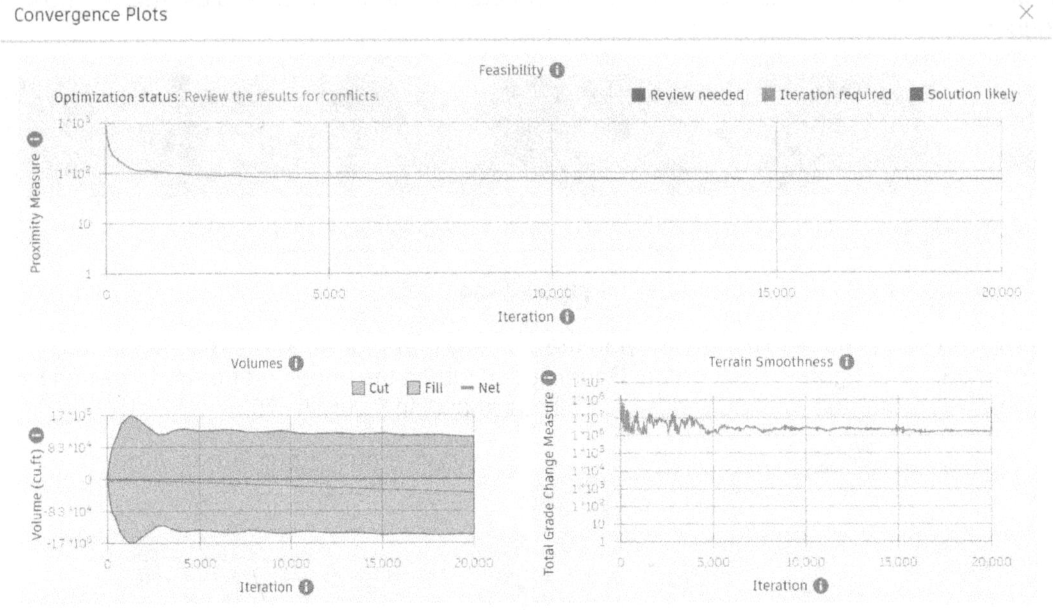

Figure 6–71

The window offers three graphs with important analytical data:

- **Feasibility**: Plots the fluctuations of the Optimization with regard to feasibility of the Grading Object and the Optimization options (constraints). Left Axis: **Proximity Measure,** which compares the current Optimization solution to the Optimization constraints and thresholds.

💡 **Hint: Convergence Plot**

If the overall direction of the graph is flat or heading upwards, then there are unsolvable conflicts and the grading objectives cannot be met. At this point, it is recommended to stop the Optimization process and check the setting and constraints to find and resolve the conflict.

- **Volumes**: Provides a running report as per the resulting earthwork at the point of the iteration. If you hover over the graph, a tooltip with tabular totals displays, as shown in Figure 6−72. Left Axis: **Volume**, which is the earthwork volume. The 0 axis is the net line, the upper portion represents the Cut volumes in red, the lower portion represents the Fill volumes in green. The resulting daylight line is plotted as an orange line.

Cut Volume: 2487.346 cu.ft
Fill Volume: -1886.227 cu.ft
Net Volume: 601.119 cu.ft

Figure 6−72

- **Terrain Smoothness:** The *Total Grade Change Measure* (Left Axis) is calculated comparing the grade change between adjacent surface triangles. The lower and smoother the graph is, the smoother the resulting surface is.

The three graphs all have **Iterations** as the bottom axis, which is graduated into the amount of iterations set in the *Optimization Options* dialog box.

Practice 6e
Grading Optimization: Parking Lot

Practice Objectives

- Create Curb Grading Objects for the parking lot.
- Create Drain Lines and Low points within the parking lot.
- Establish a retaining wall to ease the grading restrictions.
- Use the Grading Object to grade the parking lot.
- Create a Parking Lot surface.

The Grading Optimization process can be time consuming, and you may require additional time to complete the process than the estimated 30 minutes. In this practice, you will use the outline of a sketched parking lot layout to create and grade a parking lot with proper drainage. You will create a variety of Civil 3D COGO points to act as bounded points for the Grading Optimization process.

A new surface named **Pond-N** surface has been referenced via data-shortcuts into this drawing. It has been renamed to **Park-N-EG** and has been assigned the **ASC-Contours 2' and 10' (Background)** style.

Task 1: Create the Grading Limit and the Curb Grading Objects.

1. Open **PARK-GO-A.dwg** from the *C:\Civil 3D Grading\Working\Parking Lot* folder.

   Note: *The drawings for this practice are in a different folder than the previous practices in this chapter.*

2. In the *View* tab>*Named Views* panel, select the **Parking-North** view.

3. Study the Figure 6–73 to understand the various linear Grading Objects that need to be created.

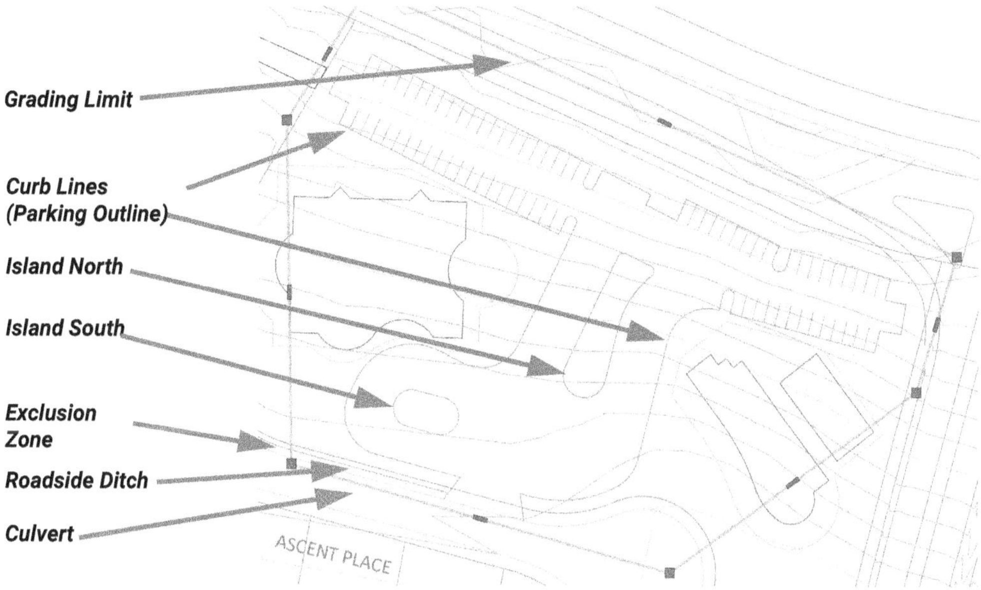

Figure 6–73

4. In the *Analyze* tab>*Grading Optimization* panel, click ▦ (Grading Objects Tools), to open up the Tool Palette with all the grading objects.

5. A yellow polyline representing the grading limit is already created, as shown in Figure 6–73.

6. In the Tool Palette, select **Grading Limit**, as shown in Figure 6–74. Select the proper polyline and press <Enter>.

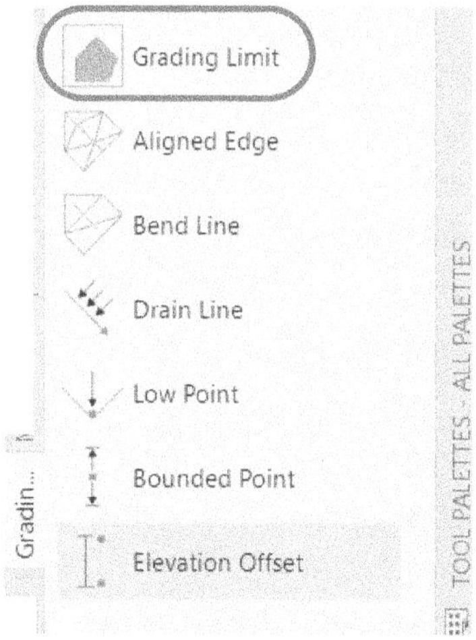

Figure 6–74

7. In the *Grading Limit Properties* dialog box, complete the following, as shown in Figure 6-75:

   * *Name:* **Parking Limit**
   * **Customize slope constraints**: toggle **on**
   * *Max Slope:* **8%**
   * *Min drain slope:* **1%**
   * **Exclusive Drainage**: toggle **on**
   * Leave the rest as defaults.

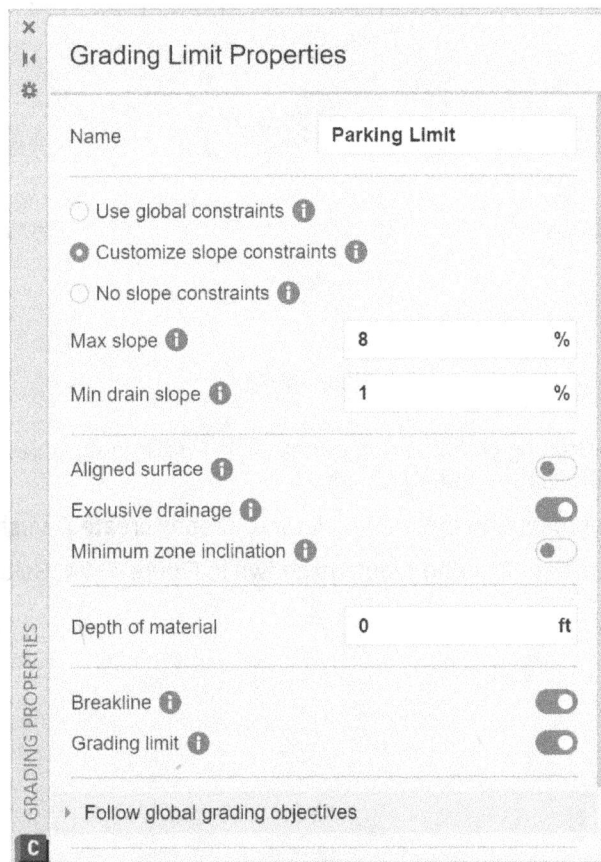

Grading Limit Properties

Name	**Parking Limit**

- Use global constraints ⓘ
- ● Customize slope constraints ⓘ
- No slope constraints ⓘ

Max slope ⓘ	8	%
Min drain slope ⓘ	1	%

Aligned surface ⓘ	◯
Exclusive drainage ⓘ	●◯
Minimum zone inclination ⓘ	◯

Depth of material	0	ft

Breakline ⓘ	●◯
Grading limit ⓘ	●◯

▸ Follow global grading objectives

GRADING PROPERTIES

Figure 6-75

8. Type **NCOPY**.., to copy plines labeled as Island North, Island South and Parking Outline. *For more information on the **NCOPY** command, refer to the AutoCAD Help documentation.*

9. For the three plines, there is no displacement, so they remain in the same place. Therefore, simply press the <Enter> key twice to accept the <Displacement> default and the (0,0,0) default.

10. Change the layer of the three plines to the C-Grad-Park layer.

11. Select the **Island South** pline and open the *AutoCAD Properties* palette. In the Geometry, *Current Vertex* section, click in the *Value* section and notice the **X** on the corresponding pline. Use the up arrow to go to Vertex #2 and notice the **X** in the drawing, as shown in Figure 6–76. Note that the pline is moving counter clockwise (CCW).

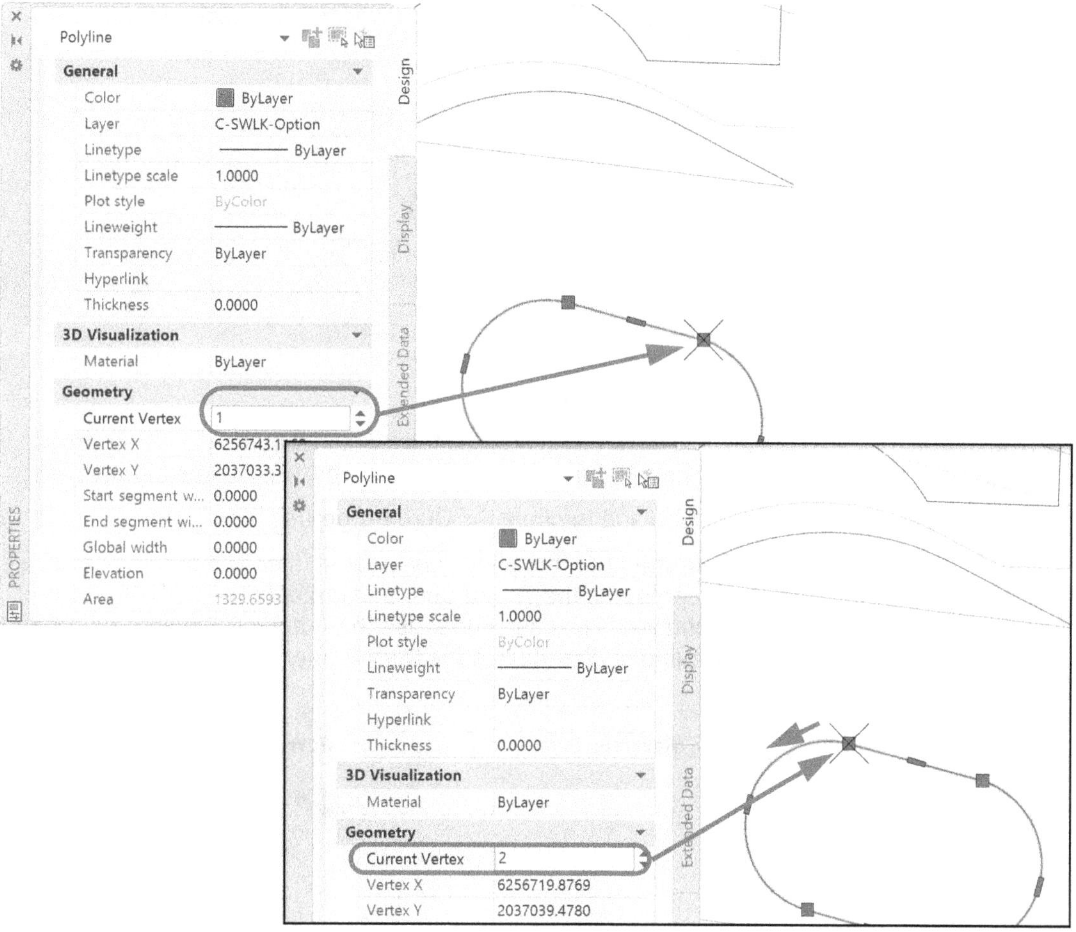

Figure 6–76

12. Repeat the same procedure on the other pline labeled Island North. You will note that this pline is also going in a CCW direction.

13. For the Parking Outline pline, we will use the Curb Grading Object properties to determine its direction. Press <Esc> to clear the selection and to close the dialog boxes.

14. In the Tool Palette, select **Curb**, as shown in Figure 6–77. Select the three polylines you copied from the base file and press <Enter>.

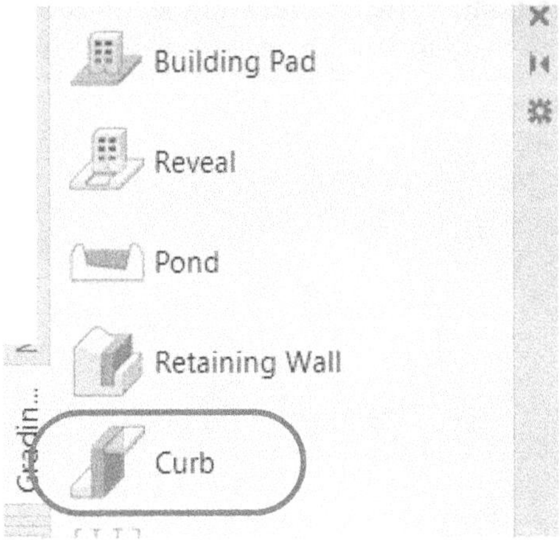

Figure 6–77

15. Notice that the three plines now have a two-shaded thick outline. In the Curb Properties dialog box, you could change the parameters for all three curbs, but not the names.

16. Press <Esc> to clear the selection and to close the Curb Properties dialog box.

17. Select the Island South curb. Remember this pline was created in a Counter-clockwise direction, therefore the pline represents the *Top of Curb* and projects the curb object downward. This needs to be changed. You can either use the AutoCAD **Reverse** command to reverse the direction of the pline or change it in the Curb Properties dialog box, as shown in Figure 6–78.

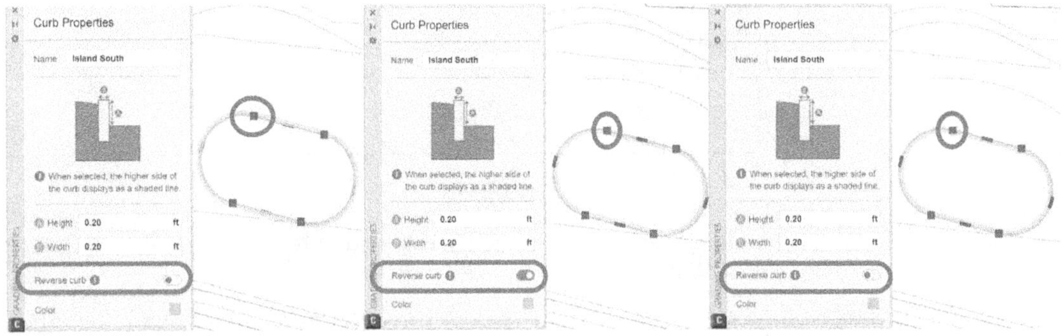

Original Clockwise Curb   *Reversed Curb*   *Reversed Pline*

Figure 6–78

18. In the Curb Properties dialog box, enter **Island-South** for the *Name*. Toggle **on** the **Reverse curb** to change the *Top of Curb*.

19. Press <Esc> to clear the selection and to close the Curb Properties dialog box.

20. Select the **Island North curb**. Remember this pline was also created in a Clockwise direction.

21. Type in **Reverse** at the command line to launch the AutoCAD command. Since the pline was already selected, its direction is reversed, as shown on the command line, which states "Object direction has been reversed."

22. In the *Curb Properties* dialog box, enter **Island-North** for the *Name*.

23. Press <Esc> to clear the selection and to close the *Curb Properties* dialog box.

24. Select the *Parking Outline* curb and name it **Parking Outline** in the *Curb Properties* dialog box. (Its direction is already proper - no need to change it).

25. Press <Esc> to clear the selection and to close the *Curb Properties* dialog box.

Task 2: Create bounded point Grading Objects (Optional).

In this task, you create four bounded points where the elevations of the entrances to the parking lot and the pond access roads must be maintained.

> *Note: In the next two tasks, Civil 3D COGO points and point groups will be created and modified. If you are not comfortable with these Civil 3D features, you can skip the next two tasks and go to Task 4. These Civil 3D features are covered in the Civil 3D Essentials course by Ascent.*

1. In the *Home* tab>*Create Gound Data* panel, expand *Points>Miscellaneous* and select **Manual** to create four Civil 3D points as follows (shown in Figure 6–79).

   - **Point 101, Entrance-West.** Elev:**None**
   - **Point 102, Entrance-East.** Elev:**None**
   - **Point 103, Pond-Access-South.** Elev:**None**
   - **Point 104, Pond-Access-North.** Elev:**None**

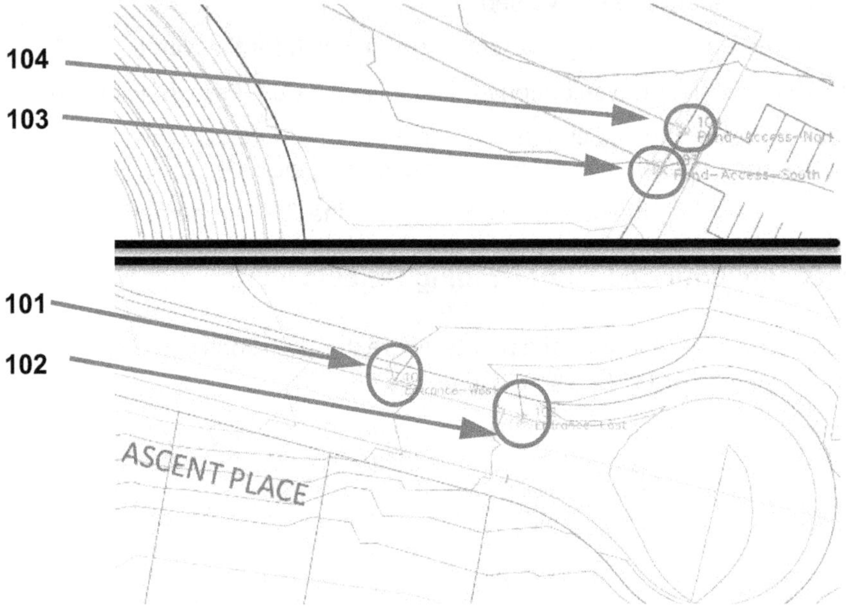

Figure 6–79

2. Create a point group of these 4 points (Point Number 101-104), as follows:

   - *Name*: **Bounded Points**
   - *Point Style:* **ASC-Grad-Opt**
   - *Point Label Style*: **ASC-Point# and Description**
   - *Include> With numbers matching*: **100-110**

3. In the Tool Palette, select **Bounded Point**. Select the four points and press <Enter>.

4. Select **Park-N-EG** as the EG surface.

5. Press <Esc> to clear the selection and to close the *Bounded Points Properties* dialog box.

6. Select each point in turn and give it a proper name and verify the elevation:

   * **Point 101, Entrance-West.** Elev: **187.73**
   * **Point 102, Entrance-East.** Elev: **188.06**
   * **Point 103, Pond-Access-South.** Elev: **170.73**
   * **Point 104, Pond-Access-North.** Elev: **169.05**

7. Save the drawing.

Task 3: Parking Drainage.

In this task, you create drainage lines and low points Grading Objects.

1. Open **PARK-GO-B.dwg** from the *C:\Civil 3D Grading\Working\Parking Lot* folder. This contains more linework and points which will be assigned to various Grading Objects. Do not continue from the previous drawing.

2. Study Figure 6–80 for the location of the drain lines and low points to be added to control the parking drainage.

3. Set layer to **C-Grad-Dran** for the drainage lines.

4. Draw AutoCAD plines for the drainage lines as shown in Figure 6–80. The start point of the pline will become the high point of the drainage line. (Hint, use the "mid between 2 points" in the right-click menu to position it properly).

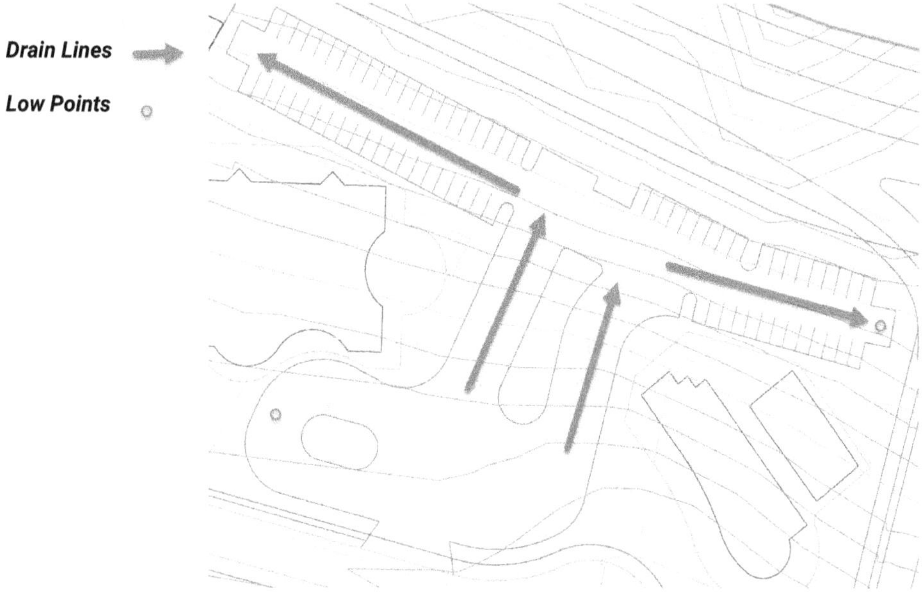

Figure 6–80

5. In the Tool Palette, select **Drain Line**. Select the four polylines you just drew and press <Enter>.

6. In the *Drain Line Properties* dialog box, review all the information. You will keep everything as the defaults.

   Note: You will leave the defaults to save time. However, in practice, it is recommended to name the Grading Objects with logical names for easier identification

7. Press <Esc> to clear the selection and to close the *Drain Line Properties* dialog box.

8. On the *Home* tab>*Create Gound Data* panel, expand *Points>Miscellaneous* and select **Manual** to create two Civil 3D points for low points as follows (shown in Figure 6–80).

   • **Point 50, Park-Low-W.** Elev:**None**

   • **Point 51, Park-Low-E.** Elev:**None**

9. Create a point group of these 2 points, as follows:

   • *Name*: **Park-Drainage**

   • *Point Style*: **ASC-Grad-Opt**

   • *Point Label Style*: **ASC-Point# and Description**

   • *Include: **With numbers matching**: 50-60*

10. In the Tool Palette, select **Low Point**. Select the two points you just created and press <Enter>.

11. In the *Low Point Properties* dialog box, review all the information. You will keep everything as the defaults.

12. Press <Esc> to clear the selection and to close the *Low Point Properties* dialog box.

13. Save the drawing.

Task 4: Drainage control at entrance (Optional).

In this task, you will create a swale and grading representing a culvert at the parking lot entrance. You will create another Grading Object in the *Grading Object* Tool Palette for the culvert, based on the Curb Grading Object. Depending on time constraints, this task can be skipped.

1. Continue working on the same drawing from the previous task. If you did not complete the previous task, you can open **PARK-GO-C.dwg** from the *C:\Civil 3D Grading\Working\Parking Lot* folder.

2. Study the figure Figure 6–81. The aligned edges on either side of the parking lot entrance represent the top-of-swale and the drain lines represent the toe-of-swale.

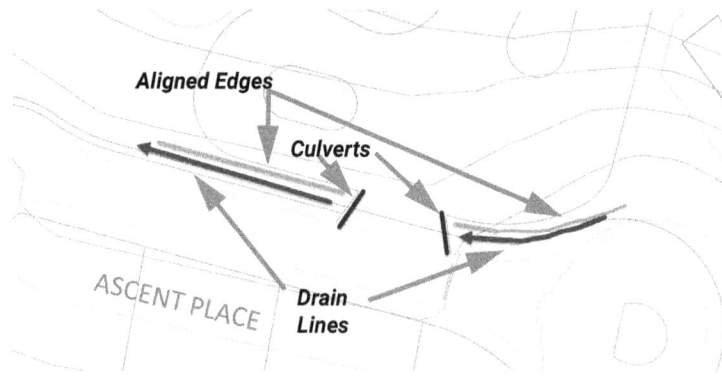

Figure 6-81

3. In the Tool Palette, select **Aligned Edge**. Select the two polylines representing the top-of-swale and press <Enter>.

4. In the *Aligned Edge Properties* dialog box, review all the information. You will keep all the default values as such and make no changes.

5. Press <Esc> to clear the selection and to close the *Aligned Edge Properties* dialog box.

6. In the Tool Palette, select **Drain Line**. Select the two polylines representing the toe-of-swale and press <Enter>.

7. In the *Drain Line Properties* dialog box, review all the information. You will keep all the default values as such and make no changes.

8. Press <Esc> to clear the selection and to close the *Drain Line Properties* dialog box.

9. In the Tool Palette, select **Curb**, as shown in Figure 6-82. In the right-click menu, select **Copy**.

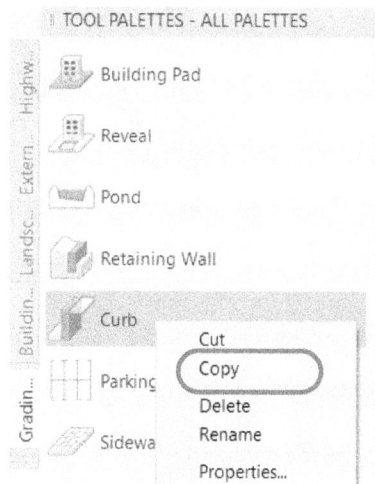

Figure 6-82

10. In the right-click menu, select **Paste** to create another Curb tool in the palette. It gets positioned at the bottom of the palette.

11. Right-click on the new *Curb* tool and select **Properties**. In the *Tool Properties* dialog box, set the following, as shown in Figure 6–83:

   - *Name:* **Culvert**
   - *Description:* **Culvert Wings**
   - *Width:* **0.2 ft**
   - *Height:* **2.2 ft**
   - *Reverse Curb Direction:* **No**
   - Click **OK**.

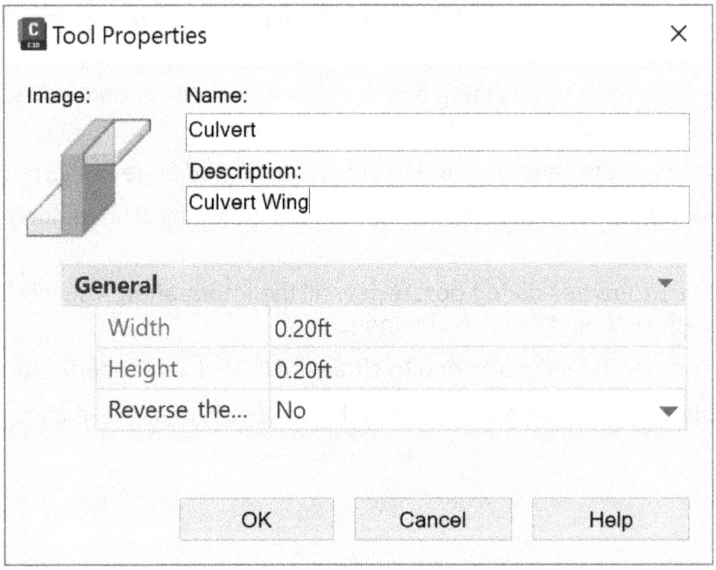

Figure 6–83

12. In the Tool palette, select the new **Culvert tool**. Select the two polylines representing the culvert edges and press <Enter>.

   Note: *The dialog box is still labeled as* **Curb** *rather than* **Culvert***.*

13. In the *Curb Properties* dialog box, review all the information, as shown in Figure 6–84. You will keep everything as the defaults, except naming them **Culvert-E** and **Culvert-W** respectively.

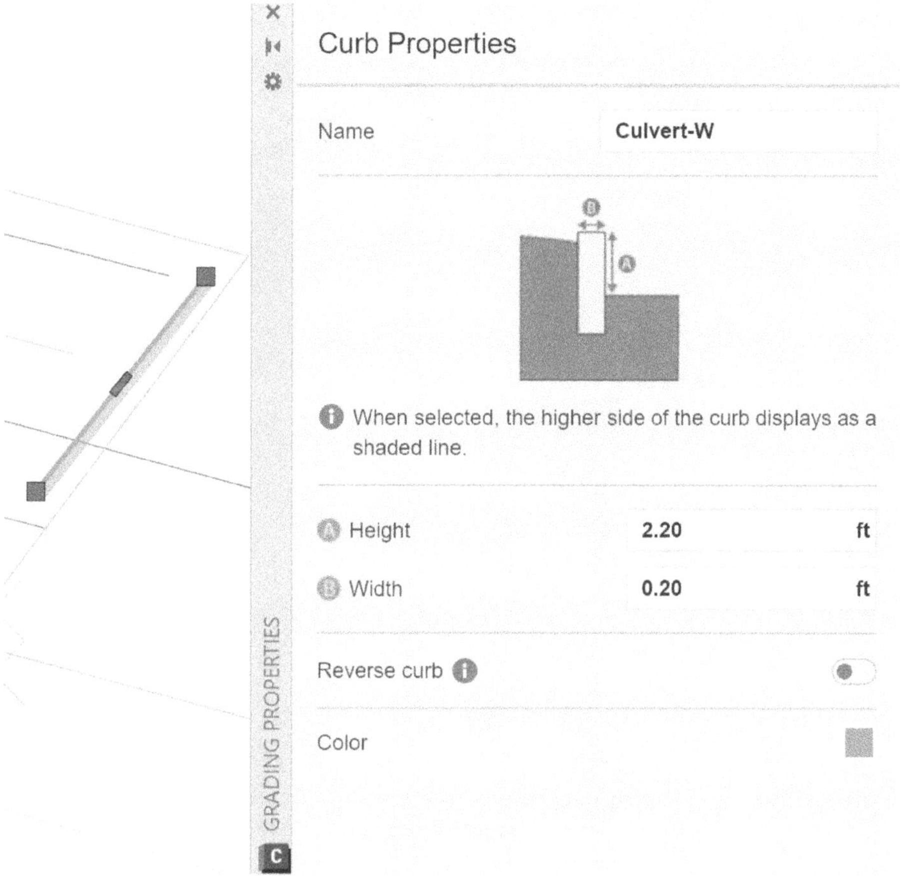

Figure 6–84

14. Press <Esc> to clear the selection and to close the *Curb Properties* dialog box.

15. Select the retaining wall to the north of the site, as shown in Figure 6−85. This is already defined as a **Retaining Wall** Grading Object through regular means to save some time and effort.

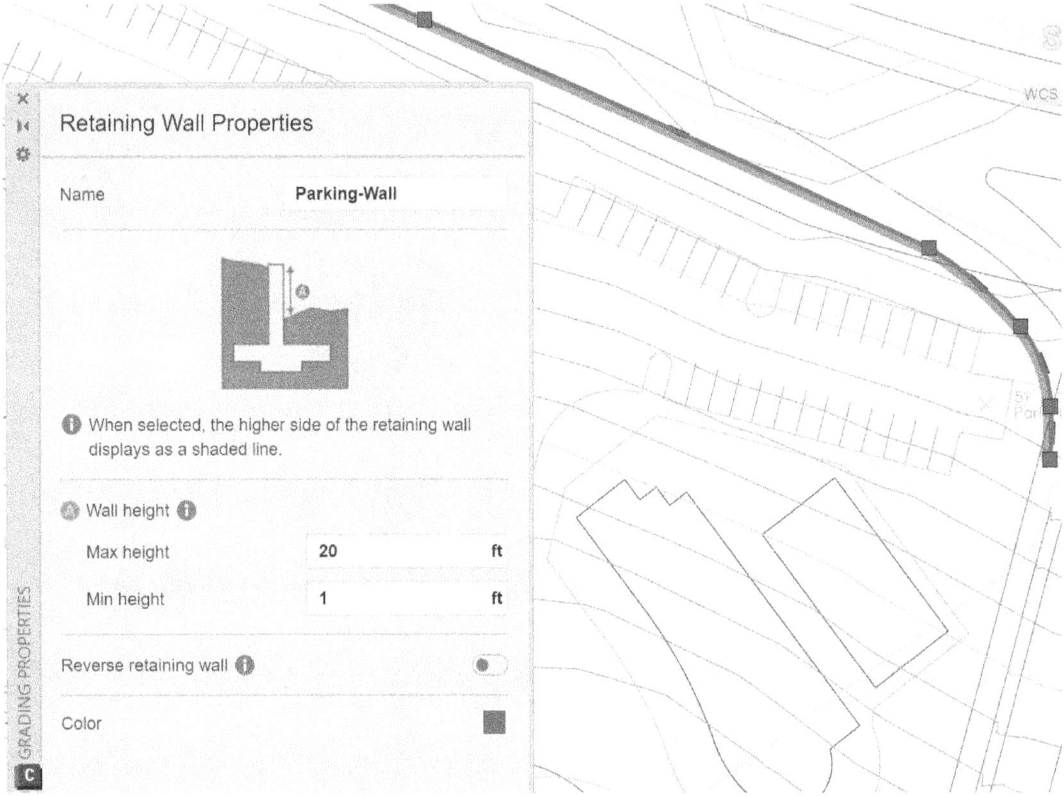

Figure 6−85

16. Save the drawing.

Task 5: Launch the Grading Optimization program.

1. Continue working on the same drawing from the previous task. If you did not complete the previous task, you can open **PARK-GO-D.dwg** from the *C:\Civil 3D Grading\Working\Parking Lot* folder.

2. In the *Analyze* tab>*Grading Optimization* panel, click (Optimize).

3. Select **Park-N-EG** as the EG surface.

4. It may take a while for the Grading Optimization program to launch. Once it launches, the grading objects will be listed in the *Grading Optimization* browser on the left side. Navigate around the model so that your vantage point is similar to that shown in Figure 6–86.

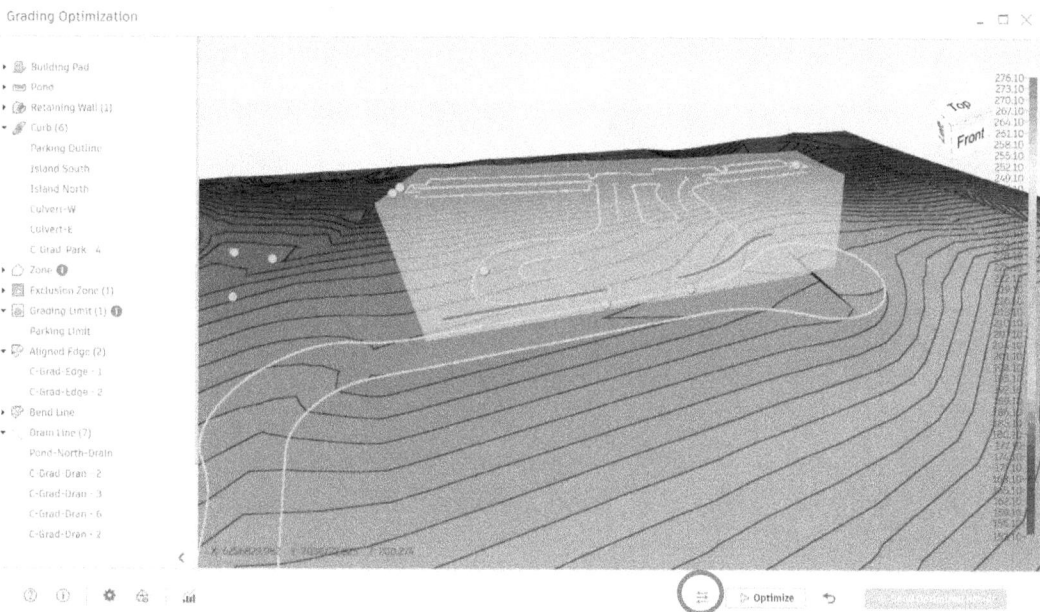

Figure 6–86

5. At the bottom of the *Grading Optimization* window, click ⇌ (Optimization Options), as shown in Figure 6–86.

6. In the *Optimization Options* window, verify that the following is set, as shown in Figure 6–87, and modify if necessary:

- *Min drain slope*: **0**
- *Max slope*: **33**
- *Cut and fill constraint*: **None**
- *Iteration*: **20000**
- *Balance cut and fill*: **15**
- *Minimize earthworks*: **20**
- *Smooth surface*: **90**

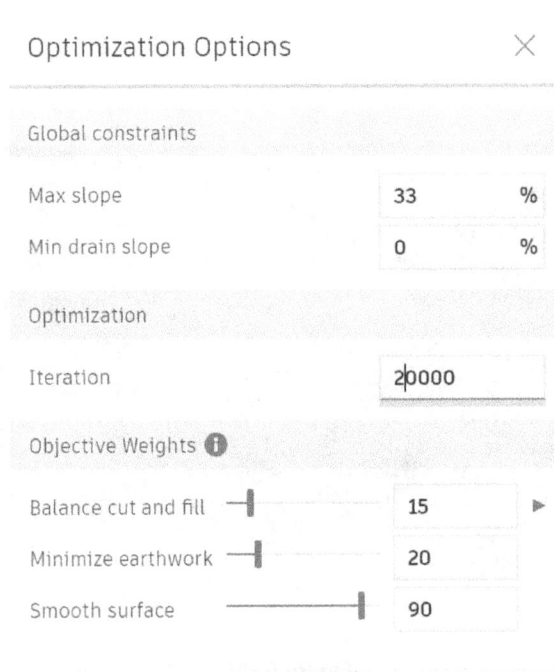

Figure 6–87

7. Close the *Optimization Options* window by clicking on the **X** in the top-right corner.

8. At the bottom of the *Grading Optimization* window, click **Optimize**.

9. There are three warnings, two about steep slopes which are due to an existing wall embedded in the surface to the north of the site, and one about grading objects (for the pond) lying outside the grading limit, as shown in Figure 6–88. These can be dismissed by clicking the **Close** button.

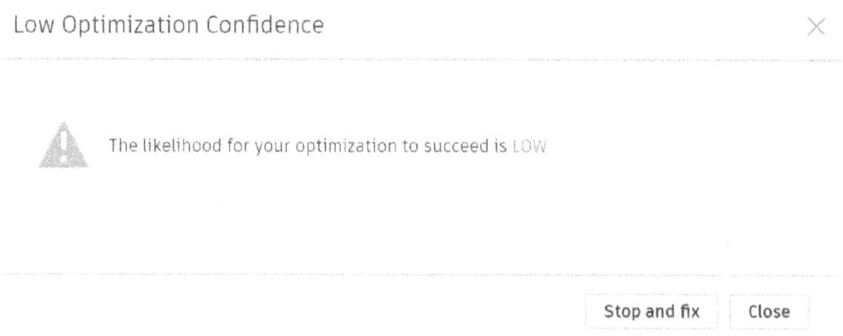

Figure 6–88

10. The drainage lines on either side of the central island are superfluous and cause too much grading, as shown in Figure 6–89. These will need to be disabled.

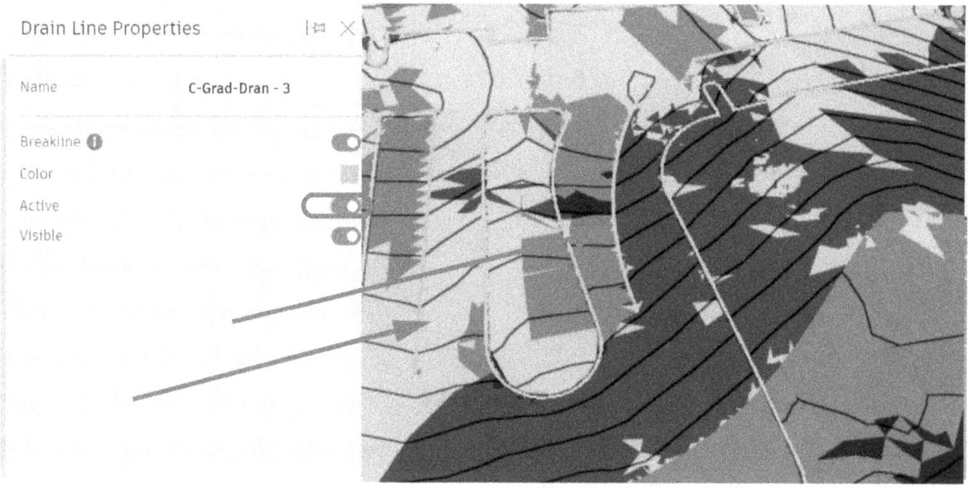

Figure 6–89

11. At the bottom of the *Grading Optimization* window, click **Stop**.

12. In the graphics area, select one of the drainage lines. In the *Drainage Line Properties* dialog box, toggle **off** the **Active** option. If you wish, you can also toggle **off** the **Visible** option.

13. Do the same for the second superfluous drainage line.

14. At the bottom of the *Grading Optimization* window, click **Optimize** again. This will reset and restart the optimization process.

*Note: It can take some time to go through these iterations. If you do not have enough time, you can click Stop and review the results in the **PARK-GO-Z-Complete.dwg** drawing.*

15. Once the optimization is complete, click **Update Drawing**. This will send the optimization results back to the Civil 3D drawing where Grading Optimization was originally launched from, and update the drawing.

16. In the Civil 3D drawing, in the *Save Optimization Result* window, ensure that the **Create new surface** option is selected to create a new surface. Enter **Park-N** for the *Name* and click on

    ▤ (Surface Style) to select a surface *Style*. In the *Surface Styles* dialog box, select **ASC-Contours 2' and 10' (Design)** and click **Finish** to close the *Surface Style selection* box, as shown in Figure 6−90.

Figure 6−90

17. In the *Save Optimization Results* window, click **Feature Lines**. Set the *Name Prefix* to **Park-**. Set the *Feature Line Style* to **ASC-Basic**.

18. In the *Save Optimization Results* window, click **Points**. Select the **Create new point group** option to create a new point group and name it **Park-N**. Leave the *Point Style* as is.

19. Click **Finish**. Civil 3D will create a new surface, site, and point group for the information retrieved from the Grading Optimizer.

    Note: It can take some time to create a new surface, point group, and site.

20. The *Events* panel of the Panorama may open to warn of duplicate points which are ignored.

    Dismiss the Event Viewer by clicking on the green check mark ☑.

21. Save and close the drawing.

Task 6: *Optional*: More Parking Lot practices for the Southern Site.

1. Open the **South-Park-GO-A.dwg** the *C:\Civil 3D Grading\Working\Parking Lot* folder.

2. Repeat the same process for the southern section to create parking lots.

3. There are two suggested parking lot layouts that you may choose to use, as shown in Figure 6–91.

Figure 6–91

4. You can either create a new surface and site and point group for the pond (suggested name: **Park-S**), or create one overall design surface for the southern site (suggested name: **Southern Site**), along with a new point group and site for the feature lines.

5. Save the drawing.

End of practice

Chapter Review Questions

1. Which of the following items must you have before you can create a corridor model? (Select all that apply.)

    a. Assembly

    b. Grading object

    c. Survey database

    d. Alignment or feature line

2. Where would you go to create a surface representing the finished ground of a corridor model?

    a. Toolspace, *Prospector* tab>*Surfaces* collection

    b. *Home* tab>*Create Ground Data* panel

    c. *Home* tab>*Create Design* panel

    d. Corridor Properties

3. How do you create a polyline from a corridor line efficiently?

    a. Manually draw it over the corridor.

    b. Use the Pline Follower.

    c. Extract a feature line from the corridor and explode it.

    d. Export the corridor to LandXML.

4. Can corridor bowties be restored once they are cleared?

    a. Only by undoing the Clear Bowtie command.

    b. No, it will corrupt the corridor.

    c. By using the Restore Bowtie command.

    d. By unchecking the cleared bowtie in Corridor Properties.

5. What direction do curbs need to be created in to represent the Top of Curb?

   a. Clockwise

   b. Counter Clockwise

   c. It doesn't matter

6. **Retaining Walls** are simply a subset of Curb Grading objects?

   a. True

   b. False

7. **Bounded Points** can be assigned an elevation.

   a. True, the default is the EG surface elevation but can be overridden.

   b. False, it is bounded by the EG surface.

8. What are **Bend Lines** used for? (Select all that apply) Bend Line objects in Grading Optimization can be used to:

   a. Serve as a top of swale

   b. Control where slope constraints need to be relaxed

   c. Assign different elevations at either end of the line

   d. Help reduce unnecessary earthwork

Command Summary

Button	Command	Location
	Assembly Properties	• **Contextual Ribbon:** *Assembly* tab> *Modify Assembly* panel • **Command Prompt:** editassemblyproperties
	Clear Bowties	• **Contextual Ribbon:** *Corridor* tab> *Corridor Tools* panel • **Command Prompt:** ClearCorridorBowTie
	Corridor Properties	• **Contextual Ribbon:** *Corridor* tab> *Modify Corridor* panel • **Command Prompt:** editcorridorproperties
	Create Corridor	• **Ribbon:** *Home* tab>*Create Design* panel • **Command Prompt:** createcorridor
	Create Feature Line	• **Ribbon:** *Home* tab>*Create Design* panel, expand *Feature Line* drop-down list • **Command Prompt:** DrawFeatureLine
	Create Infill	• **Ribbon:** *Home* tab>*Create Design* panel, expand *Grading* drop-down list • **Toolbar:** *Grading Creation Tools* (*contextual*), expand *Create Grading* drop-down list
	Delete Elevation Point	• **Ribbon:** *Feature Line* contextual tab> *Edit Geometry* panel • **Command Prompt:** DeleteElevPoint
	Restore Bowties	• **Contextual Ribbon:** *Corridor* tab> *Corridor Tools* panel • **Command Prompt:** RestoreCorridorBowTie
	Reverse Feature Line	• **Ribbon:** *Feature Line* contextual tab> *Edit Geometry* panel • **Command Prompt:** ReverseFeature
	Tool Palettes	• **Ribbon:** *Home* tab>*Palettes* panel • **Command Prompt:** <Ctrl>+<3>

Pond Design

Grading ponds can be some of the most challenging grading projects. Ponds often require grading individual objects and combining multiple feature lines to create a baseline. Various feature line editing tools and techniques are used when working with complex grading groups.

Learning Objectives

- Create a grading object from another previously created grading object.
- Create stormwater controls.
- Calculate pond staging quantities.
- Understand the different types of ponds.
- Create preliminary Pond, complete with a low point.
- Examine the Grading Object's Violation view.
- Calculate pond staging quantities.
- Add a pathway to service the pond's outfall.
- Create an interim design surface containing the conceptual pond.

7.1 Pond Design

Ponds used for irrigation, decorative features, or wild-life reserves are relatively easy to design and are handy when seeking to balance out the cut / fill materials on a site.

However, when ponds become part of the Hydrology model to use for detention or retention purposes, the storage capabilities of the pond become paramount.

Detention ponds are designed to detain the water flow so it discharges at a controlled rate and volume (ideally to meet the pre-construction typical water flow to adjoining properties). Detention ponds are also referred to as Dry ponds, depending on their design.

Retention ponds retain the water through a variety of means, with no discharge onto neighboring properties, stream or natural water ways. Retention Ponds are also referred to as Wet ponds, depending on their design.

For this dataset, the desired pond profile is shown in Figure 7–1. While this level of detail is too complex for a preliminary design, it does demonstrate a typical pond design.

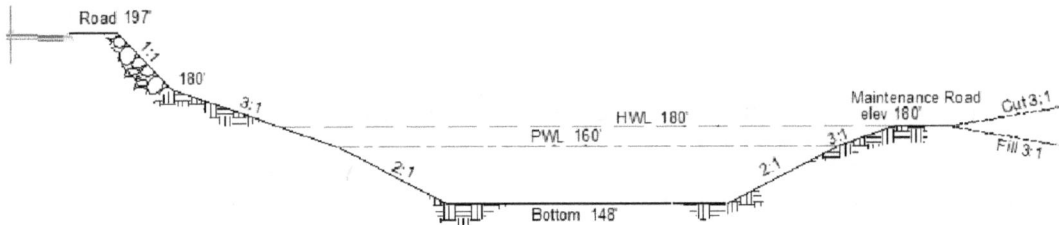

Figure 7–1

Ponds may have multiple basins with flow between the basins controlled by berms or channels. If it is a detention pond, then some type of outfall or weir is designed to control the drainage of the pond.

Calculations can be done within the Civil 3D software for *staged storage*, which show the storage capacity for the pond at various depth levels of the pond.

7.2 Feature Line Review

There are times when you cannot create a simple grading object. For example, the design criteria required for the pond cross-section shown in Figure 7−1 is too complex for just a grading group.

Each side of the pond requires different grading criteria:

- At the **South end** of the pond site is a road which has an elevation of 197'. The road is elevated at an average of 20' above the adjacent parcels. As a result, you use a 1:1 slope from the road so that you can create a pond base elevation of 180'.

- At the **North end** of the pond site, a maintenance access road is designed that is elevated 3' above the Permanent Water Level (PWL).

To grade the pond as shown in the cross-section, you must establish a base feature line that uses a common grading criteria. This involves the following:

- Creating a base feature line to the South (1:1 to elev 180').

- Creating a base feature line to the North (3:1 to elev 164').

- Joining the trimmed east and west feature lines to the north and south control feature lines.

- Grading the pond based on this new combined feature line.

7.3 Creating Complex Grading Groups

An example of grading groups that use one baseline and project specific slopes until they find daylight (called *grading to a surface*) is shown in Figure 7–2.

Figure 7–2

Unfortunately, real world grading projects are not always that simple. That is why the Autodesk® Civil 3D® provides a way to grade one grading object from another within the same site. When reviewing the pond grading parameters for the project, note that you need multiple grades for the interior of the pond, a maintenance road running along part of the pond, and then daylight from the maintenance road, as shown in Figure 7–3.

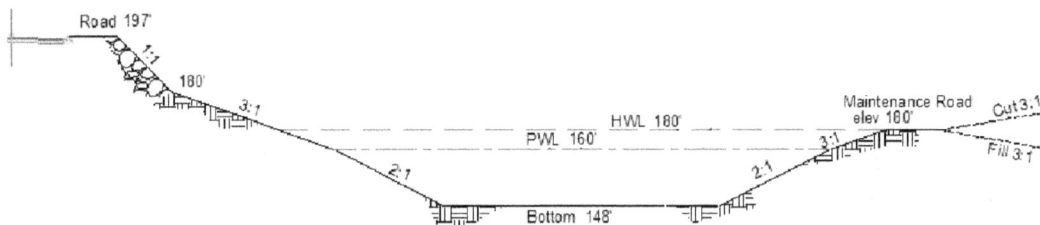

Figure 7–3

It is quite typical that pond grading projects use a minimum of three or four different grading criteria. Four types of grading criteria are available.

Grade to Elevation

When you need to keep a specific grade or slope to a specified elevation, the **Grade to Elevation** criteria is used. This enables you to set the target to be a specific elevation. It is often used in pond grading because the top of the pond needs to be level, as shown in Figure 7–4. Note in the front view that the pond bottom is sloped while the top is level.

Top view

Front view

Figure 7–4

Grade to Relative Elevation

Sometimes you need to project a grade up or down a specific vertical distance. In this case, you would use the **Grade to Relative Elevation** criteria. Note that in the front view, both the top and bottom have the same slope (as shown in Figure 7–5), unlike the Grade to Elevation in which they had differing slopes.

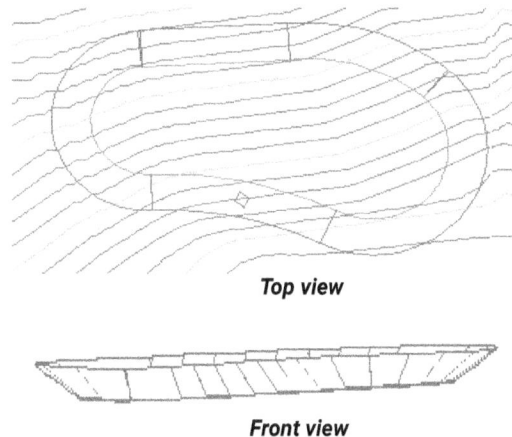

Top view

Front view

Figure 7–5

Grade to Distance

When you need to keep a specific grade or slope for a specified horizontal distance, you can use the **Grade to Distance** criteria. In pond grading, you might need to use this criteria to grade a maintenance road around the perimeter of the pond, as shown in Figure 7–6.

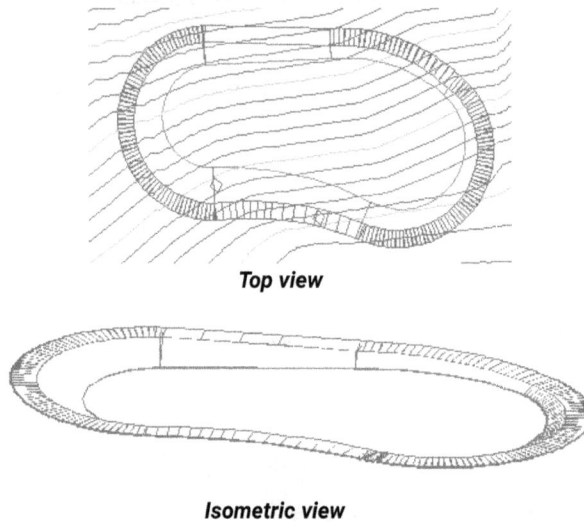

Top view

Isometric view

Figure 7–6

Grade to Surface

When you need to keep a specific slope until the projection finds daylight, you can use the **Grade to Surface** criteria. In pond grading, this is sometimes the first grading object that you create if you are starting from the outside and grading in. The pond in Figure 7–7 was graded from the inside out.

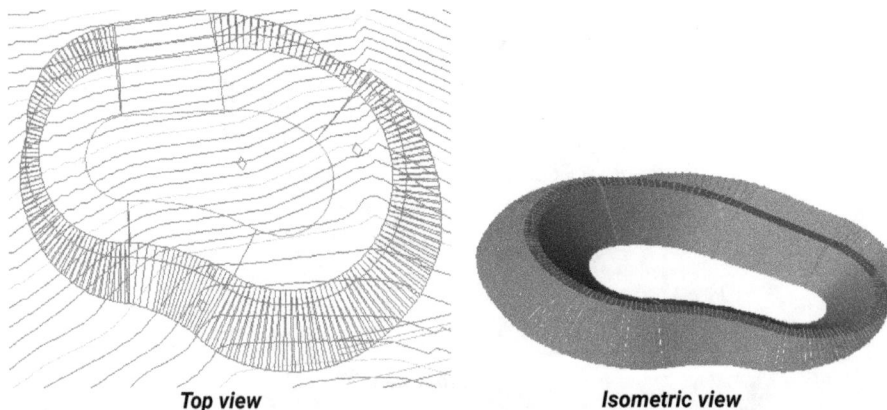

Top view

Isometric view

Figure 7–7

Practice 7a
Pond Grading - Feature Line (Create Base Line)

Practice Objective

*   Create and modify feature lines using grading objects and feature line editing tools.

In this practice, you will establish control feature lines at the north and south ends, as shown in Figure 7−8, and then create the pond outside rim feature line. The existing feature line was created in previous practices in this course.

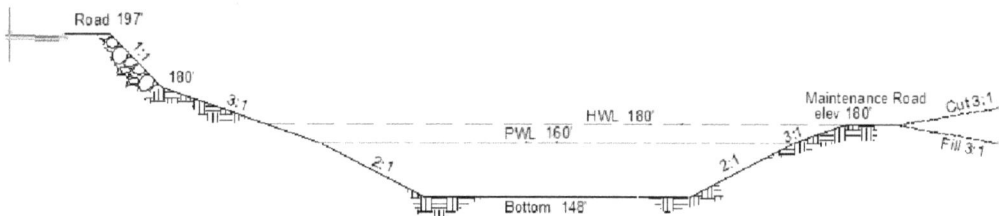

Figure 7−8

Task 1: Establish control feature lines (south end).

1. Open **POND-C.dwg** from the *C:\Civil 3D Grading\Working\Pond* folder.

2. In the *View* tab>*Named Views* panel, select the **Storm Pond** view.

3. In the *Home* tab>*Create Design* panel, expand the *Grading* drop-down list and click

    (Grading Creation Tools).

4. In the *Grading Creation Tools* toolbar, click (Set the Grading Group). Select **Pond Site** for the site, as shown in Figure 7−9, and click **OK**.

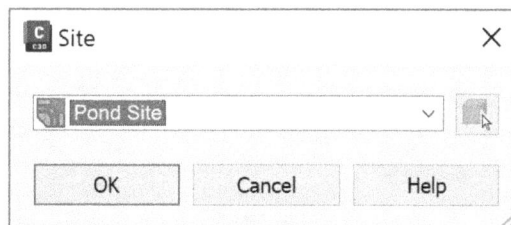

Figure 7−9

Note: You will create a temporary grading object that creates pre-design information.

---

5. In the *Create Grading Group* dialog box, for the *Name*, enter **Temp**, as shown in Figure 7–10. Clear the **Automatic surface creation** option and click **OK**.

Figure 7–10

6. In the *Grading Creation Tools* toolbar, click (Set Surface). In the *Select surface* dialog box, select **Existing-Site**, as shown in Figure 7–11.

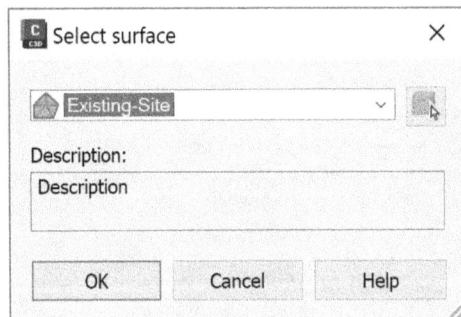

Figure 7–11

7. Establish a feature line with a **1:1** slope to an elevation of **180'** as follows.

8. In the *Grading Creation Tools* toolbar, set the *Criteria* as **Grade to Elevation** and click

   (Create Grading), as shown in Figure 7–12.

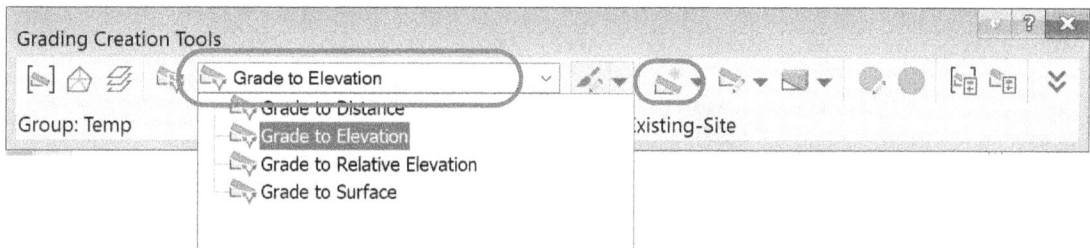

Figure 7–12

9. When prompted to select a feature, select the green pond boundary feature line that defines the perimeter pond site, as shown in Figure 7–13. If prompted to weed the feature line, select **Continue grading without feature line weeding**.

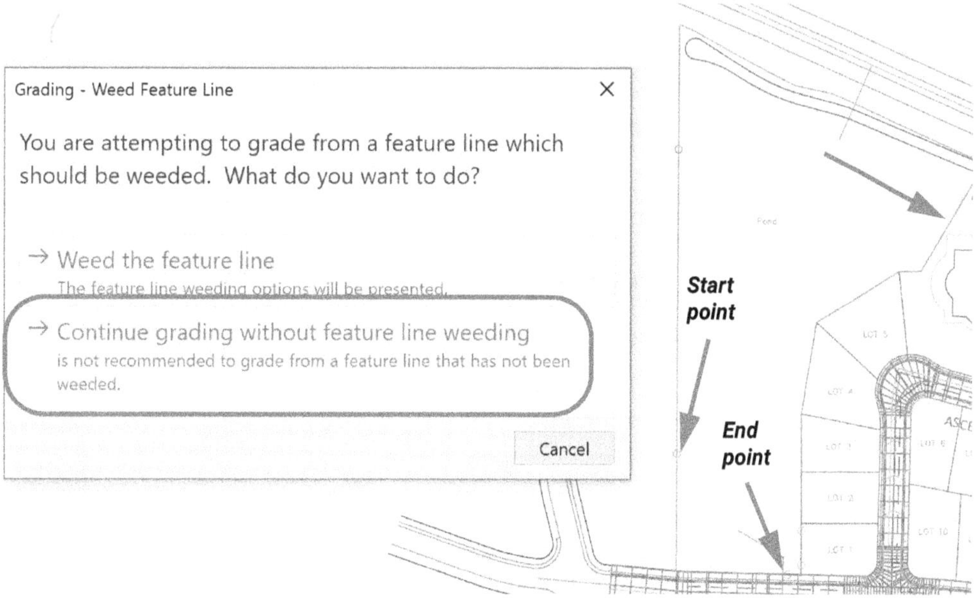

Figure 7–13

10. When prompted for the side to grade, select a point inside of the pond.

11. Select **No** when prompted to *Apply to the entire length*.

12. When prompted for the start point, select the center of the green circle located on the west feature line and press <Enter> to accept <20+09.87'> for the station.

13. When prompted for the end point or length, select the center of the green circle located on the south feature line and press <Enter> to accept <23+77.50'> for the station, as shown in Figure 7–14.

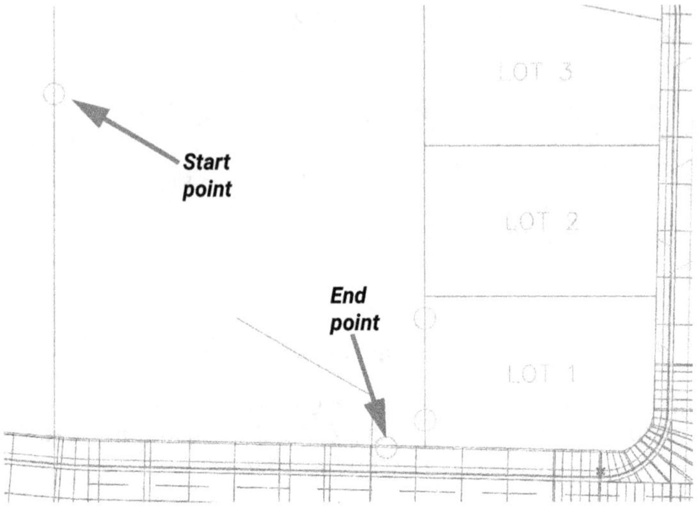

Figure 7–14

14. When prompted for the elevation, type **180** and press <Enter>.

15. When prompted for the cut format, select **Slope**. Type **1** and press <Enter> to indicate a cut slope of 1:1.

16. When prompted for the fill format, select **Slope**. Type **1** and press <Enter> to indicate a fill slope of 1:1.

17. This defines the 1:1 slope from the road, as shown in Figure 7–15.

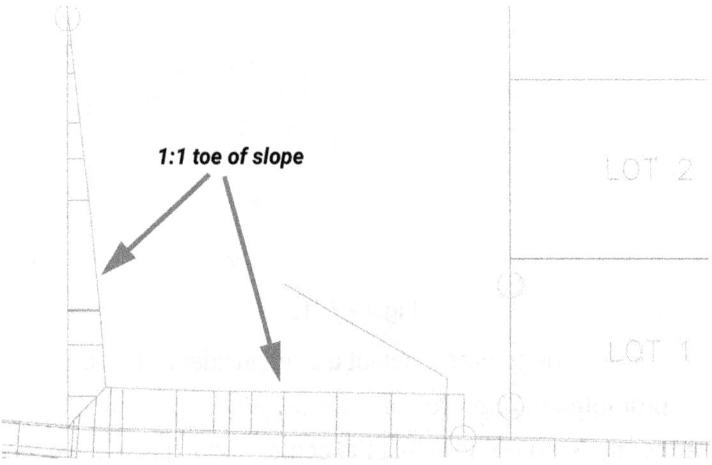

Figure 7–15

Next, you will determine where the 3:1 slope (from the parcels to the east) intersects the 1:1 slope of the pond.

> *Note: At any time, if you accidentally close the **Grading** command, you just need to click*
>
> (Create Grading).

18. When prompted to select a feature line, select the pond boundary feature line, which is the green line that defines the outer perimeter of the pond site.

19. When prompted for the grading side, select a point inside the pond.

20. When prompted for the start point, select the center of the southern-most cyan circle located on the east feature line and press <Enter> to accept <0+14.89'> for the station.

21. When prompted for the endpoint or length, select the center of the northern-most cyan circle located on the east feature line and press <Enter> to accept <0+69.25'> for the station, as shown in Figure 7−16.

Figure 7−16

22. When prompted for the elevation, type **165** and press <Enter>.

23. When prompted for the cut format, select **Slope**. Type **3** and press <Enter> for a cut slope of 3:1.

24. When prompted for the fill format, select **Slope**. Type **3** and press <Enter> for a fill slope of 3:1.

> *Note: This establishes the toe of slope where the 1:1 slope intersects the 3:1 slope.*

25. Press <Esc> to end the feature line selection and select the **X** in the *Grading Creation Tools* toolbar to close the toolbar.

> *Note: To use the toe of slope for further grading, the feature line that represents the toe of slope must be extracted from the grading object.*

26. In Model Space, select the toe of slope feature line, right-click, and select **Move to Site...**, as shown in Figure 7–17.

Figure 7–17

27. In the *Move to Site* dialog box, click **OK** to accept the default site, as shown in Figure 7–18.

Note: It does not matter which site you place it in. By moving the feature line to a different site, the grading object is deleted, leaving just the toe of slope.

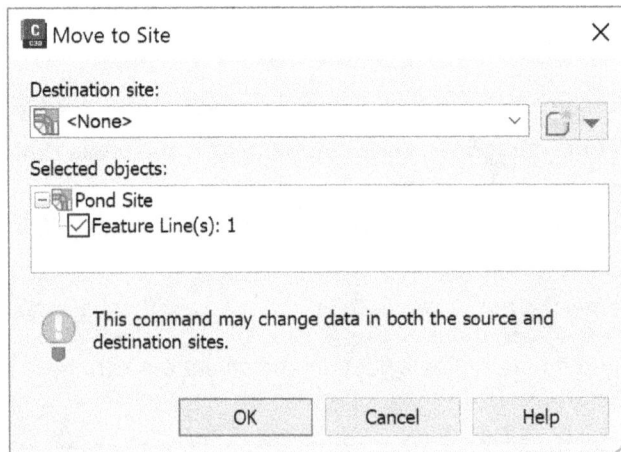

Figure 7–18

28. Select the feature line again and move it back to the **Pond Site**, as shown in Figure 7–19.

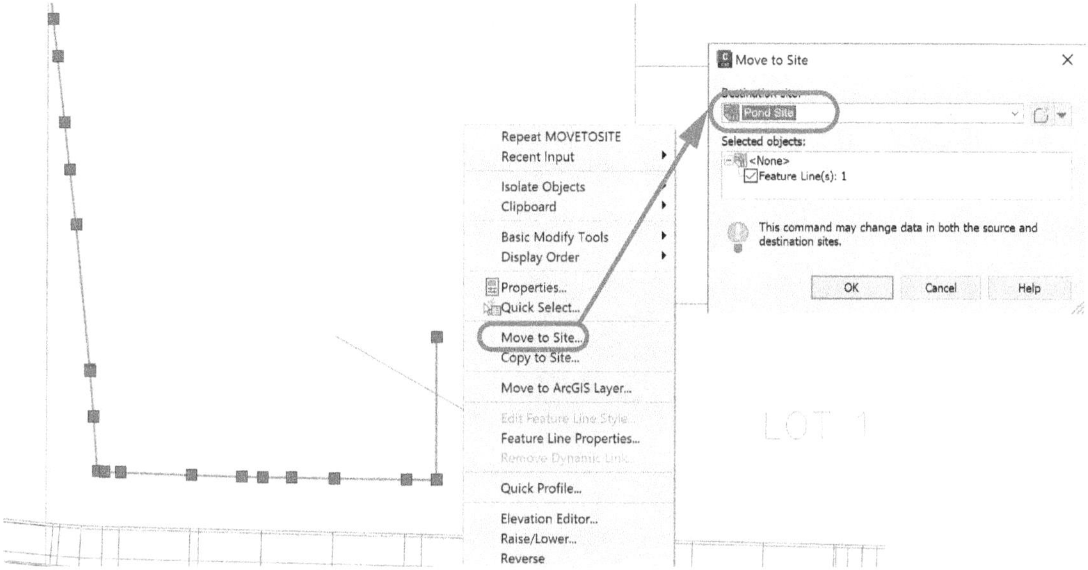

Figure 7–19

29. In Model Space, select the feature line. In the *Feature Line* contextual tab>*Modify* panel, click (Feature Line Properties).

30. In the *Feature Line Properties* dialog box, select the **Name** option and type **Toe of slope** in the *Name* field.

31. Stay in the *Feature Line Properties* dialog box and select the **Style** option. In the *Style* drop-down list, select the **ASC-Basic** style, as shown in Figure 7–20. Click **OK**.

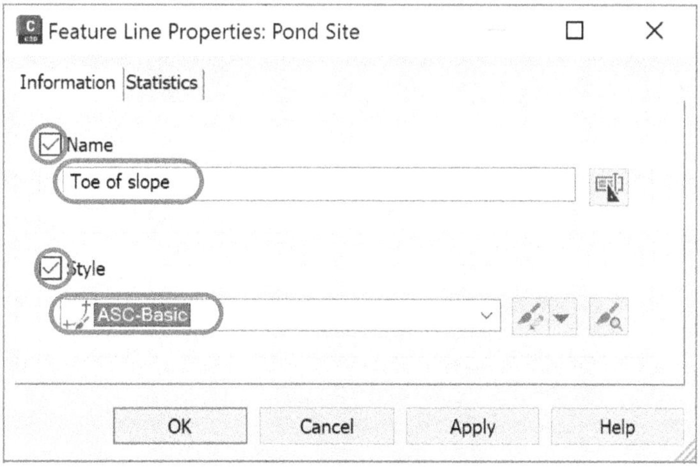

Figure 7–20

32. In Model Space, select the toe of slope feature line. In the *Feature Line* contextual tab>*Modify* panel, click ⬚ (Edit Elevations). In the *Edit Elevations* panel, click ⬤ (Elevation Editor).

In the *Grading Elevation Editor* vista, the elevation shown for station 2+84.74' is 172.50', as shown in Figure 7–21. The correct elevation is 180'.

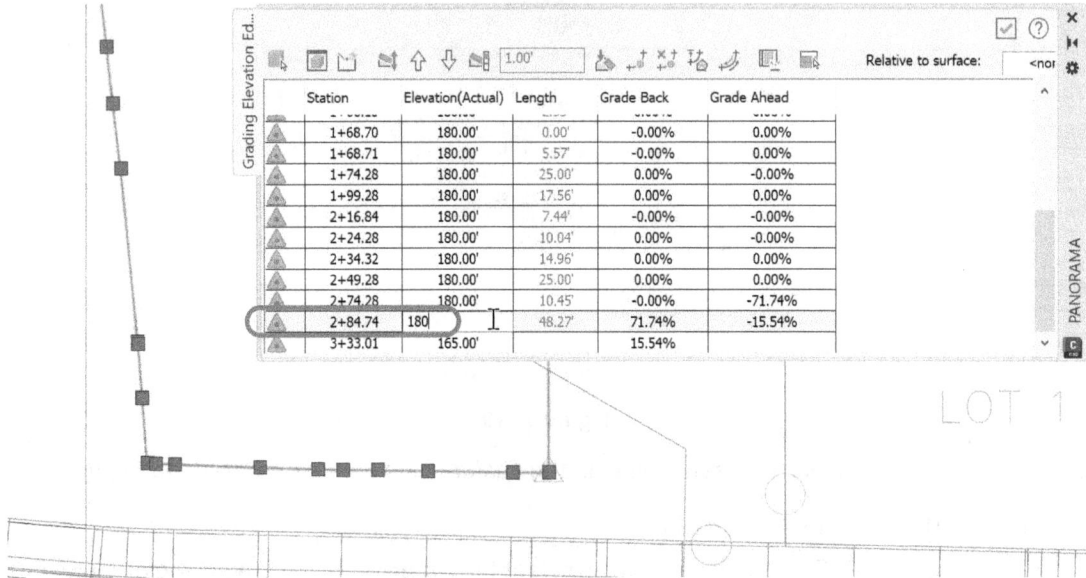

Station	Elevation(Actual)	Length	Grade Back	Grade Ahead
1+68.70	180.00'	0.00'	-0.00%	0.00%
1+68.71	180.00'	5.57'	-0.00%	0.00%
1+74.28	180.00'	25.00'	0.00%	-0.00%
1+99.28	180.00'	17.56'	0.00%	0.00%
2+16.84	180.00'	7.44'	-0.00%	-0.00%
2+24.28	180.00'	10.04'	0.00%	-0.00%
2+34.32	180.00'	14.96'	0.00%	0.00%
2+49.28	180.00'	25.00'	0.00%	0.00%
2+74.28	180.00'	10.45'	-0.00%	-71.74%
2+84.74	180	48.27'	71.74%	-15.54%
3+33.01	165.00'		15.54%	

Figure 7–21

33. Select the elevation field for station 2+84.74, type **180**, and press <Enter>.

34. Click ✔ to close the *Elevation Editor* vista.

35. To join the toe of slope feature line to the east pond boundary, select the toe of slope feature line and select the east feature line to display all of the grips.

36. Select the last grip on the toe of slope feature line and drag it to the intermediate point (as marked by the blue circular grip) on the east feature line, as shown in Figure 7–22.

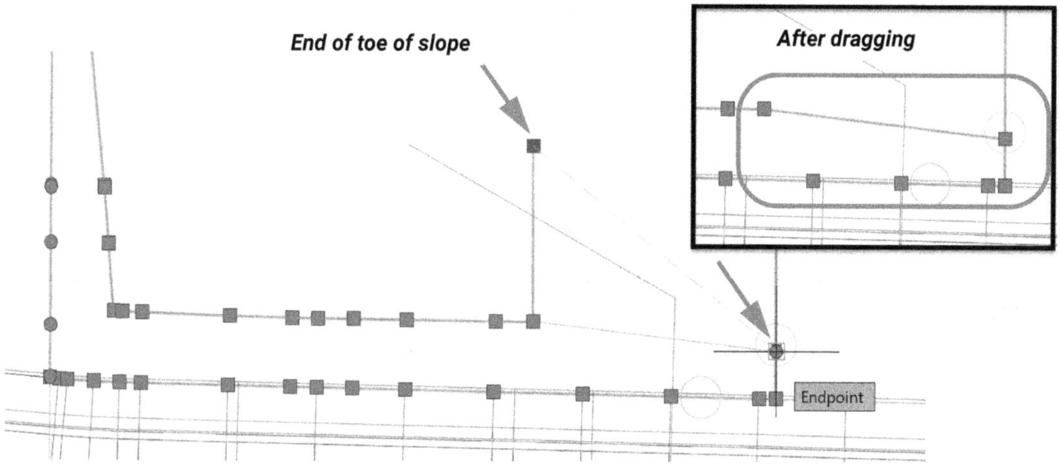

Figure 7–22

37. You have now defined the south pond feature line.

38. Save the drawing.

Task 2: Establish control feature lines (north end).

In this task, you will define the north pond feature line by determining the location of the pond maintenance access road, based on a 3:1 grade from the existing boundary.

1. Continue working with the drawing from the previous task.

2. In the *View* tab>*Named Views* panel, select the **Storm Pond** view.

3. In the *Home* tab>*Create Design* panel, expand the *Grading* drop-down list and click

   (Grading Creation Tools).

4. In the *Grading Creation Tools* dialog box, set the *Grading Group* name to **Temp** (if not already set) and ensure that the grading criteria is set to **Grade to Elevation**.

5. Click (Create Grading), as shown in Figure 7-23, and select the **Pond Boundary** feature line, which is the green line that represents the perimeter of the pond site.

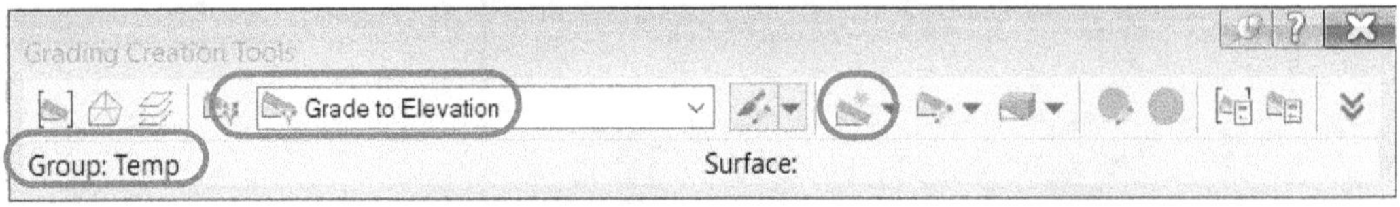

Figure 7-23

6. When prompted to weed the feature line, select **Continue grading without feature line weeding**.

7. When prompted for the side to grade, select a point inside the pond. Select **No** when prompted to *Apply to the entire length*.

8. When prompted for the start point, select the center of the magenta circle located on the northeast corner of the feature line, as shown in Figure 7-24. Press <Enter> to accept <7+88.94'> for the station.

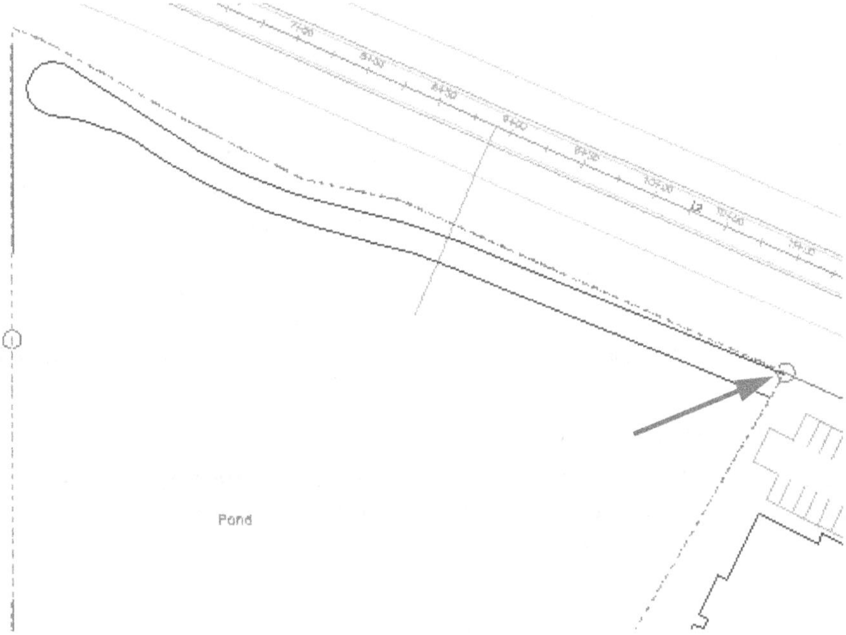

Figure 7-24

9. When prompted for the endpoint or length, select the center of the magenta circle located on the northern part of the west feature line, as shown in Figure 7–25. Press <Enter> to accept <15+31.82'> for the station.

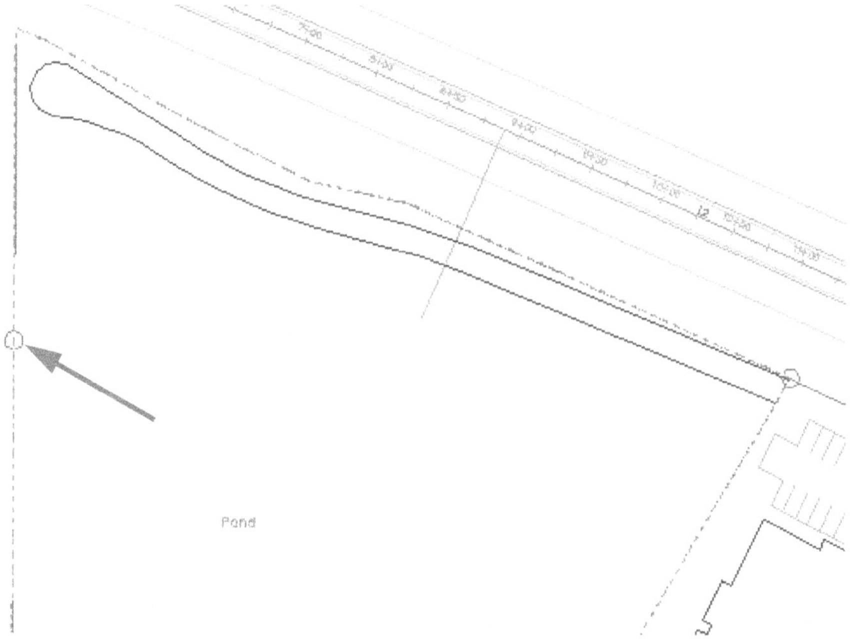

Figure 7–25

10. When prompted for the elevation, type **165.0** and press <Enter>.

11. When prompted for the cut format, select **Slope**. Type **3** and press <Enter> for a cut slope of 3:1.

12. When prompted for the fill format, select **Slope**. Type **3** and press <Enter> for a fill slope of 3:1.

13. Press <Esc> to exit the feature line selection. Select the **X** in the *Grading Creation Tools* toolbar to close the toolbar.

This grading object defines a 3:1 slope from the existing boundary and establishes the approximate location of the maintenance road. To save time, the access road has already been designed, as shown in Figure 7–26.

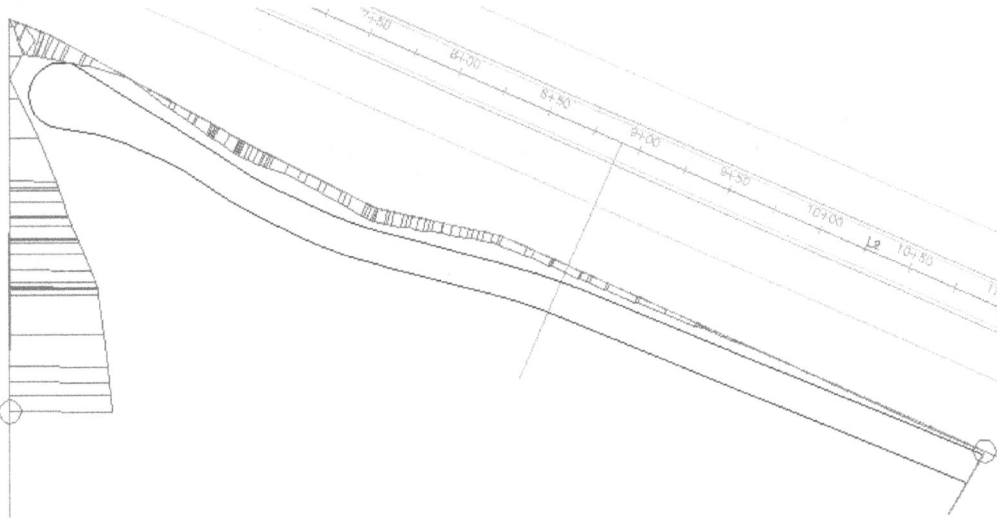

Figure 7–26

Based on the 3:1 cut and fill slope to an elevation of 164.4', you now have a feature line representing the access road. This access road has a maximum side slope of 3:1 to existing ground on the north side of the road. On the south side of the road, you continue to grade based on the design criteria for the pond.

14. You can erase the grading 3:1 maximum slope because it is no longer needed. In Model Space, select the grading object. In the *Grading* contextual tab>*Modify* panel, click

    (Delete Grading).

15. Save the drawing.

Task 3: Create the pond's outside rim feature line.

1. Continue working with the drawing from the previous task.

2. In the *View* tab>*Named Views* panel, select the **Storm Pond** view.

3. In the *Prospector* tab, expand the *Sites>Pond Site* collection. Select **Feature lines** and note the grid view that is usually at the bottom of the pane. This list displays the names of the feature lines, style, layer, and 2D length.

4. Select **Toe of slope** from the list, right-click, and select **Select**, as shown in Figure 7–27.

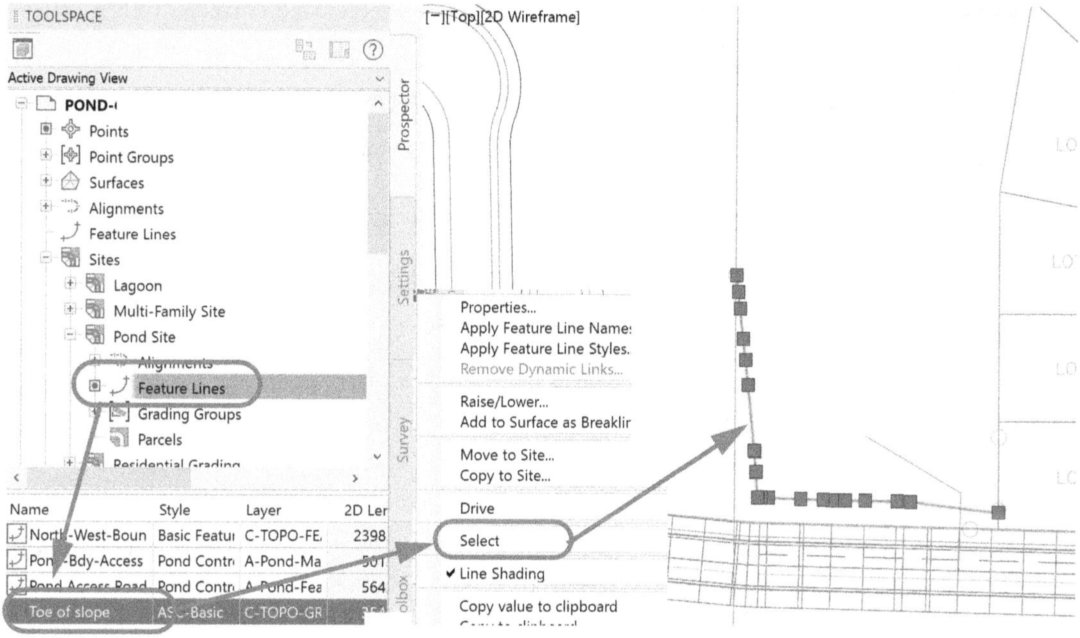

Figure 7–27

5. In the *Feature Line* contextual tab>*Modify* panel, click (Feature Line Properties).

6. In the *Feature Line Properties* dialog box, complete the following, as shown in Figure 7–28:

   - Change the *Name* to **Pond-Bdy-Control**.
   - Set the *Style* to **Pond Control Feature Line**.
   - Click **OK**.

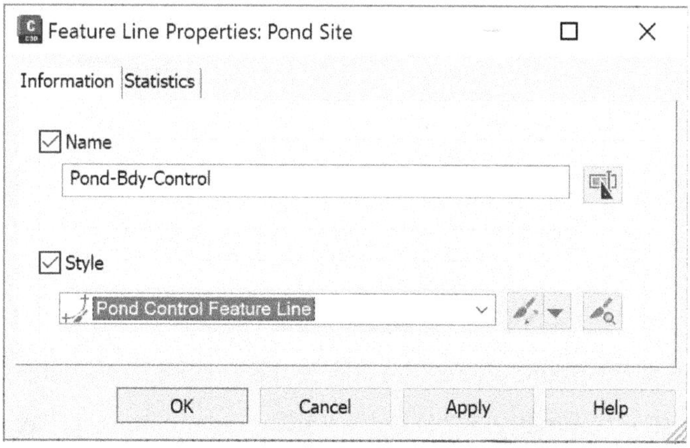

Figure 7–28

7. Press <Esc> to release the feature line.

8. Zoom in on the south end of the pond.

9. Select the feature line named **North-West-Boundary** that surrounds the pond.

10. In the *Feature Line* contextual tab>*Modify* panel, click ⬚ (Edit Geometry) if it is not already displayed. In the *Edit Geometry* panel, click ⬚ (Break), as shown in Figure 7−29.

Figure 7−29

11. Select the **North-West-Boundary** feature line again. Type **F** at the Command Line so that you can select the first and second point of the break. Select a point south of the cyan circle to the south of the control feature line for the first point, then select the endpoint of the control line using Osnaps, as shown in Figure 7−30.

Figure 7−30

12. Select the **North-West-Boundary** feature line. In the *Feature Line* contextual tab>*Modify* panel, click ⬚ (Edit Geometry) if it is not already visible. In the *Edit Geometry* panel, click ⬚ (Break).

13. Select the **North-West-Boundary** feature line again. Type **F** at the Command Line so that you can select the first and second point of the break.

14. Select a point inside the green circle to the south of the control feature line for the first point. Then select the endpoint of the control line using Osnaps, as shown in Figure 7–31.

Figure 7–31

15. In the *View* tab>*Named Views* panel, select the **Storm Pond** view. Zoom in to the northeast corner of the pond.

16. Select the **North-West-Boundary** feature line. In the *Feature Line* contextual tab>*Modify* panel, click ⬚ (Edit Geometry) if it is not already displayed. In the *Edit Geometry* panel, click ↵ (Break).

17. Select the **North-West-Boundary** feature line again just north of the south line of the maintenance road (this is also the first point), as shown in Figure 7–32. Select the endpoint of the south line of the maintenance road using Osnaps for the second point.

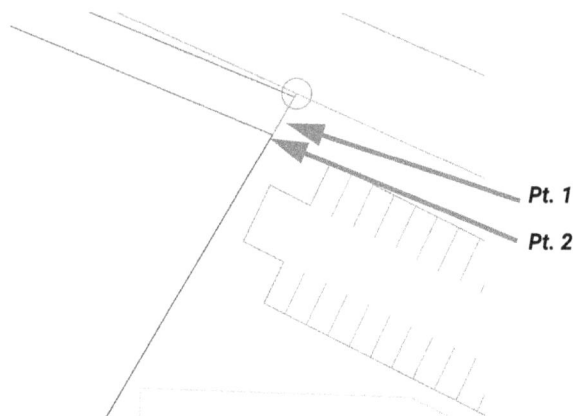

Figure 7–32

18. In the *View* tab>*Named Views* panel, select the **Storm Pond** view. Zoom in to the northwest corner of the pond.

19. Select the **North-West-Boundary** feature line. In the *Feature Line* contextual tab>*Modify* panel, click 🖾 (Edit Geometry) if it is not already displayed. In the *Edit Geometry* panel, click ↵⁺ (Break).

20. Select the **North-West-Boundary** feature line again near the northwest corner of the pond (this is also the first point), as shown in Figure 7–33. Then, select the endpoint near station 5+98.05' (using Osnap) for the second point.

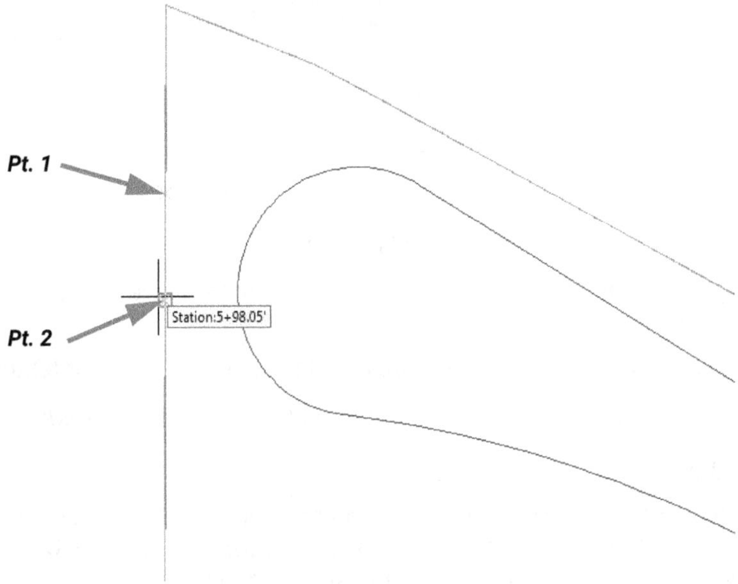

Pt. 1

Pt. 2

Station:5+98.05'

Figure 7–33

21. Select the west feature line. In the *Feature Line* contextual tab>*Modify* panel, click 🖾 (Edit Elevations). In the *Edit Elevations* panel, click ⚫ (Elevation Editor).

22. In the *Elevation Editor* vista, note that an elevation point is located at station **0+20.17** with an elevation of **170'**, as shown in Figure 7–34. You will turn this into a regular vertex.

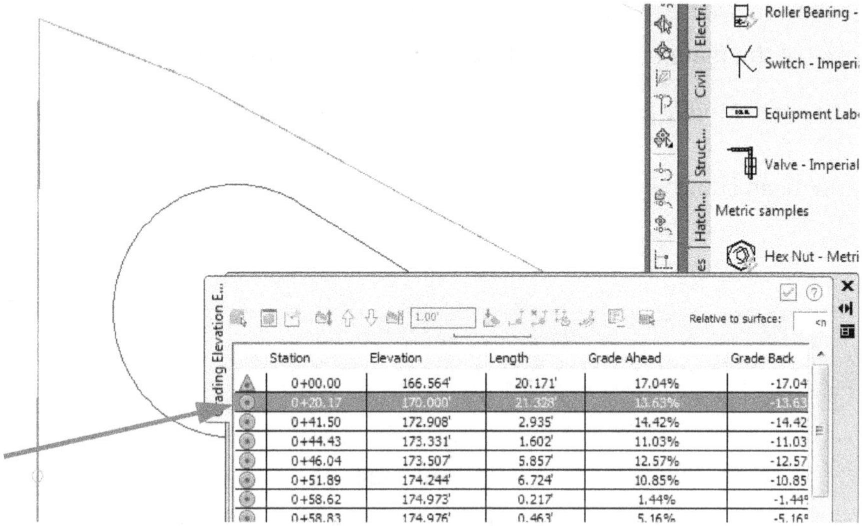

Figure 7–34

23. Select the feature line again. In the *Feature Line* contextual tab>*Modify* panel, click

    (Edit Geometry). In the *Edit Geometry* panel, click (Insert PI).

24. At the Command Line, type **D** for *Distance* and press <Enter>. For the *Distance* value, type **20.17** and press <Enter>. For the *Elevation*, type **170** and press <Enter>. Press <Esc> to end the command.

25. Click to close the *Elevation Editor* vista.

26. Select the feature line. Using grips, move the first vertex to the endpoint of the southern boundary line of the maintenance road using Osnaps, as shown in Figure 7–35.

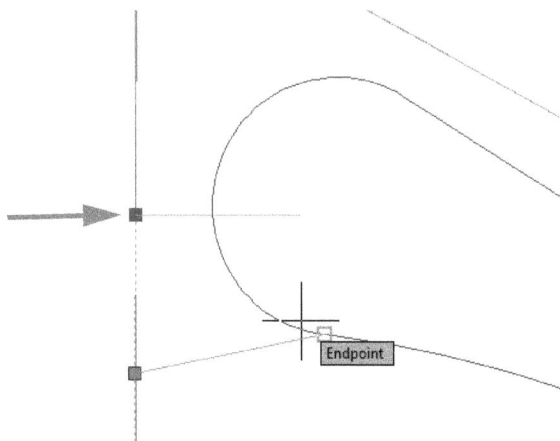

Figure 7–35

27. In the *View* tab>*Named Views* panel, select **Storm Pond** to restore the view.

28. To join all of the feature lines, select the feature line **Pond-Bdy-Control**. In the *Feature Line* contextual tab>*Modify* panel, click (Edit Geometry). In the *Edit Geometry* panel, click (Join), as shown in Figure 7–36.

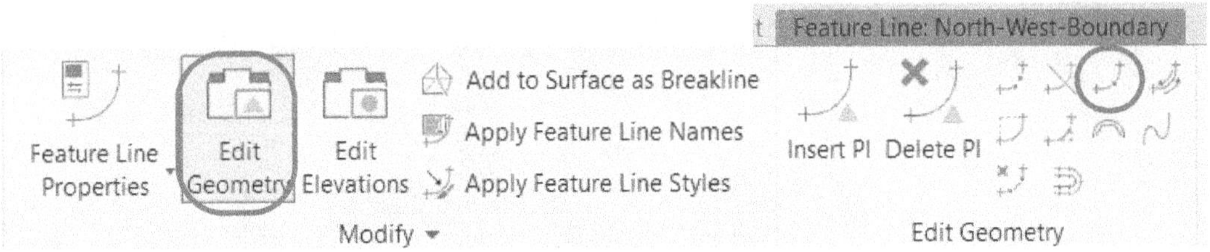

Figure 7–36

29. When prompted to select the connecting feature lines, select the feature line **Pond-Bdy-East** (2), **Pond-Bdy-North** (3), and **Pond-Bdy-West** (4), as shown in Figure 7–37. If you receive an error that they cannot be joined, you might need to grip edit the feature lines to snap them end to end.

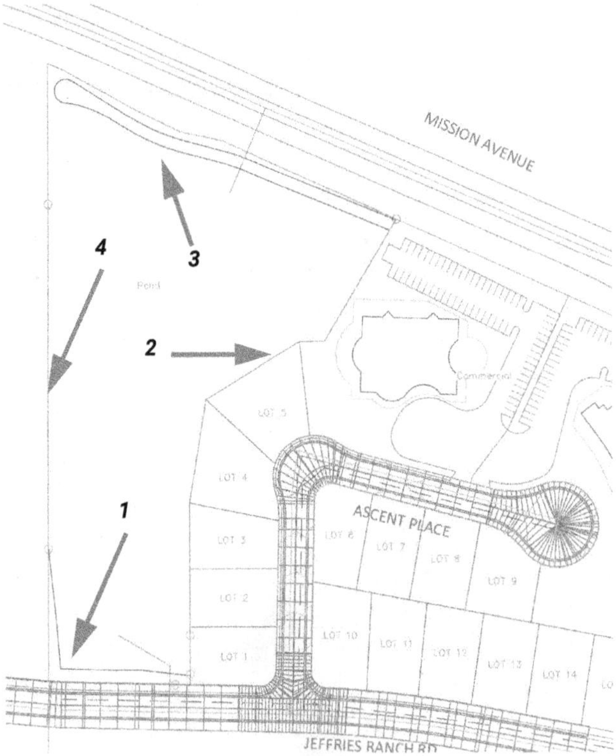

Figure 7–37

30. Press <Esc> to exit the feature line selection.

31. Select the feature line that runs along the **Jeffries Ranch Road** corridor to the south.

32. In the *Feature Line* contextual tab>*Modify* tab, click (Feature Line Properties).

33. In the Feature Line Properties, for the *Name*, type **Pond-Bdy-South**. Click **OK**.

34. Select the feature line that runs along the north of the pond.

35. In the *Feature Line* contextual tab>*Modify* panel, click (Feature Line Properties).

36. In the *Feature Line Properties*, for the *Name*, type **Pond-Bdy-North**. Click **OK**.

37. Save the drawing.

End of practice

Practice 7b
Pond Grading - Grading Object (Grading the Proposed Pond)

Practice Objective

- Create a complex grading group by grading one grading object from another.

In this practice, you will create a stormwater detention pond with feature lines and grading tools. With the control feature lines created, you can continue to grade the storm pond.

Task 1: Create pond grading.

With the pond boundary established, the rest of the pond can now be graded as specified in the cross-section.

1. Open **POND-D.dwg** from the *C:\Civil 3D Grading\Working\Pond* folder.

2. In the *Home* tab>*Create Design* panel, expand the *Grading* drop-down list and click

    (Grading Creation Tools), as shown in Figure 7–38.

Figure 7–38

3. Ensure that the grading group is set to **Temp** (within the Pond Site site).

4. In the *Grading Creation Tools* toolbar, click   (Set the Grading Group), as shown in Figure 7–39.

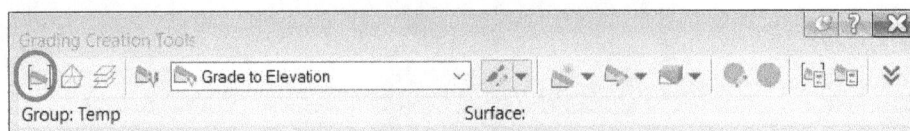

Figure 7–39

5. In the *Select Grading Group* dialog box, set the *Site name* to **Pond Site**, as shown on the left in Figure 7–40. To create a new group, click [icon] (Create a Grading Group). In the *Create Grading Group* dialog box, for the *Name*, type **Pond** and clear the **Automatic surface creation** option, as shown on the right in Figure 7–40. Click **OK**.

Figure 7–40

6. In the *Select Grading Group* dialog box, click **OK**.

7. In the *Grading Creation Tools* toolbar, set the grading criteria to **Grade to Elevation** and click [icon] (Create Grading), as shown in Figure 7–41. The first step is to grade to the permanent water level of **160.76** at a slope of 3:1.

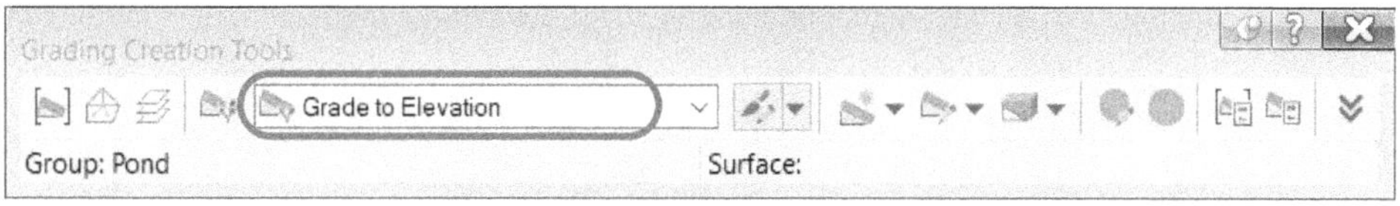

Figure 7–41

8. When prompted to select the feature line, select the **Pond-Bdy-Control** feature line. This feature line defines the inside rim of the pond.

9. When prompted to weed the feature line, select **Continue grading without feature line weeding**.

10. When prompted to select the side to grade, select the inside of the pond. Type **Yes** when prompted to *Apply to entire length*.

11. Type **160.76** for the elevation.

12. When prompted for the *Cut* format, type **Slope** and press <Enter>. For the *Slope* value, type **3** and press <Enter> to signify a 3:1 slope.

13. When prompted for the *Fill* format, type **Slope** and press <Enter>. For the *Slope* value, type **3** and press <Enter> to signify a 3:1 slope.

14. You now need to grade to the bottom of the pond, which is 13' deep at a slope of 2:1. In the *Grading Creation Tools* toolbar, change the criteria to **Grade to Relative Elevation**, as shown in Figure 7-42.

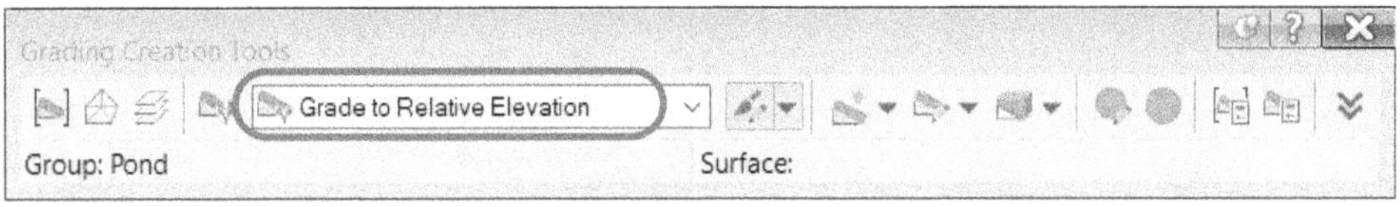

Figure 7-42

15. When prompted to select the feature line, select the inside of the pond feature line created by the last grading object, as shown in Figure 7-43. Type **Yes** when prompted to *Apply to entire length*.

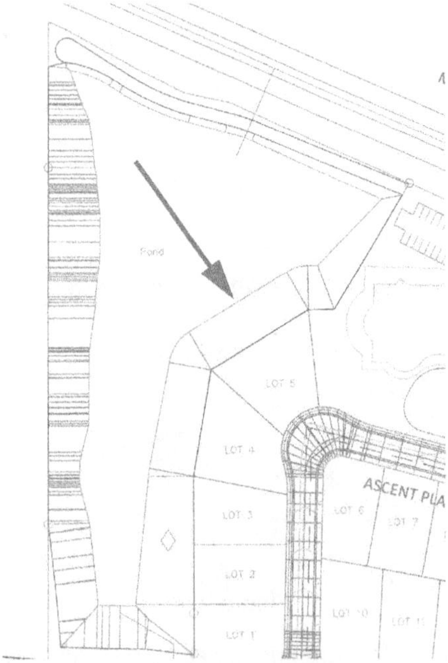

Figure 7-43

16. If prompted to select the side to grade, select the inside of the pond.

17. When prompted for the relative elevation, type **-13** and press <Enter>.

18. When prompted for the format, type **Slope** and press <Enter>. For the *Slope* value, type **2** and press <Enter> to signify a 2:1 slope.

19. In the *Grading Creation Tools* toolbar, expand the *Create Grading* drop-down list and click (Create Infill).

20. When prompted to select an area to infill, select the center of the pond, and press <Esc> to exit the command.

21. Select the diamond at the center of the infill that you just created.

22. In the *Grading* contextual tab>*Modify* panel, click (Grading Group Properties).

23. In the *Grading Group Properties* dialog box, select the **Automatic Surface Creation** option to automatically create the surface, as shown in Figure 7−44.

Grading Group Properties - Pond

Information | Properties

Name:

Pond

Description:

Automatic Surface Creation

☑ Pond

Tessellation spacing:

10.00'

Tessellation angle:

3.0000 (d)

Figure 7−44

24. Click **OK** to close the dialog box. Click **OK** in the *Create Surface* dialog box. (If the *Event* vista displays, close it.)

25. Select the **Pond** surface (select one of its contour lines).

26. In the *Surface* contextual tab, click ▨ (Object Viewer). Set the view direction to
    SW Isometric and the style to **Conceptual**. Note the hole in the surface, as shown in
    Figure 7–45. If you prefer, you can also view it through the *Model Viewer* by selecting **Add to
    Model Viewer** via the right-click menu.

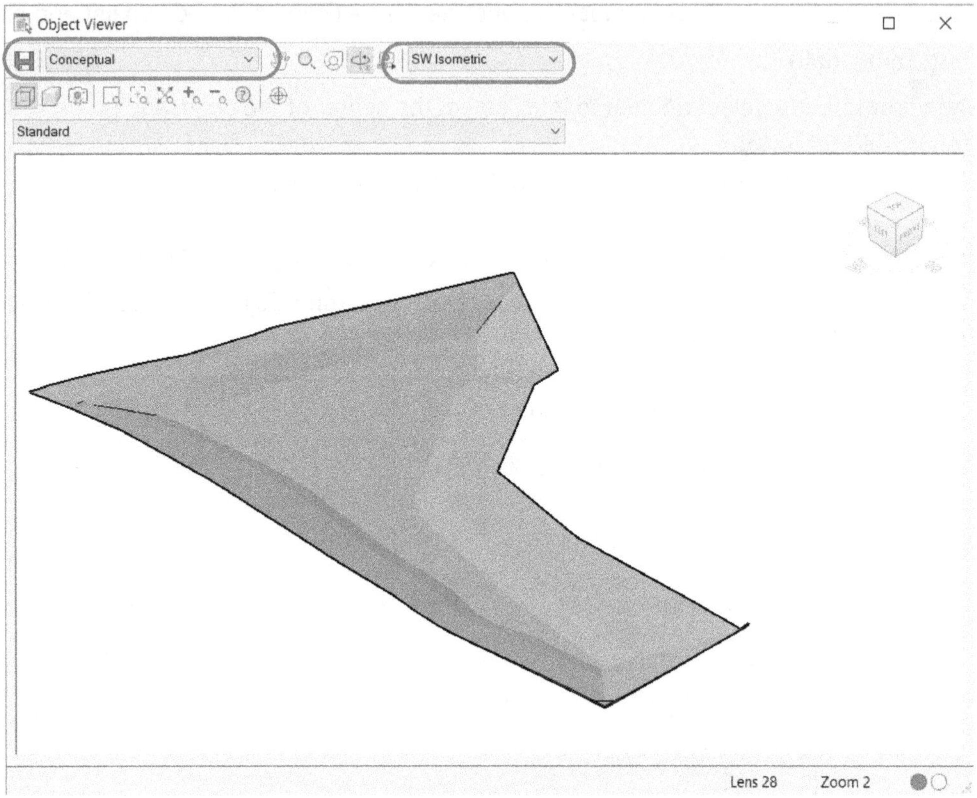

Figure 7–45

27. Press <Esc> twice to close the Object Viewer and release the selection.

Task 2: Supplement the surface with feature lines.

Add feature lines to represent critical grade breaks and other important elevation breaklines on
the surface. These lines accentuate the geometry and make the surface more accurate. In this
task, you will add feature lines at the north and south ends of the site.

1. Continue working with the drawing from the previous task.

2. In the *View* tab>*Named Views* panel, select the **Storm Pond** view.

3. In the *Prospector* tab, expand the *Sites* collection, expand the site *Pond Site* collection, and select **Feature Lines**. In the grid view at the bottom, select the three feature lines **Pond-Bdy-North**, **Pond-Bdy-South**, and **Pond-Access Rd-North** using <Ctrl>. Right-click and select **Select**, as shown in Figure 7–46.

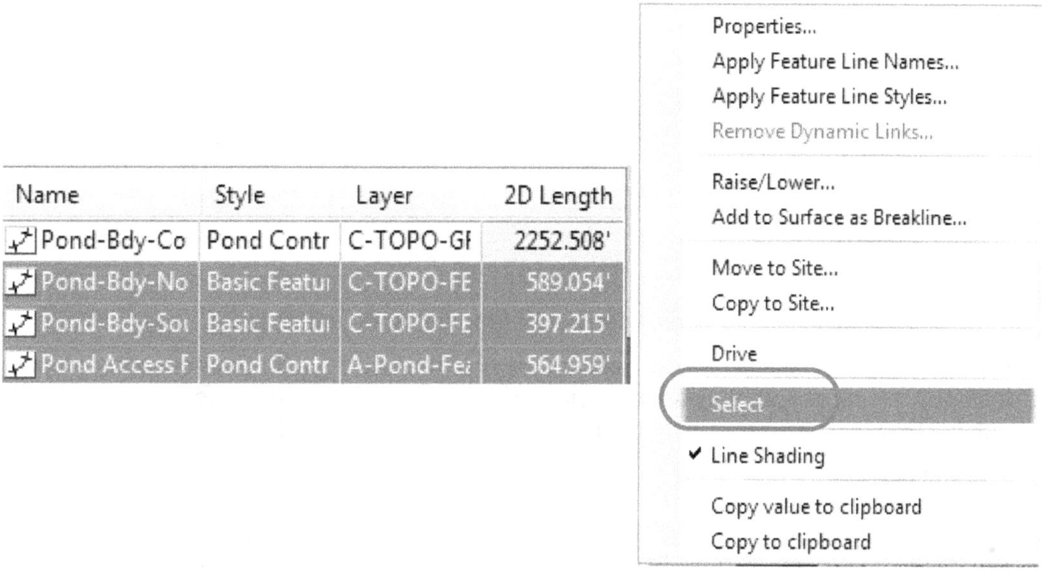

Name	Style	Layer	2D Length
Pond-Bdy-Co	Pond Contr	C-TOPO-GF	2252.508'
Pond-Bdy-No	Basic Featur	C-TOPO-FE	589.054'
Pond-Bdy-Soi	Basic Featur	C-TOPO-FE	397.215'
Pond Access F	Pond Contr	A-Pond-Fea	564.959'

Properties...
Apply Feature Line Names...
Apply Feature Line Styles...
Remove Dynamic Links...

Raise/Lower...
Add to Surface as Breakline...

Move to Site...
Copy to Site...

Drive

Select

✓ Line Shading

Copy value to clipboard
Copy to clipboard

Figure 7–46

4. Once selected, the feature lines can be added to the surface as breaklines. In the *Feature Line* contextual tab>*Modify* panel, click  (Add to Surface as Breakline), as shown in Figure 7–47.

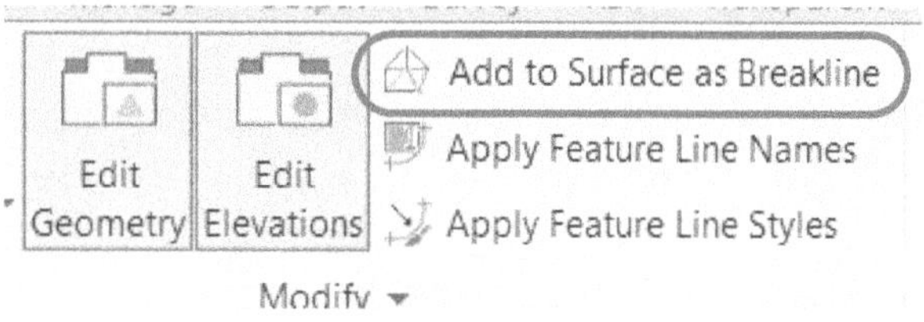

Edit Geometry   Edit Elevations

Add to Surface as Breakline
Apply Feature Line Names
Apply Feature Line Styles

Modifv ▼

Figure 7–47

5. In the *Select Surface* dialog box, select the **Pond** surface, as shown in Figure 7–48. Click **OK**.

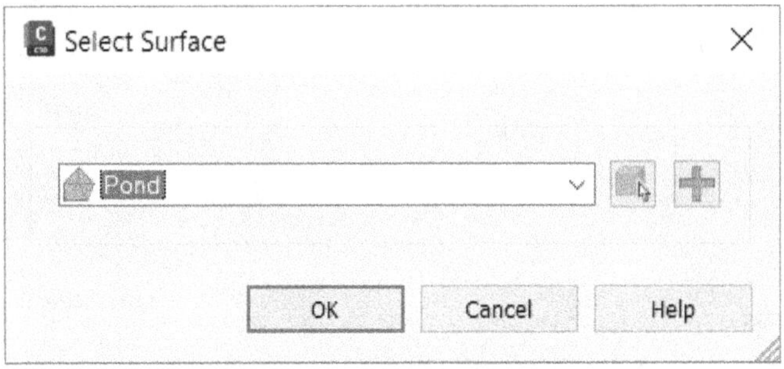

Figure 7–48

6. In the *Add Breaklines* dialog box, accept all of the defaults and click **OK**.

7. Press <Esc> to end the selection. You now have a pond surface that matches the proposed design of the parcels on the east side and **Jeffries Ranch Road** on the south side. The north and west sides of the pond have been graded to match the existing ground.

8. Save the drawing.

End of practice

7.4 Stormwater Controls

Civil 3D has recently added objects for stormwater controls, as shown in Figure 7–49.

- Channels
- Ponds
- Underground Storage

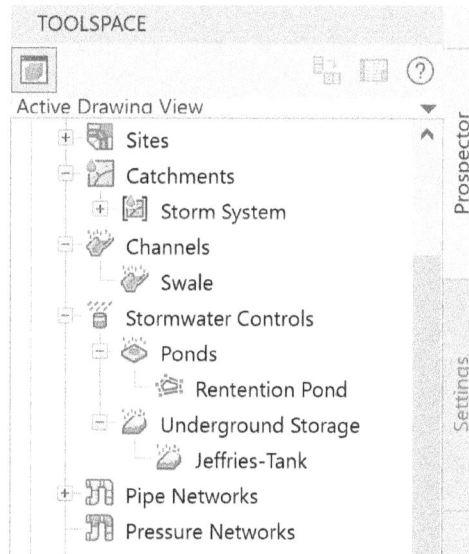

Figure 7–49

These objects are created and controlled through a series of tools for stormwater management. They integrate drainage design with analysis capabilities powered cloud-services without leaving Civil 3D, providing a more efficient and elegant workflow for such stormwater control items such as ponds, underground storage tanks, and channels. Delineation of catchments, including enhanced runoff methods, provide necessary data for analysis of multiple storm event simulations. When satisfactory results are achieved, the designs of the components can be updated to reflect the results of the analysis within the drawing. Reports can be created as well.

Channels

Channels are used to control stormwater runoffs through engineered waterways. They prevent flooding, sediment buildup and erosion for roadways and urban settings. They are designed to channel excessive runoffs to natural or man-made bodies of water.

In Civil 3D, Channel objects are derived from sketched feature lines or alignments and profiles. The Channel is a specific Civil 3D object, as shown in Figure 7–50.

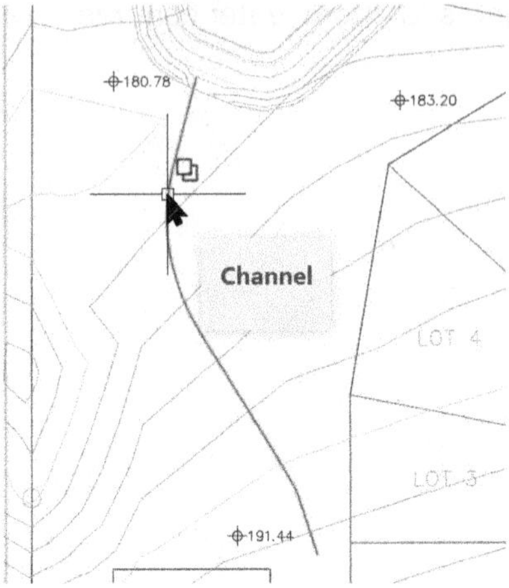

Figure 7–50

In the Channel Properties, you can assign the cross section by selecting a predefined shape (trapezoidal, triangular, rectangular or custom) and modifying its parameters. As you change the parameter values, the preview is updated, as shown in Figure 7–51.

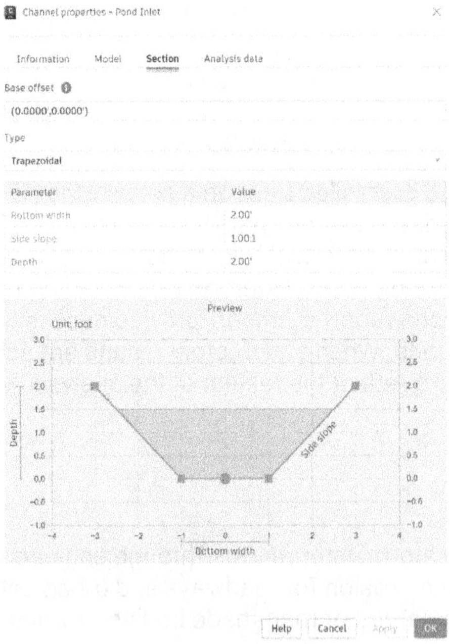

Figure 7–51

Channels are only linear representations and do not reflect their actual shape or section in Civil 3D. Their primary function is to provide analytical data for establishing comprehensive drainage systems.

The Channel style controls the settings for its Baseline and the Longitudinal Line.

Ponds

Ponds occur naturally as small bodies of water, but they are also designed and created as an effective means to capture and control stormwater runoffs. They can be fed by channels or storm sewer outfalls. They are designed to capture significant volumes of water, which they can either retain or discharge at a controlled rate through various means to maintain an optimum water level. By retaining stormwater runoff for extended periods, these systems effectively remove contaminants and sediment before discharging the treated water through weirs, orifices, or other controlled outlets.

Creating a pond

Civil 3D provides three methods for creating ponds:

1. Sketching the pond outline.

2. Selecting an outline from an existing:

    • Polyline (2D or 3D)

    • Feature Line

    • Alignment

    • Parcel segment

    • Survey figure.

3. From a surface. You either need to specify the top elevation of the pond and Civil 3D will find all depressions in the surface rimming at that elevation, or you can select a closed contour that is the top of pond.

The Pond is a specific Civil 3D object, as shown in Figure 7–52.

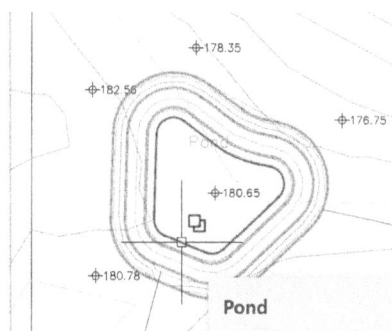

Figure 7–52

When creating a pond, the following is required, as shown in Figure 7–53:

- Name
- Description (optional)
- Depth
- Inside Slope
- The starting elevation (either Top or Bottom elevation)
- The Layer it resides on
- The Pond Style

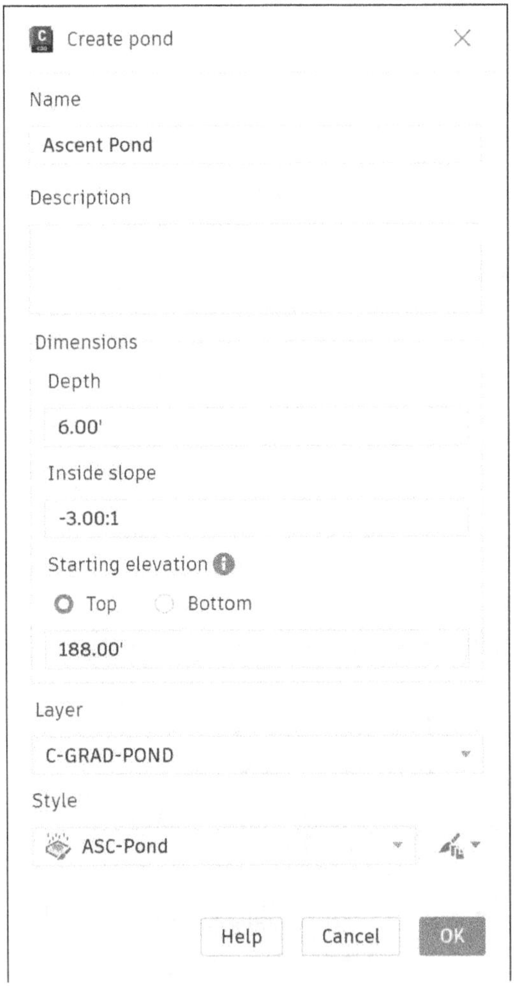

Figure 7–53

The Pond style controls the settings for its Top, Interior Contours, and its Bottom, as shown in Figure 7–54.

Component display

Component type	Visible	Layer	Color
Top	💡	C-POND-TOPB	▨ BYLAYER
Interior Contours	💡	C-POND-CONT	▨ BYLAYER
Bottom	💡	C-POND-EDGE	▨ BYLAYER

Figure 7–54

Pipes from gravity pipe network and channels can be connected to a pond, and will display on the *Inflows* tab of the *Pond Properties* dialog box. The connection is not dynamic, so moving the pond may disconnect pipes or channels and trigger a warning in the *Event Viewer*.

Pond edits and properties

Once a pond is defined, it can be refined using grips. Hover over these grips to see the following tool-tips:

- 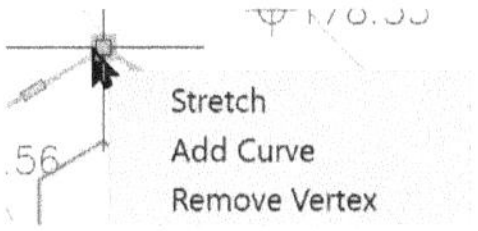 Square grip on a vertex.

- 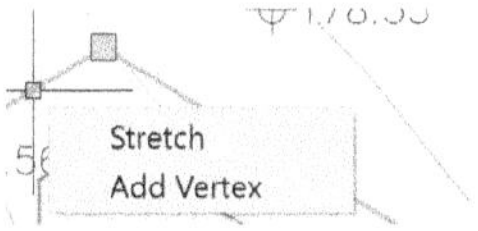 Rectangle grip at midpoint of a line segment.

- 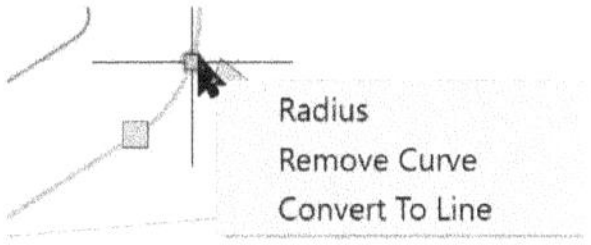 Circular grip on midpoint of a curve segment.

-  Triangular grip beyond the circular grip of a curve segment.

- 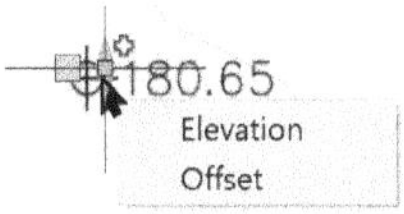 Diamond grip at the centroid of the pond. Allows you to change the elevation or provide an offset in elevation.

Furthermore, there are tools within the contextual ribbon, as shown in Figure 7-55.

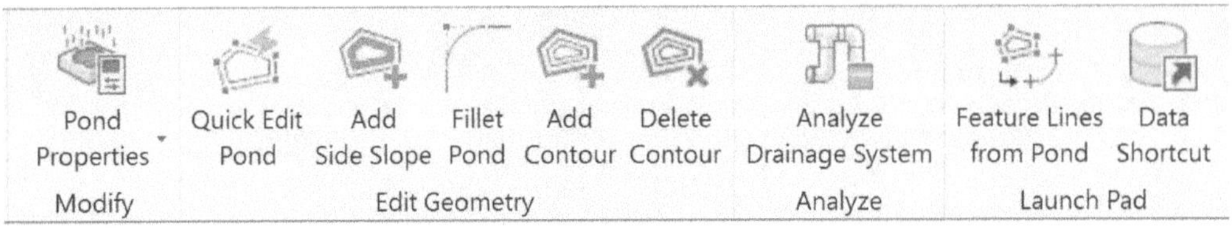

Pond Properties	Quick Edit Pond	Add Side Slope	Fillet Pond	Add Contour	Delete Contour	Analyze Drainage System	Feature Lines from Pond	Data Shortcut
Modify		Edit Geometry				Analyze	Launch Pad	

Figure 7-55

The **Pond Properties** display the properties of the pond and is divided into four categories:

- **Information**

- **Storage**

- **Inflows**: Provides key information (such as Description, Size, Elevations (Invert, Centerline, and Crown), Slope) about pipes entering the pond as well as the structures at the other end of the pipe.

- **Outflows**: Provides key information (similar to the *Inflows* tab) about pipes leaving the pond, and the structures following the pipe. In the outlets section, you can specify the outlet type (Weir, Orifice, Free discharge), diameter, invert elevation, and discharge coefficient.

All but the *Information* tab are read only (the *Freeboard* value is an exception) and derived from the overall drainage system, but you can add Outlets in the *Outflows* tab.

Note: Freeboard will be discussed later in the Grading Optimization section.

Quick Edit: Displays information of the Pond components, such as slopes / grades and widths, as you hover over them and allows you to change the values as you select them.

Add Slide Slope: You can add slide slopes to the pond by clicking on a contour (top, bottom or intermittent) and selecting the desired slope width. The new slope area is then highlighted in a blue shade.

Fillet Pond: Allows you to place curves between all vertices of the pond at a given radius.

Add Contours / Delete Contours allows you to add more contours to the pond or delete existing contours.

Feature Lines from Pond: To create a surface for the pond, you can extract feature lines directly from the pond—select either all available contours or only the top and bottom ones. Additionally, you have the option to create a dynamic link, so that both the feature lines and the resulting surface get updated automatically whenever changes are made to the pond.

Data Shortcuts: If you are working with data shortcuts, you can create a shortcut for the pond (as shown in Figure 7–56). In a referenced drawing, you can then extract the feature lines from this shortcut and build the corresponding surface.

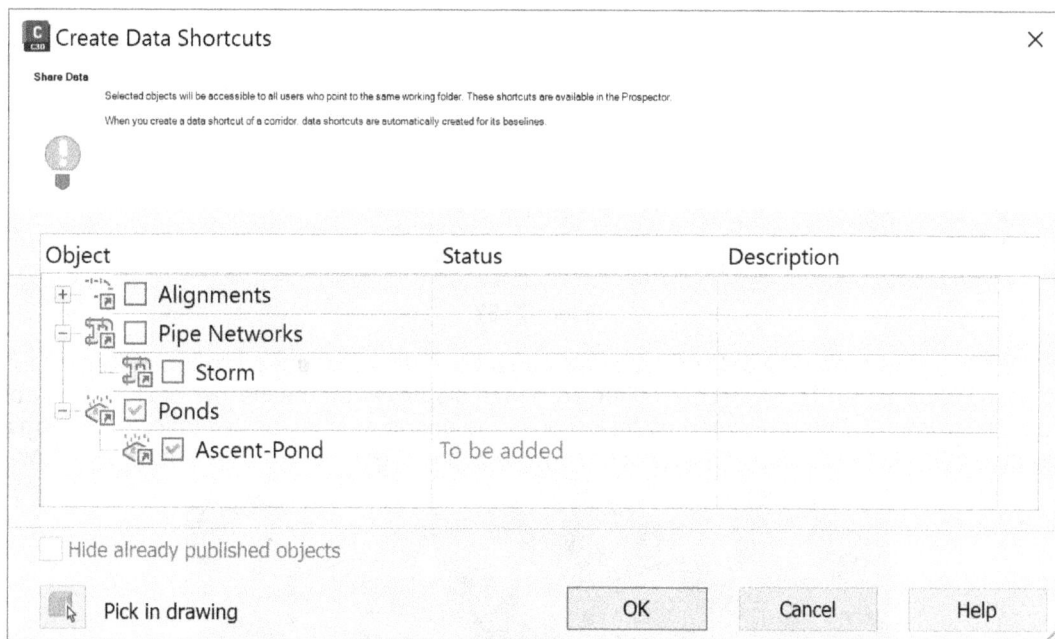

Figure 7–56

Underground Storage

Underground storage uses hidden tanks or chambers built below the surface to temporarily collect and store rainwater, releasing it gradually in a controlled way. These systems can be at multiple levels with varying amounts of voids such as gravel or rocks.

Civil 3D provides three methods for creating underground storage tanks:

1. Sketching the tank outline.

2. Selecting an outline from an existing:

   - Polyline (2D or 3D)

   - Feature Line

   - Alignment

   - Parcel segment

   - Survey figure.

The Underground Storage is a specific Civil 3D object, as shown in Figure 7-57.

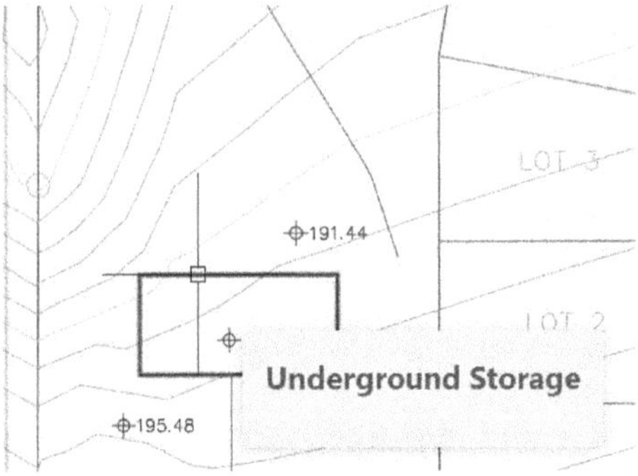

Figure 7-57

Pipes from gravity pipe network and channels can be connected to underground storage, as shown in Figure 7-58. The pipe connections are then displayed on the *Inflows* or *Outflows* tabs of the *Underground Storage Properties* dialog box. The connection is not dynamic, so moving a storage unit in plan or elevation may disconnect pipes and trigger a warning in the *Event Viewer*.

Figure 7-58

Once a storage unit is defined, it can be refined through grips. When hovering over them, the following tool-tips are displayed:

- 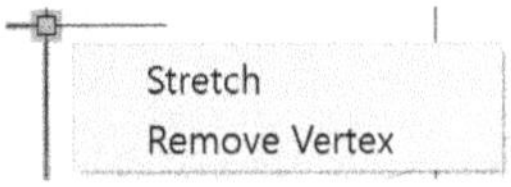 Square grip on a vertex.

- 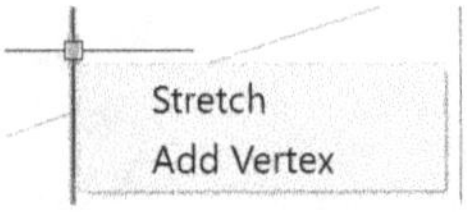 Rectangle grip at midpoint of a line segment.

- 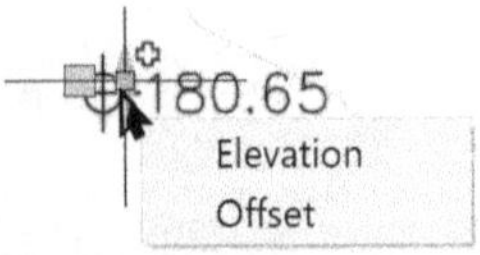 Diamond grip at the centroid of the tank. Allows you to change the elevation or provide an offset in elevation.

The **Underground Storage Properties** display the properties of the unit and is divided into five categories:

- **Information**

- **Dimensions**: Displays the depth layers; you can add or remove depth layers, or adjust the depth and the voids for each layer. The footprint area of each depth layer is displayed, as shown in Figure 7–59.

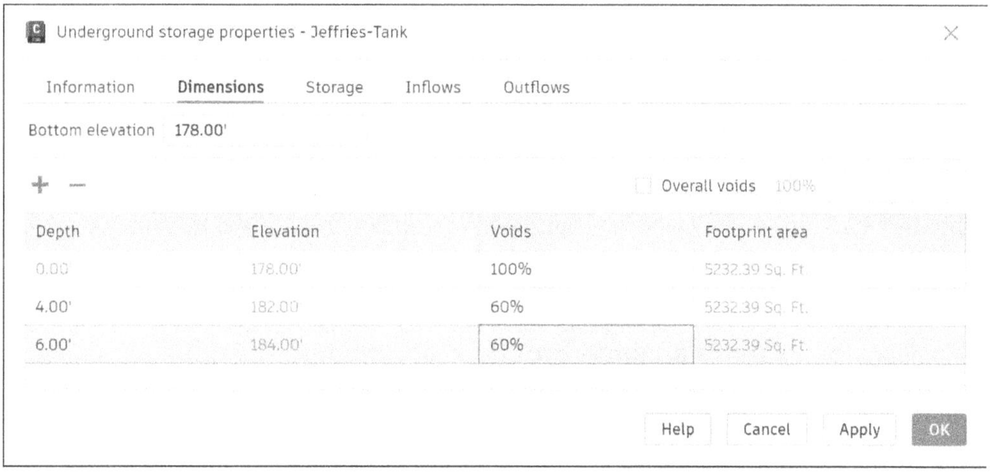

C	Underground storage properties - Jeffries-Tank				×

| Information | **Dimensions** | Storage | Inflows | Outflows |

Bottom elevation   178.00'

+ —   ☐ Overall voids   100%

Depth	Elevation	Voids	Footprint area
0.00'	178.00'	100%	5232.39 Sq. Ft
4.00'	182.00'	60%	5232.39 Sq. Ft.
6.00'	184.00'	60%	5232.39 Sq. Ft.

Help   Cancel   Apply   OK

Figure 7–59

- **Storage**: Displays the volumes of each depth layer. These values can be modified or imported from a manufacturer's *.csv file containing storage data.

- **Inflows**: Provides key information (such as Description, Size, Elevations (Invert, Centerline, and Crown), Slope) about pipes entering the storage unit as well as the structure at the other end of the pipe.

- **Outflows**: Provides key information (similar to the *Inflows* tab) about pipes leaving the storage unit, and the structure following the pipe.

Practice 7c
Stormwater Controls

Practice Objectives

- Create an underground Storage unit.
- Connect the tank to a pipe network
- Create a pond using the Civil 3D Pond tools.
- Connect to a drainage system.

In this practice, you will create an underground storage tank and a stormwater detention pond using the Civil 3D Stormwater Control tools. Then you will connect them to a stormwater drainage system. There is a pipe network with two flared end discharge points. One will connect to a new underground storage tank, the other will act as an inflow to the new pond.

Task 1: (Optional) Create an underground storage tank.

> *Note: Underground Storage Tanks are not part of the grading process but are related to ponds. Therefore, this first task is optional. If you skip this task entirely or are unable to complete it, you can use a drawing with the finished tank for the subsequent pond creation task.*

You will sketch in a Storage Tank with a given elevation, study its properties and connect it to the pipe-network.

1. Open **POND_Obj-A.dwg** from the *C:\Civil 3D Grading\Working\Pond* folder.

2. In the top left corner of the drawing window, select the - (minus) symbol for Viewport Control, expand *Viewport Configuration List* and select **U-Tank**, as shown in Figure 7−60.

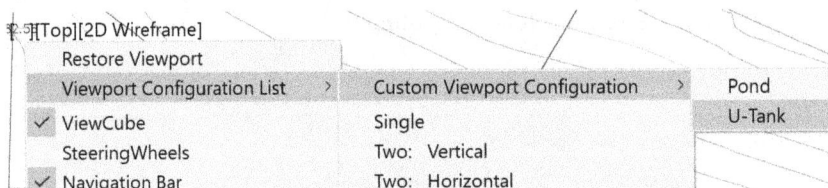

Figure 7−60

3. Make the plan viewport (the left one) active by clicking in it.

4. In the *Home* tab>*Create Design* panel, expand the *Underground Storage* drop-down list and click (Create Underground Storage).

5. In the *Create underground storage* dialog box, complete the following as shown in Figure 7–61:

    a. Set the *Name* to **Jeffries-Tank**.

    b. Set the *Depth* to **6.00'**.

    c. Set the *Starting Elevation* to **Top**, then type **184.0'** as the top elevation.

    d. Select **C-HYDR-TANK** as the layer.

    e. Confirm that **ASC-TANK** is the style.

    f. Click **OK** to close the *Create underground storage* dialog box.

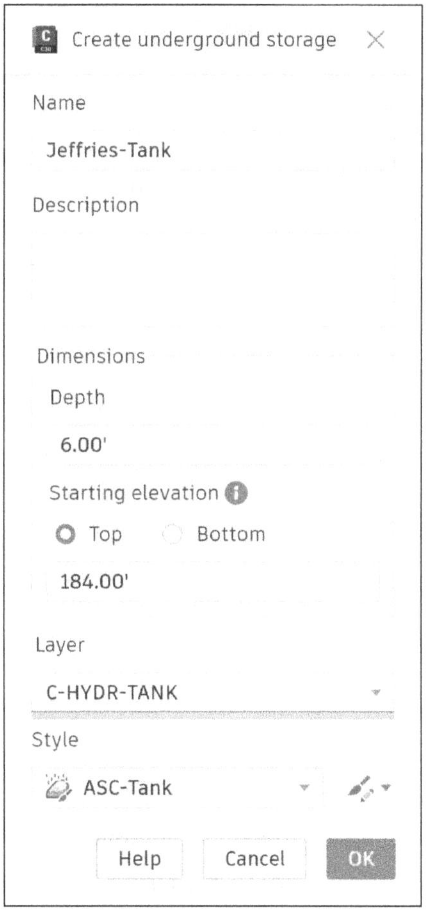

Figure 7–61

6. Sketch a rectangle roughly enclosing the blue oval, as shown in Figure 7–62.

193.09
Center
195.48

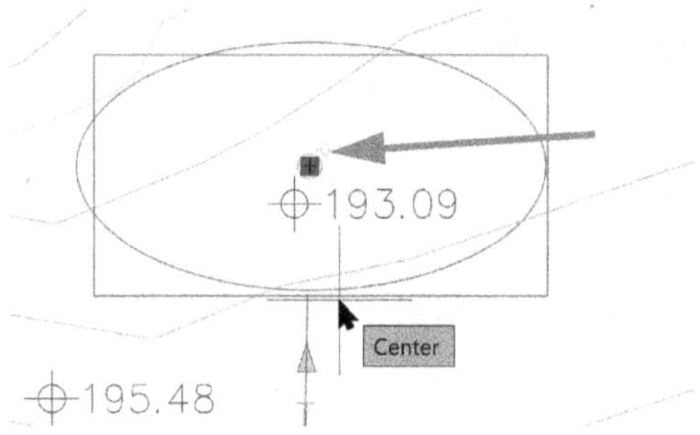

Figure 7–62

7. Select the tank, and either through the contextual ribbon or the right-click menu, select **Underground Storage Properties.**
8. On the *Dimensions* tab, click the **+** in the upper left corner to add another depth level. Change the *Depth* of the second level to **4.00'** and that of the last depth to **6.00'**, and change the *Void* to **60%**, as shown in Figure 7–63.

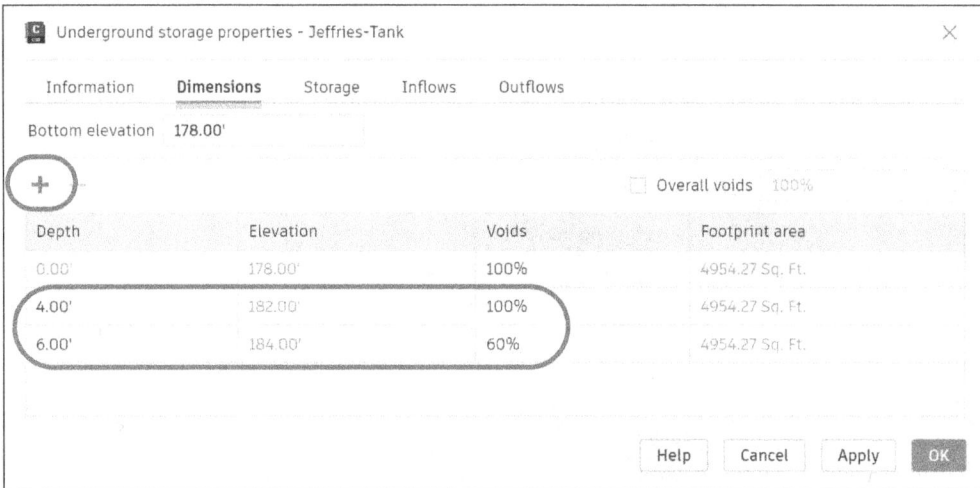

Underground storage properties - Jeffries-Tank
Information
Dimensions
Storage
Inflows
Outflows
Bottom elevation
178.00'
Overall voids
Depth
Elevation
Voids
Footprint area
0.00'
178.00'
100%
4954.27 Sq. Ft.
4.00'
182.00'
100%
4954.27 Sq. Ft.
6.00'
184.00'
60%
4954.27 Sq. Ft.
Help
Cancel
Apply
OK

Figure 7–63

9. Look at the other tabs. There are no inflows or outflows.
10. Click **OK** to close the *Underground storage properties* dialog box.
11. Press the <Esc> key to deselect the tank.
12. Select the existing Flared End Section at the end of the pipe and erase it.
13. Select the unconnected pipe. Use the square grip at the end of the pipe to drag the pipe to the tank. Wait until you see the yellow round connection icon (as shown in Figure 7–62) as you intersect the tank before releasing the pipe to ensure a connection.

14. Press the <Esc> key to deselect the pipe.

15. Select the tank and hover over the green diamond grip, then select **Offset** from the tool-tip menu, as shown in Figure 7–64. Type **10** and <Enter> to raise the tank by 10'. The *Event Viewer* is triggered explaining the pipe got disconnected from the tank; the connection is not dynamic, compared to other pipe network structures.

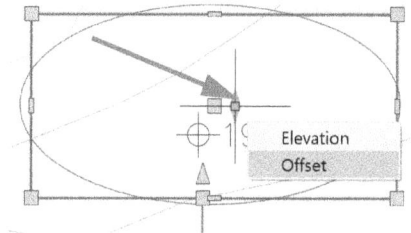

Figure 7–64

16. Close the *Event Viewer* vista.

17. Press the <Esc> key to deselect the tank.

18. Undo the last command. Check in the right viewport that the tank is back to its original location.

19. Select the tank, and either through the contextual ribbon or the right-click menu, select **Underground Storage Properties**. On the *Inflows* tab, note that there is now an inflow listed.

20. Click **OK** to close the *Underground storage properties* dialog box.

21. Erase the blue oval which served as a guideline for the underground storage tank's location.

22. Save the drawing.

Task 2: Create a pond with Civil 3D tools.

You will create a pond using the *Pond* tools within Civil 3D by selecting a pline which represents the pond's top elevation. If you didn't complete the previous task you can open a drawing in which that task has been completed.

1. Continue working with the drawing from the previous task or open **POND_Obj-B.dwg** from the *C:\Civil 3D Grading\Working\Pond* folder.

2. In the top left corner of the drawing window, select the - (minus) symbol for Viewport Control, expand *Viewport Configuration List* and select **Pond**, as shown in Figure 7–65.

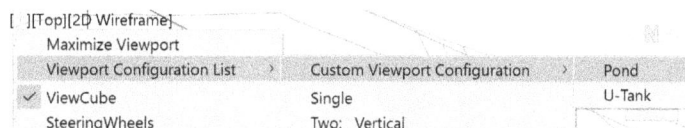

Figure 7–65

3. Make the plan viewport (the left one) active by clicking in it.

4. In the *Home* tab>*Create Design* panel, expand the *Pond* drop-down list and click ![icon] (Create Pond from Object).

5. When prompted, select the blue closed pline placed in the center of the left viewport.

6. In the *Create pond* dialog box, complete the following as shown in Figure 7–66:

    a.   Set the *Name* to **Ascent-Pond**.

    b.   Set the *Depth* to **6.00'**.

    c.   Leave the *Inside slope* at **-3.00:1**.

    d.   Set the *Starting Elevation* to **Top**, then type **183.0'** as the top elevation.

    e.   Select **C-HYDR-POND** as the layer.

    f.   Confirm that **ASC-Pond** is the style.

    g.   Select the **Erase existing entity** checkbox

    h.   Click **OK** to close the *Create pond* dialog box.

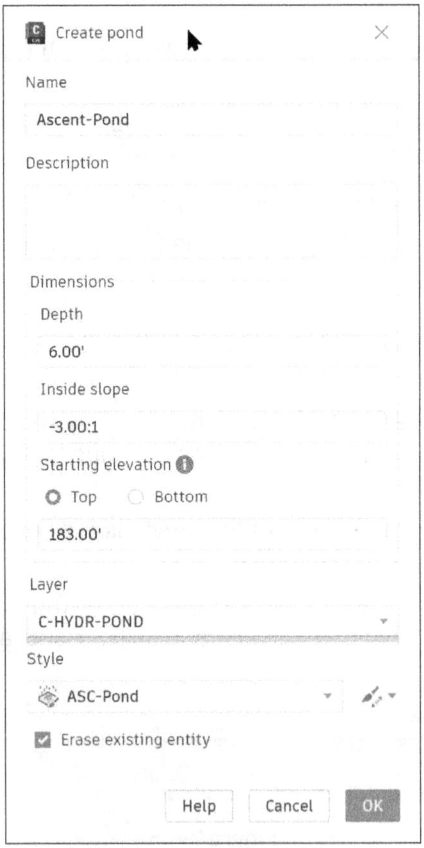

Figure 7–66

7. Select the new pond, and either through the contextual ribbon or the right-click menu, select **Pond Properties.**

8. Look at all the tabs. On the *Storage* tab, there are only two depth levels. There are no inflows or outflows.

9. Click **OK** to close the *Pond properties* dialog box.

10. In the *Pond* contextual ribbon>*Edit Geometry* panel, select (Fillet Pond) and type **50** as the radius and press <Enter> to accept the value. All vertices of both the top and bottom are rounded to a 50 foot radius.

11. In the *Pond* contextual ribbon>*Edit Geometry* panel, select (Add Side Slope) and select the bottom edge. Move the cursor towards the center and note in the right viewport how the pond shape changes. Select a point as noted in Figure 7–67.

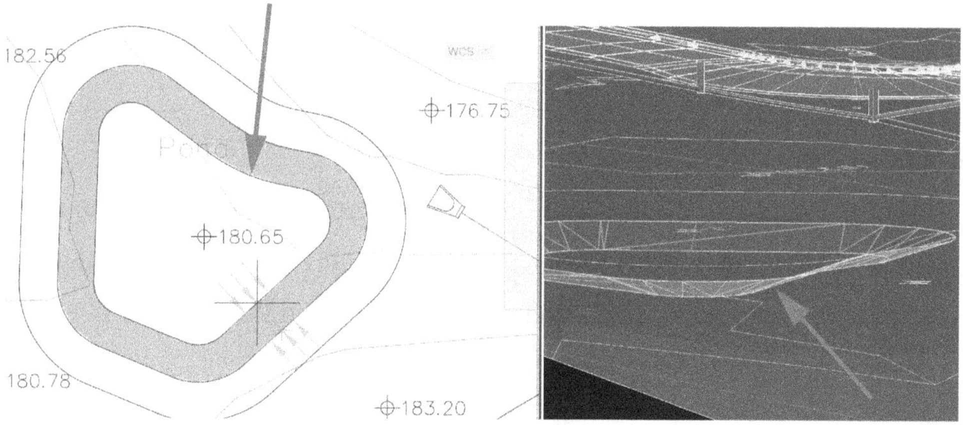

Figure 7–67

12. In the *Pond* contextual ribbon>*Edit Geometry* panel, select (Add Contour) and move the cursor between the existing pond contours. Note in the right viewport how the pond contour is displayed. Select a point to add a contour. Add two more contours.

13. Use the (Delete Contour) to delete all but two pond contours.

14. Select ⬚ (Quick Edit Pond) and hover the cursor between the existing pond contours, which highlights the area between the contours. Tooltips display the current *Width* and *Slope* of the side slope, as shown in Figure 7−68. When you select a side slope (the highlighted area), you are prompted for a new width, or specify a new slope or grade.

Figure 7−68

15. Do the following:

    • Change the *Width* of the outer most side slope to **12.0'** and the *Slope* to **2:00:1**.

    • For the next lower side slope, change the *Slope* to **4:00:1** and the *Width* to **16.0'**.

    • For the lowest side slope, change the *Width* to **8.0'** and the *Slope* to **3:00:1**.

    • Press the <Esc> key to finish the **Quick Edit Pond** command.

    Note: The whole pond is one object. As you change side slopes, other side slope values or widths will change in relation to other changes.

16. Press <Esc> to deselct the pond.

17. Select the existing Flared End Section at the end of the pipe and erase it, as shown in the upper panel of Figure 7−69.

30.65

Figure 7−69

18. Select the unconnected pipe. Use the square grip at the end of the pipe to drag it to the tank. Wait to you see the yellow round connection icon (as shown in the lower panel of Figure 7−69) as you intersect the pond contour before releasing the pipe to ensure a connection.

19. Press the <Esc> key to deselect the pipe.

20. Select the pond and hover over the green diamond grip, then select **Offset** from the tool-tip menu, as shown in Figure 7−70. Type **10** to raise the tank by 10'. The *Event Viewer* is triggered explaining the pipe got disconnected from the pond; the connection is not dynamic, compared to other pipe network structures.

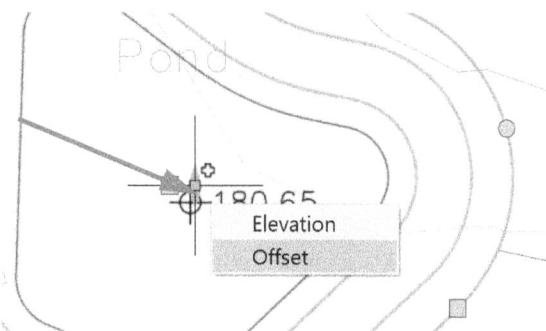

Pond

180.65

Elevation

Offset

Figure 7−70

21. Close the *Event Viewer* vista.

22. Press the <Esc> key to deselect the pond.

23. Undo the last command. Check in the right viewport that the pond is back to its original location.

24. Select the pond, and either through the contextual ribbon or the right-click menu, select **Pond Properties**. In the *Inflows* tab, note that there is now an inflow listed. On the *Storage* tab, you will see the multiple stage storages you had set up earlier. Change the *Freeboard* width to **2.50'**, as shown in Figure 7–71.

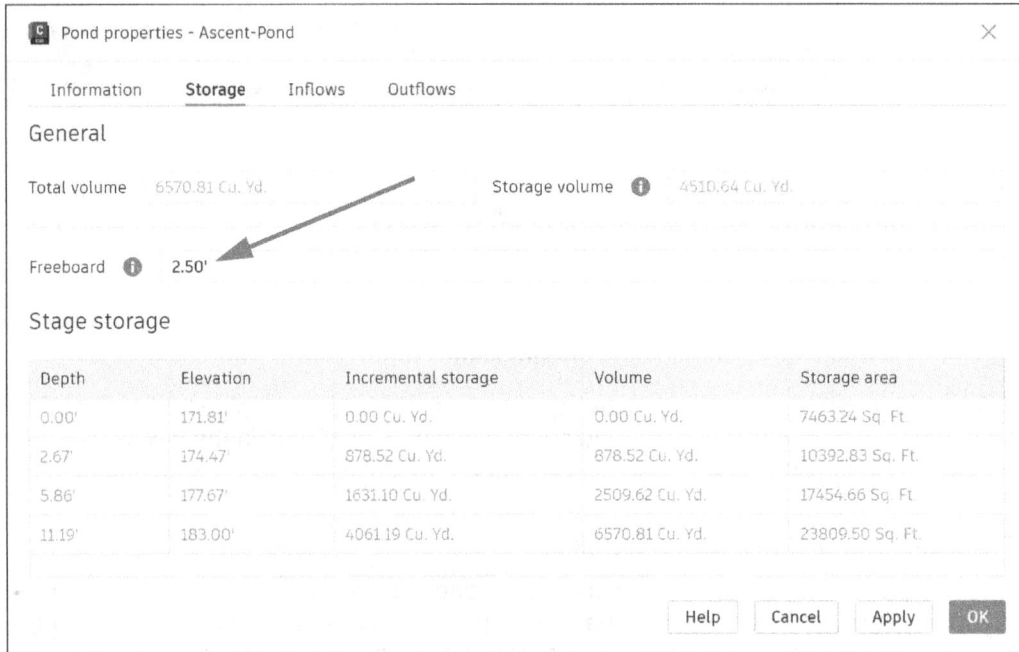

Figure 7–71

25. Click **OK** to close the *Pond properties* dialog box.

26. Save the drawing.

Task 3: Create a pond surface.

You will create a surface from feature lines extracted from the new pond.

1. Continue working with the drawing from the previous task or open **POND_Obj-C.dwg** from the *C:\Civil 3D Grading\Working\Pond* folder.

2. In the *Pond* contextual ribbon>*Edit Geometry* panel, select ⬚ (Feature Lines from Pond).

3. In the *Feature lines from pond* dialog box, do the following, as shown in Figure 7–72.

    *   For the *Style*, select **ASC-Pond** from the drop-down menu.
    *   For *Conversion options*, select **Extract all** and **Create dynamic link to the pond**.
    *   Click **OK** to close the *Feature lines from pond* dialog box.

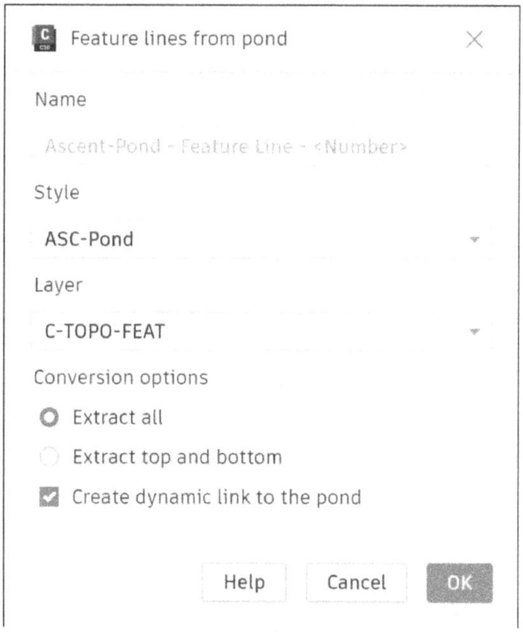

Figure 7–72

There is no site associated with the extracted feature lines. It is good practice to have sites for different design options. Therefore you need to create a site and move the feature lines to that site.

4. In the *Prospector* tab of the Toolspace, right-click on the *Sites* branch and select **New...** to create a new site.

5. In he *Site Properties* dialog box, name the site **Pond_Object** and click **OK** to close the *Site Properties* dialog box.

6. In the *Prospector* tab click on *Feature Lines,* and then in the preview section below, right-click and select **Move to Site**..., as shown in Figure 7–73.

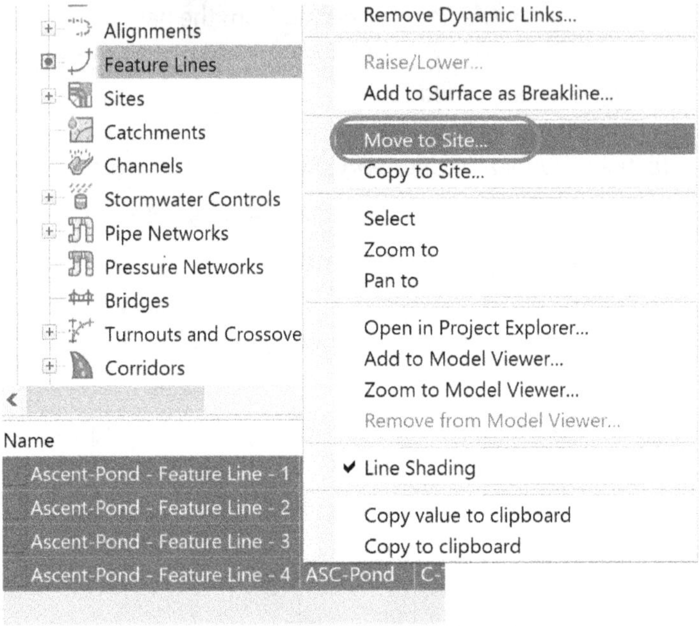

Figure 7–73

7. In the *Move to Site* dialog box, select **Pond-Object** from the *Destination site* drop down menu. Click **OK** to close the *Move to Site* dialog box.

8. In the *Prospector* tab of the Toolspace, right-click on the *Surfaces* branch and select **Create Surface...** to create a new surface for the pond. Name the surface **Ascent-Pond**, and ensure the style is set to **ASC-Contours 2' and 10' (Design).** Click **OK** to close the *Create Surface* dialog box.

9. Expand the Surfaces>*Ascent-Pond* >*Definitions* branch, then right-click on *Breaklines* and select **Add...**

10. In the *Add Breaklines* dialog box, provide a description for **From Pond**. Leave all other options as their defaults and click **OK**.

11. Select the four features lines in the drawing, taking care to select the proper ones, not the contours of the pond. You can enable *Selection Cycling* (CTRL- W keyboard shortcut) to assist.

12. Press <Enter> to finish the selection and the surface is built.

13. Select the surface either in the drawing or in the *Prospector* and through the right-click menu, select **Add to Model Viewer...**

14. Examine the surface in the *Model Viewer,* as shown in Figure 7–74.

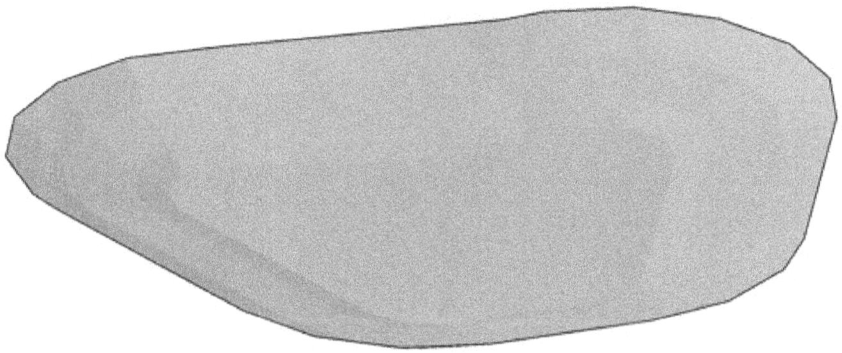

Figure 7–74

15. Close the *Model Viewer* and save the drawing.

Task 4: (Optional) Create a drainage channel into the pond.

You will create a channel from feature lines flowing to the new pond. Channels are an integral tool for stormwater management, however they are represented as a single linear object and do not reflect the actual shape or section in Civil 3D.

1. Continue working with the drawing from the previous task or open **POND_Obj-D.dwg** from the *C:\Civil 3D Grading\Working\Pond* folder.

2. Turn on the **C-HYDR-LINE** layer.

3. In the *Home* tab>*Create Design* panel, expand the *Feature Line* drop-down list and select

 (Create Feature Lines from Objects).

4. In the *Create Feature Lines* dialog box, complete the following, as shown in Figure 7–75:

   - Set *Site* to **Pond_Object**.
   - For *Name*, type **Channel to Pond**.
   - Leave the *Style* as **ASC_Basic Feature Line.**
   - Set *Conversion options* to **Erase existing entities**, **Assign elevations** and **Weed points.**
   - Click **OK** to close the dialog box.

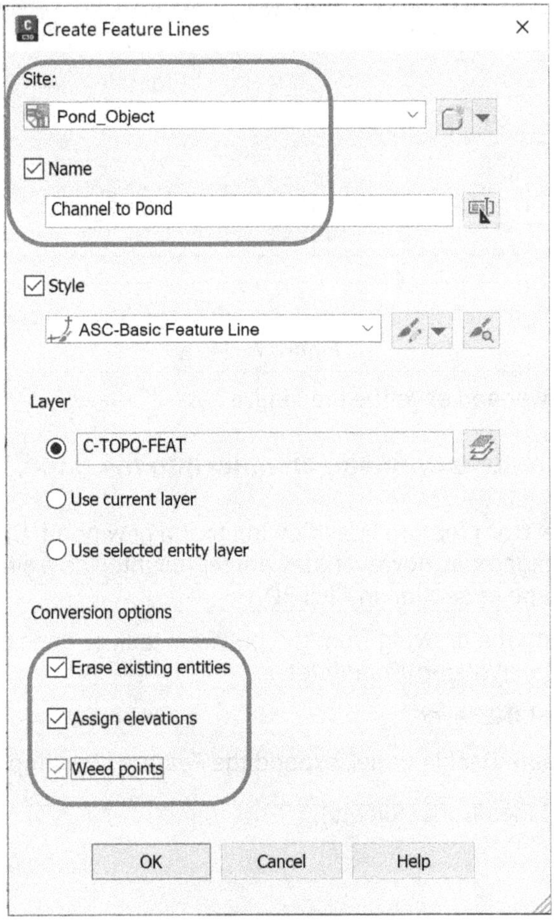

Figure 7–75

5. In the *Assign Elevations* dialog box, complete the following, as shown in Figure 7−76:

- Select **From Surface** for the surface.
- Select **Existing-Site**.
- Select the **Insert intermediate grade break points** checkbox.
- Select the **Relative elevation to surface** checkbox.
- Type in **-0.5** as the relative distance.
- Click **OK** to close the dialog box.

Figure 7−76

6. In the *Weed Vertices* dialog box, experiment with changes values for **Angle, Grade; Length** and **3D distance** and note how many vertices will be weeded. Return the values to their default values, as shown in Figure 7−77 and click **OK** to close the dialog box.

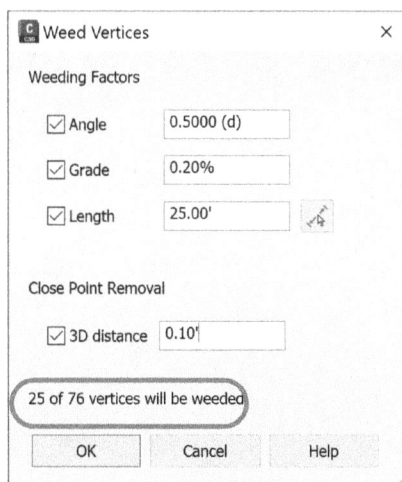

Figure 7−77

7. Yellow alerts now mark the *Ascent-Pond* surface since a new feature line is now intersecting the surface. Right-click on the surface and select **Rebuild.**

8. In the *Home* tab>*Create Design* panel, expand the *Pond* drop-down list and click

    (Create Channel).

9. In the *Create channel* dialog box, set the following as shown in Figure 7–78:

    a. Set the *Name* to **Channel to Pond**.

    b. Set the *style* to **ASC-Channel**.

    c. Toggle on Feature line.

    d. Select **Channel to Pond** as the feature line from the drop-down menu.

    e. Click **OK** to close the *Create channel* dialog box.

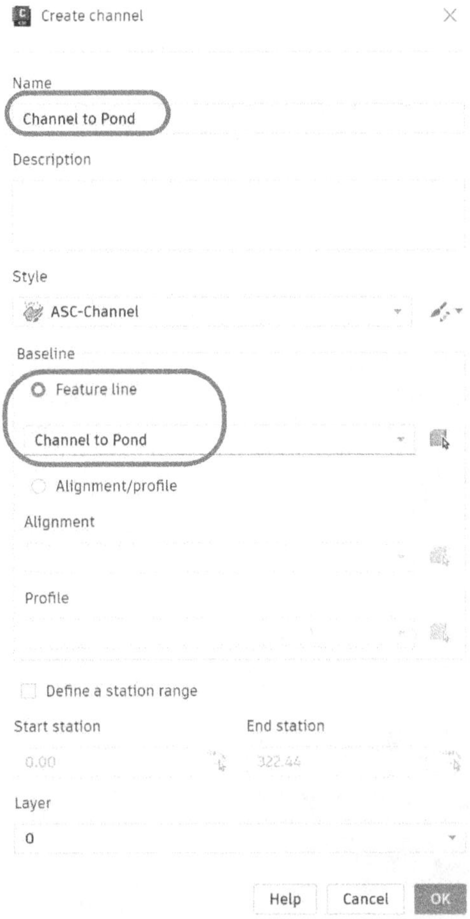

Figure 7–78

10. The channel is represented as a single linear object and does not reflect the actual shape or section in Civil 3D. Its primary use is for providing analytical data for establishing comprehensive drainage systems.

11. Select the new channel, and either through the contextual ribbon or the right-click menu, select **Channel Properties.**

12. Review all the tabs. On the *Section* tab, experiment with entering different parameter values and observe the changes in the preview section. Change the parameter settings back to the original values (Bottom width: 2.00', Side slope 1:00:1, Depth 2.00').

13. On the *Analysis data* tab, for *Outlet,* select **Ascent Pond** from the drop-down menu, as shown in Figure 7–79 and click **OK** to close the dialog box.

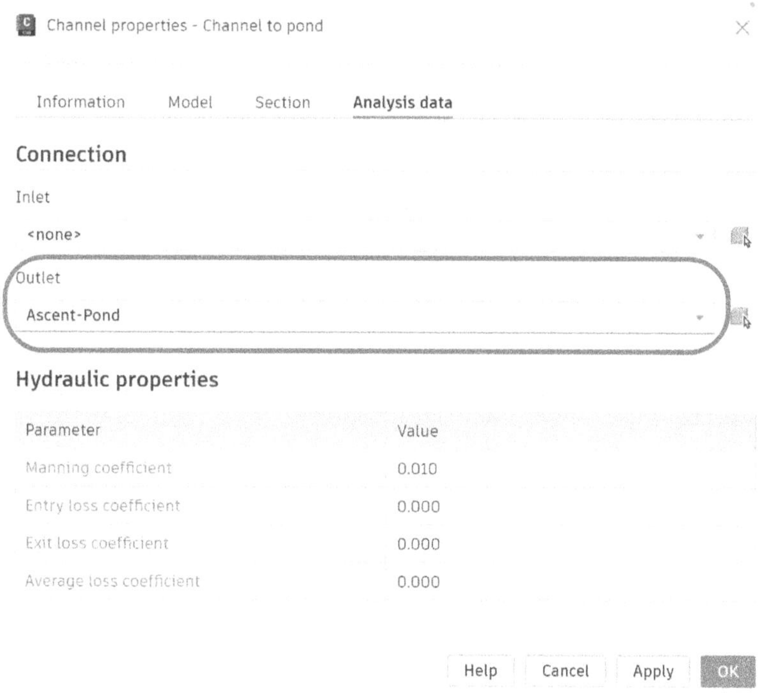

Figure 7–79

14. Click **OK** to close the *Channel properties* dialog box.

15. Save the drawing.

End of practice

7.5 Pond Staging Volumes

An important part of designing ponds or basins is ensuring that the pond can hold the volume of water anticipated. This is often done using stage-storage calculations. Stage-storage defines the relationship between the depth of water and storage volume in the storage basin or pond.

Within the Autodesk Civil 3D software, you can calculate incremental and cumulative volumes using two different calculations, as shown in Figure 7–80 and described below. Whichever method is chosen, the **Stage Storage** command is used to complete the stage storage volume analysis.

- Average End Area: Calculates the volume between two cross sections
- Conic Approximation: Calculates the volume between two sectional areas

$$V = \left(\frac{A_1 + A_2}{2}\right)L \qquad V = \left(\frac{h}{3}\right)(A_1 + A_2 + \sqrt{A_1 A_2})$$

Average End Area Method Equation　　**Conic Approximation Method Equation**

Figure 7–80

How To: Calculate the Stage Storage Volumes of a Pond or Basin

1. Ensure that the contours are visible for the surface to analyze. This is done in the surface properties by selecting an appropriate surface style.

2. In the *Analyze* tab, expand the *Design* panel and click (Stage Storage).

3. In the *Stage Storage* dialog box, set the following, as shown in Figure 7–81:

   * Enter a *Report Title*.

   * Enter a *Project Name*.

   * Enter a *Basin Description*.

   * For the *Volume Calculation Method*, select either **Average End Area**, **Conic Approximation**, or **Both**.

   * For the *Basin Definition Options*, select either **Define Basin from Entity** or **Use Manual Contour Data Entry**, then click **Define Basin**.

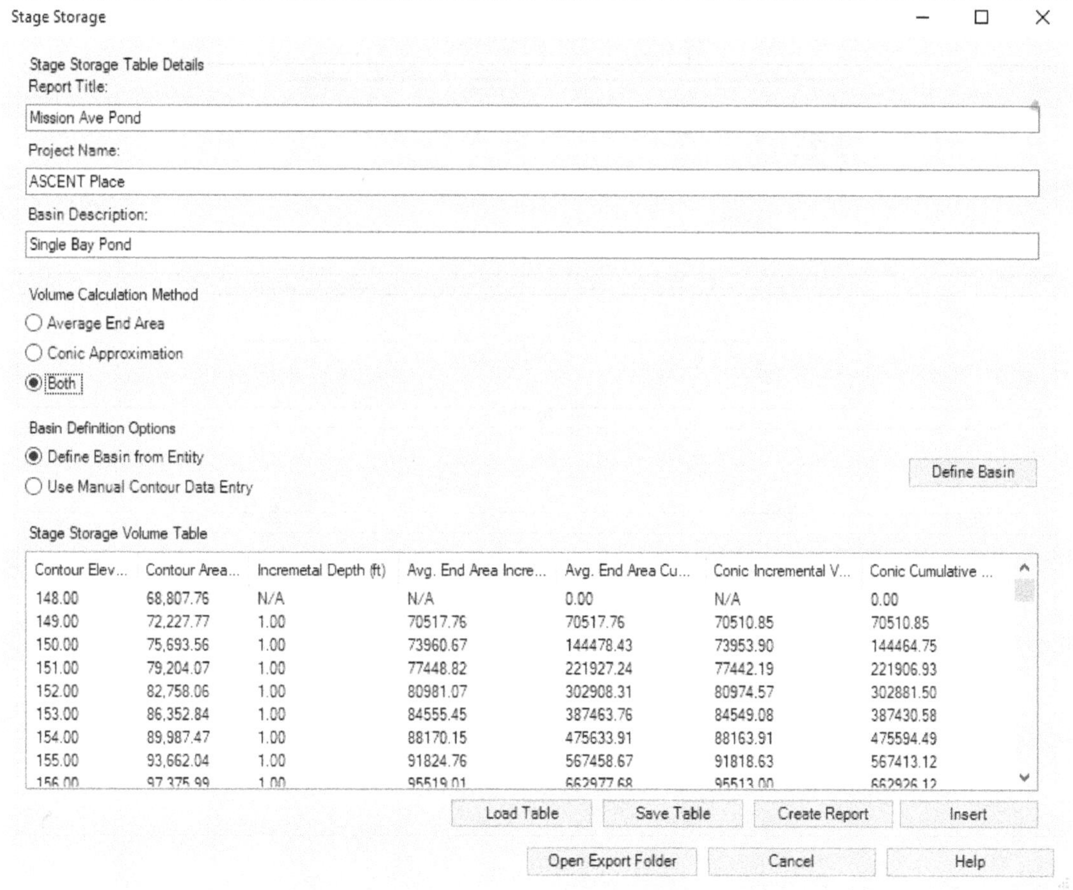

Stage Storage						− □ ✕

Stage Storage Table Details
Report Title:

Mission Ave Pond

Project Name:

ASCENT Place

Basin Description:

Single Bay Pond

Volume Calculation Method
○ Average End Area
○ Conic Approximation
◉ Both

Basin Definition Options
◉ Define Basin from Entity
○ Use Manual Contour Data Entry

[Define Basin]

Stage Storage Volume Table

Contour Elev...	Contour Area...	Incremetal Depth (ft)	Avg. End Area Incre...	Avg. End Area Cu...	Conic Incremental V...	Conic Cumulative ...
148.00	68,807.76	N/A	N/A	0.00	N/A	0.00
149.00	72,227.77	1.00	70517.76	70517.76	70510.85	70510.85
150.00	75,693.56	1.00	73960.67	144478.43	73953.90	144464.75
151.00	79,204.07	1.00	77448.82	221927.24	77442.19	221906.93
152.00	82,758.06	1.00	80981.07	302908.31	80974.57	302881.50
153.00	86,352.84	1.00	84555.45	387463.76	84549.08	387430.58
154.00	89,987.47	1.00	88170.15	475633.91	88163.91	475594.49
155.00	93,662.04	1.00	91824.76	567458.67	91818.63	567413.12
156.00	97,375.99	1.00	95519.01	662977.68	95513.00	662926.12

[Load Table] [Save Table] [Create Report] [Insert]

[Open Export Folder] [Cancel] [Help]

Figure 7–81

- If the **Use Manual Contour Data Entry** option is selected, a dialog box displays that enables you to manually enter the contour elevation and area, as shown in Figure 7–82.

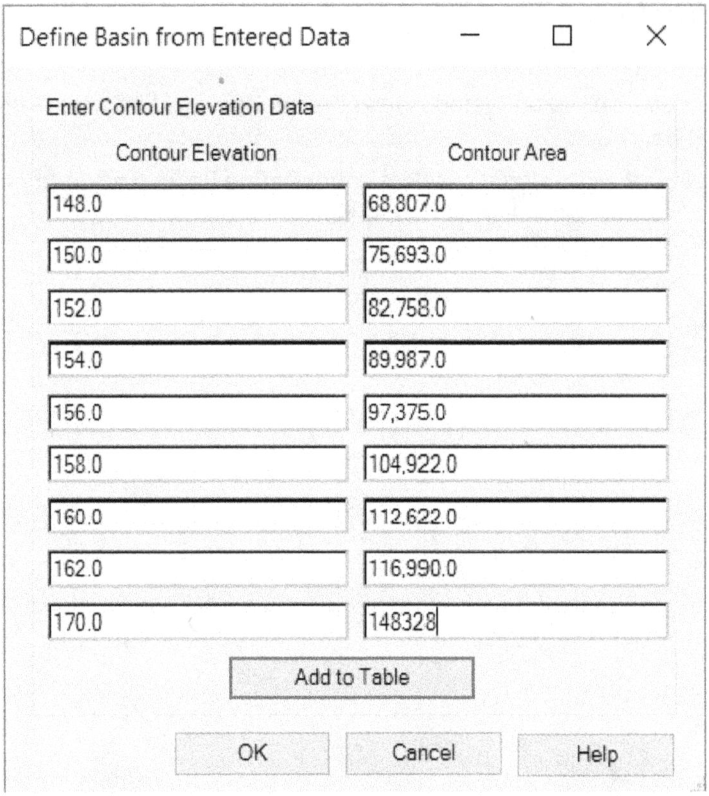

Figure 7–82

4. In the *Define Basin from Entities* dialog box, enter a *Basin Name,* and select one of the following options, as shown in Figure 7–83.

- **Define Basin from Surface Contours:** Enables you to select a surface
- **Define Basin from Polylines:** Enables you to select polylines representing surface contours

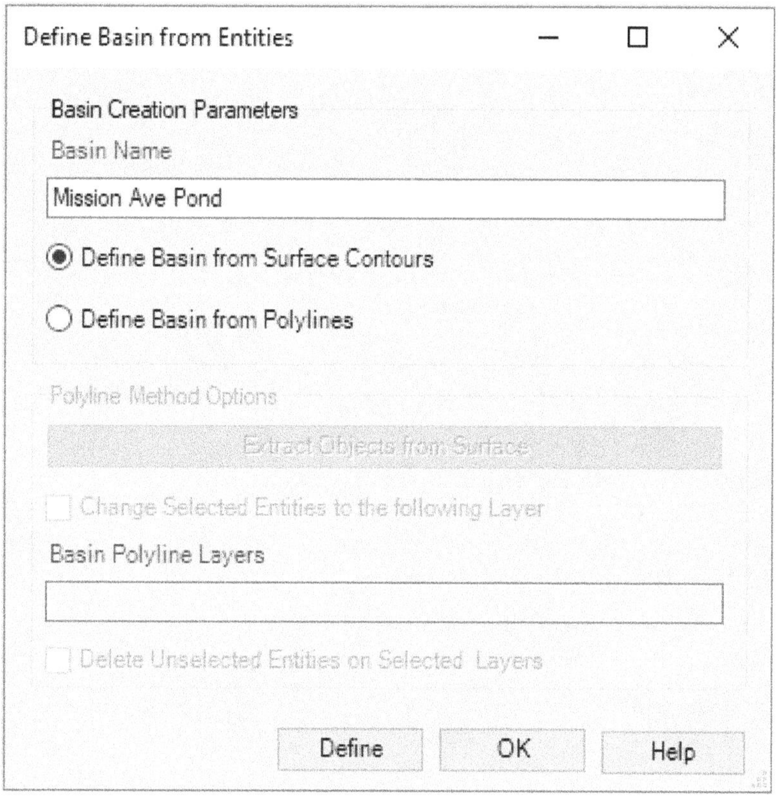

Figure 7–83

5. Click one of the following options to show the results:

- **Create Report:** Prompts you to save a *.txt file.
- **Insert:** Prompts you to select a point in the model to place the top-left corner of the volume table.

Practice 7d
Calculate Pond Staging Volume

Practice Objective

- Calculate the staging volume of the pond.

In this practice, you will calculate the volume of the pond at various depths, as shown in Figure 7–84, and then create a table showing those volumes.

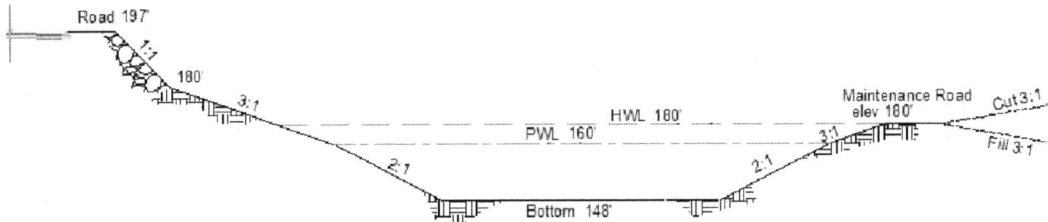

Figure 7–84

Task 1: Calculate the staging volume for the pond.

1. Continue working with the drawing from the previous practice or open **POND-E.dwg** from the C:\Civil 3D Grading\Working\Pond folder.

2. Ensure that the contours are visible for the pond surface.

3. In the *Analyze* tab>expand the *Design* panel, and click ⬚ (Stage Storage).

4. In the *Stage Storage* dialog box, do the following, as shown in Figure 7–85:

   - For the *Report Title*, type **Mission Ave Pond**.
   - For the *Project Name*, type **ASCENT Place**.
   - For the *Basin Description*, type **Single Bay Pond**.
   - For the *Volume Calculation Method*, select **Both**.
   - For the *Basin Definition Options*, select **Define Basin from Entity**, then click **Define Basin**.

Figure 7–85

5. In the *Define Basin from Entities* dialog box, enter **Mission Ave Pond** for the *Basin Name*. Select **Define Basin from Surface Contours**, as shown in Figure 7–86, and click **Define**.

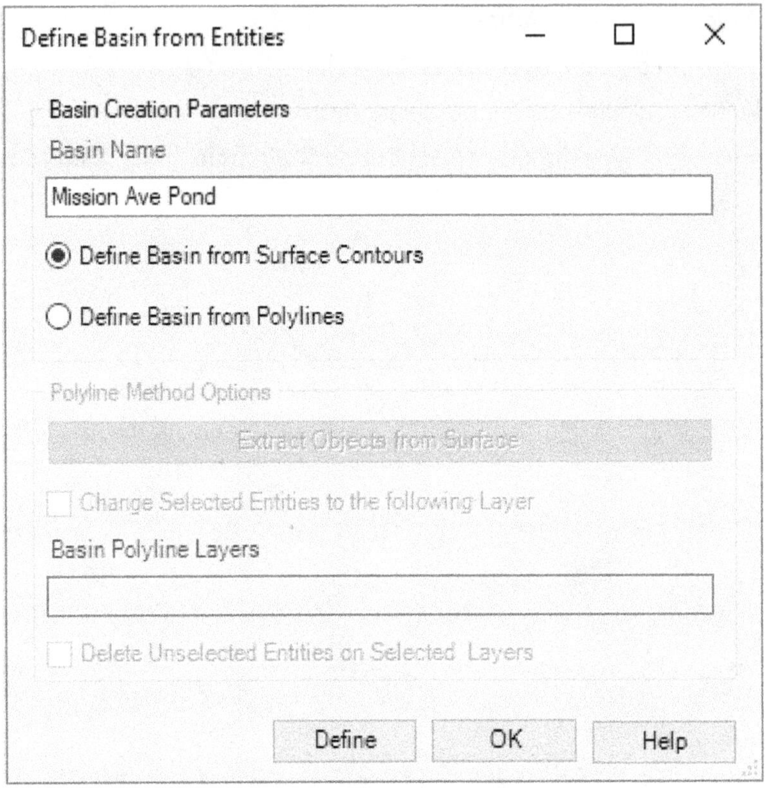

Figure 7–86

6. In the model, select the contours representing the pond surface.

7. In the *Stage Storage* dialog box, click **Insert**.

8. In the model, click to place the top-left corner of the table.

9. Close the *Stage Storage* dialog box.

10. Save the drawing.

End of practice

7.6 The Grading Optimization Pond Object

With the traditional Civil 3D grading tools, it takes some effort to come up with even a preliminary pond layout with a proper range of storage capacity.When applying a Pond Grading Object to a closed polyline, the *Pond Properties* dialog box displays. This is perhaps the most complex dialog box of all the Grading Objects, as shown in Figure 7–87.

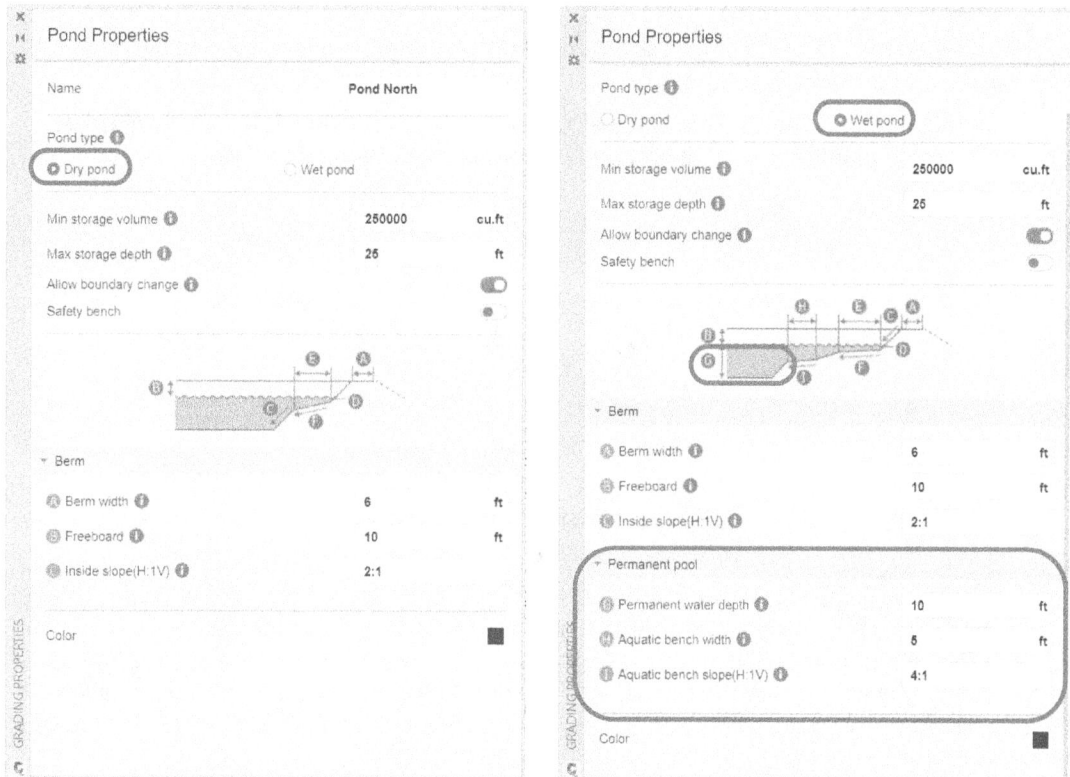

Figure 7–87

Dry vs Wet pond

A dry pond is designed to retain water only for enough time for the contents to be discharged with a calculated flowrate. It can retain the runoff from the developed site long enough for sediments to settle; the pond may remain dry the rest of the time.

A wet pond is designed to maintain some or all of the water throughout the year. It allows sediment to settle and can contain multiple basin along with plants at various levels to absorb the sediment.

When a Grading Object pond is designated as a wet pond, parameters for the permanent pool are entered, and the corresponding graphics change, as shown on the right in Figure 7–87. Both types of pond can have **berms** and **safety benches**, it is only the wet pond that has additional parameters for a permanent pool.

The **Aquatic Bench** is an area of shallow depth and minimal slope inside the perimeter of a wet pond and inside the safety bench, if so equipped. It is designed to house aquatic and wetland plants.

When designating a pond as a wet pond, the following information is required, as shown in Figure 7–88:

- **Permanent Water Depth (G)**: This is the depth of the pond bottom to the bottom of the freeboard.
- **Aquatic Bench Width (H)**: This is the width of the aquatic bench. It is usually quite shallow to promote plant growth.
- **Aquatic Bench slope (I)**: This is the slope of the aquatic bench. It is usually quite gentle to promote plant growth. It is entered as Horizontal to Vertical (H:1V)

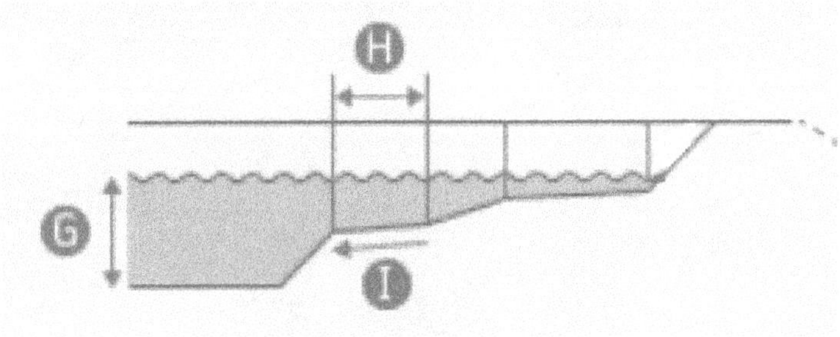

Figure 7–88

Storage Capacity

Storage capacities for ponds are essential. They are derived from complex calculations involving the area of planned hard surfaces, the varying levels of absorption, the rainfall data, the corresponding volumes of the runoff, etc. The ponds must be capable of holding such volumes based on 10, 50, or 100 year storms. If the ponds are dry ponds, then some type of discharge, outfall, or output system must be designed as well.

For either a wet or dry pond, the following information is required:

- **Minimum storage volume**: This is the minimum storage capacity of the pond, either wet or dry.
- **Maximum storage depth**: This is the sum of the Freeboard depth (B) and the permanent water depth (G) (if a wet pond), as shown in Figure 7–89.
- **Allow Boundary Change:** A toggle to determine if the outline of the pond as designated by the closed polyline can be altered to accommodate the required volumes.

Min storage volume 🛈		250000	cu.ft
Min storage volume 🛈		30000	cu.ft
🛇 Max storage depth 🛈		5	ft
Allow boundary change 🛈			🔘
Safety bench			⦿

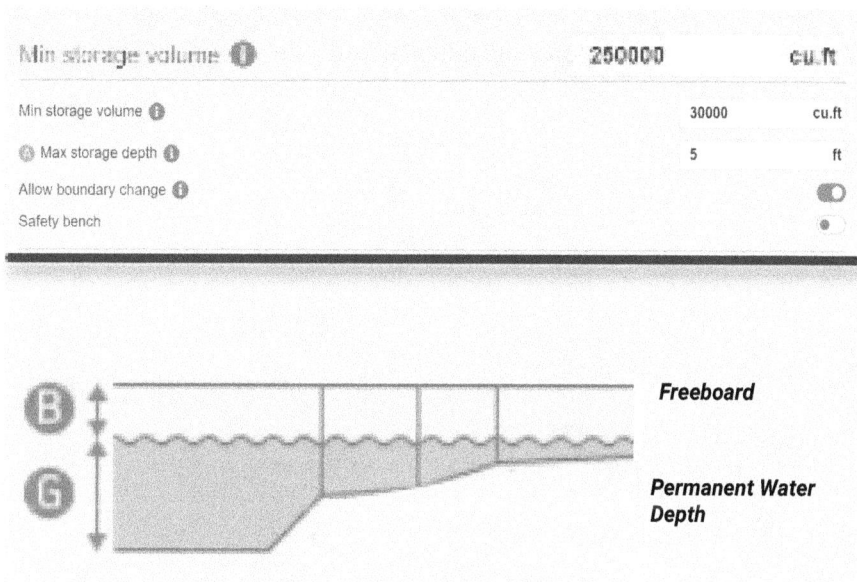

Figure 7–89

Ponds now have a property to define the maximum storage depth of both wet and dry ponds.

Berms, Safety Benches, and Freeboards

Berms, Safety Benches, and Freeboards are part of a pond's safety features designed to keep accidents to a minimum.

* A **Berm** will offer an incline up to the rim of the pond.

* A **Freeboard** is the distance between the designed maximum capacity water elevation of the pond and the top of the berm. 3 feet (1 meter) is a standard value, which means at maximum capacity, the water elevation is 3 feet (1 meter) below the top of the berm, as shown in Figure 7–90.

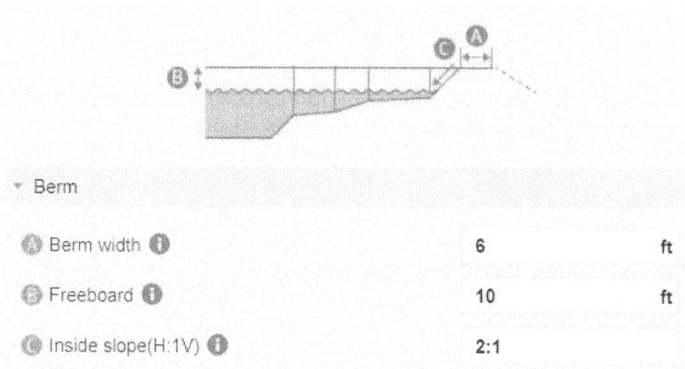

▾ Berm		
Ⓐ Berm width 🛈	6	ft
Ⓑ Freeboard 🛈	10	ft
Ⓒ Inside slope(H:1V) 🛈	2:1	

Figure 7–90

- A **Safety Bench** is on the inside of a berm. It is a slightly inclined bench with minimal depth for maintenance access to the pond and doubles as a safety zone, as shown in Figure 7−91.

Figure 7−91

Further Grading Objects can be used in Grading Object to fine tune the preliminary pond.

Visualization Toolbar

There are some great tools to aid in the understanding and analysis of the Grading Optimization processing. Many of these are available in the *Visualization* toolbar. The toolbar contains a collection of tools for changing the display of the surface for a variety of purposes, as shown in Figure 7−92.

Figure 7−92

Note: A cyan sheen on the icon means that this is the current option.

In the *Grading Object* interface, the [icon] *Visualization* toolbar in the lower left corner toggles the *Visualization* toolbar. The toolbar is divided into four sections:

1. Results:

[icon] **Cut-Fill** - Displays the area of removed material (Cut) and areas of added material (Fill) in color, as shown in Figure 7−93.

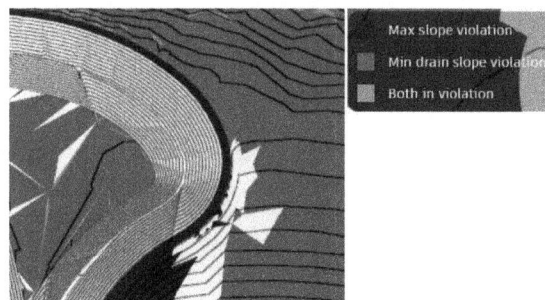

Figure 7–93

Violations - Displays the area where the given slope constraints cannot be met, in shades of red, as shown in Figure 7–94. The categories are:

- Dark Red - for the maximum slope violation
- Medium Red - for the minimum drain slope violation
- Bright Red - for both minimum and maximum slope in violation. It exceeds the maximum slope and it does not meet with minimum drainage slope.

Figure 7–94

Hint: Tooltips in Violation View

When in the *Violation* view, you can hover over a red area, and a tooltip explains the violation for that area, as shown in Figure 7–95.

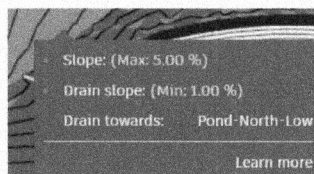

Figure 7–95

⊘ **None** - Turns off any results being displayed.

2. Theme:

(Note that with the different themes, the scale on the right side changes accordingly.)

Elevation - Displays the surface in elevation ranges, as shown in Figure 7–96.

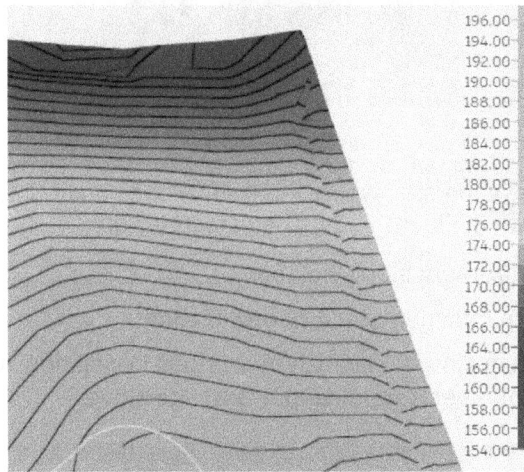

Figure 7–96

Constant - Displays the surface as a constant with no themes applied, as shown in Figure 7–97.

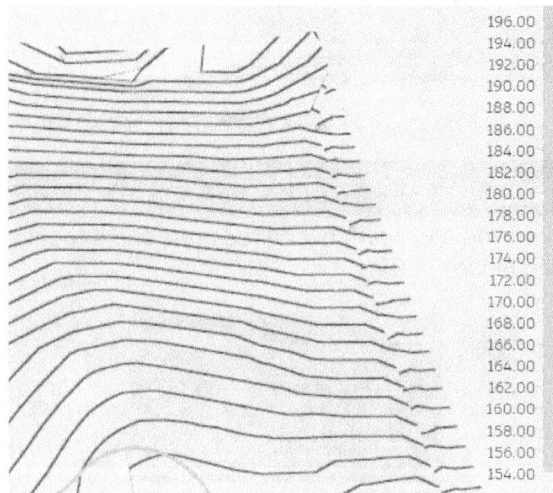

Figure 7–97

Grayscale - Displays the surface in elevation ranges in grayscale, as shown in Figure 7–98.

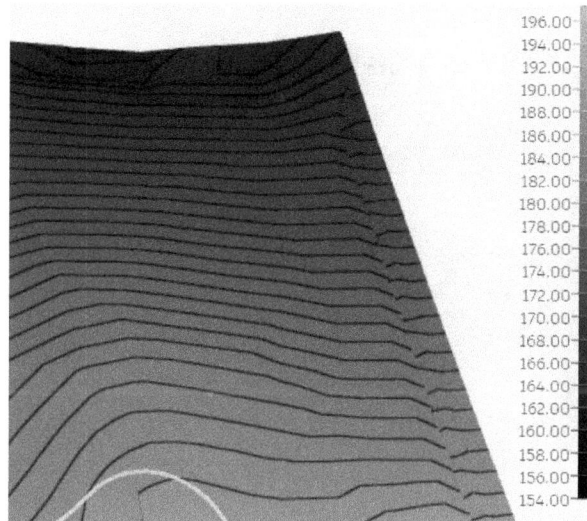

Figure 7–98

Slope - Displays the surface with slope ranges, as shown in Figure 7–99.

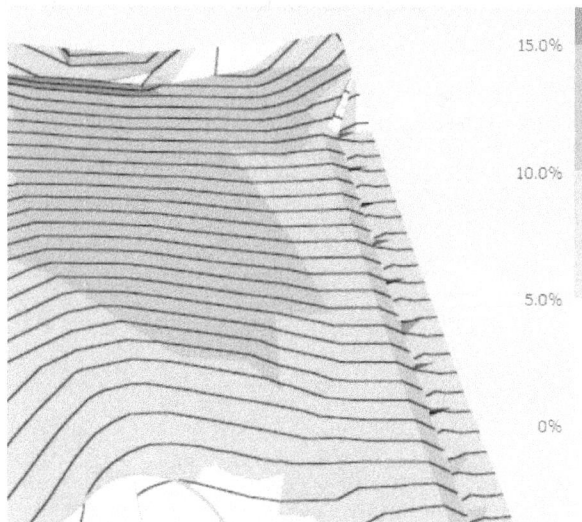

Figure 7–99

Aspect - Displays the surface with aspect ranges, as shown in Figure 7–100. Aspect refers to the compass direction.

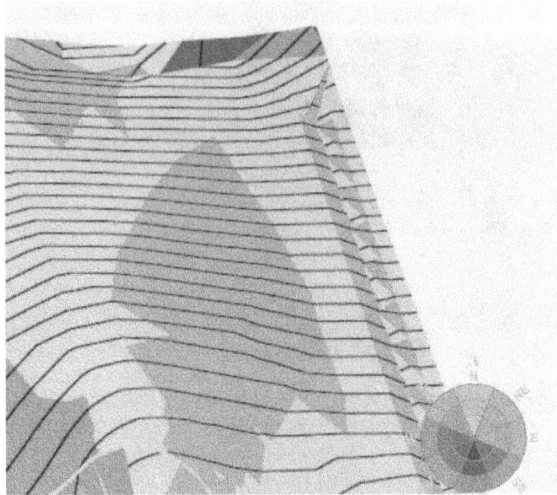

Figure 7–100

3. Topology:

Contours - Represents the surface as contour lines, as shown in Figure 7–101.

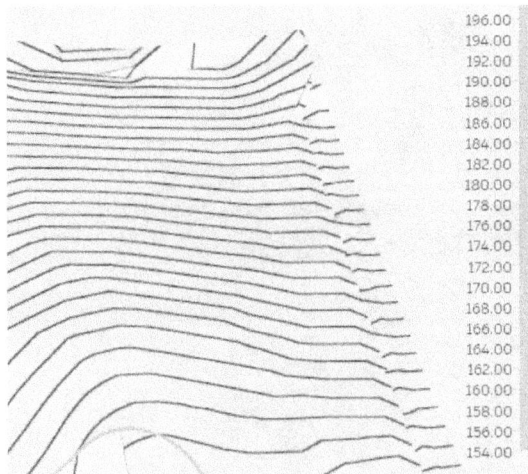

Figure 7–101

Wireframe - Represents the surface as TIN (Triangulated Irregular Network) lines, as shown in Figure 7–102.

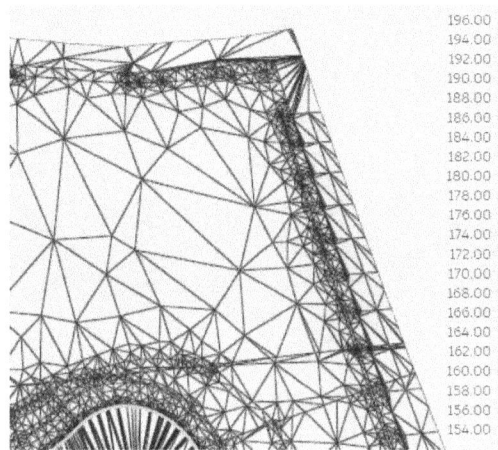

Figure 7–102

4. Hydrology:

Direction Arrows - Displays small cyan arrows on each underlying TIN triangle indicating its slope direction, as shown in Figure 7–103. These arrows are difficult to see, so zooming in is required. However, when Direction Arrows are enabled, panning and zooming become much slower; therefore, it is recommended to zoom and pan to the desired location before enabling the Direction Arrows.

Figure 7–103

None - Turns off the Direction Arrows.

⚙ **Visualization Settings** - Sets the ranges for the Contour and Slope themes, as shown in Figure 7–104. Under *Advanced Settings* (when toggled **on**), you can change the values for the slope analysis.

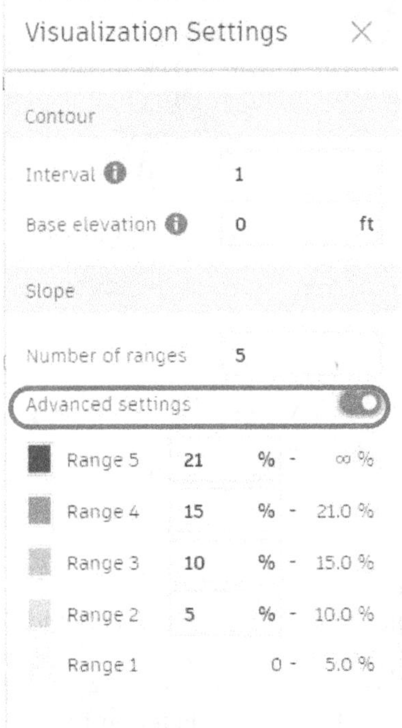

Figure 7–104

By clicking on a color box in the *Advanced Settings* section, you can change the color used for that particular slope range, as shown in Figure 7–105.

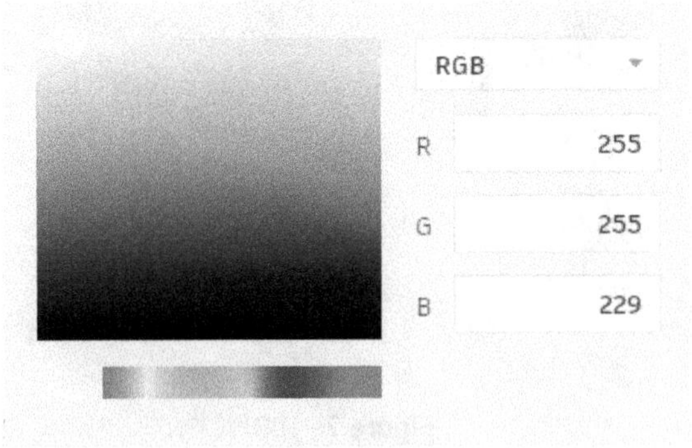

Figure 7–105

Practice 7e
Preliminary Pond Design with Grading Optimization

Practice Objectives

- Create a pond based on preliminary calculations.
- Add a drain line and a low point within the pond.
- Design a maintenance road for the pond.
- Calculate stage storage volumes.

The Grading Optimization process can be time consuming, and you may require additional time to complete the process than the estimated 30 minutes. In this practice, you will create a pond based on preliminary calculations. You will add a drain line and a low point within that pond, and then design a maintenance road for the pond. Finally, you will calculate stage storage volumes for the pond.

The surface IDG-North, which was created earlier, has been referenced into this drawing through data shortcuts. The Ascent-Development project is current for this drawing.

Task 1: Create preliminary pond.

In this drawing, you will copy the pond outline from a reference drawing into your current drawing. You will create a pond grading object from it and assign certain parameters. You will also add a drain line at a low point for the pond and then process it in the grading optimization program.

1. Open **POND-GO-A.dwg** from the *C:\Civil 3D Grading\Working\Pond* practice files folder.

2. In the *View* tab>*Named Views* panel, select the **Pond-North** view.

3. There is a suggested pond outline drawn on the **Base-Proposed Engineering|L-Watr-N** layer that is turned off. Turn this layer on.

4. A blue polyline displays along the north and west property lines, as shown in Figure 7–106.

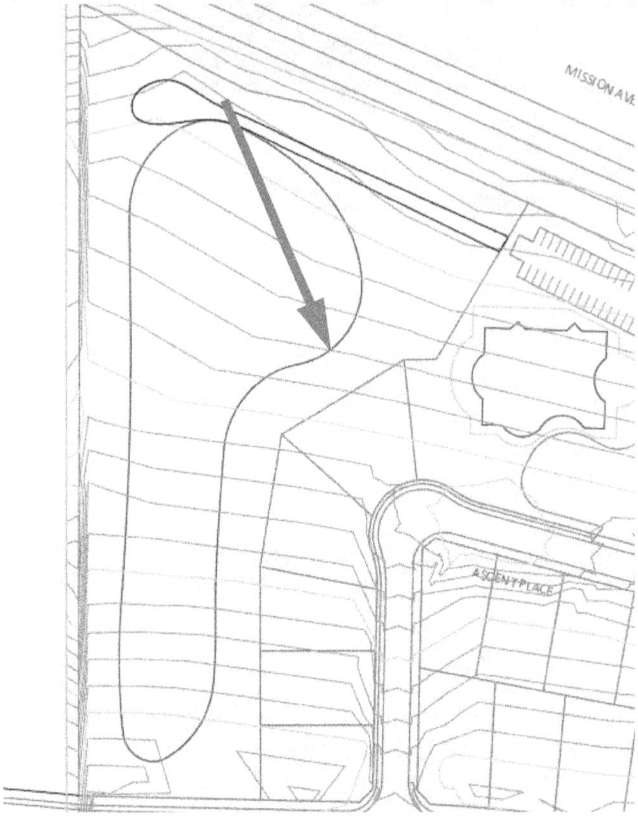

Figure 7–106

5. Type **NCOPY**.

   *Note: For more information on the **NCOPY** command, refer to the AutoCAD Help documentation.*

6. Select the blue outline of the pond as shown in Figure 7–106. Press <Enter> to finish your selection set.

7. Press <Enter> for **Displacement** and press <Enter> again for **0,0,0**. This means that there is no displacement and the polyline that you copied will be in the same place as the original XREF.

8. Select the polyline that was just generated.

9. Use the <Ctrl>+<1> keyboard shortcut to invoke the AutoCAD Properties, or invoke it from the right-click menu.

10. In the AutoCAD Properties, change the *Layer* of the polyline to **C-Grad-Pond**, as shown in Figure 7–107.

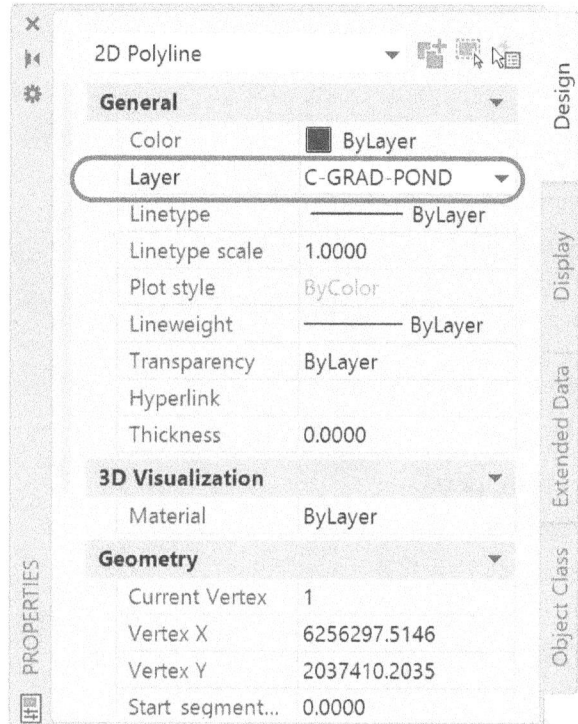

Figure 7–107

11. In the *Analyze* tab>G*rading Optimization* panel, select ▢ Grading Object Tools) to open up the Tool Palette.

12. In the *Grading Objects* Tool Palette, select **Pond**. In the drawing, select the polyline that you have just added and press <Enter>.

13. Press <Enter> again.

14. In the *Pond Properties* dialog box, set the following, as shown in Figure 7–108:

- *Name:* **Pond North**
- *Pond type:* **Wet pond**
- *Min storage volume:* **250,000 cu.ft**
- *Max storage depth:* **25 ft**
- *Allow boundary change:* toggled **on**
- *Safety bench:* toggled **off**

Expand the *Berm* section and set the following:

- *Berm width:* **6 ft**
- *Freeboard:* **10 ft**
- *Inside slope(H:1V):* **2:1**

Expand the *Permanent pool* section and set the following:

- *Permanent water depth:* **10 ft**
- *Aquatic bench width:* **3 ft**
- *Aquatic bench slope (H:1V):* **4:1**

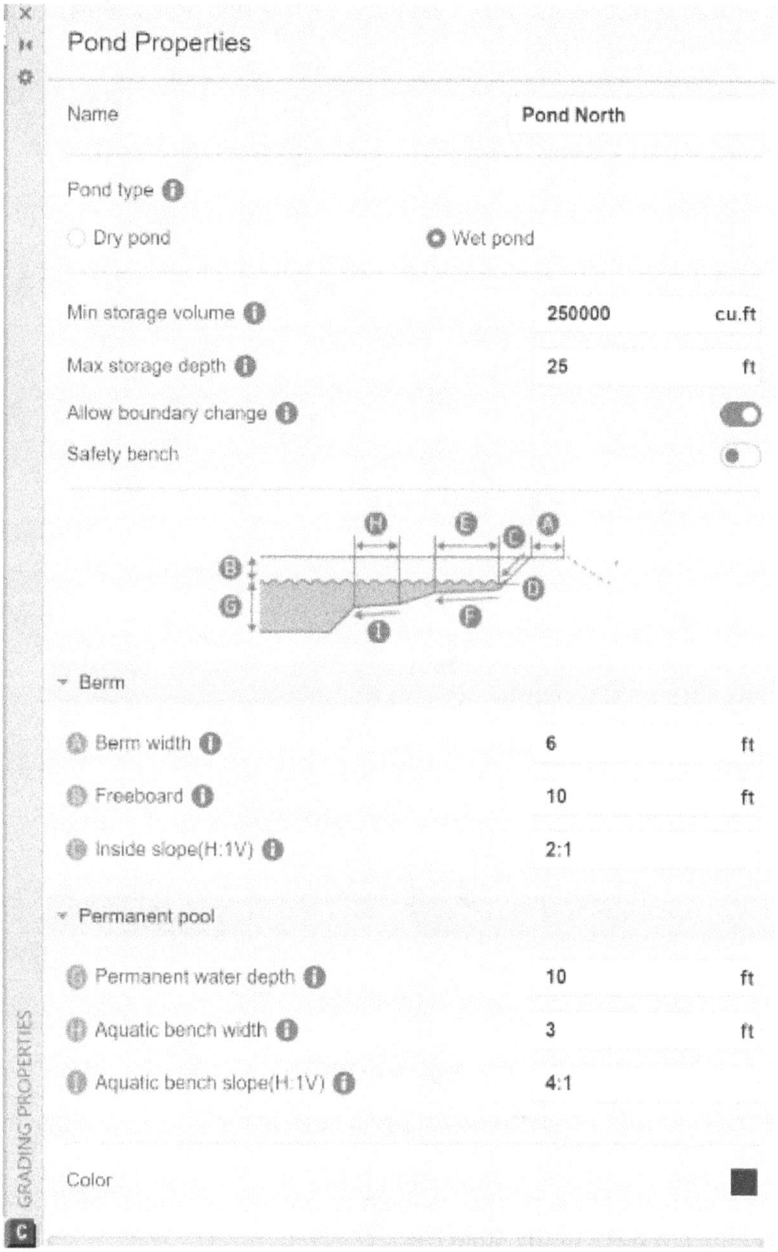

Pond Properties

Name	**Pond North**

Pond type ⓘ

◯ Dry pond   ◉ Wet pond

Min storage volume ⓘ	250000	cu.ft
Max storage depth ⓘ	25	ft
Allow boundary change ⓘ		⬤
Safety bench		⬤

▾ Berm

Ⓐ Berm width ⓘ	6	ft
Ⓑ Freeboard ⓘ	10	ft
Ⓒ Inside slope(H:1V) ⓘ	2:1	

▾ Permanent pool

Ⓖ Permanent water depth ⓘ	10	ft
Ⓗ Aquatic bench width ⓘ	3	ft
Ⓘ Aquatic bench slope(H:1V) ⓘ	4:1	

Color	⬛

Figure 7–108

15. Press <Esc> to deselect the pond and close the *Pond Properties* dialog box.

16. Set the current layer to **C-Grad-Dran**.

17. Zoom in to the pond.

18. Create an AutoCAD polyline, as shown in Figure 7–109, and press <Enter>. The polyline should go from south to north.

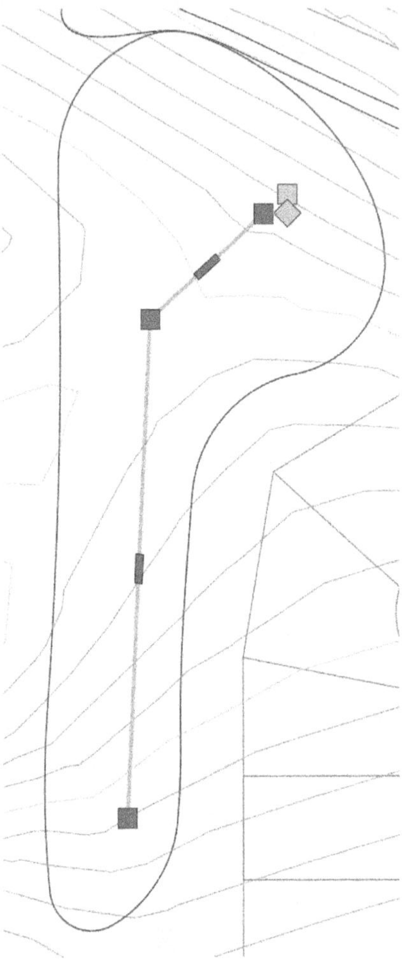

Figure 7–109

19. In the *Grading Objects* Tool Palette, select **Drain Line**. In the drawing, select the polyline that you just drew.

   • Note: The start point of the polyline is the high point of the drain line. The end of the polyline is the low point of the drain line.

20. Press <Enter>.

21. In the *Drain Line Properties* dialog box, change the *Name* to **Pond North Drain**. Press <Enter> to confirm the name, then press <Esc> to deselect the polyline and close the *Drain Line Properties* dialog box.

22. In the *Home* tab>*Create Ground Data* panel, expand **Points** and select **Create Points - Miscellaneous>Manual**.

23. Zoom in to the northern portion of the pond and create a point as shown in Figure 7–110.

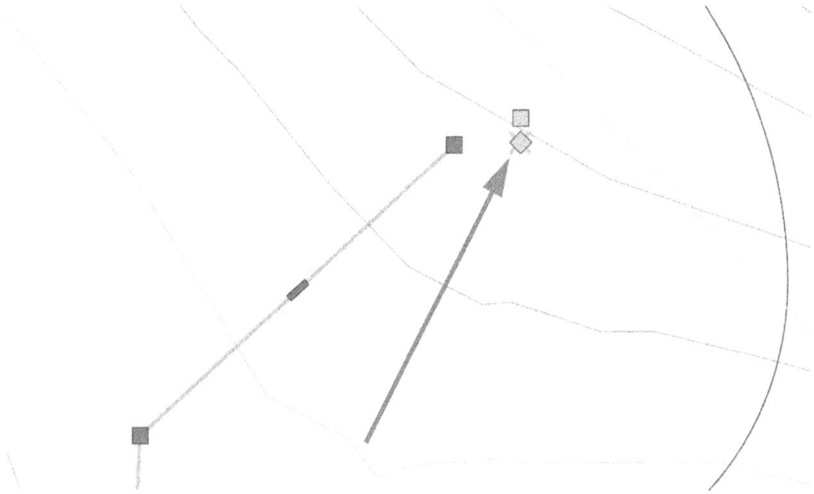

Figure 7–110

24. Enter **Low Pond Point** for the description.

25. For the elevation, press <Enter> to assign no elevation.

26. Press <Esc> to finish creating points.

27. Close the *Create Points* dialog box.

28. In the *Grading Objects* Tool Palette, select **Low Point**. In the drawing, select the point that you just created and press <Enter>.

29. In the *Low Point Properties* dialog box, change the name to **Pond-N-Low**.

   • Note the *Diamond shape* option. You can toggle the diamond shape **on** and **off**. When toggled **on**, you can set the angle of the diamond. In this case, leave it toggled **off**.

30. Save the drawing.

Task 2: Assign more grading objects.

1. Continue working on the same drawing from the previous task. If you did not complete the previous task, open **POND-GO-B.dwg** from the *C:\Civil 3D Grading\Working\Pond* practice files folder.

2. In the drawing, select the yellow polyline that outlines the two existing corridors, as shown in Figure 7–111.

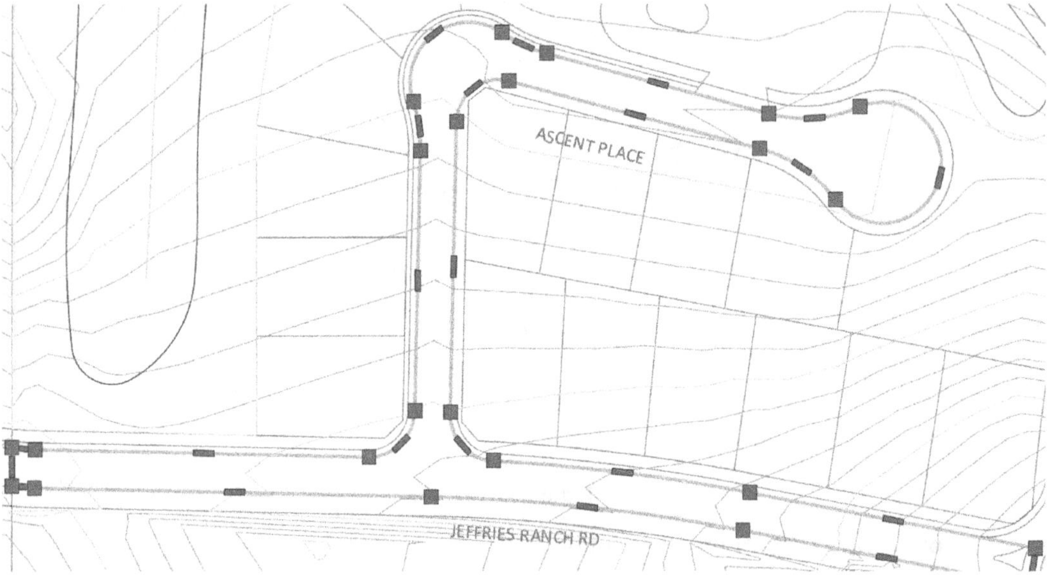

Figure 7–111

3. In the *Grading Objects* Tool Palette, select **Exclusion Zone**. Note that since the polyline was already selected, the exclusion zone is automatically assigned to the selected object.

4. In the *Exclusion Zone Properties* dialog box, change the name to **Existing Corridors** and press <Enter>.

5. Press <Esc> to clear the selection.

6. Change the current layer to **C-Grad-Limt**.

7. Draw an AutoCAD polyline, as shown in Figure 7–112. Use the AutoCAD endpoint snap to select the blue parcel line in the XREF. Close the polyline.

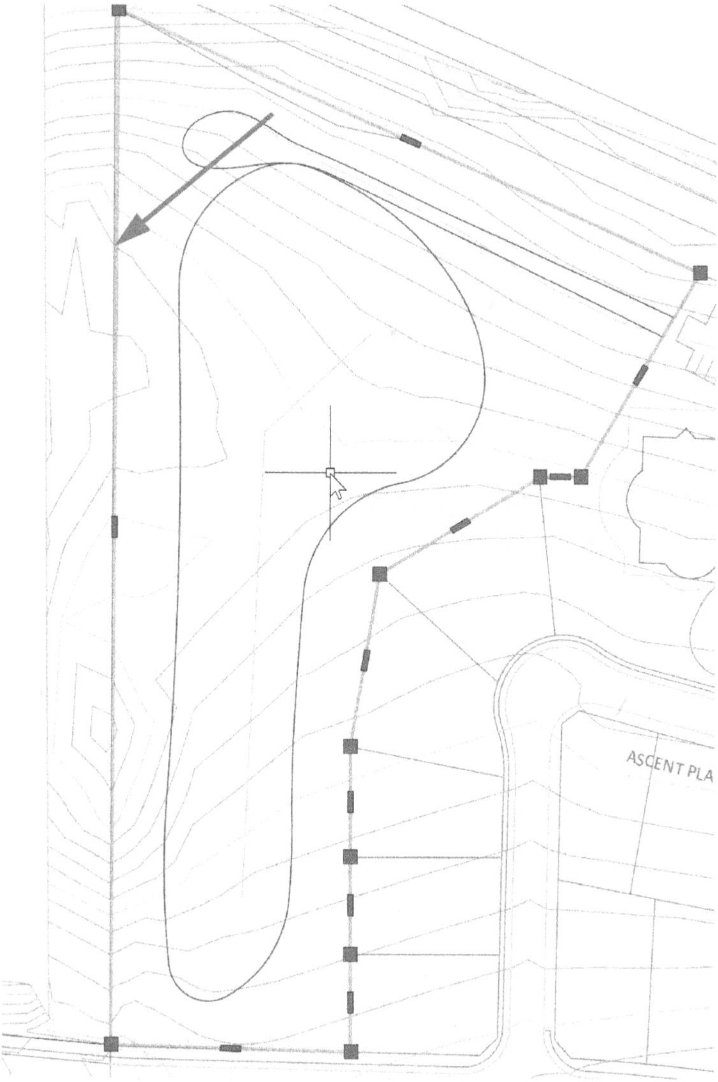

Figure 7–112

8. Select the polyline that you just drew.

9. In the *Grading Objects* Tool Palette, select **Grading Limit**.

10. In the *Grading Limit Properties* dialog box, set the following, as shown in Figure 7–113:

- *Name:* **Pond Limits**
- *Min drain slope:* **0.5%**
- *Max slope:* **12%**
- **Exclusive drainage**: toggled **on**
- *Depth of material:* **2 ft**

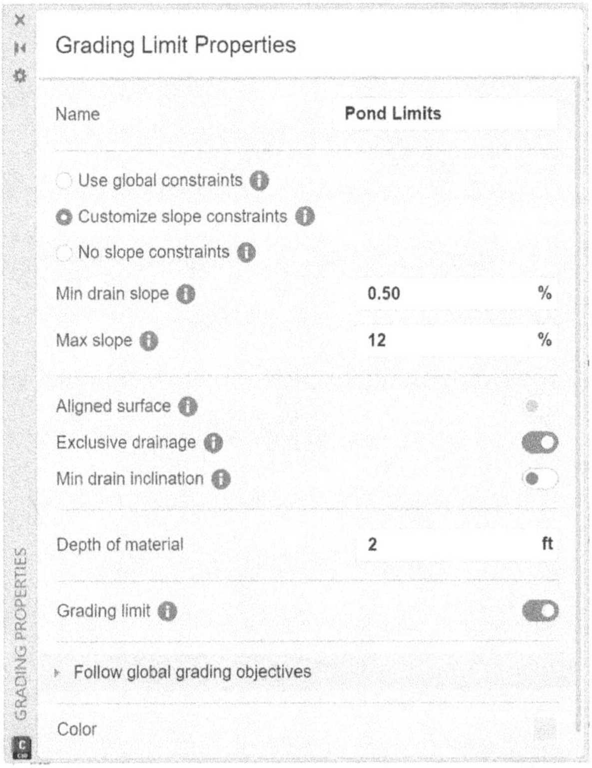

Figure 7–113

11. Toggle **on** the **Aligned surface** option and note that **Aligned surface** and **Exclusive drainage** cannot be toggled on simultaneously. Toggle **Exclusive drainage** back **on** (which automatically toggles **off** the **Aligned surface** option).

12. Press <Esc> to clear the selection.

13. In the *Analyze* tab>*Grading Optimization* panel, click ⊟ (Grading Objects Browser).

14. In the *Grading Objects Browser,* expand **Pond** and select **Pond North**. Review the information, then close the *Pond Properties* dialog box.

15. In the *Grading Objects Browser,* expand **Grading Limit** and select **Pond Limits**. Review the information, then close the *Grading Limit Properties* dialog box.

16. Save the drawing.

17. In the *Analyze* tab>*Grading Optimization* panel, click (Optimize). Note that no EG surface needs to be selected, as IDG-North is the only surface in the drawing.

18. At the bottom of the *Grading Optimization* window, click (Optimization Options).

19. In the *Optimization Options* window, set the following, as shown in Figure 7–114:

   * *Min drain slope*: **0.05**
   * *Max slope*: **33**
   * *Cut and fill constraint*: **None**
   * *Iteration:* **10000**
   * *Balance cut and fill:* **10**
   * *Minimize earthwork:* **40**
   * *Smooth surface:* **75**

Optimization Options   ✕

Global constraints

Min drain slope	0.05	%
Max slope	33	%
Cut and fill constraint	None	▾

Optimization

| Iteration | 10000 |

Objective Weights ⓘ

Balance cut and fill	10	▸
Minimize earthwork	40
Smooth surface	75

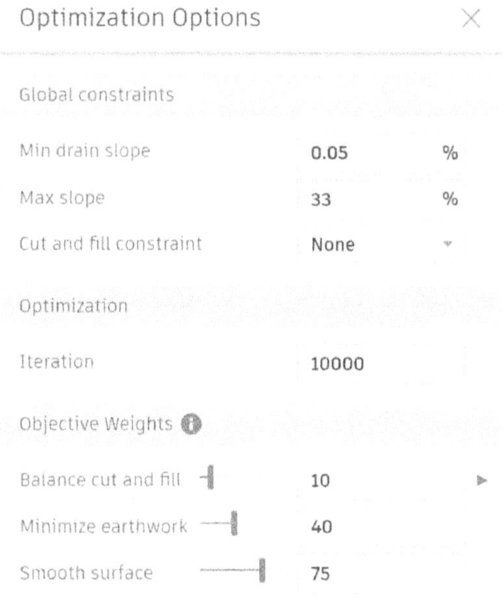

Figure 7–114

20. Close the *Optimization Options* window.

21. Click (Visualization Toolbar) in the lower-left corner to launch the *Visualization* toolbar.

22. Click **Optimize** to start the optimization process.

23. There are three warnings (as shown in Figure 7–115) - two about steep slopes due to an existing wall to the north of the property, and one about grading objects (for the pond) lying outside the grading limit. These can be dismissed by clicking the **Close** button.

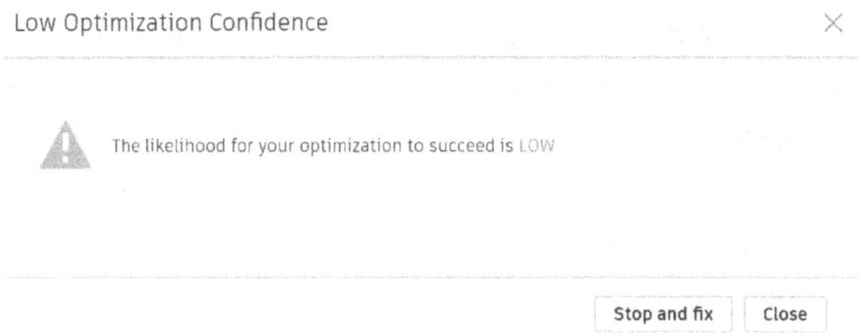

Low Optimization Confidence   ✕

⚠   The likelihood for your optimization to succeed is LOW

Stop and fix   Close

Figure 7–115

24. During the optimization, in the *Visualization* toolbar, change the *Topology* from Contours to **Wireframe**, as shown in Figure 7–116.

Result 🔻 ⨁ ⊘ | Theme 🔳 🔲 🔳 ⚞ ❇ | Topology 🔳 ⨁ | Hydrology ≋ ⊘   ⚙ ✕

Figure 7–116

25. Zoom in where the pond is being generated. Note that the processing only takes place within the grading limit.

26. In the *Visualization* toolbar, turn on the **Direction Vectors** for the *Hydrology*, as shown in Figure 7–117.

Result 🔻 ⨁ ⊘ | Theme 🔳 🔲 🔳 ⚞ ❇ | Topology 🔳 ⨁ | Hydrology ≋ ⊘   ⚙ ✕

Figure 7–117

Note: Zooming and panning become slower once the direction vectors are displayed. It is recommended that you zoom first before turning on the direction vectors.

27. Zoom in to see the various direction arrows for the hydrology.

28. In the *Visualization* toolbar, turn on **Violations**, as shown in Figure 7–118. Note the various triangles changing colors between bright red, red, and dark red.

Result 🔻 ⨁ ⊘ | Theme 🔳 🔲 🔳 ⚞ ❇ | Topology 🔳 ⨁ | Hydrology ≋ ⊘   ⚙ ✕

Figure 7–118

29. Hover over a red triangle and note the explanation within the tooltip, as shown in Figure 7–119.

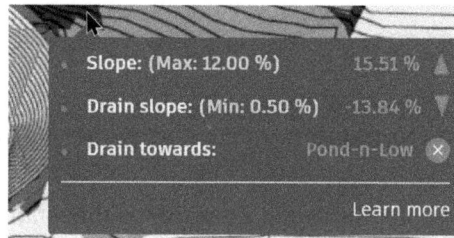

Figure 7–119

30. When the grading optimization is complete, click **Update Drawing.**

   *Note: If grading optimization takes too long, you can click **Stop** and move on to the next task, where you open a drawing that has already been optimized.*

31. Back in Civil 3D where the drawing originated, in the *Save Optimization Results* dialog box, select **Create new surface** and name the surface **Pond-N.**

32. Next to the *Style* field, click the **Surface Styles** button to select a surface style.

33. In the *Surface Styles* dialog box, select **ASC-Contours 1' and 5' (Design) with Slope Arrows**, as shown in Figure 7–120, and click **Finish** to close the *Surface Styles* dialog box.

Figure 7–120

34. In the *Save Optimization Results* window, click **Feature Lines**. Set *Name Prefix* to **Pond-**. Leave the Feature Line Style as is.

35. Click **Finish**. The surface is created with the designated surface style.

36. Save the drawing.

Task 3: Grade the maintenance access road for the pond (Optional).

1. Continue working on the same drawing from the previous task. If you did not complete the previous task, open **POND-GO-C.dwg** from the *C:\Civil 3D Grading\Working\Pond* practice files folder. Depending on time constraints, this task can be skipped.

2. In the *Grading Objects Tool* palette, select **Zone**. In the drawing, select the polyline on the C-ROAD layer, as shown in Figure 7–121.

   Note: The Pathway grading object is not ideal for the access road since the shape is not symmetrical, due to the cul-de-sac at the end.

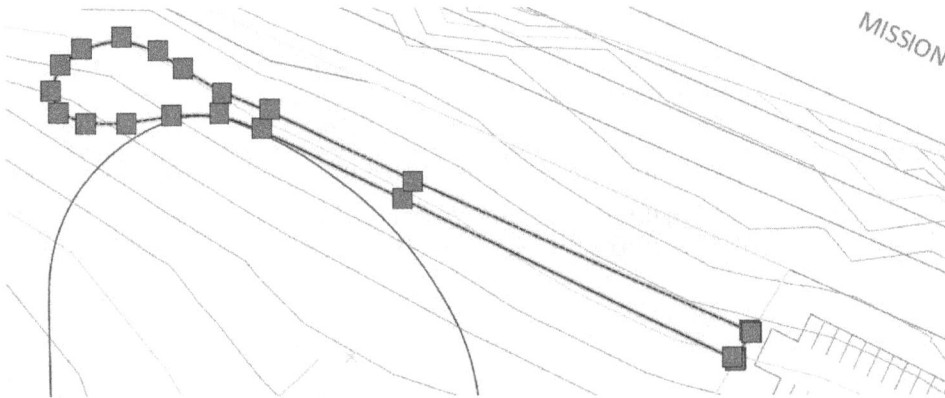

Figure 7–121

3. Press <Enter>. Note that even though you selected the Pathways grading object, it is merely a zone with some predefined parameters.

4. In the *Zone Properties* dialog box, change the following, as shown in Figure 7–122.

    *   *Name:* **Access-Road N**
    *   *Customize slope constraints*: toggle **on**
    *   *Min drain slope:* **1%**
    *   *Max slope:* **5%**
    *   *Aligned surface:* toggle **off**
    *   **Exclusive drainage***:* toggle **off**
    *   **Min drain inclination***:* toggle **on**
    *   *Inclination direction*: Click the pencil icon (✏). In the drawing, select a point perpendicular to the access road in a north-east bearing (or type in **55**).
    *   *Depth of material:* **0.75 ft**
    *   **Breakline***:* toggle **on**
    *   **Grading limit***:* toggle **off**

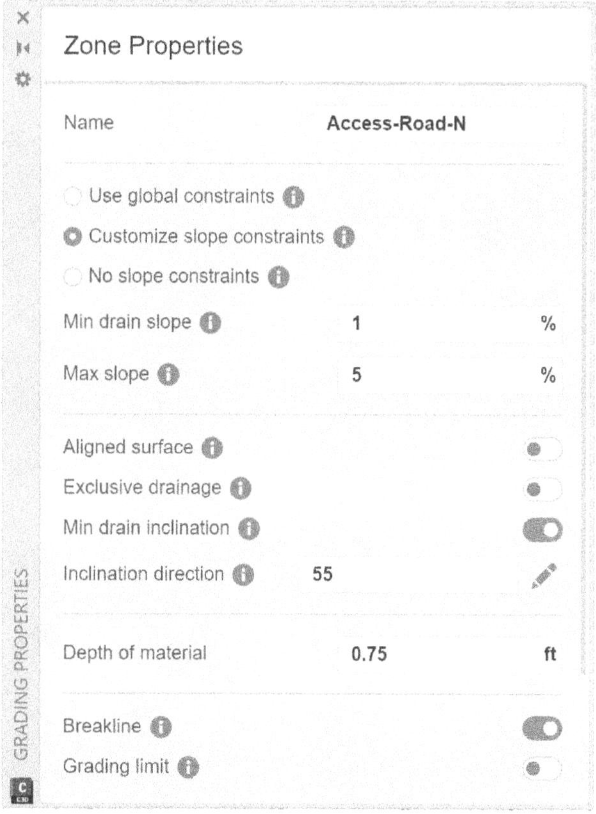

Figure 7–122

5. Press \<Esc\> to release the selection and close the *Zone Properties* dialog box.

6. Save the drawing.

7. In the *Analyze* tab>*Grading Optimization* panel, click ✦ (Optimize).

8. You are prompted to select a surface. Select the **Pond-N** surface by selecting a red contour in the drawing.

9. In the *Grading Optimization* window, verify that the *Optimization Options* are as follows (i.e., they are still set as before):

   * *Min drain slope*: **0.05**
   * *Max slope*: **33**
   * *Cut and fill constraint*: **None**
   * *Iteration:* **30000**
   * *Balance cut and fill:* **10**
   * *Minimize earthwork:* **40**
   * *Smooth surface:* **75**

   *Note: You will be updating the Pond-N surface when optimized. Previously, you had the iterations set to **10000**, to check the viability of the design of the pond. This time, we set the iterations higher for a more refined result.*

10. Click **Optimize**. You can dismiss the warning in the *Low Optimization Confidence* dialog box by clicking on the **Close** button.

11. Open the *Visualization* toolbar.

12. Zoom in to the pond access road.

13. Set the *Results* to **None**, as shown in Figure 7–123.

14. Change the *Theme* to **Grayscale**, as shown in Figure 7–123.

Figure 7–123

15. Change the *Theme* to **Slope** and note how the legend changes, as shown in Figure 7–124.

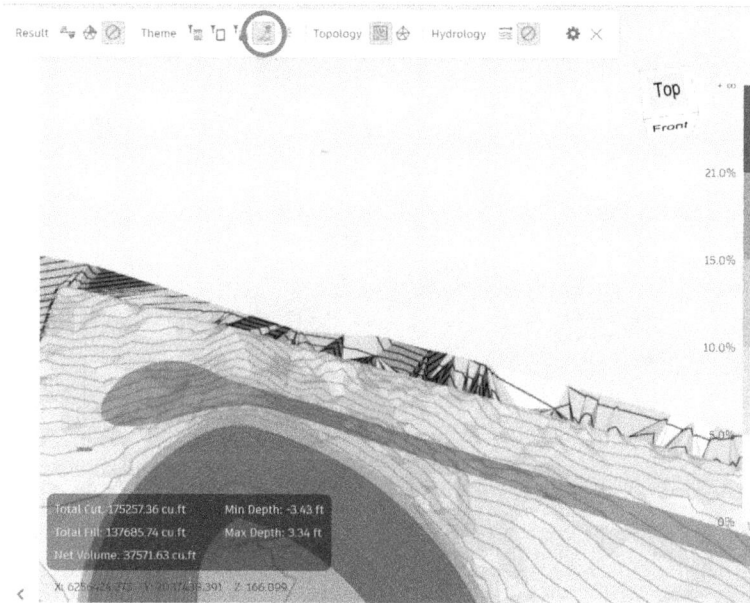

Figure 7–124

16. Change the *Theme* to **Aspect** and note the change in the legend, as shown in Figure 7–125.

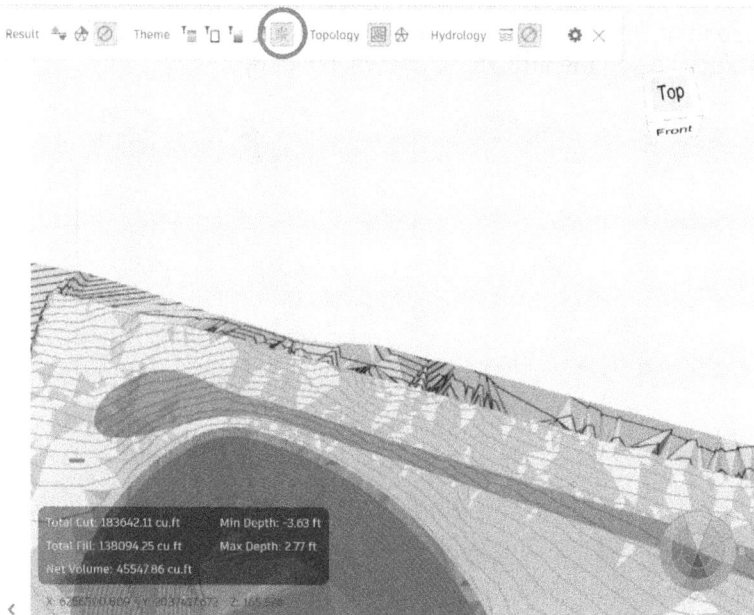

Figure 7–125

17. Change the *Theme* to **Constant** and note the change in the legend, as shown in Figure 7–126.

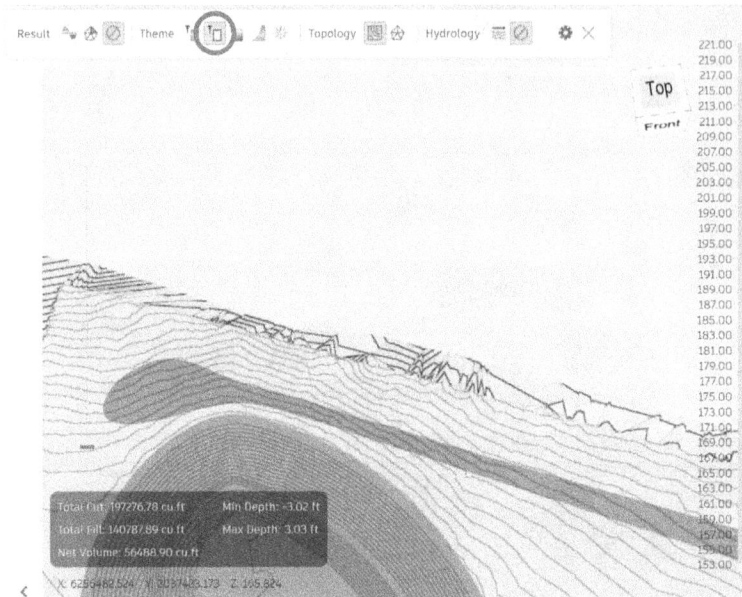

Figure 7–126

18. Change the *Theme* back to **Elevation**.

19. Zoom in close to an area. With the *Topology* set to **Contours**, turn on the **Direction Vectors** for the *Hydrology*, to see the arrows, as shown in Figure 7–127.

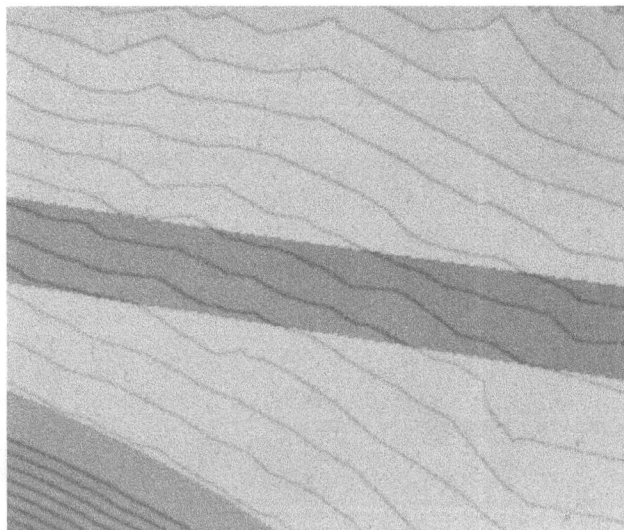

Figure 7–127

20. Change the *Topology* to **Wireframe** and note that the arrows tend to be more visible in this mode, as shown in Figure 7–128.

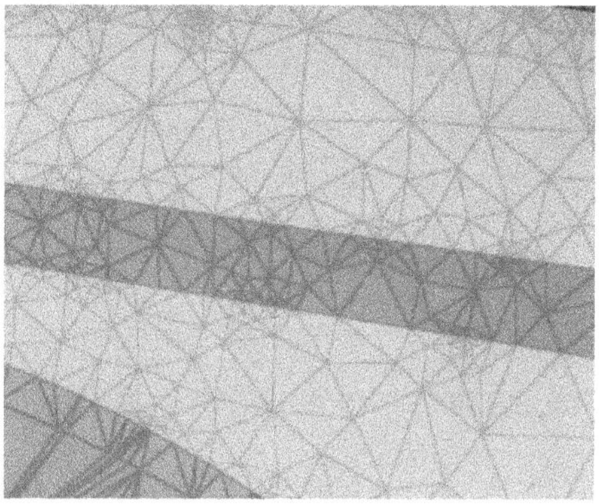

Figure 7–128

21. When the grading optimization is complete, click **Update Drawing**.

   *Note: If grading optimization takes too long, you can click **Stop** and move on to the next task, where you open a drawing that has already been optimized and surface imported.*

22. In the *Save Optimization Result* window, verify that the following are set:

   • *Surfaces*: **Update an existing surface** for **Pond-N**

   • *Feature Lines*: **Update existing feature lines** for the prefix of **Pond-**

   • *Points*: **Update an existing point group** for **Pond-N**

23. Click **Finish**.

24. The *Events* panel of the Panorama may open to warn you of duplicate points which are ignored. Dismiss the Event Viewer by clicking on the green check mark ☑.

25. Save the drawing.

Task 4: Review the surface.

1. Continue working on the same drawing from the previous task. If you did not complete the previous task, open **POND-GO-Z-Complete.dwg** from the *C:\Civil 3D Grading\Working\Pond* practice files folder.

2. Select the surface. In the right-click menu, click **Add to Model Viewer**.

3. In the *Model Viewer*, examine the surface. Change the view style to **Shaded with edges**.

4. Save and close the drawing.

End of practice

Chapter Review Questions

1. Which of the following is NOT part of a pond?

   a. Berm

   b. Bounded Point

   c. Freeboard

   d. Aquatic bench

2. A RETENTION pond discharges water from the pond at a controlled rate?

   a. False

   b. True

   c. Only in Northern climates

   d. Only in drought situations

3. Which of the following is NOT a surface theme in the Grading Optimization?

   a. Slope

   b. Wireframe

   c. Aspect

   d. Constant

4. Which of the following are a Result display in the Grading Optimization (Select all that apply)?

   a. Cut / Fill

   b. Wireframe

   c. Aspect

   d. Violation view

5. How can you calculate the storage capacity of a pond at different elevation stages?

    a. Within the Pond Grading Object

    b. You must use a third party Program

    c. Through the Civil 3D Stage Storage command

    d. Through the Grading Optimization interface

6. How do you calculate how much volume a pond can hold?

    a. This must be done manually since there is no way to do it in the software.

    b.

    c.

    d.

Command Summary

Button	Command	Location
	Add to Surface as Breakline	• **Ribbon**: *Feature Line* contextual tab>*Modify* panel • **Command Prompt**: FeatureAddAsBreakline
	Break	• **Ribbon**: *Feature Line* contextual tab>*Edit Geometry* panel • **Command Prompt**: BreakFeatures
	Create Feature Line from Corridor	• **Ribbon**: *Home* tab>*Create Design* panel, expanded *Feature Line* drop-down list • **Command Prompt**: FeatureLinesFromCorridor
	Delete Elevation Point	• **Ribbon**: *Feature Line* contextual tab>*Modify* panel, click **Edit Elevations** to display the *Edit Elevations* panel • **Toolbar**: *Elevation Editor* (*contextual*) • **Command Prompt**: DeleteElevPoint
	Feature Line Properties	• **Ribbon**: *Feature Line* contextual tab>*Modify* panel
	Insert Elevation Point	• **Ribbon**: *Feature Line* contextual tab>*Modify* panel, click **Edit Elevations** to display the *Edit Elevations* panel • **Toolbar**: *Elevation Editor* (*contextual*) • **Command Prompt**: InsertElevPoint
	Insert PI	• **Ribbon**: *Feature Line* contextual tab>*Edit Geometry* panel • **Command Prompt**: InsertFeaturePI
	Join	• **Ribbon**: *Feature Line* contextual tab>*Edit Geometry* panel • **Command Prompt**: JoinFeatures
	Stage Storage	• **Ribbon**: *Analyze* tab>*Design* panel • **Command Prompt**: _AeccStageStorage
	Trim	• **Ribbon**: *Feature Line* contextual tab>*Edit Geometry* panel • **Command Prompt**: TrimFeatures

Managing Surfaces

Grading objects can increase the size of your drawing and slow down your computer. For grading projects, it is important to plan ahead and decide how to best organize your drawings before you begin designing. The topics explore different methods for organizing Autodesk® Civil 3D® projects and explain how to use Data Shortcuts to create a final grading plan.

Learning Objectives

- List the ways in which teams can collaborate with each other and share design information in the Autodesk Civil 3D software.
- Share design information with other members of a design team using Data Shortcuts.
- Create a data shortcut.
- Transmit a drawing with all its references.
- Create the Finished Ground / Finished Grade.
- Create a Volume Surface and label the surface.

8.1 Autodesk Civil 3D Projects

There are multiple ways of organizing Autodesk Civil 3D project drawings, depending on the size and location of the project team, drawing / document control requirements and what type of access multiple offices / consultants require.

Single-Design Drawing Projects

Since Autodesk Civil 3D surfaces, alignments, and other AEC objects can be entirely drawing-based, you can have a single drawing file act as the repository for all design data. Realistically, this might only be feasible for smaller projects and/or those worked on by only one person. The only external data might be survey databases and externally referenced (XREF) drawings.

Multiple Drawings Sharing Data Using Shortcuts

This approach permits multiple existing conditions and design drawings to share data. For example, a surface could exist in one drawing and an alignment in another. A third could contain a surface profile based on the alignment and terrain model, and all could be kept in sync with each other using data shortcuts. This approach is usually preferable to the single-drawing approach, because this permits more than one user to work on the project (in different design drawings) at the same time and keeps the drawings at more manageable sizes. Using data shortcuts is essential in larger projects to ensure that the regeneration time for drawings is at an acceptable speed. This approach does not create any external project data other than survey databases and XML data files that are used to share data between drawings.

Once an object has been referenced into the drawing and the drawing has been saved, the object is saved in the drawing. Therefore, it only needs access to the source drawing for validation and synchronization purposes if the source object changes. This makes it easy to share drawings with others because it ensures that the referenced objects display even if the source drawings are not available.

Shortcuts tend to be efficient for projects with a small number of drawings and project team members. Since the XML data files that connect drawings must be managed manually, keeping a large number of drawings and/or people in sync with shortcuts can be cumbersome. It is recommended that your BIM manager establishes procedures to ensure that data is not unintentionally deleted or changed. These procedures need to be properly documented.

Autodesk Docs Design Collaboration

The Autodesk Docs cloud software enables Civil 3D to share external reference files (XREFs) and data shortcuts (DREFs) to be stored and shared within a project in an Autodesk Docs Hub. This enables you to collaborate your Civil 3D design, through these references in the cloud, with anyone anywhere.

Autodesk Docs makes extensive use of the Autodesk Desktop Connector, which serves as a traffic director between the Autodesk Docs project files in the cloud and the local caches on your hard drive.

When opening an Autodesk Docs-based drawing for the first time (or after a long interlude), the Desktop Connector checks the local cache of the drawings and reference files to see if they are up to date. If not, the Desktop Connector downloads a fresh copy of the files. This can take some time, depending on the file sizes, your download speeds, and the traffic in the Autodesk Docs cloud.

Multiple Drawings Sharing Data with Autodesk Vault

The Autodesk Vault software is a data and document management system (ADMS). It is used in conjunction with other Autodesk applications in different industries. When working with the Autodesk Vault software, all project drawings, survey databases, and references are managed and stored inside an SQL-managed database. Autodesk Vault includes user-level access permissions, drawing check-in/out, project templates, automated backups, data versioning, etc. These benefits are offset by the additional time required to manage and administer the database and, in some cases, needing to purchase additional hardware and software. If you work on large projects with multiple design drawings or have many team members (more than ten), you might find that Autodesk Vault is the best way to keep those projects organized.

8.2 Sharing Data

In the Autodesk Civil 3D workflow, you can use two methods of project collaboration to share Autodesk Civil 3D design data: data shortcuts (local-based or through Autodesk Docs) and Vault references.

Autodesk Vault and data shortcuts can be used to share design data between drawing files in the same project, such as alignment definitions, profiles, corridors, surfaces, pipe networks, pressure networks, sample line groups, and view frame groups. They do not permit the sharing of profile views, assemblies, or other Autodesk Civil 3D objects. Drawing sets using shortcuts typically use XREFs and reference other line work and annotations between drawings. Whether using Vault shortcuts or data shortcuts, the process is similar.

The example in Figure 8-1 shows the sharing of data in a project collaboration environment. The data is divided into three distinctive levels. Using either data shortcuts or Autodesk Vault, these levels can be accessed and contributed to on a local or remote server or across a wide area network (WAN).

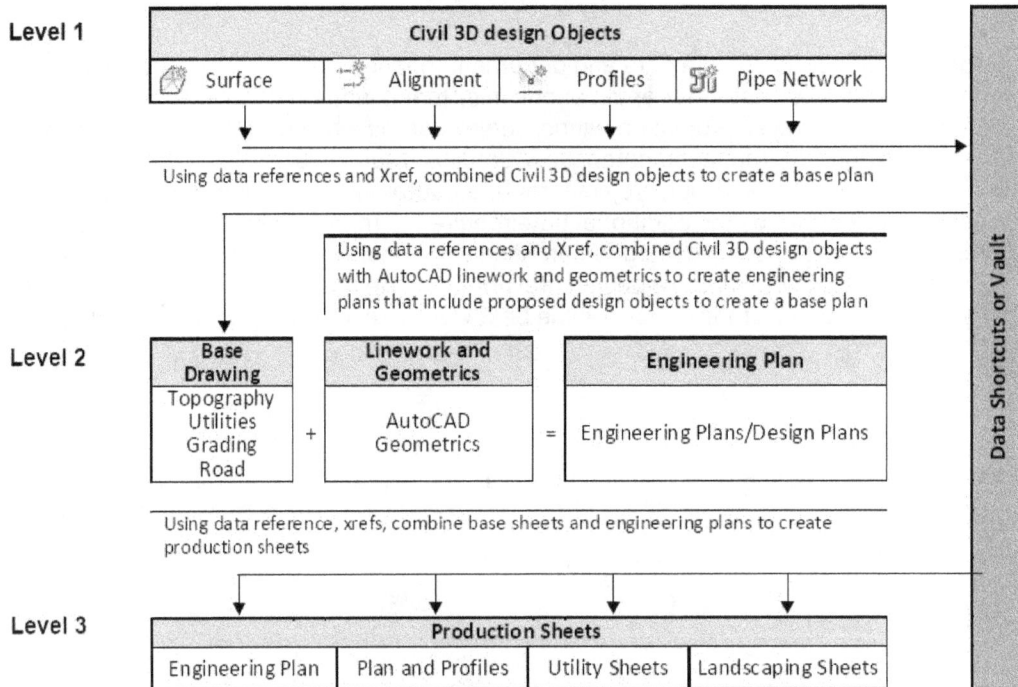

Figure 8-1

8.3 Using Data Shortcuts for Project Management

Data shortcuts can be used to share design data between drawing files through the use of XML files. Using data shortcuts is similar to using the Autodesk Vault software, but does not provide the protection of your data or the tracking of versions the way the Autodesk Vault software does.

Data shortcuts are managed using the *Toolspace>Prospector* tab, under the *Data Shortcuts* collection, or in the *Manage* tab>*Data Shortcuts* panel, as shown in Figure 8–2. The shortcuts are stored in XML files in one or more working folders that you create. They can use the same folder structure as the Autodesk Vault software. This method simplifies the transition to using the Autodesk Vault software at a future time.

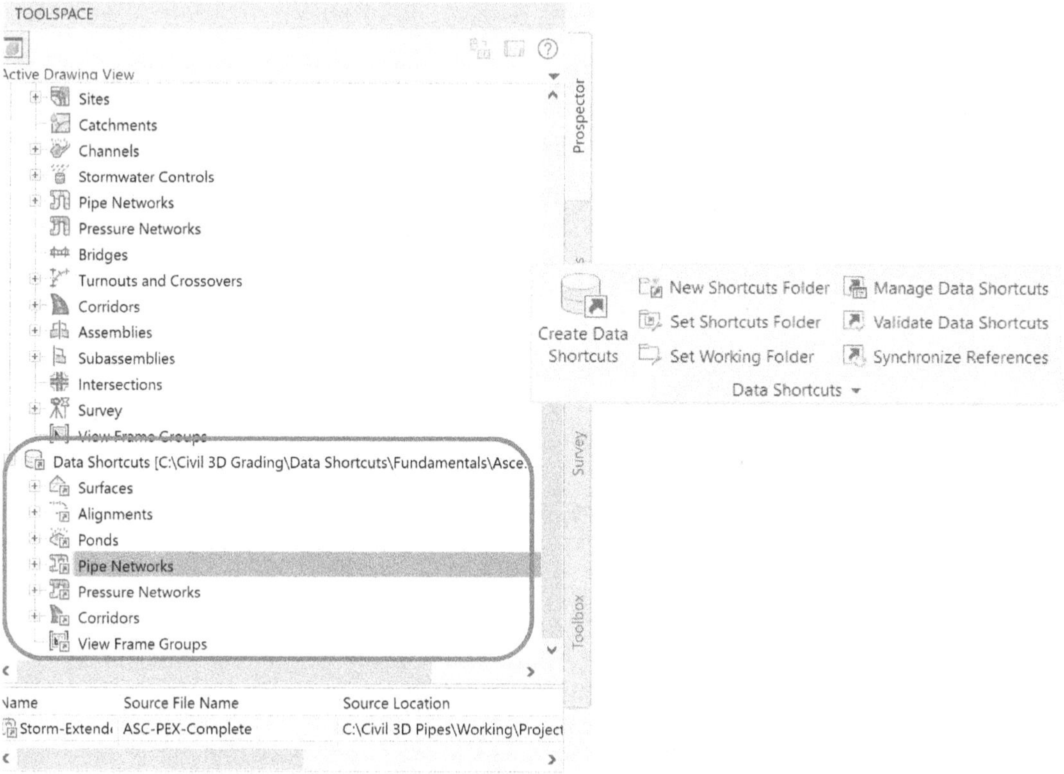

Figure 8–2

When the data shortcuts reside in an Autodesk Docs project in the cloud, it is designated as such in the *Toolspace>Prospector* tab with a small cloud symbol and a path pointing to the Autodesk Docs project, as shown in Figure 8–3.

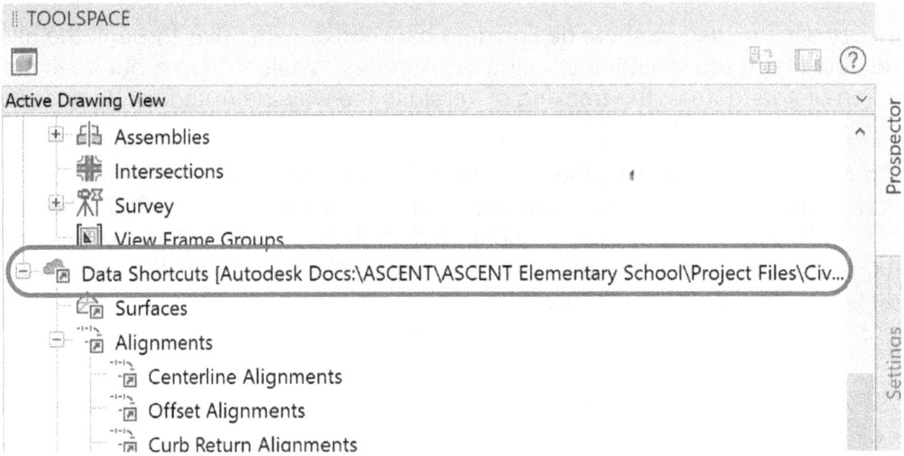

Figure 8–3

Similarly, when you are working in a drawing that resides in an Autodesk Docs project, in the *Toolspace>Prospector* tab, the drawing has a cloud symbol as a prefix, as shown in Figure 8–4.

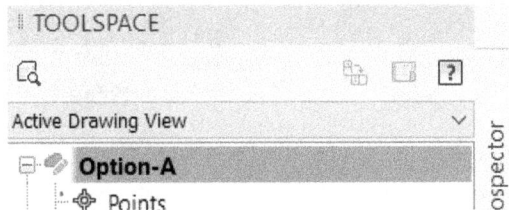

Figure 8–4

Whether using the Autodesk Vault software or data shortcuts (local based or through Autodesk Docs), the intelligent Autodesk Civil 3D object design data can be consumed and used on different levels. However, this referenced data can only be edited in the drawing that contains the original object. As referenced data can be assigned a different style than those in the source drawing, you can separate the design phase (where drawing presentation is not critical) from the drafting phase (where drawing presentation is paramount). Therefore, after the styles have been applied at the drafting phase, any changes to the design have minimal visual impact on the completed drawings.

Changing the name of a drawing file that provides data shortcuts or the shortcut XML file itself invalidates the shortcut. In the *Manage* tab, there is a *Data Shortcut Manager* that is used to correct such issues. It is used to repair references broken through renamed drawings or re-pathing drawings containing the Civil 3D objects.

Update Notification

If the shortcut objects are modified and the source drawing is saved, any drawings that reference those objects are updated when opened. If the drawings consuming the data referenced in the shortcuts are open at the time of the edit, a message displays to warn you of the changes, as shown in Figure 8−5.

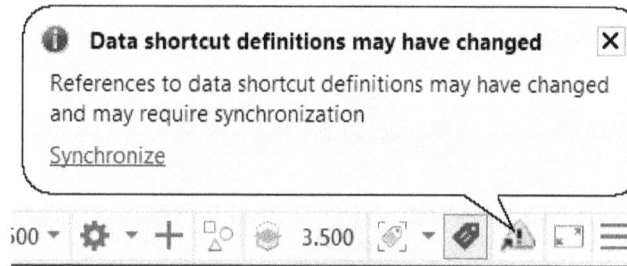

Figure 8−5

The following modifier icons help you to determine the state of many Autodesk Civil 3D objects.

▽	The object is referenced by another object. In the *Toolspace>Settings* tab, this also indicates that a style is in use in the current drawing.
↰	The object is being referenced from another drawing file (such as through a shortcut or Autodesk Vault reference).
⚠	The object is out of date and needs to be rebuilt, or is violating specified design constraints.
◣	A Vault project object (such as a point or surface) has been modified since it was included in the current drawing.
◢	You have modified a Vault project object in your current drawing and those modifications have not yet been updated to the project.

Figure 8–6 shows how the modifier icons are used with an Autodesk Civil 3D object as it displays in the *Toolspace>Prospector* tab.

Figure 8–6

To update the shortcut data, click **Synchronize** in the balloon message or right-click on the object in the *Toolspace>Prospector* tab and select **Synchronize**.

Autodesk Docs Notification

In the current release of Autodesk Docs, there is no standard Civil 3D notification indicating that the data shortcuts have changed. For that, you need to go to the *Collaborate* tab and click

(Check Reference Status). It will examine if any of the referenced data items have changed and need updating.

Removing and Promoting Shortcuts

Shortcut data can be removed from the Shortcut tree in the *Toolspace>Prospector* tab by right-clicking on it and selecting **Remove**; however, this does not remove the data from the drawing. To do so, right-click on the object in the *Toolspace>Prospector* tab and select **Delete**. This removes the shortcut data from the current list so that the item is not included if a data shortcut XML file is exported from the current drawing.

You can also promote shortcuts, which converts the referenced shortcut into a local copy without any further connection to the original. You can promote objects by right-clicking on them in the *Toolspace>Prospector* tab and selecting **Promote**.

Reference Part of a Surface

If you have a large surface and only need a part of it, you can create a boundary for the surface and only that portion will be referenced. This boundary acts like a Data Clip boundary for the surface in that only the data within the boundary is referenced, thus not bogging down the drawing with extraneous data.

When creating the Data Shortcut for the surface, in the *Create Surface Reference* dialog box, select the **Reference part of the surface** checkbox as shown in Figure 8–7.

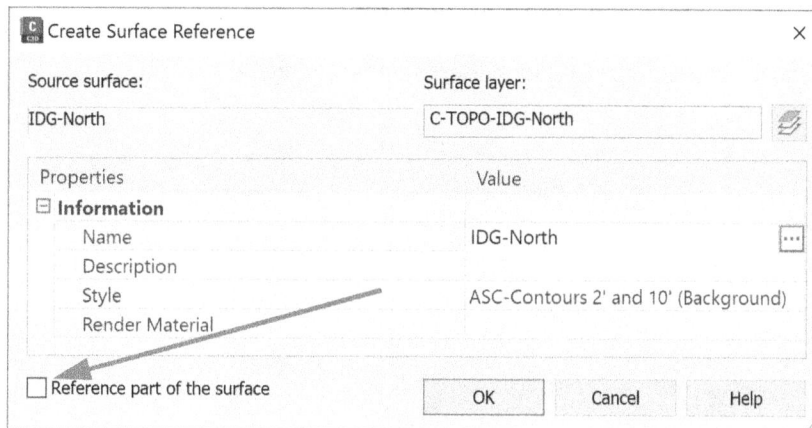

Figure 8–7

Data Shortcut Workflow

1. In the *Toolspace>Prospector* tab, right-click on **Data Shortcuts** and select **Set the Working Folder...**.

2. In the *Toolspace>Prospector* tab, right-click on **Data Shortcuts** and select **New Data Shortcuts Folder...** to create a new project folder for all of your drawings.

   Note: Whenever Civil 3D is searching for folders, you can use the Autodesk Desktop Connector to browse to the local cache folders of files that reside in an Autodesk Docs project.

3. Create or import the data that you want to share in the source drawing and save it in the current working folder under the correct project folder.

4. In the *Toolspace>Prospector* tab, right-click on **Data Shortcuts** and select **Associate Project to Current Drawing**.

5. In the *Toolspace>Prospector* tab, right-click on **Data Shortcuts** and select **Create Data Shortcuts**.

6. Select all of the items that you want to share, such as surfaces, alignments, profiles, etc., and click **OK**.

7. Save the source drawing (and close, as required).

8. Create and save a new drawing or open an existing drawing to receive the shortcut data. Expand the *Data Shortcuts* collection and the relevant object trees (*Surfaces*, *Alignments*, *Pipe Networks*, *View Frame Groups*, etc.).

9. Highlight an item to be referenced, right-click, and select **Create Reference....** Repeat for all of the objects, as required. You are prompted for the styles and other settings that are required to display the object in the current drawing.

10. (Optional) Add an XREF to the source drawing if there is additional AutoCAD® objects that you want to display in the downstream drawing.

-   The Autodesk Civil 3D tools for data shortcuts are located in the *Manage* tab>*Data Shortcuts* panel (as shown in Figure 8–8) and in the *Toolspace>Prospector* tab.

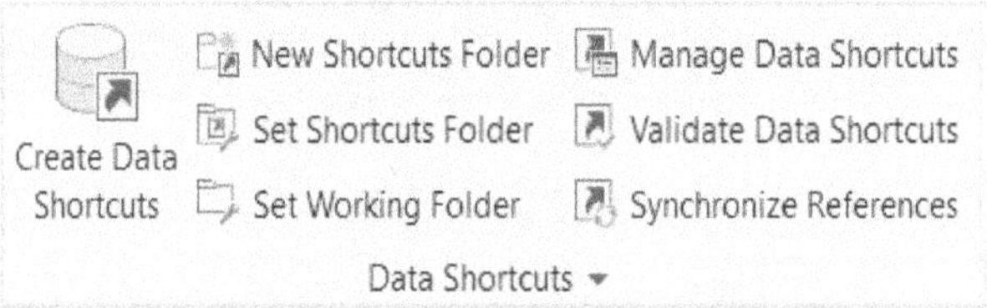

Figure 8–8

Workflow Details

-   **Set Working Folder** sets a new working folder as the location in which to store the data shortcut project. The default working folder for data shortcut projects is *C:\Users\Public\Documents\Autodesk\Civil 3D*.

    -   In a shared working environment, the working folder needs to be accessible by all project team members. Often working folders are named for the year of the project, or perhaps the major clients for the project.

    -   For project team members who reside outside of your firewall, consider setting up an Autodesk Docs project for design collaboration and file referencing.

    -   The default working folder is also used for Autodesk Vault projects and local (non-Vault) Survey projects. If you work with the Autodesk Vault software, local Survey, and Data Shortcut projects, you should have separate working folders for each project type for ease of management.

-   **New Shortcuts Folder** creates a new folder for storing a set of related project drawings and data shortcuts.

-   **Create Data Shortcuts** creates data shortcuts from the active drawing.

Data shortcuts are stored in the *_Shortcuts* folder for the active project and used to create data references to source objects in other drawings. Each data shortcut is stored in a separate XML file.

Advantages of Data Shortcuts

*   Data shortcuts provide a simple mechanism for sharing object data, without the added system administration needs of the Autodesk Vault software.

*   Data shortcuts offer access to an object's intelligent data while ensuring that this referenced data can only be changed in the source drawing.

*   Referenced objects can have styles and labels that differ from the source drawing.

*   When you open a drawing containing revised referenced data, the referenced objects are updated automatically.

*   During a drawing session, if the referenced data has been revised, you are notified in the Communication Center and in the *Toolspace>Prospector* tab.

*   When data shortcuts reside in an Autodesk Docs project, design collaboration and file referencing can be done beyond the firewall of your organization.

Limitations of Data Shortcuts

*   Data shortcuts cannot provide data versioning.

*   Data shortcuts do not provide security or data integrity controls.

*   Unlike the Autodesk Vault software, data shortcuts do not provide a secure mechanism for sharing point data or survey data.

*   Maintaining links between references and their source objects requires fairly stable names. However, most broken references can be repaired using the tools in the Autodesk Civil 3D software.

Practice 8a
Data Shortcuts

Practice Objectives

- Create a new drawing for the design surfaces.

- Associate a Data Shortcuts project with the drawing.

- Reference a variety of surfaces from the project.

In this practice, you will create a new drawing and associate a Data Shortcuts project with the drawing. Then you will reference surfaces into this drawing.

In a subsequent practice, these surfaces will be combined into the final design ground (FG) surface.

Task 1: Start a new drawing and set the Shortcuts.

In this task, you will set up a new working folder as the location in which to store Data Shortcuts projects and select a Shortcuts folder. The default working folder for Data Shortcuts projects is *C:\Users\Public\Documents\Autodesk\Civil 3D Projects*.

1. Start a new drawing from **ASC-GRD (CA83-VIF) NCS.dwt** from the *C:\Civil 3D Grading* *\Ascent-Config* folder.

2. If the *Geolocation - Online Map Data* dialog box opens, answer **No** to using Online Map Data, and also select the **Remember my choice** checkbox, as shown in Figure 8−9.

Geolocation - Online Map Data

Do you want to use Online Map Data?

Online Map Data enables you to use an online service to display maps in AutoCAD. Please sign into your Autodesk account to access online maps.

By accessing or using this service, you understand and agree that you will be subject to, have read and agree to be bound by the terms of use and privacy policies referenced therein: Online Map Data - Terms of Service.

☑ Remember my choice   Yes   No

Figure 8−9

3. Erase the message about the set coordinate system in the center of the screen.

4. Save the file in *C:\Civil 3D Grading\References\DWG\Proposed* folder and name it **XXX-Design-Surfaces.dwg** (substituting your initials for XXX).

5. In the *Manage* tab>*Data Shortcuts* panel, select **Set Working Folder**, as shown in Figure 8–10.

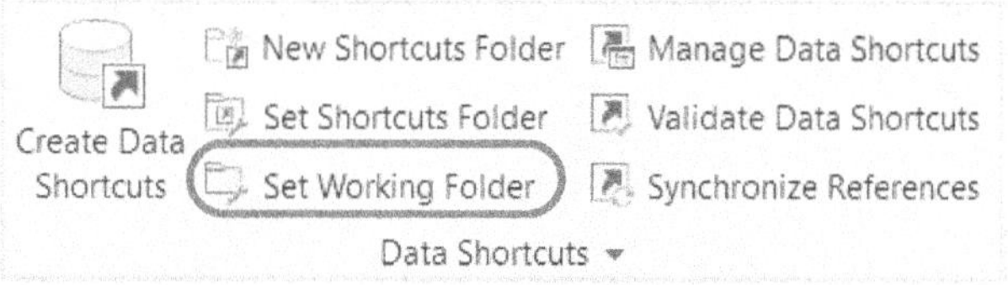

Figure 8–10

6. In the *Browse For Folder* dialog box, select the *C:\Civil 3D Grading\Data Shortcuts\Fundamentals* folder and click **Select Folder**.

7. In the *Manage* tab>*Data Shortcuts* panel, click (Set Shortcuts Folder), as shown in Figure 8–11.

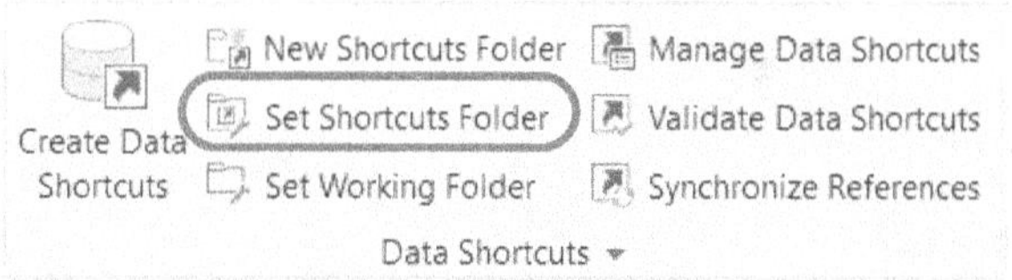

Figure 8–11

8. In the *Set Data Shortcut Folder* dialog box, select the **Ascent-Development** project, as shown in Figure 8–12.

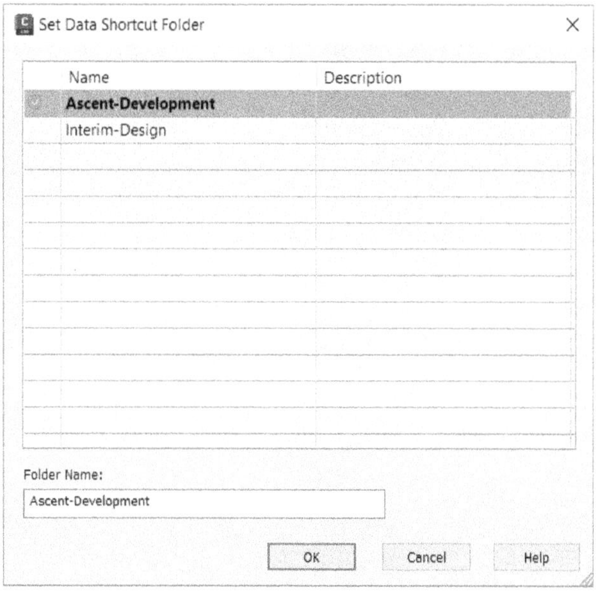

Figure 8–12

9. Click **OK**.

10. In the *Toolspace>Prospector* tab, verify that the Data Shortcuts point to the correct folder, as shown in Figure 8–13. You can hover over the *Data Shortcuts* heading, to see the full path displayed in the tooltip.

Figure 8–13

11. In the *Prospector* tab, right-click on *Data Shortcuts* and select **Associate Project to Current Drawing**, as shown in Figure 8–14.

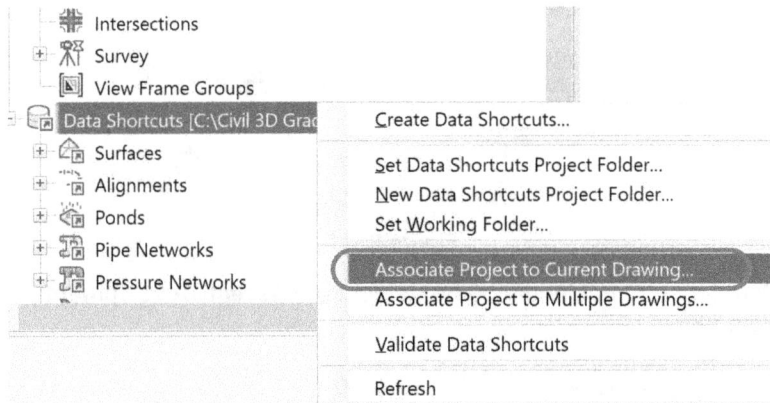

Figure 8–14

12. In the *Associate Project to Current Drawing* dialog box, click **OK** to accept the default working folder and project, as shown in Figure 8–15.

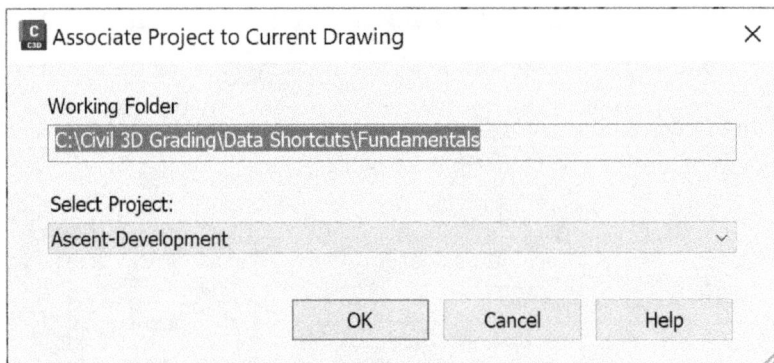

Figure 8–15

13. Under the *Surfaces* collection, right-click on the surface **Existing Ground** and select **Create Reference**, as shown in Figure 8–16.

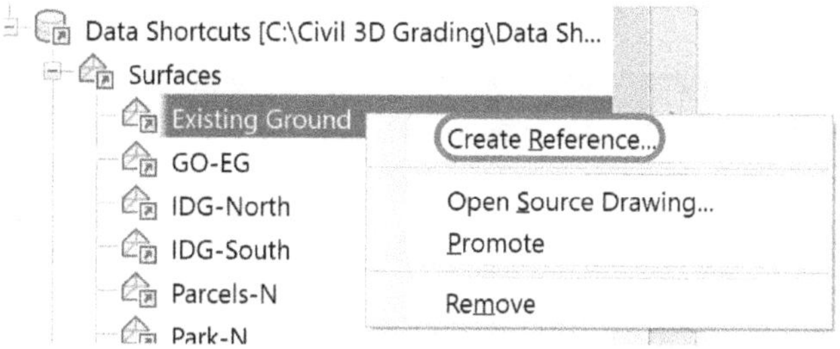

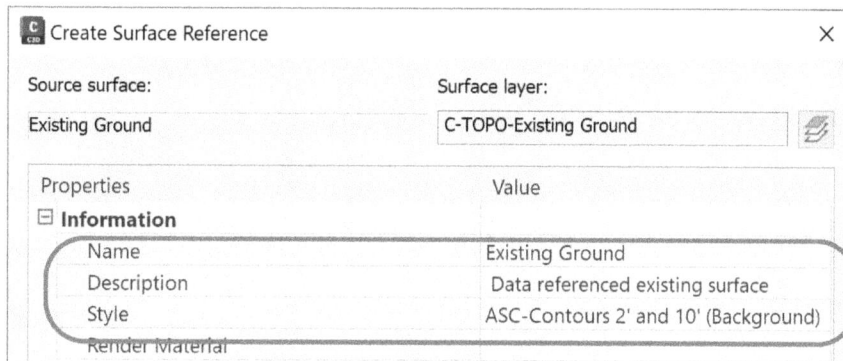

Figure 8–16

14. In the *Create Surface Reference* dialog box, complete the following, as shown in Figure 8–17:

* For the *Name:* Type **Existing Ground**

* For the *Description:* Type **Data referenced existing surface**.

* For the *Style:* Set **ASC-Contours 5' and 25' (Background)**.

Figure 8–17

15. Click **OK** to close the dialog box.

16. Repeat Steps 9 to 11 to create references to the following:

* **Ascent-Pond**
* **Parcels-N**
* **Park-N**
* **Pond-N**
* **Road-Tops**

Leave the names as default, provide appropriate descriptions, and set the surface style to **ASC-Contours 5' and 25' (Design)**.

17. Type **ZE** and press <Enter> to display the surface reference. The only surface to be displayed is the Existing Site, all others have been set to the _No Display style.

18. Save the drawing.

End of practice

8.4 Surface Editing

There are three ways of adjusting surfaces graphically:

1. Lines edit tools (Add, Delete, Swap Edge)

2. Points edit tools (Add, Delete, Modify, Move)

3. Area edit tools (Minimize, Raise/Lower, Smooth, Paste, Simplify)

All of these tools are available by right-clicking on the *Edits* heading in a surface's *Definition* area (*Toolspace>Prospector* tab), as shown in Figure 8–18. These editing tools are also available through the contextual tab of the surface.

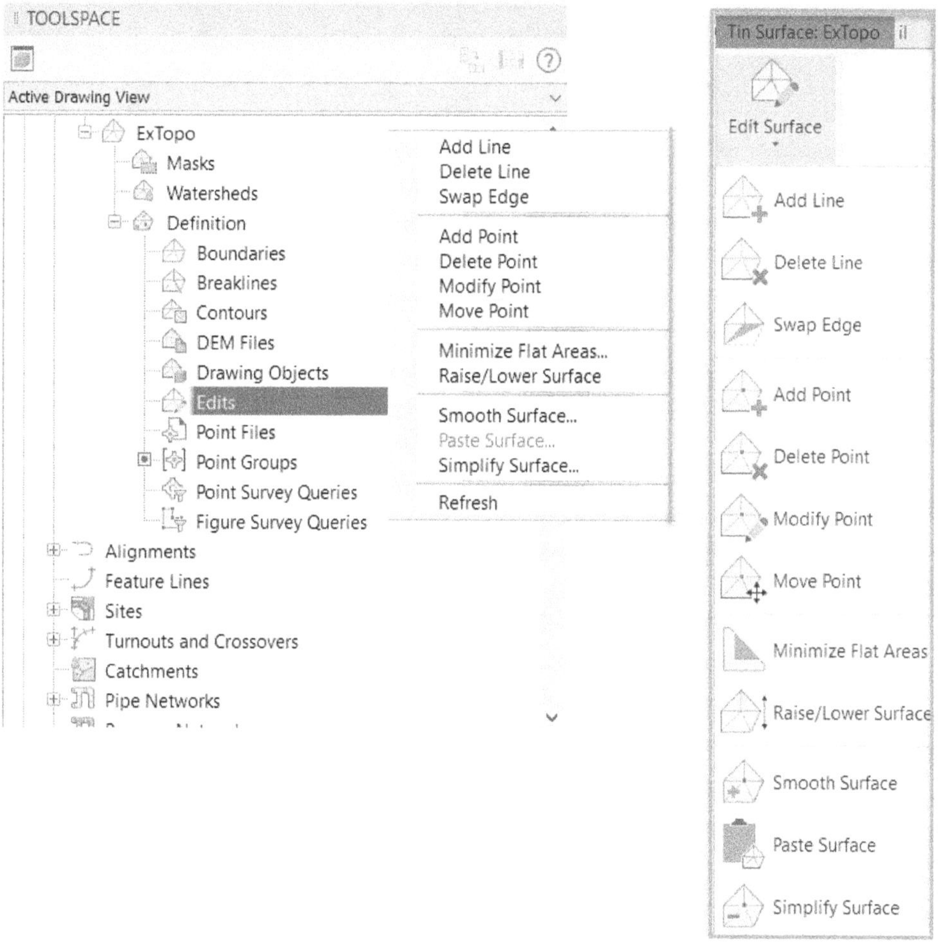

Figure 8–18

*   The Autodesk Civil 3D software considers each graphical surface edit to be an additional data item that can be removed or restored.

- Most surface edits apply immediately. If the drawing item modifier icon displays (as shown in Figure 8–19), it means that an edit has rendered the surface out of date. When this happens, a surface should be rebuilt by right-clicking on the surface name in the *Prospector* tab and selecting **Rebuild**.

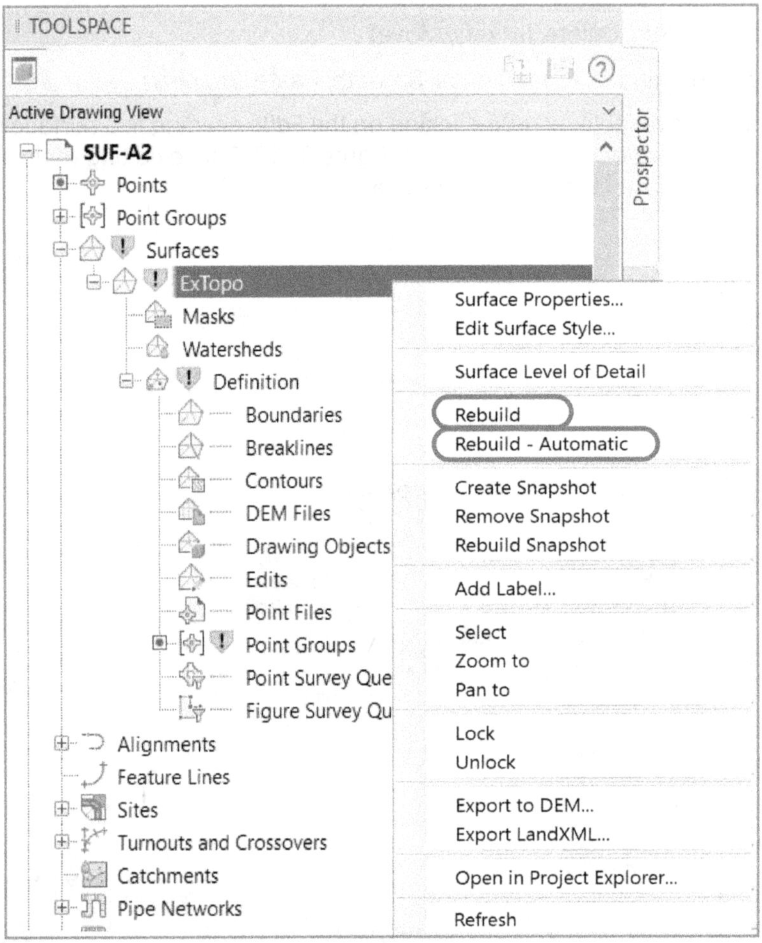

Figure 8–19

- To automatically rebuild a surface as required, right-click on the surface name in the *Prospector* tab and select **Rebuild-Automatic**. However, toggling this option on increases the use of computer resources and graphics capabilities, depending on the complexity of the surface and your computer's hardware.

Copy Surface

The Autodesk Civil 3D software does not have a copy surface command, but surface objects can be copied using the AutoCAD **Copy** command (**Modify>Copy**). When copying surface objects, select the same base and then a second point to ensure that the surface is not moved during the copy. Another option is not to specify a base point, but simply give it a Displacement distance of 0,0,0, which means there is no displacement. If you want to raise or lower the surface, the displacement distance would be 0,0,0.5 to give it a 6" grubbing surface.

After a copy, a duplicate surface is created and displays in the *Toolspace>Prospector* tab. The copy has the same name as the original followed with a number in parenthesis, such as (1). These copied surfaces can be renamed as required. Surface copies are independent of each other and can be edited independently.

Surface Paste

The **Surface Paste** command enables the Autodesk Civil 3D software to combine multiple surfaces into a single surface. You might want to paste into a copy of a surface if you want to keep the original unmodified. For example, a finished condition surface is needed that includes a proposed surface (**Proposed**) along with the existing ground (**EG**). In this situation, you would first create a new surface and name it **Finished Ground**. In the *Surfaces* collection in the *Toolspace>Prospector* tab, right-click on the **Finished Ground** surface's *Edit* collection and select **Paste** to merge in the **Existing ground (EG)** and **Proposed** surfaces.

Once the command has executed, the surface's **EG** and **Proposed** surfaces are left unchanged, and the **Finished Ground** surface represents a combination of the two. If you did not create the **Finished Ground** surface, but pasted the **Proposed** surface into the **EG** surface, you would not have the original **EG** surface for reference in profiles and other places (unless you copied the **EG** surface as explained above). If surfaces are pasted in the wrong order, the order can be rearranged using the *Definition* tab in the *Surface Properties* dialog box.

Surfaces remain dynamically linked after pasting. Therefore, if the **Proposed** surface changes, the **Finished Ground** surface updates to display the change, when the **Finished Ground** surface is set to Rebuild Automatically.

> *Note: The industry uses **Finished Ground** and **Finished Grade** interchangeably, as well as **Final Ground** / **Final Grade** both abbreviated as **FG**.*

Raise/Lower Surface

The **Raise/Lower Surface** command adds or subtracts a specified elevation value. This adjustment is applied to the entire surface. It is useful for modeling soil removal (grubbing surface) and changing a surface's datum elevation.

> *Note: You can also move the surface up or down similar to copying a surface as explained previously.*

Level of Detail

Civil 3D surfaces can become very complex. Displaying large surfaces with many contours can drag down the performance of Civil 3D. To simplify the display of such surfaces, you can reduce the level of detail of specific surfaces displayed in the drawing.

Each surface can apply a level of detail, either through the right-click menu or the contextual tab when the surface is selected, as shown in Figure 8-20.

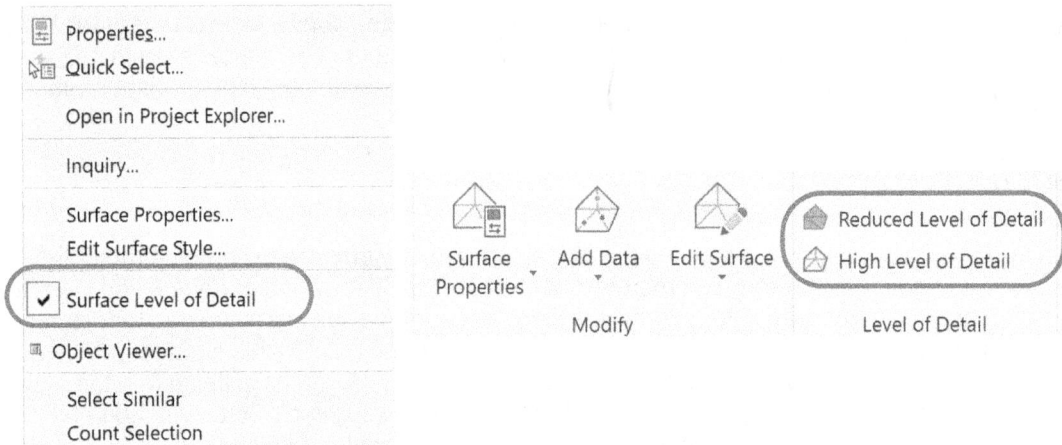

Figure 8-20

When the **Surface Level of Detail** is enabled, the displayed amount of drawing data decreases as the zoom level decreases. This will reduce the level of detail and improve the performance of Civil 3D. Conversely, as the zoom level increases, the displayed amount of drawing data increases. However, when a drawing is plotted, the full detail of all the surfaces will be plotted, even if the *level of detail* mode is only on for some of the surfaces.

Surfaces are the only objects that can apply the *level of detail* aspect. When applied, surface borders, user-defined contours, and watersheds are not affected; these items are always displayed in full detail.

Editing an Object in Level of Detail View

When a surface has the *level of detail* enabled, some editing tools will not be available if the drawing display's zoom factor is low. In this case, the cursor is displayed as a red icon indicating that the zoom factor needs to increase (zoom further in) to the true level of detail, or disable the level of detail (High Level of Detail) for the surface.

> *Note: Previously in Civil 3D, the **Level of Detail** was a system-wide setting, meaning that once it was enabled, it was enabled for all drawings you would open in Civil 3D. There were two commands to control the Level of Detail (which are now obsolete), namely **LEVELOFDETAIL** and **LEVELOFDETAILOFF**.*

Viewing a Surface in 3D

AutoCAD's default view, the overhead or plan view, is not the only way to view a surface. The AutoCAD **3D Orbit** command and the Autodesk Civil 3D **Object Viewer** tilt the coordinate space to display a 3D surface model. How the surface displays is dependent on the assigned style. You can view a surface in 3D using the **Object Viewer** or directly in the drawing window using the **3D Orbit** command. Both have similar navigation controls, but the **Object Viewer** enables you to review only your surface in 3D without changing your current view.

Both **Object Viewer** and **3D Orbit** can display visual styles such as **3D Wireframe**, **3D Hidden**, **Conceptual**, **Realistic**, etc. By default, a **Conceptual** style is a cartoon-like rendering without edge lines, while **Realistic** has material styles with edge lines. Both viewing methods use the AutoCAD ViewCube, which uses labels and a compass to indicate the direction from which you are viewing a model.

The **Object Viewer** method is shown in Figure 8-21.

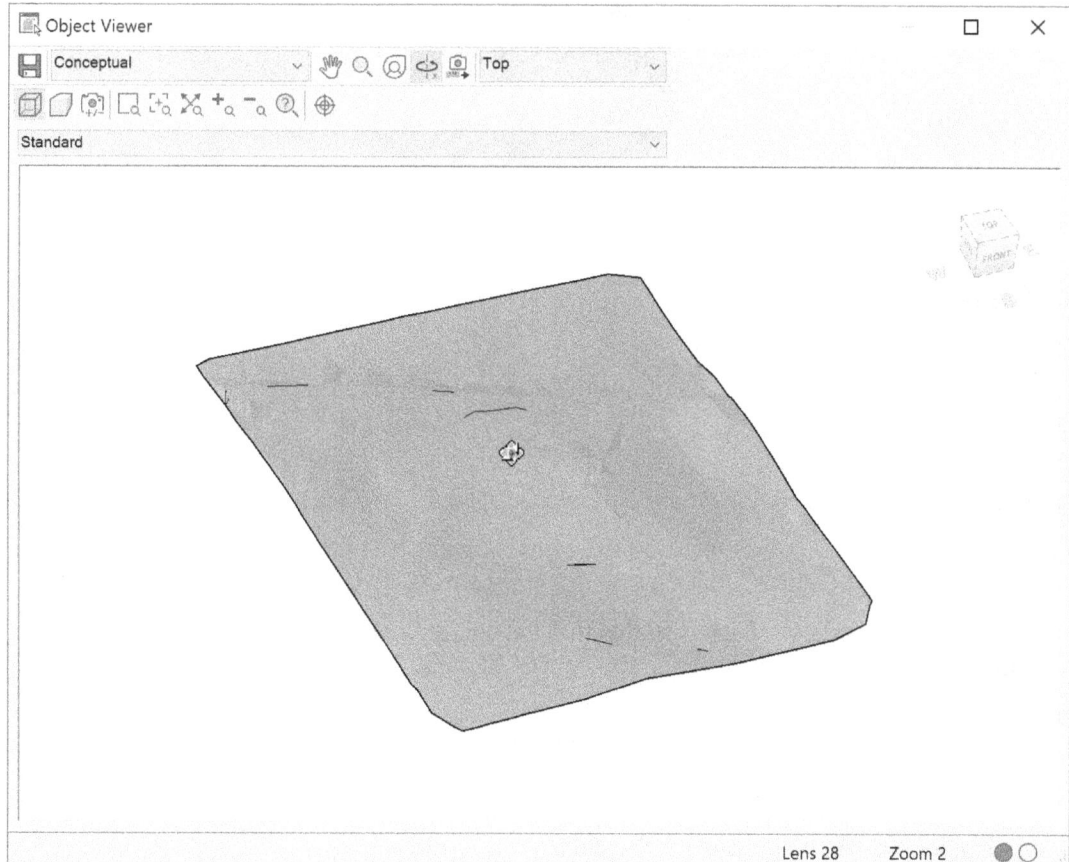

Figure 8-21

Model Viewer

The Model Viewer is similar to the Object Viewer in that you can view Civil 3D objects in 3D, render it to a chosen visual style, orbit, pan and zoom or use the view cube for predefined views, as shown in Figure 8–22.

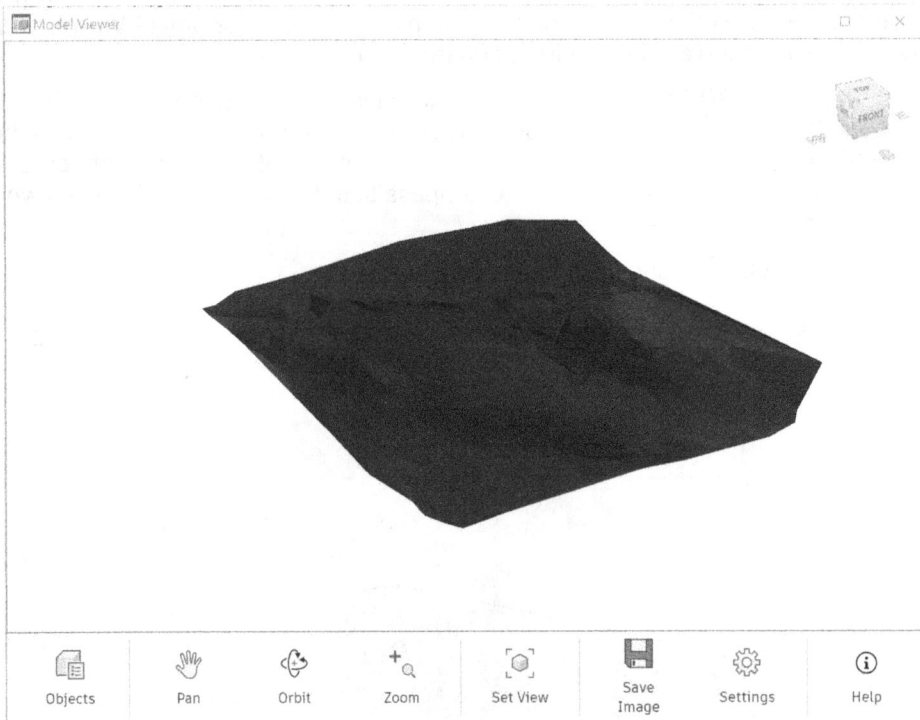

Figure 8–22

However, it contains additional enhancements as follows:

- **Modeless Window**: Allows the window to remain open while you continue to work in Civil 3D. The window can be moved to a second monitor so as to be less obtrusive.

- **Adding Components**: Any object within the drawing area or listed in the Prospector can be added to the Model Viewer through the right-click menu. You can also remove objects from the Model Viewer.

- **Component Visibility**: Objects within the Model Viewer can be turned off or on by selecting (Objects), as shown in Figure 8–23. The objects are grouped via type, and the entire types or individual objects can be 👁 (Visible) or 🚫 (Invisible).

Figure 8–23

- **Transparency**: For the surfaces displayed in the Model Viewer, you can set various levels of transparency. Right-click on the surface and select **Transparent**. When you do, a slider is displayed allowing you to set the transparency level between **0** to **90**. When a surface has transparency enabled, a symbol (⬚) is listed next to the surface name, as shown in Figure 8–24.

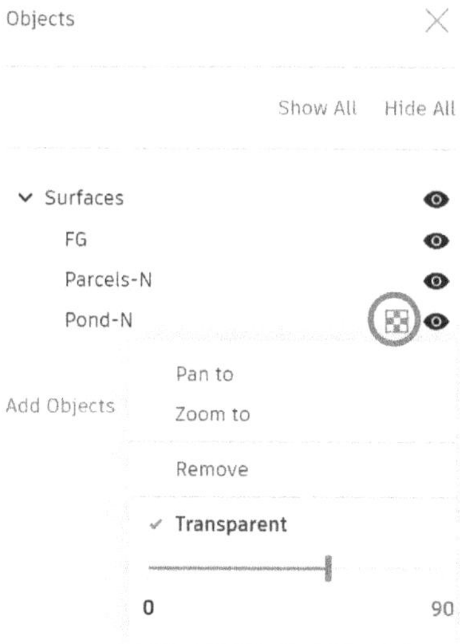

Figure 8–24

- **Set View**: You can set the view in Modelspace to match the vantage point set in the Model Viewer by selecting ⬡ (Set View).

- **Visual Style Settings**: You can set the visual style in the Model Viewer by selecting ⚙ (Settings), as shown on the left in Figure 8–25. You can also choose to display corridor feature lines, corridor sections and/or rendered surfaces, as shown on the right in Figure 8–25.

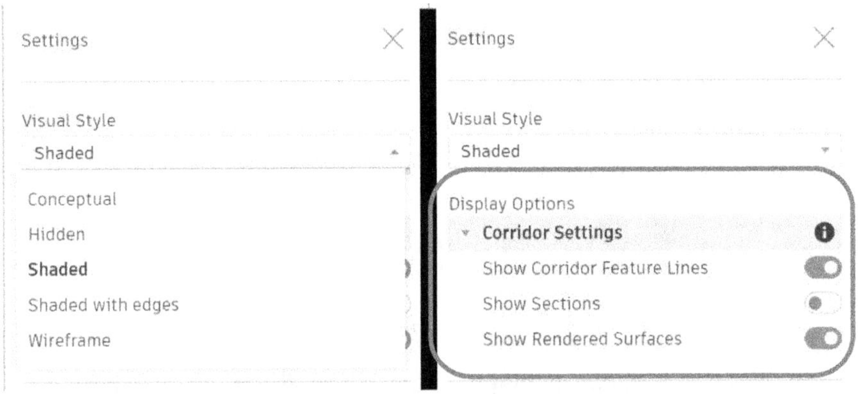

Figure 8–25

- **Performance improvement**: Launching the Model Viewer and navigating within it is faster than similar operations in the Object Viewer.

Practice 8b
Create the Final Ground Surface

Practice Objectives

- Create a copy of the existing surface as the Final Ground surface.
- Paste other design surfaces into the FG surface
- View the FG surface in 3D to check for validity.

In this practice, you will create a Final Ground(FG) surface by making a copy of the **Existing Ground** (EG) surface and raising it 6" in order to accommodate a topsoil layer that will need to be added to the site.

Task 1: Copy the Existing surface to create the Final Ground surface.

1. Continue working in the drawing from the previous practice or open **ASC-Design-Surfaces.dwg** from the C:\Civil 3D Grading\References\DWG\Proposed folder.

2. If there are errors with the referenced surfaces through data shortcuts, you can open **ASC-Surfaces-Promoted.dwg** from the C:\Civil 3D Grading\References\DWG\Proposed folder instead.

3. Select the **Existing Ground** surface.

4. From the Home Tab>Modify panel, select ⌗ (Copy).

5. In the Command Line, you are prompted to Specify base point or [Displacement/mOde] <Displacement>. Press <Enter> to accept the default, which is **Displacement**.

6. For the displacement distance, type **0,0,0.5,** to copy the existing surface to the same position but 6" higher.

7. Note the surfaces now listed in the Prospector tab, as shown in Figure 8–26. **Existing Ground (1)** has been added and it is still a referenced surface (unless you opened the **ASC-Surfaces-Promoted.dwg).**

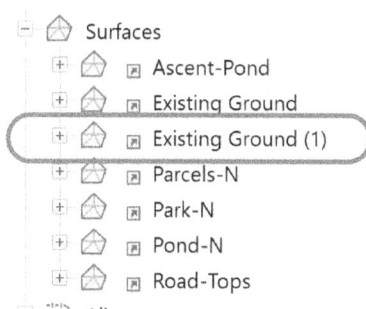

Figure 8–26

8. Click on **Existing Ground**, and in the right-click menu, select **Surface Properties**.

9. In the *Surface Properties* panel, on the *Information* tab, change the surface style to **_NoDisplay**.

10. Click **OK** to close the *Surface Properties* panel.

11. Click on **Existing Ground (1)**, and in the right-click menu, click **Select**.

12. For making any changes to the surface, you need to promote it so it is no longer a reference from a data shortcut. In the contextual ribbon, select ⌐🗐 (Promote Data Reference) as shown in Figure 8–27. Notice how the *Modify* panel of the contextual ribbon has changed after the surface has been promoted, as shown in Figure 8–27.

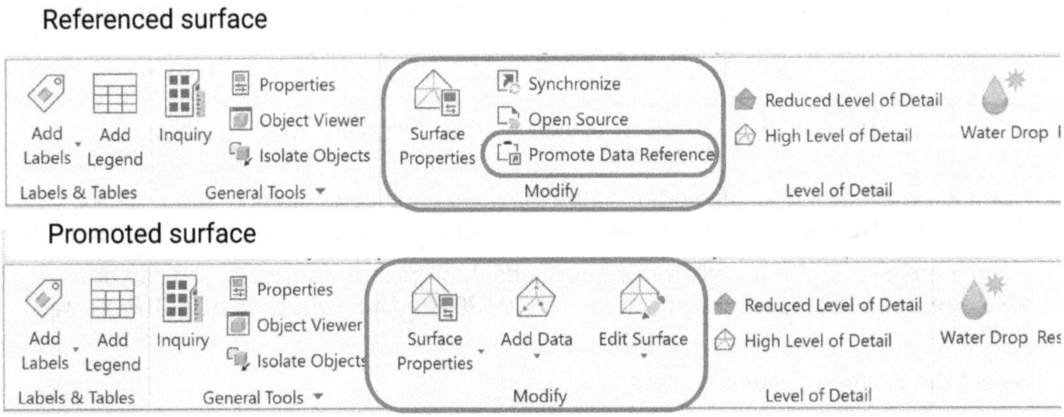

Referenced surface

Promoted surface

Figure 8–27

13. In the *Modify* panel of the contextual ribbon, select ⌂🖽 (Surface Properties).

14. In the *Surface Properties* panel, on the *Information* tab, rename the surface to **FG** and enter **Finished Ground** as the description. Change the surface style to **ASC-Contours 2' and 10' (Design)**, as shown in Figure 8–28.

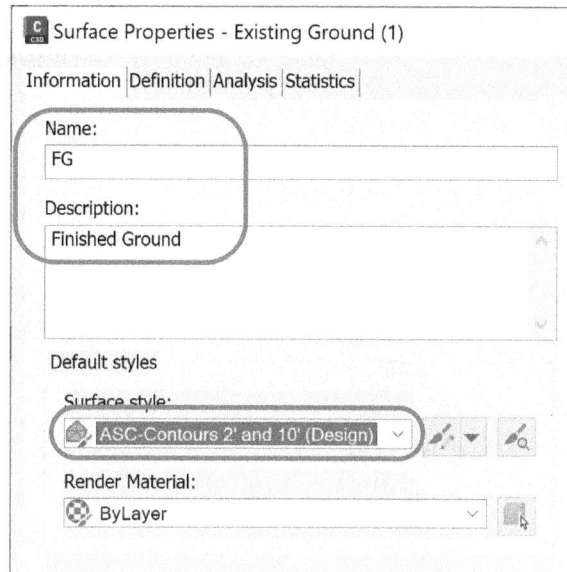

Figure 8–28

15. Click **OK** to close the *Surface Properties* panel.

16. In the *Modify* panel > *Edit Surface* drop-down menu, select 📋 (Paste Surface).

17. In the *Select Surface to Paste* dialog box, select the surfaces shown in Figure 8–29. Press and hold down the <Ctrl> key or the <Shift> key to select multiple surfaces in the list.

- **Parcels-N**
- **Park-N**
- **Pond-N**
- **Road-Tops**

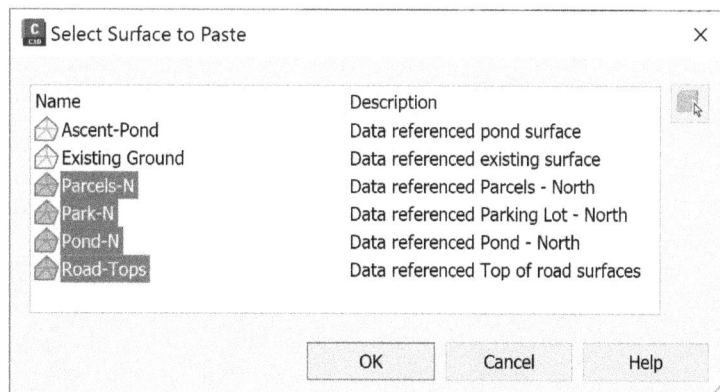

Figure 8–29

18. Click **OK** to close the dialog box.

19. In the *Prospector* tab, select the *Surfaces* collection. In the preview list area, press <Ctrl> and select all the surfaces except for **FG**. Right-click on the *Style* column heading and select **Edit**, as shown in Figure 8–30.

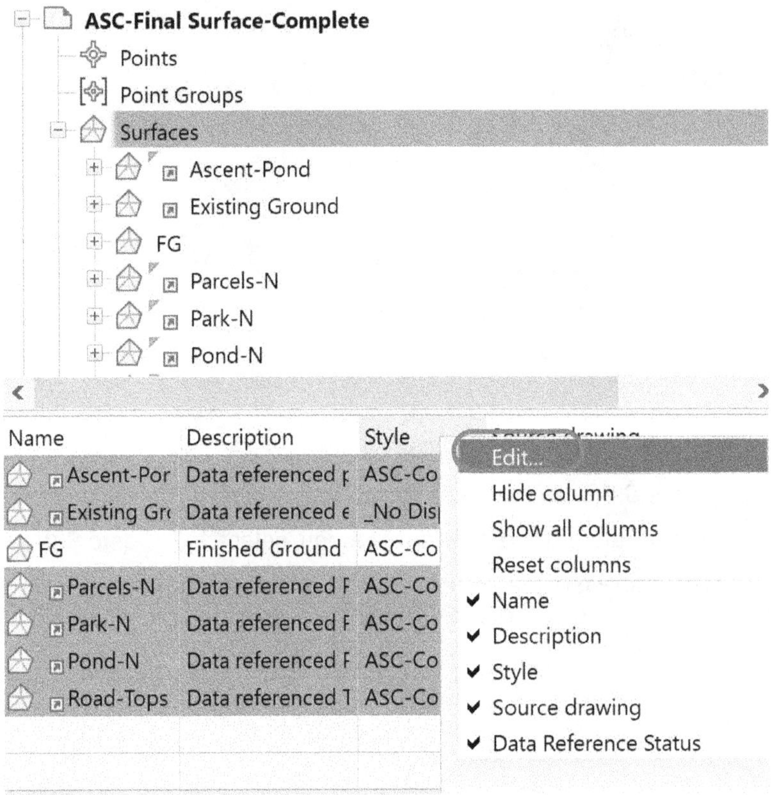

Figure 8–30

20. Set the surface style to **_No Display** and click **OK** to accept the changes and close the dialog box.

21. Select the **FG** surface. In the right-click menu, click **Add to Model Viewer** to study it. Set the *Visual Style* to **Conceptual** and navigate to the area of interest, as shown in Figure 8–31. Leave the *Model Viewer* window open so you can see the changes while you perform the next steps.

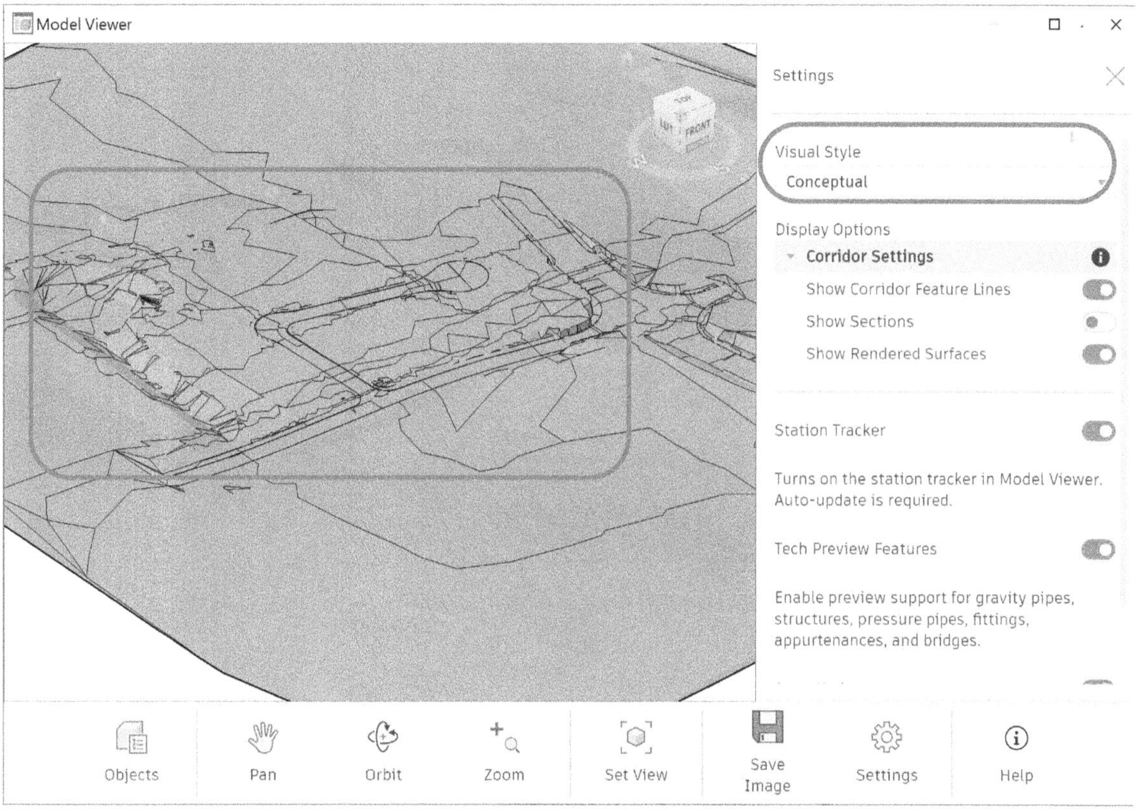

Figure 8–31

22. The surface is incorrect; the parking lot and building pads are missing. To check the order in which the surfaces were pasted, select the **FG** surface in the drawing, then go to the *Tin Surface* contextual tab>*Modify* panel, and click ▣ (Surface Properties).

23. In the *Surface Properties>Definition* tab, note the pasted surfaces order (this is the order in which they were initially selected), as shown in Figure 8–32.

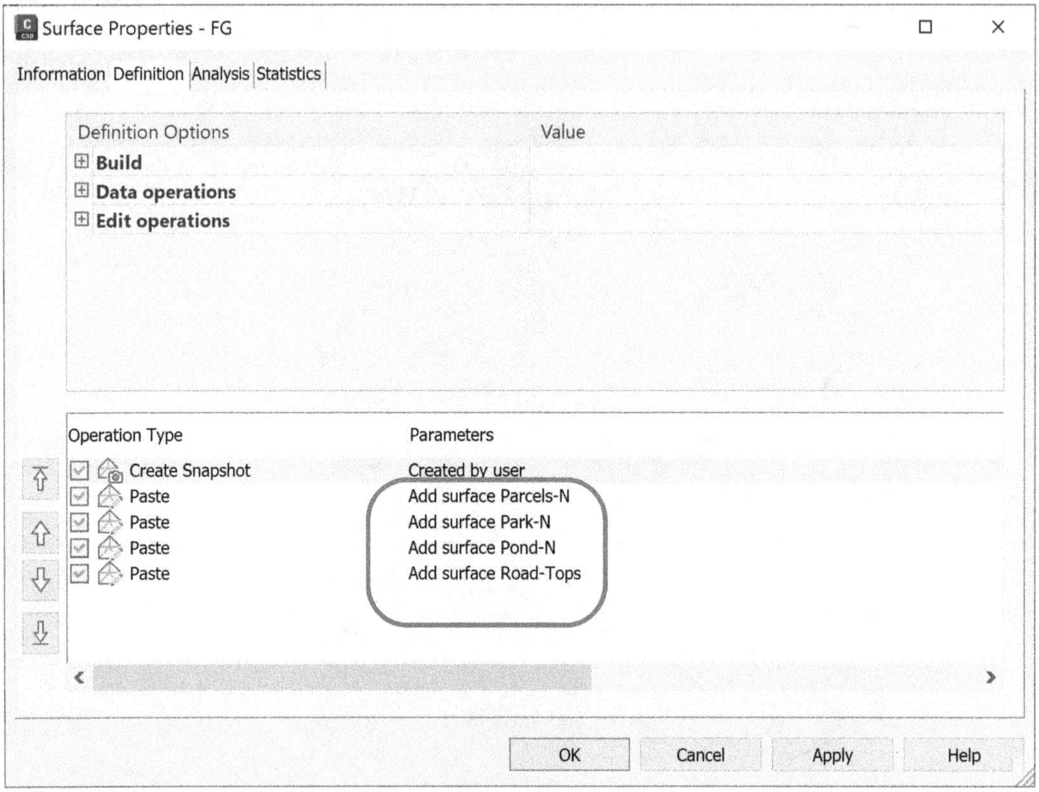

Figure 8–32

24. Arrange the *Operation Type* in the sequence that they would be created on the construction site. You can change the sequence by selecting a **Paste** operation and moving it up or down with the arrows on the left, as shown in Figure 8–33.

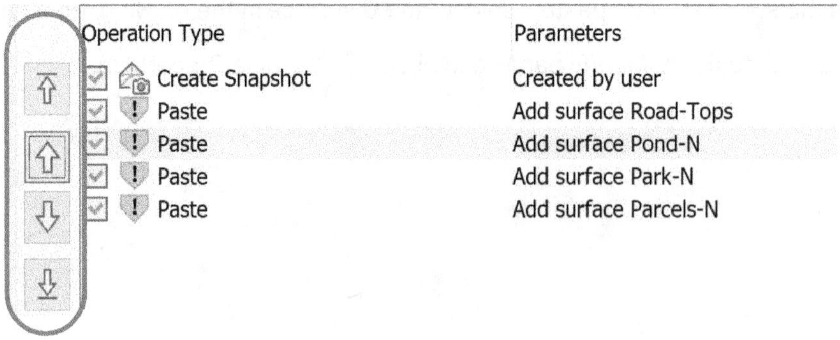

Figure 8–33

Each time you move an entry, a yellow alert icon displays. The final sequence should be:

- **Pond-N**
- **Park-N**
- **Parcels-N**
- **Road-Tops**

25. Click **OK** to close the dialog box. Select **Rebuild the Surface** when prompted.

26. Note the difference in the surface in the *Model Viewer*. The building pads and parking lot are now apparent, as shown in Figure 8–34.

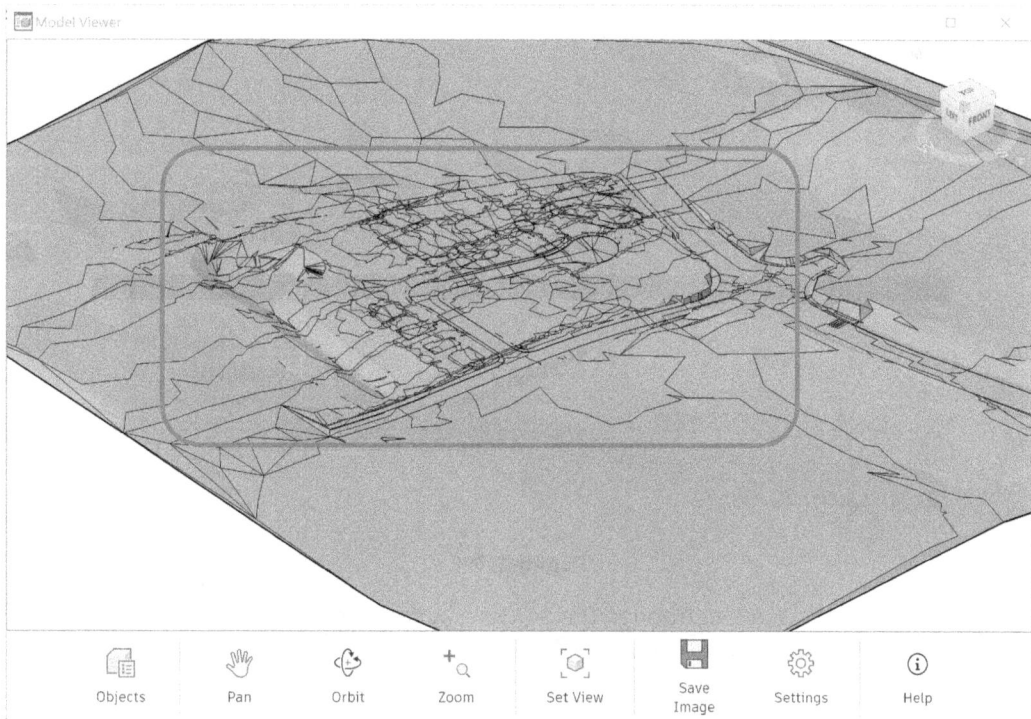

Figure 8–34

27. There are two options for the pond, represented by the **Pond-N** and the **Ascent-Pond** surfaces. To evaluate these options, do the following:

    • Paste the **Ascent-Pond** surface into the **FG** surface as you had done previously.

    • In the *Surface Properties* dialog box>*Definitions* panel, select only the option you want to study. Make sure that the other option is cleared, as shown in Figure 8–35.

    • Ensure that the **Pond-N** checkbox is selected and the **Ascent-Pond** checkbox cleared, prior to continuing.

Operation Type		Parameters
☐ Create Snapshot		Created by user
☐ Paste		Add surface Ascent-Pond
☑ Paste		Add surface Pond-N
☑ Paste		Add surface Park-N
☑ Paste		Add surface Parcels-N
☑ Paste		Add surface Road-Tops

Operation Type		Parameters
☑ Create Snapshot		Created by user
☐ Paste		Add surface Ascent-Pond
☐ Paste		Add surface Pond-N
☑ Paste		Add surface Park-N
☑ Paste		Add surface Parcels-N
☑ Paste		Add surface Road-Tops

Figure 8–35

28. Apply a level of detail, either through the right-click menu or the contextual tab when the surface is selected, as shown in Figure 8–36.

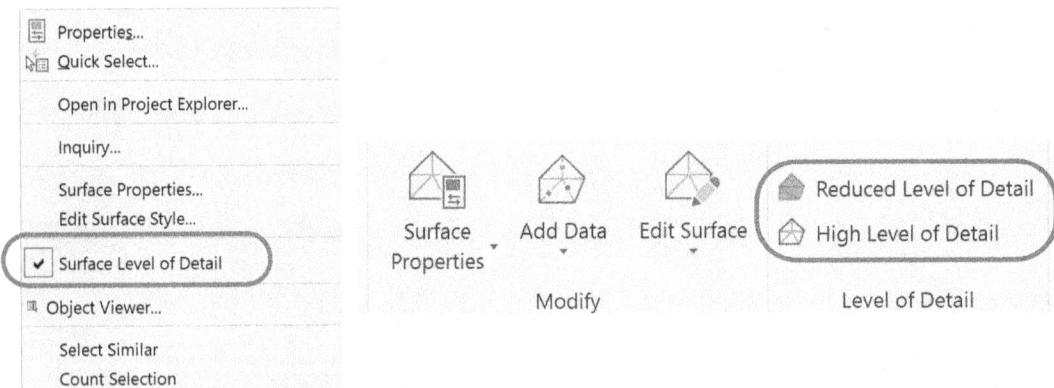

Figure 8–36

29. Zoom out and notice how the further you zoom out, the contours are reduced. Turn on the **High Level of Detail** again and notice how even at a reduced zoom level, all contours are displayed as shown in Figure 8–37.

Figure 8–37

30. Save the drawing.

Task 2: Create a data shortcut of the surface (Optional).

1. In the *Manage* tab>*Data Shortcuts* panel, click  (Create Data Shortcuts).
2. If you receive a message that the drawing has not yet been saved, click **OK**. Save the drawing and start the **Create Data Shortcuts** command again.

3. In the *Create Data Shortcuts* dialog box, select the **FG** surface, as shown in Figure 8–38, and click **OK**.

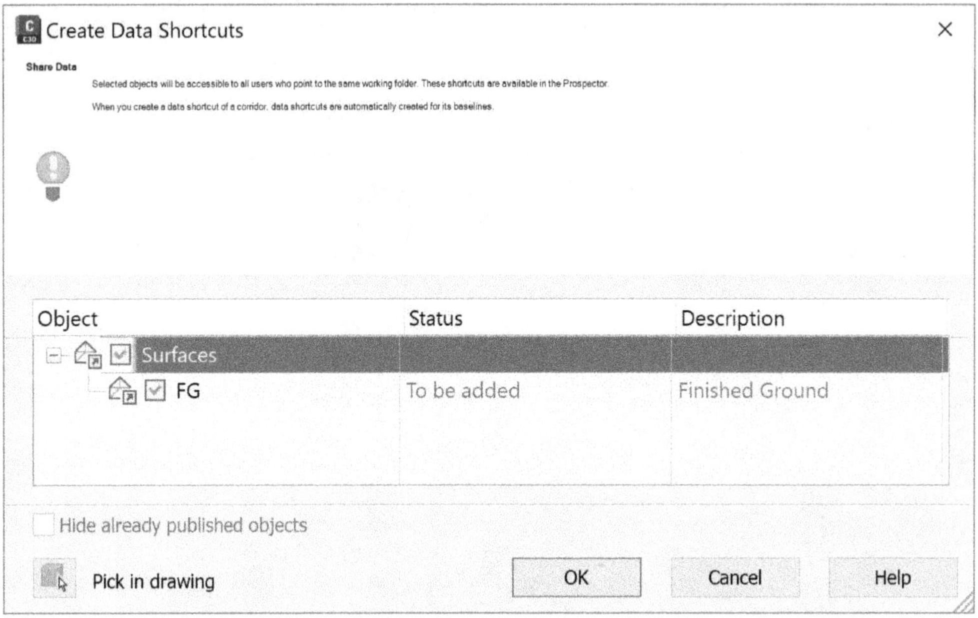

Figure 8–38

4. Note that the surface now displays in the lower surface listing as shown in Figure 8–39.

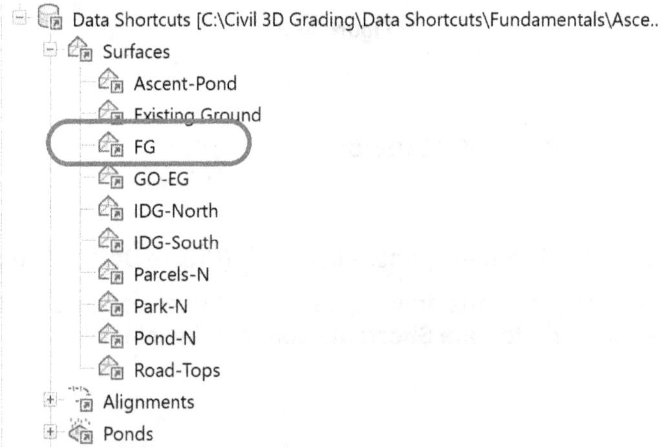

Figure 8–39

5. Save the drawing.

End of practice

8.5 eTransmit Data References

Projects that use Data Shortcuts can be packaged and sent to reviewers, clients, and other consultants using the AutoCAD **eTransmit** command. With this command, all of the related dependent files (such as XML files, XREFs, and text fonts) are automatically included in the package. This reduces the possibility of errors and ensures that the recipient can use the files you send them. A report file can be included in the package explaining what must be done with drawing-dependent files (e.g., XML or XREFs) so that they are usable with the included files. The *Create Transmittal* dialog box is shown in Figure 8-40.

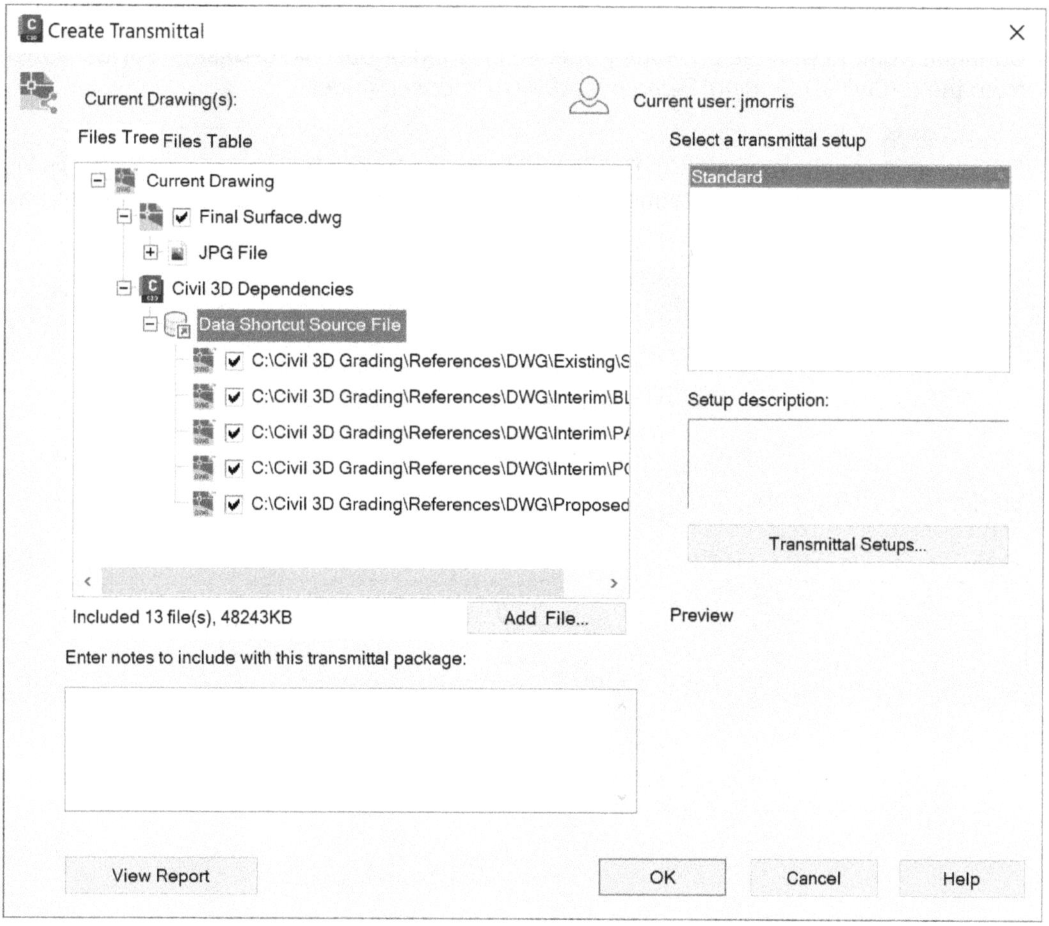

Figure 8-40

Practice 8c
Share Projects Outside the Office Network

Practice Objective

- Create a transmittal package to send to other design professionals on the project team, which includes all of the referenced object drawings, XREFs, and other required files.

In this practice, you will create a transmittal to send the drawing and all its dependencies to other interested parties.

1. Continue working with the previously opened drawing or open **ASC-Design-Surfaces.dwg** from the *C:\Civil 3D Grading\References\DWG\Proposed* folder.

2. Expand ![C] (Application Menu)>**Publish** and select **eTransmit**, as shown in Figure 8–41. If a warning dialog box opens stating that the current drawing is not saved, click **Yes** to save the drawing.

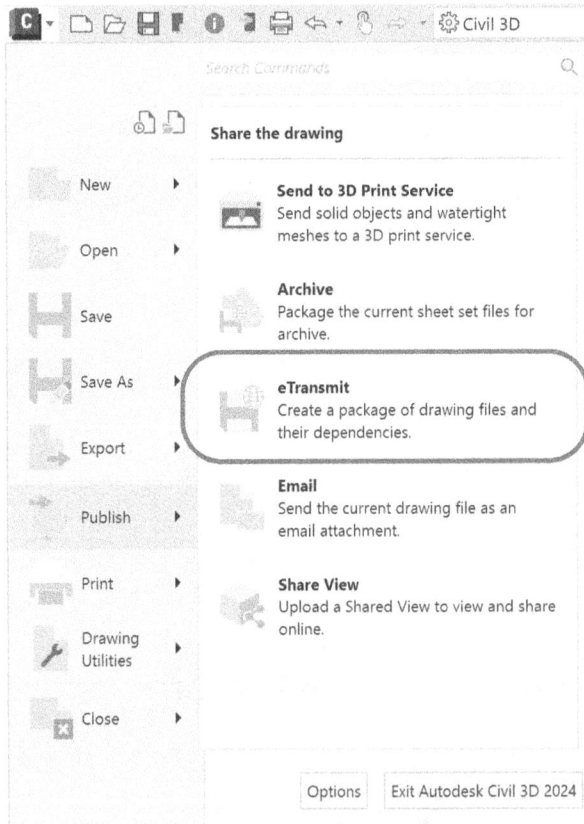

Figure 8–41

3. In the *Create Transmittal* dialog box, click **Transmittal Setups,** as shown in Figure 8–42.

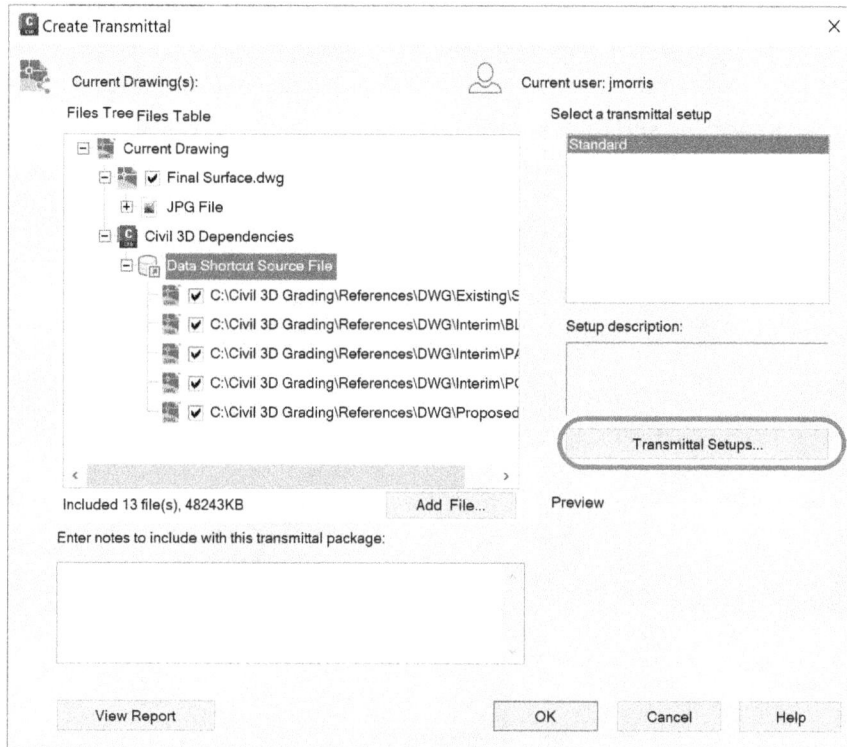

Figure 8–42

4. In the *Transmittal Setups* dialog box, select the **Standard** setup and click **Modify,** as shown in Figure 8–43.

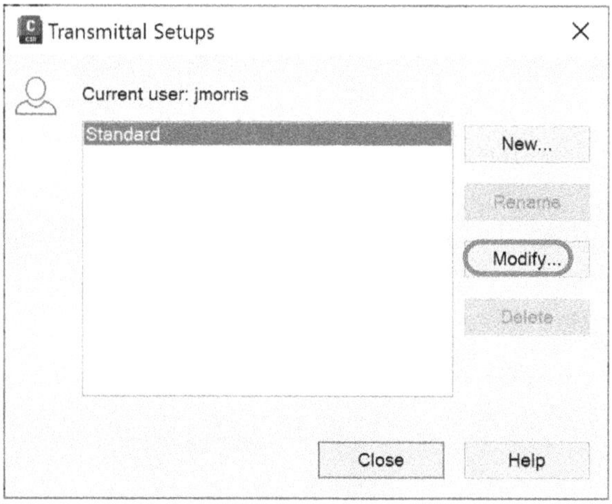

Figure 8–43

5. In the *Modify Transmittal Setup* dialog box, complete the following (as shown in Figure 8–44):

- Accept the default for *Transmittal file folder*.

- Expand the *Transmittal file name* drop-down list and select **Prompt for a filename**.

- Select the **Keep files and folders as is** option.

- In the *Include options* area, select all of the options **except** the **Include unloaded file references** option.

- Type **Submittal for Municipality review** in *Transmittal setup description*.

- Accept the remaining defaults and click **OK** to close the dialog box.

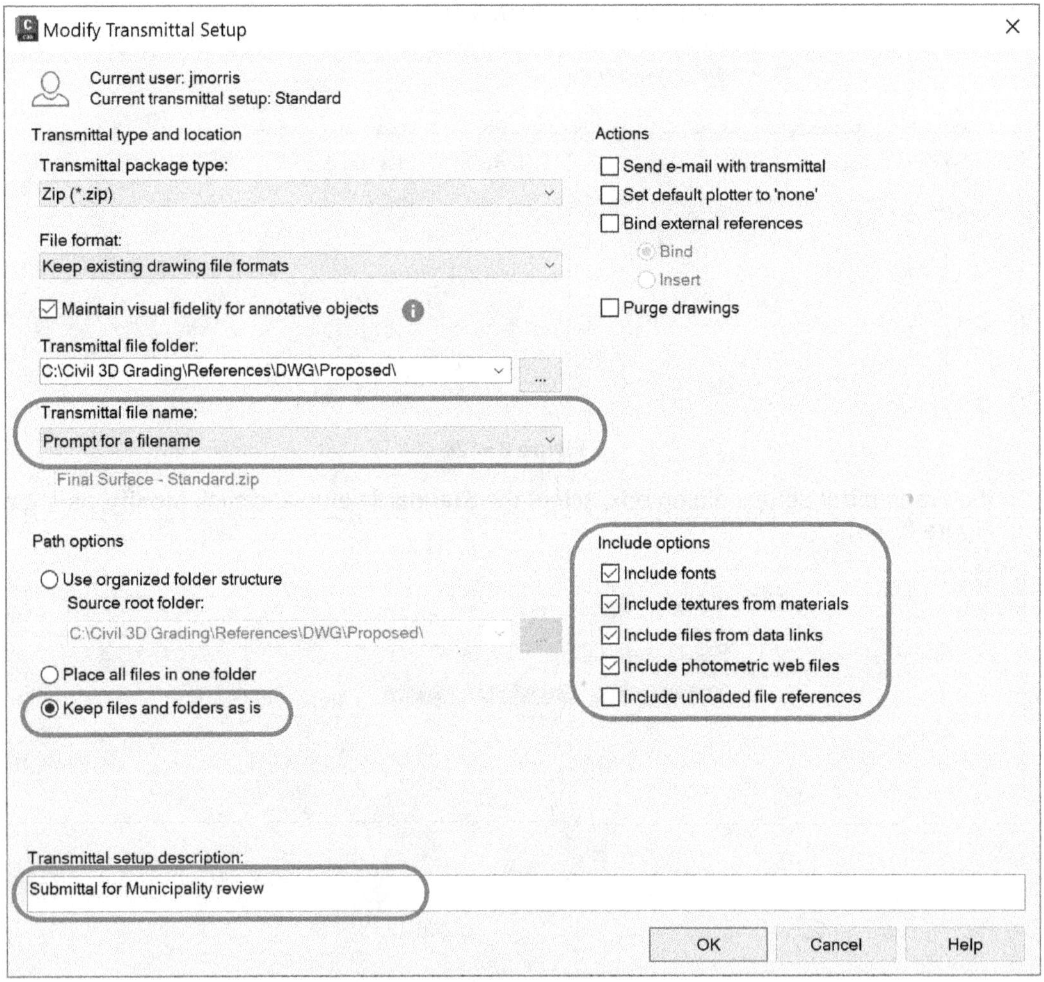

Figure 8–44

6. Close the *Transmittal Setups* dialog box.

7. Click **OK** to close the *Create Transmittal* dialog box and create the transmittal.

8. When prompted for the file name for the transmittal file, accept the default location and file name and save it. The Autodesk Civil 3D software will create a compressed file of all of the relevant data.

9. Save and close the drawing.

End of practice

8.6 Surface Volume Calculations

You can generate volume calculations in the Autodesk Civil 3D software in many ways. Surface-to-surface calculations are often used to compare an existing ground surface to a proposed surface to determine cut and fill quantities. In the Autodesk Civil 3D software, quantities can be adjusted by an expansion (cut) or a compaction (fill) factor. Surfaces representing different soil strata can be compared to each other to determine the volume between the soil layers. There are multiple ways of comparing surfaces to each other in the Autodesk Civil 3D software.

Volumes Dashboard

In the *Analyze* tab>*Volumes and Materials* panel, click 📊 (Volumes Dashboard). The *Volumes Dashboard* creates a volume surface based on a graphical subtraction of one surface from the other, as shown in Figure 8−45.

Figure 8−45

The *Net Graph* column color displays in red if the surface difference results in a net cut, and it displays in green if it is a net fill. You can have multiple volume entries listed if you are comparing multiple surfaces. If any surfaces change, return to this vista and click

🔄 (Recompute Volumes) to update the calculations. Alternatively, you can add another volume entry. Select the same two surfaces and compare before and after volume calculations.

Bounded Volumes

The area to calculate cut and fill can be limited by clicking 🗺 (Add Bounded Volume). This limits the calculations to the area defined by a polyline, polygon, or parcel.

Volume Reports

The dashboard's cut/fill summary contents can be placed directly into the drawing by clicking

A₊ (Insert Cut/Fill Summary) inside the *Volumes Dashboard*. In addition, you can create a volume report from the dashboard contents to include in specifications or other project

documents, by clicking 📋 (Generate Volume Report) inside the *Volumes Dashboard*.

Alignment labels fall into two general categories: those controlled as a group using the **Edit Alignment Labels** command (referred to here as *Alignment Point Labels*), and those managed individually (referred to here as *Independent Alignment Labels*). Alignment labels of both types can be selected, repositioned, and erased separate from the alignment object itself.

Spot Elevation Labels

The Spot Elevation labels for volume surfaces do not specify an actual elevation, rather the amount of cut or fill at that particular spot, as shown in Figure 8–46.

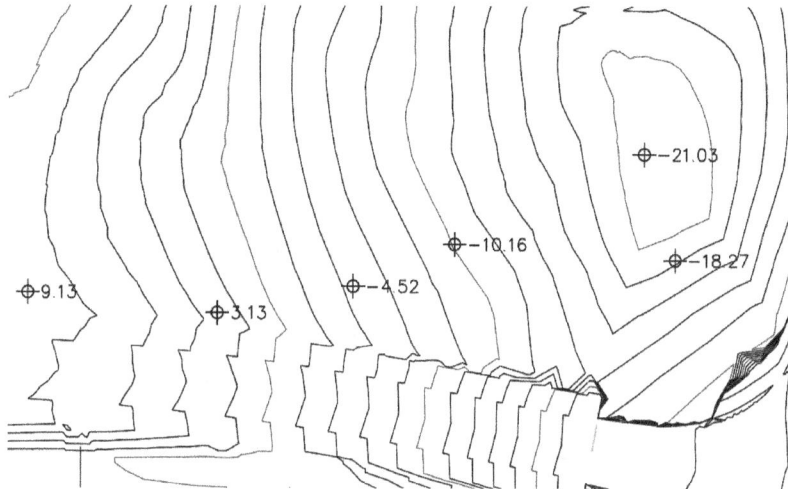

Figure 8–46

A positive value indicates that fill is required by that amount, whereas a negative value indicates that the area will need to be cut or excavated by the amount shown.

A grid of spot elevation labels that lists the elevation differences between two surfaces can also be generated. In the *Annotate* tab>*Labels & Tables* panel, expand **Add Labels>Surface** and select **Spot Elevations on Grid**, as shown in Figure 8–47.

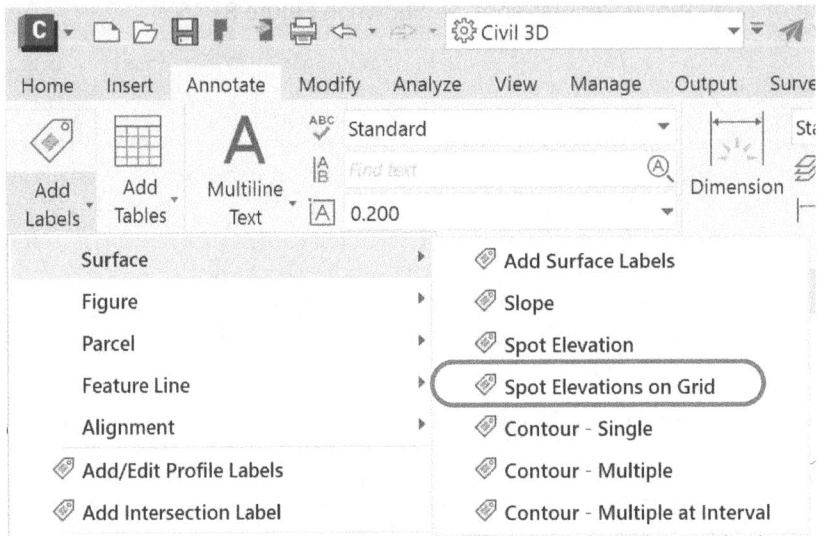

Figure 8–47

Volume Table

With the standard "out-of-the-box" Civil 3D installations, there are no "*Volumes Table*" for volume surfaces. There is a "*Total Volume Table*" for earthwork quantities for corridors, but that is not suitable for volume surfaces.

One can make a copy of the standard *Elevations Table* and modify it to show the *Minimum Depth* and *Maximum Depth* of the cut/fill within a range and the accompanying volume within that range, as shown in Figure 8–48.

Figure 8–48

In the *Toolspace>Settings* tab, navigate to *Surface>Table Styles>Elevations* and right-click on the **Standard** *Table Style* and select **Copy...**, as shown in Figure 8–49.

Figure 8–49

On the *Information* tab, give it a proper name and description. On the *Data Properties* tab, change the name of the table title, change *Maximum* and *Minimum Elevation* to *Maximum* and *Minimum Depths* respectively, delete the existing *Area* column and add the *Volume* column, as shown in Figure 8–50.

Figure 8-50

Calculate Surface Volumes

Practice Objectives

- Create a volume surface.
- Analyze the Volume surface.
- Communicate information about the surface by labeling.

A primarily final surface has been established, so now you can get an idea of the overall volumes for the entire site. This surface will calculate the volumes of the extents of the final ground you have established. Then you will create a table showing the volumes and some spot elevations noting the amount of cut or fill at certain spots.

Task 1: Create a volume surface.

1. Continue working in the drawing from the previous practice or open **ASC-Volume-Surfaces.dwg** from the *C:\Civil 3D Grading\References\DWG\Proposed* folder.

2. In the *Analyze* tab>*Volumes and Materials* panel, click ╤ (Volumes Dashboard).

3. In the *Volumes Dashboard*, click ⬤ (Create new volume surface), as shown in Figure 8–51.

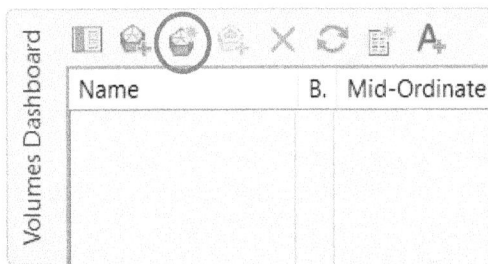

Figure 8–51

4. In the *Create Surface* dialog box, enter the following values, as shown in Figure 8–52:

   - *Name:* **Site-Volume**
   - *Description:* **Volume of EG-FG for project site**
   - *Style:* **ASC-Cut and Fill BandingInterval (2D)**
   - *Base Surface:* **Existing Ground**
   - *Comparison Surface:* **FG**

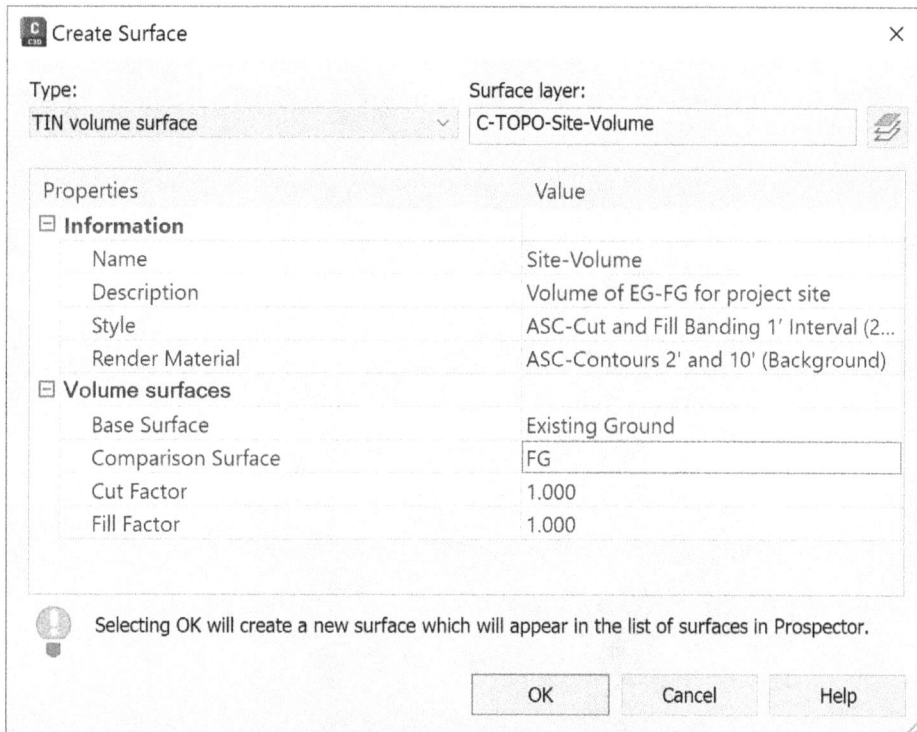

Figure 8–52

5. Click **OK** to close the *Create Surface* dialog box.

6. Use the green check mark in the upper right corner to close the *Volumes Dashboard.*

7. The new volume surface is displayed in a series ofblue blotches. The reason is the intervals for the elevation ranges are too small.

8. Select the volume surface and launch **Surface Properties**.

9. In the *Surface Properties* dialog box, select the *Analyze* tab and complete the following (as shown in Figure 8–53):

   - Set the *Analysis type* to **Elevations**.

   - Set *Create ranges by* to **Range interval with datum** and the number of intervals to **5**. *Important: Do not press <Enter> after typing as this will close the dialog box.*

   - Click (Run Analysis) to run the analysis.

Figure 8–53

10. Click **OK** to close the *Surface Properties* dialog box. The surface will rebuild, as shown in Figure 8–54.

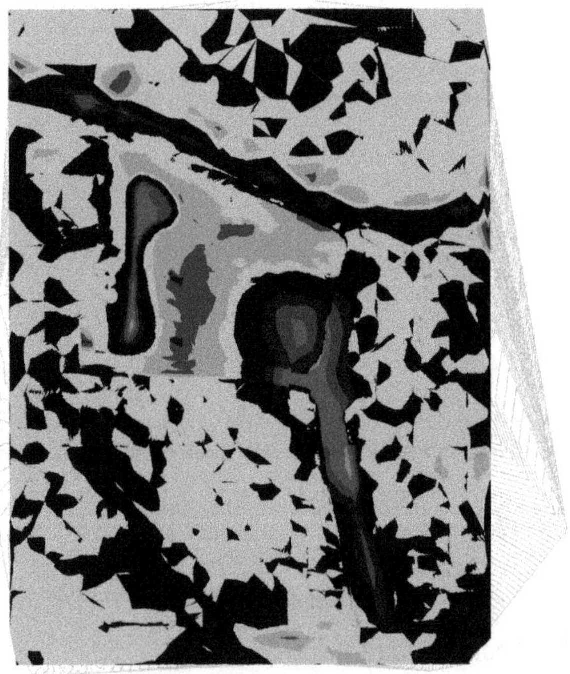

Figure 8–54

11. Save the drawing.

Task 2: Create tables and labels for the volume surface.

1. Select the **Site-Volumes** surface.

2. In the *Surfaces* contextual tab>*Labels & Tables* panel, in the *Add Labels* pull-down menu, select **Spot Elevations**.

3. Select a few spots in the various green areas and the red areas, then press the <Enter> key or the <Esc> key to finish. A positive value indicates that fill is required by that amount, whereas a negative value indicates that the area will need to be cut or excavated by the amount shown.

4. In the *Surfaces* contextual tab>*Modify* panel, select ⬆️ (Surface Properties).

5. In the *Information* tab, change the *Surface Style* of the *Site-Volume* surface to **_NoDisply** and click **OK** to close the *Surface Properties* panel. Now you can see the spot elevations better. An example is shown in Figure 8–55.

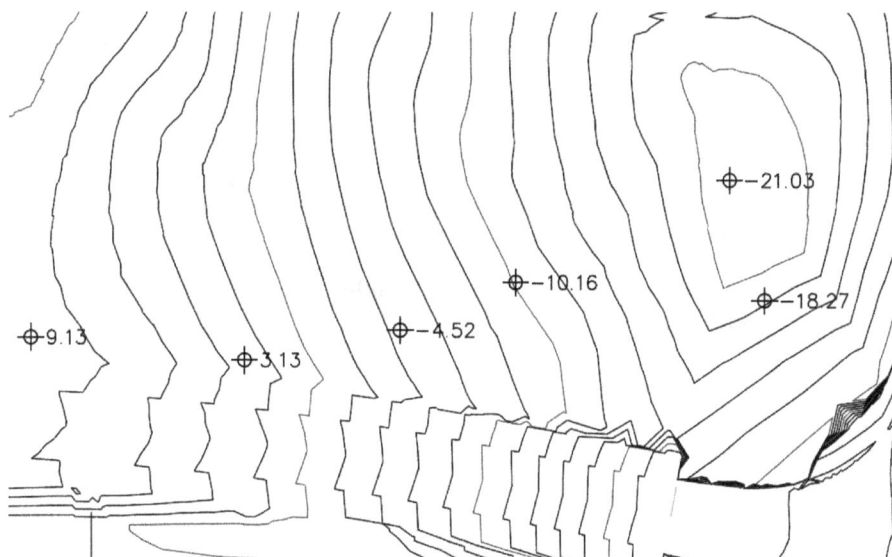

Figure 8–55

6. With the surface still selected, in the *Surfaces* contextual tab>*Labels & Tables* panel, select ▦ (Add Legend).

7. When prompted for the *Table Type*, select **Elevations**.

8. When prompted for the *Behavior*, select **Dynamic**.

9. Select a point somewhere in the drawing for the upper left corner of the table.

10. The table is placed in the drawing, but it is the standard elevation table. You need to change the Table Style. Select the elevation table.

11. In the *Tables* contextual tab>*Modify* panel, select ▦ (Table Properties)

12. In the *Table Properties* panel, from the *Table style* drop-down, select **ASC-Volumes**, as shown in Figure 8–56.

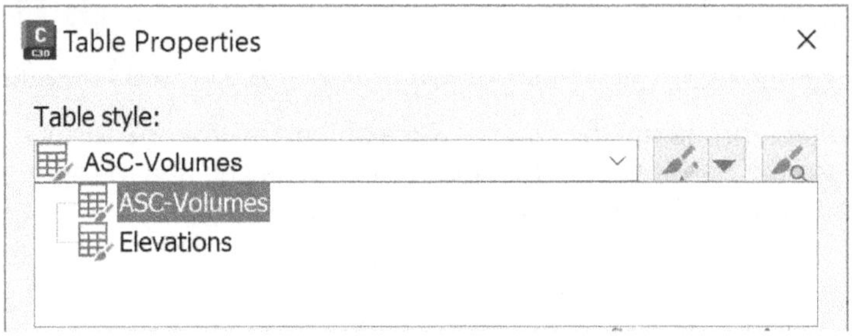

Figure 8–56

*Note: The **ASC-Volumes** table style was created for this course and is stored in the **ASC-Grading-Styles.dwg** reference template.*

13. Click **OK** to close the *Table Properties* panel.

14. The table changes from the standard elevations table shown on the left of Figure 8–57 to display the *Volume* as shown on the right.

Elevations Table				
Number	Minimum Elevation	Maximum Elevation	Area	Color
1	−30.00	−25.00	3516.21	
2	−25.00	−20.00	68407.30	
3	−20.00	−15.00	79814.42	
4	−15.00	−10.00	131120.14	
5	−10.00	−5.00	190235.43	
6	−5.00	0.00	1581291.58	
7	0.00	5.00	2390834.00	
8	5.00	10.00	292758.88	
9	10.00	15.00	74880.46	
10	15.00	20.00	3347.71	

Volumes Table				
Number	Minimum Depth	Maximum Depth	Volume	Color
1	−30.00	−25.00	155.89	
2	−25.00	−20.00	6054.60	
3	−20.00	−15.00	20577.18	
4	−15.00	−10.00	39168.00	
5	−10.00	−5.00	68529.94	
6	−5.00	0.00	144267.44	
7	0.00	5.00	160973.13	
8	5.00	10.00	39823.47	
9	10.00	15.00	3915.79	
10	15.00	20.00	74.49	

Figure 8–57

15. Save the drawing.

16. Open **ASC-Final Surface-Complete.dwg** from the *C:\Civil 3D Grading\References\DWG\ Proposed* folder to see the final result.

17. Close the drawing(s).

End of practice

Chapter Review Questions

1. In the Autodesk Civil 3D workflow, what are the two main methods of project collaboration (or the sharing of intelligent Autodesk Civil 3D design data)?

    a. Windows Explorer and XREFs.

    b. Data Shortcuts and Vault references.

    c. XREFs and Data Shortcuts.

    d. Vault references and XREFs.

2. Why would you want to use Vault references over Data Shortcuts?

    a. Added security and version control.

    b. Permit more people to have access.

    c. It works more like the Autodesk® Land Desktop software.

    d. It works better with multiple offices.

3. How can you edit an object referenced through Data Shortcuts?

    a. Open the source drawing.

    b. With grips.

    c. Using the Panorama view.

    d. You cannot do it.

4. What is the file format that Data Shortcuts use to share design data between drawing files?

    a. SHP

    b. DWT

    c. DWG

    d. XML

5. How do you calculate the volume between two surfaces in a specific parcel?

    a. Bounded Volumes

    b. Grid Volume Surface

    c. TIN Volume Surface

    d. Show Cut/Fill Labels in a grid pattern

6. Which of the following is NOT a standard "out-of-the-box" Civil 3D table style?

    a. Elevations

    b. Volumes

    c. Contours

    d. Slopes

Command Summary

Button	Command	Location
	Create Data Shortcuts	• **Ribbon:** *Manage* tab>*Data Shortcuts* panel • **Command Prompt:** CreateDataShortcuts
	New Shortcuts Folder	• **Ribbon:** *Manage* tab>*Data Shortcuts* panel • **Command Prompt:** NewShortcutsFolder
	Set Shortcuts Folder	• **Ribbon:** *Manage* tab>*Data Shortcuts* panel • **Command Prompt:** SetShortcutsFolder
	Set Working Folder	• **Ribbon:** *Manage* tab>*Data Shortcuts* panel • **Command Prompt:** SetWorkingFolder
	Surface Properties	• **Contextual Ribbon:** *Surface* tab>*Modify* panel • **Command Prompt:** EditSurfaceProperties
	Volumes Dashboard	• **Ribbon:** *Analyze* tab>*Volumes and Materials* panel • **Contextual Ribbon:** *Surface* tab>*Analyze* panel • **Command Prompt:** VolumesDashboard
	Level of Detail Reduced	• **Contextual Ribbon:** *Surface* tab>*Level of Detail* panel • **Command Prompt:** AeccSurfaceLODLow
	Level of Detail High	• **Contextual Ribbon:** *Surface* tab>*Level of Detail* panel • **Command Prompt:** AeccSurfaceLODHigh
	Add Legend	• **Contextual Ribbon:** *Surface* tab>*Level of Detail* panel • **Command Prompt:** AeccAddSurfaceLegendTable

Parcel Grading

Site properties enable you to assign elevations to lot lines or treat them as simple 2D parcel outlines. Assigning elevations to parcel lines can make it faster to build a grading model and create the finished ground surface.

You will create a residential grading plan where the front of the lots use elevations from the corridor model. The rear of the lots will follow the existing ground surface elevations and designed elevations to accommodate walk-out basements. Retaining walls and other feature lines will also be added to mark areas where the building footprint creates a significant change in grade.

Learning Objectives

- Set parcel line elevations using the feature line Edit Elevation tools.
- Create wall breaklines representing large grade breaks to add definition to the site.
- Edit surfaces to make them more accurate.
- Create split points where parcel lines cross feature lines or share elevation points.
- Create drainage at parcel boundaries, Building Pads and Reveals with Grading Optimization.
- Establish Pathways for sidewalks and zones for driveways.
- Create controlled grading spaces around commercial buildings.

A.1 Setting Parcel Line Elevations

You can create and edit parcel lines in the Autodesk® Civil 3D® software. If site properties are set correctly, parcels can be assigned elevations. Once parcel lines have been assigned elevations, they can be added to a surface as breaklines to grade a site. The tools that are used to edit feature lines can also be used to assign elevations to parcel lines.

There are two places that enable you to edit parcel, feature line, or survey figure elevations. The first is in the *Parcel Segment* contextual tab>*Edit Elevations* panel and the second is in the *Parcel Segment* contextual tab>*Edit Elevations* panel in the *Edit Elevations* vista. You can also use the Quick Elevation Tool.

Site Properties

Before you can edit parcel line elevations, you need to ensure that the site they are in is set up to use the elevations you assign. In the *Prospector* tab, expand the Sites tree, right-click on the site in which the parcels reside, and select **Properties**, as shown in Figure A–1.

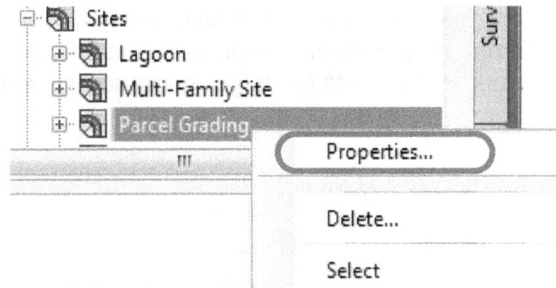

Figure A–1

In the *Site Properties* dialog box, go to the *3D Geometry* tab. Change the *Site Display Mode* to **Use elevation**, as shown in Figure A–2.

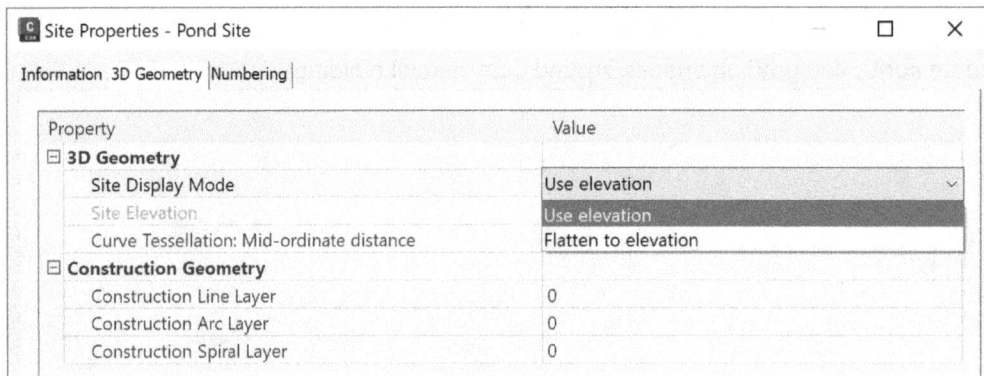

Figure A–2

Practice A1
Set Parcel Line Elevations

Practice Objective

- Assign elevations to parcel lines using the Edit Elevation tools.

For the land development drawings in this guide, much of the preliminary work has already been done for the site development.

The completed corridors for **Jeffries Ranch Road** and **Ascent Place**, the **Ascent Place** knuckle and cul-de-sac target alignments, the **Mission Avenue** alignment, and the **Existing Ground** surface have been referenced through Data Shortcuts.

Another surface that has been referenced is **Road-Tops**, which is a combination of all the corridor top surfaces, including **Jeffries Ranch Road**, **Ascent Place**, **Rand Boulevard** and the roundabout at the juncture of **Jeffries Ranch Road** and **Rand Boulevard**.

In this practice, you will review the site and prepare the drawing. You will then set the parcel elevations by design, and set parcel elevations by reference.

Task 1: Set parcel elevations by design.

The lots on the west side of Ascent Pl have been assigned elevations to ensure that the pond grading elevations to their west coordinate with each other.

1. Open **PARCELS-B.dwg** from the *C:\Civil 3D Grading\Working\Parcels* folder.

2. In the *View* tab>*Named Views* panel, select **Storm Pond** to zoom in on the pond area.

3. In the drawing, select the parcel segments representing the pond boundary. In the right-click menu, expand the *Display Order* drop-down list and select **Bring to Front**, as shown in Figure A–3. This will make the selection of lines later easier.

Figure A–3

4. In the drawing, select the pond's parcel segments again if you released the selection.

5. In the *Parcel* tab>*Edit Elevations* panel, click (Edit Elevations). Press <Enter> until the green triangle displays at the northernmost vertex of Lot 5, as shown in Figure A–4.

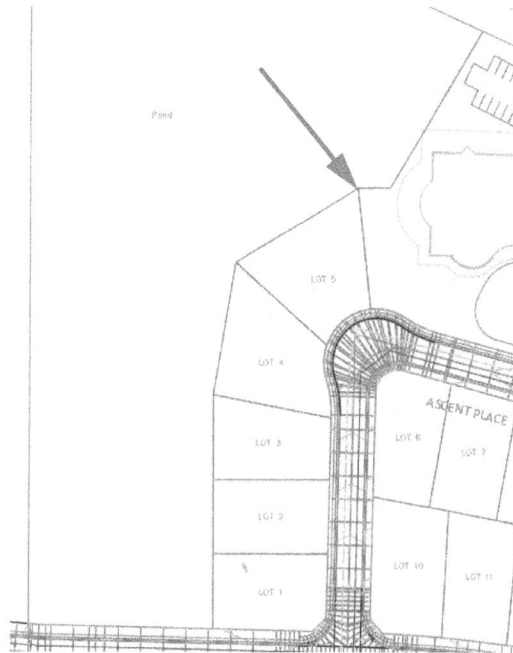

Figure A–4

6. Type **180.5** and press <Enter> for the elevation. The green triangle should move to the next vertex when you press <Enter> to assign the remaining elevations, as shown in Figure A–5. Press <Esc> twice when done to release the pond segments.

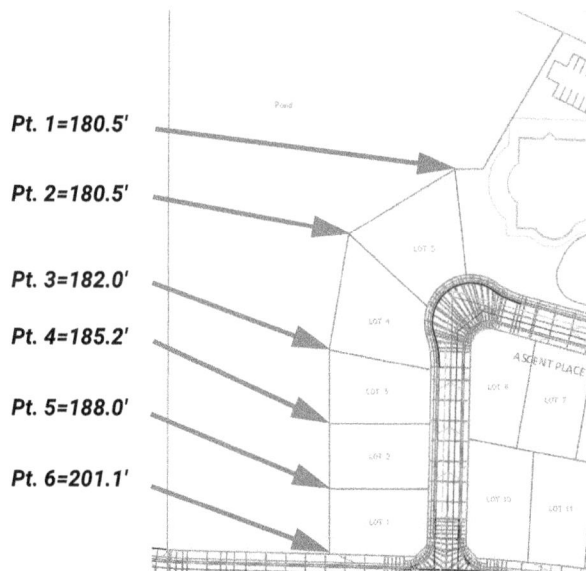

Pt. 1=180.5'
Pt. 2=180.5'
Pt. 3=182.0'
Pt. 4=185.2'
Pt. 5=188.0'
Pt. 6=201.1'

Figure A–5

7. **Lots 1-5,** in the Residential Grading site, share these vertices. Therefore, their elevations also update. Verify this by opening the *Elevation Editor* vista and selecting the parcel segments of one of the parcels. In the *Parcel* contextual tab>*Edit Elevations* panel, click

    ⬤ (Elevation Editor) to open the *Elevation Editor* vista.

8. Save the drawing.

Task 2: Set parcel elevations by reference.

> *Note: Setting elevations by reference does not create a link. If the corridor design changes, the parcel lines need to be updated manually.*

In this task, you will assign elevations to the front of the lots according to the corridor elevations. At vertices that do not fall directly on the corridor model, use a -2% grade if it falls outside the corridor and a 2% grade if it falls inside the corridor model.

1. Continue working in the drawing from the previous task.

2. In the *View* tab>*Named Views* panel, select **Lot 1** to zoom in on the area to be graded.

3. In the drawing, select the Corridor models (**Ascent Pl** and **Jeffries Ranch Rd**). In the

    Corridors contextual tab>expanded *General Tools* panel, click 🖫 (Bring to Front). Press <Esc> to end the selection.

    > *Note: If you have difficulty selecting the **Lot 1** parcel segments, turn on Selection Cycling with the **<CTRL> W** keystrokes.*

4. In the drawing, select the **Lot 1** parcel segments. In the *Parcel* tab>*Edit Elevations* panel,

    click ↗ (Set Elevations by Reference).

5. In the drawing, select the endpoint of the corridor section line directly north of the first parcel corner for the reference point marked as **A** in Figure A–6.

Figure A–6

6. In the drawing, select the parcel vertex near the corridor section line that you selected for the reference point marked as **B** in Figure A–6.

7. In the Command Line, verify that it is prompting you for the grade. If not, type **G** and press <Enter>. Since the parcel line is down slope from the end of the corridor, type **2** (for upslope) to maintain the corridor grade of 2%. Press <Esc> to end the command.

8. Repeat Steps 5 to 7 to set the elevation for the next vertex running counter-clockwise along the Lot 1 perimeter, as shown in Figure A−7.

Figure A−7

9. In the drawing, select the **Lot 1** parcel segments again. In the *Parcel* tab>*Edit Elevations* panel, click (Set Elevations by Reference).

10. In the drawing, select the nearest point on the corridor feature line at the north-east parcel corner for the reference point, using the **NEAR** Osnap setting, as shown in Figure A−8.

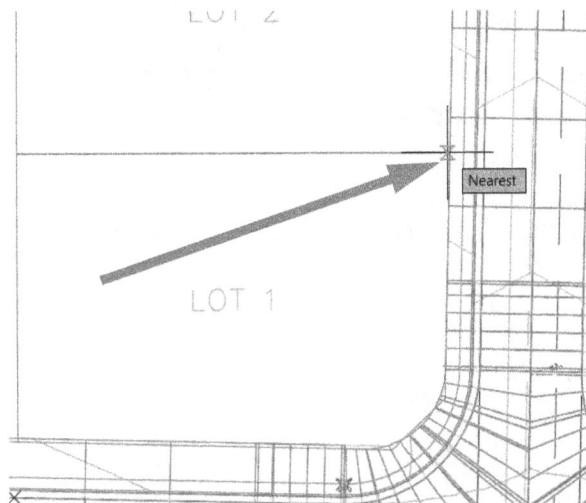

Figure A−8

11. In the drawing, select the parcel corner near the reference point for the vertex to change.

12. Since the parcel line falls directly on the corridor being referenced, type **0** for the grade to indicate that there is no change in elevation. Press <Esc> to end the command.

Task 3: (Optional) More elevation referencing.

More elevations need to be set along the vertices of the feature lines. Time permitting, set the following, otherwise you can open a drawing with the completed task for the next practice.

1. Repeat this process for all of the lot corners adjacent to or touching the corridor model, including the Commercial parcel.

    *   At vertices that do not fall directly on the corridor model, ensure that you pick points that are perpendicular to the corridor model and then use a -2% grade if it falls outside of the corridor and a 2% grade if it falls inside the corridor model.

2. Lot 4 has some additional vertices. Select the **Lot 4** Parcel lines.

3. In the *Parcel* contextual tab>*Edit Elevations* panel, click ⬤ (Elevation Editor) to open the *Elevation Editor* vista to see what elevations are now assigned to the parcel segments.

4. Note that the elevations and grades are acceptable, as shown in Figure A–9.

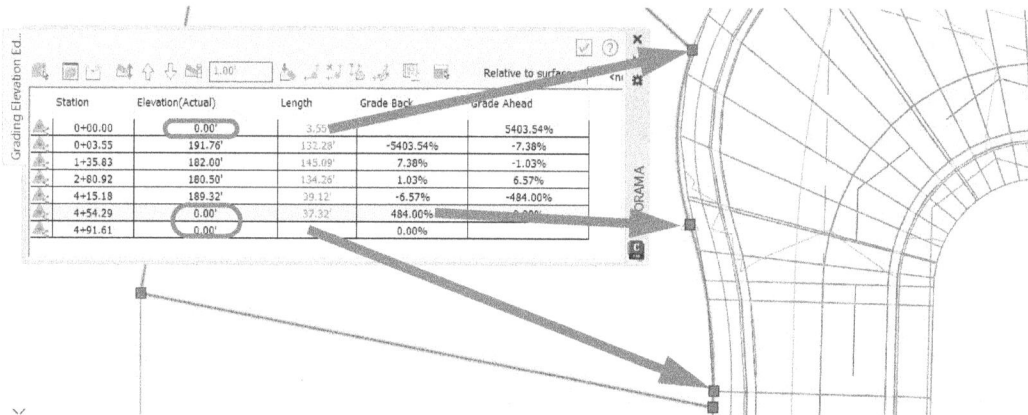

Station	Elevation(Actual)	Length	Grade Back	Grade Ahead
0+00.00	0.00'	3.55'		5403.54%
0+03.55	191.76'	132.28'	-5403.54%	-7.38%
1+35.83	182.00'	145.09'	7.38%	-1.03%
2+80.92	180.50'	134.26'	1.03%	6.57%
4+15.18	189.32'	39.12'	-6.57%	-484.00%
4+54.29	0.00'	37.32'	484.00%	0.00%
4+91.61	0.00'		0.00%	

Figure A–9

5. Repeat the ⤴ (Set Elevations by Reference) process for these three vertices, while keeping the *Elevation Editor* open.

6. When done, the results are shown in Figure A-10.

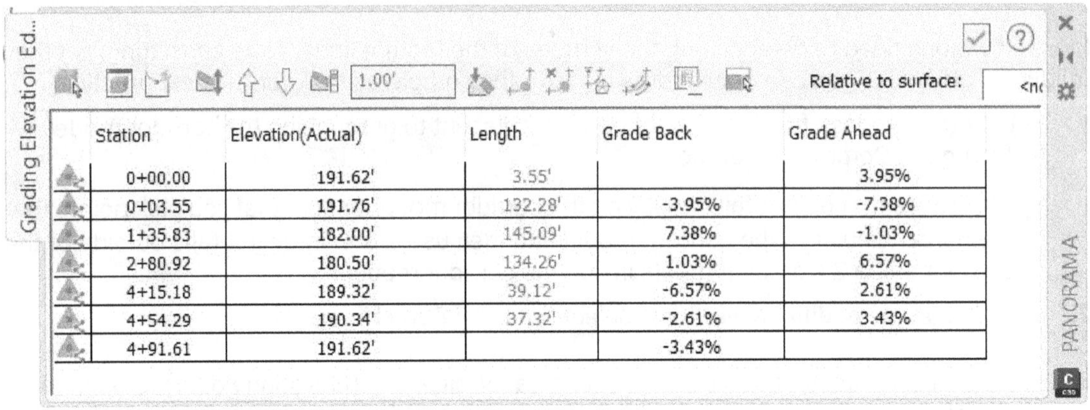

Station	Elevation(Actual)	Length	Grade Back	Grade Ahead
0+00.00	191.62'	3.55'		3.95%
0+03.55	191.76'	132.28'	-3.95%	-7.38%
1+35.83	182.00'	145.09'	7.38%	-1.03%
2+80.92	180.50'	134.26'	1.03%	6.57%
4+15.18	189.32'	39.12'	-6.57%	2.61%
4+54.29	190.34'	37.32'	-2.61%	3.43%
4+91.61	191.62'		-3.43%	

Relative to surface:

Figure A-10

7. Time permitting, check the other lots - 1 through 5.

8. Save the drawing.

End of practice

A.2 Retaining Walls

Adding elevations to parcel segments helps define the finished grade. However, it does not do anything until you add them to a surface. This section covers adding breaklines to a surface since you add parcel segments to surfaces as breaklines.

Breaklines created by Proximity leave the original polylines in the drawing even though they are defined as a Standard breakline. This Standard definition can be inserted into the drawing and manipulated. The original line can be deleted.

A breakline created as a Standard breakline is linked to the original line in the drawing. If this line is deleted, the breakline definition is also deleted. The different breakline definitions are as follows:

Breakline Type	Description
Standard	Creates a breakline that is defined by selecting 3D lines, feature lines, parcel segments, survey figures, and 3D polylines.
Proximity	Creates a breakline that is defined by drawing or selecting a feature line, parcel segment, survey figure, or polyline within the extents of the surface boundary. The location and elevation of each vertex is determined by the nearest surface point.
Wall	A wall breakline is stored as a standard breakline but is defined differently. You provide an offset side, elevation difference at each vertex or along the entire breakline.
Non-destructive	Creates a breakline that is defined using grading feature lines and open or closed AutoCAD® objects. A non-destructive breakline does not affect the original surface.

How To: Add Parcel Segments to a Surface

1. To create a surface, in the *Home* tab>*Create Ground Data* panel, expand the *Surfaces* drop-down list and click (Create Surface).

2. In the *Create Surface* dialog box, type a name and description, and select a style. Click **OK** to close the dialog box.

3. In the *Prospector* tab, expand *Surfaces*>[Surface you are working with]>*Definition*. Right-click on **Breaklines** and select **Add**, as shown in Figure A–11.

Figure A–11

4. In the *Add Breaklines* dialog box, type a description and set the type to **Standard**, if elevations are already assigned to the parcels. Add weeding and supplementing factors as required. Click **OK** to close the dialog box.

5. Select the parcel segments in the drawing. Press <Enter> when done.

How To: Add Wall Breaklines to a Surface

1. Draw a feature line, parcel line, survey figure, or 3D Polyline.

2. In the *Prospector* tab>expand *Surfaces*>[Surface you are working with]>*Definition*. Right-click on **Breaklines** and select **Add**, as shown in Figure A–12.

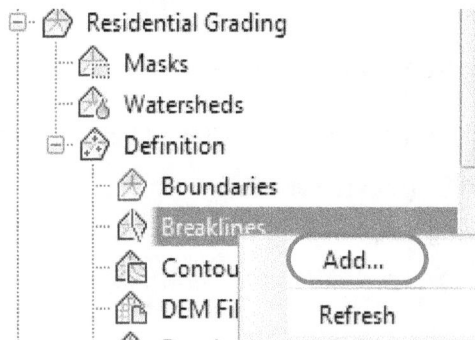

Figure A–12

3. In the *Add Breaklines* dialog box, type a description and set the *Type* to **Wall**, as shown in Figure A–13.

Figure A–13

4. Add weeding and supplementing factors as required. Click **OK** to close the dialog box.
5. In the drawing, select the object you drew in Step 1. Press <Enter> when done.
6. Pick a point on the side to offset the original feature line.
7. Type **I** to set the height of the wall at each individual vertex or press <Enter> to accept the default **All** to set the height of all of the vertices at the same time.
8. In the Command Line, type a value for the difference in elevation or type **E** to set the actual elevation.

A.3 Editing Surfaces

Once the basic information has been added to a surface definition, you might need to edit the surface to make it more accurate. Surface edits can be done by selecting the surface. Then, in the *Tin Surface* contextual tab>*Modify* panel, expand ✎ (Edit Surface) to display the available tools, as shown in Figure A–14.

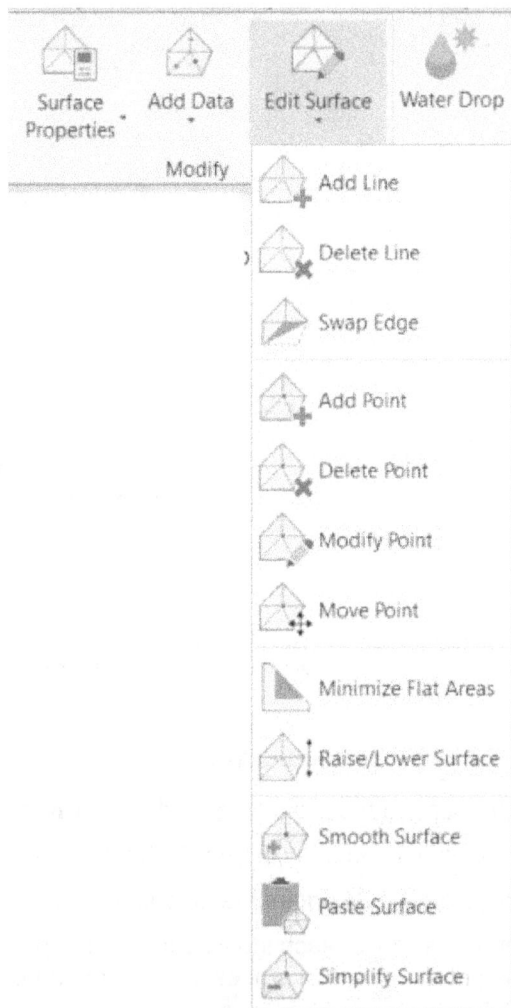

Figure A–14

The tools in the *Edit Surface* drop-down list are as follows:

Icon	Command	Description
	Add Line	Adds additional triangle line to a surface to modify how the surface triangulates. Note that the surface triangles must be visible in the style to use this command.
	Delete Line	Removes triangle or grid lines from a surface to modify how the surface triangulates. Note that the surface triangles or grid lines must be visible in the style to use this command.
	Swap Edge	Changes the direction of two triangle faces within a surface to modify how the surface triangulates. Note that the surface triangles must be visible in the style to use this command.
	Add Point	Adds a point to a surface to modify how the surface triangulates. Note that the surface points must be visible in the style to use this command.
	Delete Point	Removes unnecessary or inaccurate points from a surface to modify how the surface triangulates. Note that the surface points must be visible in the style to use this command.
	Modify Point	Modifies the elevation of a surface point to modify how the surface triangulates. Note that the surface points must be visible in the style to use this command.
	Move Point	Moves a surface point to a new location without changing its elevation to modify how the surface triangulates. Note that the surface points must be visible in the style to use this command.
	Minimize Flat Areas	Reduces the number of adjacent triangles containing the same elevation and modifies how the surface triangulates to make it more accurately represent a real-world surface.
	Raise/Lower Surface	Adds/Subtracts a specified distance to a surface and changes the elevations of every triangle by the same amount.
	Smooth Surface	Adds points at system-determined elevations using Natural Neighbor Interpolation (NNI) or Kriging methods to smooth contour lines without making them overlap.
	Paste Surface	Combines two surfaces by overriding triangles in the destination surface with triangles from the pasted surface. Note that the paste order is key because elevations are taken from the last surface pasted.
	Simplify Surface	Removes unnecessary points from a surface to reduce its size while preserving its accuracy.

How To: Paste Surfaces Together

1. In the drawing, select the destination surface (it is going to be overridden by another surface.
2. In the *Tin Surface* contextual tab>*Modify* panel, expand the *Edit Surface* drop-down list and click 🗋 (Paste Surface).
3. In the *Select Surface to Paste* dialog box, select the surface(s) to paste into the destination surface, as shown in Figure A–15.

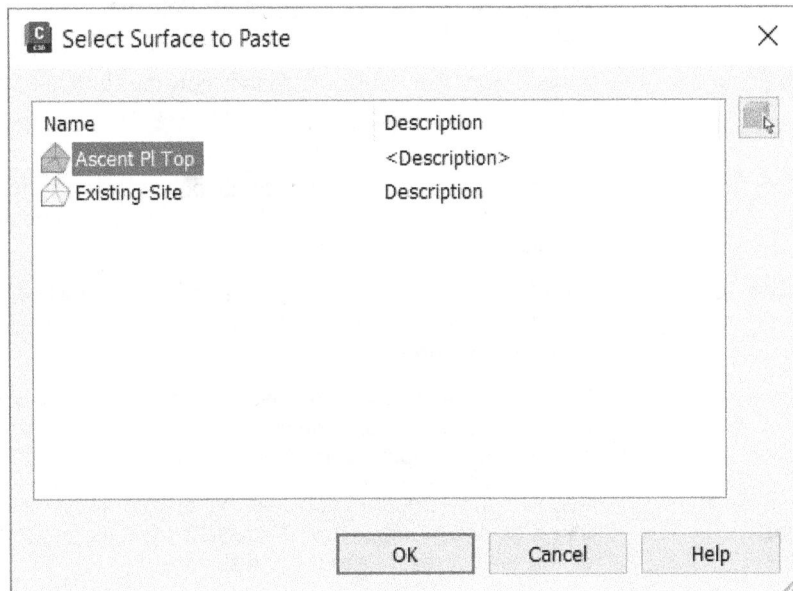

Figure A–15

4. Click **OK** to close the dialog box.

Practice A2
Create a Surface and Add Retaining Walls

Practice Objective

* Create wall breaklines to display drastic grade breaks and create a 7' minimum wall.

In this practice, you will create a finish ground surface to grade the single-family area. You will then paste the surfaces together and add wall breaklines to the surface.

Task 1: Create a finish ground surface to grade the single-family area.

1. Open **PARCELS-C.dwg** from the *C:\Civil 3D Grading\Working\\Parcels* folder. Do not continue working in the drawing from the previous practice, the parcel elevations have been fine-tuned in this drawing. Some more feature lines have been added as well.

2. In the *View* tab>*Named Views* panel, select **Single Family Lots** as the view to zoom into the residential area.

3. In the *Home* tab>*Create Ground Data* panel, click (Create Surface).

4. In the *Create Surface* dialog box, set the following as shown in Figure A–16.

   * *Name:* Type **Residential Grading**.
   * *Description:* Type **Grading from parcel segment elevations and additional breaklines**.
   * *Style:* Select **ASC-Temporary Grading View**.

Figure A–16

5. Click **OK** to close the dialog box.

6. In the *Prospector* tab, expand **Surfaces>Residential Grading>Definition**. Right-click on Breaklines and select **Add**.

7. In the *Add Breaklines* dialog box, for the *Description,* type **Residential Parcels**, as shown in Figure A−17. Click **OK** to accept the other defaults and close the dialog box.

Figure A−17

8. Select the 15 single-family parcel segments and the one Commercial parcel segment to the north (16 total), as shown in Figure A−18. Press <Enter> to end the selection.

Figure A−18

9. Save the drawing.

Task 2: Paste the surfaces together.

1. Continue working in the drawing from the previous task.

2. In the drawing, select the **Residential Grading** surface.

3. In the *Tin Surface* contextual tab>*Modify* panel, expand the *Edit Surface* drop-down list and click (Paste Surface).

---

4. In the *Select Surface* dialog box, select the **Road-Tops** surface, as shown in Figure A–19.

Figure A–19

5. Click **OK** to close the dialog box.
6. Save the drawing. The drawing displays as shown in Figure A–20.

Figure A–20

Task 3: Add wall breaklines to the surface.

1.   Continue working in the drawing from the previous task.

The feature lines for the top of the walls have already been created for you to speed up the process. This was done by creating stepped offsets of the parcels lines 55' from the back of lot at a positive 2% slope to ensure that the water drains away from the house toward the back property line and 30' from the street at a positive 4% grade to ensure that the water drains toward the street in front. At the front of the property, the wall is a minimum of 7' and tapers down from there. Figure A–21 shows a cross section of a typical wall breakline.

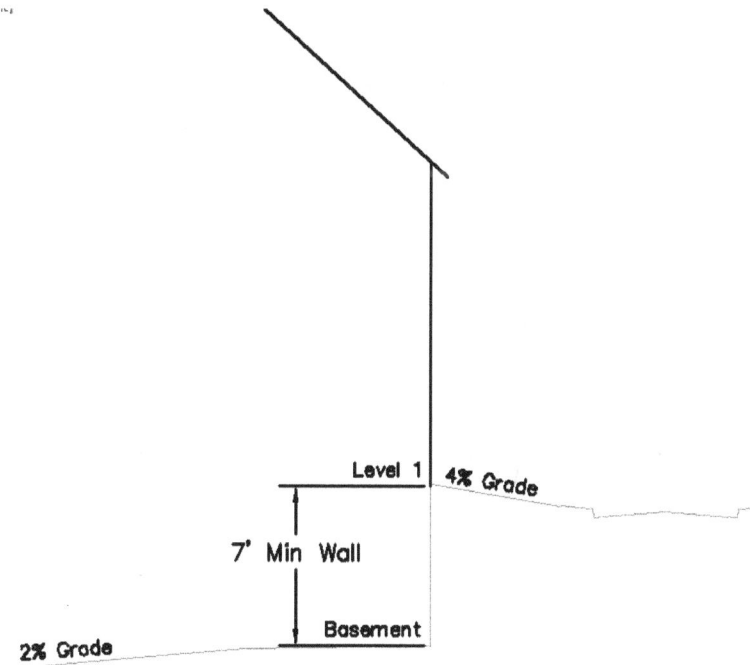

Figure A–21

2.   Thaw the **C-GRAD-BREK** layer which contains feature lines which you will convert to breaklines.

3.   In the *View* tab>*Named Views* panel, select **Lot1** as the view to zoom into the first lot to grade.

4. Select the **Residential Grading** surface in the drawing. In the *Tin Surface* contextual tab>*Modify* panel, expand the *Add Data* drop-down list and click 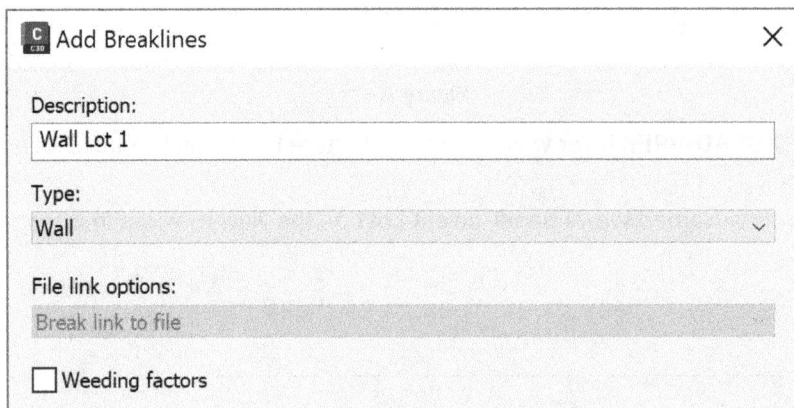 (Breaklines), as shown in Figure A–22.

Figure A–22

5. In the *Add Breaklines* dialog box, set the following (as shown in Figure A–23) and click **OK**, to accept all of the other defaults and close the dialog box.

   • *Description:* Type **Wall Lot 1**.

   • *Type:* Select **Wall**.

Figure A–23

6. In the drawing, select the green C-shaped feature line inside Lot 1 and press <Enter>.

7. Pick a point to the inside of the C-shaped feature line for the offset side. Press <Enter> to accept the **All** option to set the height for all of the vertices at the same time.

8. In the Command Line, select the **Elevation** option.

9. For the elevation value, type **196**. Note that the arrows on the surface indicate the direction in which the water will flow, as shown in Figure A–24.

Figure A–24

10. Repeat Steps 5 to 9, to add a retaining wall to Lots 2 to 5 using the following value for the target elevation in each lot.

Area	Target Elevation
Lot 2	188
Lot 3	186
Lot 4	183
Lot 5	182

Once all of the wall breaklines are in the surface, add the back of lot breaklines to set the back yard grades at 2%.

11. In the *View* tab>*Named Views* panel, select **Single Family Lots** as the view to zoom into.

12. Select the **Residential Grading** surface in the drawing. In the *Tin Surface* contextual tab>*Modify* panel, expand the *Add Data* drop-down list and click ⬙ (Breaklines).

13. In the *Add Breaklines* dialog box, set the following and click **OK**, to accept all of the other defaults and close the dialog box.

    - *Description:* Type **Backyard Grade**.
    - *Type:* Select **Standard**.

14. In the drawing, select the black feature lines in each lot, as shown in Figure A–25. Press <Enter> to end the selection.

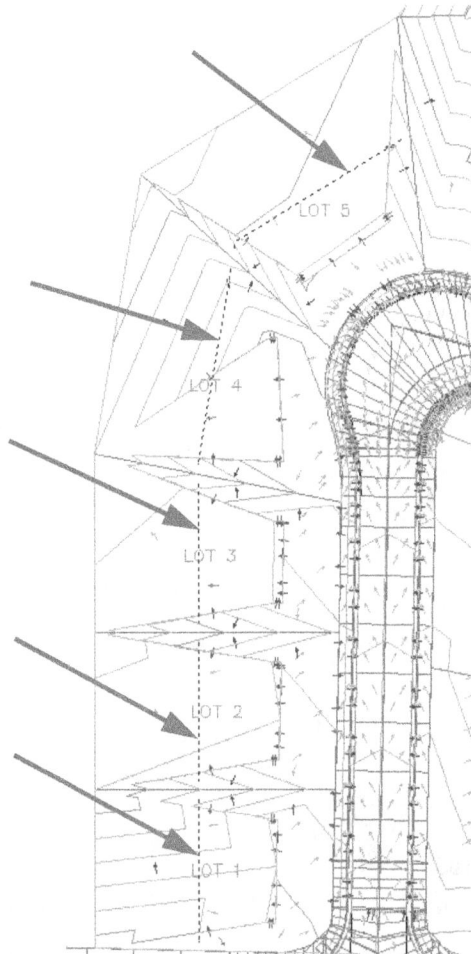

Figure A–25

15. Press <Esc> to release the surface and then save the drawing.

End of practice

A.4 Feature Line Interactions with Parcel Lines

When parcel lines and feature lines reside in the same site and intersect each other or share vertices, one line overrides the elevations of the other and creates a split point at the shared point of intersection. The last object edited automatically edits the elevations of the first. This is called the *last one wins* rule. Therefore, it is recommended that you create multiple sites for a grading plan. Keeping parcels in one site and feature lines in another site ensures that they do not unintentionally override each other as you are working.

When parcels share line segment(s), any edits to the elevations of one parcel affect the elevations of the second parcel along the shared segment(s). This includes any elevation points that might be added. Figure A–26 shows the elevations of two lots that share a common segment. Elevation points have been inserted along the shared segment in Lot 1 (marked with circular symbols). Note that Lot 2 automatically picked up the same elevation points (marked with empty triangles) along the shared segment. These are known as split points.

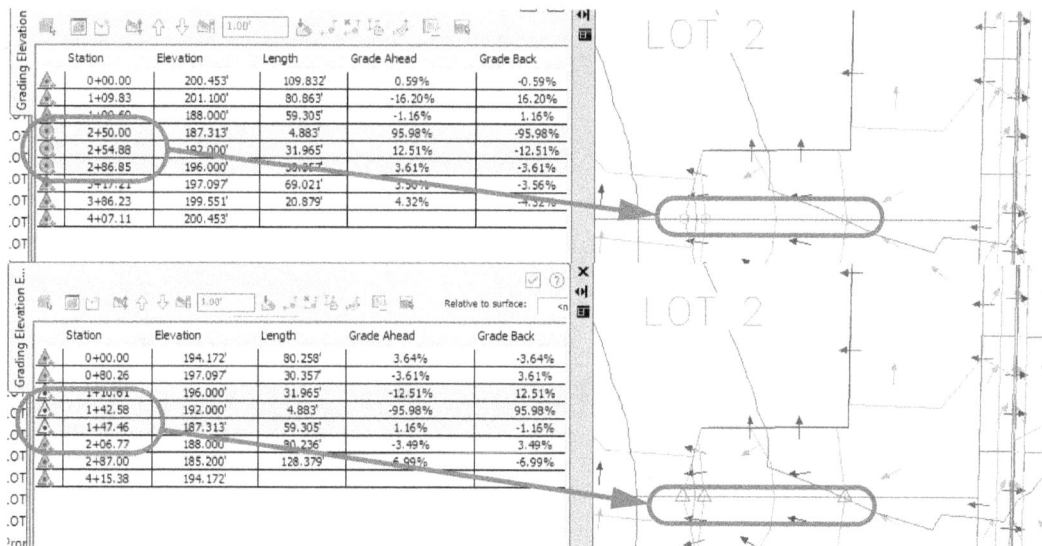

Figure A–26

Practice A3
Add Elevation Points to Parcels

Practice Objective

- Create split points along parcel lines by adding elevations to adjacent parcel segments.

In this practice, you will insert elevation points along the parcel segments.

1. Continue working in the drawing from the previous practice or open **PARCELS-D.dwg** from the *C:\Civil 3D Grading\Working\Parcels* folder.

2. In the *View* tab>*Named Views* panel, select **Lot1** as the view to zoom into the first lot to grade.

3. In the *Prospector* tab, expand *Surfaces*, right-click on **Residential Surface** and select **Rebuild - Automatic**, as shown in Figure A−27.

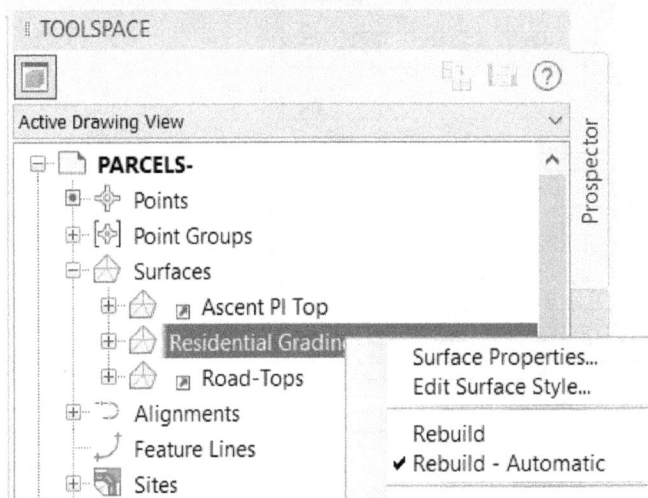

Figure A−27

4. In the drawing, select the Lot 1 parcel segments. In the *Parcel Segments* contextual tab>*Modify* panel, click ⬛ (Edit Elevations). In the *Edit Elevations* panel, click ⬤ (Elevation Editor).

5. In the *Elevation Editor* vista, click ⬛ (Insert Elevation Point).

6. In the drawing, pick the endpoint of the walls at the front corner of the house in Lot 1, as shown in Figure A–28.

Station	Elevation(Actual)	Length	Grade Back	Grade Ahead
0+00.00	200.20'	109.83'		0.82%
1+09.83	201.10'	80.86'	-0.82%	-16.20%
1+90.69	188.00'	126.51'	16.20%	7.20%
3+17.21	197.11'	69.02'	-7.20%	3.52%
3+86.23	199.54'	20.88'	-3.52%	3.16%
4+07.11	200.20'		-3.16%	

Insert PVI

Station: 2+86.85   Elevation: 194.92'

OK   Cancel   Help

Figure A–28

7. In the *Insert PVI* dialog box, for the *Elevation* type **198**. Click **OK**. (This dialog box might not open. If it does not, keep an eye on the Command Line because it will prompt you for the elevation instead.)

8. Repeat Steps 4 to 7, to add an elevation at the endpoint of the backyard feature lines for Lot 1 with an elevation of **190**. When finished, the Lot 1 elevations in the *Elevation Editor* vista should be as shown in Figure A–29.

Station	Elevation(Actual)	Length	Grade Back	Grade Ahead
0+00.00	200.20'	109.83'		0.82%
1+09.83	201.10'	80.86'	-0.82%	-16.20%
1+90.69	188.00'	55.00'	16.20%	3.64%
2+45.70	190.00'	41.15'	-3.64%	19.44%
2+86.85	198.00'	30.36'	-19.44%	-2.94%
3+17.21	197.11'	69.02'	2.94%	3.52%
3+86.23	199.54'	20.88'	-3.52%	3.16%
4+07.11	200.20'		-3.16%	

Figure A–29

9. In the *Elevation Editor* vista, click 📷 (Select Feature).

10. In the drawing, select the Lot 2 parcel segments. Note the three split points marked with triangles along the south boundary line, as shown in Figure A–30.

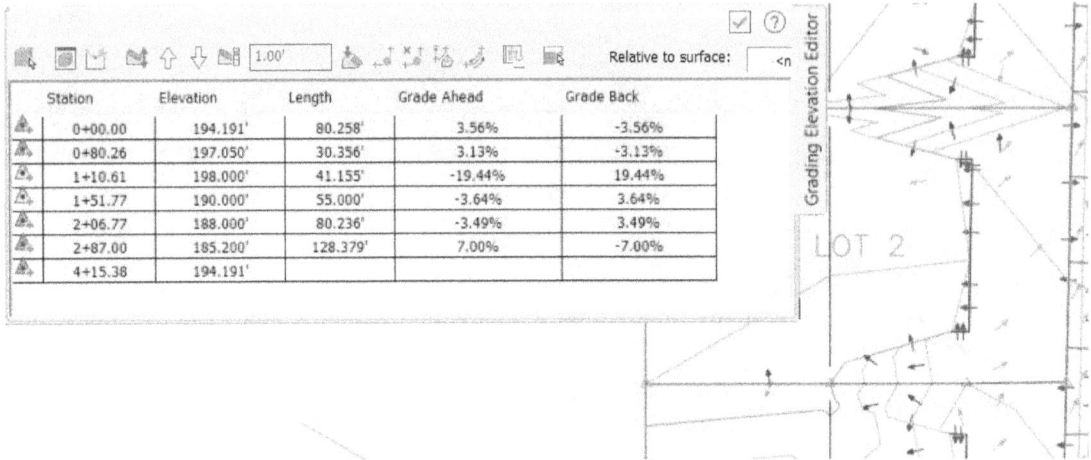

Station	Elevation	Length	Grade Ahead	Grade Back
0+00.00	194.191'	80.258'	3.56%	-3.56%
0+80.26	197.050'	30.356'	3.13%	-3.13%
1+10.61	198.000'	41.155'	-19.44%	19.44%
1+51.77	190.000'	55.000'	-3.64%	3.64%
2+06.77	188.000'	80.236'	-3.49%	3.49%
2+87.00	185.200'	128.379'	7.00%	-7.00%
4+15.38	194.191'			

Figure A–30

11. Repeat Steps 4 to 8, to add elevation points to the north line of Lot 2, as shown in Figure A–31.

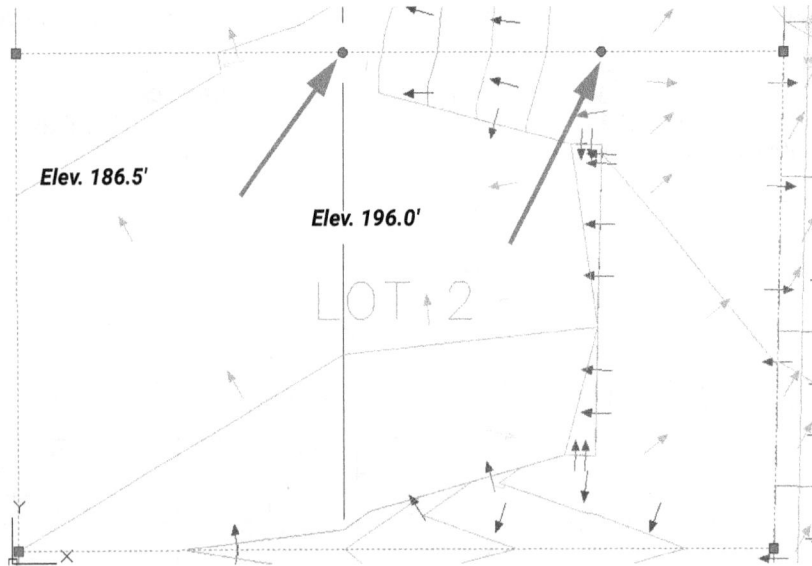

Figure A–31

12. Repeat Steps 4 to 8, to add elevation points to the north line of Lot 3, as shown in Figure A-32.

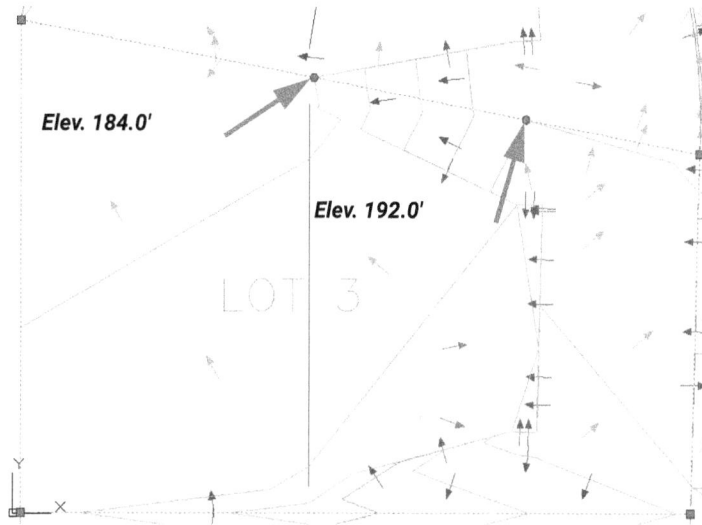

Figure A-32

13. Repeat Steps 4 to 8, to add elevation points to the north line of Lot 4, as shown in Figure A-33.

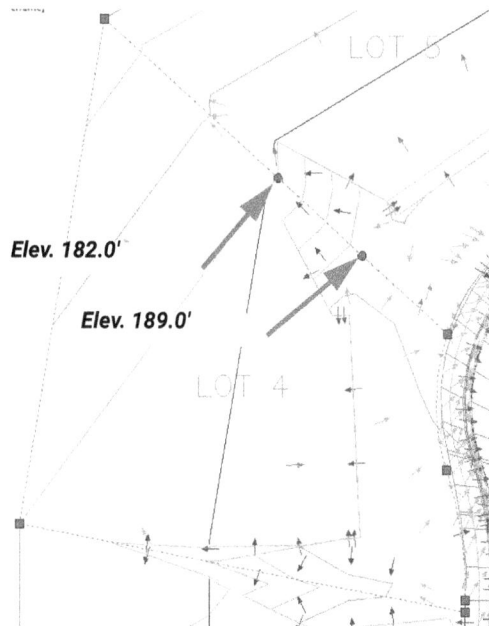

Figure A-33

14. Repeat Steps 4 to 8, to add elevation points to the north line of Lot 5, as shown in Figure A–34.

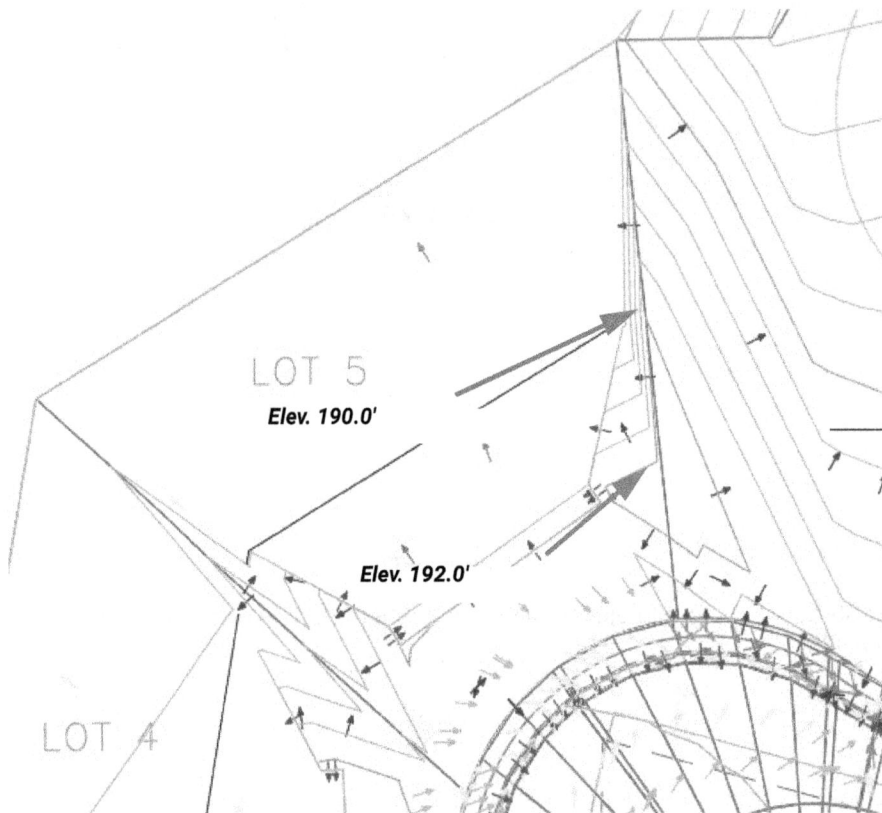

Figure A–34

15. Select the **Residential Grading** surface (select one of its contour lines).

16. In the *Surface* contextual tab, click [icon] (Object Viewer). Set the view direction to **SW Isometric** and the style to **Conceptual**, as shown in Figure A–35. If you prefer, you can also view it through the *Model Viewer* by selecting **Add to Model Viewer** via the right-click menu.

Figure A–35

17. Press <Esc> twice to close the *Object Viewer* and release the selection.

End of practice

A.5 Grading Optimization: Parcels and Building Pads

Site properties enable you to assign elevations to lot lines or treat them as 2D representations of parcels. The advantage of assigning elevations to parcel lines is that it helps to speed up the building of a grading model and to finish the ground surface. In this section, you will create a residential grading plan in which the front of the lots take on elevations in reference to the corridor model. The back of the lots take on the existing ground surface elevations and designed elevations to accommodate walk out basements. Finally, retaining walls and other feature lines will be added to indicate where the building footprint causes a drastic change in grade.

Building Pads

Building pads are at the top of the Grading Object hierarchy. This means that they take precedence over the other Grading Object and will always "come out on top".

When defining a building pad, give it a meaningful name for easy identification, especially if there are multiple building pads in the project.

You can either define an elevation range or a fixed elevation to constrain the building pad. Or you can omit entering any elevation constraints to let the Grading Optimization come up with an elevation.

To specify an elevation range, type in values for the minimum and maximum elevations for the constraints, as shown in Figure A–36. For the minimum, if you type in a greater value than is in the maximum field, Grading Optimization will simply ignore it and revert back to the previous value (and vice versa).

For a fixed elevation, toggle **on** the **Fixed elevation value**. This will hide the *Min* and *Max elevation* fields and reveal the *Elevation* field, where you can type in the fixed elevation for a constraint, as shown in Figure A–36.

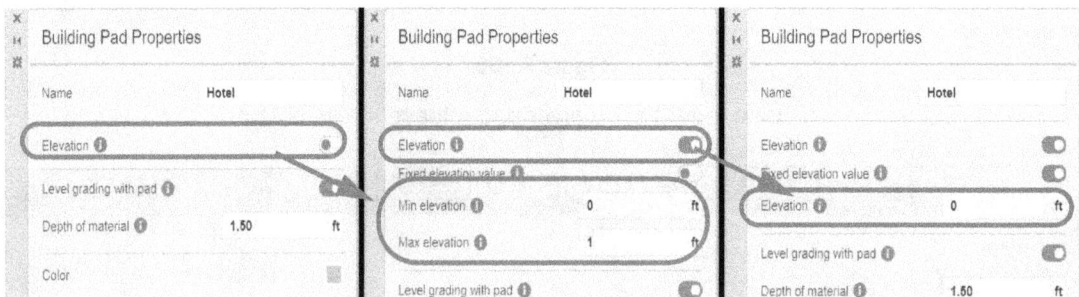

Figure A–36

When the **Level grading with pad** toggle is **on**, the Grading Optimization will attempt to have the building pad to be "draped" over the surface, allowing the pad's edges to be on the same elevation as the surface. When the **Level grading with pad** toggle is **off**, there will be squared off with hard edges, as shown in Figure A–37.

Level grading is ON　　　　　　　**Level grading is OFF**

Figure A–37

The **Depth of Material** can be thought of as the surface depth between the building pad and the surface comprising of composition base materials, such as crushed stone, concrete slab, etc. that should not be considered when calculating the cut and fill material.

Building pads now have a specific property to drain water away from the pad.

A building pad Grading Object can be considered the exact building footprint, in which case foundations and footings can be considered. However, for such granular grading, it is recommended to be done in Civil 3D with its more traditional grading tools.

A building pad can also be considered the area on the surface that the building will occupy. One can give it the desired elevation for the pad, representing the ground level of the building, or even an extended pad encompassing the building's immediate flattened vicinity. For such situations, the elevation range for the pad may be more appropriate.

Pathways

The **Pathways** Grading Object is a linear object to define a pathway. It is ideal for sidewalks, accessible walkways, and other forms of areas used for pedestrian or even vehicular travel.

After a linear object is assigned with the **Pathway** Grading properties, it is displayed as a thick line with two colors, representing both sides of the walkway. However if the object is deselected, only the original object is displayed, as shown in Figure A–38.

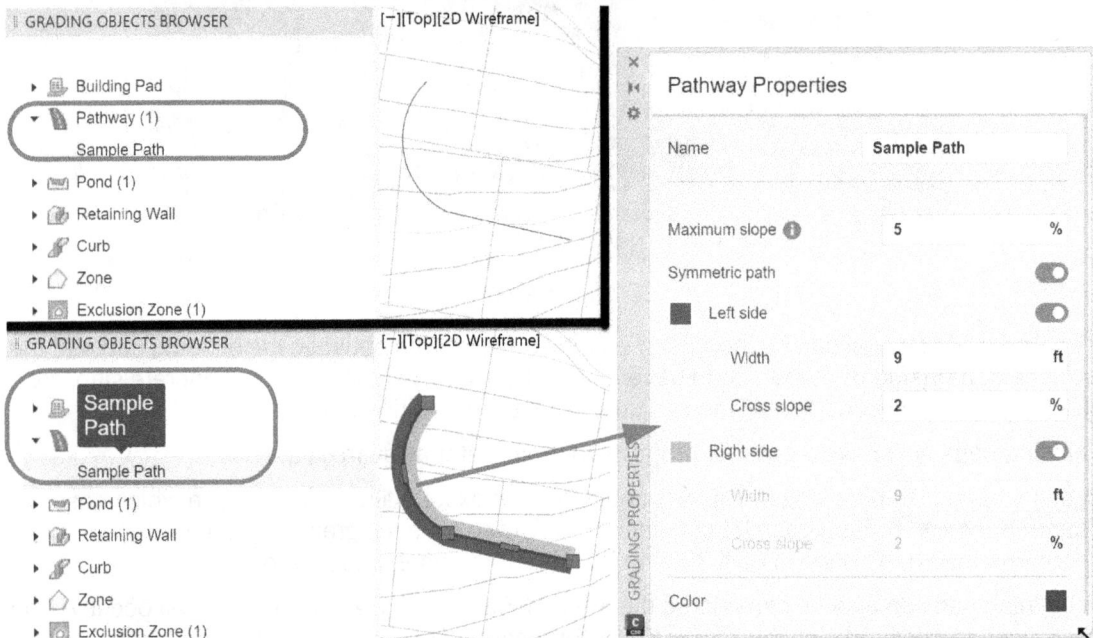

Figure A–38

The options for are a pathway are a name and the maximum slope of the path, along the length of the path. You can specify individual values for width of the sides and cross slopes if you deselect the **Symmetric path** toggle.

The **Color** option is how the linear object is represented in the Grading Optimization program. To change the color of the pathway sides, click on the color square next to Left side or Right side to select a different color.

The Grading Optimization will reshape the terrain to accommodate the pathway within the given parameters as best as it can and provide feedback as to when the parameters cannot be met, as shown in Figure A–39.

Figure A–39

Offset Points

The **Offset Points** Grading Object is a handy tool to control elevation of two points defined by the start point and end point of a linear object. (Therefore, the object must be open, it cannot be closed). Grading Object will slope the surface between these two points.

You can assign a fixed elevation difference between the two points, or supply a range for Grading Object to work with. The start point of the line will be the higher elevation for positive elevation differences; if the elevation difference is negative, the start point will be lower than the endpoint, forcing an uphill slope of the surface, as shown in Figure A–40.

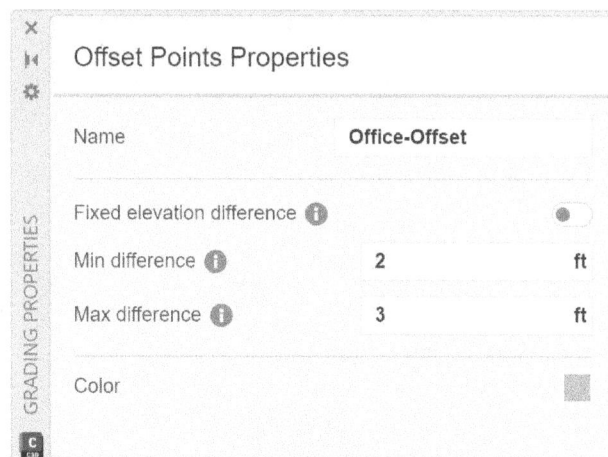

Figure A–40

If you want to control the elevation difference between Grading Objects, you need to ensure that the start and endpoints of the line snap to the Grading Object's geometry are using the appropriate AutoCAD Object Snaps.

The **Offset Points** Grading Object applies the elevation of the start point to the grading surface, and then the elevation difference at the endpoint of the Offset Points object to the grading surface, as shown in Figure A–41.

Offset Point to a Building Pad

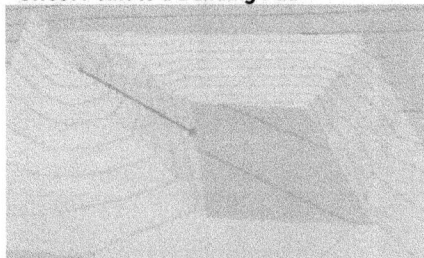

Offset Point to an Inclined Zone

Figure A–41

By itself on a surface, this feature is rather unexciting, however, it can be useful when used with other Grading Objects. If you target a building pad or a zone (with **Aligned Surface** option toggled **on**), then it becomes quite valuable in coordinating building elevations, as shown in Figure A–42.

Before Optimization

After Optimization

Figure A–42

> **Hint: Elevation Difference**
>
> Be careful of the elevation difference you provide. If the resulting slopes are greater than those provided in the Optimization Options in the Grading Optimization interface, then Grading Optimization will not be able to solve the conflict. The Violation view is a great tool to monitor such conflicts.

Reveals

A **Reveal** is a Grading Object attached to a building pad. It is defined along the edge of a building pad and is given an elevation difference, which represents the depth of how much of the building pad is to be revealed for the length of the reveal, as shown in Figure A–43.

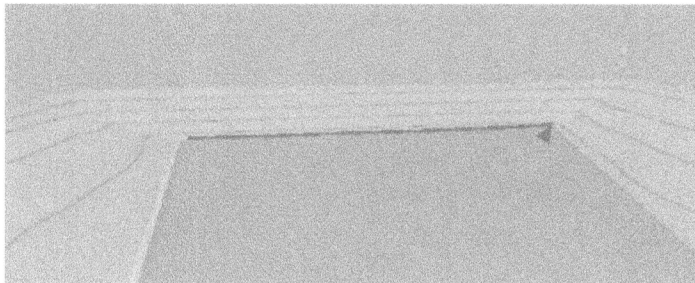

Figure A–43

How To: Create a Reveal Grading Object.

1. Create a **Building Pad** Grading Object.

2. You can select ![Reveal icon] Reveal (Reveal) in the *Grading Optimization Tool Palette* to assign it to a **Building Pad**, or you can select the **Building Pad** Grading Object and use the right-click menu to assign a **Reveal** as shown in Figure A–44.

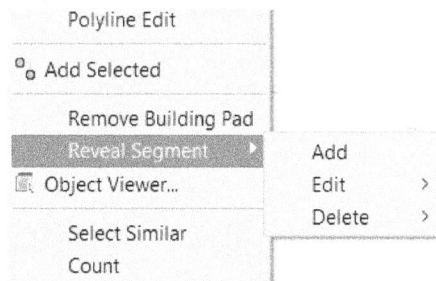

Figure A–44

3. In the *Reveal Properties* dialog box, you assign the elevation values, which is how the depth of the building pad is to be revealed for that segment.

4. You can assign fixed elevation values for the length of the reveal, or toggle **off** the **Fixed elevation value** option to assign minimum and maximum distance.

5. The End elevation difference can be the same as the Start elevation difference when the **Same as start elevation** is toggled **on** (as shown in Figure A–45), or it can contain its own values.

Figure A–45

6. Once Reveals are assigned to Building Pads, they can be edited, either through the right-click menu or by selecting it in the *Grading Objects Browser*.

7. You can delete a **Reveal**, either through the right-click menu or when selected in the *Grading Objects Browser*, a red **X** appears on the screen, as shown in Figure A–46. When you select the red X, the **Reveal** is removed from the **Building pad**, without any confirmation or warning.

Figure A–46

8. A **Reveal** in conjunction with an inner and outer zone adjoining the reveal is an ideal situation to create truckwell to lower the terrain at the building pad to allow trucks to load and unload their cargo.

Aligned Edges

As parking lots merge into roadways, the transition can create a challenge drainage wise. Roadways usually have a gutter line to carry away the rainwater into catch basins. Such lines can get disrupted by a merging parking lot. Or if the parking lot lies beyond a contiguous sidewalk along the road, some type of ridge or sag line needs to be defined for proper drainage.

The **Aligned Edge** Grading Object is used to create such edges. It is assigned to a line or polyline or feature line. During the Grading Object process, the resulting triangle edges of the TIN surface align with this feature to form a smooth edge, like a fold or crease on the surface, as shown in Figure A–47.

Contours - edge not aligned

Contours - edge aligned

TIN triangles - edge not aligned

TIN triangles - edge aligned

Figure A–47

To assign, select the Aligned Edge (Aligned Edge Grading Optimization) from the *Grading Optimization* Tool Palette. You can either select all the linework first and then select the **Aligned Edge** Grading Object in the palette, or vice versa. When done, the *Aligned Edge Properties* dialog box displays.

The *Aligned Edge Properties* dialog box is quite simple, as shown in Figure A–48. It requires a name. The default name is the name of the layer the object resides on. It is recommended that you give it a proper name for easier identification.

When the **Breakline** toggle is **on**, the aligned edge object will become part of the surface in the form of a breakline, resulting in a consistent slope along the line.

Figure A–48

Practice A4
Grading for Buildings

Practice Objectives

- Create drainage at parcel boundaries.
- Create Building Pads and Reveals.
- Create a Pathway.
- Establish zones for driveways.
- Create controlled grading spaces around commercial buildings.

he Grading Optimization process can be time consuming, and you may require additional time to complete the process than the estimated 30 minutes. Parcels for single family housing and commercial building pads make up much of the buildings in this development. In this practice, you will grade these properly with the Grading Optimization tools.

The **Park-N** surface created in the Parking Lot chapter has been referenced via data-shortcuts into this drawing.

A lot of linework has been created for this practice to save some time and effort. Building Footprints for single family housing have been added, as well as drainage lines between the parcels, as shown in Figure A–49.

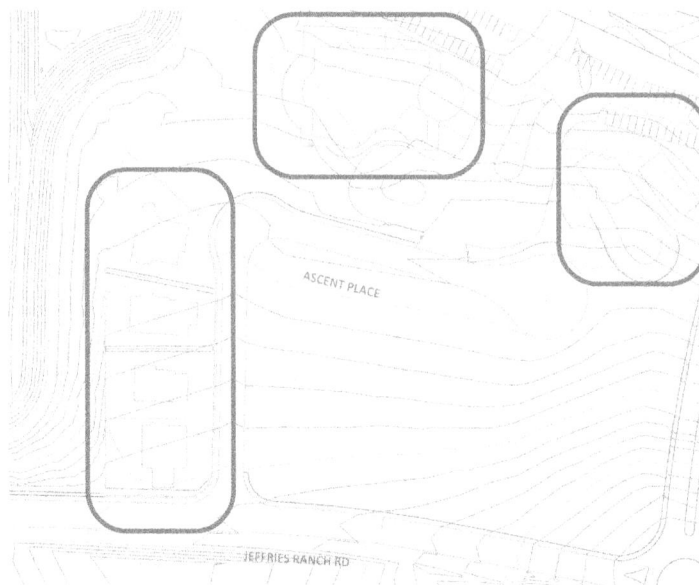

Figure A–49

Task 1: Residential lots and site preparation.

1. Open **BLDG-GO-A.dwg** from the *C:\Civil 3D Grading\Working\BLDG Pad* folder.

2. In the *View* tab>*Named Views* panel, select the **Residential** view.

3. In the Tool Palette, select **Building Pad.** Select the lowest building pad, as shown in Figure A–50 and press <Enter>.

Figure A–50

4. In the *Building Pad Properties* dialog box, set the following:

   - *Name:* **Lot-1**
   - **Elevation**: toggle **off** (to let Grading Optimization determine the best elevation)
   - **Level grading with pad**: toggle **on**
   - Leave the rest as defaults.

5. With the building pad still selected, in the right-click menu, select *Reveal Segment>Add*, then draw a line on the left side of the building, as shown in Figure A–51.

Figure A–51

6. In the *Reveal Properties* dialog box, set the following:

   * *Name:* **Lot 1 Reveal**
   * *Min difference:* **6 ft**
   * *Max difference:* **8 ft**
   * Leave the rest as defaults.

7. Press <Esc> to clear the selection and to close the dialog boxes.

8. In the *Grading Objects Browser*, expand *Building Pad>Lot-1* and select as shown in Figure A−52. Here, you can review and change the information you had entered earlier.

Figure A−52

9. Repeat the same steps for the next building pad and enter the following, as shown in Figure A−53.

- Building Pad:
    - *Name:* **Lot-2**
    - **Elevation**: toggle **on**
    - *Min difference:* **193 ft**
    - *Max difference:* **196 ft**
    - Leave the rest as defaults.
- Reveal:
    - *Name:* **Lot-2-Reveal**
    - *Min difference:* **3 ft**
    - *Max difference:* **5 ft**
    - Leave the rest as defaults.

10. Press <Esc> to clear the selection and to close the dialog boxes.

Building Pad Properties

Name	Lot-2
Elevation ⓘ	
Fixed elevation value ⓘ	
Min elevation ⓘ	193 ft
Max elevation ⓘ	196 ft
Level grading with pad ⓘ	
Depth of material ⓘ	1.50 ft
Color	

Reveal Properties

Name	Lot-2-Reveal
Fixed elevation value ⓘ	
▾ Start elevation difference	
Min difference ⓘ	3 ft
Max difference ⓘ	5 ft
▾ End elevation difference	
Same as start elevation	
Min difference ⓘ	7 ft
Max difference ⓘ	9 ft

Figure A–53

11. Select the light-blue pline, representing the sidewalk as shown in Figure A–54 and assign it to the **Pathway** Grading Object from the tool palette. Change the following:

- *Name*: **Sidewalk**
- *Maximum slope*: **5%**
- *Symmetric path*: toggle **on**
- *Width*: **2ft**
- *Cross slope*: **2%**

12. Press <Esc> to clear the selection and to close the dialog boxes.

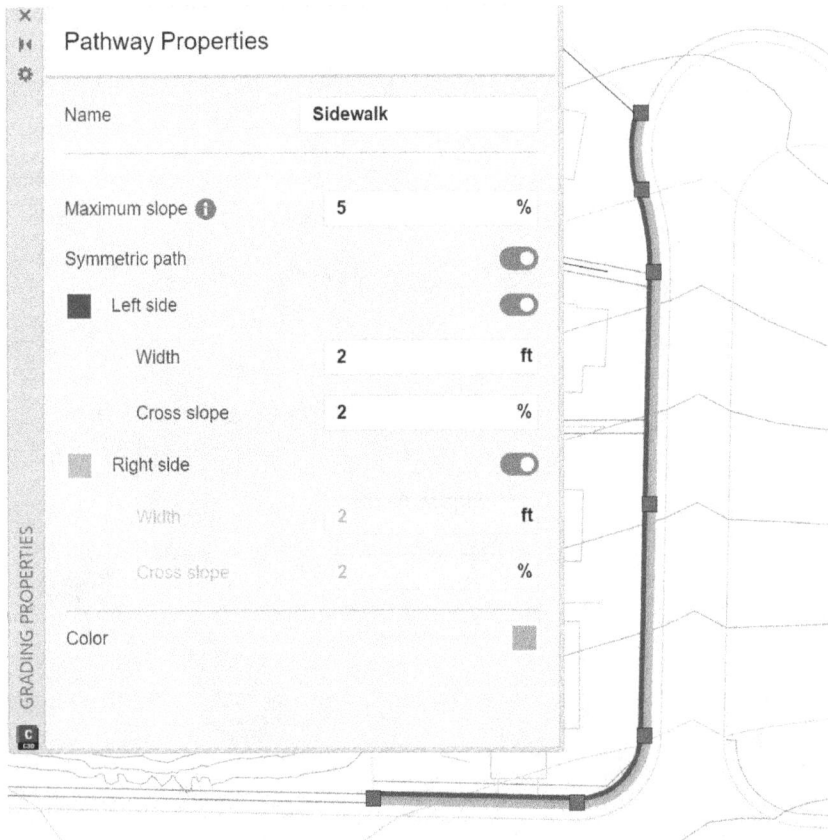

Figure A–54

13. Select the pline representing the driveway for Lot 1, as shown in Figure A–55 and assign it the **Parking Lot** Grading Object from the tool palette. This tool is another **Zone** Grading Object with preconfigured parameters. Therefore, you only need to change the following:

- *Name:* **Lot-1-Drive**
- *Exclusive Drainage:* **off**
- Leave the rest as defaults.

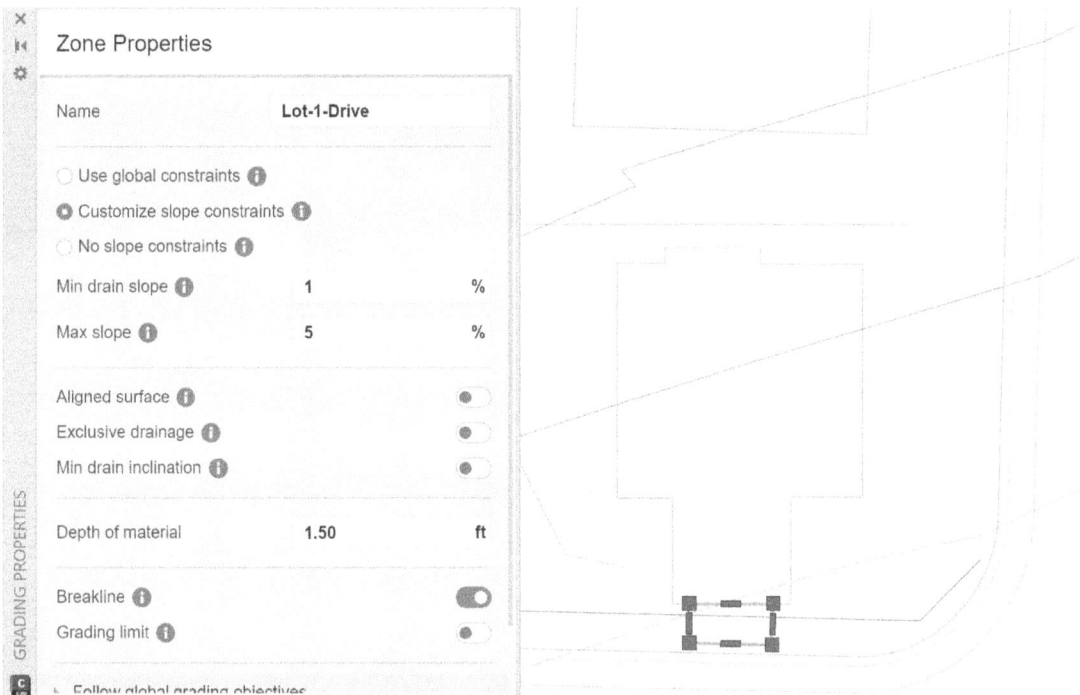

Figure A–55

14. Press <Esc> to clear the selection and to close the dialog boxes.
15. Save the drawing.

Task 2: Create drainage control between the parcels.

You will create three different drainage situations to see how the Grading Optimization process handles different situations.

1. Assign drainage lines to the four cyan plines shown in Figure A–56. Select the Drain Line from the Grading Object Tool Palette and select the highlighted lines. Keep all the defaults as they are.

    Note: You will leave the defaults to save time. However, in practice, it is recommended to name the Grading Objects with logical names for easier identification.

Figure A–56

2. Press <Esc> to clear the selection and to close the dialog boxes.

3. Now you assign a generic zone around a drainage line, as shown in Figure A–57. Select the Zone from the Grading Object Tool Palette and select the highlighted magenta pline and enter the following:

- **Customized slope constraints**: toggle **on**
- *Max slope:* **50%**
- *Min drain slope:* **2%**
- Leave the rest as defaults.

Figure A–57

4. Press <Esc> to clear the selection and to close the dialog box.

5. Now assign Bend lines as those shown in Figure A–58. Select the Bend Line from the *Grading Object* Tool Palette and select the highlighted lines. Leave all the defaults as they are.

Figure A–58

6. Press <Esc> to clear the selection and to close the dialog box.

7. Select the yellow pline shown in Figure A−59. Select the **Grading Limit** Grading Object from the *Grading Object* Tool Palette. Since the pline was already selected, it is assigned the Grading Limit. In the *Grading Limit Properties* dialog box, set the following:

- *Name:* **Residential-Limit**
- **Customized slope constraints**: toggle **on**
- *Max slope:* **18%**
- *Min drain slope:* **0.5%**
- Leave the rest as defaults.

Figure A−59

8. Press <Esc> to clear the selection and to close the dialog box.
9. Save the drawing.

Task 3: (Optional) Prepare the Hotel site and study the Office site.

You will create a few Grading Object for the Hotel site, and then review the other Grading Objects for both the hotel and the office tower. Depending on time constraints, you can skip this task and proceed to the next task.

1. Continue working on the same drawing from the previous task. If you did not complete the previous task, you can open **BLDG-GO-B.dwg** from the *C:\Civil 3D Grading\Working\BLDG-Pad* folder.

2. In the *View* tab>*Named Views* panel, select the **Hotel-Pad** view.

3. Select the cyan pline shown in Figure A–60. Select the **Zone** Grading Object from the *Grading Object* Tool Palette. In the *Zone Properties* dialog box, set the following:

    - *Name:* **Hotel Greenspace**
    - **Customized slope constraints**: toggle **on**
    - *Max slope:* **3%**
    - *Min drain slope:* **0%**
    - **Aligned Surface**: toggle **on**
    - Leave the rest as defaults.

Figure A–60

4. Press <Esc> to clear the selection and to close the dialog box.

5. Select the magenta pline shown in Figure A–61. Select the **Retaining Wall** Grading Object from the *Grading Object* Tool Palette. In the *Retaining Wall Properties* dialog box, enter the following:

- *Name:* **Hotel-Parking**
- *Max Height:* **6 ft**
- *Min Height:* **1 ft**
- **Reverse Retaining Wall**: toggle **on** (so the non-shaded side and the grips are pointing north for the low point of the wall)
- Leave the rest as defaults.

Figure A–61

6. Press <Esc> to clear the selection and to close the dialog box.

7. Select the blue pline representing the hotel building footprint shown in Figure A–62. Select the **Building Pad** Grading Object from the *Grading Object* Tool Palette. In the *Building Pad Properties* dialog box, set the following:

- *Name:* **Hotel**
- **Elevation**: toggle **on**
- **Fixed elevation value**: toggle **on**
- *Elevation:* **181 ft**
- Leave the rest as defaults.

Figure A–62

8. Press <Esc> to clear the selection and to close the dialog box.

9. Select the light-blue pline shown in Figure A-63. Select the **Zone** Grading Object from the *Grading Object* Tool Palette. In the *Zone Properties* dialog box, set the following:

- *Name:* leave as default
- **Customized slope constraints**: toggle **on**
- *Max slope:* **2%**
- *Min drain slope:* **0.25%**
- **Aligned Surface**: toggle **on**
- **Minimum zone inclination**: toggle **on**
- *Inclination:* **35** (for a 35 degree angle - roughly Northeast)
- *Depth:* **0.50 ft**
- Leave the rest as defaults.

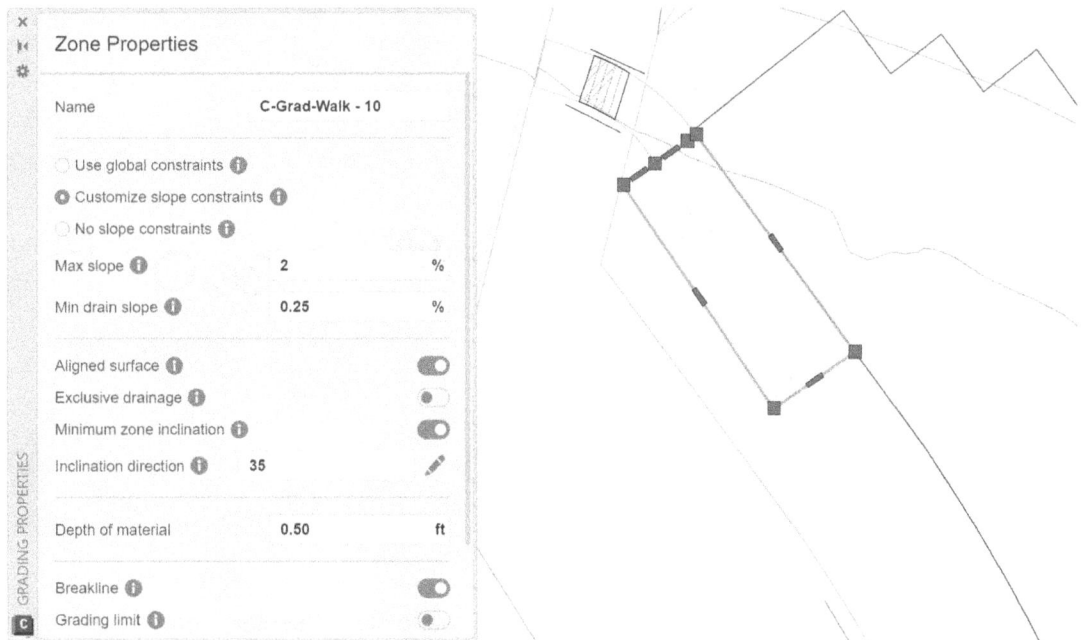

Figure A-63

10. Press <Esc> to clear the selection and to close the dialog box.
11. Save the drawing.
12. Zoom out to see both the hotel and the office.

13. Study all the Grading Objects listed in Figure A–64. Select each object and examine the corresponding *Grading Object Properties* dialog box.

(A) Office Building Pad & Reveal
(B) Office "Path"
(C) Office Walkout
(D) Office Retaining Walls
(E) Office Grading Limit

(F) Pool Building Pad
(G) Hotel Retaining Wall
(H) Steps (Zones) & Aligned Edges
(I) Hotel Grading Limit
(J) Drain Line
(K) Offset Points

Figure A–64

14. Remember to press <Esc> to clear each selection and to close the dialog box.

15. Save the drawing when done.

Task 4: Launch the Grading Optimization program.

1. Open **BLDG-GO-C.dwg** from the *C:\Civil 3D Grading\Working\BLDG-Pad* folder. This contains more linework which has already been assigned to various Grading Objects. Do not continue from the previous drawing.

2. In the *Analyze* tab>*Grading Optimization* panel, click ◇ (Optimize).

3. Select **IDG-North** as the EG surface.

4. It may take a while for the Grading Optimization program to launch. Once it launches, the grading objects will be listed in the *Grading Optimization* browser on the left side. Navigate around the model so your vantage point is similar to that shown in Figure A–65.

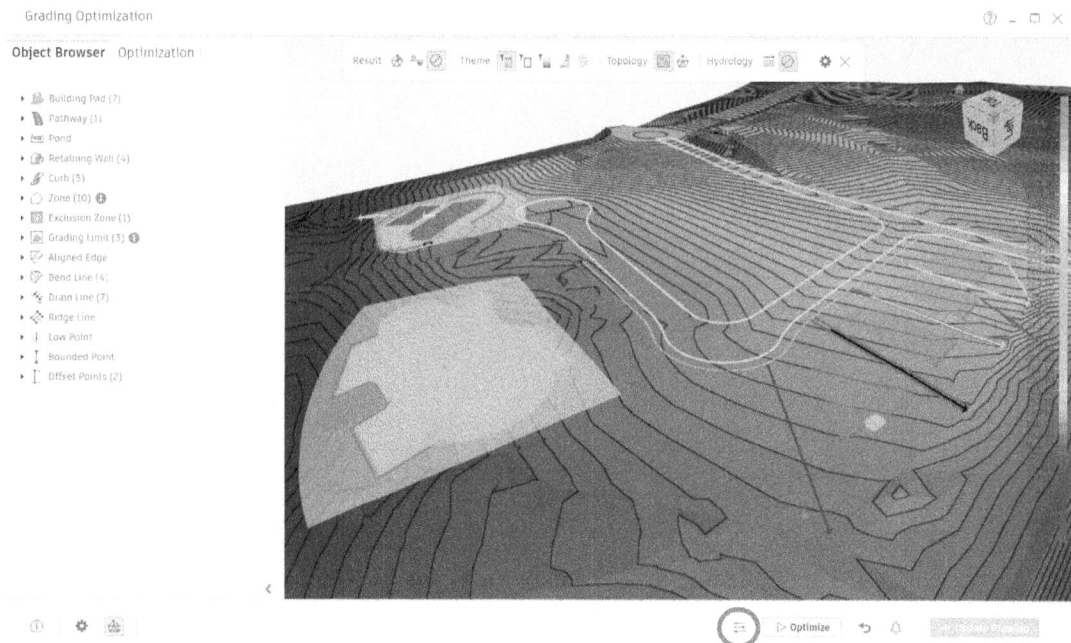

Figure A–65

5. At the bottom of the *Grading Optimization* window, click ⇌ (Optimization Options).

6. In the *Optimization Options* window, confirm that the following are set, and modify if need be as shown in Figure A–66:

- *Min drain slope:* **0**
- *Max slope:* **60**
- *Cut and fill constraints:* **Fill Only**
- *Iteration:* **20000**
- *Balance cut and fill:* **15**
- *Cut - fill =* **-10000 cu. ft.** (Accessible by clicking on right arrow)
- *Minimize earthwork:* **15**
- *Smooth surface:* **90**

Optimization Options   ✕

Global constraints

Min drain slope	0	%
Max slope	60	%
Cut and fill constraint	Fill only ▾	

Optimization

Iteration	20000

Objective Weights ⓘ

Balance cut and fill ⊢	40	▼
Cut - fill =	-10000	cu.ft
Minimize earthwork ⊢	15	
Smooth surface ⊢	90	

Figure A–66

7. Close the *Optimization Options* window by clicking on the **X** in the top-right corner. Ensure that all the Grading Limits are on by hovering over each one and noting their *On* and *Visibility* status, as shown in Figure A–67.

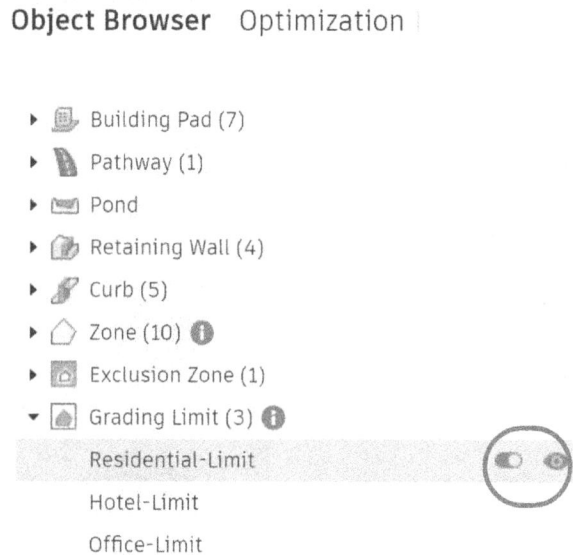

Object Browser   Optimization

▶ 🏬 Building Pad (7)
▶ 📄 Pathway (1)
▶ 📬 Pond
▶ 🎯 Retaining Wall (4)
▶ 🖊 Curb (5)
▶ ⬠ Zone (10) ℹ
▶ 🏠 Exclusion Zone (1)
▼ 🏠 Grading Limit (3) ℹ
    Residential-Limit
    Hotel-Limit
    Office-Limit

Figure A–67

8. At the bottom of the *Grading Optimization* window, click **Optimize**.

9. The various warning signs deal with an existing wall at the north of the property that has excessive slopes, the hotel steps (which are actually curb objects) which only have three points, and the sidewalk that lies outside of one of the grading limits. The sidewalk will still be graded. The warnings can be dismissed.

10. In the *Visualization* toolbar, turn on **Violations**, as shown in Figure A–68. Note the various triangles changing colors between bright red, red, and dark red.

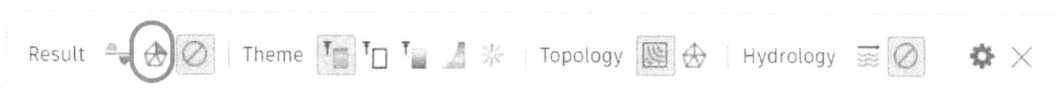

Figure A–68

11. In the *Visualization* toolbar, turn off **Violations**, as shown in Figure A–69.

Figure A–69

12. Notice how the optimization proceeds simultaneously in all thee grading limits. If you want to grade only in one area, you could disable the other grading limits. For now, let them all proceed.

13. Set the *Theme* to **Slopes** and the *Display* to **Wireframe**, then adjust your view so it is similar to that in Figure A–70.

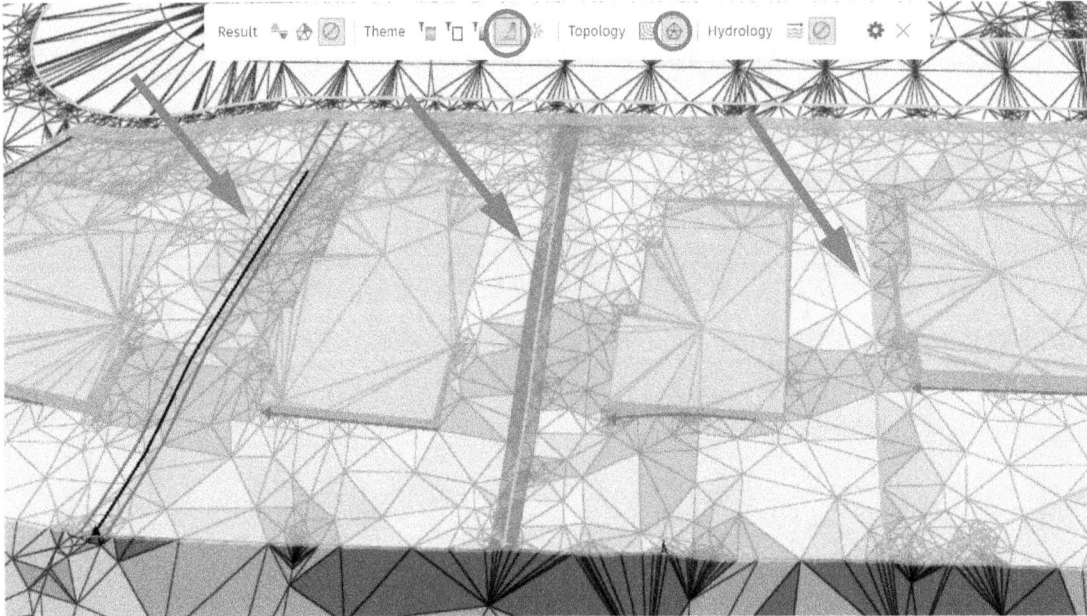

Figure A–70

14. Study how the triangulation is affected by the three different treatments we did surrounding the drain lines in the previous steps, one with no treatment, one with a zone, and one with two Aligned Edges.

   *Note: It can take some time to go through these iterations. If you do not have enough time, you can click Stop and review the results in the **BLDG-GO-Z-Complete.dwg** drawing.*

15. Once the optimization is complete, click **UpdateDrawing**. This will send the optimization results back to the Civil 3D drawing where Grading Optimization was originally launched from and update the drawing.

16. In the Civil 3D drawing, in the *Save Optimization Result* window, ensure that the **Create new surface** option is selected to create a new surface.

- Enter **Parcels-N** for the *Name* and click on ≡ (Surface Style) to select a surface style.
- In the *Surface Styles* dialog box, select **ASC-Contours 2' and 10' Design** and click **Finish** to close the *Surface Styles* selection box, as shown in Figure A–71.
- Leave the *Save Optimization Result* window open.

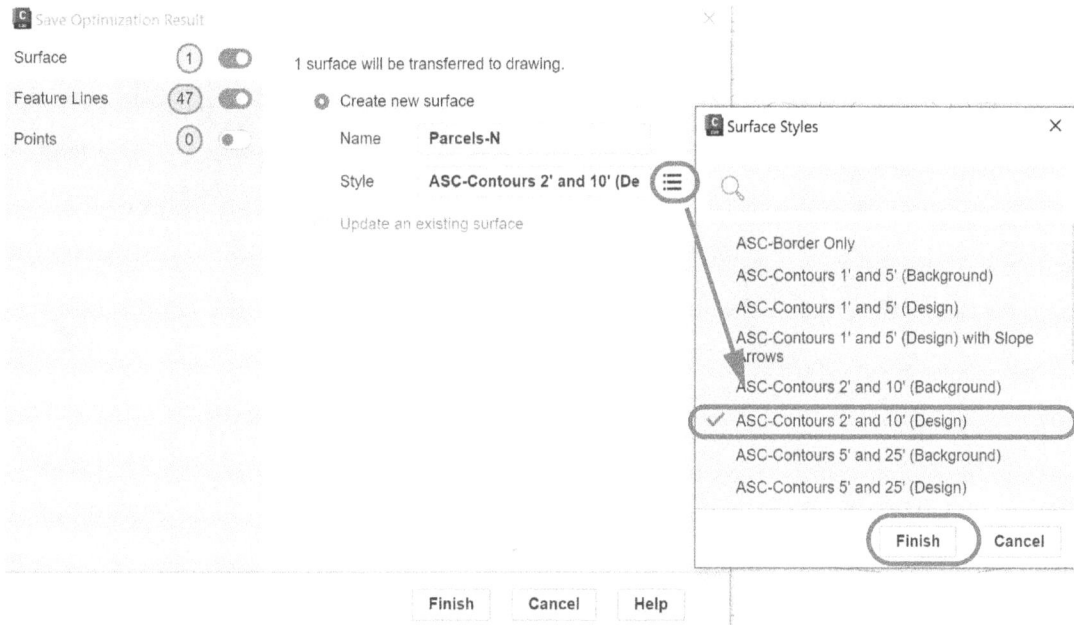

Figure A–71

17. In the *Save Optimization Results* window, click **Feature Lines**. Set the *Name Prefix* to **Parcels-**. Set the *Feature Line Style* to **ASC-Basic**.

18. Click **Finish**. Civil 3D will create a new surface, site, and point group for the information retrieved from the Grading Optimizer.

    Note: It can take some time to create a new surface, point group, and site.

19. The *Events* panel of the Panorama may open to warn of duplicate points which are ignored.

    Dismiss the *Event Viewer* by clicking on the green check mark ☑.

20. This time, you will examine the surface with the *Model Viewer*. Select the **Parcels-N** surface and launch the Model Viewer from the right-click menu.

21. The *Model Viewer* is displayed. Zoom and orbit to examine the surface, as in Figure A–72.

Figure A–72

22. Close out of the *Model Viewer*. through the **X** in the top right corner.

23. Save the drawing.

Task 5: *Optional*: More building / platform practices for the Southern Site.

1. Open the *C:\Civil 3D Grading\Working\\BLDG-PAD***South-BLDG-GO-A.dwg.**

2. Repeat the same process for the southern section to create a building pad for the school, and level areas for the sports fields, picking **IDG-South** as the Existing surface.

3. There are two suggested parking lot layouts you may choose to use as shown in Figure A–73.

Figure A–73

4. You can either create a new surface and site and point group for the pond (suggested name: **BLDG-S**), or create one overall design surface for the southern site (suggested name: **Southern Site**), along with a new point group and site for the feature lines.

5. Save the drawing.

End of practice

Chapter Review Questions

1. Where do you set the option to use parcel elevations in the drawing?

    a. Parcel Properties

    b. Site Properties

    c. Drawing Properties

    d. Feature Line Properties

2. When using 🢒 (Edit Elevations) in the *Parcel Segments* contextual tab>*Edit Elevations* panel, how many vertices' elevations do you set at a time?

    a. One

    b. Any selected

    c. All

3. When using 🢒 (Set Elevations by Reference) in the *Parcel Segments* contextual tab>*Edit Elevations* panel, how many vertices' elevations do you set at a time?

    a. One

    b. Any selected

    c. All

4. When creating a wall breakline, you can use the following to set the elevations of the offset points at each vertex? (Select all that apply.)

    a. Elevation

    b. Difference in Elevation

    c. By Reference

    d. Surface

5. When feature lines, parcel segments, or survey figures cross each other, what is the elevation point assigned called?

   a. Point of Intersection

   b. Crossing Point

   c. Elevation Point

   d. Split Point

6. Which of the following is NOT a member of the *Grading Optimization* tool palette?

   e. Retaining Wall

   f. Building Pad

   g. Reveal

   h. Foundation

7. Is **Reveal** listed in the *Grading Optimization* browser?

   a. Yes

   b. No

   c. It is listed under the Building Pad.

8. The **Pathways** Grading Object is a type of which Grading Object?

   a. Curbs

   b. Zone

   c. Sidewalk

   d. Exclusion Zone

9. Do **Building Pads** require a fixed elevation?

   a. No, the Grading Optimization will always determine the elevation.

   b. Yes

   c. It is optional.

   d. No, it has to be an elevation range.

10. Can **Reveals** be found on the *Grading Objects* tool palette?

    a. Yes

    b. No

Command Summary

Button	Command	Location
	Breakline	• **Ribbon**: *Tin Surface* contextual tab>*Modify* panel, expanded *Add Data* drop-down list • **Command Prompt:** AddSurfaceBreaklines
	Bring to Front	• **Ribbon**: *Parcel Segments* contextual tab>expanded *General Tools* panel • **Command Prompt:** DrawOrder
	Edit Elevations	• **Ribbon**: *Parcel Segments* contextual tab>*Edit Elevations* panel • **Command Prompt:** EditFeatureElevs
	Elevations from Surface	• **Ribbon**: *Parcel Segments* contextual tab>*Edit Elevations* panel • **Command Prompt:** FeatureElevsFromSurf
	Move to Site	• **Ribbon**: *Parcel* contextual tab>*Modify* panel • **Command Prompt:** MoveToSite
	Paste Surface	• **Ribbon**: *Tin Surface* contextual tab>*Modify* panel, expanded *Edit Surface* drop-down list • **Command Prompt:** EditSurfacePaste
	Send to Back	• **Ribbon**: *Parcel Segments* contextual tab>expanded *General Tools* panel • **Command Prompt:** DrawOrder
	Set Elevations by Reference	• **Ribbon**: *Parcel Segments* contextual tab>*Edit Elevations* panel • **Command Prompt:** SetFeatureRefElev

Using InfraWorks for Visualization

You will learn about Building Information Modeling (BIM) and how it is used in the Autodesk®
InfraWorks® software. You will learn how to bring in a Civil 3D drawing and other source files,
add details to the file, add visualization, and create a storyboard for output.

Learning Objectives

- Locate basic features and commands in the Autodesk InfraWorks software interface.
- Navigate a model.
- Connect to select data source types to display the model.
- Create water features in a model to represent a pond.
- Add predefined 3D buildings to a model.
- Create city furniture to add bike racks and other 3D models to a model.
- Add landscaping details to a model using trees and other vegetation.

B.1 Building Information Modeling

The Autodesk InfraWorks software is a powerful Building Information Modeling (BIM) program that streamlines site design and the design process for different types of infrastructure projects using a 3D model. The BIM process supports the ability to coordinate, update, and share design data with team members throughout the design, construction, and management phases of a project's life cycle.

The Autodesk InfraWorks software creates data-rich models using information about the existing environment. Using these models supports more informed decision-making and an accelerated site design process. You can create multiple design alternatives in one model, enabling you to quickly estimate the budget, scope, and schedule with an appropriate level of detail from the beginning of a project. The high-impact visuals that are automatically created during the design process better communicate the design intent to stakeholders.

The Autodesk InfraWorks software coordinates with other software, such as the Autodesk® Civil 3D® software and the Autodesk® Revit® software, to reduce rework and seamlessly enable coordination between project team members.

Launching the Software

The Autodesk InfraWorks software can be launched by double-clicking on (Autodesk InfraWorks) on the desktop or selecting it from the Start menu.

When you open the software for the first time (and periodically thereafter), you must sign in to the Online Autodesk Account. The Autodesk Account Sign In screen displays automatically, as shown in Figure B-1. Enter your username and click **NEXT**. Enter your password and click **SIGN IN**.

Figure B-1

B.2 Overview of the Interface

The Autodesk InfraWorks user interface is designed for intuitive and efficient access to commands and views. It includes the *Home Screen* and the *Model View*.

Home Screen

When Autodesk InfraWorks is initially launched, the *Home Screen* displays, as shown in Figure B–2. This screen enables you to:

- Preview recent models

- Access Model Builder

- Open existing or create new models

- Toggle on and off available feature previews

- Collaborate with others

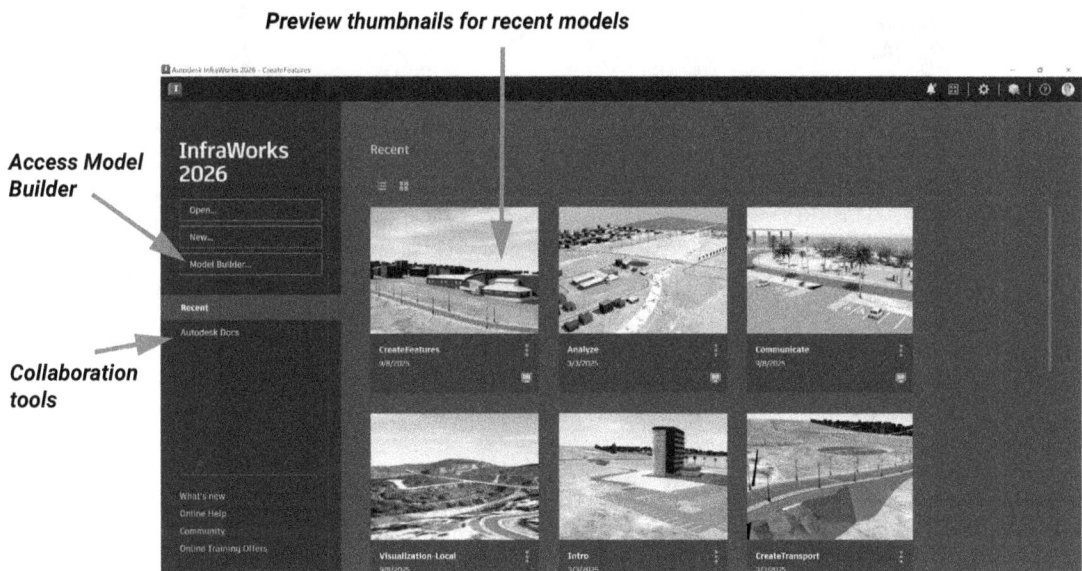

Figure B–2

- Various icons display on each preview thumbnail, as shown in Figure B–3.

Figure B–3

*Note: A **Save** option is not available because the model is a database file (SQLite), which saves after every action. The **Duplicate** command, found under Settings and Utilities, enables you to save an existing model to a new file.*

When you hover over a thumbnail, ellipses (three dots) appear in the lower left corner of the thumbnail. Upon clicking on the ellipses, options become available to:

- Open the model
- Duplicate (copy) the model
- Delete the model
- Remove the model from the Recent list

How To: Open a Model

1. In the *Home Screen*, select tile or list view by clicking the required button at the top, as shown in Figure B–4.

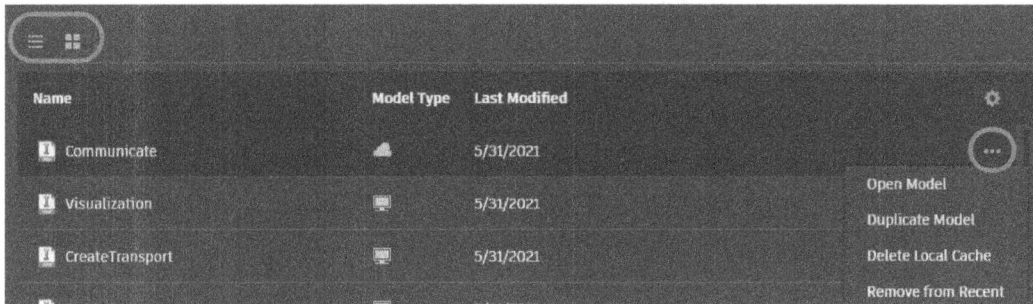

Figure B–4

2. Click the preview thumbnail of the model you wish to work with.

   - If the model is not visible on the *Home Screen*, click the **Open** button at the top. Then browse for the file location and click **Open**.

   - If the model was saved in an older version of the software, you can either **Upgrade** the model or **Create a Copy**, as shown in Figure B–5. All team members should sync their changes before any cloud model is upgraded.

Figure B–5

   - If the model was saved in a more recent version of the software, you cannot open the model, as shown in Figure B–6. A model cannot be saved to an earlier version, therefore you must upgrade your software to open the model.

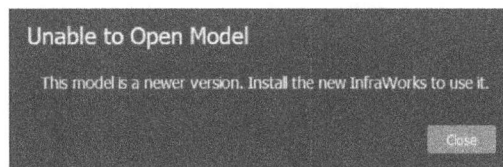

Figure B–6

Model View

The Model View displays when a model is created or opened from the *Home Screen*. Figure B–7 shows the components in the Model View user interface.

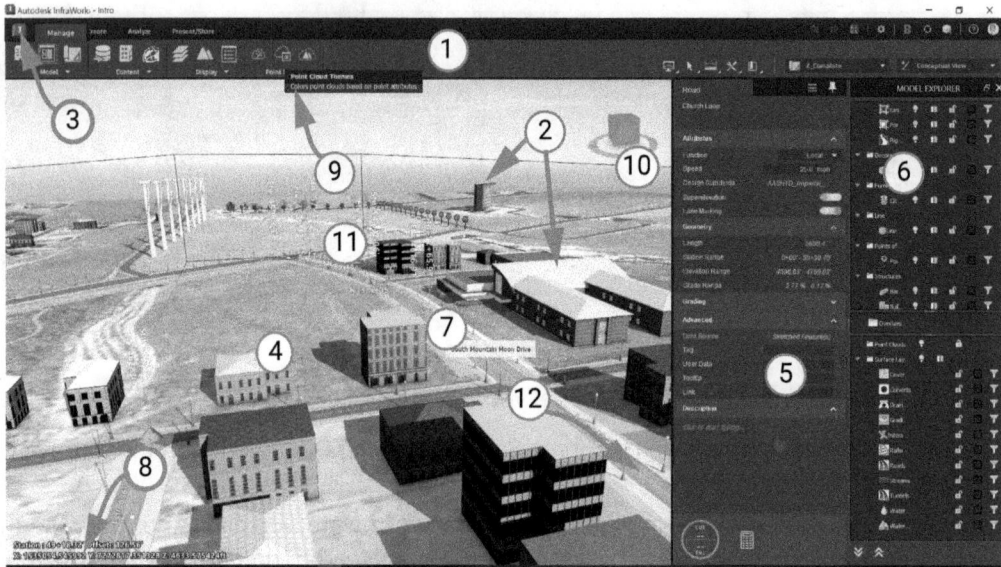

Figure B–7

1. Toolbar	5. Asset Card	9. Tooltips
2. Buildings from Revit	6. Model Explorer	10. ViewCube
3. Switch to Home	7. Automatic Labels	11. Station labels
4. Buildings from Model Builder	8. Model Coordinates	12. Selected Feature

*Note: For more information on InfraWorks, refer to the ASCENT **Autodesk InfraWorks Fundamentals** guide.*

1. Toolbar

The Toolbar provides a variety of frequently used tools. These tools are distributed over a series of tabs on the left side (shown in Figure B–8). These tabs contain tools for a specific phase of work, coinciding with the workflow of a typical project – from left to right vis-a-vis from start to finish. These tabs are further separated into panels and drop-down menus, similar to those in the Civil 3D and a variety of other Autodesk programs.

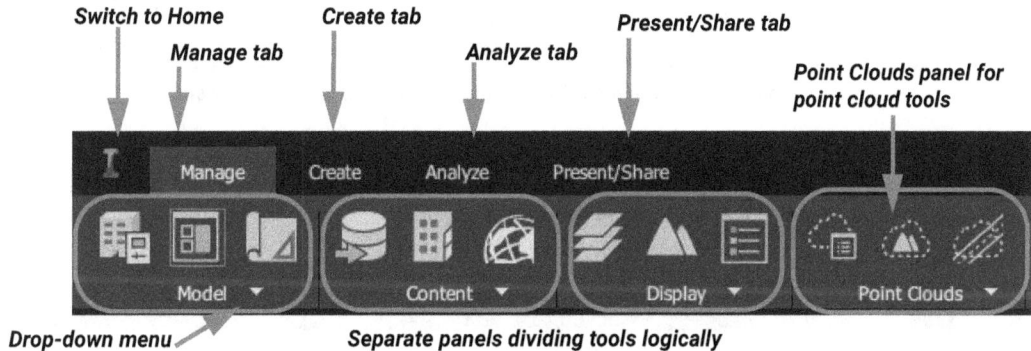

Figure B–8

On the right side of the toolbar are Common Tools (shown in Figure B–9), which enable you to switch views and proposals, undo/redo commands, and select or edit model components.

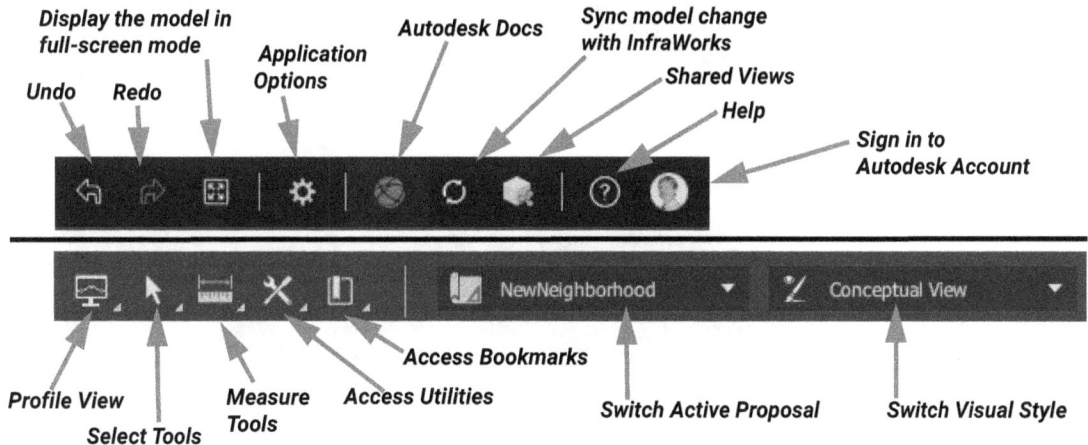

Figure B–9

2. Toolbar Tabs

The tabs across the top contain a variety of tools for the creation, development, modification, analysis, presentation, and sharing of the InfraWorks model, as shown in Figure B–10.

Manage tab: Tools for adding content to the model, controlling the display, and point clouds.

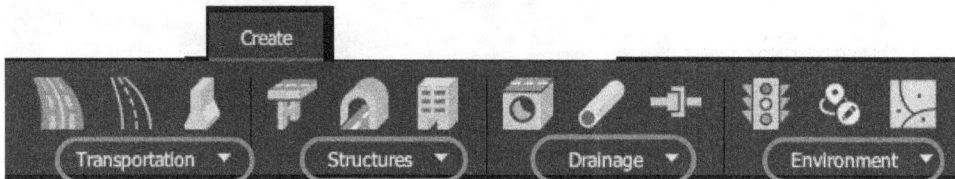

Create tab: Tools for creating and editing roads, bridges, and misc model content.

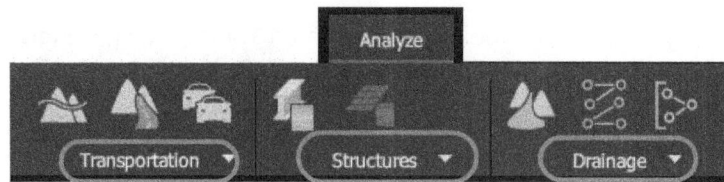

Analyze tab: Tools for analyzing roads, bridges, and drainage.

Present/Share tab: Tools for creating images/video, export and sharing options.

Figure B–10

3. Toolbar Panels

Each tab is divided into panels, as shown above in Figure B–10. These panels contain the most commonly used tools for the task that the panel is named for. The panel is limited to three tools, but there are more tools available in the drop-down menu, which is accessible by clicking on the down arrow next to the panel name (Drainage ▼).

4. Drop-down Tool Menus

Within the drop down menus, as shown in Figure B–11, are more tools available for the task at hand. Some drop-down menu may only contain three tools, while others can contain many more. Some tools may be grayed out because the tool is not valid for the present state of the model. For example, **Quantities** in the Structures drop-down list would be grayed out if there are no bridges or other structural objects in the model to quantify.

Some drop-down menus with only three tools seem redundant, since the panel is already populated with those three tools. However, the drop-down menus reveal keyboard shortcuts available for these tools. These shortcuts are not visible in the panel itself.

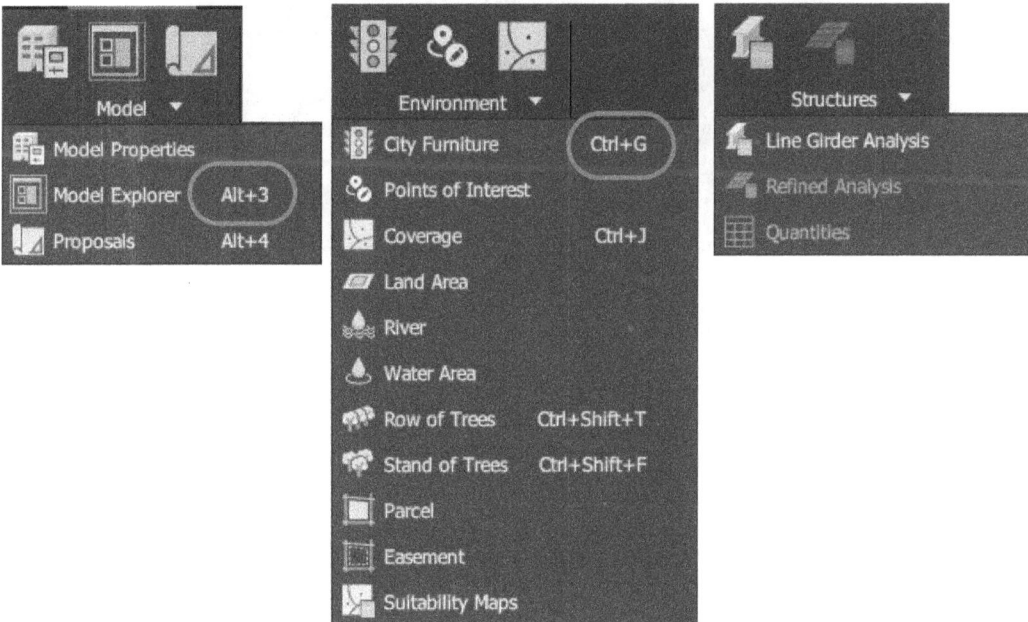

Figure B–11

The contents within the panels can be rearranged. The panels are limited to three tools, however you can choose the tools.

How To: Add Tools to a Panel

1. In the drop-down menu, hover over a tool, which causes vertical ellipses (⋮) button to be revealed.

2. Click on the vertical ellipses and select **Pin to Toolbar** to put the tool in the panel, as shown in Figure B–12.

Figure B–12

*Note: You can also use the **Pin to Toolbar** method to rearrange the sequence of the tools in the panel. The tool that you select will be pinned as the first tool in the panel.*

5. Model Window

The Model Window (shown in Figure B–13) is the working area in which you create model elements.

Figure B–13

How elements display in the Model Window depends on the visual style selected in the Toolbar. Different view settings can be set up to support different work flows, as shown in Figure B–14. When working on design roads, you might want to display the surface and buildings in wireframe in order to view their triangular irregular network (TIN). In contrast, when you are communicating the design to stakeholders, you might want a more realistic appearance to communicate what the design should look like when the construction is complete.

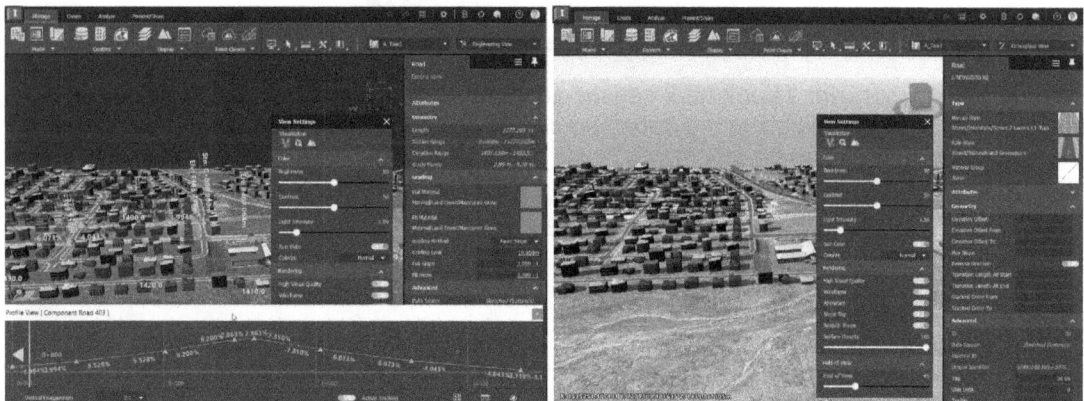

Engineering view style used for creating design elements

Conceptual view style used for communicating the design

Figure B–14

6. Bookmarks

Bookmarks are saved views that quickly reorient the view from one location of the model to another. You can create, preview, and search bookmarks. In addition, you can share bookmarks via Shared Views. Just to the left of the *Proposals* drop-down list, selecting 🔲 (View bookmarks) displays a list of bookmarks with preview thumbnails, as shown in Figure B–15.

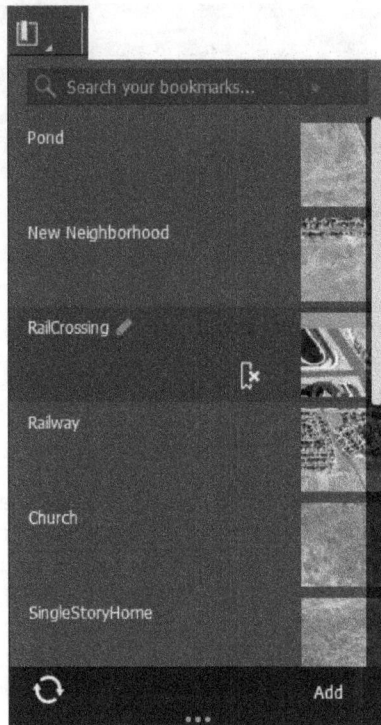

Figure B–15

Hovering the cursor over a bookmark causes additional tools to display. The table below describes each tool available in the *Bookmarks* drop-down list.

Icon	Description
✏️	Enables you to rename a specific Bookmark.
📑✕	Deletes the specific Bookmark.
🔄	Refreshes the preview thumbnails for all Bookmarks according to what displays in the current proposal.
Add	Adds a new Bookmark for the current model view.

B.3 Creating an InfraWorks Model

All Autodesk InfraWorks models begin by importing existing data from various sources. These sources include building outlines, roads, utilities, terrain, images, etc.

Model Builder

The easiest way to find GIS data is to use the Model Builder. The Model Builder creates a new model and includes existing datasets from the following sources:

Note: Internet access is required to use this feature.

Data Type	Source
Elevation	Terrain data for the United States and its territories uses 10 and 30 meter DEMs from the National Elevation Dataset (NED). The rest of the globe uses SRTM 90m DEM data processed by CIAT-CSI.
Imagery	Satellite imagery from Microsoft® Bing® Maps is draped over the model terrain.
Roads and Highways	OpenStreetMap's (OSM) Highway and Railway datasets are readily available. They are used to create roads and railway features in the model. If feature names are available from OSM, they appear as tooltips and provide a hyperlink to the source feature that opens in the default web browser.
Buildings	The building data is also from the OpenStreetMap dataset.

How To: Create a New Model Using Model Builder

1. In the *Home Screen,* click **Model Builder**.

2. In the *Model Builder* dialog box, type the project address in the *Search by Location* field or zoom in on the project area using the map in the left pane, as shown in Figure B–16.

Figure B–16

3. Use one of the Select tools to define the area of interest (AOI) to include in the model. (Note: There is a 200 sq. km maximum area limit.) You can choose between the following:

   • Select current map extents.

   • Draw a rectangle to select an AOI.

   • Draw a polygon to select an AOI.

   • Import a polygon to select an AOI.

4. Type a name for the model.

5. Type a description for the model.

6. Assign a **coordinate system** by opening the *Select Coordinate System* dialog box. You can type in the coordinate system's abbreviation, shown in Figure B–17, or browse through the available systems in the list. Click **OK** when one is selected.

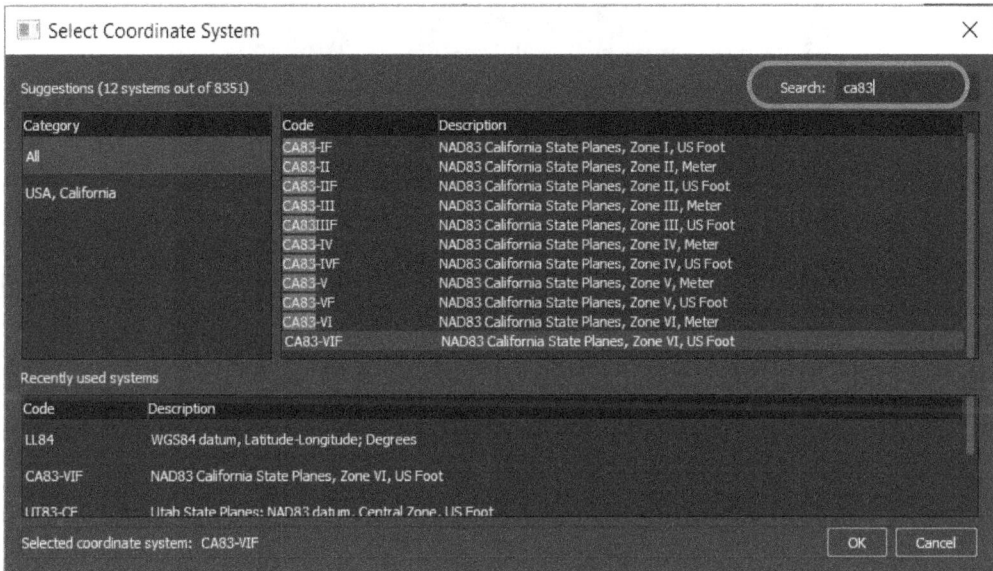

Figure B–17

7. Click **Create Model**. The model is created in the background. Click **Close** in the *Model Builder* message box.

8. Close the Model Builder.

Note: You are notified by email when the model is ready.

9. In the *Home Screen*, click on the newly created model to open it, as shown in Figure B–18.

Figure B–18

10. In the dialog box requesting where to store the model, click **Local** to save it to your computer's C Drive or **Autodesk Docs** to save it in a predefined Autodesk Docs project, as shown in Figure B–19.

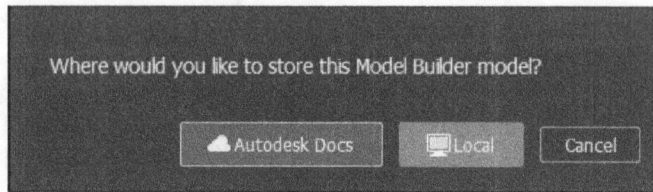

Figure B–19

11. If you choose **Local**, the model will be stored in the default location with a cryptic folder name. The default location is C:\Users\login-name\Documents\Autodesk InfraWorks Models\Autodesk 360.

B.4 Share Design Elements with Autodesk Civil 3D

Autodesk InfraWorks models can be opened directly in the Autodesk Civil 3D software. Therefore, you do not have to recreate these design elements for the detailed design phase of the modeling process. Additionally, Autodesk Civil 3D drawing files can be imported into an Autodesk InfraWorks model to help communicate the final design to stakeholders by taking advantage of the high-definition graphics. In order to import an Autodesk Civil 3D DWG file directly, you must have the Autodesk Civil 3D software installed on your computer.

How To: Import Autodesk Civil 3D AEC Objects from DWG Files

1. In the *Manage* tab>*Content* panel, select ![icon](Data Sources).

2. In the *DATA SOURCES* palette, expand ![icon](Add file data source) and select **Autodesk Civil 3D DWG**.

3. In the *Select Files* dialog box, browse to the Autodesk Civil 3D DWG file, select it and click **Open**.

4. In the *Choose Data Sources* dialog box, select all of the AEC objects you want in the Autodesk InfraWorks model, as shown in Figure B−20. Click **OK**.

Figure B−20

5. In the *DATA SOURCES* palette, note that all of the imported AEC objects display under their appropriate source type and are selected, as shown in Figure B–21. Click (Refresh data source).

Figure B–21

Civil 3D "Roads"

There are two types of roads that can be created in the Autodesk InfraWorks software: **planning roads** (existing roads) and **component roads** (proposed design roads). You can use the component roads to add engineering parameters to road designs and the rule-based tool sets to lay out a preliminary roadway design.

Visually, the unselected roads look similar, as seen in Figure B–22.

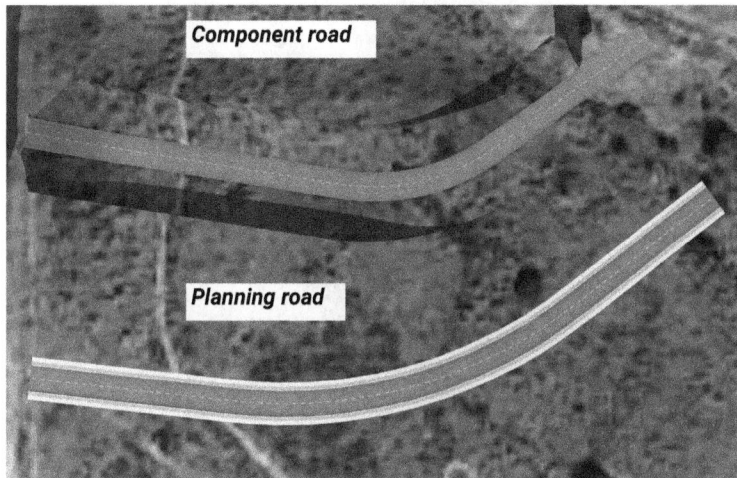

Figure B–22

However, when selected, the grip clearly distinguish between the two types, as seen in Figure B–23.

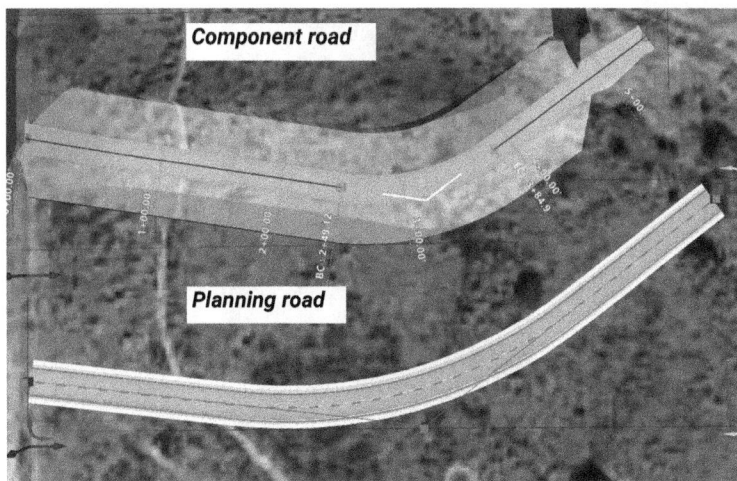

Figure B–23

You can create either type of road in InfraWorks. However, when roads are created in the Model Builder, they are Planning Roads. You can convert Planning Roads to Component Roads. Planning Roads have road styles assigned to them, which can be swapped. Planning roads can be split into different parts, with the individual parts having different styles. There are several planning road styles set up in InfraWorks, as shown in Figure B–24, and more can be created.

Figure B–24

When roads are imported from Civil 3D (either alignments or corridors), they are Component Roads. Component Roads consist of *Road Assemblies* that can be replaced for sections of the road, and more components can be added, replaced, or deleted. There are Road Assemblies set up in InfraWorks, as shown in Figure B–25, and more can be created.

Figure B–25

Drawing Overlays

When the Autodesk Civil 3D DWG data source type is selected, only the AEC objects are imported into the Autodesk InfraWorks model. In order to import other linework (such as parcel lines and utilities other than pipe networks), you can use an *AutoCAD DWG as 2D Overlay* data source type.

When working with terrain overlays, you can:

- Move
- Rotate
- Scale
- Control selectability
- Control transparency, as shown in Figure B–26.

Figure B–26

How To: Import Autodesk Civil 3D DWG File Linework

Note: Internet access and an Autodesk 360 account are required to use this feature.

1. In the *Manage* tab>*Content* panel, select ![icon](Data Sources).

2. In the *DATA SOURCES* palette, expand ![icon] (Add file data source) and select **AutoCAD DWG as 2D Overlay**.

3. In the *Select Files* dialog box, browse to the AutoCAD DWG file, select it, and click **Open**.

4. In the *Data Import* dialog box, when the following warning displays, click **Send**:

   - *This feature requires an Internet connection and an Autodesk 360 account. By clicking "Send", you will be transmitting data to InfraWorks 360 cloud-based services.*

5. In the *DATA SOURCES* palette, under *Terrain Overlays*, double-click on the imported DWG data source.

6. In the *Data Source Configuration* dialog box, adjust the **Scale** and **Rotation** as necessary. Click **Interactive Placing...** and double-click on a point in the model where the drawing should be located, as shown in Figure B–27.

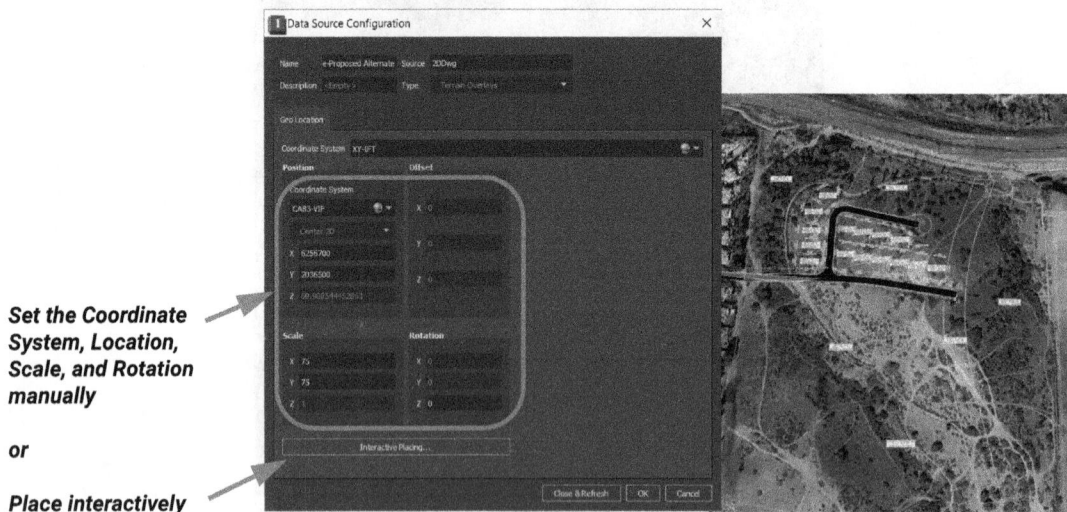

Set the Coordinate System, Location, Scale, and Rotation manually

or

Place interactively

Figure B–27

7. In the *Data Source Configuration* dialog box, click **Close & Refresh**.

8. In the model, select the overlay, then use the gizmos to move, scale, or rotate the overlay as required.

Practice B1
Create a New Model Using Model Builder

Practice Objectives

* Create a new model with existing GIS data.

* Import Civil 3D and AutoCAD data.

Note: Internet access is required to complete this practice.

In this practice, you will create a new model using the Model Builder and add existing GIS data to it automatically during the creation process. Then, you will import Civil 3D data and AutoCAD 2D underlays.

Task 1: Create a new model.

1. In the *Home Screen*, click **Model Builder**.

2. In the *Model Builder* dialog box, in the *Search by Location* field, type in the following address: **Jeffries Ranch Road, Oceanside, CA**. Pan over and click the Area of Interest and draw a rectangle as shown in Figure B−28.

3. In the *Model Name* field, type **Visualization**. Provide an appropriate description of your choice.

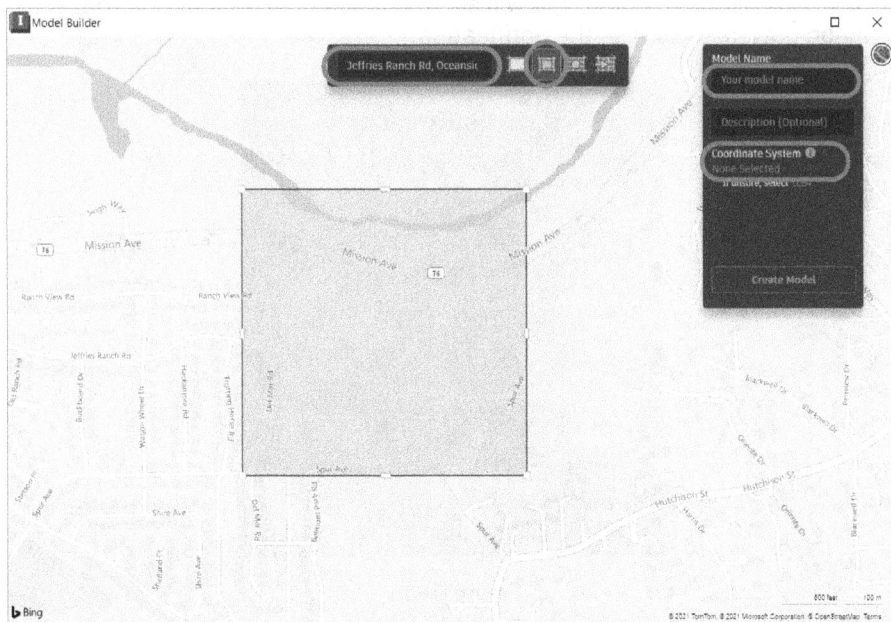

Figure B−28

4. Under *Coordinate System*, click **None Selected**. In the *Select Coordinate System* dialog box, in the *Search* area, type **CA83** to narrow the selection choices, then select **CA83-VIF** at the bottom of the selection list, as shown in Figure B–29.

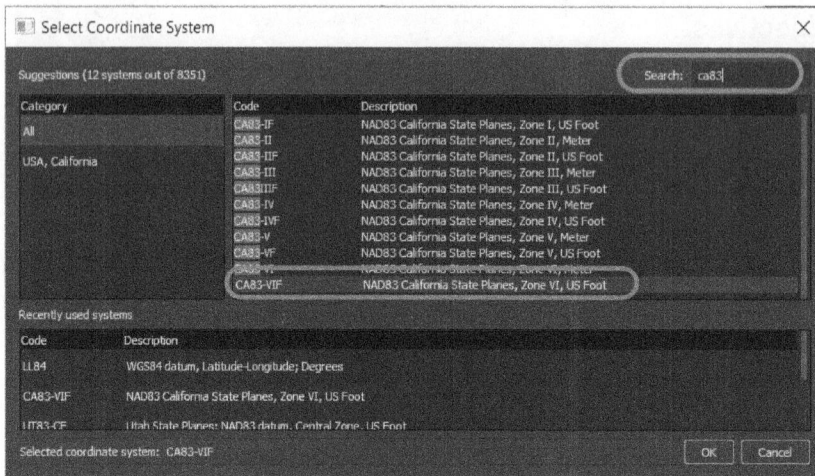

Figure B–29

5. Click **OK** to close the *Select Coordinate System* dialog box.

6. In the *Model Builder* dialog box, click **Create Model**.

7. You are notified that the model is being prepared, as shown in Figure B–30. When you expand the *Show details* section, you will see the tracking ID and other information. Click the **Continue** button to dismiss the notification.

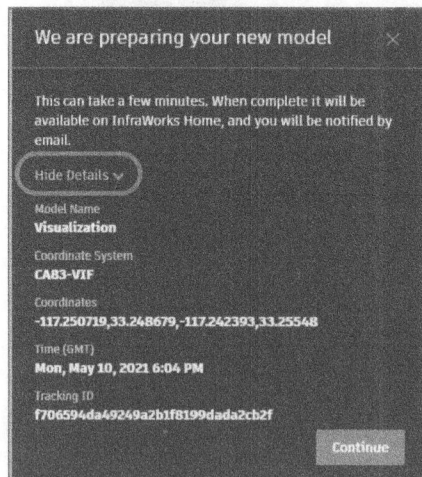

Figure B–30

8. Close the *Model Builder* dialog box by clicking on the **X** in the upper right corner.

9. After a while, you will receive notification that your model is complete, and it is displayed on the *Home Screen*.

10. On the *Home Screen*, select the **Visualization.sqlite** model that was created in the cloud. If it is taking too long, you can open **Visualization-Local.sqlite** from *C:\Civil 3D Grading\Working\Visualization* and, in the main Toolbar on the right side, expand *Switch Active Proposal* and select proposal **A_Task1**.

11. When initially opening a model created in *Model Builder*, select **Local** when prompted to select a location to store the model, as shown in Figure B−31.

Figure B−31

12. On the upper right corner of the Toolbar, click ⚙ (Application Options).

13. In the *Application Options* dialog box, select **Unit Configuration**. Expand the *Default Units* drop-down list and ensure that **Imperial is selected,** as shown in Figure B−32.

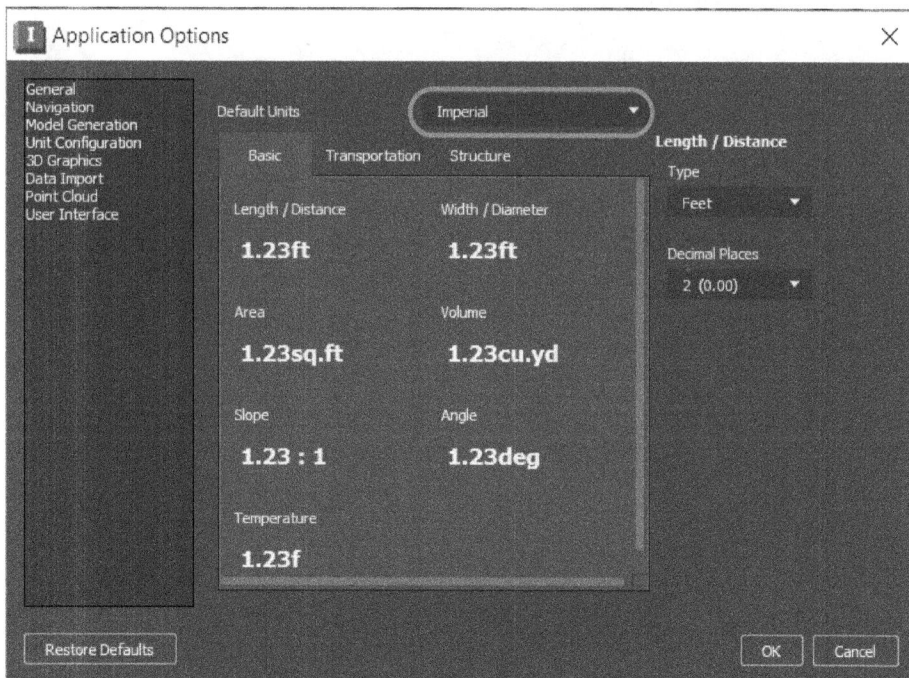

Figure B−32

14. Click **OK**.

Task 2: Open local file and import Autodesk Civil 3D data.

In this task, you will import the Autodesk Civil 3D surfaces, pipes, and roads from the detailed design phase of the project. Do not continue working on the previous file you created in Model Builder as there are proposals and adjustments made in the **Visualization-Local.sqlite** file contained in your practice files folder.

1. Open **Visualization-Local.sqlite** from *C:\Civil 3D for Land Dev\Working\Visualization*. It may take some time for the model to open.

2. In the main Toolbar on the right side, expand *Switch Active Proposal* and select proposal **A_Task1**.

3. In the *DATA SOURCES* palette, expand  (Add file data source) and select **Autodesk Civil 3D DWG**.

    *   If the Data Sources palette is not open, in the *Manage* tab>*Content* panel, select

        (Data Sources) to open it, as shown in Figure B–33.

Figure B–33

4. In the *Select Files* dialog box, browse to the *C:\Civil 3D Grading\Working\Visualization* folder, select **VIZ-to-IWX.dwg**, and click **Open**. It may take some time for the drawing to be added.

    Note: The Top Corridor surfaces have already been pasted into the FG surface, so you need not import them.

5. In the *Choose Data Sources* dialog box, click the **Exclude All** button, then select the **VIZ-to-IWX-Roads**, **VIZ-to-IWX-FG**, and **VIZ-to-IWX-CORRIDOR-COVERAGES** objects, as shown in Figure B–34. Click **OK**.

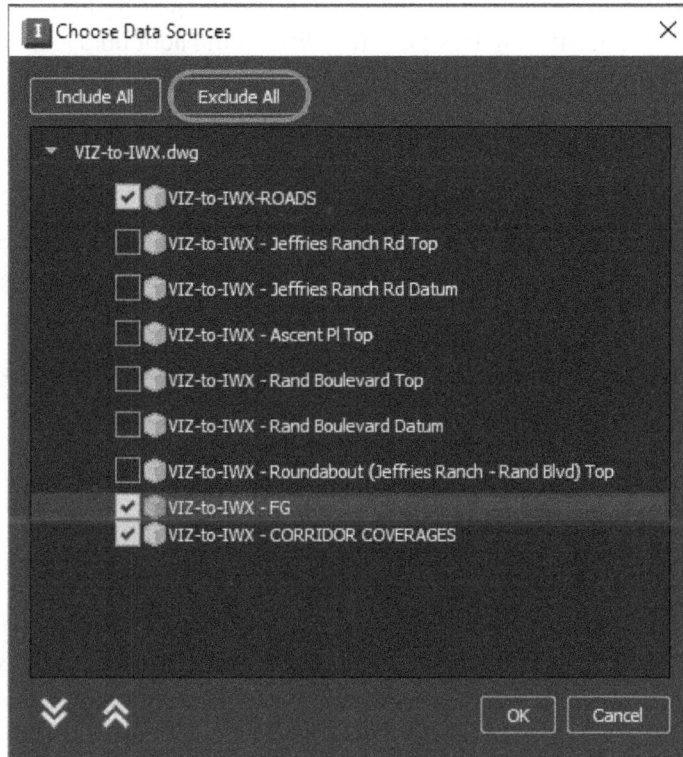

Figure B-34

6. In the *DATA SOURCES* palette, click (Refresh). This can take a while.

    Note: *If this message does not display, in the Manage tab>Display panel, select*

     (Surface Layers).

7. In the dialog box, select **Yes** to open the *Surface Layers* panel, as shown in Figure B-35.

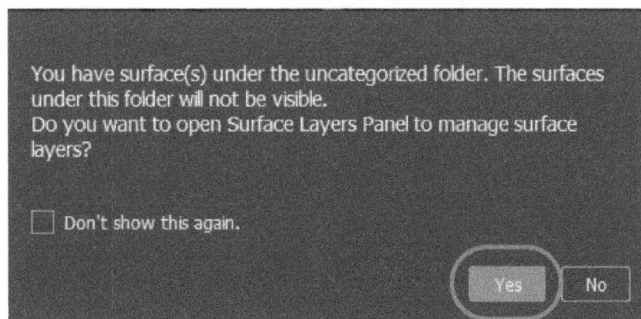

Figure B-35

---

8. In the *Surface Layers* dialog box, drag the *FG* surface above *elevation1* and *elevation2*, as shown in Figure B–36, and make it visible (by clicking the light bulb icon to turn it yellow).

Before | **After**

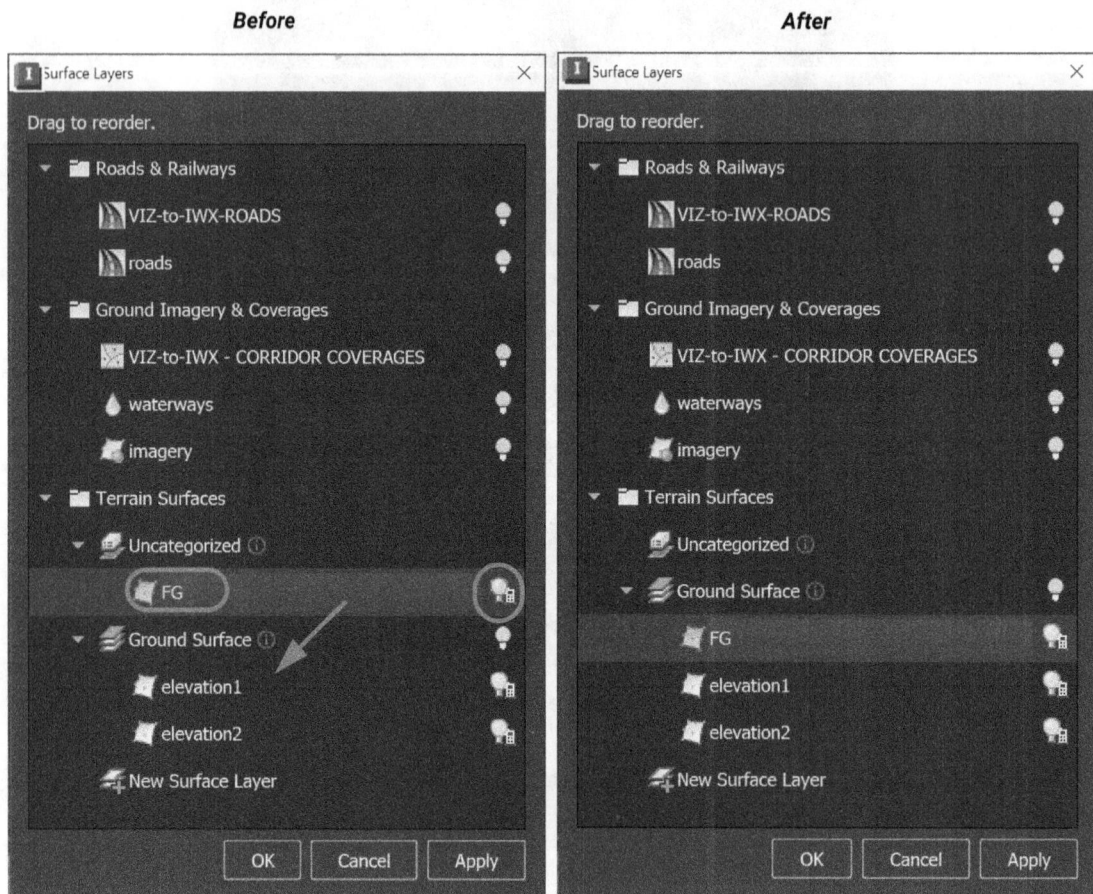

Figure B–36

9. Click **OK** to close the *Surface Layers* dialog box.

10. The **Civil 3D** corridors and **FG** surface are imported, as shown in Figure B–37. Note that the corridors are imported as Component Roads, as well as alignments without corridors (such as Mission Avenue to the north).

Figure B-37

11. The **Jeffries Ranch Road** corridor overlaps the **Jeffries Ranch Rd Planning Road** (created from *Model Builder*), as shown above in Figure B-37. This needs to be adjusted. Select the **Jeffries Ranch Rd Planning Road** by clicking on it.

12. Select the second last grip and in the right-click menu, select **Remove Vertex**, as shown in Figure B-38.

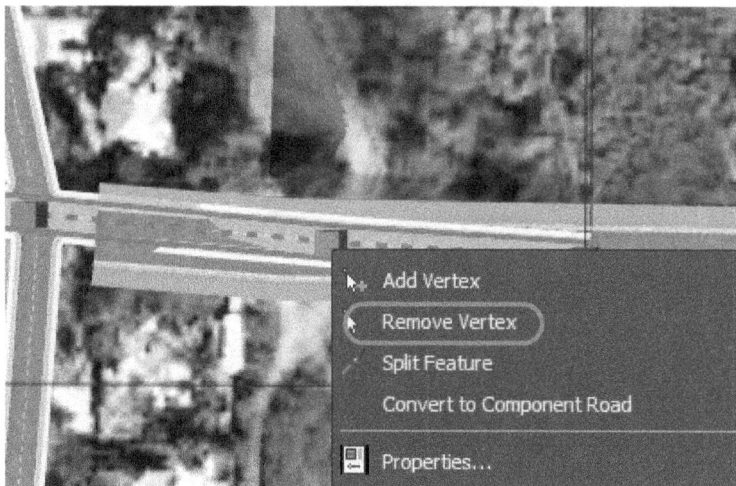

Figure B-38

---

13. Now select the last grip and drag it to the beginning of the **Jeffries Ranch Road** corridor, as shown in Figure B–39.

Figure B–39

14. The **Roundabout** corridor was imported with a default Four-Lane Roadway assembly, which needs to be replaced for the **Jeffries Ranch Road** corridor sections. Pick on the **Jeffries Ranch Road** corridor and in the right-click menu, expand **Road Assembly** and select **Replace Assembly**, as shown in Figure B–40.

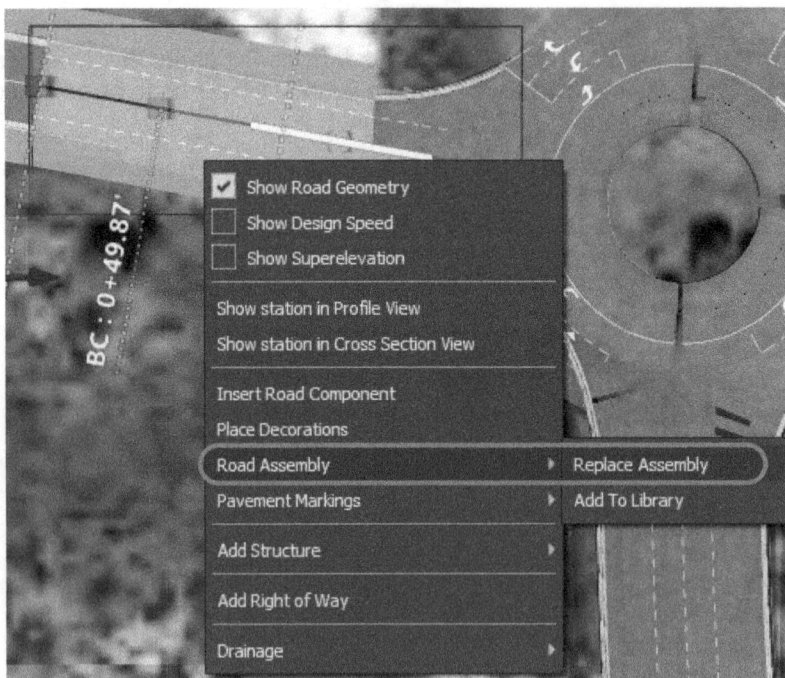

Figure B–40

15. In the *SELECT DRAW STYLE* window, select the **Two Lanes** assembly (at the bottom of the list), as shown in Figure B−41.

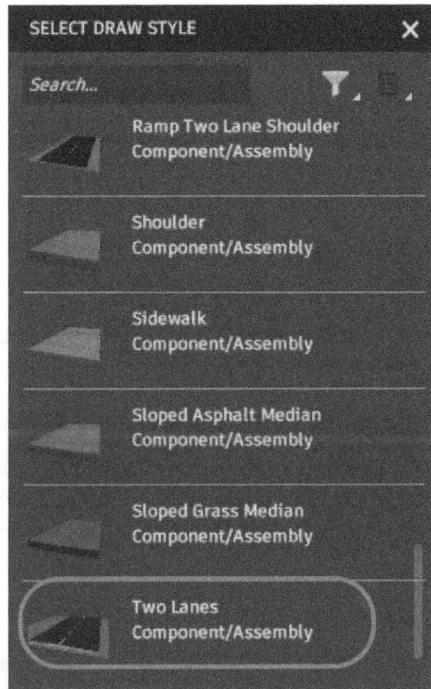

Figure B−41

16. You are prompted for the range. Select the beginning and then drag it to the end, as shown in Figure B−42. Press <Enter> to apply the assembly.

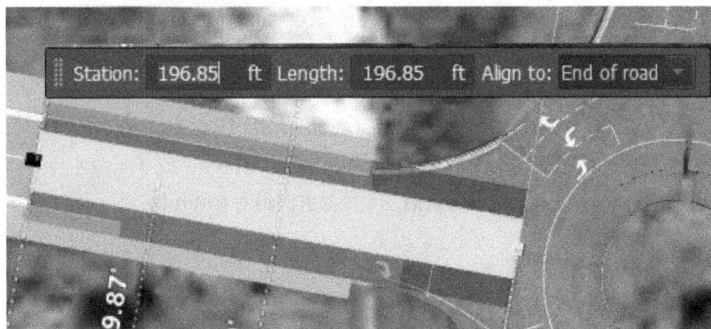

Figure B−42

17. Time permitting, repeat the procedure for the other end of **Jeffries Ranch Road** corridor and the **Roundabout**.

Note: Even though you haven't made any changes, InfraWorks still considers the terrain to be configured.

Task 3: Import a drawing overlay.

In this task, you will import a drawing overlay to display the linework created in a CAD drawing.

1. Continue working in the **Visualization-Local.sqlite** model from the last task.

2. In the main Toolbar on the right side, expand *Switch Active Proposal* and select the **A_Task2** proposal. Here the Roundabout Lanes were also replaced with the **Two Lanes** assembly as you had done earlier.

3. In the *Manage* tab>*Content* panel, select (Data Sources).

4. In the *DATA SOURCES* palette, expand (Add file data source) and select **AutoCAD DWG as 2D Overlay,** as shown in Figure B–43.

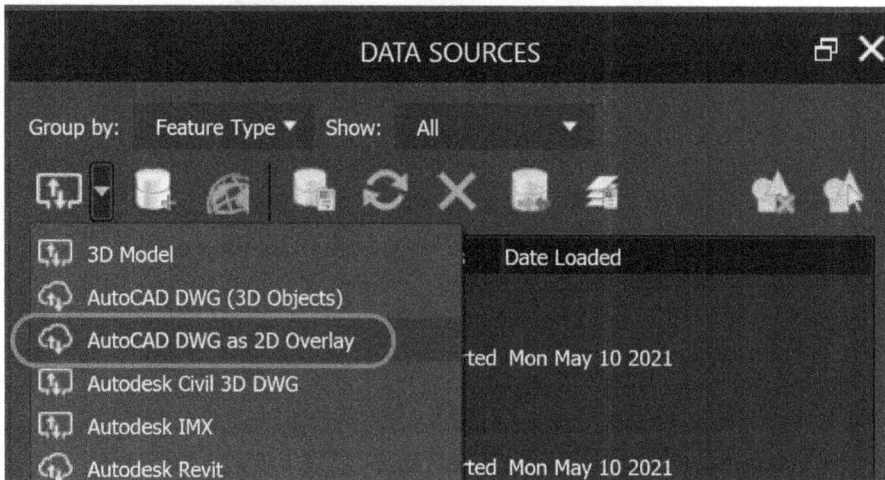

Figure B–43

5. In the *Select Files* dialog box, browse to the *C:\Civil 3D Grading\Working\Visualization* folder, select **Base-Proposed for IWX.dwg**, and click **Open**.

6. In the *Data Import* dialog box, click **Send**. This can take a while.

7. Once you note that the *Status* is no longer showing **Processing**, in the *DATA SOURCES* palette, under T*errain Overlays*, double-click on the **VIZ-to-IWX** data source, as shown in Figure B–44.

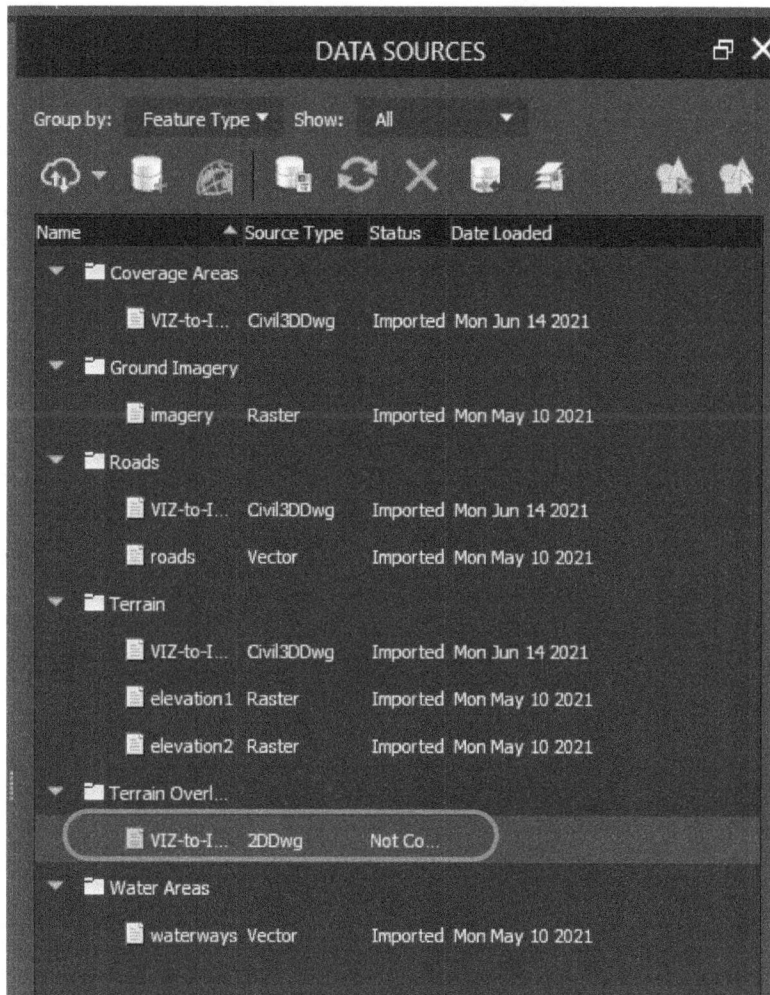

Figure B–44

8. In the *Data Source Configuration* dialog box, complete the following, as shown in Figure B–45:

   Note: If **CA83-VIF** *is not in the drop-down list, click* 🌐 *(Choose Coordinate System) and search for it.*

   - Leave the first *Coordinate System* as is (as **XY-M**).
   - In the *Position* area, under *Coordinate System*, expand the drop-down list and select **CA83-VIF**.
   - In the *X* field, type **6256700**.
   - In the *Y* field, type **2036500**.
   - In the *Scale* area, for both the *X* and *Y* fields, type **75**.

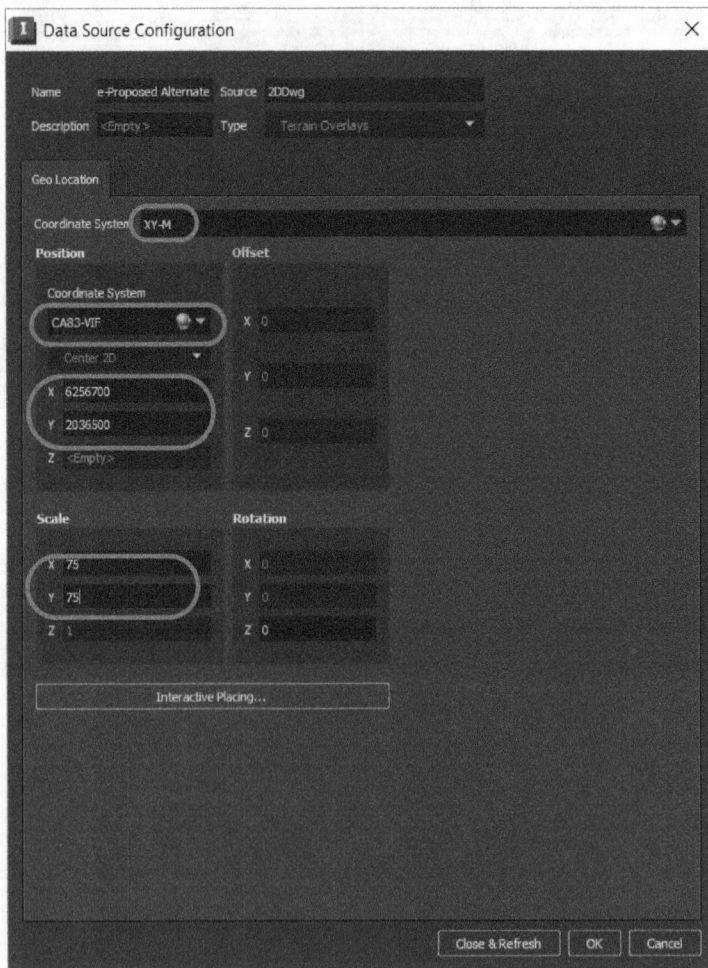

Figure B–45

9. Click **Close & Refresh.**

10. You will notice the overlay is not lined up perfectly. Zoom into the intersection of **Jeffries Ranch Rd** and **Ascent Place**, as shown in Figure B−46.

Figure B−46

Note: Experiment with pick points as suggested. Accuracy is not required here because the image will be properly positioned and scaled in the next practice.

11. Select the overlay and right-click to select **Place by Reference Point.** This command will allow you to select reference and destination points to move, rotate, and scale the overlay at once.

12. When asked to pick *point 1*, double-click on the point, and then double-click where that point belongs in the model, as shown in Figure B−47.

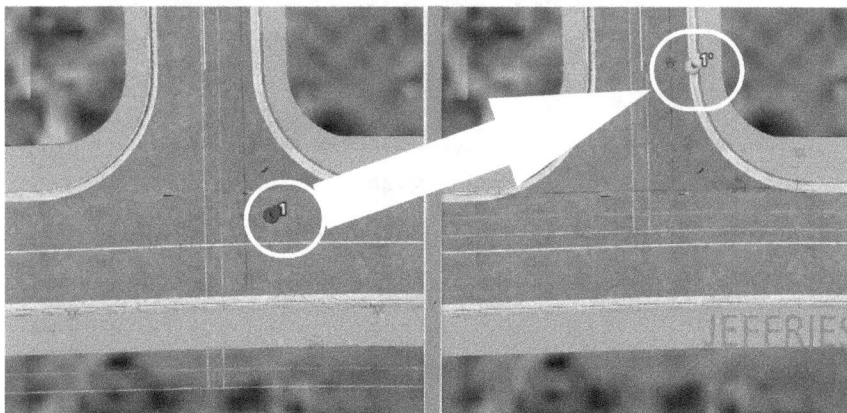

Figure B−47

13. The command will stay active to select up to three references and destination points. Repeat this process two more times, selecting corners of the parking lot on the west and east sides, as shown in Figure B–48 and Figure B–49.

Figure B–48

Figure B–49

14. Review the overlay and notice it lays much better over the existing area.

15. Keep the InfraWorks model open for the next exercise. Remember, there is no *"Save"* command within InfraWorks.

End of practice

B.5 Create Water Features in a Model

When designing a new community, water features are often required. Water features have a number of purposes. They can act as a water retention area that is used by local residents for drinking water, such as a reservoir. They can also be used to divert excess water away from homes and businesses to avoid flooding. This is often required when new hard surfaces prevent water from being absorbed into the ground, as it did before the land was developed. Finally, water areas can be used to provide recreation and make an area more visually appealing.

Water areas are a surface layer in the Model Explorer. You can create the following two types of water features:

- **Water Areas:** Enables you to create bodies of water, such as ponds, lakes, and wetlands. To create a body of water, you click to create points that will act as a boundary for the water area. Figure B–50 shows a small pond water area.

Figure B–50

- **Rivers:** Enables you to create linear water features, such as canals, rivers, and streams. To create a river, you click to create points along a linear path. A buffer surrounds the water on either side. The buffer width is set in the Water asset card.

How To: Create Lakes or Ponds

1. In the *Create* tab>*Environment* drop-down panel, select ![water drop icon] (Water Areas).
2. In the *Select Draw Style* asset card, select the required water style, as shown in Figure B–51.

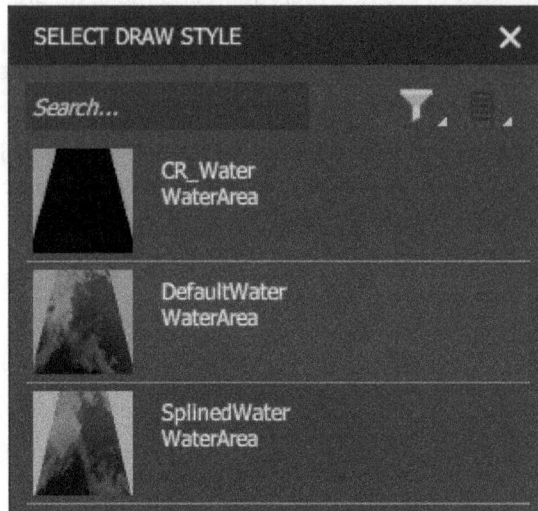

Figure B–51

3. Click in the model to start the creation of the water boundary.
4. Move the cursor in the direction that you want the water boundary to follow. Type a distance for the length to the next point on the boundary and press <Enter> to set the distance. Click in the model to place the boundary point.
5. Continue clicking in the model until all of the boundary points have been created for the water area.
6. Double-click to place the last boundary point and end the command.

B.6 Create City Furniture in a Model

If you need to create multiple predefined 3D buildings or other 3D models in your model, it is recommended that you use ![traffic light icon] (City Furniture).

This command enables you to create multiple 3D models spaced along a path or a single feature at the location specified. Any type of 3D model style can be selected as city furniture, including trees and railway models. However, these models display in the *Furniture* category in the Model Explorer and are furniture features in the database.

The following 3D models can be added as city furniture to a model:

- **Buildings:** There are a number of predefined 3D building models. They fall into three categories from which you can select:
- **Furniture:** 3D models of roof-top items, such as solar panels and HVAC units.
- **Neighborhood:** A few common building types that are found in a typical city, such as gas stations, churches, and post offices.
- **Residential:** Multiple single-family home models.

These 3D model options are located in the *3D Model* tab of the Style Palette. The **Neighborhood** and **Residential** style options are shown in Figure B−52.

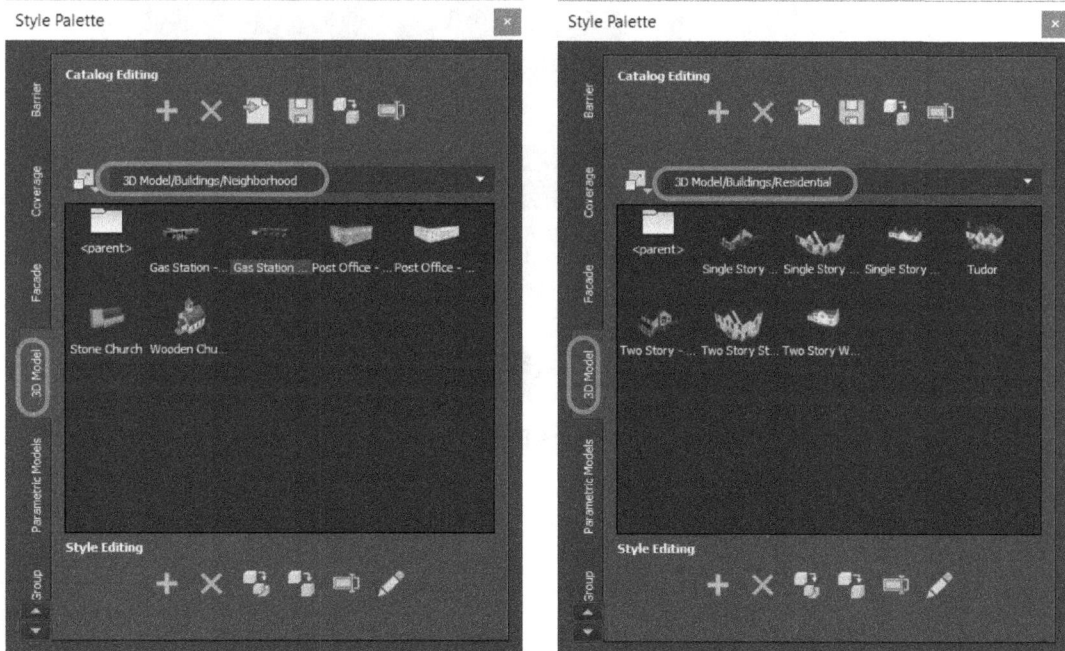

Figure B−52

- **City Furniture:** Objects found in a city, including signs, fences, bike stands, parking meters, dumpsters, etc., as shown in Figure B–53.

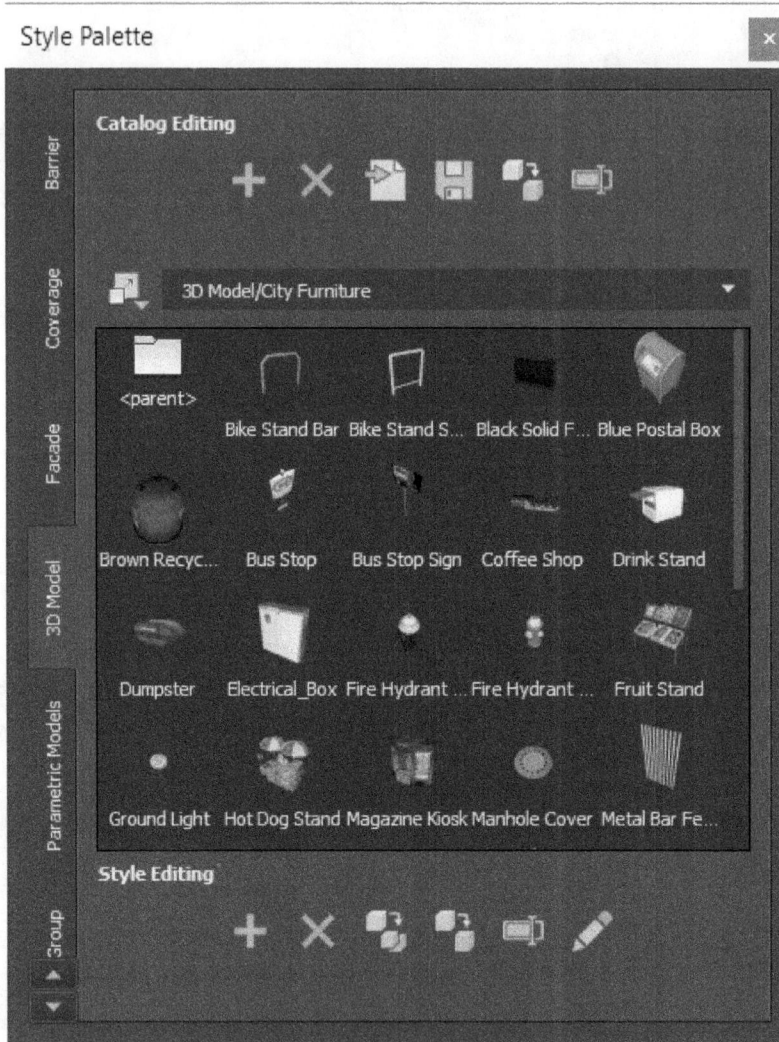

Figure B–53

How To: Add One Predefined 3D Building or Single Piece of City Furniture

1. In the *Create* tab>*Environment* panel, select ![traffic light icon] (City Furniture).
2. The *Select Draw Style* asset card displays, as shown in Figure B–54. You can search for an asset by typing its name in the *Search* field.

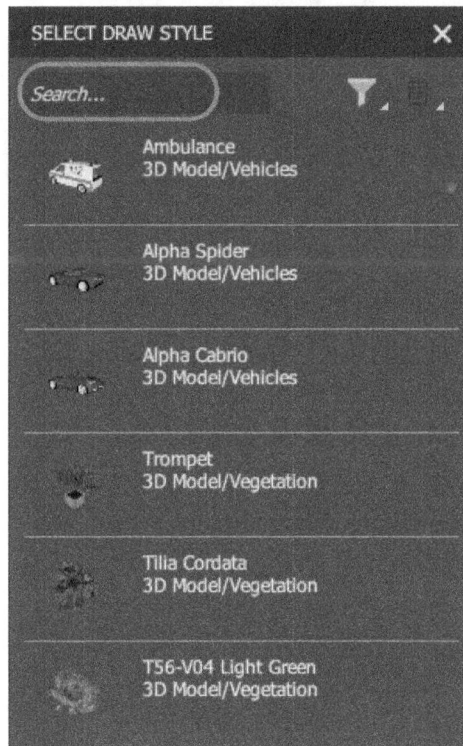

Figure B–54

Hint: Change Asset Card Thumbnail display

You can change the way the thumbnails are displayed in the asset card by clicking the view icon drop-down in the upper right corner (as shown in Figure B–55) and selecting the desired option from the list.

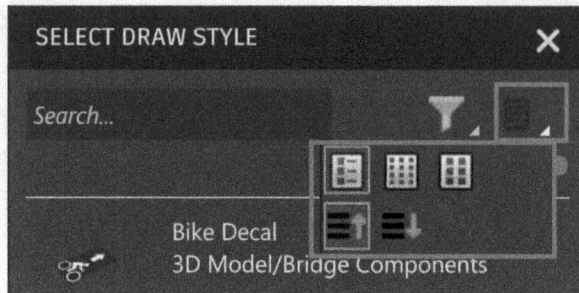

Figure B–55

a. The upper row icons can be used for changing the display of the assets:

   • content items with thumbnails and text

   • content items with small thumbnails only

   • content items with large thumbnails only

b. The lower row icons can be used for changing the sorting order:

   • sort in the ascending order

   • sort in the descending order

3. Select a 3D model.

4. In the model, double-click to place the 3D model and end the command. The size is not important because the 3D model size and shape are predetermined as part of the 3D model.

5. Press <Esc> to clear the selection of the newly created building.

B.7 Add Vegetation to a Model

Adding vegetation can add privacy, shade, noise barriers, and landscape appeal to a project. Trees and other vegetation can also help stakeholders to better understand how the project could look when completed. You can add vegetation in three different ways:

- **Single Plant:** A single plant is placed in the model when you double-click on an insertion point, no matter which vegetation tool is used. Figure B–56 shows a single tree.

Figure B–56

- **Row of Trees:** A group of plants are placed in the model along a line, as shown in Figure B–57.

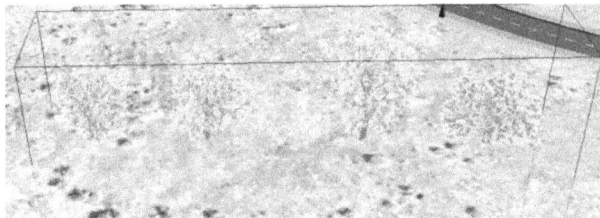

Figure B–57

- **Stand of Trees:** A group of randomly spaced plants are placed in the model inside a polygon, as shown in Figure B–58.

Figure B–58

If you create vegetation along a line or in a polygon, you can set the number of plants that display using the Density Slider, as shown in Figure B-59. The higher the density (slider moved to the right), the more plants that display.

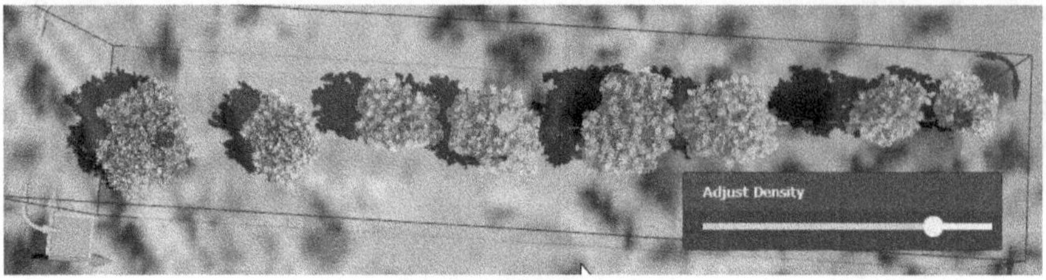

Figure B-59

How To: Create Vegetation in a Group

1. In the *Create* tab>*Environment* drop-down panel, select ![icon] (Stand of Trees).

2. In the *Select Draw Style* asset card, select the type of plant required, as shown in Figure B-60.

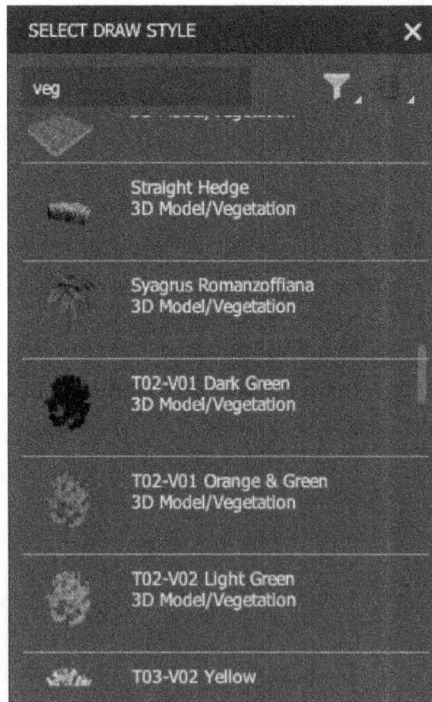

Figure B-60

3. In the model, click to create the corners of a polygon for the vegetation group area. Remember to double-click on the final corner to finish the polygon.

4. Press <Esc> to make the Feature Density bar display. Slide the Density Slider (as shown in Figure B−61) until the required number of plants displays in the model.

Figure B−61

5. Press <Esc> to clear the selection of the newly created trees.

Edit Vegetation

When you select vegetation, gizmos display to enable you to modify the plants. ● (Elevation Gizmo) enables you to adjust the height of the plants, while ▣ (Height Gizmo) enables you to change the size and scale of the plants.

If you select a vegetation group (row or stand of trees), the Density Slider displays, enabling you to change the number of plants that display in the group. Move the slider left or right until the required number of plants displays in the model. If the Density Slider is not displayed, orbit the view to a plan view to make it display, as shown in Figure B−62.

Figure B−62

Practice B2
Add Details to the Site

Practice Objectives

* Add a pond water area.
* Add predefined buildings.
* Add vegetation and other city furniture.

In this practice, you will enhance the site with a pond, buildings, trees and shrubs, and other details. An office building, hotel, and school have already been added to the site, as well as coverage areas to place homes along the pond area.

Task 1: Add a water retention pond.

1. Continue working in the same model as the previous practice. If you did not finish the previous exercise, open **Visualization-Local.sqlite** from *C:\Civil 3D for Land Dev\Working\ Visualization*.

2. In the main Toolbar on the right side, expand *Switch Active Proposal* and select proposal **B_Task1**.

3. Just to the left of the *Proposals* drop-down list, click ▥ (View bookmarks) and select **Pond**.

4. In the *Create* tab>*Environment* drop-down panel, select ◉ (Water Areas).

5. In the *Select Draw Style* asset card, select **Splined Water**, as shown in Figure B−63.

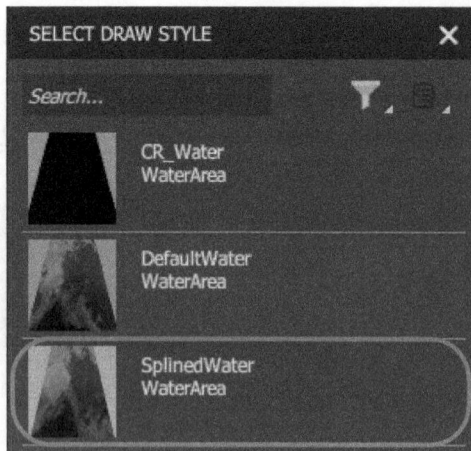

Figure B−63

6. Trace around the red polyline representing the pond, placing vertices as shown in Figure B–64. If you can offset your picks inside the pond by about 3 feet, the pond will look better.

Figure B–64

7. Double-click to finish the pond definition. Press <Esc> to exit the command (rather than creating another water area).

8. Right-click on the pond to edit vertices and adjust vertices, if needed, to make sure the pond is not overlapping any parcels or the office building (as shown in Figure B−65).

Figure B−65

The AutoCAD Overlay may prevent you from selecting the pond. You may need to lock the overlay in the Model Explorer to prevent it from being selected. Also lock the Coverage Areas to avoid their selection.

9. In the *Manage* tab>*Model* panel, click (Model Explorer).

10. In the Model Explorer, in the *Overlays* section, click on the light bulb beside **Base-Proposed for IWX** to turn off the overlay, as shown in Figure B–66.

Figure B–66

Task 2: Add predefined buildings to the site.

1. Continue working in the same model as the last task.

2. In the main Toolbar on the right side, expand *Switch Active Proposal* and select the **B_Task2** proposal.

3. Just to the left of the *Proposals* drop-down list, click (View bookmarks) and select **Subdivision**.

4. In the *Create* tab>*Environment* panel, select (City Furniture).

5. In the *Select Draw Style* asset card that displays, type **two stor** in the search field. Select the **Two Story Stucco** building, as shown in Figure B–67.

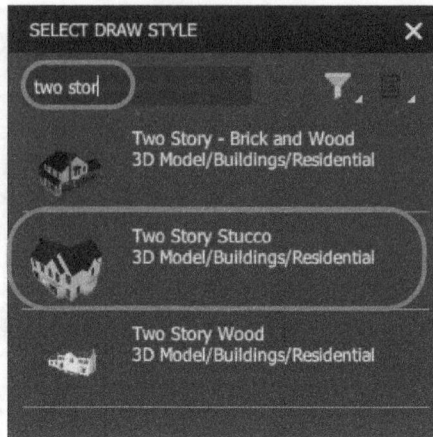

Figure B–67

6. In the model, in the first lot, double-click in the center of the green coverage area to place the building, as shown in Figure B–68. Press <Esc> to exit the command (rather than placing more buildings).

Figure B–68

7. Use (Rotate Gizmo), (Height Gizmo), and (Move Gizmo) as required to relocate it.

8. These lots were graded as walk-out basements and the city furniture buildings are slab-on-grade. Therefore, you won't be able to place the houses correctly on the surface as graded.

9. Continue this process for the other four lots, adjusting the building types as you add them. One example is shown in Figure B–69.

Figure B–69

Task 3: Add vegetation to the site.

1. Continue working in the same model as the last task.

2. In the main Toolbar on the right side, expand *Switch Active Proposal* and select the **B_Task3** proposal.

3. Just to the left of the *Proposals* drop-down list, click ⬛ (View bookmarks) and select **Tree**.

4. In the *Create* tab>*Environment* drop-down panel, select 🌳 (Stand of Trees).

5. You can use the search window at the top of the asset card to find the proper tree if needed. The previous filter is still active; you need to change it. In the *Select Draw Style* asset card, in the search field, type **veg** and scroll to select the **Syagrus Romanzoffiana** tree, as shown in Figure B–70.

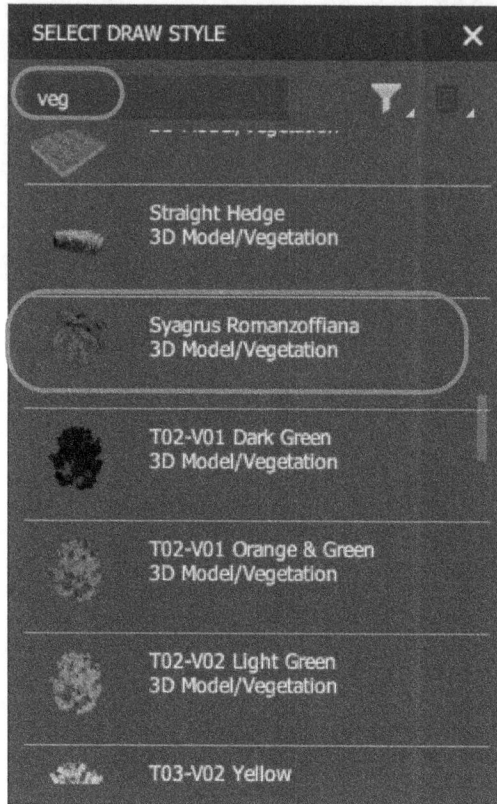

Figure B–70

6. In the first lot, double-click at the corner of the lot to add a tree, as shown in Figure B–71. Press <Esc> once to finish the command. The gizmos of the tree are now visible.

    Note: Be sure to double-click on the spot rapidly, otherwise you will have to draw a line for a row of trees, which is covered later in the practice.

Figure B–71

7. Use 🔲 (Height Gizmo) to adjust the height of the tree as needed. Press <Esc> when done, to deselect the tree.

8. In another lot of your choice, add some shrubs along the house. Select 🔲 (Stand of Trees) again. In the *Select Draw Style* asset card, type **hedge** in the search field. Select the **Straight Hedge**, as shown in Figure B–72.

Figure B–72

9. Double-click to add the first hedge at the front corner of one of the houses. Add five more hedges to the front of the house, as shown in Figure B−73. You will need to use

    (Rotate Gizmo) and (Move Gizmo) to properly place the hedges along the front of the house.

Figure B−73

10. Just to the left of the *Proposals* drop-down list, click (View bookmarks) and select **Open Lot**.

11. In the *Create* tab>*Environment* drop-down panel, select (Stand of Trees).

12. In the *Select Draw Style* asset card, in the search field, type **Ded** and scroll to select **Deciduous-V01 Tree**.

13. Create a polygon, as shown in Figure B−74, to place an area of trees. Double-click to end the polygon. Press <Esc> when done.

Figure B−74

14. To adjust the density of the trees, click once on a tree, then click again. This will bring up the Density Slider (as shown in Figure B–75). Adjust the slider until you have the amount of trees you like.

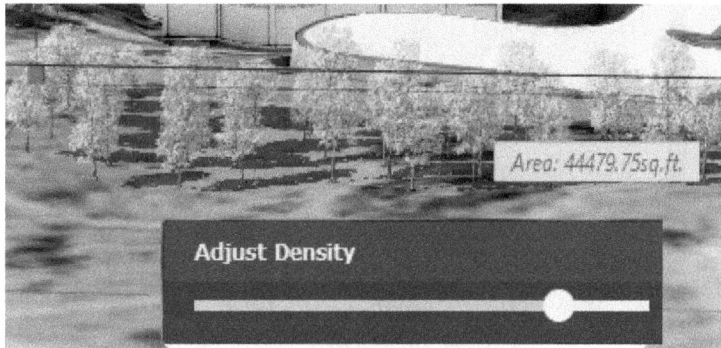

Figure B–75

Task 4: Enhance the site with city furniture.

1. In the main Toolbar on the right side, expand *Switch Active Proposal* and select proposal **B_Task4**.

2. Just to the left of the *Proposals* drop-down list, click (View bookmarks) and select **Church**.

3. In the *Create* tab>*Environment* panel, select (City Furniture).

4. In the *Select Draw Style* asset card that displays, type **church** in the search field. Select the **Wooden Church**, as shown in Figure B–76.

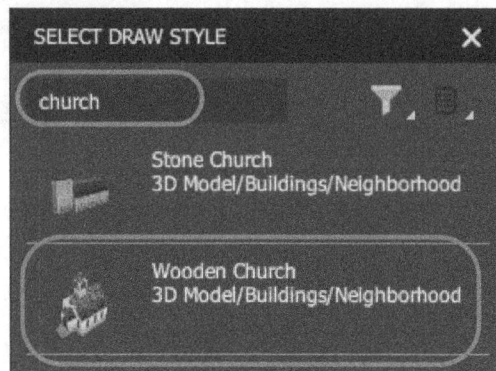

Figure B–76

5. Double-click in the area shown in Figure B–77 to add the church. You may need to use the Gizmos to adjust the rotation and position.

Figure B–77

6. Click ⬛ (View bookmarks) and select **Open Lot**.

7. In the *Create* tab>*Environment* panel, select ⬛ (City Furniture).

8. In the *Select Draw Style* asset card, type **gas** in the search field. Select the **Gas Station with Convenience Store**, as show in Figure B–78.

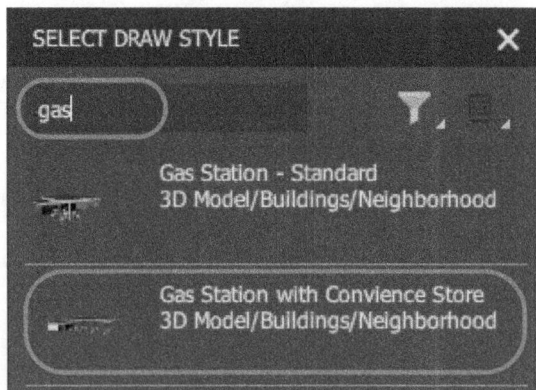

Figure B–78

9. Double-click in the area shown in Figure B–79 to add the gas station. You may need to use the Gizmos to adjust the rotation and position.

Figure B–79

10. Time permitting, continue to add city furniture elements to the open lot, similar to those shown in Figure B–80.

Figure B–80

Task 5: Hide CAD overlay.

1. In the main Toolbar on the right side, expand *Switch Active Proposal* and select proposal **B_Task5**.
2. In the *Manage* tab>*Model* panel, click ▦ (Model Explorer).
3. In the Model Explorer, in the *Overlays* section, click the light bulb beside **Base-Proposed for IWX** to turn off the overlay, as shown in Figure B–81.

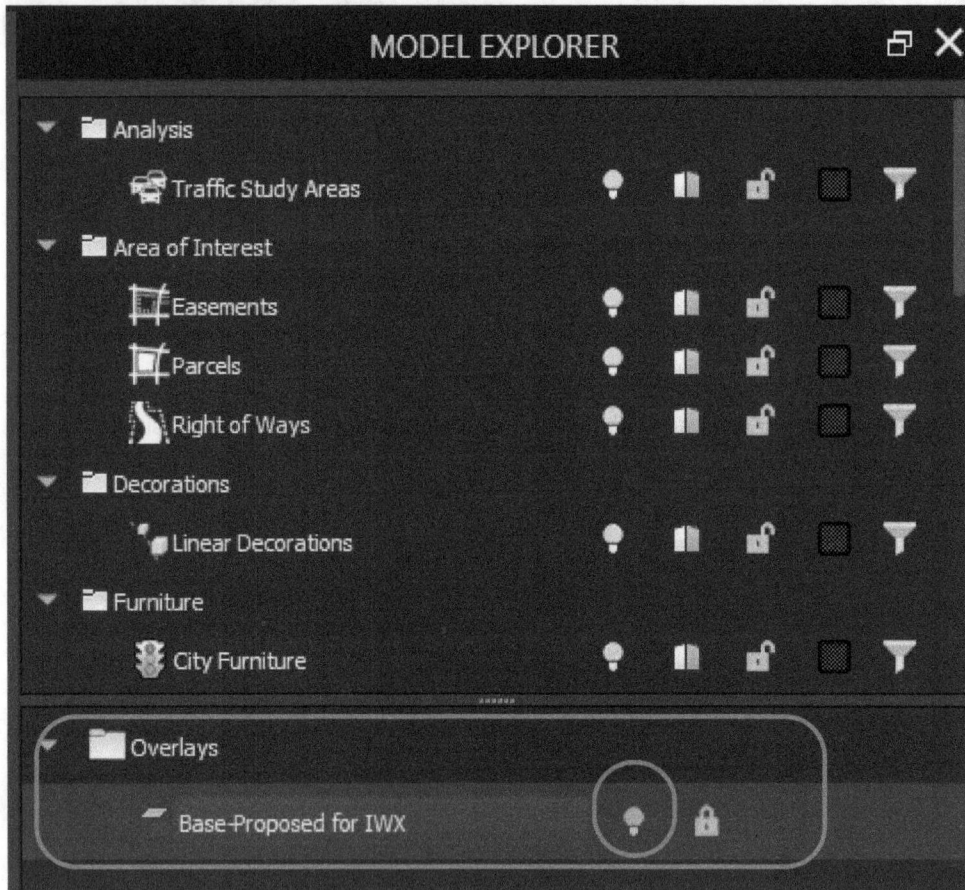

Figure B–81

End of practice

Chapter Review Questions

1. Which part of the user interface would you use to quickly change to an isometric view, for example a view from the upper north-east corner?

    a. In Canvas Tools

    b. ViewCube

    c. Model Explorer

    d. Model Window

2. How do you change the density of a Row of Trees?

    a. By changing the style of the trees.

    b. By using the Properties palette.

    c. Select the tree row, then select it again and use the slider to adjust the density.

    d. Once placed, you cannot change the density.

3. Which of the following should be used to display different design variations for the project?

    a. Bookmarks

    b. Proposals

    c. Coverages

    d. Model Explorer

4. Which of the following is not a category for a predefined 3D building model?

    a. Furniture

    b. Residential

    c. Neighborhood

    d. Commercial

5. Once placed, you can change the footprint of a building that has been created from a 3D model.

    a. True

    b. False

Command Summary

Button	Command	Location
⚙	**Application Options**	• **Home Screen** • **In Canvas Tools:** Settings and Utilities
▯	**Bookmark**	• **Toolbar**
N/A	**Elevate Camera Down**	• **Mouse:** Hold scroll wheel • **Shortcut Key**: <E> or <0> (zero)
N/A	**Elevate Camera Up**	• **Mouse:** Hold scroll wheel • **Shortcut Key**: <Q> or <1>
▮ / ⌂	**Home**	• **ViewCube** • **Keyboard:** <Home> or <F4>
N/A	**Lock Above Terrain**	• **View Settings>Interaction stack**
▣	**Model Explorer**	• **Toolbar** • **In Canvas Tools:** Build, manage, and analyze your infrastructure model>Create and manage your model
N/A	**Open**	• **Home Screen**
N/A	**Pitch Down**	• **Shortcut Key**: <W>
N/A	**Pitch Up**	• **Shortcut Key**: <S>
▤	**Proposals**	• **Toolbar** • **In Canvas Tools**: Build, manage, and analyze your infrastructure model>Create and manage your model
N/A	**Tooltips**	• **View Settings>Interaction stack**
N/A	**ViewCube**	• **View Settings>Interaction stack**
N/A	**Zoom In**	• **Mouse:** Scroll wheel • **Shortcut Key**: <+>
N/A	**Zoom Out**	• **Mouse:** Scroll wheel • **Shortcut Key**: <->
🔍	**Zoom Selected**	• **Shortcut Key**: <F> • **In Canvas Tools:** Build, manage, and analyze your infrastructure model>Select model features • **In Model**: Double-click on point of interest

More Grading with Corridor Models

The Autodesk® Civil 3D® software provides tools that enable you to create multiple design scenarios quickly. An added advantage is how easily you can make changes to a design. You can create a finished ground surface using parcel lines, feature lines, and grading objects; however, these methods sometimes lack the flexibility needed for certain projects.

As an alternative to standard grading tools, you can use Autodesk Civil 3D corridors for grading design. Corridors and their related features make designing and editing straightforward. While this is not the typical way to grade in Civil 3D, corridor subassemblies offer more options for daylighting and allow you to add conditional grades to a finished ground surface. This method can help you redesign areas, such as converting a pond site into a two-chamber lagoon, with greater control over the grading process.

Learning Objectives

- Create corridor baselines that can be used for a grading solution rather than a road design.

- Create profiles to be used in grading solutions.

- Determine the best subassembly to use for the type of grading being created.

- Create multiple baselines and regions in a corridor model to include multiple alignments, profiles, and assemblies in the grading solution.

- Modify a grading solution by changing the alignments, profiles, assemblies, target surface, or corridor parameters.

- Add feature lines to the corridor surface for additional grading control.

C.1 Create Grading Assemblies

The next elements to define are assemblies with associated subassemblies that create a grading solution from the previously defined baselines. There are three generic subassemblies that accomplish the same results as grading criteria would in a grading group. The three subassemblies and their grading criteria equivalent are as follows:

1. Link Width and Slope = Grade to Distance

2. Link Slope to Surface = Grade to Surface

3. Link Slopes to Elevations = Grade to Elevation or Grade to Relative Elevation

These subassemblies are accessed in the *Generic* tab in the Tool Palettes, as shown in Figure C-1.

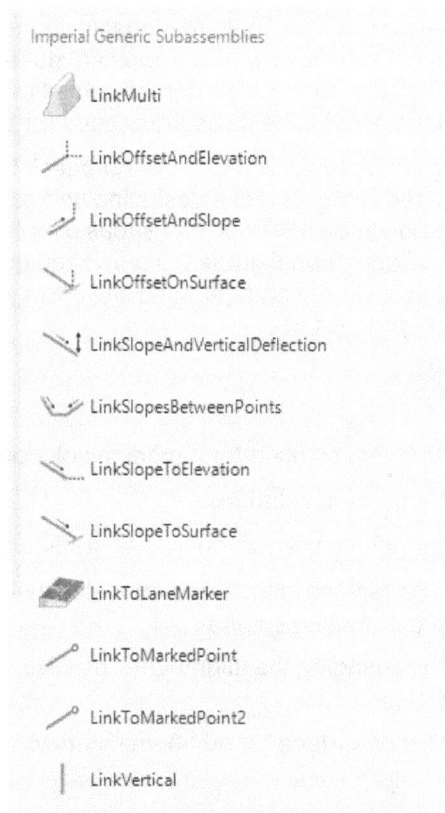

Imperial Generic Subassemblies

- LinkMulti
- LinkOffsetAndElevation
- LinkOffsetAndSlope
- LinkOffsetOnSurface
- LinkSlopeAndVerticalDeflection
- LinkSlopesBetweenPoints
- LinkSlopeToElevation
- LinkSlopeToSurface
- LinkToLaneMarker
- LinkToMarkedPoint
- LinkToMarkedPoint2
- LinkVertical

Figure C-1

The Tool Palettes contains numerous subassemblies that act like grading scenarios. The subassembly used depends on the grading task, and the task determines when and how to use each subassembly. Most grading projects use link and/or daylight subassemblies. However, a grading solution may be more complex; for example, if a grading project is a parking lot, the design may include curb, sidewalk, and other specialized subassemblies.

Link Subassemblies

The Civil 3D Subassemblies Tool Palettes, *Generic* tab contains 14 subassemblies that create surface links between a grading alignment/profile and other drawing objects. Other Civil 3D objects may include offsets, elevations, alignments, profiles, surfaces, etc. These link subassemblies only have a top or datum link to create a surface and may not even have a point code. For more information on the link subassembly's parameters, right-click on the subassembly in the Tool Palette and select **Help**.

Link Width and Slope

The Link Width and Slope subassembly creates a link by specifying a link width and a link slope parameter. The link's inside point, closest to the assembly, is its attachment point. The link's fixed width and slope parameters can be overridden by targeting alignments, polylines, feature lines, or survey figures. The subassembly applies to an assembly's left or right side. An example is shown in Figure C-2.

Figure C-2

Link Slope to Surface

The Link Slope to Surface subassembly creates a link by specifying a link slope parameter. The link's inside point, closest to the assembly, is its attachment point. The link's slope parameter is a pre-defined fixed value. The width of the link is determined by the link intersection with the closest target surface. The subassembly applies to an assembly's left or right side. An example is shown in Figure C-3.

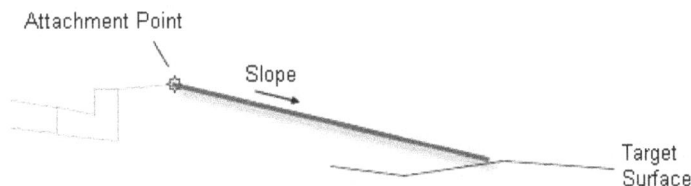

Figure C-3

Link Slope to Elevation

The Link Slope to Elevation subassembly creates a link to a user-specified target elevation, using a specified slope and elevation parameter. The link's length depends on the specified slope and target elevation. The link's inside point, closest to the assembly, is its attachment point. The link's elevation parameter can be overridden by targeting profiles, 3D polylines, feature lines, or survey figures. The subassembly applies to an assembly's left or right side. An example is shown in Figure C−4.

Figure C−4

Link Offset on Surface

The Link Offset on Surface subassembly creates a link by specifying an offset parameter and a target surface. The link's inside point, closest to the assembly, is its attachment point. The offset parameter is the distance from the assembly's baseline to a target surface. A positive value sets the offset to the baseline's right and a negative value sets the offset to the baseline's left. The link's offset parameters can be overridden by targeting alignments, polylines, feature lines, or survey figures. An example is shown in Figure C−5.

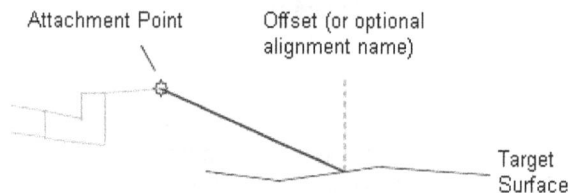

Figure C−5

Link to Marked Point

The Link to Marked Point subassembly creates a link from a subassembly point to a previously named marked point. The link's beginning point is a selected subassembly point. The link can go in any direction to connect to the named marked point. The link is to another subassembly within the assembly. An example is shown in Figure C–6.

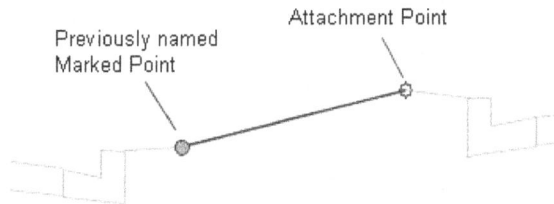

Figure C–6

Link to Marked Point 2

The Link to Marked Point 2 subassembly enables a link from the attached point to a previously named marked point. The link's beginning is the attachment point and the link can go in any direction. The named marked point's location determines the link's direction. The marked point can be on an adjacent corridor model. An example is shown in Figure C–7.

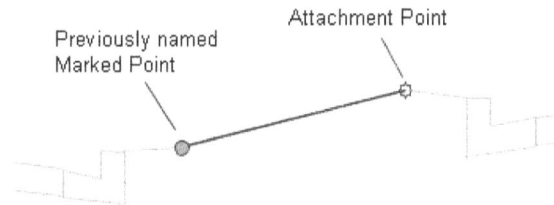

Figure C–7

Daylight Subassemblies

The *Daylight* tab in the Civil 3D Subassemblies Tool Palettes contains 17 subassemblies that create surface links between the grading alignment/profile and other objects in the drawing. In addition to creating links, materials can be assigned to the links to help with quantity calculations and visualization of the grading model. For more information on each daylight subassembly's parameters, right-click on the subassembly in the Tool Palette and select **Help**.

Daylight General

The Daylight General subassembly is a generalized solution to create cut and fill slopes from the edge of the grading design out to a target surface. This is the most commonly used daylight subassembly. However, it is seldom used to its full potential because many people do not realize the variety of cut and fill slope conditions it contains.

By default, the Daylight General subassembly attempts to create a cut first according to the parameter settings. The parameters can include up to eight different cut slopes, each with their own assigned material, before reaching the Cut Hinge Point, as shown in Figure C–8. You do not have to use all eight cut parameters. If only one slope is required, you can leave all of the other Cut Slope Width and Slope parameters set to zero. The slope after the Hinge Point can be set to define the final slope out to the target surface. It can vary according to the Max Cut Height settings. Therefore, the Flat Cut Slope (6:1 by default) is used if the height of the cut is less than the Flat Cut Height (5' by default). If the height of the cut from the Hinge Point to the surface is greater than the Flat Cut Height, but less than the Max Cut Height, the Medium Cut conditions are used automatically. The Medium Cut Slope enables the slope to be slightly more steep (4:1) than the Flat Cut Slope up to the Medium Cut Max Height (10'). If the cut is greater than the Medium Cut Max Height, the Steep Cut Slope (2:1) is used. The Steep Cut Slope does not have a maximum height parameter.

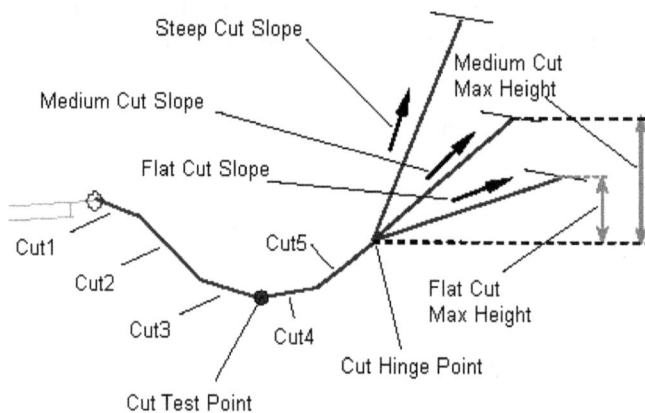

Figure C–8

If a cut condition is not found, a fill condition is used. Multiple fill conditions can be set similar to setting a cut condition, except that only three Fill Slopes can be set before the Fill Hinge Point. As with cut conditions, the fill conditions can include a Flat Fill Slope (6:1 by default) for a Maximum Height (5' by default), a Medium Fill Slope (4:1 by default) for a Maximum Height (10' by default), and a Steep Fill Slope (2:1) with no height restrictions, as shown in Figure C–9.

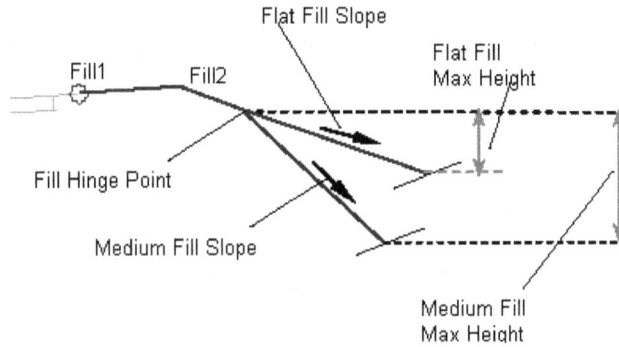

Figure C–9

If the Steep Slope is used in a cut situation, a guardrail can be incorporated into the design automatically by setting the guardrail parameter to **Include**. You can then set the slope, width, and post position parameters, as shown in Figure C–10.

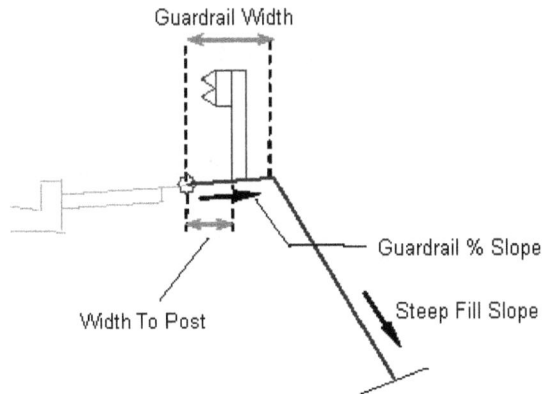

Figure C–10

Daylight Max Width

The Daylight Max Width subassembly creates a link that daylights to a target surface. The slope used is determined by the Maximum Width permitted. If the daylight link can touch the target surface within the Maximum Width parameter set, the slope is defined by the Slope parameter entered. If the daylight link cannot touch the target surface within the Maximum Width parameter set, the Slope parameter is ignored and the slope is defined by the Width parameter and the difference in elevation from the Hinge Point and the Target Surface at the Maximum Width permitted, as shown in Figure C–11.

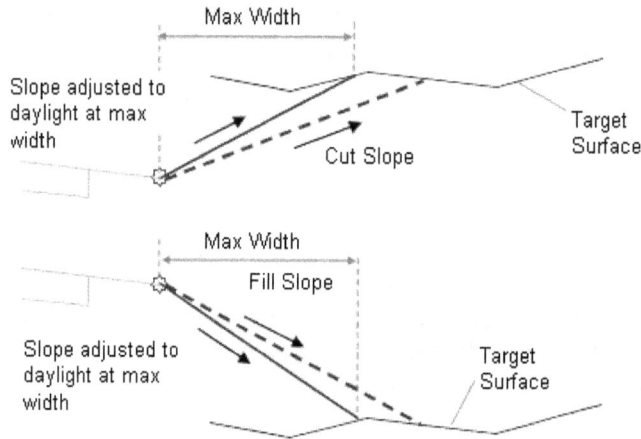

Figure C–11

Daylight to Offset

The Daylight to Offset subassembly creates a daylight link from the attachment point to a set offset from the baseline. This offset can be parallel to the baseline or target an alignment, polyline, feature line, or survey figure. Material types and depths can be assigned to the daylight link based on the slope's ranged values, as shown in Figure C–12.

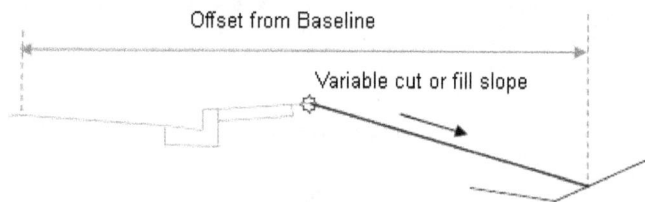

Figure C–12

Daylight Bench

The Daylight Bench subassembly creates repeating benches as needed at specified heights, widths, and slopes until it finds daylight on a target surface. The cut benches can have different parameters than fill benches if required, as shown in Figure C-13.

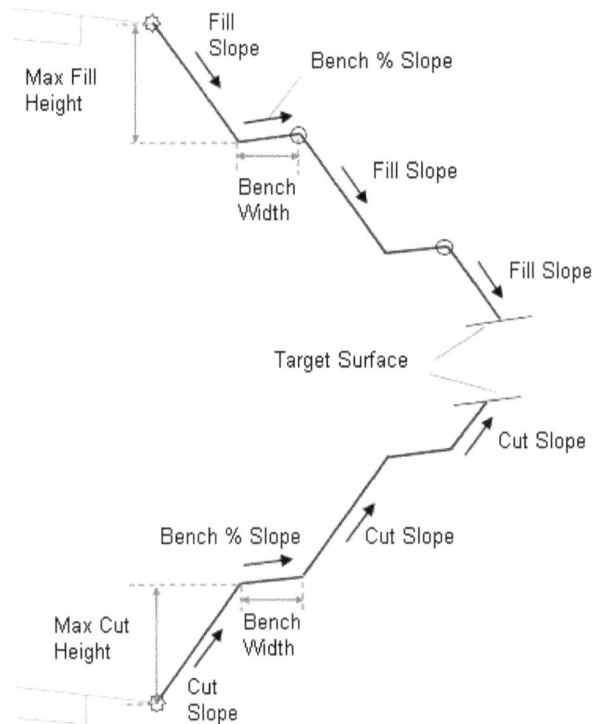

Figure C-13

How To: Create an Assembly for a Grading Solution

1. In the *Home* tab>*Create Design* panel, expand the *Assembly* drop-down list and click
   (Create Assembly).
2. In the *Create Assembly* dialog box, type a name.
3. Set the *Assembly Type* to **Other**.
4. Click **OK** to accept all of the other defaults and close the dialog box.
5. In the drawing, select a point as the insertion point.
6. In the *Home* tab>*Create Design* panel, click   (Tool Palettes).
7. Select the required subassembly.

8. In the *Properties* palette, set the parameters in the *Advanced* area, as shown in Figure C–14.

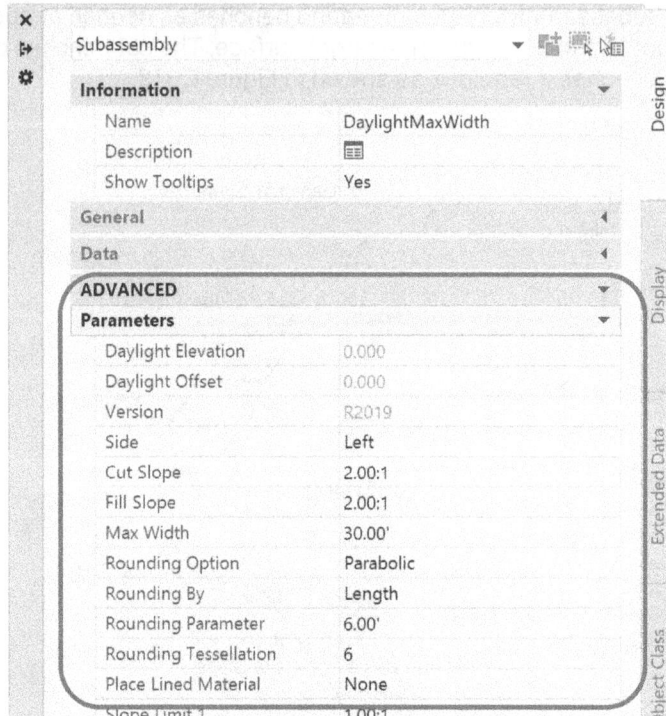

Figure C–14

9. In the drawing, select the assembly marker to which to connect the subassembly. Press <Enter> to end the command.

10. In the Tool Palettes, select another required subassembly.

11. In the *Properties* palette, set the parameters in the *Advanced* area.

12. In the drawing, select the required connection point, as shown in Figure C–15. Press <Enter> to end the command.

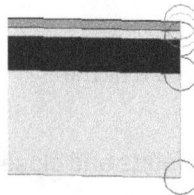

Figure C–15

13. Continue adding additional subassemblies as required.

Practice C1
Create Grading Assemblies

Practice Objective

* Create typical grading corridor cross-sections by using assemblies and selecting appropriate subassemblies from the design specifications.

In this practice, you will create multiple assemblies for the pond grading.

Task 1: Create assemblies for the outer rim of the pond.

In this task, you will create an assembly that represents the outer rim of the pond and daylights to the existing ground surface.

1. Open **LAGOON-C.dwg** from the *C:\Civil 3D Grading\Working\Lagoon* folder.

2. In the *Home* tab>*Create Design* panel, expand the Assembly drop-down list and click

   (Create Assembly).

3. In the *Create Assembly* dialog box, complete the following:

   * For the *Name*, type **Pond Outer Rim**.
   * Set the *Assembly Type* to **Other**.
   * Set the *Code Set Style* to **ASC-View-Edit**.

4. Click **OK** to accept all of the other defaults and close the dialog box.

5. In the drawing, select a point to the right of the **Pond Outer Rim Profile** view as the insertion point, so it visually relates to that profile.

   Note: The Autodesk Civil 3D software automatically zooms in on the assembly marker.

6. In the *Home* tab>*Palettes* panel, click (Tool Palettes) to display the Tool Palettes.

7. In the *Daylight* tab in the Tool Palettes, select **Daylight Max Width** to display the Properties palette.

8. In the *Properties* palette, set the parameters according to those shown in Figure C-16.

    *   *Side:* **Right**
    *   *Max Width:* **25'**
    *   *Rounding Parameter:* **3'**
    *   *Material 1 Thickness:* **1'**
    *   *Material 2 Thickness:* **0.5'**
    *   *Material 3 Thickness:* **0.33'**

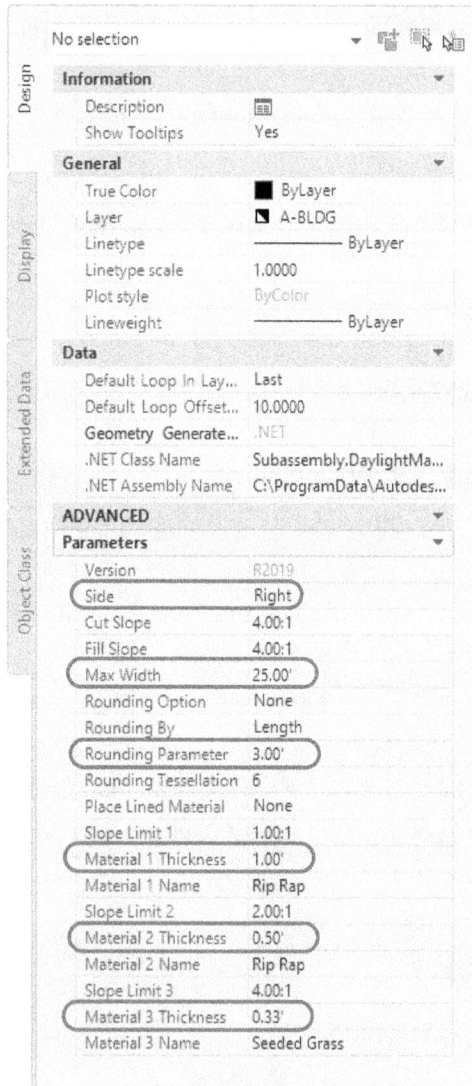

Figure C-16

9. In the drawing, select the **Pond Outer Rim** assembly marker to connect the subassembly.

10. Press <Enter> to end the command.

11. Save the drawing.

Task 2: Create the north bay assemblies.

In this task, you will create three assemblies that represent the interior of the pond's north bay rim and daylights to the existing ground surface.

1. Continue working in the drawing from the previous task.

2. In the *Home* tab>*Palettes* panel, expand the *Assembly* drop-down list and click (Create Assembly).

3. In the *Create Assembly* dialog box, complete the following:

    * For the *Name*, type **Pond North Bay 33 percent**.

    * Set the *Assembly Type* to **Other**.

    * Click **OK** to accept all of the other defaults and close the dialog box.

4. In the drawing, select a point to the right of the **Pond North Bay** profile view as the insertion point.

5. If the Tool Palettes is not already displayed, in the *Home* tab>*Palettes* panel, click  (Tool Palettes).

6. In the *Generic* tab in the Tool Palettes, select **Link Slope To Elevation**.

7. In the *Properties* palette, set the following parameters (as shown in Figure C–17).

    *   *Side:* **Right**
    *   *Slope:* **33%**
    *   *Target Elevation:* **165'**

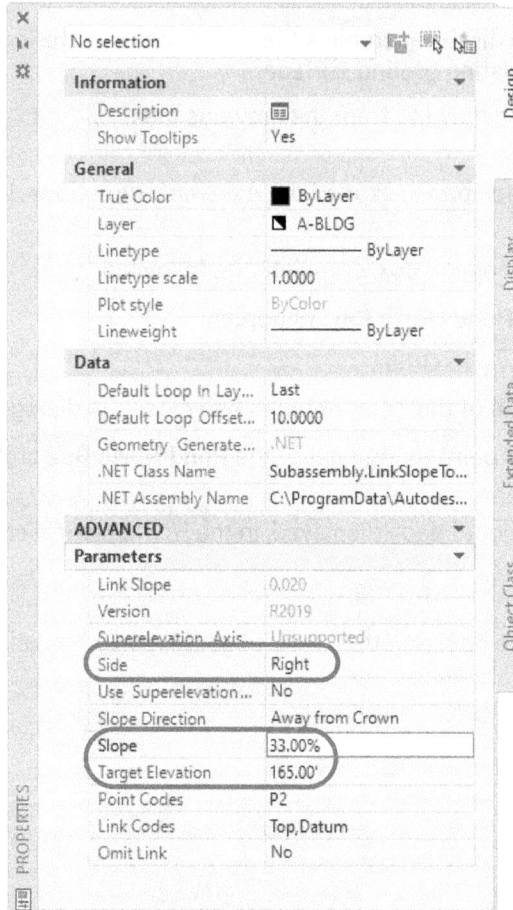

Figure C–17

8. In the drawing, select the **Pond North Bay 33** percent assembly marker to attach the subassembly, then press <Enter> to end the command.

Now you will create a copy of the **Pond North Bay 33** assembly and change the slope for part of the north interior rim grading.

9. In the *Home* tab>*Modify* panel, click ⟳ (Copy).

10. In the drawing, select the **Pond North Bay 33** assembly marker. Press <Enter> to end the selection.

11. In the drawing, pick two points of displacement to copy the assembly below the original, as shown in Figure C–18.

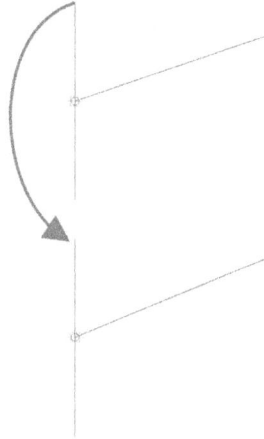

Figure C–18

12. Select the bottom assembly marker, in the *Assembly* contextual tab>*Modify Assembly* panel and click (Assembly Properties).

13. In the *Assembly Properties* dialog box, in the *Information* tab, for the *Name*, type **Pond North Bay 40 percent**.

14. In the *Construction* tab, complete the following:

   • Select **LinkSlopeToElevation**.

   • For *Input values*, for the *Slope Value,* type **40**.

   • Click **OK** to close the dialog box.

15. Press <Esc> to release the selection.

Now you will create an assembly with two links for part of the north interior rim grading.

16. In the *Home* tab>*Create Design* panel, expand the *Assembly* drop-down list and click (Create Assembly).

17. In the *Create Assembly* dialog box, complete the following:

   • For the *Name,* type **Pond North Bay - Double slope**.

   • Set the *Assembly Type* to **Other**.

   • Set the *Code Set Style* to **ASC-View-Edit**.

   • Click **OK** to accept all of the other defaults and close the dialog box.

18. In the drawing, select a point in the vicinity of the two existing pond north bay assemblies to locate the assembly in the drawing.

19. In the Tool Palettes>*Generic* tab, select **Link Width And Slope**.

20. In the *Properties* palette, set the following parameters (as shown in Figure C−19):

- *Side:* **Right**
- *Width:* **30'**
- *Slope:* **-10%**

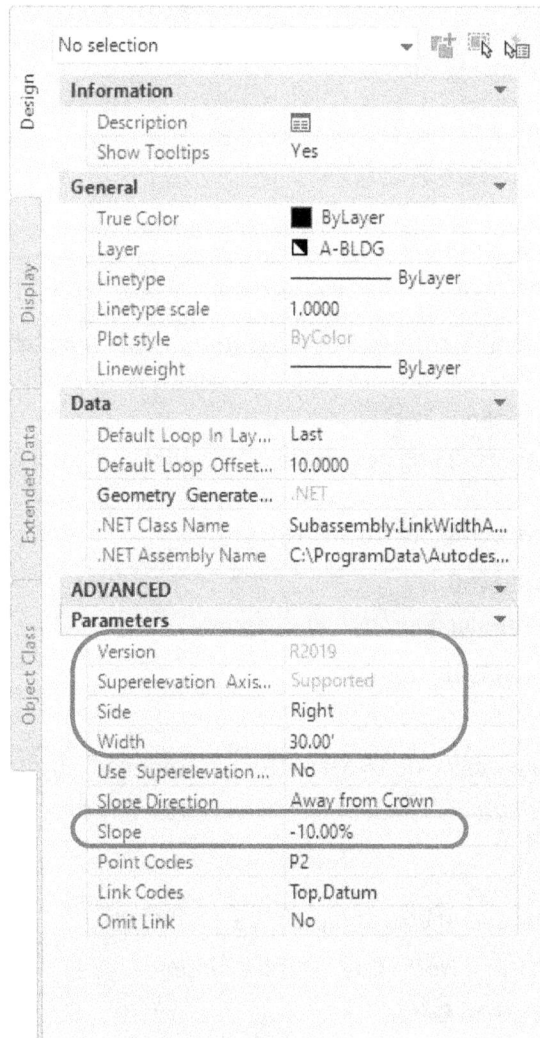

Figure C−19

21. In the drawing, select the **Pond North Bay - Double slope** assembly marker to attach the subassembly. Press <Enter> to end the command.

22. In the Tool Palettes>*Generic* tab, select **Link Slope to Elevation**.

23. In the *Properties* palette, set the following parameters (as shown in Figure C–20):

- *Side:* **Right**
- *Slope:* **50%**
- *Target Elevation:* **165'**

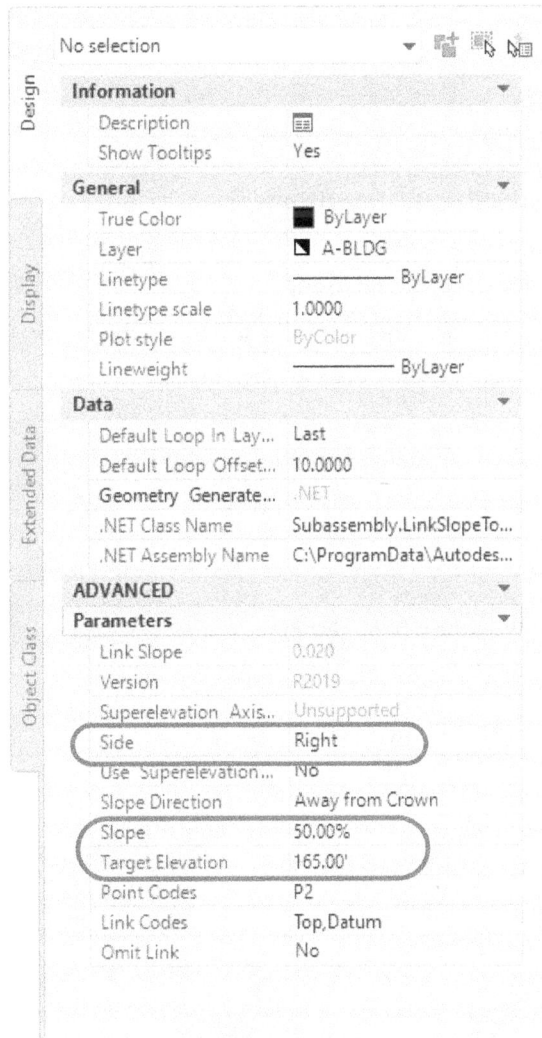

Figure C–20

24. In the drawing, select the **Pond North Bay - Double slope** assembly's *Link Width* and *Slope* subassembly to connect the new subassembly.

25. Press <Enter> to end the command.

26. Save the drawing.

Task 3: Create the pond's south bay assemblies.

In this task, you will create four assemblies for the pond's south bay assemblies.

1. Continue working in the drawing from the previous task.

2. In the *Home* tab>*Create Design* panel, expand the *Assembly* drop-down list and click

    (Create Assembly).

3. In the *Create Assembly* dialog box, complete the following:

    • For the *Name,* type **Pond South Bay Bench**.

    • Set the *Assembly Type* to **Other**.

    • Set the *Code Set Style* to **ASC-View-Edit**.

    • Click **OK** to accept all of the other defaults and close the dialog box.

4. In the drawing, select a point below the **Pond North Bay** assemblies as the location for this assembly.

5. In the *Daylight* tab in the Tool Palettes, select **Daylight Bench**.

    Note: *If the Tool Palettes is not already displayed, in the Home tab>Palettes panel, click*

    (Tool Palettes).

6. In the *Properties* palette, set the following parameters (as shown in Figure C–21):

    • *Side:* **Left**

    • *Cut Slope:* **3:1**

    • *Max Cut Height:* **4'**

    • *Max Fill Height:* **3'**

    • *Bench Width:* **2'**

    • *Bench Slope:* **-5%**

    • *Rounding Parameter:* **1.5'**

    • *Material 1 Thickness:* **1'**

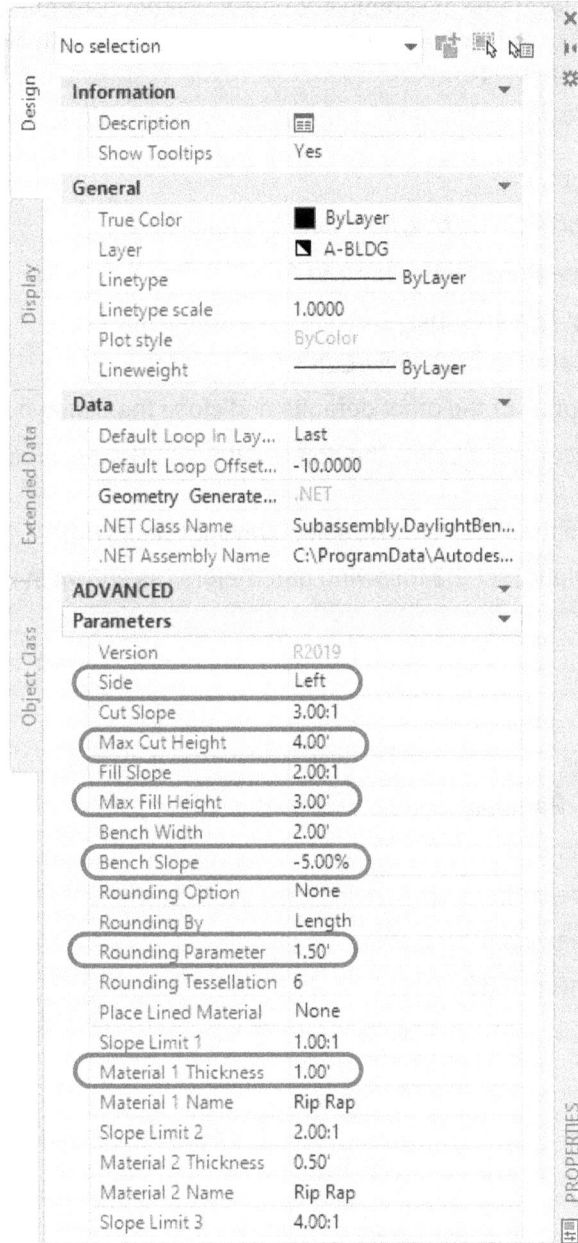

Figure C–21

7. In the drawing, select the **Pond South Bay Bench** assembly marker to attach the subassembly. Press <Enter> to end the command.

Now you will create the last three assemblies for the south bay. The first uses the *Daylight Max Width* subassembly and the other two are copies of the assembly with different slopes for part of the south interior rim grading.

8. In the *Home* tab>*Create Design* panel, expand the *Assembly* drop-down list and click

    (Create Assembly).

9. In the *Create Assembly* dialog box, complete the following:

    *   For the *Name,* type **Pond South Bay 2 to 1**.
    *   Set the *Assembly Type* to **Other**.
    *   Set the *Code set style* to **ASC-View-Edit**.
    *   Click **OK** to accept all of the other defaults and close the dialog box.

10. In the drawing, select a point below the first Pond South Bay assembly as the insertion point.

11. In the *Daylight* tab in the Tool Palettes, select **Daylight Max Width**.

12. In the *Properties* palette, set the following parameters (as shown in Figure C–22):

    *   *Side:* **Left**
    *   *Cut Slope:* **2:1**
    *   *Fill Slope:* **2:1**
    *   *Max Width:* **30'**
    *   *Rounding Option:* **Parabolic**
    *   *Rounding Parameter:* **6'**
    *   *Material 1 Thickness:* **1'**
    *   *Material 2 Thickness:* **0.5'**
    *   *Material 3 Thickness:* **0.33'**

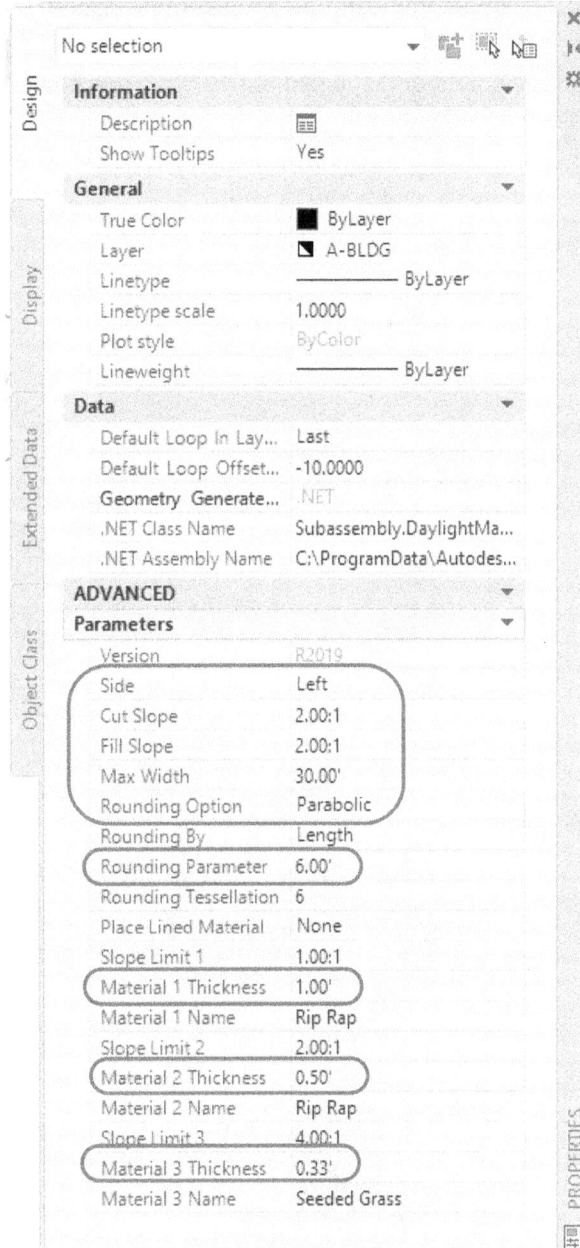

Figure C–22

13. In the drawing, select the **Pond South Bay 2 to 1 slope** assembly marker to attach the subassembly. Press <Enter> to end the command.

14. In the *Home* tab>*Modify* panel, click (Copy).

15. In the drawing, select the **South Bay 2 to 1 slope** assembly marker. Press <Enter> to end the selection process.

16. In the drawing, pick three points of displacement to make two copies of the assembly below the original, as shown in Figure C−23.

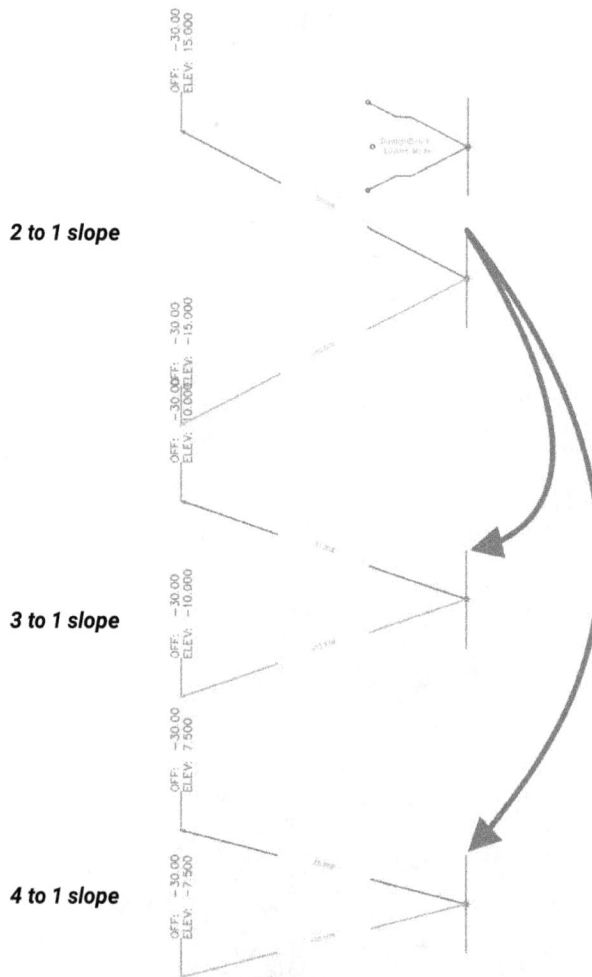

2 to 1 slope

3 to 1 slope

4 to 1 slope

Figure C−23

17. Select the middle assembly marker. In the *Assembly* contextual tab>*Modify Assembly* panel, click (Assembly Properties).

18. In the *Assembly Properties* dialog box, complete the following:

    - In the *Information* tab, for the *Name*, type **Pond South Bay 3 to 1 slope**.
    - In the *Construction* tab, select **DaylightMaxWidth**.
    - In *Input values*, for the *Cut Slope* and *Fill Slope* values, type **3.0**.
    - Click **OK** to close the dialog box.

19. Press <Esc> to release the selection.

20. Select the bottom assembly marker, in the *Assembly* contextual tab>*Modify Assembly* panel, click (Assembly Properties).

21. In the *Assembly Properties* dialog box, complete the following:

    - In the *Information* tab, for the *Name*, type **Pond South Bay 4 to 1 slope**.
    - In the *Construction* tab, select **DaylightMaxWidth**.
    - In *Input values*, for the *Cut Slope* and *Fill Slope* values, type **4.0**.
    - Click **OK** to close the dialog box.

22. Press <Esc> to release the selection.

    - *Since you're done with using the Tool Palettes, it can be closed now.*

23. Save the drawing.

End of practice

C.2 Creating Complex Corridors

A complex corridor model is created by combining surfaces, baselines, assemblies, and subassembly targets. A simple corridor model uses one of each these Civil 3D objects. A complex corridor may contain several objects to create a corridor. For example, the Intersection Wizard creates an intersection that contains multiple baselines, regions, and assemblies. Each baseline and region may in turn use different assemblies and targets to create the intersection.

Corridor grading projects also create complex corridors that use multiple baselines, regions, and targets to create the grading solution. A grading solution can contain multiple grading slopes and non-parallel paths.

Baselines

Baselines represent a corridor model's path and are based on an alignment and profile or a feature line. The alignment controls the horizontal path, and the profile controls the vertical path. A corridor combines these two alignment types, horizontal and vertical, into a single string known as a baseline.

If a baseline is a feature line, it is a 3D object that control the path of the corridor in three dimensions, which defines both the horizontal and vertical paths.

A corridor may have multiple baselines and/or regions to permit multiple assemblies in the corridor's area or to change a corridor model's design elements.

How To: Add Baselines to a Corridor

1. In the *Home* tab>*Create Design* panel, click ![icon] (Corridor).
2. In the *Create Corridor* dialog box, you can add multiple baselines of either type (alignments and profiles or feature lines) by doing the following, as shown in Figure C−24:
   * Type a *Name* and *Description*.
   * Assign the appropriate *Code set style*.
   * Select the *Alignment* or *Feature line*. You can do this by using the drop-down lists or selecting it from the drawing.
   * Select the *Profile* (if an alignment baseline was selected). A most suitable profile is selected, however you can change it by using the drop-down lists or selecting it from the drawing.
   * Select the *Assembly*.
   * Select the *Target Surface*.
   * Select **Set baseline and region parameters**. This is optional.
   * Click **OK** to close the dialog box.

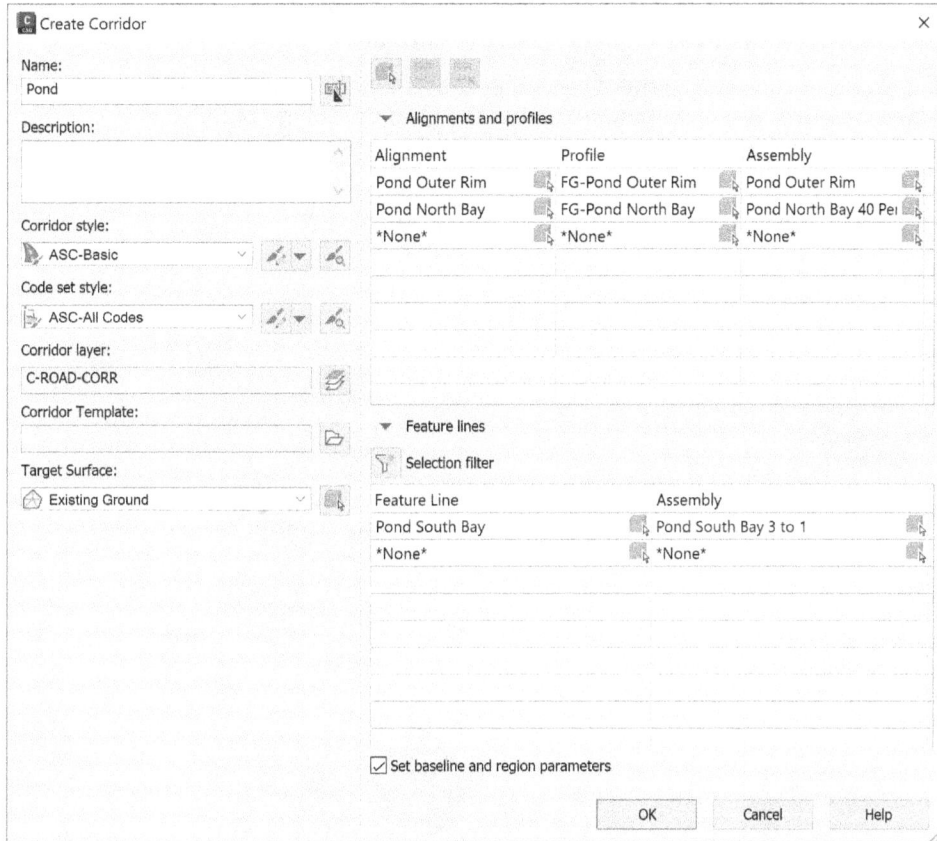

Figure C–24

3. In the *Baseline and Region Parameters* dialog box, you can adjust the *Frequency Target* and the *Start* and *End Stations*. You can also add more baselines if required, as shown in Figure C–25.

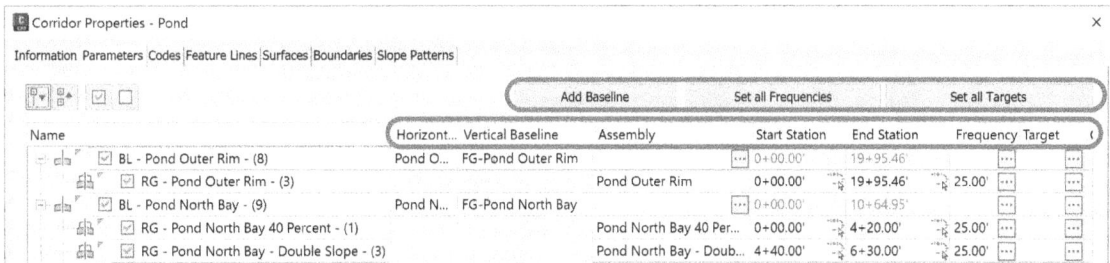

Figure C–25

4. To add baselines, in the *Baseline and Region Parameters* dialog box, click **Add Baseline**, or pick (Add Baseline) from the contextual ribbon.

5. In the *Add Baselines* dialog box, select the *Alignment* or *Feature line*. You can do this using the drop-down lists or by selecting it from the drawing.

6. Select the *Profile* (if an alignment baseline was selected). A most suitable profile is selected, however you can change it using the drop-down lists or by selecting it from the drawing, as shown in Figure C−26. Click **OK** to close the dialog box.

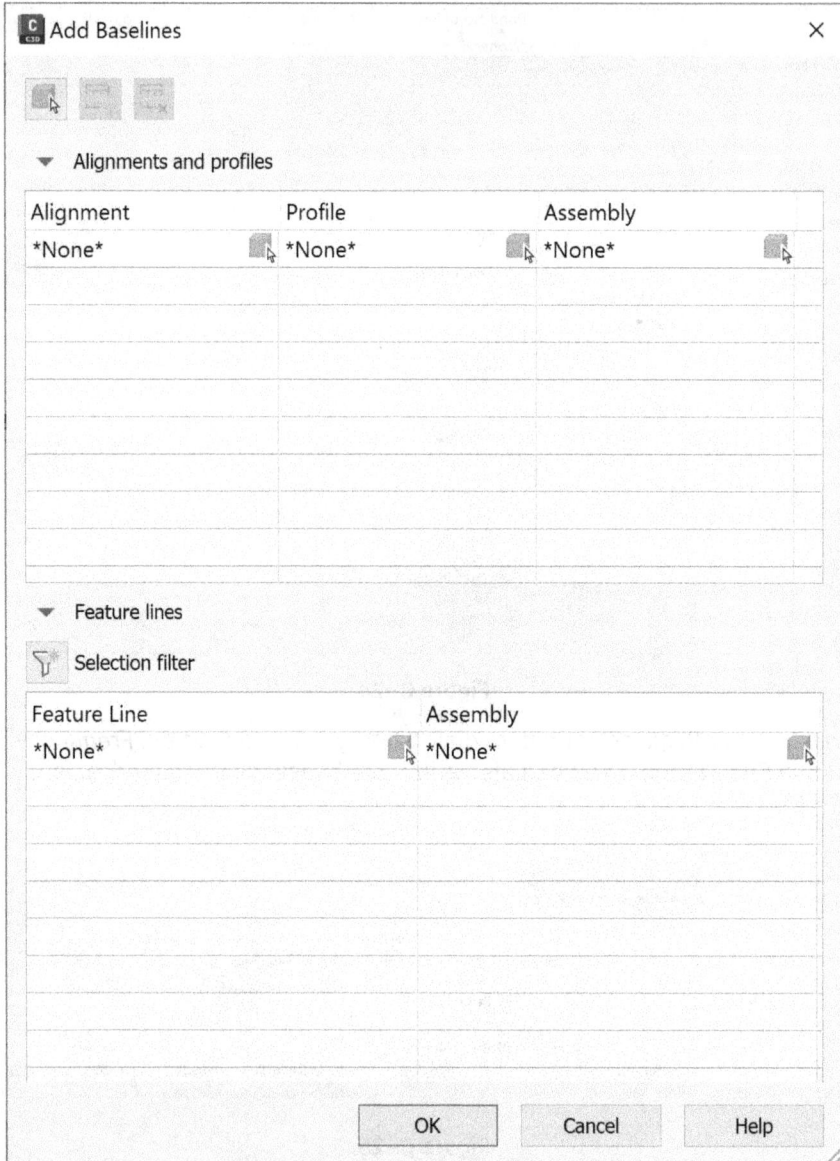

Figure C−26

Regions

Baselines consist of one or more regions. Each region is assigned its own assembly and provides a way to transition from one typical cross-section to another along the baseline. In addition, each region can target different subassembly points to modify an assembly's behavior.

How To: Add Regions to a Corridor

1. In the drawing, select the corridor. In the *Corridor* contextual tab>*Modify Region* panel, click (Add Regions).

2. In the drawing, select the baseline alignment, as shown in Figure C–27.

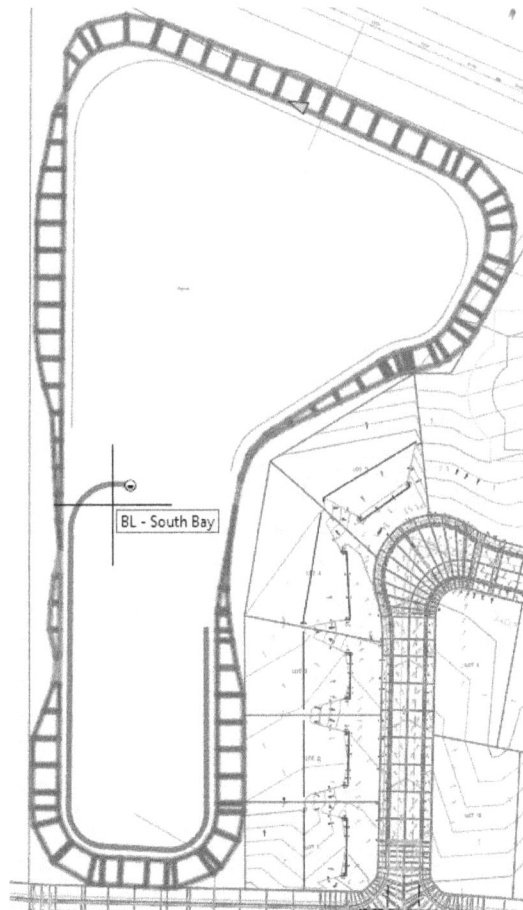

Figure C–27

3. In the drawing, select a point or type a station number and press <Enter> for the beginning station, then select a point or type a station number and press <Enter> for the ending station.

4. In the *Create Corridor Region* dialog box, type a *Region name* and select an *Assembly*, as shown in Figure C–28.

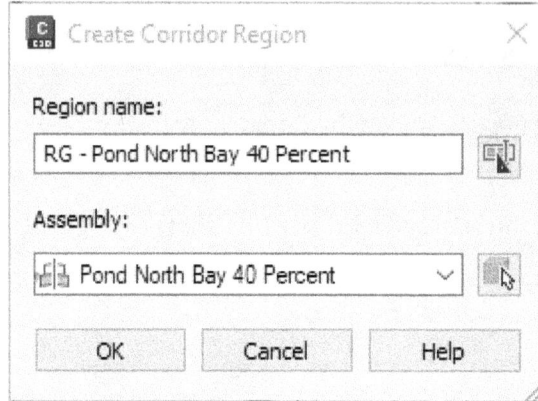

Figure C–28

5. In the *Target Mapping* dialog box, set the required targets, as shown in Figure C–29. Click **OK**.

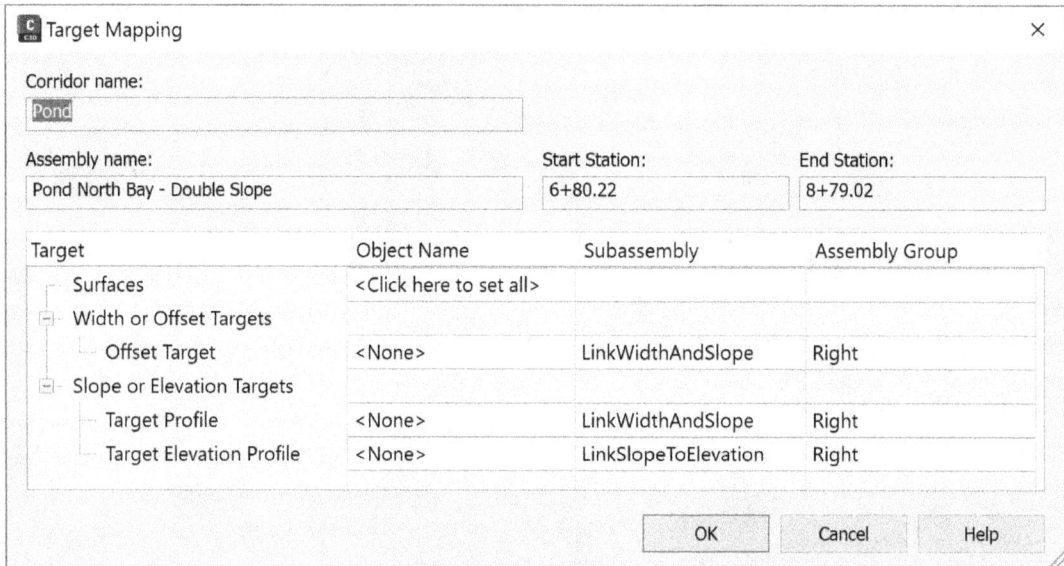

Figure C–29

When you pick an alignment from the drop-down menu, Civil 3D finds the most appropriate profile, however you should verify that it is the correct profile. If you pick the alignment from the drawing, Civil 3D will display a list in the drawing of the available profiles for that alignment, as shown in Figure C–30.

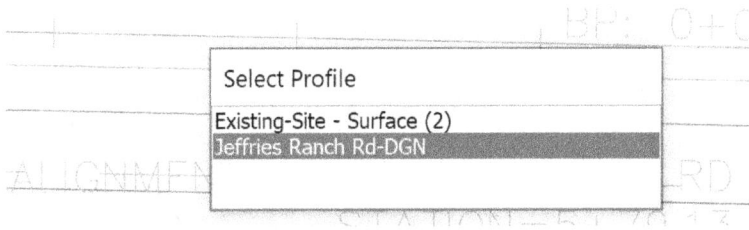

Figure C–30

You can add multiple alignments to create the corridor, and even combine alignments and feature lines to create a single corridor!

Practice C2
Create Complex Corridors

Practice Objective

- Create a corridor model with multiple baselines and regions in the grading solution.

In this practice, you will create a corridor model with multiple baselines and regions to create a grading solution.The initial corridor is a single baseline and region. The corridor is made more complex by edits to the corridor that add additional baselines as alignments, profiles, or feature lines, regions, targets, and assemblies for each region. The corridor additions produce a corridor-based pond grading model.

You will create the initial corridor with multiple baselines and regions. Then you will adjust the region.

Task 1: Create a corridor with multiple baselines.

1. Continue working in the drawing from the last practice or open **LAGOON-D.dwg** from the *C:\Civil 3D Grading\Working\Lagoon* folder.

2. In the *View* tab>*Named Views* panel, select **Storm Pond.**

3. In the *Home* tab>*Create Design* panel, click (Corridor).

4. In the *Create Corridor* dialog box, complete the following, as shown in Figure C–31:

    - For the *Name*, type **Pond.**
    - Ensure that the *Alignment and profiles* panel is not collapsed.
    - In the first row, use the drop-down list for the *Alignment*, and select **Pond Outer Rim.**
    - Check to see if **FG-Pond Outer Rim** is selected as the *Profile*.
    - For the *Assembly*, from the drop-down menu, select **Pond Outer Rim.**
    - In the second row, use the drop-down list for the *Alignment*, and select **Pond North Bay.**
    - Check to see if **FG-Pond North Bay** is selected as the *Profile*.
    - For the *Assembly*, from the drop-down menu, select **Pond North Bay 40 Percent.**
    - Ensure that the *Feature lines* panel is not collapsed.
    - In the first row, use the drop-down list for the *Feature Line* and select **Pond South Bay.**
    - For the *Assembly*, from the drop-down menu, select **Pond South Bay 3 to 1.**
    - For the *Target Surface*, select **Existing Ground.**
    - Clear the **Set baseline and region parameters** checkbox.

Figure C–31

5. Click **OK** to close the *Create Corridor* dialog box. The corridor is built.

6. If the *Event Viewer* displays some errors, close the *Event Viewer*. Such errors can be ignored for now, they will be dealt with later.

7. Save the drawing.

Task 2: Add regions to the corridor to accommodate varying slopes around the north bay of the pond.

1. Continue working in the drawing from the last practice or open **LAGOON-D1.dwg** from the *C:\Civil 3D Grading\Working\Lagoon* folder.

2. In the drawing, select the **Pond** corridor. In the *Corridor* contextual tab>*Modify Corridor* panel, click (Corridor Properties), as shown in Figure C–32.

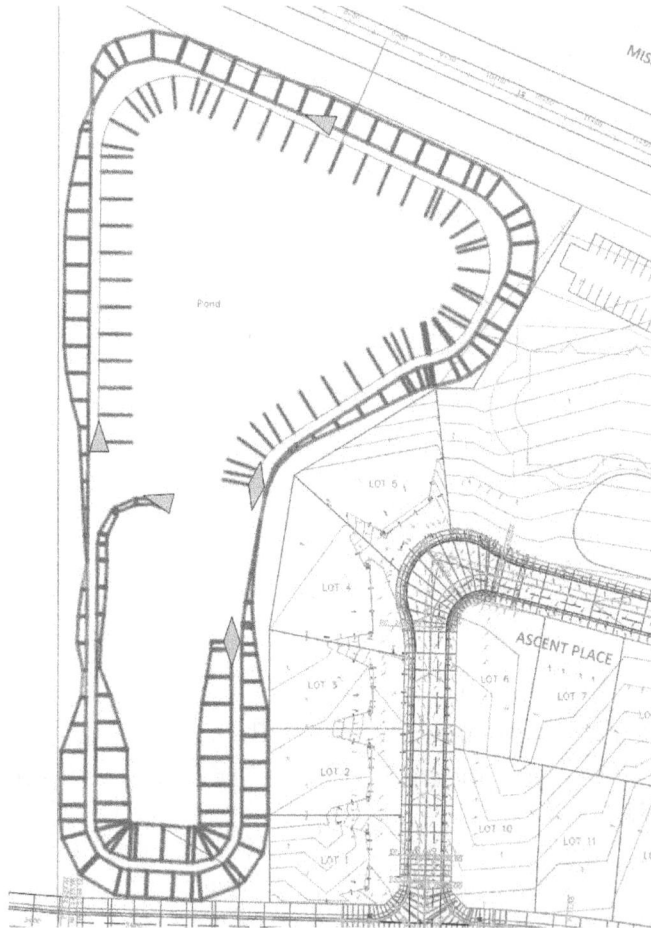

Figure C–32

3. In the *Corridor Properties* dialog box>*Parameters* tab, select the **BL-North Bay -(10)** baseline. Notice how the baseline is highlighted in red in the drawing when you select it, as shown in Figure C–33.

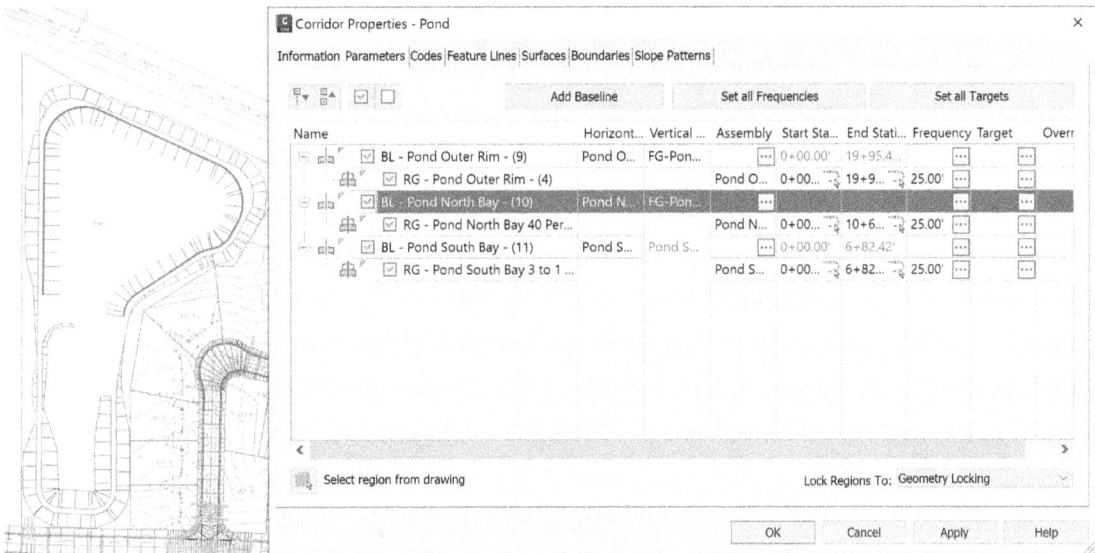

Figure C–33

Note: Throughout these practices, the numbering suffix of the region names may differ from the numbers printed here.

4. Select the **RG - Pond North Bay 40 Percent - (1)** region and notice how it is highlighted in the drawing.

5. For the *Ending Station*, type **420** and press <Enter>, as shown in Figure C–34.

6. Right-click on **BL-North Bay -(10)** and pick **Add Region...**, as shown in Figure C–34.

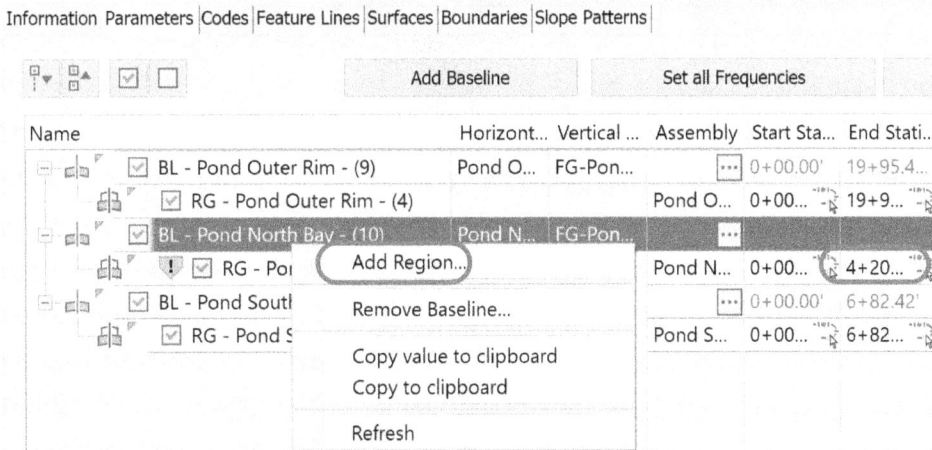

Figure C–34

7. In the *Create Corridor Region* dialog box leave the name as the default and for the *Assembly*, select **North Pond Bay - Double Slope** as shown in Figure C–35.

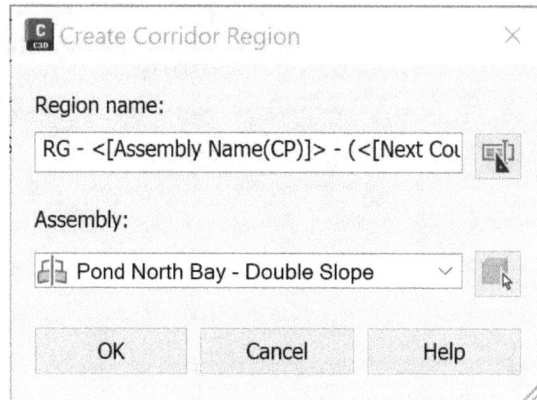

Figure C–35

8. Click **OK**.

9. You return to the *Corridor Properties* dialog box>*Parameters* tab. Change the *Start Station* of the newly created region to **4+40.00.** Type **440** and press <Enter>.

10. Change the *End Station* of the newly created region to **6+30.00.** Type **630** and press <Enter>.

11. Repeat the same procedure for creating a new region in the **BL-North Bay -(10)** baseline with the following parameters:

    * For the *Region name*, **leave as default**.

    * For the *Assembly*, select **Pond North Bay 33 percent**.

    * Adjust the *Start Station* to **6+50.00.** (Type **650** and press <Enter>).

    * Leave the *End Station* as is.

12. Click **OK** to close the *Corridor Properties* dialog box.

13. In the *Corridor Properties - Rebuild* dialog box, click **Rebuild the corridor**.

14. Save the drawing.

Task 3: Create a surface to set the pond bottom slope in the south bay.

In this task, you will create a pond bottom target surface for the pond's south bay area as a target for the correct slopes in this pond area. Feature lines in the pond's central area have already been drawn to aid in the design process.

1. Continue working in the drawing from the previous task.

2. In the *Home* tab>*Layers* panel, expand the layers and scroll down to the layer **C-TOPO-POND BOTTOM**. Select the light bulb to turn on the layer, as shown in Figure C−36.

   *Note: You may have to enter **RE** in the command line to regenerate the drawing and display all the feature lines.*

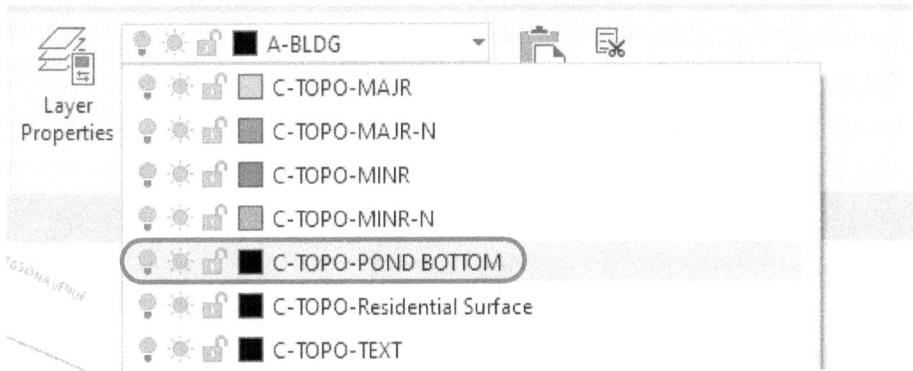

Figure C−36

3. In the *Home* tab>*Create Ground Data* panel, expand the *Surfaces* drop-down list and click

   (Create Surface).

4. In the *Create Surface* dialog box, complete the following:

   * For the *Name*, type **Pond Bottom**.
   * For the *Style*, select **ASC-Border Only**.
   * Click **OK** to close the dialog box.

5. In the drawing, zoom in on the south bay of the pond.

6. In the *Prospector* tab, expand **Sites>Lagoon** and select **Feature Lines**. In the preview window below, select **Feature1** and **Feature2**, right-click and select **Add to Surface as Breakline**.

7. In the *Select Surface* dialog box, select the **Pond Bottom** surface as shown on left of Figure C–37 and click **OK**.

8. In the *Create Breaklines* dialog box, set the following as shown on right of Figure C–37:

   • *Description*: **Pond Bottom FLs**

   • *Breakline type*: **Standard**

   • *Supplementing factors*: **25**

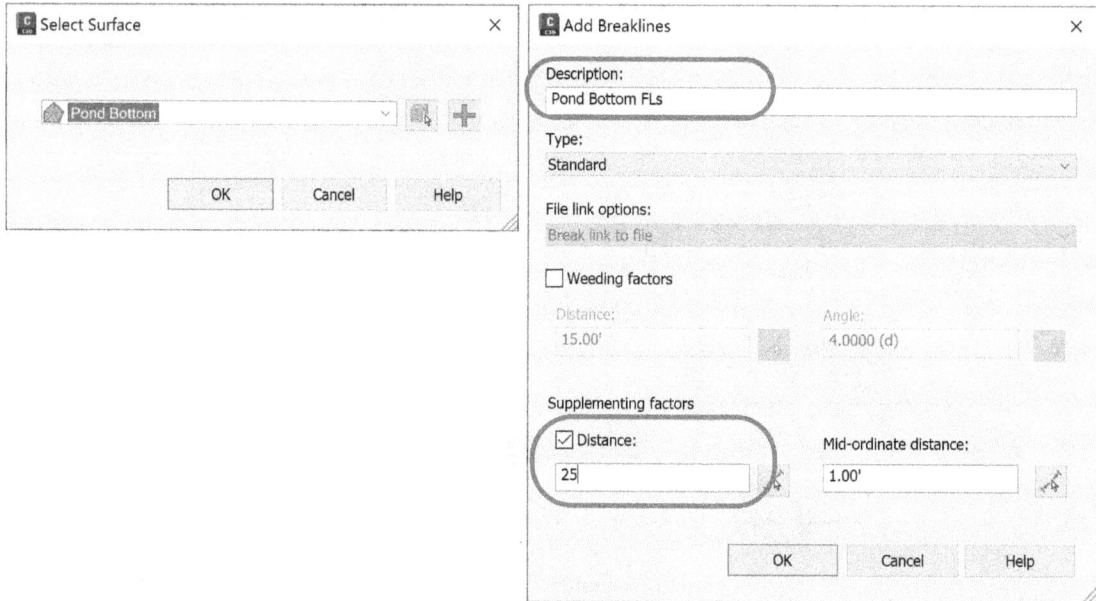

Figure C–37

9. Click **OK** to close the *Add Breaklines* dialog box. A surface is created.

10. Save the drawing.

Task 4: Add baseline regions to define varying slopes around the south bay of the pond.

1. Continue working in the drawing from the last practice or open **LAGOON-D2.dwg** from the *C:\Civil 3D Grading\Working\Lagoon* folder.

2. In the *View* tab>*Named Views* panel, select **South Pond**.

3. In the drawing, select the **Pond** corridor. In the *Corridor* contextual tab>*Modify Corridor* panel, click (Corridor Properties).

4. In the *Corridor Properties* dialog box>*Parameters* tab, select the **RG - Pond South Bay 3 to 1 - (1)** region and notice how it is highlighted in the drawing.

---

5. Adjust its *End Station* to **1+30.00**.

6. From the right-click menu, pick **Insert Region - After...**, as shown in Figure C–38.

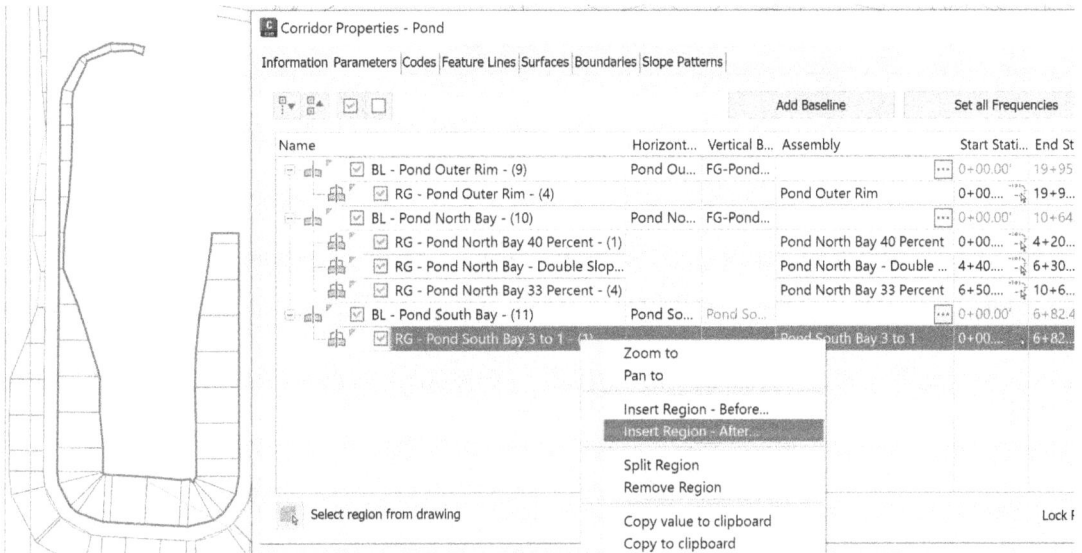

Figure C–38

7. In the *Create Corridor Region* dialog box, leave the name as the default and for the *Assembly*, select **Pond South Bay 2 to 1 slope** as shown in Figure C–39.

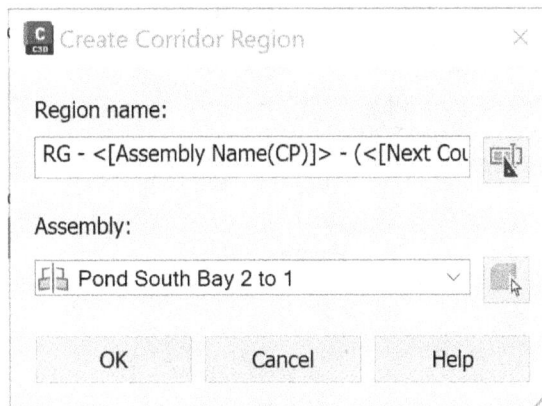

Figure C–39

8. Click **OK**.

9. You return to the *Corridor Properties* dialog box, *Parameters* tab. Change the *Start Station* of the newly created region to **1+50.00.** Type **150** and press <Enter>.

10. Change the *End Station* of the newly created region to **3+10.00**. Type **310** and press <Enter>.

11. Repeat the same procedure for creating a new region after the
    RG - Pond South Bay 2 to 1 - (5) region with the following parameters:

    • For the *Region name*, leave as default.

    • For the *Assembly*, select **Pond South Bay Bench.**

12. Adjust the *Start Station* to **3+20.00** and the *End Station* to **5+50.00.**

13. Repeat the same procedure for creating a new region after the **RG - Pond South Bench - (6)**
    region with the following parameters:

    • For the *Region name*, leave as default.

    • For the *Assembly*, select **Pond South Bay 4 to 1 slope**.

14. Adjust the *Start Station* to **5+60.00.** (Type **560** and press <Enter>), and leave the *End Station*
    as is.

15. Select the **BL - Pond South Bay - (10)** region, click on the *Target* ellipses (...), as shown in
    Figure C–40.

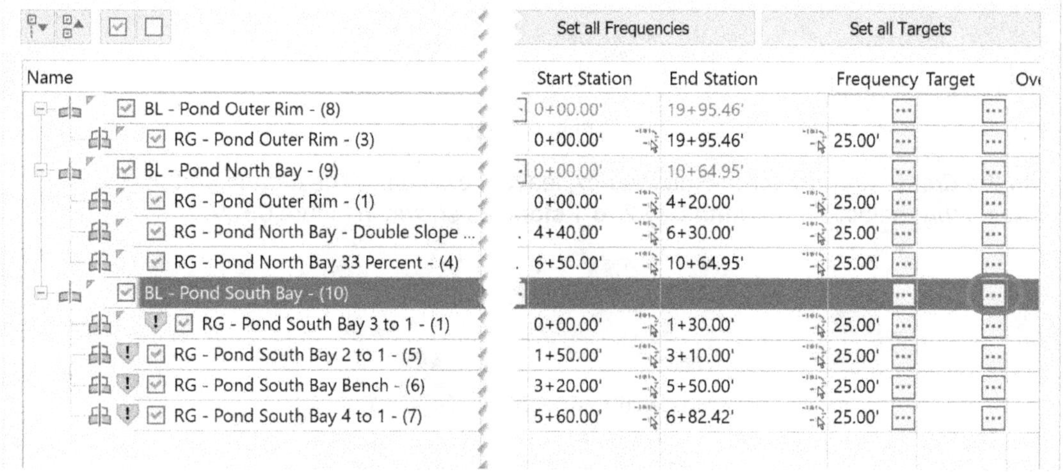

Name	Start Station	End Station	Frequency	Target	Ov
⊟ ☑ BL - Pond Outer Rim - (8)	0+00.00'	19+95.46'		...	...
☑ RG - Pond Outer Rim - (3)	0+00.00'	19+95.46'	25.00'	...	...
⊟ ☑ BL - Pond North Bay - (9)	0+00.00'	10+64.95'		...	...
☑ RG - Pond Outer Rim - (1)	0+00.00'	4+20.00'	25.00'	...	...
☑ RG - Pond North Bay - Double Slope ...	4+40.00'	6+30.00'	25.00'	...	...
☑ RG - Pond North Bay 33 Percent - (4)	6+50.00'	10+64.95'	25.00'	...	...
⊟ ☑ BL - Pond South Bay - (10)				...	...
☑ RG - Pond South Bay 3 to 1 - (1)	0+00.00'	1+30.00'	25.00'	...	...
☑ RG - Pond South Bay 2 to 1 - (5)	1+50.00'	3+10.00'	25.00'	...	...
☑ RG - Pond South Bay Bench - (6)	3+20.00'	5+50.00'	25.00'	...	...
☑ RG - Pond South Bay 4 to 1 - (7)	5+60.00'	6+82.42'	25.00'	...	...

Set all Frequencies   Set all Targets

Figure C–40

16. In the *Target Mapping* dialog box, on the *Surface* tab, select **Pond Bottom** from the drop-down list, as shown in Figure C–41.

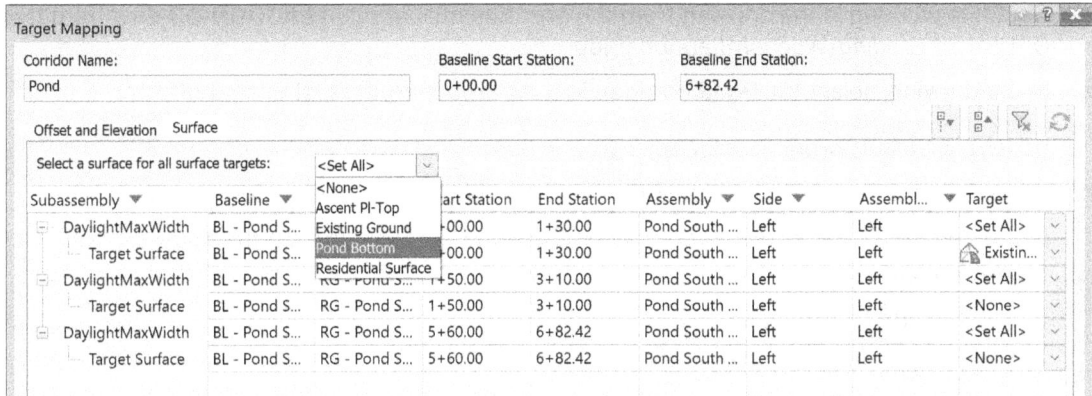

Subassembly ▼	Baseline ▼	... art Station	End Station	Assembly ▼	Side ▼	Assembl... ▼	Target
DaylightMaxWidth	BL - Pond S...	+00.00	1+30.00	Pond South ...	Left	Left	<Set All>
Target Surface	BL - Pond S...	+00.00	1+30.00	Pond South ...	Left	Left	Existin...
DaylightMaxWidth	BL - Pond S...	RG - Pond S... 1+50.00	3+10.00	Pond South ...	Left	Left	<Set All>
Target Surface	BL - Pond S...	RG - Pond S... 1+50.00	3+10.00	Pond South ...	Left	Left	<None>
DaylightMaxWidth	BL - Pond S...	RG - Pond S... 5+60.00	6+82.42	Pond South ...	Left	Left	<Set All>
Target Surface	BL - Pond S...	RG - Pond S... 5+60.00	6+82.42	Pond South ...	Left	Left	<None>

Drop-down list showing: <None>, Ascent PI-Top, Existing Ground, Pond Bottom, Residential Surface

Corridor Name: Pond
Baseline Start Station: 0+00.00
Baseline End Station: 6+82.42
Offset and Elevation | Surface
Select a surface for all surface targets: <Set All>

Figure C–41

17. Click **OK** to close the *Target Mapping* dialog box.

18. Click **OK** to close the *Corridor Properties* dialog box.

19. In the *Corridor Properties - Rebuild* dialog box, click **Rebuild the corridor**.

20. Save the drawing.

21. Select the **Pond** corridor model, right-click, and select **Object Viewer** or **Add to Model Viewer**. Set the *Visual Style* to **3DWireframe**. Note that the pond is missing the weir between the two ponds, as shown in Figure C–42. The feature lines define the weir and are to be added as breaklines to the surface in the next task.

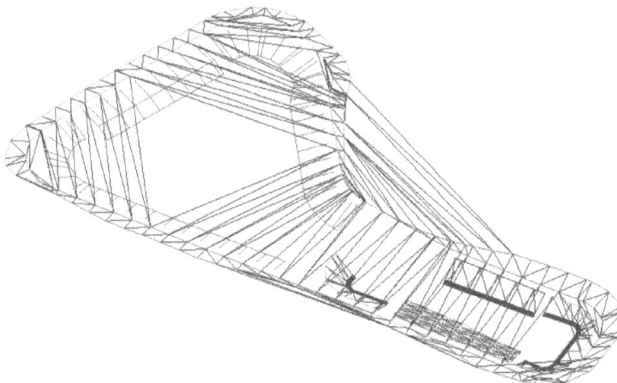

Figure C–42

22. Close the *Object Viewer*.

Task 5: Create a surface from the corridor and add weir feature lines.

1. Continue working in the drawing from the previous task or open **LAGOON-D3.dwg** from the C:\Civil 3D Grading\Working\Lagoon folder.

2. In the drawing, select the **Pond** corridor. In the *Corridor* contextual tab>*Modify Corridor* panel, click 🏠 (Corridor Surfaces).

3. In the *Corridor Surfaces* dialog box>*Surfaces* tab, click 🏠 (Create Corridor Surface).

4. In the *Corridor Surfaces* dialog box, select the **Pond Surface**, and set the following, as shown in Figure C–43:

   • Set the *Data type* to **Links**.

   • Set the *Specify code* to **Top**.

   • Click ➕ (Add surface item) to add the top codes to the surface.

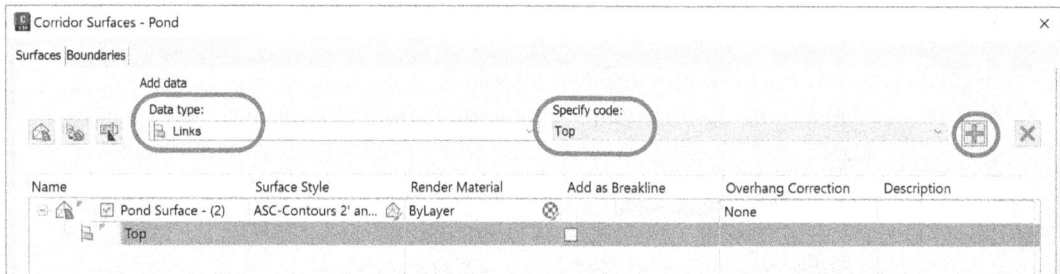

Figure C–43

5. In the *Corridor Surfaces* dialog box>*Boundaries* tab, right-click on the Pond surface, and select **Corridor extents as outer boundary**, as shown in Figure C–44.

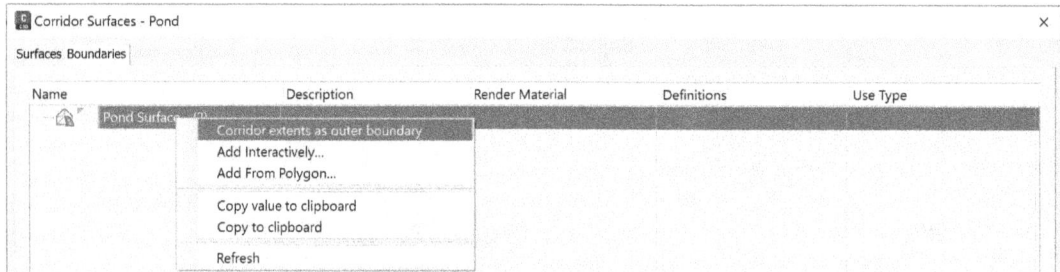

Figure C–44

6. Click **OK** to close the *Corridor Surfaces* dialog box and create the surface.

7. Click **Rebuild Corridor Model**.

8. In the *Prospector* tab, expand **Sites>Lagoon**, and select **Feature Lines**. In the preview window, select **Feature3**, then hold down <Shift> and select **South bay bottom**, and right-click and select **Add to Surface as Breakline**.

9. In the *Select Surface* dialog box, select the **Pond Surface** surface and click **OK**.

10. In the *Create Breaklines* dialog box, set the following:

   - *Description*: **Pond FLs**
   - Type: **Standard**
   - Supplementing factors: **25**
   - *Mid-ordinate distance:* **0.1**

11. Click **OK**. A surface is created that you control by modifying the two feature lines.

12. Press <Esc> twice to deselect everything.

13. Save the drawing.

14. Select the **Pond** surface, right-click and select **Object Viewer** (or *Model Viewer*, if you prefer). Set the *Visual Style* to **Conceptual**. **Zoom** and **Orbit** around the pond, as shown in Figure C–45.

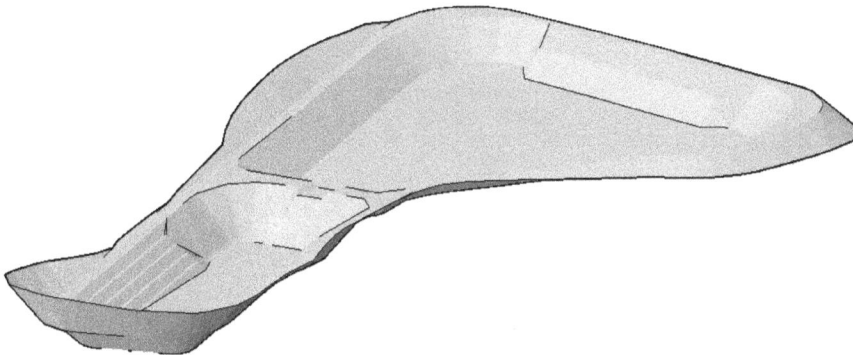

Figure C–45

15. Close the *Object Viewer*.

End of practice

C.3 Modify Corridor Grading

Change occurs in any project. Using corridor models for grading projects speeds up the change process and makes it easier to edit slope values. A corridor provides additional tools to modify a grading solution.

Grip Editing

Grips can be used to edit a corridor model quickly. The ▷ (Triangle Grip) grips are located at the beginning and ending of regions and enable you to adjust the regions' stations.

The ◁▷ (Diamond Grip) grip that is located between two regions enables the station adjustment of both regions' stationing at the same time. Triangular grips located at the diamond grip's location modify one region's stationing separately from the adjacent region's stationing.

Modify Regions

The *Modify Region* panel in the *Corridors* contextual tab provides all of the required tools for making changes to corridor regions, as shown in Figure C–46. The following table describes each command.

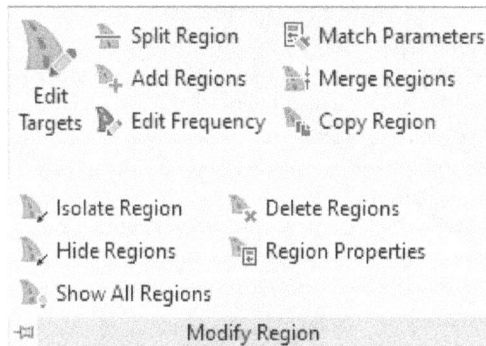

Figure C–46

Icon	Command	Description
	Edit Targets	Sets the targets for the assembly along the specific region only.
	Split Region	Splits a corridor region into multiple regions enabling different assemblies to be applied to a corridor.
	Add Regions	Enables an assembly to be applied to a gap on a corridor.

Icon	Command	Description
	Edit Frequency	Changes the frequency that an assembly is applied to a corridor within a region.
	Match Parameters	Match the assembly, target, and/or frequency of selected corridor regions.
	Merge Regions	Merges corridor regions along the same baseline.
	Copy Region	Copies regions along the same baseline.
	Isolate Region	Sets the visibility of all regions except the selected one to off.
	Hide Region	Sets the visibility of the selected region to off.
	Show All Regions	Sets the visibility of all regions to on.
	Delete Region	Removes a region from a corridor.
	Region Properties	Edits the assembly, beginning and ending stations, frequency, targets, and station overrides of a selected region.

Modify Corridor

The *Modify Corridor* panel in the *Corridors* contextual tab provides all of the tools required to make changes to the entire corridor at the same time, as shown in Figure C–47. The table below lists each command and describes what they do.

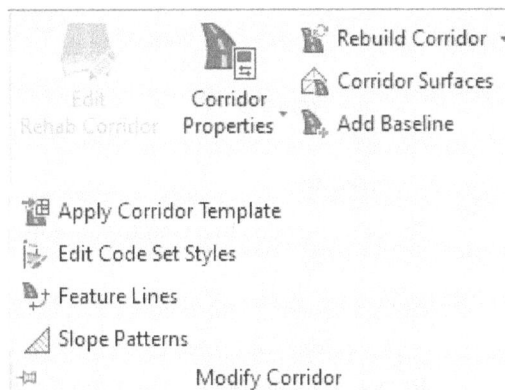

Figure C–47

Icon	Command	Description
	Corridor Properties	Edits corridor properties including *Name*, *Description*, *Object style*, Baselines, Regions, Targets, *Frequencies*, *Code sets*, *Feature lines*, *Surfaces*, *Boundaries*, and *Slope patterns*.
	Rebuild Corridor	Applies changes to a corridor that is out of date.
	Corridor Surface	Creates and manages surfaces built from links and codes assigned to assemblies used in the corridor.
	Add Baseline	Attaches alignments to a corridor to accommodate widening and non-parallel designs in road and grading projects.
	Edit Code Set Styles	Edits code set styles assigned to points, links, and shapes within subassemblies used in the corridor.
	Feature Lines	Edits feature line connections by indicating the point codes that are connected.
	Slope Patterns	Edits the patterns that are applied between any two feature lines.

Modify Corridor Sections

The *Modify Corridor Sections* panel in the *Corridors* contextual tab provides all of the tools required to make changes to the entire corridor at the same time, as shown in Figure C–48. The following table describes each command.

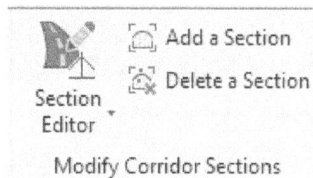

Figure C–48

Icon	Command	Description
	Section Editor	Applies overrides to assembly parameters at specific stations.
	Add Section	Adds a section to the corridor at a defined location.
	Delete Section	Removes a selected section from a corridor.

Practice C3
Modify Corridor Grading

Practice Objective

- Modify the corridor using grips and corridor parameters.

In this practice, you will create a new assembly for the outer rim of the pond, modify the corridor, and modify the frequency of the corridor and edit the corridor sections.

Task 1: Create an assembly for the outer rim of the pond.

In this task, you will create an assembly that represents the outer rim of the pond and daylights to the Residential Grading surface.

1. Continue working in the drawing from the previous practice or open **LAGOON-E.dwg** from the *C:\Civil 3D Grading\Working\Lagoon* folder.

2. In the *Home* tab>*Create Design* panel, expand the *Assembly* drop-down list and click

   (Create Assembly).

3. In the *Create Assembly* dialog box, enter the following:

   - *Name*: **Pond Rim to Surface**
   - *Description:* **Pond Outer Rim-Tie to Residential Surface**
   - *Assembly Type*: **Other**
   - *Code set style*: **ASC-View-Edit**

4. Click **OK** to accept all of the other defaults and close the dialog box.

5. In the drawing, select a point near the **Pond Outer Rim Profile** view as the insertion point to remember which profile it goes with.

   Note: The Autodesk Civil 3D software automatically zooms in on the assembly marker.

6. In the *Daylight* tab in the Tool Palettes, select **Daylight to Offset** to display the *Properties* palette.

   Note: If the Tool Palettes is not already displayed, in the Home tab>Palettes panel, click

   (Tool Palettes).

7. In the *Properties* palette, set *Rounding Option* to **Circular**, and leave all of the other parameters as their default value, as shown in Figure C-49.

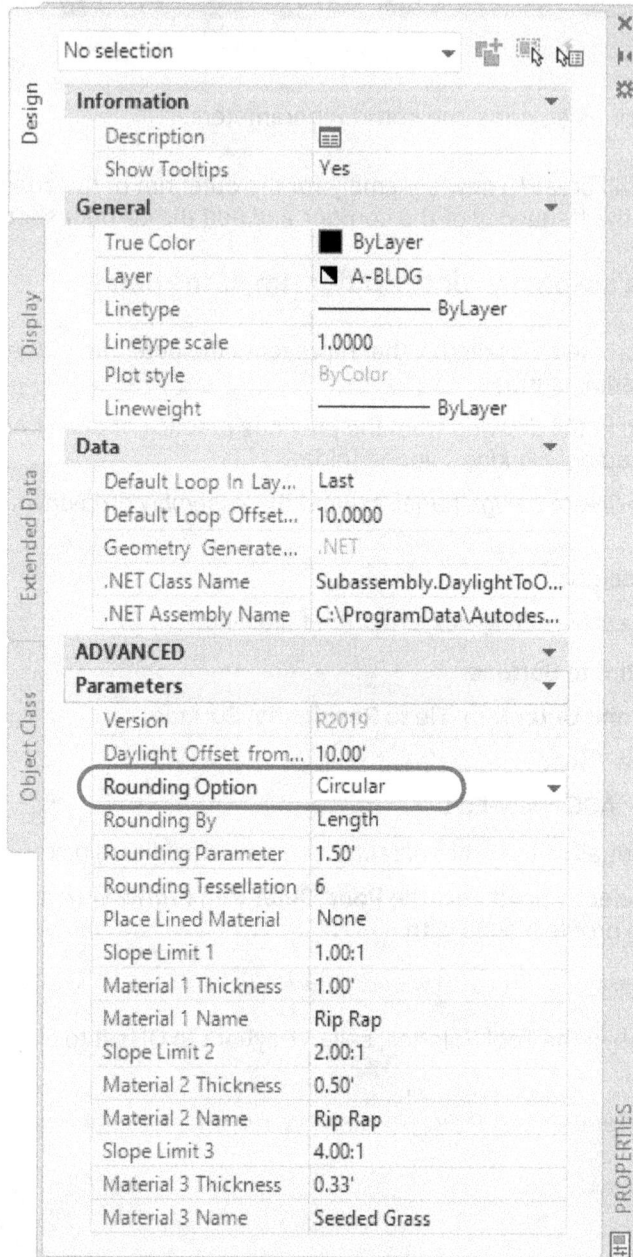

No selection	▼
Information	▼
Description	▦
Show Tooltips	Yes
General	▼
True Color	■ ByLayer
Layer	◣ A-BLDG
Linetype	——— ByLayer
Linetype scale	1.0000
Plot style	ByColor
Lineweight	——— ByLayer
Data	▼
Default Loop In Lay...	Last
Default Loop Offset...	10.0000
Geometry Generate...	.NET
.NET Class Name	Subassembly.DaylightToO...
.NET Assembly Name	C:\ProgramData\Autodes...
ADVANCED	▼
Parameters	▼
Version	R2019
Daylight Offset from...	10.00'
Rounding Option	**Circular** ▼
Rounding By	Length
Rounding Parameter	1.50'
Rounding Tessellation	6
Place Lined Material	None
Slope Limit 1	1.00:1
Material 1 Thickness	1.00'
Material 1 Name	Rip Rap
Slope Limit 2	2.00:1
Material 2 Thickness	0.50'
Material 2 Name	Rip Rap
Slope Limit 3	4.00:1
Material 3 Thickness	0.33'
Material 3 Name	Seeded Grass

Figure C-49

8. In the drawing, select the **Pond Rim to Surface** assembly marker to attach the subassembly, as shown in Figure C–50.

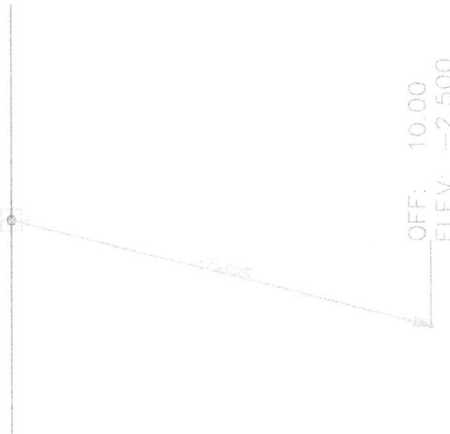

Figure C–50

9. Press <Enter> to end the command.

    Note: Since you're done with using the Tool Palettes, it can be closed now.

10. Save the drawing

Task 2: Modify the corridor.

In this task, you will adjust the corridor using grips. You will then create a polyline 6" inside the residential parcels to target and add the **Pond Rim to Surface** assembly to the corridor.

1. Continue working in the drawing from the previous practice or open **LAGOON-E1.dwg** from the *C:\Civil 3D Grading\Working\Lagoon* folder.

2. In the *View* tab>*Named Views* panel, select **Weir** to view where the corridor encroaches on the feature lines that create the weir on the east side of the north bay.

3. Select the **Pond** corridor model.

4. Select the region grip at the endpoint of the *North Bay* baseline.

5. Using the **Midpoint** Osnap, move the grip to the midpoint of the curve, as shown in Figure C–51 and Figure C–52.

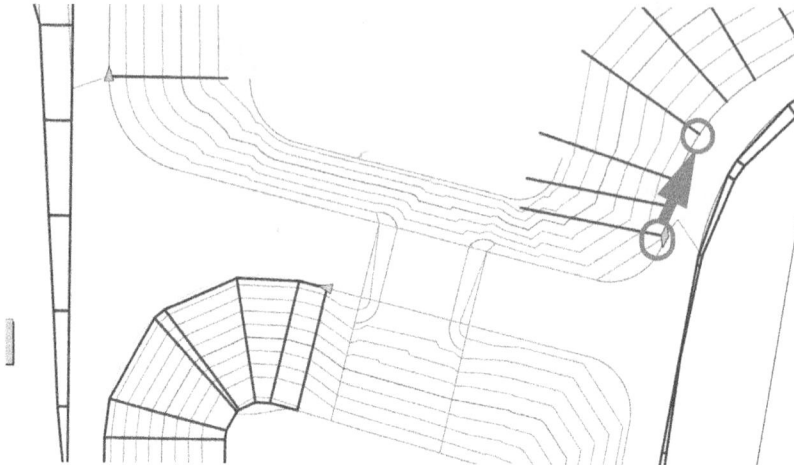

Figure C–51

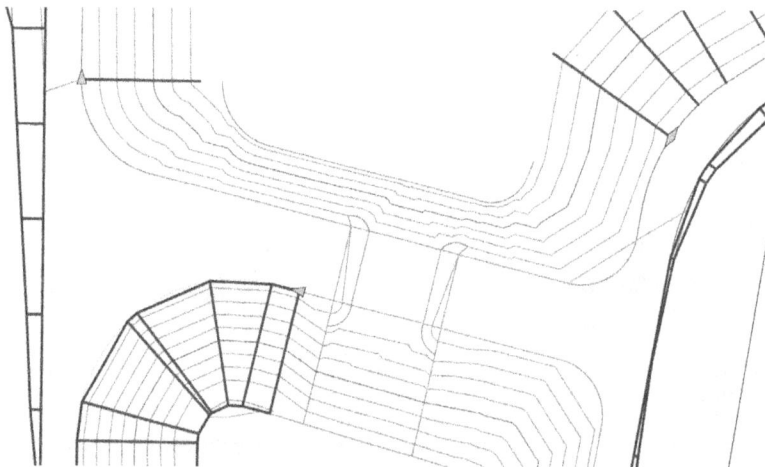

Figure C–52

6. Press the **<Esc>** key to clear the selection.

Now you will create a target polyline that daylights the pond outer rim to the residential grading surface. To create the target, offset the pond parcel segment by half a foot and trim the offset at Lot 1's northern boundary and Lot 5's northern boundary. This leaves a polyline target between Lots 1 to 5.

7. In the *View* tab>*Named Views* panel, select **Storm Pond.**

8. In the *Home* tab>*Modify* panel, click ⊆ (Offset). In the Command Line, for the *Offset distance,* type **.5**.

9. In the drawing, select the **Pond** parcel segments, as shown in Figure C–53.

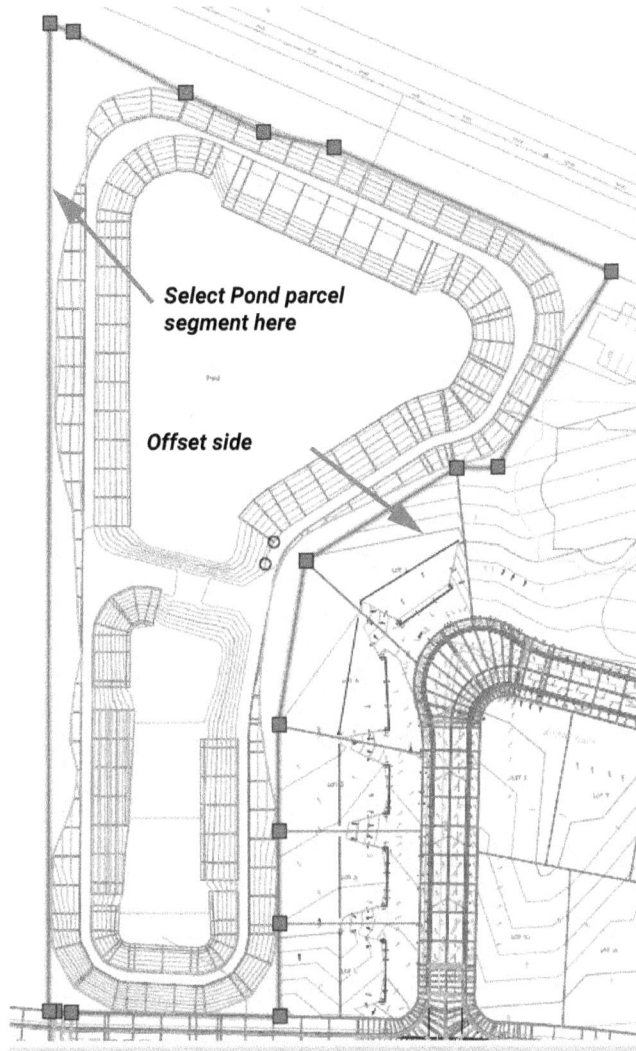

Figure C–53

10. In the drawing, pick an offset point outside the pond.

11. Press <Enter> to end the **Offset** command.

12. In the *Home* tab>*Modify* panel, click ✂ (Trim).

13. In the drawing, select the short segment to the east of Lot 5 and the southern segment bordering the road, as highlighted with red lines in Figure C–54. Press <Enter> to finish the **Trim** command.

Figure C–54

14. In the drawing, erase the trimmed polyline that is in the northwest of the pond, so the only polyline that remains is the one to the rear of Lots 1 through 5, as highlighted with a red line in Figure C–55.

Figure C–55

15. Save the drawing.

Task 3: Create a region for Pond Outer Rim.

1. Continue working in the drawing from the previous task or open **LAGOON-E2.dwg** from the
    C:\Civil 3D Grading\Working\Lagoon folder.

2. In the drawing, select the **Pond** corridor. In the *Corridor* contextual tab>*Modify Region* panel,

    click (Split Region).

3. In the drawing, select the **Outer Rim** region for the region to be split, as shown in
    Figure C–56.

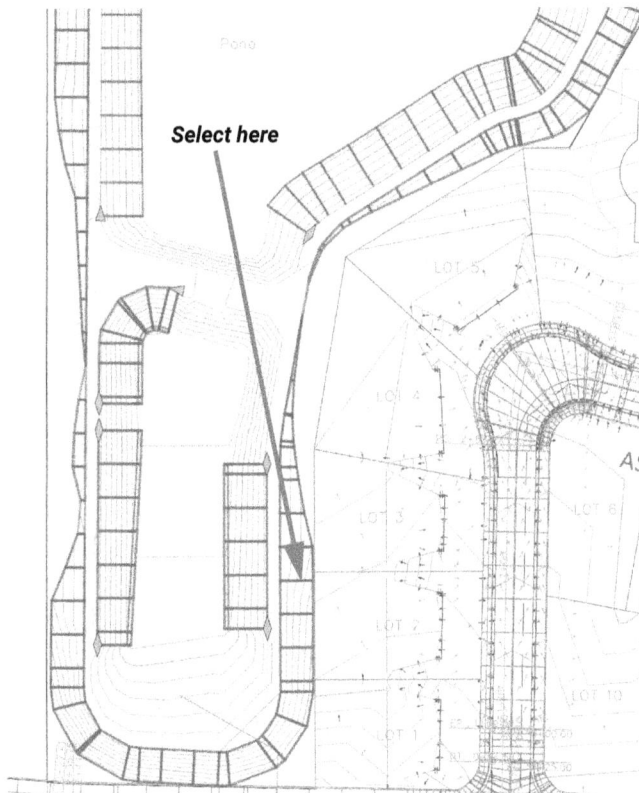

Figure C–56

4. For the split point in the drawing use the **Endpoint** Osnap to select the endpoint of the offset line at Lot 1's northern boundary as a region split point, as shown in Figure C–57.

5. You are prompted for another region to split. Select the same one as you did previously (as shown in Figure C–56) for the region to be split, and then select at the northern boundary of Lot 5, as shown in Figure C–57 as the location of the split.

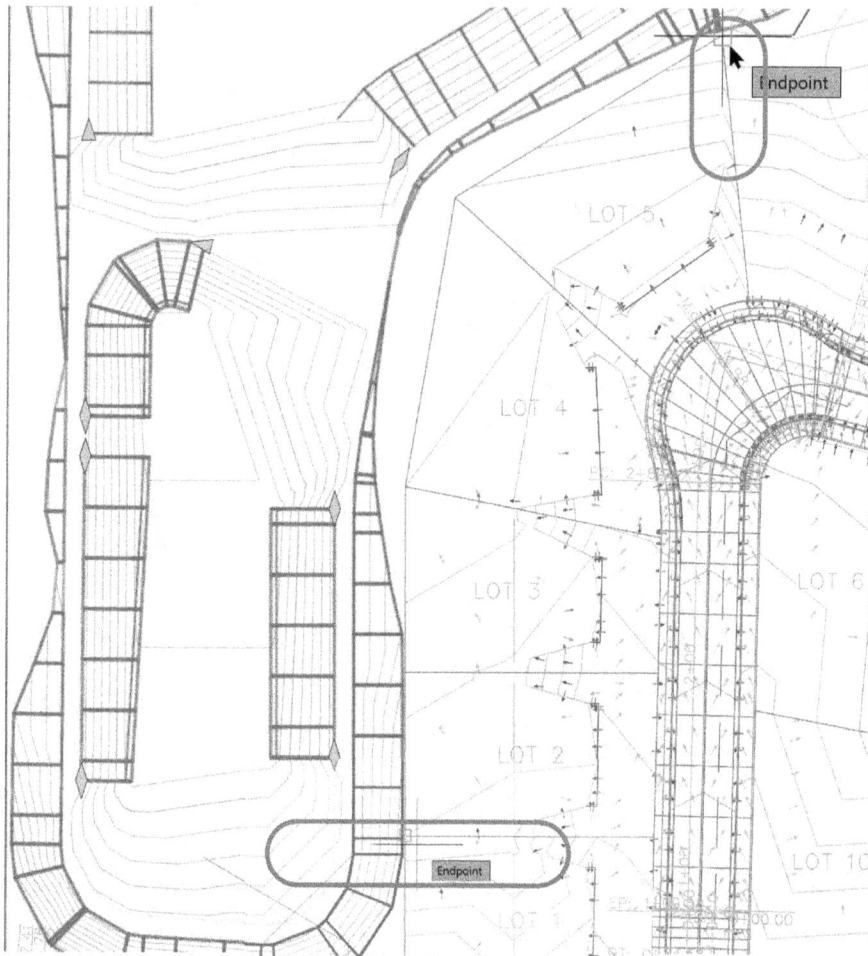

Figure C–57

6. Press <Enter> to end the **Split** command.

7. In the drawing, select the **Pond** corridor if no longer selected. In the *Corridor* contextual tab, expand the *Modify Region* panel and click (Region Properties), as shown in Figure C–58.

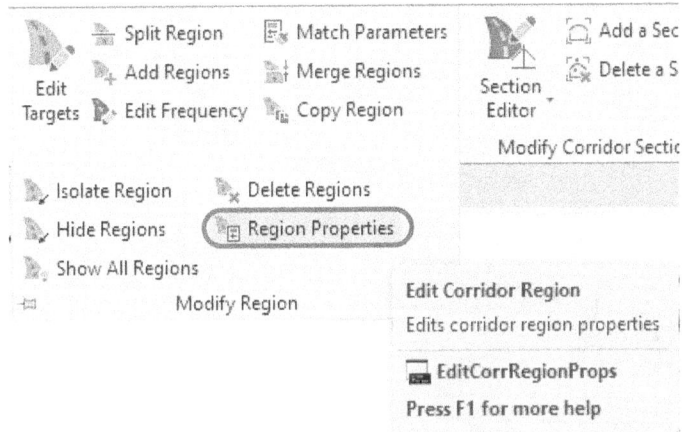

Figure C–58

8. In the model, click the **Outer Rim Region** on the east side of the pond, as shown in Figure C–59.

Figure C–59

9. In the *Corridor Region Properties* dialog box, in the *Assembly value* field, click ⬚ to open the *Edit Corridor Region* dialog box.

10. In the *Edit Corridor Region* dialog box, for the *Region name*, type **Residential Daylight**. For the *Assembly*, select **Pond Rim to Surface**, as shown in Figure C-60. Click **OK**.

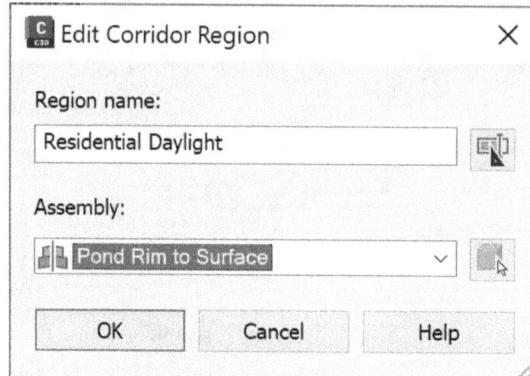

Figure C-60

11. In the *Target value* field, click ⬚ to open the *Target Mapping* dialog box.

12. In the *Target Mapping* dialog box, set the *Target Surface* to the **Residential Surface**. Click **OK**.

13. Select the *Object Name* field currently marked as *<None>*, as shown in Figure C-61.

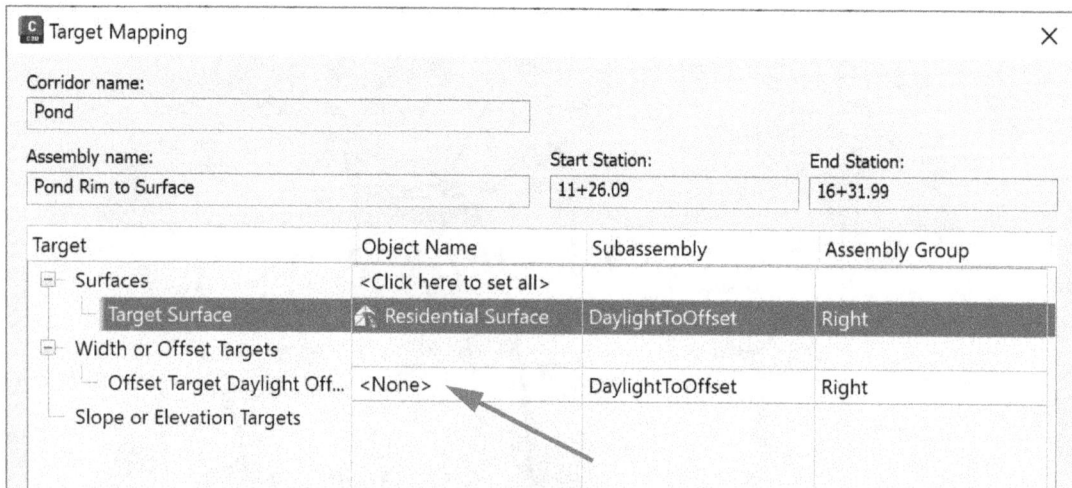

Figure C-61

14. In the *Set Width or Offset Target* dialog box, expand the *Select object type to target* drop-down list and select **Feature lines, survey figures and polylines**, as shown in Figure C-62. Click **Select from drawing**.

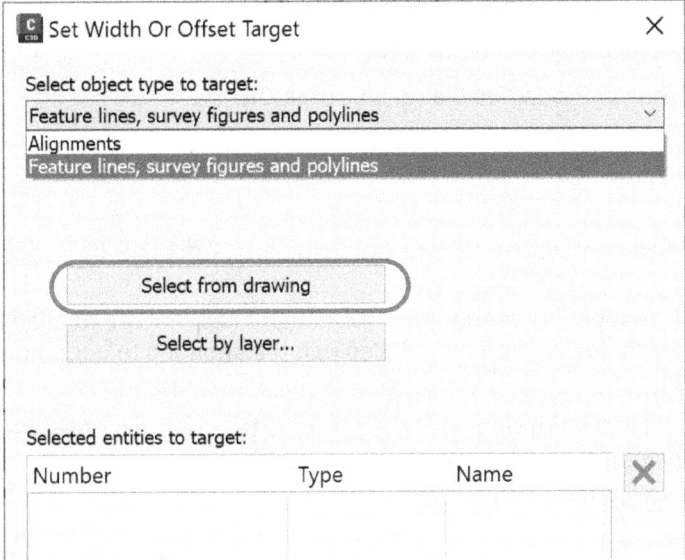

Figure C-62

15. In the drawing, select the polyline that was created from the Pond boundary offset, as shown in Figure C-63, and press <Enter> to finish the selection.

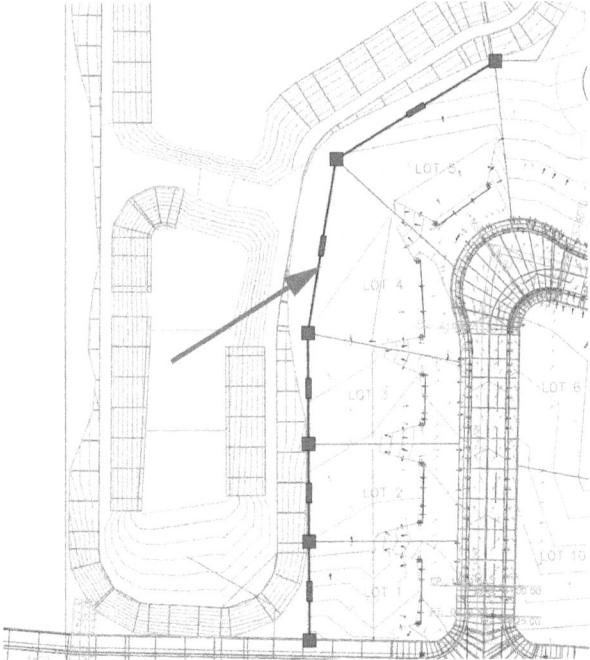

Figure C-63

16. In the *Set Width or Offset Target* dialog box, click **OK**.

17. In the *Target Mapping* dialog box, click **OK**.

18. In the *Corridor Region Properties* dialog box, click **OK**.

19. Press the **<Esc>** key to clear the selection.

20. Save the drawing.

Task 4: Modify the frequency of the corridor and edit the corridor sections.

In this task, you will change the frequency of the assemblies that are applied to the corridor to smooth transitions around curves. You will also edit the sections to accommodate another design change.

1. Continue working in the drawing from the previous task or open **LAGOON-E3.dwg** from the *C:\Civil 3D Grading\Working\Lagoon* folder.

2. In the drawing, select the **Pond** corridor.

3. In the *Corridor* contextual tab>*Modify Corridor* panel, click (Corridor Properties).

4. In the *Parameters* tab or the *Corridor Properties* dialog box, click **Set all Frequencies**.

5. In the *Frequencies to Apply Assemblies* dialog box, complete the following, as shown in Figure C–64:

    * Set *Along tangents* to **10**.

    * Set *Curve increment* to **3**.

    * Click **OK** twice to close the dialog boxes.

    * When prompted, rebuild the corridor.

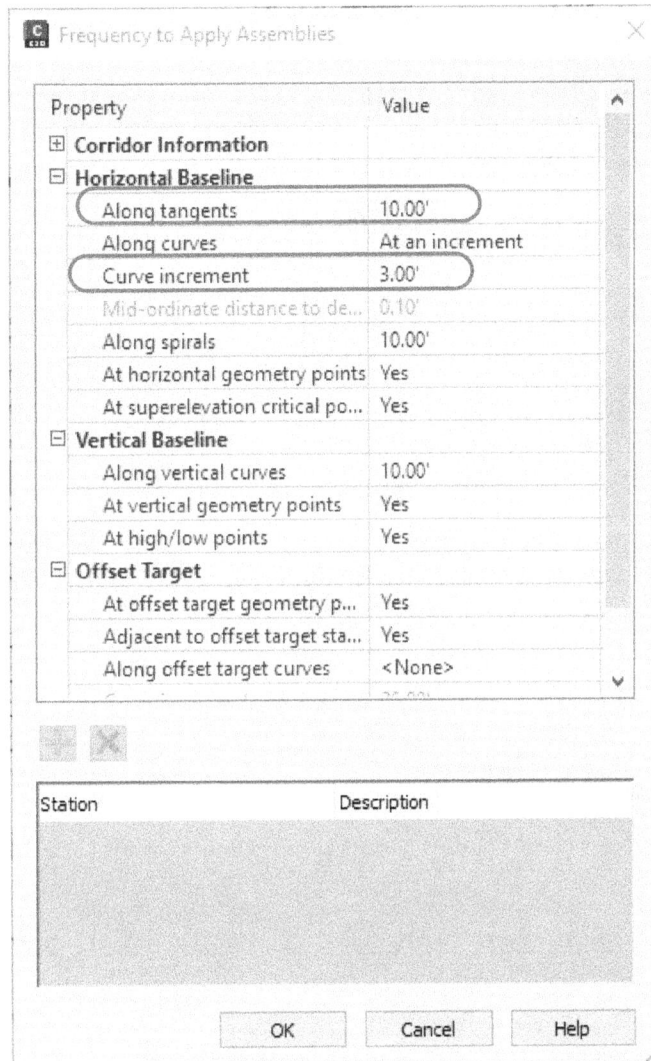

Figure C–64

Now you will edit a small section of the pond to extend the grade into the pond with less slope.

6. If deselected, select the **Pond** corridor again. In the *Corridor* contextual tab, click

    (Section Editor). This splits the drawing area into three viewports.

7. In the *Section Editor* contextual tab>*Baselines & Offsets* panel, complete the following, as shown in Figure C–65:

   - In the *Baselines & Offsets* panel, expand the *Select a Baseline* drop-down list and select **BL - North Bay**.

   - In the *Station Selection* panel, expand the *Select a Station* drop-down list and select **5+00.00'**.

   - In the *Corridor Edit Tools* panel, click (Parameter Editor).

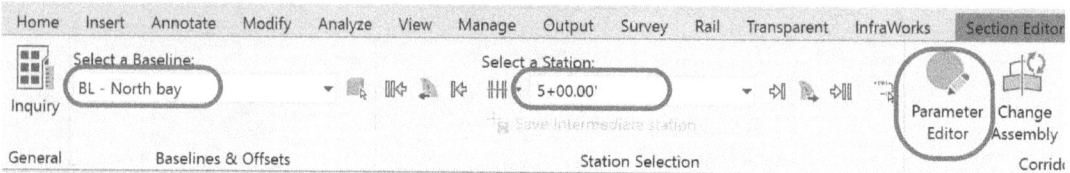

Figure C–65

8. In the *Parameter Editor* vista, expand the subassemblies. Under the *LinkWidthAndSlope* subassembly, change the *Value* of the *Slope* to **-3%** and the *Width* to **50.00'**, as shown in Figure C–66.

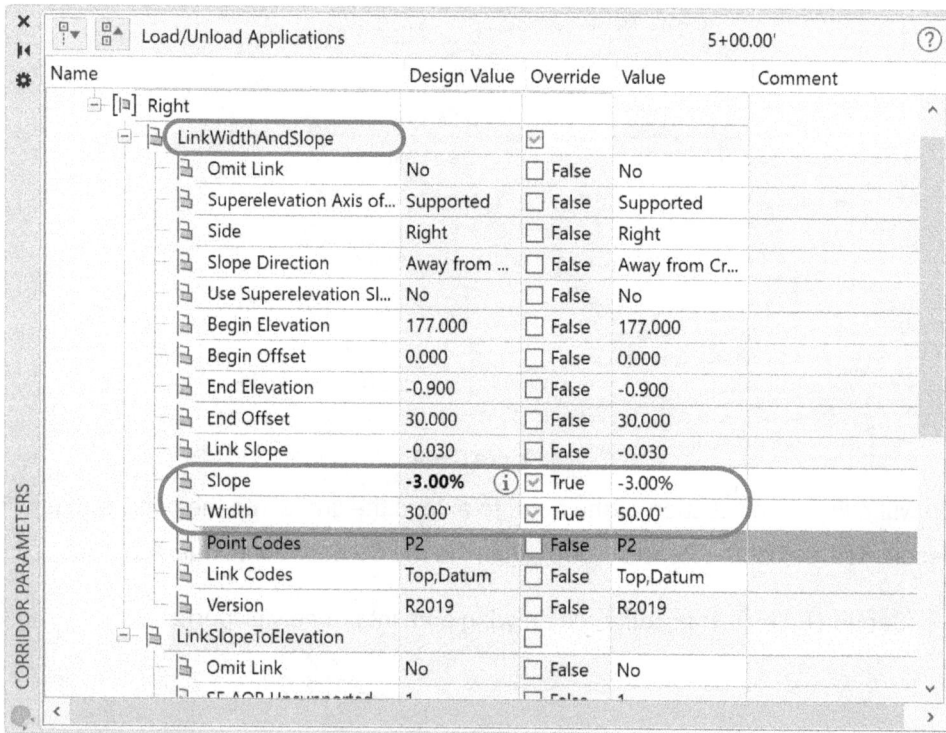

Figure C–66

9. In the *Section Editor* contextual tab>*Corridor Edit Tools* panel, click 🖼 (Apply to a Station Range).

10. In the *Apply to a Range of Stations* dialog box, for the *End station* value, type **530**, as shown in Figure C−67. Click **OK**.

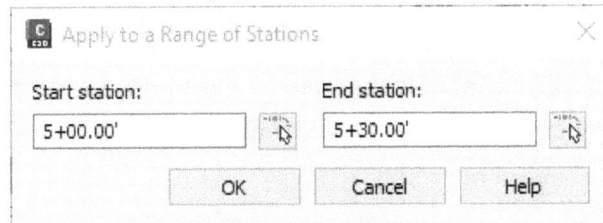

Figure C−67

11. In the *Edit Corridor Tools* panel, select **Update Corridor**.

12. In the *Section Editor* contextual tab, click the ✓ icon to close the *Section* editor.

13. Save the drawing.

14. In the drawing, select the **Pond** surface, right-click, and select **Object Viewer** (or *Model Viewer*, if you prefer). Zoom and orbit around the pond, as shown in Figure C−68.

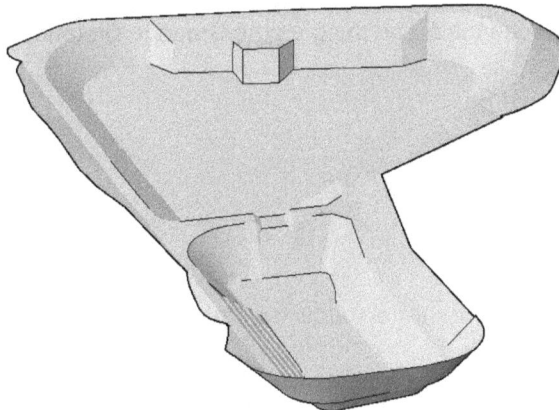

Figure C−68

15. Close the *Object Viewer*.

16. Close the drawing.

17. To view the final solution, open **LAGOON-ZZ-Complete.dwg** from the *C:\Civil 3D Grading\Working\Lagoon* folder.

End of practice

Chapter Review Questions

1. Which of the following is important to remember when grading an enclosed area with a corridor model?

    a. You cannot grade enclosed areas with corridor models.

    b. Begin and end the alignment for the corridor at a corner.

    c. Begin and end the alignment or feature line for the corridor along a straight segment.

    d. Begin and end the alignment for the corridor along a curve.

2. Which of the following is important when creating a profile for an enclosed area grading corridor model? (Select all that apply.)

    a. Begin and end the profile at the same elevation.

    b. Extend the design profile approximately 200 feet beyond the alignment to accommodate changes in length.

    c. End the profile with a tangent rather than a vertical curve.

    d. You cannot grade enclosed areas with corridor models.

3. Which subassembly does the same thing as the Grade to Distance grading criteria?

    a. Daylight General

    b. Link Width and Slope

    c. Daylight to Offset

    d. Link to Surface

4. If you need to have a corridor model follow multiple alignments or feature lines, which would you do?

    a. Add Baselines.

    b. Add Regions.

    c. Create a second corridor model.

    d. Split Regions.

5. What is assigned to a corridor region?

    a. Alignment

    b. Profile

    c. Subassembly

    d. Assembly

6. Which tool would you use to add a corridor region to a corridor to which an assembly has already been applied to its entire length?

    a.

    b.

    c.

    d.

Command Summary

Button	Command	Location
	Add Baseline	• **Ribbon:** *Corridor* contextual tab>*Modify Corridor* panel • **Command Prompt:** AddCorrBaseline
	Add Regions	• **Ribbon:** *Corridor* contextual tab>*Modify Region* panel • **Command Prompt:** AddCorrRegions
	Alignment Creation Tools	• **Ribbon:** *Home* tab>*Create Design* panel • **Command Prompt:** CreateAlignmentLayout
	Alignment Grid View	• **Toolbar:** Alignment Layout Tools (*contextual*)
	Assembly Properties	• **Ribbon:** *Assembly* contextual tab>*Modify* panel • **Command Prompt:** EditAssemblyProperties
	Corridor Properties	• **Ribbon:** *Corridor* contextual tab>*Modify Corridor* panel • **Command Prompt:** EditCorridorProperties
	Create Alignment from Objects	• **Ribbon:** *Home* tab>*Create Design* panel • **Command Prompt:** CreateAlignmentEntities
	Create Assembly	• **Ribbon:** *Home* tab>*Create Design* panel • **Command Prompt:** CreateAssembly
	Create Corridor	• **Ribbon:** *Home* tab>*Create Design* panel • **Command Prompt:** CreateCorridor
	Create Profile from Surface	• **Ribbon:** *Home* tab>*Create Design* panel • *Command Prompt:* CreateProfileFromSurface
	Draw Tangents	• **Toolbar:** Profile Layout Tools (*contextual*)
	Edit Alignment Style	• **Ribbon:** *Alignment* contextual tab>*Modify* panel>*Alignment Properties* drop-down list • **Command Prompt:** EditAlignmentStyle
	Geometry Editor	• **Ribbon:** *Alignment* contextual tab>*Modify* panel • **Command Prompt:** EditAlignment
	Profile Creation Tools	• **Ribbon:** *Home* tab>*Create Design* panel • **Command Prompt:** CreateProfileLayout
	Profile Station Elevation	• **Toolbar:** Transparent commands • **Command Prompt:** 'PSE
	Region Properties	• **Ribbon:** *Corridor* contextual tab>*Modify Region* panel • **Command Prompt:** EditCorrRegionProp

Button	Command	Location
	Section Editor	• **Ribbon:** *Corridor* contextual tab>*Modify Corridor Sections* panel • **Command Prompt:** ViewEditCorridorSection
	Split Region	• **Ribbon:** *Corridor* contextual tab>*Modify Region* panel • **Command Prompt:** SplitCorrRegion
	Tool Palettes	• **Ribbon:** *Home* tab>*Palettes* panel • **Command Prompt:** ToolPalettes, <Ctrl>+<3>

Index

www.ingramcontent.com/pod-product-compliance
Lightning Source LLC
Chambersburg PA
CBHW080343220326
41598CB00030B/4594